LILACS
The Genus Syringa

Lilacs

The Genus Syringa

by

FR. JOHN L. FIALA

TIMBER PRESS
Portland, Oregon

Paperback edition printed 2002, reprinted 2002

TIMBER PRESS, INC.
The Haseltine Building
133 S.W. Second Avenue, Suite 450
Portland, Oregon 97204, U. S. A.

Printed through Colorcraft Ltd, Hong Kong

Library of Congress Cataloging-in-Publication Data

Fiala, John L.
    Lilacs, the genus Syringa / John L. Fiala.
        p.   cm.
    Bibliography: p.
    Includes index.
    ISBN 0-88192-530-6 (paperback)
    1. Lilacs. I. Title.
QK495.O44F53 1988
583'.74—dc19   87-36094
                                                CIP

Contents

Author's Notes

Mon bon Jardinier;

In writing this volume I have been engaged for a little more than ten years in a labor of love. I have tried to write all about what might interest anyone who loves lilacs, from the home gardener to the connoisseur, from the park superintendent to the scientific hybridizer. May it bring you new ideas on growing them—a single bush, or as many as your garden can respectfully contain. The lilac is a simple plant to grow and needs very little extra care for so much beauty!

This volume began back when I was a boy of six or seven and oft visited my Grandmother's country home in Gladwin, Michigan—some ten miles out of town amid the most beautiful pines, balsams and firs of the northwoods. A clear trout stream meandered about fifty feet from her house, splashing along at hurried pace over green-mossed boulders in whose shadows the swift trout would hide as we tried to catch them by hand, rarely successful. All along this lovely river, the Sugar River, on both sides grew venerable old bushes of lilacs my Aunts and Uncle had planted for Grandmere. How she loved lilacs! There were more lilac bushes than I had ever seen anywhere. In bloom they were a marvelous sight! Heaven must be something like this, I thought. Ah, and their fragrance—like none other!

Grandmere was a true pioneer; she once lived with her growing family in a real log house! Now her house was a saltbox by the stream and my Uncle Leo and two early-widowed Aunts Marie and Amelia, who were some of the greatest gardeners I ever knew, transformed the acres of lawn and gardens around Grandmere's house into one grand seed catalogue come suddenly to life and bloom! Now they are all long gone—but it was from them at the age of six that I had to learn the common as well as the Latin name for all their flowers. The house, too, is gone, but some of the gardens still remain. The lilacs, moss covered from the mists of the running waters (that never froze even in winter), their old trunks more ancient than ever, continue to bloom each spring and make me a boy again. Perhaps in these pages, in your love for lilacs, you will experience some memories of youth and family. Hopefully it will bring you to love the lilacs as I do.

Few books have been written in English about the Lilac. Most are long out of print and are now collector's items. A lovely little book called *Lilacs,* written by N. Hudson Moore and beautifully illustrated by Frederick G. Hall, was published in 1904. Probably few lilac authorities have ever seen this little volume. It is filled with nostalgic tales about lilacs. If you have a copy, treasure it! A famous monograph by Susan Delano McKelvey, *The Lilac,* was published in 1928. It is a most prestigious and scholarly book about lilacs and their species origins.

Two practical guides for those who grow lilacs were published in the 1930s. John C. Wister, an outstanding horticultural scholar, professor and landscape designer, wrote *Lilac Culture.* He was later responsible for the *Lilac Checklist* of 1941 and *Lilacs for America,* which have been the backbone of lilac cultivar evaluation and knowledge ever since. *Lilacs in My Garden* was written by the famous gardener and horticulturist, Mrs. Edward (Alice) Harding. The well-known hybridizers Victor and Emile Lemoine named two fine lilacs in Mrs. Harding's honor. One is a beautiful double white called 'Souvenir de Alice Harding'; the other a double deep red-budded pink called 'Mrs. Edward Harding'. Both are as lovely as the grand lady they commemorate!

Written by an Englishman, Douglas Bartrum, *Lilacs and Laburnum* (1959) has never been widely distributed in the U.S.A. It is also well done, but in a more limited fashion. In recent years three other important publications on the Lilac have been printed. The *Tentative Checklist of the Genus Syringa* by Dr. Owen Rogers, which updates to 1976 the Checklist of John Wister, is a wonderful compilation of all known lilac cultivars and species. The monograph of Joseph Dvorak, Jr., *A Study of the Lilacs of Morton Arboretum and Lilacia Park*, contains marvelous line drawings. Finally, *The Edward A. Upton Scrapbooks of Lilac Information* was published by the International Lilac Society through the efforts of Dr. Owen Rogers and Isabel Zucker. It is a compilation of articles on the Lilac from Upton's Books I and II (published in one volume). These books, together with many individual articles published in various journals, magazines and newspapers, have constituted all we have on the Lilacs.

There has been no comprehensive volume on the many aspects of lilac species, cultivars, hybrids, the growing and propagation, landscaping with and the hybridizing and hybridizers of lilacs, and above all, the newer lilacs and where one may view outstanding lilacs at close hand. I have undertaken to write this long journey of the Lilacs. Their history is bound up with famous places, towns and above all historic men and women of science who searched out and hybridized to improve the Lilac. The story of the Lilac is one of stamina and beauty. It is a part of our lives and world heritage! Should I have omitted some elements of value I beg your forgiveness; should I have favored too much the newest introductions, I ask your indulgence. This I have done to show you that the Lilac is not a shrub of the past but is ever new and vibrant in its development and adaptations.

In my quest for knowledge and in working to improve the Lilac over the past forty years, I have made many wonderful horticultural friends. I wish I could mention each by name, but that would be another adventure book! I am, however, indebted to several whom I must recognize, for without their efforts this book would never have been written.

To Robert B. Clark, whom I met while he was taxonomist for the Rochester Parks and who has been a loyal and wonderful friend, a guiding hand in my lilac work, a source of constant knowledge and prodding, and in my illness edited for me the bibliography of this book, I owe a deep personal gratitude. Much of this volume is from his knowledge and research, reworked to fit the present needs. Now retired, he lives at Birchwood Gardens, his delightful retreat at Meredith, New Hampshire.

To Dr. Donald Egolf of the U.S National Arboretum for his many sharings of his genius in hybridizing and knowledge of horticulture, especially in lilacs, I am ever grateful. I firmly believe he is one of the world's outstanding hybridizers and plantsmen. He has been to me a friend, teacher, and guide.

To Arch McKean of Grand Beach, Michigan, a treasured friend, lilac specialist and promoter of lilacs and lilac parks for his friendship and knowledge of lilacs over the past decade and for sharing his lilacs with others.

There are others who have shared much with me to whom I am likewise grateful:

To Clare Short of Elyria, Ohio, friend and traveling companion, who with his sister Mary (after whom I have named a lovely early hybrid lilac) have been wonderful friends who have shared their home and their hearts over many years.

To Marty Martin, Superintendent at Holden Arboretum, who is both friend and font of knowledge on how to do things in my own little garden and an expert on lilacs and rhododendrons, and to his wonderful family.

To Joseph Dvorak, Jr., who, through his drawings and skill, has shared his fine perceptions on lilacs that are partially presented in this volume.

To Charles Holetich, Horticulturist at the Royal Botanical Gardens at Hamilton, Ontario, Canada, for his knowledge of lilacs and for the use of the many colored pictures he has so skillfully taken at the Royal Botanical Gardens. I am deeply grateful for his permission to use them.

To Isabel Zucker, friend, scholar, author and professional photographer who has encouraged me to complete this volume before my dotage sets in. A grand person and lady of horticulture and knowledge in whose honor an equally grand lilac will soon be named.

Again, I must give credit to the Royal Botanical Gardens at Hamilton, Ontario, for a truly dedicated and magnificent staff who love the lilac and upon whom I have greatly depended: its former Director, Dr. Leslie Laking; Charles Holetich who, as Horticulturist, has kept up a wonderful lilac collection; the Registrar of Lilacs, Freek Vrutgman; and Dr. James Pringle, taxonomist, who has untangled many lilac 'gordian knots' as to the species that are recorded in this book.

I am deeply indebted to the Arnold Arboretum of Harvard University for its pre-eminent place in lilacdom—its expeditions into China seeking new plant materials, its scholarly preservation and descriptions of lilac species and especially for the use of its historic archives and the permission to reproduce several photographs from its files.

Dear to me also, because it is so near and so much a part of my horticultural experiences, is the Holden Arboretum at Kirtland, Ohio. To the former Director, R. Henry Norweb Jr. and the Norweb Family of visionary horticulturists, to the Arboretum Superintendent, Marty Martin and his staff, and to Peter 'China' Bristol for his knowledge, I am ever grateful. I have sought to honor the great Holden-Norweb Family by naming some of my finest lilacs after them: 'Emery Mae Norweb' to honor the grand lady of the family, and 'Albert F. Holden' to honor the founder of the Arboretum. They are one of America's great horticultural families and deeply fond of the Lilac.

Very specially I must thank my family who have encouraged me, been my companions on lilac conventions, trips and who have worked so diligently in my garden to tend and prune when I was not able and after whom I sometimes name my best lilacs and who also share my love of lilacs from our childhood. A grateful 'thanks for being you'—my sisters and in-laws, Marie and Ben Chaykowski, Mollie Ann and Pat Pesata, Elsie Lenore Meile and my sister-in-law, Pauline Fiala. They have been my finest critics and helpers filling the gardens of my lifetime with their love as the lilacs do with their fragrance and bloom!

To Dr. Karen and Peter Murray of Ameri-Hort Research who are continuing my work and through whose nursery my introductions are available.

(Rev. Father) John L. Fiala

P.S. And you, *mon bon jardinier,* read this volume carefully for in it I share with you some of my life and my love in our common friends—the Lilacs!

New names published in this work

Syringa × *clarkiana* Fiala	page 7, 81
Syringa debelderi Fiala	page 48
Syringa × *fialiana* Clark	page 7
Syringa × *lemoineiana* (Lemoine) Fiala	page 7
Syringa oblata var. *donaldii* Clark & Fiala	page 62
Syringa × *pringleiana* Fiala	page 7, 73
Syringa × *quatrobrida* Fiala	page 7
Syringa × *tribrida* Fiala	page 7

Carolus Linnaeus—Carl von Linne, 1707–1779

CHAPTER ONE

The Taxonomy and Technical Considerations of the Lilac Species

Lilacs, to the botanists called *Syringa,* have a fascinating history when one considers their origins, their great variety and the migrations that have made them at home in all the colder regions of the earth. They are not children of the very warm climates nor of the tropical sun. They are natives, mountain dwellers, of the colder regions requiring a length of cold weather to set their fat buds for bloom. Recent experiments show that they will grow in some of the southerly regions where frost and drought are minimal. They are best where winters are cold but not arctic.

All the 23 species, more or less accepted today, have marvelous tales to tell of their native lands and the progress made in their development as garden shrubs. Some, like the common lilac, *Syringa vulgaris,* are well known by almost every gardener and loved for their beauty, fragrance and dependability. The other species, beautiful in their own way, are far less known and most would not be recognized by many people as belonging to the family of lilacs. By careful examination and consideration of each classification we shall seek, as we unfold this unique lilac family history, to appreciate the beauty they bring to gardens throughout the world. By understanding them, knowing them well and seeing their ease of culture, we shall find them both a garden companion and a mainstay of beauty in our landscapes.

In Greek legend the nymph Syrinx was pursued by the god Pan and turned into a hollow reed from which Pan made his first flute or pan-pipe. The name *Syringa* derives from the Greek word 'syrinx' meaning 'hollow stem'. One of the first names for the lilac in English was the 'Pipe Tree' or 'Blow Stem'. We are told ancient Greek doctors used its stem to inject medications into their patients or to bleed them. 'Pipe Tree' was an old English name for both *Syringa vulgaris* and *Philadelphus coronarius.* John Claudius Loudon, the English botanist (1783–1843), stated in his famous work on trees and shrubs that the best Turkish pipes were made from the straight stems of the lilac. The name 'pipe-stem' did not prevail for so lovely a shrub. Everywhere today it is known by some form of the word 'lilac' (perhaps from the Persian 'Lilak' or 'Lilaf' meaning bluish); 'Lilas' in French; 'der Flieder' or more rarely 'Lilak' in Germany; 'Holler' in Viennese; 'Lilza' in Portugal; while in Spain it is 'Lila'. The old English called it 'Laylock', 'Lilack' or 'Lilock'. Although we know it universally by some form of the common name 'Lilac', the botanical name *Syringa* prevails whenever we speak of it in scientific terms.

Without names the world would be a most confusing place. Names are as important to plants as they are to people, since they designate to which species or named cultivar we wish to refer. A 'cultivar' is an individual plant of a species or a hybrid cross usually named for some particular characteristic, e.g. color. (The terms variety and cultivar are for all practical purposes interchangeable.) By this name we are immediately aware that we mean a particular plant with all its characteristics, inherent traits and nature. It was not until the time of the great Swedish botanist, Carolus Linnaeus (Carl von Linne, 1707–1779), who established a system of binomial nomenclature in Latin, that plants began to have universal, specific, scientific names. Linne was an orderly man with a super-orderly mind that categorized all known plants into 'families', 'genera' and 'species'. He placed the lilacs among the *OLEACEAE* (Olive family) because of certain similarities to that ancient group of trees and shrubs, then into the special category called *Syringa* (the pipe-stems or hollow stems).

Today, opinions differ among scholars as to where one taxonomically places Lilac. For simplicity we shall follow the more common view and place it among the seed plants in the traditional Order of Gentianales (Order Contorta by other authorities), then in the Family of Oleaceae, distinguished by its two's (two-merous flowers, two anthers with two cells back to back, two-loculed superior ovary, generally with two ovules per locule). Dr. Owen Rogers, an outstanding taxonomist and authority on present day lilacs, in speaking of the Family Oleaceae cautions that, "While the 2-s hold the family together, there are serious questions as to whether the whole assemblage is a natural evolutionary grouping. Should *Fraxinus* be included in the family at all? Suffice it to mention the problem as the first of several areas needing further work and careful study in any consideration of the Family."

The Family Oleaceae is one of considerable importance in economics, history and aesthetics. Generally the Family is divided into the subfamilies of Jasminoideae (with the 3 genera *Jasminum, Mendora, Nyctanthes*) and the subfamily of Oleoideae with its 20 or so genera that include *Olea* (the Olive), *Fraxinus* (the Ash), *Chionanthus* (the Fringe Tree), *Osmanthus* (the Fragrant Olive), *Ligustrum* (the Privet), *Forsythia* (the Golden Bell) and *Syringa* (the Lilacs). So we have the plant family relatives of the Lilac, near and far! Whatever the taxonomical route to *Syringa*, once there the genus unfolds in a very natural order.

In the past the genus *Syringa* had been divided into two sub-genera: *Eusyringa*, with its three series of *Villosae, Vulgares* and *Pinnatifoliae;* and *Ligustrina*, which included all the tree lilacs. Today the noted taxonomist who has done so much to clarify the various species of lilacs, Dr. James Pringle, has given us a more accurate and updated classification. We prefer his classification with one exception; we do not believe *S. afghanica* has ever existed or been a valid species. (It is included in Pringle's classification only for its historic value and not because he believes it to have been a valid but a doubtful species. We do not include it as a valid species in this work). Dr. Pringle ends his taxonomical listing with the traditional names for hybrid crosses. I have added several for clarification purposes, i.e. *S.* × *pringleiana* Fiala, *S.* × *fialiana* Clark, *S.* × *lemoineiana* Fiala, *S.* × *tribrida* Fiala and *S.* × *quatrobrida* Fiala, realizing these have not been taxonomically described.)

GENUS *SYRINGA*

Subgenus *Syringa*

Series *Pinnatifoliae* Rehder
S. *pinnatifolia* Hemsley

Series *Pubescentes* (C. K. Schneider) Lingelsheim
S. *debelderi* Clark & Fiala
S. *julianae* C. K. Schneider
S. *meyeri* C. K. Schneider
S. *microphylla* Diels
S. *patula* Nakai
S. *potaninii* C. K. Schneider
S. *pubescens* Turczaninow

Series *Syringa*
S. *laciniata* Miller (S. *protolaciniata* Green, 1988)
S. *oblata* Lindley
var. *oblata*
var. *alba* Rehder
var. *dilatata* (Nakai) Rehder
var. *donaldii* Clark & Fiala
S. *vulgaris* Linnaeus
var. *vulgaris*
var. *alba* Weston 1770
var. *brevilaciniata* Jovanovic & Vukicevic 1980
var. *coerulea* Weston 1770
var. *forsythiodes* Jovanovic & Vukicevic 1980
var. *hyacinthoides* Jovanovic & Vukicevic 1980
var. *macrantha* Borbas 1882
var. *parviflora* Jovanovic & Vukicevic 1980

           var. *pulchella* Velenovsky 1894
           var. *purpurea* Weston 1770
           var. *rhodopea* Velenovsky 1922
           var. *rubra* Loddiges 1836
           var. *transsilvanica* Schur 1866
           var. *violacea* Aiton 1789
    S. × *chinensis* Wildenow (pro sp.) (*S. laciniata* × *S.vulgaris*)
    S. × *hyacinthiflora* Rehder (*S. oblata* × *S. vulgaris*)
    'Hyacinthiflora Plena'
    S. × *persica* Linnaeus (pro sp.) (*S.?* × *S. laciniata*)

  Series *Villosae* C. K. Schneider
    S. emodi Wallich ex Royle
    S. josikaea Jacquin f. ex Reichenbach
    S. komarowii C. K. Schneider
    S. reflexa C. K. Schneider
    S. sweginzowii Koehne & Lingelsheim
    S. tigerstedtii H. Smith
    S. tomentella Bureau & Franchet
    S. villosa Vahl
    S. wolfii C. K. Schneider
    S. yunnanensis Franchet
    S. × *clarkiana* Fiala (*S. komarowii* × *S. wolfii*) 'Spellbinder'
    S. × *pringleiana* Fiala (*S. reflexa* × *S. yunnanensis*)
    S. × *fialiana* Clark ([*S. sweginzowii* × *S. tomentella*] × *S. wolfii*) 'Springtime'
    S. × *henryi* C. K. Schneider (*S. josikaea* × *S. villosa*) 'Lutece'
    S. × *josiflexa* Preston ex Pringle (*S. josikaea* × *S. reflexa*) 'Guinevere'
    S. × *nanceiana* McKelvey (*S.* × *henryi* × *S. sweginzowii*) 'Floreal'
    S. × *prestoniae* McKelvey (*S. reflexa* × *S. villosa*) 'Isabella'
    S. × *swegiflexa* Hesse ex Pringle (*S. reflexa* × *S. sweginzowii*)
    S. × *lemoineiana* (Lemoine) Fiala (*S. sweginzowii* × *S. tomentella*) 'Albida'
    S. × *tribrida* Fiala (*S.* × *lemoineiana* × *S. komarowii*) 'Lark Song'
    S. × *quatrobrida* Fiala (*S.* × *lemoineiana* × *S.* × *clarkiana*) 'Quartet'
  Interseries hybrid
    S. × *diversifolia* Rehder (*S. pinnatifolia* × *S. oblata*)
Subgenus *Ligustrina* (Ruprecht) K. Koch
    S. pekinensis Ruprecht
    S. reticulata (Blume) Hara
        var. *reticulata*
        var. *amurensis* (Ruprecht) Pringle

    So we find in this classification of *Syringa* 22 valid species which are readily accepted by all present day authorities, plus the new species *S. debelderi*, which is first mentioned in this book, bringing the total number of lilac species to 23. Some would add the *S. afghanica* (for historical reasons if for no other) and *S. pinetorum*, for either of which no cultivated plants can be found. Most would agree that these two are questionable names. Fifty years ago E. H. Wilson, quoted by Mrs. McKelvey, mentions 28 possible species. Lingelsheim in his 1920 monograph describes 30 species. With more extensive data and the scholarship available to present day taxonomists, plants once thought to be species have been reduced to what they really are, varietal forms or introgressive hybrids of a species. There are also educated differences of opinion in regard to various species or varietal forms. In the past, hybrids were at times given species rank; for example, *S. chinensis* really a hybrid of *S. laciniata* ✕ *S. vulgaris*, or *S. persica* which is probably a hybrid of *S. vulgaris* (or *oblata*) ✕ *S. laciniata.* (It was thought to be a cross of the so called *S. afghanica* ✕ *S. laciniata.*)

These are not only difficulties of the past but many present-day problems are being created when every species cross is given a new name, e.g. *S.* ✕ *henryi*, or *S.* ✕ *nanceiana*, that must be validated in botanical journals. There are many unnamed hybrids involving 3, 4 and even 5 species on the market which have never been botanically named. This problem and that of tetraploids (plants with increased numbers of chromosomes) is discussed in a later chapter, as is introgressive hybridization.

Species names no longer accepted as valid include: *amurensis, japonica, chinensis, fauriei, persica* var. *laciniata, affinis, buxifolia, palibiniana, reticulata mandschurica, rhodopea, rothomagensis, rugulosa* and *velutina.* Some of these are found today under varietal names but do not hold species status. Many other names are found in the historic descriptions of lilacs by plant explorers, who were not aware that the same species had already been discovered and named by someone else. Mrs. McKelvey in her outstanding monograph *THE LILAC* has throughly documented this historical-taxonomical data. Her work should be consulted by all interested in the details of naming lilac species.

As a group lilacs are not very old in botanical history. The discovery and introduction of the various species have been largely limited to the past 100 years, with few exceptions. *S. vulgaris* which has been known and cherished for over 500 years, and the hybrid *S.* ✕ *persica* (probably *S. vulgaris* ✕ *S. laciniata*), often called the 'Persian Lilac', has been around for nearly 300 years, whereas *S.* ✕ *chinensis*, a natural hybrid between *S. laciniata* ✕ *S. vulgaris* discovered in a Rouen garden in 1777, has been around for over 200 years.

Some would argue that we have not explored native habitats sufficiently to locate living specimens of *S. afganica, S. pinetorum* or the fabled *S. fauriei.* Perhaps, somewhere a last plant or two may yet be found. Others do not see them as species, but as invalid names or varietal forms of existing species. So in this rather large genus of *Syringa* we find a number of reductions to varietal status or non-existence of what were once cherished names. As hybridizers plant larger populations of the various species, they are finding more varietal forms in their seedlings.

But enough of all of this. In considering the various species of lilacs we seek to present them as 'garden plants', not to belabor their taxonomical status exhaustively covering all historical aspects of their introduction—Mrs. McKelvey has done this job so well. We wish only to give accurate and pertinent historical data for research on the lilacs, and a fuller picture of their native habitat and the events and people who brought them onto the modern horticultural scene as one of our foremost garden shrubs.

Before closing this section we wish to warn, again, of the area of developing confusion caused by the vast and multiplying number of 'new hybrids'—especially among those containing several species, in some of which 4 or 5 species contribute to a single hybrid. It is becoming more and more difficult to ascertain (unless careful and extensive records are available) the species used in developing these modern lilac beauties. For example, amoung *S. vulgaris* hybrids we now have early hybrids using *S. vulgaris* ✕ *S. oblata* Giraldi ✕ *S. oblata dilatata.* Among the late blooming hybrids are multibrids involving a complex cross of 4, 5 and even 6 species, especially in the Villosae Series.

In the chapters ahead we will describe all the species and varietal forms of existing lilacs that are prominent today (with the exception of *S. vulgaris* and its hybrids which includes nearly 2,000 varieties). We seek to present them as your garden companions. We do not wish to make a controversial botanic tract but to whet your appetite to love, to plant and cherish the Lilac around your homes and in your city parks. To know them is to love them! (*Bon jardinage!*)

On Naming and Registering New Lilacs

The genus *Syringa* is neither the largest nor the smallest in terms of the number of species, 23. But from these species a great number of new cultivars have been derived through hybridization or selection. Plants of a single species displaying some difference in color, flower size, or other characteristic are called cultivars (or less formally, 'forms' of the species). Crosses between species are called 'hybrids'. Ordinarily a hybrid refers to a cross between two species. Today, however, some plants are the result of crosses involving several species. As a consequence some authors are beginning to call such multi-species plants 'tribrids, quatrobrids, quintobrids, sextobrids, septobrids, octobrids' and so on, to designate succinctly the number of species in a given hybrid plant.

From the single species of the common lilac, *S. vulgaris*, nearly 2,000 individually named cultivars have been derived, most of them since 1900. Each is supposed to be a bit different from all the others, in color, form, growth habit or some other way that has been signaled out as a 'special quality worthy of being named and recognized'. (Many are so similar they should never have been named in the first place. Some are actually inferior to the original species.)

At first these differences were mostly in flower color, and the earliest named lilacs had simple names (Blue Lilac, White Lilac or Purple Lilac). Then special qualities began to appear and be recognized, e.g. *S. vulgaris* 'Alba Grandiflora' (Large Flowered White Lilac), and so on. As new cultivars proliferated, with increased refinement, lilacs began to be named after famous personages, ('Princess Clementine', 'Leopold II', 'Duc de Massa'); friends and family members, ('Madame Lemoine', 'Elsie Lenore', 'Prof. Robert B. Clark'); special events, ('Bright Centennial', 'Russkii Suvenir'); or places, (Rochester', 'Belorusskie Zori', 'Krasnay Moskva', 'City of Gresham'); or some natural resemblance, ('Sunset', 'Snowdrift', 'Sovetskaya Arktika'). The International Lilac Society requested Dr. Owen Rogers, University of New Hampshire, to prepare and publish an updated, tentative *Lilac Checklist* of all known lilac names up to 1975 (a sort of Who's Who in Lilacs). It is an update of previous lilac checklists published in 1941 and 1953 by the late John C. Wister, then of the Arthur Hoyt Scott Horticultural Foundation, Swarthmore College, Swarthmore, Pennsylvania, U.S.A.

To be worthy of a name a plant should be a "notable improvement" over already existing named cultivars. The assessment of the true qualities of a lilac should be based on observations over a period of several years of bloom and trial in different areas of cultivation. To name a cultivar on the basis of color alone simply does not take into consideration questions of the plant's growth qualities, disease resistance, height, and many other necessary garden features.

It is required that each cultivar name be registered by an accepted and recognized system and horticultural authority. The principles governing acceptance or rejection of cultivar names for registration are laid down by the International Code of Nomenclature of Cultivated Plants. This Code of Regulations for botanical names is revised periodically by a world botanical body. The Royal Botanical Gardens in Hamilton, Ontario, Canada, has been designated as the International Registration Authority for all new cultivar names for the Genus *Syringa* (Lilacs). Freek Vrugtman is the Official Registrar.

Freek Vrugtman, Royal Botanical Gardens, Hamilton, Ontario, Canada, is the first official Registrar for the Genus *Syringa*. His is the task of compiling the official listing of all recognized and registered lilacs of all species.

Chromosome Counts for the Lilac Species and Principal Hybrids

Although the specific chromosome counts of the lilac species are not of primary interest to the general lilac fancier, they are of interest to those who deal with them from a scientific aspect or who hybridize them scientifically. Generally species will cross only within their own series and with species having identical chromosome counts. The ordinary number of chromosomes found in *Syringa* are diploid (the lowest possible for the species). Under certain conditions arising either naturally or by the use of specific chemicals, the count on occasion can be doubled, tripled or quadrupled, etc. Thus we would have 2n=diploid, 3n=triploid, 4n=tetraploid, etc., increasing the number of the total chromosomes proportionately. In these induced states of higher polyploidy, certain changes are effected by the increased number of chromosomes, although the character genetically remains constant—only more genes are available to the plant. In the tetraploid state the tissue is heavier, color somewhat deeper (because of the heavier tissue), growth thicker and leaves thicker. It is a complicated process, difficult to obtain polyploids, and takes a long time for results to be evident. Elsewhere we have discussed the process more in detail. For those interested in lilac polyploids we would suggest advanced Botany courses or the study of texts such as *'Colchicine'* by Dustin & Egesti.

Today, with advanced techniques, electron microscopes, and instant photography, the process of counting is much easier and more accurate than before. Since the chromosome counts are important in any complete consideration of the lilac, we present the table of available counts for the various species.

All the lilac species chromosomes that have been counted are presented in the following table. The few tetraploids, although so far unpublished, follow the tetraploid number for their diploid counterpart. In *S. vulgaris* we find varying diploid counts from 46, 47 to 48. One must be aware that very little chromosome counting is done once the number has been officially published. It may be that there are certain groups, especially in *S. vulgaris* and perhaps in *S. oblata,* that vary from the given count. Recently, a magnificent cultivar of *S. vulgaris* named 'Rochester' was introduced that gives every indication from external characteristics that it could well be a natural tetraploid. As yet no one has done for *Syringa* what the Japanese have done for *Paeonia* in counting most of the individual cultivars. It would be an enormous task, but perhaps only the most outstanding cultivars could be counted. Undoubtedly variations will be found. As yet the field of tetraploid lilacs is an uncharted area that could add another dimension to this already magnificent shrub. The cost of research and the time and tedious work involved are not appealing to most younger botanists. Perhaps lilac fanciers might make grants available to interested colleges for some of this type of work.

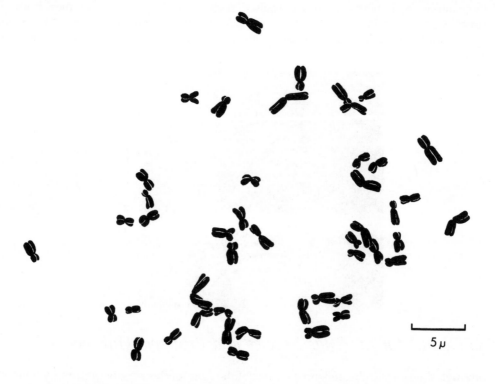

5 µ

S. tigerstedtii is the latest species to be counted; chromosome sketch made by Dr. James Pringle, R.B.G., 1979.

PLATE 1

Class I—White: 'Angel White' (Lammerts)

Class II—Violet: 'Marechal Lannes (Lemoine)

Class III—Blue: 'Tiffany Blue' (Fiala)

Class IV—Lilac: 'Aleksei Mares'ev' (Kolesnikov)

Class V—Pink: 'Mrs. Watson Webb' (Havemeyer)

Class VI—Magenta: 'Rochester Hybrid #307' (Fenicchia)

Class VII—Purple: 'Frank Paterson' (Paterson)

TODAY WE CLASSIFY LILACS BY THE WISTER COLOR CODE

Many lilacs of various hues defy accurate color classification. Much depends on the soil, weather and at what stage of open florets the color is determined. Many in the classification listing have been poorly determined as to predominant color. We accept them as they are—all are lovely!

LILACS WITH AUTUMN COLORED LEAVES

S. patula (all forms)

S. oblata 'Wildfire'

S. meyeri 'Palibin'

LILACS WITH VARIEGATED OR GOLD LEAVES

S. emodi 'Aurea'

S. tomenella 'Kum-Bum'

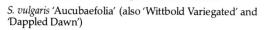

S. villosa 'Aurea'. Fine bloom.

S. vulgaris 'Aucubaefolia' (also 'Wittbold Variegated' and 'Dappled Dawn')

PLATE 3

S. vulgaris, the finest and best known of all the species of lilacs. Today it still can be found growing wild in Yugoslavia, Bulgaria and the mountains of that area of southeastern Europe. Several wild forms of this species have been recorded, called varieties. Many are beautiful in their wild form, but over the centuries in the hands of hybridizers marvelous shrubs of many colors are to be had in the lilacs of today. Pictured below is the wild form of *S. vulgaris* var. *purpurea* described by Weston in 1770. It is probably the most distributed form of the common lilac by nurserymen today.

PLATE 4

Among some of the oldest varieties of S. vulgaris are *S. vulgaris* var. *alba* which in time becomes a huge tree-like shrub with many smaller heads of fragrant blooms. This old centenarian is growing at Grape Hill Gardens lilac collection, Clyde, N.Y..

S. vulgaris var. *rubra* (rosea) described by Loddiges in 1836 certainly existed nearly 50 years before his time and an excellent form of it can be seen in the Governor Wentworth Estate, Portsmouth, New Hampshire.

The twisted ancient trunks of the Wentworth lilacs, probably dating to 1775 or earlier, showing the vine-like, twisting with age and the peeling bark.

S. vulgaris 'Pyrimadalis Alba' one of the earliest named cultivars, a selection from seedlings by Oudin offered in his catalogue in 1845.

PLATE 5

SOME OF THE OLDEST NAMED LILAC CULTIVARS

'Croix de Brahy' (Brahy pre 1850)

Marie Legraye' (Legraye 1840)

'Erzherzog Johann' (Petzold and Kirchner pre 1864)

Languis' (Mako pre 1862)

Gigantea' (Ellwanger 1867)

'Macrostachya'. Very old yet one of the fine light pinks, attributed to Lafievre around 1874.

PLATE 6

S. vulgaris **'Rochester'** (1971). Pre-eminent among white flowering lilacs. Perhaps one of the finest white cultivars ever produced but a very slow grower and difficult to propagate. This magnificent, multipetaled white seedling of 'Edith Cavell' is the work of Alvan Grant. It is an hybridizer's dream that has ushered in a whole new race of heavy textured, multi-petaled lilacs called the 'Rochester Strain'.

PLATE 7

A half-dozen fine white lilacs from Lemoine & Fils that have been around for decades and are still good selections for the garden. The plant of 'Monument' is on the lower right (1934). Photos by C. Holetish, R.B.G.

PLATE 8

SOME OUTSTANDING NEWER SINGLE WHITE LILACS

'Sovietskaya Arktica' (Koles. 1976)

'Slater's Elegance' (Slater 1975)

'Käete Häerlin' (Pfitzer 1910)

'Gertrude Clark' (Fiala 1984)

'Independence' (Fennichia 1987)

PLATE 9

MORE OUTSTANDING WHITE LILACS

'Carley' (Havemeyer 1953)

'Saint Margaret' (Blacklock 1955)

'Mme. Felix' (Felix 1924)

'Souviner de Mme. Louis Giellis' (Giellis 1950)

'Avalanche' (Fiala 1983)

PLATE 10

One of the finest new lilacs, **'Flower City'**, a Rochester Strain Hybrid introduced by the Highland Parks Department of Parks, Rochester, N.Y. in 1983, is the hybridizing work of Richard Fenicchia. A wonderful deep violet, very floriferous and extremely showy, it will be one of the lilacs of the future. The large florets of deep violet have a light silvery reverse. The fine bush form is also shown.

PLATE 11

Many new and improved lilacs in Color Class II (Violet) have been recently introduced. These would be among them. Few new introductions have been made in this color. 'Dr. John Rankin' (Fiala 1979) is a fine single in this class.

'Hosanna' (Fiala 1969)

'Agincourt Beauty' (Slater 1969)

'Marie Marcelin' (Unknown, 1953)

'Marechal Lannes' (Lemoine 1910)

'Lullaby' (Fiala 1983)

PLATE 12

A triumph among blue colored lilacs is **'Dwight D. Eisenhower'** introduced by R. Fenicchia, Rochester Parks, N.Y., in 1968. It is a beautiful pale blue to medium blue, multipetaled 'Rochester Strain' hybrid, ranking among the finest blues thus far produced.

PLATE 13

Five outstanding blue lilacs from Victor Lemoine & Fil—older but still beautiful! Although most of the Lemoine blues were the work of Emile Lemoine, it was his father, Victor, who established the genetic blue line for their breeding. (See chapter on Hybridizers)

'Emile Gentile' 1915. Fine double.

'Jules Simon' 1908. One of Victor Lemoines first double blues.

'Firmament' 1932. Excellent blue single, very blue.

'Ami Schott' 1933. Very blue, heavy double, very beautiful.

'President Grevy' 1886. One of the finest double blues in existence, even today after 100 years!

PLATE 14

Since 1970 many new, truly blue lilacs have been introduced by hybridizers. Most of these are excellent blue lilacs without lavender shades and although difficult, as yet, to obtain they are very worth seeking out by name from nurseries. Other excellent blues are Berdeen's 'Lynette Sirois', 'Irene Berdeen' and 'Kathleen Cowan'.

'Blue Danube' (Fiala 1985) one of the newest is a deep, clear blue, multipetaled 'Rochester Strain' hybrid.

'President Lincoln' (Dunbar 1916) once considered the 'bluest' today is not highly recommended being far surpassed in 'blueness' and because it is such a tall, rampant grower hiding the bloom.

'Margot Grunewald' (Grunewald 1913) is somewhat old but a fine lilac.

'Bluets' (Fiala 1979) is a unique small floret pale blue heavy bloomer.

'Blue Delight' (Castle 1969) is a lavender toned blue.

PLATE 15

Class IV. 'Lilac' colored lilacs is a difficult color in which to find good cultivars. 'Sonnet' (Fiala 1982) is a very heavy bloomer, showy and fragrant. A good grower, it should be better known.

PLATE 16

Color IV—Lilac—is a difficult one in which to find the best flowering cultivars. The finest are among the newest introductions and yet-to-be-named seedlings seen in hybridizer's gardens. Other fine cultivars not pictured include Berdeen's 'Beth Morrison' and 'James Berdeen'. 'Anna Nickels' (Stone) and 'Alice Chieppo' (× hyacinthiflora, Fiala) are excellent cultivars.

'Silver King' (Lemke 1953). A fine cultivar with shades of pale lavender-silver.

'Mollie Ann' (Fiala 1981). A clear color with large heads of bloom, very showy.

An outstanding, still to-be-named 'Rochester Strain' seedling of Richard Fenicchia.

The Chromosome Counts (X) for the Genus *Syringa*

Subgenus *Syringa*   X = 22, 23, 24
    Series *Pinnatifoliae*
        S. pinnatifolia   48 Sax & A. 1932
    Series *Pubescentes*
        S. debelderi   not counted
        S. julianae   not counted
        S. meyeri   46–48 Sax & A. 1932
        S. microphylla   48 Taylar 1945
        S. patula   46 Sax & A. 1932
        S. potaninii   46 Taylor 1945
        S. pubescens   48 Sax & A. 1932
    Series *Vulgares*
        S. laciniata   44 Sax & A. 1932
        S. oblata   46 Taylor 1945
        S. vulgaris   46,47,48 Taylor 1945
        S. X *chinensis*   not counted
        S. X *hyacinthiflora*   not counted
        S. X *persica*   44 Sax & A. 1932
    Series *Villosae*
        S. emodi   44 Tischler 1930
        S. josikaea   46,48 Sax & A. 1932
        S. komarowii   46,48 Sax & A. 1932
        S. reflexa   46 Taylor 1945
        S. sweginzowii   46 Taylor 1945
        S. tigerstedtii   46 Pringle 1979
        S. tomentella   46,48 Sax & A. 1932
        S. villosa   46,48 Sax & A. 1932
        S. wolfii   46 Sax 1930
        S. yunnanensis   48 Sax 1930
        S. X *prestoniae*   not counted
    Interseries hybrid *S.* X *diversifolia*   not counted
Subgenus *Ligustrina*
        S. pekinensis   not counted
        S. reticulata   46 Sax & A. 1932

Classification of Lilac by Season of Bloom

To plan a garden wisely a knowledge of the season of bloom of each plant is required. Various Lilac species bloom for a combined period of about 6 weeks in an ordinary season. A very warm spring will, however, bring out flowers ahead of schedule which will remain in bloom for about 4 weeks rather than 6. Bloom also depends upon the climatic conditions in which they are grown. Spring in North America (Canada and the United States) is vernal-centrifugal; that is, springtime begins in the center of the continent continuing outward to both coasts. Likewise it travels from South to North and upward from the valleys to the mountains. Thus those living in Iowa will have lilacs in full bloom whereas in New England they are still in tight bud and will bloom a month later. In the mid-states bloomtime begins in mid-April and continues to the end of May; on the eastern coast it begins in later May and extends into June. On the West Coast the period of bloom starts in early May as in England. In Europe, May is lilac time. In mountainous areas spring is toward the end of May or early June.

Despite the intricacies of the seasons, once growing lilacs begin to bloom, they do so according to a fairly reliable pattern typical for each species. Bear in mind that the longest blooming species is *S. vulgaris*, cultivars of which are early, midseason, or late-midseason bloomers. Depending on the coolness of the weather each lilac species can be expected to have a real show of color for from 16–20 days (from full bud color to fading florets). This is quite a long season of bloom for a shrub. It is possible with thoughtful planning to have some lilacs in full bloom for at least 6 weeks. If one has only a small garden the pleasure of a single lilac blooming is well worth its care and planting.

Early Blooming Species or Selected Cultivars
S. oblata and its forms *S. oblata dilatata, alba, donaldii* and *S. oblata* 'Giraldii'
S. hyacinthiflora (the Early Hybrids of *S. vulgaris* × *S. oblata*)
S. vulgaris 'Rhodopea' (the early woods lilac)
S. pinnatifolia (bridges the early and midseasons)

Midseason Blooming Lilacs
S. vulgaris and its cultivars (bloom over a period of a month depending on cultivar)
S. × *chinensis* (hybrids between *S. laciniata* × *S. vulgaris*)
S. julianae and its cultivars
S. laciniata and its hybrids (*S.* × *chinensis* × *S.* × *persica*)
S. meyeri
S. microphylla
S. debelderi
S. × *persica* (hybrid between *S. vulgaris* or *S. oblata* × *S. laciniata*)
S. pinnatifolia (and its hybrid *S.* × *diversifolia, S. pinnatifolia* × *S. oblata*)
S. potaninii
S. pubescens
S. patula

Late Blooming Lilacs
S. emodi
S. × *henryi* (*S. josikaea* × *S. villosa*)
S. × *henryi* × *S. tomentella*
S. × *josiflexa* (*S. josikaea* × *S. reflexa*)
S. julianae and its hybrids *S.* × *julianae* × *S. microphylla*
S. komarowii and its hybrids (*S. komarowii* ×*S. wolfii*) × (*S. yunnanensis* × *S. wolfii*)
S. × *nanceiana* hybrid (*S. josikaea* × *S. villosa*) × *S. sweginzowii*)
S. × *prestoniae* (*S. reflexa* × *S. villosa*)
S. × *quatrobrida* hybrids of (*S. komarowii* × *S. wolfii*) × (*S. sweginzowii* × *S. yunnanensis*)
S. reflexa and its hybrids *S.* × *swegiflexa* (*S. reflexa* × *S. sweginzowii*)
S. sweginzowii and its hybrid *S. sweginzowi* 'Albida'
S. tigerstedtii and its hybrids
S. tomentella and its hybrid *S. tomentella* × *S.* × *prestoniae*
S. villosa and its hybrids *S.* × *prestoniae* and *S. villosa* × *S. sweginzowii*
S. wolfii and its hybrids and quatrobrids, quintobrids
S. yunnanensis and its hybrids *S. yunnanensis* × *S. wolfii, S. yunnanensis* × *S. tomentella*

Very Late Blooming Lilacs
There are a very few of the multibrids that bloom very late (and somewhat sparingly) but the tree lilacs are the last of the lilacs to bloom
S. pekinensis
S. reticulata and its variety *amurensis.*

Many of the species are not readily available, or are obtainable only from an arboretum or a special private collection. Most of the complex species hybrids are unobtainable but some day the best of these will find their way into our gardens. (*Bon jardinier,* because a plant has several different kinds of grandparents does not make it a prince! *S. vulgaris* still reigns supreme in lilacdom!)

In bloom many of the species are rather insignificant, although several are really outstanding, whereas some are not worth planting in the smaller garden and should be reserved only for the largest arboreta and historical or botanical collections of hybridizers. We have listed elsewhere the really exceptional species that are most worthy of garden space. Among the late blooming lilacs so many are quite similar that one or two suffice to represent the group in any ordinary garden.

The Fragrances of Lilacs

Fragrance is an elusive factor, very individual, emotionally colored by related experiences and extremely subtle in its presence—from highly penetrating and noticeable to distant and elusive. The fragrance of lilacs is generally considered to be that extremely pleasing scent of *S. vulgaris*. It is THE fragrant lilac above all, the best known of all lilac scents, the most cherished from early childhood memories and the one most people seek in planting lilacs. Although several of the lilac species have unique and pleasing fragrances, none can equal that of *S. vulgaris*, the common lilac. It is a strong fragrance yet not overpowering.

Not all the *S. vulgaris* cultivars are equally fragrant, in fact some of the most recently developed and largest florets are only faintly scented. The old, common lilac, *S. vulgaris purpurea* is outstanding in fragrance. Many of the older cultivars are more strongly scented than the newer doubles and latest introductions. Perhaps a special fragrance in flowers is a means of attracting insects for pollination. Could it be that in the newer, much larger flowered cultivars, color and size have gradually replaced fragrance as the attractant? However, there are new cultivars that are strongly scented and if you are demanding about fragrance, you had better investigate as to the scent of the lilac you purchase. How often one hears, "But they don't smell as strongly as the old lilacs did!"

S. oblata has a fragrance very similar to that of *S. vulgaris*, although it is not as strongly scented. Most of the Early Hybrids, *S. vulgaris* × *S. oblata*, have pleasing fragrance. To determine personal preferences, visit a nearby lilac collection or arboretum not only to see the lilacs in bloom but to smell them as well. In this way you are certain to have a cultivar pleasingly fragrant to you.

Several species have noticeable fragrance although very unlike that of *S. vulgaris*. Most of the Chinese species have a delightful spicy, cinnamon or oriental scent. *S. patula* has an excellent fragrance, not overpowering yet captivating and pleasing; *S. sweginzowii* and its hybrid *S.* × *sweginzowii* 'Albida' have an aromatic, spicy scent; *S. pubescens* is another oriental fragrance of spicy clove; *S. julianae* has its own sweet spicy scent; *S. microphylla* is somewhat similar yet less pronounced; Joseph Hers called *S. meyeri* 'very scented' whereas we find it only faintly so; McKelvey states that all the lilacs in series *villosae* are 'virtually odorless or rather ill-scented', others find them uniquely subdued, somewhat musk-like spicy to displeasing. *S. tigerstedtii* has a 'fragrance well developed, similar to that of carnations but spicier' (Smith 1948).

In the Subgenus *Ligustrinae*, the tree lilacs, both *S. pekinensis* and *S. reticulata* have a very similar fragrance. McKelvey prefers the scent of *S. pekinensis* as 'pleasing'. Both have a spicy musk-like scent, agreeable to some and not to others.

One should have both *S. vulgaris* and some of its more fragrant Chinese cousins in the garden to appreciate the differences in lilac fragrances. Each is unique and pleasing in its own way. (*Bon jardinier*, have you ever heard of *Grandames* and *belles* limiting themselves to only one fragrance? The lilacs have outdone them all!)

The Hardiness of Lilacs

Lilacs are shrubs of the colder climates. They revel in cold winters but there is a limit to their ability to endure extreme cold. They grow ideally in hardiness zones 3, 4 and 5 and reasonable well in the milder sections of zone 2. They will do fairly well in the colder regions of zones 6 and 7. The warmer zones 8 and 9 appear too tropical for lilacs, although they have been reported to bloom well in Houston, Texas and seem to grow but not bloom well in the northern parts of interior Florida (Gainesville). Their buds need some weeks of frost or drought to set them well for bloom. On occasion I have seen a specimen of *S.* × *persica* in the south and a few *S. reticulata* (Tree Lilacs). How well they bloom I cannot attest. It may be that some of the species like *S. patula* 'Palibin' or *S. potaninii*, *S. julianae* or *S. oblata* have not been sufficiently tried in the warmer areas. Some of the species exhibiting more intermittent blooming, such as *S. microphylla*, *S. potaninii* and *S. pubescens* might be candidates for southerly regions. These intermittent bloomers apparently do not need a dormant period to flower. It may be that in warmer latitudes they require far more water and heavily enriched soils than are generally available.

Lilacs do best, however, in the colder zones. There they are exceptional! Although they can withstand wintery cold, even to −35–40°F., they do need protection from wind-chill that can kill flowering buds. Too frequently lilacs are planted in sites where wet autumns leave them in a water pocket freezing them in blocks of ice. This they will not tolerate; frozen ground yes, but not frozen in ice. Come spring they will have died.

Some of the later blooming species are reputed to be less hardy than *S. vulgaris*. This may be so but they usually require a sandy-gravel soil rather than the heavier soil congenial to *S. vulgaris,* hence they freeze out in extremely cold weather. One must visit local lilac collections and arboreta to ascertain what species will withstand the climate of a particular area. Lilacs on their own root system are far more hardy than those grafted on privet stock.

In the mid-western U.S. (around Ohio, Michigan, Indiana, Illinois) lilacs have withstood temperatures in winters that have plunged to −40°F. and bloomed very well in the spring. They are an exceedingly hardy shrub and mostly bloom very well annually. It is a constant wind-chill factor that kills and desiccates flower buds when below that temperature.

At Ocala, Florida, I have tried to grow lilacs but there does not appear to be a sufficient number of frost days for them to set good flowering buds. *S. oblata,* once established in good ground and with sufficient water does manage to grow but blooms sparingly; *S. julianae* grows fairly well when once established (2 years) and blooms sufficiently to merit growing it—good enriched ground and sufficient water in the springtime are a necessity. I believe that some hybridizer using the new form of *oblata* var. *donaldii* with its enormous leaves that are as thick as leather will develop a whole new strain of lilacs that will grow and bloom heavily in southern regions. Selected cultivars of *S. vulgaris* appear to grow but do not bloom at this Florida location. For a hybridizer for the southern lilacs the *S. oblata* and the little-leaved species appear to be the most promising.

CHAPTER TWO

The Lilac Species from Europe

In presenting the individual species of *Syringa* we have chosen to discuss first the two species native to Europe, *S. vulgaris* and *S. josikaea. S. vulgaris*, the familiar Common Lilac is widely cherished as a garden shrub. Its history and characteristics are here described. No other species has been so extensively developed and been the source of so many named cultivars and specialized flower forms. The principal cultivars are described in a later chapter on Color in Lilacs. Also in this chapter we shall discuss the other, rather new, *Syringa josikaea* as the only other lilac species found in Europe. In a later chapter we shall consider the lilacs native to China, Japan, India, and Korea.

E. H. Wilson writing on the 'History and Distribution of the Lilacs' in Susan McKelvey's definitive monograph, *THE LILAC* (1928), gives an interesting account of origins of the then estimated 28 lilac species. He writes:

> Lilacs are an Old World group of shrubs and small trees confined with two exceptions to Asia and have no representatives in the New World. All the species are continental but one variety of Tree Lilac (*S. amurensis* var. *japonica*) is found on the islands of Japan, and *S. velutina (S. patula)* occurs on Dagelet Island in the Japan Sea.... Of the twenty-eight species recognized in the work two (*S. vulgaris* and *S. josikaea*) are found in central and south-eastern Europe; two (*S. emodi* and *S. afghanica*) occur in the Himalayas; two species (*S. velutina* and *S. wolfii*) of true lilacs, together with the variety *dilatata* of *S. oblata* and two Tree Lilacs (*S. amurensis* and *S. fauriei*) are indigenous in Korea and six species of true lilacs together with two varieties of the Tree Lilac (*S. pekinensis*) are found in northern China. From this analysis it would appear that western China is the headquarters of the genus but in this connection it must be remembered that a number of species from that region are little known and when properly understood it may be necessary to reduce the number. (op. cit. p. 3)

A remarkable piece of lilac information from a very knowledgeable man who spent most of his active life exploring for plants in China. Today, as Wilson predicted, the number of species has been reduced from his 28 to 23. It is still possible that in the vastness of western China there are some undiscovered native species. Two new species were discovered only a few years ago, in the mountains of South Korea.

Syringa vulgaris (The Common Lilac) Its Origins and History

Syringa vulgaris growing native in the Balkans, in Yugoslavia, Moldovia, and especially common in Serbia and Macedonia and throughout southeastern Europe, is represented by a number of unique subspecies to which little attention has been paid until most recent times. Mato Jurkovic (Dept. of Botany, University of Zagreb, Yugoslavia) draws attention to these subspecies, noting that the geological substratum upon which lilacs grow often greatly influenced their varietal differences. Grebenscikov (1963) states, ". . . the substratum is almost exclusively limestone and related stones, but sporadic cases of the occurrence of lilac have been noticed on conglomerate and on serpentine." The most recent studies of Jovanovic and Vukicevic in 1980 on the variability of the lilac in its natural habitats in Yugoslavia (Serbia—the Ibar River Ravine) where this species occurs on serpentine, describe new varieties of *S. vulgaris*. According to these authors, the specific ecological factors of that region, above all serpentine, have affected the ecological and morphological differentiation of *S. vulgaris* in comparison with the same species appearing in regions of limestone bedrock. They described 4 new subspecies of *S. vulgaris* in 1980.

Thus the recognized subspecies of *S. vulgaris* are the following:

Syringa vulgaris Linnaeus 1753
var. *vulgaris*
var. *alba* Weston 1770
var. *brevilaciniata* Jovanovic & Vukicevic 1980
var. *coerulea* Weston 1770
var. *forsythiodes* Jovanovic & Vukicevic 1980
var. *hyacinthoides* Jovanovic & Vukicevic 1980
var. *macrantha* Borbas 1882
var. *parviflora* Jovanovic & Vukicevic 1980
var. *pulchella* Velenovsky 1894
var. *purpurea* Weston 1770
var. *rhodopea* Velenovsky 1922
var. *rubra* Loddiges 1836
var. *transsilvanica* Schur 1866
var. *violacea* Aiton 1789

Taxonomists may differ on accepting all these subspecies of *S. syringa,* but I list them all for their botanical value and citation to be complete. Undoubtedly much genetic potential is contained in them for hybridizers to recombine with *S. oblata* and with newer forms of *S. vulgaris* (*Mon ami,* no one person can do it all, we must leave some things for future generations of hydbridizers!)

It was not until 1828 that the actual home of the Lilac, *S. vulgaris,* was positively identified. Anton Rochel, writing of the rare plants of Banat, in western Romania, noted lilacs growing among limestone rocks in the Alibek Mountains. Heuffel corroborated these findings in 1831, extending the lilac's native habitat to include the valley of the Czerna, Mt. Domaglett and the rocky banks along the Danube River at the military boundaries of Moldovia, Szaszka, Csiklova and Krassova. This was, as far as can be ascertained, their native land. (Although some few still claim that lilacs were the children of the cold and desolate ranges of Afghanistan and Turkey where they bedecked the festivals of robber chiefs—but this be legend!)

S. vulgaris growing naturalized on rocks in Sarajeva (Bistrik), Bosnia, Yugoslavia. (Photo Karl Maly, courtesy Archives of Arnold Arboretum.)

Centuries before the plant explorations of Rochel and Heuffel, the lilac was probably grown by local mountain herdsmen to add a touch of beauty to their otherwise drab living conditions. From these peasant homes of central Europe with their colorful spring festivals, lilacs were taken to the garden courts of Istanbul. It was from Istanbul that the Flemish scholar and traveler, Ogier Ghiselin, Count de Busbecq and Ambassador of Ferdinand I of Austria to the court of Suleyman the Magnificent, brought back to Vienna in his baggage in 1563, gifts from the Sultan's gardens. Among them was a plant called the 'lilac'. Planted in Busbecq's Viennese garden on the Bastei, the 'Lilak' or 'Turkischer Holler', as the Austrians called the lilac, attracted much attention. There the lilac bloomed for the first time in western Europe. To Ogier Ghiselin, man of gentle learning, Count, connoisseur of beauty, we owe the wisdom of again packing in his baggage in 1570 a shoot of his lilac as he, now Curator of the Imperial Court Library, prepared to accompany the Archduchesse Elizabeth from Vienna to Paris where she became the wife and queen of Charles IX of France. De Busbecq never returned to Vienna but remained in France until his death in 1592. Meanwhile his beloved lilac began to fill the gardens of Paris and be loved as the lilacs of France. They had made the long journey twice in his baggage—from Istanbul to Vienna and again from Vienna to Paris!

The Coming of Age of the Lilac in Europe   (The First White and Deep Purple Lilacs)

Beside the wild blue-flowered lilac, two color variants sprang up in European gardens; a white flowered form with olive buds and paler foliage, and a taller growing purple-flowered sort with somewhat larger petals. Literature does not provide a record of their origins, only the gardens in which they grew. Residents of Central Europe claim a wild form of the white-flowering lilac, but it appears to be known only as a cultivated plant. It is further believed that the first white lilacs were quite unlike the pure whites of today. They were instead, a milky or silvery color "which is a kinde of white, wherein is a thinne wash, or light shew of blew shed therein, coming somewhat neare unto an ash-color" (Parkinson, 1629). Some time after 1800 commercial flower and ornamental horticulture growers focused their attention on improving the lilac using these variants. Loddiges lists a large flowered 'Alba Major' lilac in his catalogue in 1826, while in the same year Noisette speaks of a 'white lilac'. In 1831 Audibert lists an 'Alba Grandiflora' which became widely cultivated. Ten years later Oudin lists the 'Alba Virginalis' with beautiful, white flowers in fragrant, dense clusters. Four years later he offered a lilac with long conical thyrses of white flowers called 'Pyramidalis Alba'.

The first white lilac raised by crossing named parents is 'Louise Marie', named for the Belgian Queen in 1851 and grown by Monsieur Brahy of Hostal near Liege.

A second variant, the deep purple lilac, was first grown by James Sutherland in the Edinburgh medicinal garden in 1683 and was, therefore, called the 'Scotch Lilac'. In France this dark flowered lilac first grew in the Chateau de Marly gardens at Marly-le-Roi in 1808 and became known as 'Lilas de Marly'. The history of this dark lilac is difficult to trace because the description of color in lilacs was not yet standardized. Moreover, it was not until recent times that lilac colors have possessed 'substance', that is, resistance to fading in strong sunlight. (There is a very pale lavender-white lilac known today as 'Marlyensis Pallida' which should not be confused with the deep purple 'Marlyensis' or 'Marly Lilac'.)

The first lilac of deep purple to bear a distinguished name was Audibert's selection named 'Charles X' to honor the then recently-abdicated French king who had survived the Revolution, the Consulate, The Empire, only to yield his throne after six years (1824–1830) to Louis Philippe, the 'Citizen King'. This 'ancient' reddish-purple lilac had always been very popular. It became the seed parent in the first recorded cross between lilacs made by the Belgian, Brahy. In 1840 he pollinated it with Noisette's white and raised 7 seedlings which he released over the following decade through the Luxembourg nursery of August Wilhelm. Brahy's lilacs were "Croix de Brahy', a clear rose in 1853; 'Charlemagne', a rose-lilac in 1854; 'Ekenholm', a delicate blue-lilac also in 1854; 'Princess Camille de Rohan', a pure clear rose in 1856; 'Archduchesse Charlotte', a magnificent rose in 1861; 'Duchesse de Brabant', a clear rose in 1861 and 'Louise Marie', a pure milky-white in 1861. Lilacs were beginning to take names, and very famous ones at that!

Meanwhile the old-fashioned 'Lilas de Marley', also known as 'Marlyensis' or 'Marly Flieder', although not distinct from the common purple *S. vulgaris* var. *purpurea* of Richard Weston's recording, over the years produced some notable progeny: 'Philemon' introduced by Pierre Cochet of Grisy Suisnes, France (1840); 'Dr. Nobbe' named by Moritz Eichler, Chemnitz, Saxony (1862); 'James Booth', 'Moritz Eichler' and 'Professor E. Stoeckhardt' all introduced the same year in 1862 by M. Eichler.

How Lilacs Became French Aristocrats

For the next three-quarters of a century (1878 to 1950) the nursery of Victor Lemoine *et fils*, at Nancy in the Province of Lorraine, France, continued the work of seriously hybridizing the lilac. The number of cultivars available to Victor Lemoine was small indeed, perhaps no more than six dozen. Only about 10 cultivars were the product of hybridization, the rest were chance seedlings, many quite similar. There was, however, one lilac which Victor Lemoine's plant genius picked out to be the 'cornerstone' of his remarkable breeding program. It was a natural sport raised in 1843 by Monsieur Libert of Liege, which bore a second corolla, one inside the other, making it the first and only double lilac and which since has been called 'Azurea Plena'.

The alert Victor Lemoine bought his plant specimen of this double lilac from Augustin Wilhelm. What a marvelous plant it turned out to be in the hands of Victor's skillful genius and that of his wife. Madame Lemoine, because her eyesight was far better and her fingers more nimble, perched high on a ladder, did the actual hybridizing under the careful direction of her husband. Together they established a whole new race of magnificent, double-flowering lilacs of indescribable beauty and color. Because of this monumental success in changing the 'ordinary' lilac into French belles, countessas, princesses and nobility, with every color-hue in lilacs, they became known as 'French Lilacs'. Lemoine's continuous stream of new lilacs named after famous personages dominated the lilac and plant world from 1878 to 1950. What marvelous work in hybridizing came forth from the genius of the Victor Lemoines and their son, Emile! To date it has been unsurpassed in lilacdom!

Versatility and the ability to adapt to new countries and climates are inherent in the common lilac. Before Victor Lemoine began his famous lilac breeding program, the plant had already spread throughout Europe. It was brought to the Russian Court by French princesses and travelers. There it found a welcome home very much to its liking in both the Russian soil and climate, and so prospered. Decades later a Russian hybridist, Leonid Kolesnikov, was to continue Lemoine's work with outstanding success.

How Lilacs Came to America

Lilacs were growing in America long before they were mentioned in the literature. Many of the oldest plants are not recorded in manuscripts but attest to their age by their gnarled trunks. Lilacs were brought by the very earliest settlers to the colonies, both in the United States and Canada. The first were probably brought by the Dutch and French who so loved them in their native land where they grew better than in England, although the English colonists also dearly cherished the common lilac. Their sturdiness fitted them to withstand the long sea voyage. The lilac has always been an ideal traveler, ever ready to be off on a new journey, needing little care and only remote concern. Once planted it could fend for itself and readily withstand the severe cold. Lilacs became perfect settlers in the new homeland of North America.

By 1652 lilacs were commonly grown all over the colonies (refer to Miss Harriet Keeler, *Our Northern Shrubs*). In 1753 we read of Collinson sending lilacs to John Bartram who complains to him. . . . "(lilacs) are already too numerous, as roots brought by the early settlers have spread enormously". (Asa Gray Bulletin III, 15, 1895) Two plantings can boast of having the oldest living lilacs in North America. The first is the Governor Wentworth Lilacs planted in Portsmouth, New Hampshire. These are among the oldest, having been planted around 1750—and still growing strongly today. They are massive old trees, gnarled and twisted with the centuries!

The other example is the group of equally old and more massive lilac patriarchs growing in Mackinac Island, Michigan. Again, their old trunks and age are sure guarantee that they have been around for centuries. Their trunks are much larger than the Wentworth Lilacs. The Mackinacs ('Meche-ne-mock-i-nog' in Indian meaning the 'Hump of the Great Turtle') are reputed to have been planted by French Jesuit missionaries working in the area as early as 1650. The first permanent white settler was a Frenchman Nicolet in 1634. In 1948 Professor LaRue, University of Michigan, made a documented study of the size of these lilac giants. Some trunks measured over 20 inches in diameter. The largest of all these *S. vulgaris* measured 23.6 inches in diameter, with several at 21.8, 20.3, 19.2 and 18.3. These would appear to be the largest in diameter of any living lilacs officially measured. It is well known they were already large trees and growing in 1760. They are truly the 'giants' of *S. vulgaris*. Do not discount their age! Susan Delano McKelvey in her monograph *THE LILAC* gives detailed citations of the lilac in America covering many pages. It is a most comprehensive survey of written evidence on the lilac. Strangely she failed to even mention these ancient giant lilacs of Mackinac Islands and many of the very old lilacs growing for centuries in historic new England towns. Obviously she was somehow not aware of them.

In 1767 Thomas Jefferson wrote . . . "planted lilacs, Spanish broom, Umbrella and laurel . . ." His lilacs do not exist today. While in 1785 George Washington recorded . . . "March 3, Thursday, Likewise took up the clumps of lilacs that stood at the corner of the South Grass plot and transplanted them to the clusters in the shrubberies and standards at the South gate." These, too, are long since gone! Undoubtedly there are family diaries and accounts which have never been made public that include mention of the lilac fellow-traveler and how it came to be so universally planted so early throughout the new land.

As early as 1800, possibly earlier, Prince Nursery, Flushing, Long Island, N.Y., offered lilacs for sale. This nursery, founded in 1737, claimed to have the largest number of rare and new plant introductions directly imported from China (McGourt 1967). It is also most probable that Colonel James L. Warren, who had previously operated the Nonantum Vale Nursery near Brighton, Massachusetts, and who arrived in San Francisco on the ship 'Sweden' in 1849, brought with him

S. vulgaris var. *violacea* forms a magnificent specimen over 100 years old, planted by William Roggenkemp at the Wishart Homestead 'Lilacland' at Bennet, Nebraska. (Photo Lourene Roggenkemp Bratt Wishart.)

lilacs for the new nursery he came to establish, James L. Warren & Sons of Sacramento and San Francisco. Certainly lilacs were growing well in California Territory long before its statehood in 1850. (Butterfield 1966).

Arrive they did, in good style and health and their progeny crossed mountains and rivers. Wrapped in burlap and wet straw, they were stowed in the wagons of immigrants on the 'Westward Ho!' march. Throughout the northern tier of states and settlements and on into western Canada, everywhere they left their progeny to grow and prosper. By saddlebag and stage; they became kin to log cabins and sod shelters, perfumed the valleys of the Rockies, pressed onward to Oregon and Washington and the colder mountain regions of California setting strong roots in a new and wonderful land! Their expansion to the newly opened lands of the West was simply their continued long trek from their homeland in Central Europe, to Istanbul and the Middle East, then back to Europe, France, Germany, England and the vast country of Russia and then onward to North America!

Floret Formation and Structure in *Syringa vulgaris* and its Hybrids

(In a monograph on the *LILACS OF LILACIA PARK AND MORTON ARBORETUM* some decades ago, Joseph Dvorak, Jr., compared *Syringa vulgaris* cultivars by floret form and thyrse structures with remarkable artistry. Permission has been granted by Mr. Dvorak to reproduce some of his magnificent line drawings in this book, for which we are grateful.)

S. vulgaris is the most showy and truly the 'Queen' of all the lilac species. No other species of lilacs has had such attention paid to selection for unusual colorations, different floret forms or diversity of structures nor has any other species had so many named cultivars propagated. It is the common lilac, *S. vulgaris,* that first comes to mind whenever we speak of lilacs. To acquaint those who love lilacs with this great diversity of bloom no better guide can be provided than the line drawings of Dvorak. Study the floret structures and begin to realize the marvels contained in the lilac's flower—then add the colors, blends and hues and the maddening fragrance! Then you can begin to appreciate *S. vulgaris,* the 'common' lilac!

The newest floret form added to the lilac by hybridization. It is a single yet multipetaled floret. Seedlings of 'Rochester', which is the genetic transmitter of this floret trait, often have several petals on one floret rather than the usual four. It is a highly desirable addition for it adds considerably to the total color mass of the thyrse. Several of these new 'multipetaled', often called 'primula flowered', lilacs have been introduced. All are exceedingly beautiful!

TYPES OF FLORETS

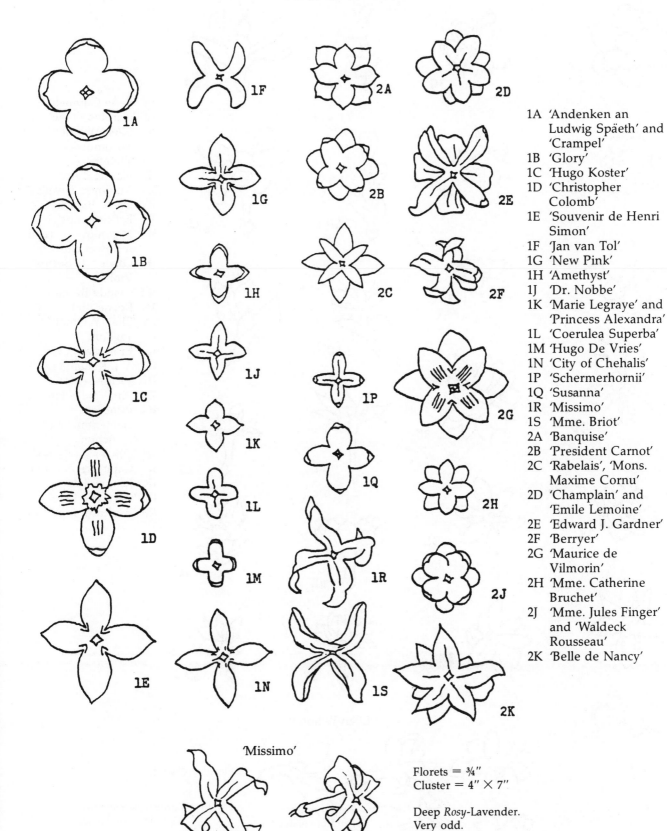

1A 'Andenken an
  Ludwig Späeth' and
  'Crampel'
1B 'Glory'
1C 'Hugo Koster'
1D 'Christopher
  Colomb'
1E 'Souvenir de Henri
  Simon'
1F 'Jan van Tol'
1G 'New Pink'
1H 'Amethyst'
1J 'Dr. Nobbe'
1K 'Marie Legraye' and
  'Princess Alexandra'
1L 'Coerulea Superba'
1M 'Hugo De Vries'
1N 'City of Chehalis'
1P 'Schermerhornii'
1Q 'Susanna'
1R 'Missimo'
1S 'Mme. Briot'
2A 'Banquise'
2B 'President Carnot'
2C 'Rabelais', 'Mons.
  Maxime Cornu'
2D 'Champlain' and
  'Emile Lemoine'
2E 'Edward J. Gardner'
2F 'Berryer'
2G 'Maurice de
  Vilmorin'
2H 'Mme. Catherine
  Bruchet'
2J 'Mme. Jules Finger'
  and 'Waldeck
  Rousseau'
2K 'Belle de Nancy'

'Missimo'

Florets = ¾"
Cluster = 4" × 7"

Deep *Rosy*-Lavender.
Very odd.

TYPES OF FLORETS

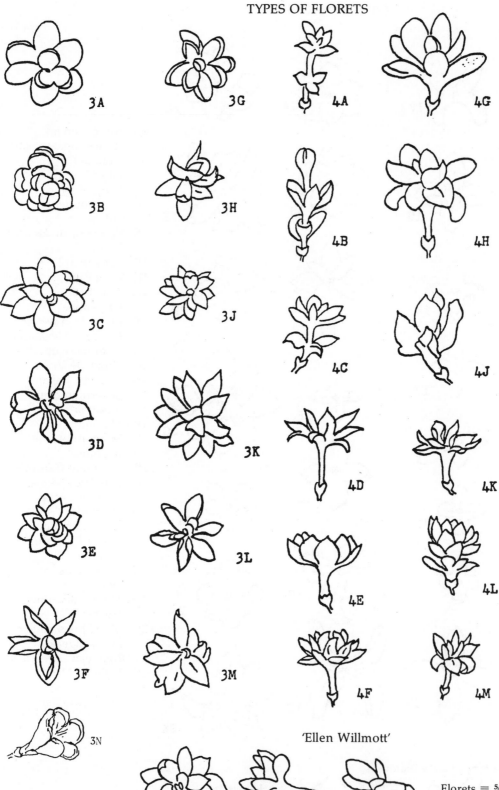

3A 'Leon Gambetta'
3B 'Carolyne Mae'
3C 'Ellen Willmott' and 'Maximowicz'
3D 'Violetta'
3E 'Jeanne d'Arc'
3F 'Alphonse Lavallee'
3G 'Dame Blanche'
3H 'LePrintemps'
3J 'Maximowicz' (end of flower cluster)
3K 'Olivier de Serres'
3L 'Violetta'
3M 'Claude Bernard'
3N 'Rochester'
4A 'Ellen Willmott'
4B 'Taglioni'
4C 'Professor E. Wilson'
4D 'A. J. Kettenberg'
4E 'Victor Lemoine'
4F 'Mme. Jules Finger'
4G 'Princess Clementine' and 'Planchon'
4H 'Olivier de Serres'
4J 'Capitaine Perrault'
4K 'Jeanne d'Arc'
4L 'Carolyne Mae'
4M 'Professor E. Wilson'

'Ellen Willmott'

This type often at end of cluster

Florets = ⅝"–¾"

2 + to 3 Corollas; sometimes triple Hose-in-Hose.
White.
Whiter than Mme. Lemoine.

TYPES OF CLUSTERS

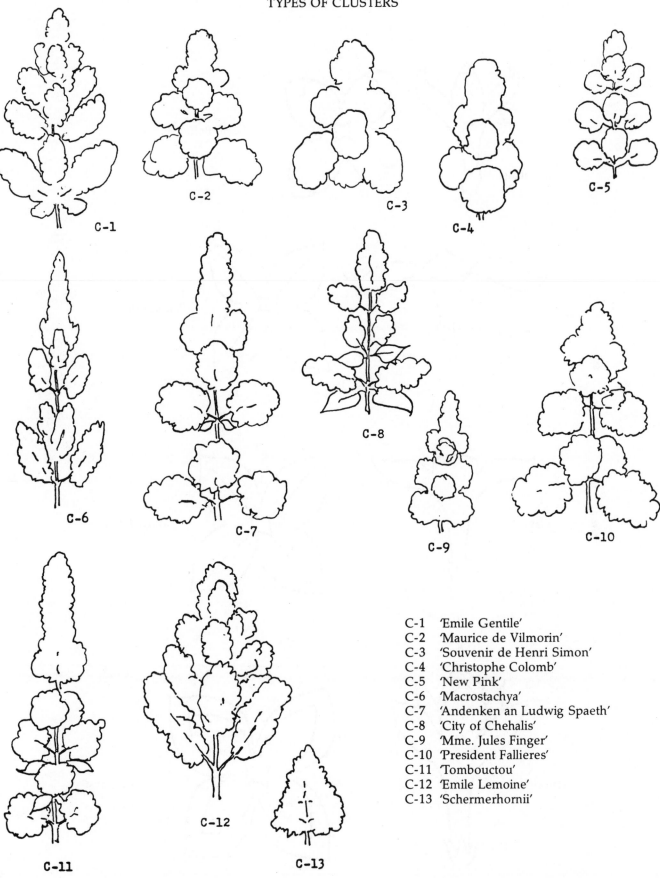

C-1   'Emile Gentile'
C-2   'Maurice de Vilmorin'
C-3   'Souvenir de Henri Simon'
C-4   'Christophe Colomb'
C-5   'New Pink'
C-6   'Macrostachya'
C-7   'Andenken an Ludwig Spaeth'
C-8   'City of Chehalis'
C-9   'Mme. Jules Finger'
C-10   'President Fallieres'
C-11   'Tombouctou'
C-12   'Emile Lemoine'
C-13   'Schermerhornii'

TYPES OF FLOWER

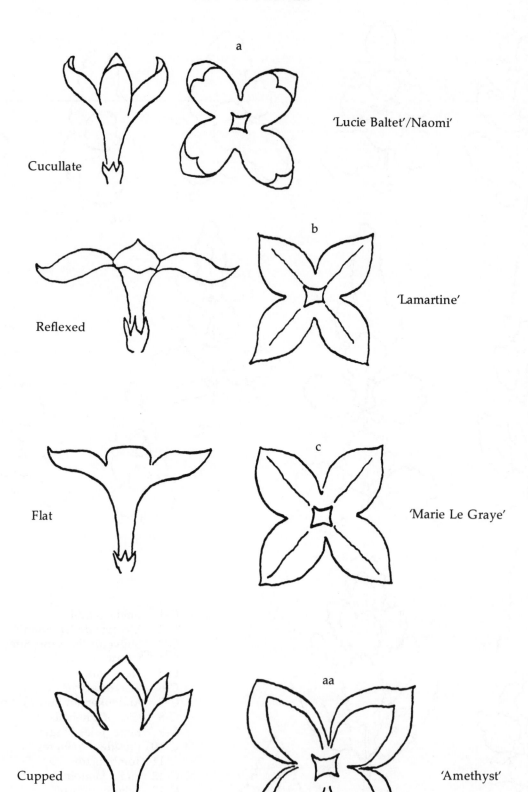

Cucullate

a

'Lucie Baltet'/Naomi'

Reflexed

b

'Lamartine'

Flat

c

'Marie Le Graye'

Cupped

aa

'Amethyst'

Syringa josikaea The Hungarian Lilac

Only two lilac species are native to Europe. The home of *S. vulgaris*, as previously noted, is in the Balkan Mountain regions of Romania, Yugoslavia and Moldovia, while the native land of *S. josikaea* appears to be in the nearby mountain country of Transylvania, more specifically what is today parts of Hungary, Czechoslovakia, Romania and Yugoslavia, some of which was formerly the Imperial Nation of Hungary or the Austro-Hungarian Empire. The roots of *S. josikaea* lie mostly in today's nations of Hungary and Romania.

S. josikaea appears to have been discovered and known by the Hungarian botanist, Paul Kitaibel, who lived from 1757 to 1817. In an undated manuscript (probably circa 1800) he states . . . "I have named temporarily so that it be not lost from memory a lilac, *S. prunifolia*, that grows along the roadside from Munkacs to Lemberg, in the county of Bereg, between Hrabonitza and Pudolocz, and according to Dr. Bulla, having leaves distinctively like those of the *Prunus*." Botanically this does not appear to have been an adequate description, so the credit for discovering this species of lilac goes to Rosalia, Baroness von Josika, nee Countess Czaky, an ardent and knowledgeable botanist, who discovered plants of this species growing on her estate in Kolosvar, Hungary (Now known as Cluj and in Romania) in 1826.

It was from plants sent by the Baroness that Baron Joseph Franz Jacquin, a botanist, first described botanically and named this species as *Syringa josikaea* before a meeting of the German Naturalists in Hamburg, September 30, 1830. Jacquin's description came from seeing several plants sent by the Baroness to the gardens of the Imperial and Royal University in Vienna, one of which bloomed for the first time in May of 1830. (Kitaibel's unpublished manuscript in the Hungarian Museum, Budapest was sent there sometime between 1800 and 1810. His name of *S. prunifolia* would certainly have been a far better botanical name for this lovely lilac.) In all honesty the Baroness von Josika only popularized a native lilac that was already well known among the regional botanists. To her must be given the credit of collecting specimens of this lilac and seeing to their distribution to botanists in other countries and calling attention to it as a species native to her country. *S. josikaea* was at one time also described under the name of *S. vincetoxifolia* at an even earlier date than Kitaibel's work in another unpublished manuscript of Baumgarten (Steudel). (*Mon ami*, who is to say who deserves to be honored in the naming of this fine species? Certainly we are happy the name *S. vincetoxifolia* did not prevail!)

Baron Joseph Jacquin described the new lilac as . . ."shrubs cultivated in our garden 4–5 feet tall, upright, branchy, the lowest part of the trunk has a smooth gray bark, the branches are terete, stiff, slightly reddish with white spots, and the younger one somewhat pubescent. The leaves are opposite and spreading, somewhat fleshy, oval, cuneate at the base and acuminate at the apex, 3–4 inches long, 2 inches or less wide, on the upper surface a saturated green, on the under-side blue-green, on both sides, however, glabrous, rugose and wrinkled, sinuated at the margins, otherwise entire; the petioles are ½ inch long, canaliculate and reddish-purple. The flower grows on the ends of branches in panicles which are a foot long, straight, stiff, and not thickly flowered; the individual peduncles and pedicles are opposite or decussate, and each is supported by a persistent heart-shaped bract, soft haired, and similar to the leaves only much smaller. The color of the flowers is blue-violet, similar to that of *S. × chinensis*, and almost wholly scentless or having only a very weak scent like Jasmine. The calyx is very small, bell-shaped, green and densely soft-pubescent with violet hairs, truncate above and indistinctly four-toothed; of the teeth the two opposite ones are almost bifid. . . . Stamens two, placed at the base of the corolla-tube, upright, terete, filaments violet and glabrous, the anthers oblong, lying open, double and yellow. The pistil is half as long as the corolla. . . . In order not to let the memory of the discoverer be lost the referent (Jacquin himself) decided to give the plant her name *Syringa josikaea* . . ." (and the entire body of assembled botanists agreed!)

Jacquin continues, "The new *Syringa* grows in Transylvania in the western part of the district of Kolos, not far from the capital of Klausenburg, on both banks of the river Szekelyo, on steep, bare, washed cliffs. . . . Its location is not on very high places, usually hardly 5 fathoms (30 feet) above the river bank, not completely dry, yet not damp, except for a few minutes of sun in the morning and as many in the afternoon, always in the shade. There are always several shrubs growing close together. . . . The trunk of this Lilac is 12–18 feet high and its circumference is about 2½ inches. The beautiful flowers are used for hair and hat decorations by the peasants of the neighborhood villages. The plant blooms in May. . . . we thought it worthwhile to be made known in our circles, and to recommend it especially to the owners of gardens as a very beautiful ornamental shrub . . ."

Dr. Graham, Royal Botanic Garden, Edinburgh, Scotland, remarks in 1833. . . . "the plant received in 1832 flowered in the end of May and beginning of June. It seems, therefore, to flower later and remain longer in bloom than the other species, but does not equal any of them in beauty. . . ." Loudon writes, "Its leaves are shining and lucid green above, and white beneath in the manner of the balsam poplar, but of a dark green . . ." (his description of white beneath is a poor choice). Professor Sargent (Garden and Forest, 1888) makes some unfounded statements that "all the plants come from a single specimen found in a Hungarian garden" (whereas they were collected in several places in the wild) . . . "but not known to be wild in Europe, and probably of Asiatic origin." This statement aroused considerable controversy as to the native habitat of *S. josikaea.*

McKelvey extensively reviews the argument current at the time of her writing. She makes only slight reference to the very close similarities between *S. josikaea* and *S. wolfii* nor does she ever consider that *S. josikaea* might have been a migrant with the Asiatic tribes moving westward and the Mongols settling in Hungary and areas of Transylvania (see *S. wolfii*). As we mention elsewhere seeds of plants often follow the migrations of nations. There have been few migrations as large, complete and total as those of these Asiatic tribes to Europe. Why could not have *S. josikaea* been naturalized centuries before it was ever discovered and be a European representative of a single species to which both *S. josikaea* and *S. wolfii* are extreme forms? Considerably more scholarly, scientific and thorough research needs to be done and it cannot be settled on ethnic pride or writings from 1890 on. More evidence such as produced by the scanning electron microscope as done recently by Peter Green, Keeper of the Herbarium and Deputy Director of the Royal Botanic Gardens, Kew, England, in work on *Papillate Leaves in Lilacs* might reveal a new matrix of scientific relationship heretofore unavailable. We are strongly in favor of such research.

S. josikaea has much to offer in hybridization; its leaves are exceptionally heavy in substance, almost leather-like, with an attractive, lustrous-green sheen much needed in some lilac species; it is one of the very few species with a dark blue-violet flower color that is also lacking in the late-blooming hybrids. Its open flowering panicles should do well when crossed with heavier blooming, tighter panicled species. *S. josikaea* crossed with *S. reflexa* has produced the fine hybrids known as *S.* × *josiflexa* of which 'Guinevere' is the type. It grows to 8–10 ft. with a somewhat modest form. *S. josikaea* crossed with *S. villosa* has given us the hybrids referred to as *S.* × *henryi* of which the cultivar 'Lutece' (the old name for the city of Paris) is an excellent example. Other named *S.* × *henryi* cultivars are 'Floreal', 'Rutilant' and 'Prairial'. The latter is a second generation hybrid much improved over the original *S.* × *henryi* hybrids and belongs to a series now called *S.* × *nanceiana* hybrids which are pregnant with hybridizing potential. Although *S. josikaea* first generation hybrids are not as showy as most other species crosses and so are in need of continued work and refinement, they are, however, excellent plants with fine leaf and deep flower color. *S. josikaea* remains one of the best sources genetically for deep violet colored hybrids, excellent glossy leaves and perhaps the only source for eventual blue flowering late-blooming lilacs.

It appears that *S. josikaea* requires far richer soil than most other species and does fairly well even where it is somewhat damp (but not swampy). As a species it is at best a mediocre bloomer but a rich green plant. It is attractive in the summer garden as a background to other plants. Space should not be used in the smaller garden for this species as it has far less to offer than others. Larger gardens and collections, especially arboreta or large parks, could well plant it in large massed groups, especially in blending wooded areas into more formal space. Mrs. McKelvey well suggests that it makes an excellent hedge. It does not do well in sandy soils. It need not be grafted as cuttings strike root easily if taken immediately after bloom. From seed it is somewhat variable but acceptable. The best seedlings should be named to retain the better blooming sorts with the deepest color and be propagated vegetatively. Too many inferior seedlings are being distributed under the species name.

PLATE 17

Some outstanding cultivars in Class IV come from the hybridization of Kolesnikov, U.S.S.R. His beautiful, heavy blooming 'Mechta', shown here, is one of the finest. It is an extremely showy, dependable bloomer ranking among the highest of this color class. (Koles. 1941)

'Pamyat O.M. Kirove' also introduced by Kolesnikov in 1963 is a fine double with shades of pink.

Kolesnikov used mostly Lemoine cultivars in his work. Shown here is one of Lemoine's fine introductions in color Class IV, 'Christophe Columbe' (Lemoine 1905). Still beautiful and worthy of any modern collection!

Notable lilacs (see recommended list) in this color classification have been introduced by Havemeyer, Fiala and Maarse. The large floret, single cultivars to many are the most attractive. One must include among the best 'Victor Lemoine', 'Emile Lemoine' (Lemoine), 'Mrs. John S. Williams' (Havemeyer) and Fenicchia's beautiful 'Sesquicentennial'.

PLATE 18

THE LOVELY PINK LILACS

These come in shades of pale true pink to beautiful pinks tinted with light lavender. 'Lois Utley' (Fiala 1985) is a pale light pink double of excellent form.

PLATE 19

The exquisite pale pink of 'Lee Jewett Walker' is one of the
finest new pinks. It was introduced by Ken Berdeen in 1981.

OME EXCELLENT 'TRUE PINKS'

he tall majestic 'Marechal Foch' (Lemoine 1924) is one of
is finest single pinks. A glorious pink!

Another excellent pink is 'Stephanie Rowe' (Berdeen 1981)

The beautiful 'Lucie Baltet' introduced by Baltet before 1888
is still one of the finest—coppery buds and a low bush form.
It is excellent!

PLATE 20

THE MIXED PINKS

Beautiful but with tints of lavender in them. Do not place these lilacs next to lavender ones as it tends to make them appear more lavender than they really are.

One of the finest of the double pinks is 'Edward J. Gardner' which should be in every lilac collection, even those of modest size. The Gardener Nursery produced several very fine lilacs.

'De Croncels' (Baltet 1876). An old cultivar but still beautiful.

'Edward J. Gardener' (Gardener 1950). Excellent in every way!

'Comte Horace de Choiseul' (Lemoine 1887)

'Catawba Pink' (Utley 1980). Very new.

PLATE 21

'Znamya Lenina', an outstanding red-red lilac of Kolesnikov introduced in 1962, is one of the finest of its class. An excellent deep red in bud and very heavy bloomer, it will be a forerunner of its class when better known.

PLATE 22

THE PINK-MAGENTA (COLOR VI)

These lilacs begin with deep red buds and open a pinkish-red washed with pale lavender. Very beautiful and showy, each is different in shading. See chapter on 'Hybridizers' for the magnificent magentas of Richard Fenicchia—some yet unnamed but excellent.

'Elsie Lenore' is a huge floreted colchicine treated seedling of 'Sensation' with petals edged light pink. (Fiala 1982).

'Atheline Wilbur'. An extraordinarily beautiful large bloom of semi-double florets. One of the newer 'Rochester Strain' lilacs from Fiala, 1980, named to honor a lovely lady who cherishes lilacs.

'Murillo' (Lemoine 1901). Double of rare beauty with large thryses of bloom.

PLATE 23

THE RED MAGENTA LILACS

Both colors are very lovely.

'Spuvenir de Louis Chasset'. The last of the lilacs of V. Lemoine & Fil (Lemoine 1953). Very showy.

'Paul Thirion'. One of the finest of this color is truly outstanding (Lemoine 1915).

'Mme. F. Morel' (Morel 1892) is a very old lilac yet one of extreme popularity and beauty. Some of the newer cultivars have surpassed it.

'Bright Centennial' (Robinson 1967) is one of the reddest and very showy. Of Canadian origin.

PLATE 24

THE RED-PURPLE LILACS (CLASS VII)

These are among the most sought after color by the public even though they have the lower carrying power as to color in the garden. They are most showy when surrounded by white or pale pink lilacs.

'Frank Paterson', shown here, the very fine introduction of Mrs. Paterson in 1961, remains one of the finest of this class. An excellent, showy bloomer, vigorous shrub, it should be on every gardener's list. There are excellent choices of cultivars in this red-purple classification.

PLATE 25

'Charles Joly' (Lemoine 1896)

'Ethiopia' (Brand 1946)

'Chris' (Berdeen 1963)

'Doctor Bretheur' (Paterson 1961)

The beautiful two-toned 'Ostrander' (also known as 'Ostrander Cooley') is one of the finest introduction of Hulda Klager, 1928.

'Reaumur' (Lemoine 1904) often listed as color VI but more appropriately VII.

PLATE 26

'**Sensation**' a 'Dutch sport' of unusual beauty of deep purple edged with white introduced by Dirk E. Maarse in 1938. A much sought after lilac it is only now being recognized by some more progressive nurserymen.

To fully appreciate its beauty it must be planted for close inspection of its unique color combination.

'Sensation' is a mutation (sport) of the old lavender 'Hugo de Vries' and was created in the forcing house for Christmas bloom of lilacs so popular in the Netherlands.

There appear to be a few different colors of purple, from a lavender-purple to a reddish-purple, found in different plants of 'Sensation' (see the reddish-purple form on left). All are very beautiful.

Mon ami et amie, you must have it for your garden!

PLATE 27

THE DEEP PURPLE AND RED-PURPLE LILACS

ochester Hybrid #173 (Fenicchia). Very beautiful but as yet nnamed.

'Mrs. W. E. Marshall' (Havemeyer 1924). Often called the darkest lilac.

Mildred Luetta' (Hertz 1951)

'Margaret Rice Gould' (Brand 1953)

PLATE 28

'Sarah Sands' (Havemeyer 1943). One of the very finest, late bloomer.

Among the deep red-purple lilacs are some of the most desired cultivars.

'Etna' (Lemoine 1927). An old favorite very hard to equal in both quality and quantity of bloom! Among other choice Lemoine dark lilacs 'Monge', 'Prodige' and 'Volcan' are outstanding. My preference is 'Monge'.

'Andenken an Ludwig Späth' (Späth 1883). One of the oldest but still good. Newer cultivars have replaced it.

'Fürst Bülow' (Späth 1920). A deep bluish purple, very fine.

'Vesper' (Fleming 1979) is a newer Canadian introduction not yet widely grown because it is difficult to obtain in nurseries.

PLATE 29

S. josikaea, named to honor the Baroness von Josika, is more famous in its hybrids than the species. It imparts to its offspring hybrids its fine glossy leaves, vigor and lavender-purple color, which is much needed in good late blooming hybrids. Hybridizers are now discovering the merits of *S, josikaea* with many new hybrids and multibrids.

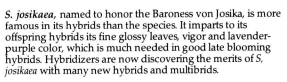

_ower and leaf of *S. josikaea*. A pinker form than the species general.

S. josikaea 'Rubra' a select deeper pink seedling dating as far back as 1885.

Bush form of 'Floreal' (Lemoine 1925). It is a *S. × nanceiana* hybrid (*S. josikaea × S. villosa*) × *S. sweginzowii,* a tribrid.

S. × henryi 'Lutece' (Lemoine 1910). A cross of *S. josikaea × S. villosa.* It is a tall shrub, rather coarse and not for the small garden but a background shrub. The newer multibrids are smaller shrubs, heavier bloomers and far more refined for the garden.

PLATE 30

'Royalty' a S. × josiflexa (Preston 1937) (*S. josikaea* × *S. reflexa*). It has been found to be quite susceptible to the virus of brooming disease.

'Prairial' a tribrid (Lemoine 1933) (*S. josikaea* × *S. villosa*) × *S. tomentella*. A lovely, heavy blooming hybrid moderate shrub.

S. × *josiflexa* 'Summer White' (Lape 1973) is an outstanding white of highest quality and heavy bloom. Remove the abundant seed pods for good annual flowering. Do so with all late lilacs.

S. × *josiflexa* 'Anna Amhoff' (Yeager 1958) is another very fine white from the University of New Hampshire. It is excellent in every way.

PLATE 31

Syringa debelderi appears to be a new species discovered by Robert and Jelena de Belder in Korea. Slow growing, rather dwarf in habit it could prove to be a treasure for hybridizers. As a species it would be well suited for the miniature or rock garden. As a parent in hybridizing it could give a whole new race of small growing lilacs. It is described for the first time here but what its eventual status will be remains for further evaluation and a wider dissemination of the plant. At Falconskeape it has produced some seed which was viable. We have only begun to cross pollenize it with other species in the pubescentes family of lilacs. *S. debelderi* may eventually prove to be another cultivar of the little-leaf lilacs which might also eventually be a single species with wide ranging variants. To date we treat it as a new species with its own unique identity. It appears to be a better grower than some of the lilacs in the pubescentes series.

Syringa debelderi in bloom showing its small pale violet bloom and leaf formation.

    Very small seed pods with gray warty appearance are characteristic of *S. debelderi* and are 1 cm. long.

PLATE 32

Syringa julianae and its named cultivars.

S. julianae. Note its more upright rather than spreading growth.

A close-up of the bloom of *S. julianae* 'Hers'.

S. julianae 'Hers Variety' discovered by Joseph Hers in China in 1923. The most beautiful from of this species in its spreading, weeping form and abundant annual bloom. It is truly outstanding!

S. julianae 'Pink Parasol' (Fiala 1983) is a cross of 'George Eastman' with 'Hers Variety' with recurved petals.

S. julianae 'Epaulettes' (Fiala 1984) a 'George Eastman' cross.

S. julianae 'George Eastman' (Clark-Fenicchia 1980). A true color break of a rosy-reddish hue, unique and beautiful. It is now being used extensively in breeding.

CHAPTER THREE

The Lilac Species from China, India, Korea and Japan

The Species Lilacs in Their Homeland of China

We have observed the facile ability of *S. vulgaris,* the common lilac, to adapt wonderfully to the colder regions of Europe and North America. This 'common lilac' of Balkan origins has some 20 Oriental cousins (species) whose native origins lay in the vast reaches of China. Of these different but beautiful lilac species, so unlike in flower, leaf and fragrance from their European relative, many deserve to be better known, appreciated and planted. Great strides are being made in their hybridization, which will lead to greater popularity. Some are wild transplants from the forests, canyons and mountain valleys of their homeland; others have graced, as ancient garden shrubs, the temples and houses of China perfuming the prayer rituals of Buddist monks or the clear mountain air.

In the cold northeastern provinces of China, Hebei Sheng (Sheng = Province, Ho-pei Sheng, Hopeh Province) and Shandong Sheng (Shan-tung Sheng, Shantung Province) in montane arboreal forests the lilac species, *S. patula* and *S. pubescens* are found growing as natives with wild roses and filberts in dense thickets of secondary growth in openings of *Picea abies* forests. While among the rich and varied shrubs of the forest floor, *S. reticulata* (The Amur Tree Lilac) vies for a place in the sun, raising its feathery white blossoms with their spicy fragrance in late June.

In the bitterly cold winter areas of the montane coniferous forests of northern Gansu Sheng (Kan-su Sheng, Kansu Province) and Shaanxi Sheng (Shaan-hsi Sheng, Shensi Province) the late lilac species *S. villosa* is one of the five most important shrubs and groundcovers. It forms thickets of mixed seedlings and older plants in full bloom. In deciduous, broad-leaved forests of mixed northern hardwoods the lilac is, again, one of the leading shrubs in the middle plant layer just below the foliage of high trees. *Syringa* holds its place among the 8 to 10 most common shrubs in the dense thickets of the shrub layer. Reaching up to 50 ft. *S. reticulata* var. *amurensis* competes with 50 species in the northeast Shandong Sheng (Shan-tung Sheng, Shantung Province). As a border thicket at the edge of the forest *S. villosa* forms random stands or invades forest clearings.

In eastern China's Hebei Sheng (Ho-pei Sheng, Hopeh Province) and around Beijing (Peking) *S. pubescens* is common as a native of the upper oak forests of *Quercus liaotungensis.* Continuing above the oaks, upward to 1400 meters, it appears in the community of linden and birch forests (*Tilia-Betula*). It grows strongly in the rich, well-drained soils of the forest clearings. In the western provinces of Shaanxi (Shaan-hsi, Shensi), Gansu (Kan-su, Kansu) and Sichuan (Seu-chu'uan, Szechwan) the tree lilac, *S. reticulata* forms dense thickets among other shrubs on sunny slopes opposite birch-aspen forests above bands of oaks. In the upper oak forest of south Shaanxi

Note: The Chinese names for areas and provinces are given in three spellings. The first is modern Pinyin, the most acceptable transliteration; the second is the older, less acceptable Wade-Giles still used in many countries; the last is the English transliteration which many of the older plant explorers used in their descriptions but not really acceptable today. I prefer the more modern Chinese designation of geographical places in Pinyin as all modern maps and explorations use this form, so the reader can readily find locations on newer maps of China. (There are a few places mentioned by the older explorers in English transliteration that I have been unable to find on modern maps so I present them as they are given.)

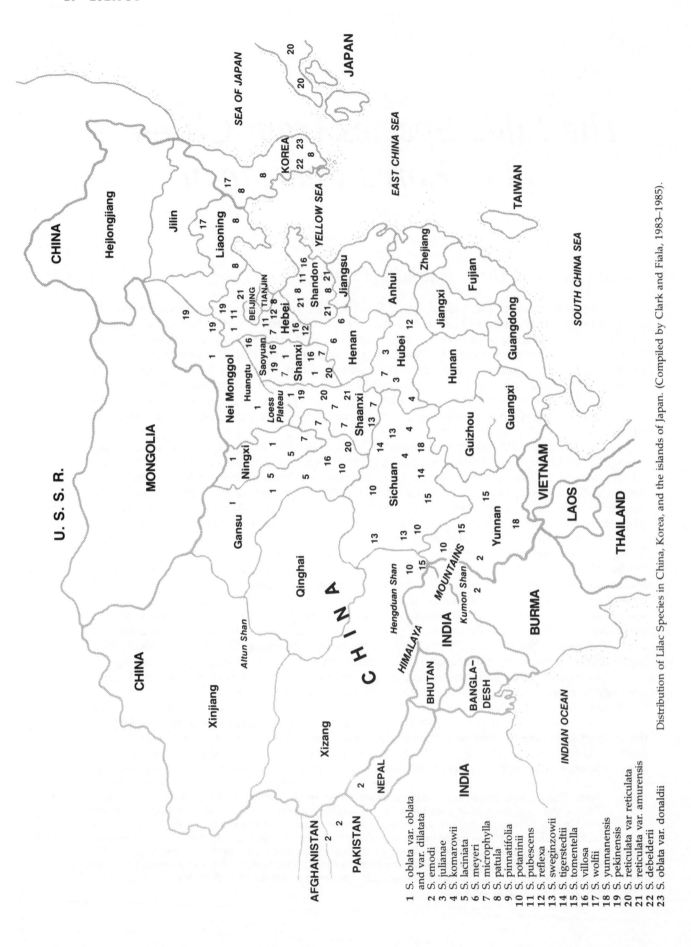

Distribution of Lilac Species in China, Korea, and the islands of Japan. (Compiled by Clark and Fiala, 1983–1985).

1 S. oblata var. oblata
   and var. dilatata
2 S. emodi
3 S. julianae
4 S. komarowii
5 S. laciniata
6 S. meyeri
7 S. microphylla
8 S. patula
9 S. pinnatifolia
10 S. potaninii
11 S. pubescens
12 S. reflexa
13 S. sweginzowii
14 S. tigerstedtii
15 S. tomentella
16 S. villosa
17 S. wolfii
18 S. yunnanensis
19 S. pekinensis
20 S. reticulata var reticulata
21 S. reticulata var. amurensis
22 S. debelderii
23 S. oblata var. donaldii

Sheng at 1400–2000 meters and at above 1500 meters in Gansu Sheng, *S. pubescens* is common in the rich understory of cane thickets and tall shrubs, many of which are evergreens. These are definitely lilacs of the high country and open forests or forest margins.

In the grasslands and deserts, *S. oblata*, the early lilac, is common in the sharply dissected loess plateau Husang-t'u Kao-yuan (Huangtu Gaoyuan) south of the Great Wall and is to be found everywhere in valleys and sheltered slopes. (Some taxonomic controversy surrounds these and their distinct forms known today.) The form *S. oblata* var. *oblata* differs considerably from *S. oblata* var. *dilatata*, whereas the newest form *S. oblata* var. *donaldii* differs from both. (I have chosen to call it *S. oblata donaldii* because it is so new and little known to distinguish it from *S. oblata* vars. *oblata* and *dilatata*. It appears to be somewhat more closely related to *S. oblata dilatata*. What taxonomists call it in the future remains to be seen. Presently the only plants are at the U.S. National Arboretum in Washington D.C.)

From our limited knowledge of Chinese horticulture it does now appear that the native lilacs were cultivated to some extent for their own sake in both private and public gardens. The tree lilac, *S. reticulata* var. *amurensis,* was probably the most commonly grown of the entire genus. It was sometimes used as a temple tree, as at the monastery of Kum-Bum, in the gardens of both the very rich and the poor, as an easily grown native for its late bloom of feathery plumes. Some find its fragrance unpleasant but its malodor cannot be compared to the offensive *Azalea mollis* or the blooming Chinese chestnut. *S. reticulata* is the most widespread of the species of China. One would expect that there would be considerably more clonal variations than we now have. Perhaps we do not have seed from the plant's diverse locations or may have taken it for granted that they are all alike.

From the mountains of Yunnan Sheng (Yunnan Province) and Tibet comes the species *S. yunnanensis*. Its flower is so insignificant that it is not cultivated even by Tibetans. Also from Yunnan Sheng comes *S. tomentella* and in the northeastern part of this province *S. potaninii* is native as it is in Xizang Sheng and Gansu Sheng.

Sichuan Sheng is the home of *S. sweginzowii, S. komarowii, S. yunnanensis* and *S. potaninii*. In neighboring Hubei Sheng, the Province to the east, *S. julianae, S. reflexa* and *S. microphylla* are all native.

Most of the lilac species of China are known in their wild state only. The sole exception is *S. meyeri* which has never been found in the wild and is known only as a Chinese garden plant.

The bulk of the Chinese species lilacs were discovered in the late 1880s to 1900 with a few as late as 1910 and 1925. The most recent introduction, *S. oblata* var. *donaldii,* was brought back as seed by the U.S. Dept. of Agriculture in 1978. *S. debelderii* was brought from South Korea by deBelder in 1977 as seed.

Gansu Sheng, the favorite plant hunting territory of E. H. Wilson. Picture of vast plains and mountains near Peitatung, Gansu Sheng. (Photo by J. F. Rock, Oct. 11, 1926, courtesy Archives of Arnold Arboretum.)

Photo of J. F. Rock on his plant explorations in 1925–26, taken by Rock, Gansu Sheng (Kansu Province), the home of at least six lilac species. (Photo, Archives of Arnold Arboretum.) The Arnold Arboretum has been a world leader in sending plant expeditions to search out new species in China for the past century.

Plant Explorations in the Orient Important to the Discoveries of New Lilac Species

It was through the efforts and knowledge of plant explorers, missionaries and botanists that the many species of lilacs native to China, Tibet, Japan and Afghanistan were discovered and introduced into the commerce of horticulture. Men and women of many countries have participated in this great lilac adventure. In the past two centuries they braved unexplored mountainous terrain, rigors of climate and journey and unfamiliar languages of hundreds of dialects to discover the beauty of the many lilac species. Adventurous men like Grigori Potanin and Ernest H. Wilson not only discovered new species of great beauty but left accounts of their exciting adventures. We owe much in modern horticulture to these plant explorers of past and present decades. The introduction of thousands of new plant species to the West resulted from their labors. There is hardly a garden today that does not have several of the plants they hunted out and introduced. Many of these earliest plant collectors travelled on their own, were missionary-botanists or were part of their country's diplomatic missions as botanical experts. Most of the more recent explorations (since 1900) have been the undertakings of the world's great horticultural institutions.

THE INITIAL ERA OF LILAC DISCOVERIES IN CHINA AND AFGHANISTAN

The history of the plant collectors and botanists in China, Tibet and India can be roughly divided by the Western War (England, France, Russia and the United States) with China in 1860. From the beginning of plant explorations in China, as early as 1742 when Pierre d'Incarville, a French Jesuit botanist missionary, discovered *S. pekinensis* in the Beijing Mountains and *S. villosa* in the same area in 1750, the history of the discovery and naming of lilac species was mostly the work of French, Russian and English botanists who travelled or were associated with China as missionaries or military attaches. From d'Incarville's first discoveries of new lilac species in the mid 1700s it was almost 80 years later, in 1831, that the Russian botanist, Alexander Bunge sent lilac specimens back home and the Englishman, R. Blinkworth, discovered another lilac species, *S. emodi*, in the mountains of the Karum Valley in Afghanistan. In the next 10 years the Russian explorer and botanist, P. V. Kirilov was to send seed home of two previously discovered species, *S. pekinensis* and *S. villosa*, and in 1840 discovered still another beautiful new lilac, *S. pubescens* in Hebei Sheng, sending back seed and plant materials.

Some few years later in his third exploration to China, Robert Fortune in 1853–1856 was to send back to England live plants of *S. oblata* and its variety *alba* which he found already growing in Chinese gardens. At this time two other Russian botanists, Richard Maack and Karl Ivan Maximowicz, independently each discovered *S. reticulata* var. *reticulata*. This first hundred years was an initial phase in the discovery and collecting of lilac species. Most of these earlier explorers, although learned and able, did not collect in the volume and thoroughness of those who were to follow them in the next century, yet they added 7 new species and outstanding cultivars to the growing list of lilacs. (*Bon jardinier*, this was only the beginning of the great lilac story!)

THE CHINA WAR WITH THE WEST AND THE OPENING OF THE INTERIOR TO PLANT EXPLORATION

As a result of the War with the West, China was obliged by treaty to open its interior and plant hunters were free to follow rivers to the western interior and highlands in search of new species and materials. It was a trying time for China with the Taiping Rebellion going on right through the War with the West. The war, itself, was a discredit to the Western Powers who made a mountain out of a mole-hill in order to squeeze concessions from a rebellion-weakened Chinese government. The Manchus and Mandarins, aware that their Empire was disintegrating, were forced to ask the help of the West under Gordon's command to overcome from within the Taiping Rebellion. It was a bad time for Chinese statesmen especially with the European powers, but it was an opportune time for plant hunters waiting to move into interior regions. This they did in increasing numbers. It was a grand time for the discovery of many new plant species, among which were the lilacs. (*Mon ami*, these were exciting times for those who loved the lilac species! What wonderful discoveries were made! You must read Tyler Whittle's exciting book on *The Plant Explorers*—it is marvelous!)

For the collectors of lilac species the very heart of the native habitat of *Syringa* was opened to explorations—Tibet and the Chinese provinces of Gansu (Kansu), Sichuan (Szechuan) and Yunnan. From these three provinces alone, 13 species of lilacs were found to be native—more than in any other area of China. To Western plant hunters the interior of China was sheer 'grandeur'. . . . "the size of the rivers and extent of their headwaters, the many breathtaking cataracts, rapids, currents, mountain gorges, the sheer mountains and their overwhelming valleys, the flat dry plateaus cut by rivers and chasms over a thousand feet below and the screes over which screaming winds howled endlessly." (Joseph Rock) This was the awe-inspiring interior of Mother China that contained in her bosom treasured lilac species unseen by the rest of the world. The famous Chinese poet, Po Chu-i, who was sent to be governor of this remote area in Sichuan, named Yunnan, "The Land South of the Cloud" and the province of Sichuan, "The Land of the Four Rivers"—all this became a mecca sacred to plant collectors, especially for the species of *Syringa*.

Some of the first of these were amateur plant collectors like the Frenchman, Prince Henry d'Orleans, and the very rich Englishman, Antwerp Pratt, who . . . 'bought a luxurious houseboat on the Yangtze, hired a German assistant collector, Kricheldorf, and went sailing into Szechuan in the grandest style possible!' The brilliant young linguist, August Margary, an Englishman, travelled from the Yangtze-kiang to Irrawaddy—over a thousand miles of unknown country on his plant collecting journey when he was only twenty-six! He suffered from toothaches, rheumatism, pleurisy and dysentery. When he completed his journey, just beyond Bhamo, he was mysteriously murdered. A British Consulate investigation indicated he was probably murdered by his own litter-bearers for insisting a dog be carried in his curtained litter, as they considered this to be a gross insult and outrage. Magary was 'out of the ordinary'—it is recorded that . . . "when he felt lonely and depressed he would stand outside his tent singing *Clementine, Polly-wolly-doodle, The Lass of Richmond Hill* and finish off with a shouting rendering of *God Save the Queen.*" Such were the lives of these free-lancers among the plant collectors. (*Mon ami*, they were an adventurous lot!) The majority who came after them were of an entirely different cast.

Under the 'Great Annexer', Lord Dalhousie, England extended its rule over India and became concerned about the extent of Csar Alexander II sending 'military botanists' into the newly opened areas of China. Despite the open outrage of the 'Widow of Windsor' he continued to send men who, though of a military commission, were well-trained botanists. High among these was the capable Russian botanist, Nikolai Mikhailovich Przewalski, whose achievements took him from the rank of a literary footsoldier to a major generalship. He was essentially a naturalist botanizing along the way in his great aim to reach Lhasa in Tibet. In his last attempt in 1888 he died of typhoid. Before his death, however, he left a lasting legacy of a collection of over 15,000 plant specimens which contained over 1,700 species of plants sent to Russia to the industrious scholar, K. I. Maximowicz, in St. Petersburg (Leningrad). Among these were many specimens of lilacs.

This doyen of Russian collectors was followed by equally illustrious quasi-military botanists that included the brilliant Grigori Potanin, Berezovski, Kashkarov and Roborovski. (Much of their great work and travels remains unknown because it has not been translated outside of Russia. Their accomplishments were extensive—including many specimens and species of lilacs.)

Beginning in 1866 with Père Armand David, a Frenchman, it was a new era. There was a notable change in the style, character and training of plant collectors from Europe and the West. Before Armand David plant collectors were adventurers (excepting the Russian military-botanists) with some basic training in collecting herbarium specimens who collected as they willed materials of their own choosing. After Armand David, with a few exceptions of self-trained or academic botanists like the Englishman, Dr. Augustine Henry, the Swedish scholar Doctor Henry Smith, Camillo Schneider and Handel Mazetti, both Austrians, and the American, Professor Liberty Hyde Bailey of Ithaca, the rest of the plant hunters were well trained plantsmen. They collected plants for botanical study and herbariums, but this was only secondary to collecting seeds and living stock for introduction to cultivation and horticultural commerce. They were men of a professionally trained and practical cut. Rather than haphazardly skimming off the best materials, they conducted a systematic and exhaustive search for anything new and different over set and well-defined areas, as Armand David had. These newer plantsmen, being better trained and more scientific, were lavishly rewarded for their efforts. There were a number of these men and the reading of their adventures

The Great Shimen, gateway to Tebbu land, Gansu. (Rock, 1925)

Pikow Bridge across the Wen Hsien iron-rod chain bridge, northwest of Pikow. (Rock, April 30, 1925)

Jupar Valley, Tibet—"valleys of magnificent vegetation". (Rock, June 27, 1926) (Photos, Archives of Arnold Arboretum.)

in quest of new plant materials, including lilacs, is fascinating and awesome.

To appreciate the great Lilac Adventure one must be aware of how and under what circumstances many of the lilac species became known and available. Each plant explorer's life is unique and fascinating; together they form the background of lilac history. I present but a thumbnail sketch of some of these great plant hunters who discovered species or cultivars of *Syringa* to give some insight and historical appreciation for the great lilac species they have bequeathed to us and the uniqueness of their own personalities. (*Mon ami et amie,* the work and lives of these adventurers make the beautiful lilacs growing in our gardens more appreciated and meaningful!)

A few stand out as 'exceptional' in their stature as plantsmen and their extensive contributions. Among these giants I would include: the Englishmen, E. H. M. Cox, Henry John Elwes and Reginald Farrer; George Forrest from Scotland and the United States, Joseph Hooker from England, Frank Meyer—a Dutchman, Carl Maximowicz—a Russian, Grigori M. Potanin—a Siberian-Russian; the Viennese-American, Joseph J. Rock; Père Jean Andre Soulie from France; Nicolai Mikhailovich Przewalski from Russia; Frank Kingdon-Ward, a Cambridge, Englishman and Ernest Henry Wilson, an English-American.

Père Armand David

Born of humble parents in 1826 in Espelette, a small town in the Pyrenees, France, David entered the Order of Lazarists and as a trained botanist was sent by his Order to China in 1866 on his first Mongolian Expedition. He carried little baggage, no food—depending on the hospitality of the people. He was methodical and painstaking as a plant collector. Although his over 2,000 species could not compare with other missionary-botanists who worked after him in the Tibetan mountains, like Abbé Jean Marie Delavay who is credited with personally collecting, drying and pressing more than 200,000 specimens, David's work was exceptionally well done and thorough. He continued collecting in China until 1874 when illness forced him to return to France where he taught botany until his death in 1900.

While collecting in the Beijing Mountains he is credited to be the discoverer of *S. pekinensis.* In his long plant expeditions he wrote, . . . "As for food I depend on the Chinese, and I believe that with a little goodwill, one man can live wherever another can. I do not burden myself with carrying food, except a bottle of cognac—for emergencies." The Abbé Jean Marie Delavay, a contemporary of David, discovered *S. yunnanensis* growing in the wooded areas around Lake Lanking in Yunnan Sheng. Abbé Jean Marie Soulie collected already discovered species of *Syringa* in Tibet where he was murdered in a military uprising of local rulers. Rev. Guiseppe Giraldi, an Italian missionary-botanist, gathered and first collected plants of *S. oblata* var. *Giraldii* in 1891 and *S. microphylla* in 1896 in Shaanxi Sheng. These missionary-botanists added 3 new species and 1 subspecies to the lilacs.

Ernest Henry Wilson

Often called 'Chinese Wilson' (which he disliked) because of his many expeditions into China, Wilson was perhaps the most outstanding of the modern plant hunters after the opening of the interior of China after the war of 1860. Born in 1876 in the small town of Chipping Camper, Glouchestershire, England, Wilson showed a love and attraction for plants as a boy working as an apprentice gardener to a Strattford nursery firm, transferring then to Birmingham Botanic Gardens and shortly to the famous Kew Gardens. He was not much attracted to teaching botany and when recommended by the Director, Sir William Thiselton-Dyer, for the job of a plant hunter in China for the firm of Veitch, although only twenty-three, he quickly accepted. It was the beginning of a fabulous career and a life of fulfillment in seeking new species and plants. Wilson was overjoyed. (*Mon ami,* he was a wonderfully inspiring and brilliant man!)

Veitch's staff instructed him for 6 months on the practical side of plant hunting—plant recognition, taking, stowing, and transport of herbarium materials, seed collecting and care of propagating stocks (these latter were their chief interest for commercial introduction of new plants). To this was added the use of a camera. The young Wilson was an astute and able student and became a plant collector of highest rank and an excellent photographer (oddly he always used a heavy, full-plate camera, tripod in brass and mahogany, despite its weight). He was instructed by Veitch to take the long route to China via the United States so he could stop at the Arnold Arboretum at Boston, Massachusetts. Here he met and formed a lasting friendship with the Arboretum Founder, Professor Charles Sargent, who gave him much valuable advice on collecting

Ernest H. Wilson, the doyen of plant collectors in China, who from 1901 to 1926 made six separate plant explorations to China. His favorite places were Gansu, Hubei, and Hebei Sheng, where he discovered *S. reflexa* growing wild in 1901. Collecting first for Veitch Nursery, England, and then making several explorations for the Arnold Arboretum, he became one of the world's foremost and famous plant collectors. Sargent's writings on the plant introductions of Wilson fill three volumes. Lilacdom owes much to this gentle and methodical man. (Photo Archives of Arnold Arboretum.)

in China. (Later this friendship was to result in his leaving the Veitch firm to work for the Arnold Arboretum.) Another instruction of his employer was to visit Dr. Augustine Henry in Yunnan, China. This meeting also proved most beneficial to Wilson as Henry was a veteran plantsman with much knowledge to offer on plant hunting in China. Wilson's first assignment from Veitch was to find the legendary or real *Davidia involucrata* (and anything of commercial value along the way). He was most successful—although not finding *Davidia involucrata* (which was to come in his second journey) he did discover *D. involucrata* var. *laeta* sending seed of it and 305 other species, plus 35 Wardian cases of tubers, corms, bulbs, rhizomes and rootstocks—together with 906 herbarium specimens of plants! An outstanding accomplishment for his first expedition into unknown China! Within 6 months of returning to England he undertook a second trip for Veitch. This time he went into the territory called Laolin (the Sichuan Sheng—Szechuan Province and Hubei Sheng—Hopeh Province—often called Wilson's exclusive territory) where he discovered rare species of poppies and many rare plant species among which were *S. julianae* (from Hebei Sheng) and the beautiful *S. reflexa* in western Hubei Sheng. Pressing deeper into Sichuan in the areas surrounding the sacred Mt. Omei he discovered *S. pinnatifolia* and took seed of the already discovered but rare *S. sweginzowii.* From this one exploration he was to return to Veitch four new and outstanding species

Tibetan bridge over the Tao River, near Choni, western Gansu. Wilson crossed here several times. Photo by William Purdom on his explorations in 1909–1911. (Photo Archives of Arnold Arboretum.)

of lilacs together with hundreds of other species. Later in his book *Aristocrats of the Garden,* Wilson gives an exciting account on this discovery of *S. reflexa,* so vivid one imagines they are actually in his company of bold adventure. His account of *S. sweginzowii* covering a hillside down to a valley stream is sheer artistry.

Nor were these explorations without personal danger. Wilson was not one to dwell upon himself or his accomplishments and tribulations. He does describe one harrowing experience: (On his second journey) — ... "while searching for the regal lily Wilson and his party of coolies, taking an unknown and narrow path where avalanches were common, were suddenly pelted with falling stones—one boulder hit Wilson breaking his leg in two places. Suffering greatly, a long distance from any doctor, surrounded only by his coolies who were ready to run away—he provided splints made from his tripod and continued carried on a litter on the narrow mountain trail. From the opposite direction they met a train of fifty mules on this high path too narrow for them to be turned—nor would the mule train wait for Wilson's small party to edge its way one-at-a-time past the mules. Wilson knew he could not turn back, racked with pain he ordered his men to lay him across the narrow path and one by one the sure-footed mules stepped over him. Such was the life of this remarkable plant-hunter. He returned with the lilacs, the regal lily and a life-long limp (which he called his Lily limp).

Upon returning from his second trip, realizing the financial difficulties being encountered at the Veitch Firm, he left them to join Professor Sargent at the Arnold Arboretum for which he made 6 more plant hunting trips to China. Here he had more financial backing, more freedom in collecting and a wider scope. Professor Sargent proved the value of Wilson's explorations in his writing on the extent of Wilson's accomplishments in *Plantae Wilsoneanae* in 9 parts and 3 volumes. In each of his trips Wilson brought back to the Arnold additional seed or new forms of lilac species. On his fifth trip in 1917 he sent back seed of *S. oblata dilatata* found in Korea, while on his sixth trip in 1924–25 he sent back seed of *S. pinnatifolia* which he had previously discovered in 1904 but had been unable to send seed.

He was outstanding in his plant explorations and was named Assistant or Keeper of the Arboretum which delighted him. He authored several books on his plant discoveries. He faced death many times in his explorations—once by near starvation, another time by nearly drowning when his boat was overturned, and again under avalanche. In 1930, while driving with his wife on a highway near Worcester, Massachusetts, he was killed in an automobile accident. Certainly he was one of horticulture's and the lilacs' outstanding plant explorers.

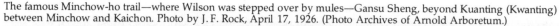

The famous Minchow-ho trail—where Wilson was stepped over by mules—Gansu Sheng, beyond Kuanting (Kwanting) between Minchow and Kaichon. Photo by J. F. Rock, April 17, 1926. (Photo Archives of Arnold Arboretum.)

Grigori A. Potanin—famous Russian plant explorer who in 1885 discovered the beautiful species *S. potaninii* in Gansu Sheng. This was the same area so well explored by E. H. Wilson in 1901 and J. F. Rock in 1925–26. (Photo from *New York Times*, Russian edition, courtesy Archives of Arnold Arboretum.)

Grigori Nikolaievich (Nikolaevitch) Potanin

This outstanding man of letters, science, travel and plant collecting was born in 1835 in the city of Tomsk in Old Siberia. As a student he was one of the enthusiastic writers in Petrograd, whose leader was the well known Belinski, who greatly influenced Russian literature and politics. He was a brilliant scholar and perhaps best known for his travels in Mongolia as a quasi-military plant collector. Between 1876 and 1893 he made as many as 4 journeys to the plateau of Central Asia, travelling extensively in the plant-rich areas of Gansu Sheng. In 1885 he collected *S. oblata* var. *giraldii* in Shaanxi Sheng and a few years later discovered the beautiful *S. potaninii* in Gansu Sheng. It was on this last rigorous journey that he discovered *S. komarowii* in Sichuan Sheng where he lost his devoted wife and fellow-worker. Although his expeditions had in mind chiefly botanical collecting and zoological observations, he brought back and wrote much ethnic material.

After his return to Tomsk he resumed his intellectual work, especially in the way of founding societies for the study of Siberia and its various aspects. In later life he married a highly gifted Siberian poetess and their Tomsk home became a center of literary and learned gatherings. He became most active in the community and together with Iadrinstov, published papers, organized intellectual circles and did much that was instrumental in opening the Irkutsk University. Potanin worked diligently to revolutionize the intellectual life of the Russians living in Siberia. Everywhere he was proclaimed as the champion of Oriental study and the intellectual life of the Sibiriaks. Much of his writings, especially his exciting accounts of plant explorations into China, have not been given the attention they deserve, chiefly because they have not been translated from Russian into other languages. He was a gifted and accomplished writer. Those who grow lilacs will remember him through the rare species, *S. komarowii* and *S. potaninii*, that bears its discoverer's name. He died, aged 85, at his celebrated home in Tomsk, Siberia, in 1920. Potanin was one of many outstanding Russian plant collectors and botanists, generally termed as quasi-military plant explorers who collected in China, Mongolia and Tibet.

Maximowicz continued his explorations and in 1875 in Japan collected *S. reticulata* var. *reticulata* calling it *S. japonica*, by which name it was known until recent taxonomical correction gave it the older name of *reticulata*. From 1893 to 1895, the distinguished Russian botanist, V. L. Komorov, sent seed of *S. wolfii* to St. Petersburg enlarging the magnificent collection gathered there by nearly a century of outstanding Russian botanists and plant collectors. Miss A. Sontag, a member of the Russian legation was the first to collect *S. patula* near Seoul, Korea in 1895. To these men and women must be accredited the discovery of at least 7 lilac species and the introduction into Europe of several others. A most outstanding contribution to the genus *Syringa*.

Gansu Sheng—Hera Rock mountains—home of species lilacs, explored briefly as early as 1885 by Grigori Potanin, a Russian botanist-writer, who discovered in its valleys the beautiful *S. potaninii.* (Photo by E. H. Wilson, Archives of Arnold Arboretum.)

Photo of plant exploration camp of J. F. Rock in Gansu Sheng in 1925, ". . . a land of wonderful scenery, mountains, cascades and majestic vistas . . ." (Photo by Rock, Archives of Arnold Arboretum.)

Joseph Rock

A prodigy as a scholar in science and an accomplished multi-language linguist, Joseph Rock was born in Vienna in 1885. In 1907 he was appointed to the Chair of Chinese and Botany at the University of Hawaii and later economic Plant Collector for the Department of Agriculture, U.S.A. Becoming an American citizen in 1913, his position enabled him to travel extensively in Yunnan, China, where his plant collecting crossed paths with George Forrest and Frank Kingdon-Ward. Rock had a great love for China especially in that area of Gansu Sheng he called "Tebbu land, that is, the country peopled by the Tepos south of the Min Shan which is divided in two by the Satani Alps". It was Tebbu Land which fired his imagination: "I have never in all my life seen such magnificent scenery! If the writer of Genesis had seen the Tebbu Country he would have made it the birth place of Adam and Eve!"

In his work as plant collector for the Arnold Arboretum he was systematic and sent back thousands of specimens, seeds and stock. Among his collections were many forms and species of lilacs already previously discovered. He worked through the entire area of Sichuan Sheng which had once been under the control of the Tibetan Prince of Litang. The thoroughness of his explorations would preclude the finding of other *Syringa* species in the areas of his endeavors. During the Chinese-Tibetan frontier quarrels, the region of Tibet became extremely lawless and in 1928 when Rock wished to botanize there, it was only through his special friendship with Drashetsongpen, a former lama monk turned robber bandit, that he was permitted to continue his work. As the frontier quarrels continued, Rock returned home to America. He has left in the Arnold Archives a vast number of photographs of the plant explorations and commentary, most of which has yet to be published. To him we owe the debt of commercializing the lilac by bringing home seed enough for many of the lesser known species to be made more widely available. (*Mon ami,* he was an excellent photographer and through the permission of The Arnold Arboretum I am using some of his pictures.)

Among the later contemporaries of Joseph Rock was Frank Kingdon-Ward, the son of a Botany professor at Cambridge, from a family of botanists. Ward plant collected in Yunnan, Sichuan Sheng, Upper Burma, French Indonesia and Southeast Tibet. Between 1909 and 1957 he introduced hundreds of new species of plants. He discovered no new species of lilacs but did send home several cultivars, one he thought to be a new species he named *S. wardii*, which later was disavowed as a species and classified as a form of *S. microphylla*. At this time another noted collector, William Purdom, an Englishman, who had collected for both Veitch and the Arnold Arboretum and who worked for one exploration with Reginald Farrer in Gansu Sheng, was actively working in the interior provinces of China. Purdom discovered no new species of *Syringa* but did collect seed of already introduced species that he thought were variations of exceptional merit. During this active time of plant explorations from 1900 to 1930 Joseph Hers, a Belgian, working in Sichuan Sheng sent home seed of *S. microphylla* and the special cultivar he called *S. julianae* 'Hers'.

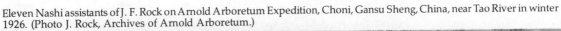

Eleven Nashi assistants of J. F. Rock on Arnold Arboretum Expedition, Choni, Gansu Sheng, China, near Tao River in winter 1926. (Photo J. Rock, Archives of Arnold Arboretum.)

Plant exploration camp of J. F. Rock, beyond Tatzutong, Gansu Sheng (Kadjaku), ". . . among birches, poplars, pines and wild apple trees . . . in the Tao River Valley, northwest of Jone (Choni), Gansu . . . elevation 9,200 feet." (Photo by J. Rock, 1925, Archives of Arnold Arboretum.)

Picture taken by Frank Meyer April 23, 1915, of *S. oblata* growing in the gardens of the German legation, Beijing, China. Meyer sent home seed from these plants. He notes: "A single well flowering shrub of a north Chinese lilac which is very resistant to drought and alkaline. May be valuable for hybridization purposes."

Frank N. Meyer

Lilacdom was enriched by another species, *S. meyeri*, discovered by Frank N. Meyer, a Dutchman by birth and later an American by choice, who had worked under and was trained by the famous botanist, Hugo de Vries. He was a man who loved the out-of-doors and travel—by the time he was 13 he crossed the Alps on foot and went down into Italy. Later he tramped through the United States dipping down to consider the plants of Mexico—ever collecting and always preferring to go on foot. By 1905 he was working for the Department of Agriculture, U.S.A. and in this office made four expeditions to China under his commission to plant-explore the Orient. He spent 3 years combing the plants and spice stalls of Northern China, Manchuria and Northern Korea, returning to Washington and a year later he left for the Caucasus, Siberia, Russian Turkestan and Chinese Turkestan after which he made 2 more expeditions to China.

In his 1909 expedition he found the beautiful *S. meyeri* growing in Chinese gardens and was responsible for its introduction abroad. This unique dwarf species has never been found in the wild, leading some to believe it is a remarkable cross of the little-leaved lilacs. Today it holds species rank. Meyer is also responsible for introducing *S. villosa*, previously discovered, into commerce. In 1915 he found *S. laciniata* . . . "growing wild at Kingchow in Gansu, China. (Kingchow is at the extreme east of Gansu, slightly south of its north and south center, and not far from the border of Gansu and Shaanxi (Shensi). It is south of the King River, a branch of the Wei which further east runs into the Huang ho, and is north of the Tsin-ling Range." There appears to be no doubt that it is indigenous there and like other plants of Chinese origin found its way from that country into Persian gardens, where, commonly cultivated, it soon came to be regarded as native to the country of its adoption. It was from this Persian adoption that early botanists (Linne and McKelvey in her monograph *The Lilac*) erroneously called it a subspecies of *S. persica*, whereas *S.* × *persica* is an hybrid of *S. laciniata*. It was in this same 1915 exploration that Meyer sent back to the National Arboretum in Washington the beautiful *S. oblata* 'Alba' (still growing magnificently to this day at the Glendale Center and considered one of the finest forms of *S. oblata*.)

Meyer was an extremely able and prolific plant collector who travelled the great plains of China, Manchuria, Korea, up by Lanchow, the Great Wall and into Wilson's Gansu Sheng. Most of his enormous collections were of economical importance rather than for beauty—soya, wheat, rice, peppers and many valuable introductions—some discovered in the open stalls of the markets. He stayed out in the open or in simple village inns . . . "with odors hanging about to make even angels procure their handkerchiefs. . . . with foreign tongues ever babbling strange languages and unknown dialects'."

He introduced the single yellow rose (*R. xanthina*) 'Canary-bird', the Chinese Elm and several ornamental shrubs. As he was preparing to leave Hebei Sheng down the Yangtze something happened—to this day no details are known but in June of 1918 his swollen body was found floating in the sluggish waters of the Yangtze, below the port of Anking, some thirty miles north of Nanking. The river he had sailed so often claimed another of its famous voyagers! (*Mon ami*, what a loss—Frank Meyer was only in his early forties!)

George Forrest

This methodical plant comber of Tibet and Yunnan Sheng was a solitary, brusque man who in 28 years sent home from the high province of Yunnan more than 31,000 herbarium sheets and an equal number of separate parcels of seed. Forrest, who was considered one of the best trained plant collectors, was of humble family, born in 1872 at Falkirk, Sterlingshire, Scotland. He went to school in Kilmarnock entering Pharmacy which he disliked. The young Forrest preferred the out-of-doors as he loved to walk and hunt. As a youth after his studies he went to Australia to work as a roustabout in the bush country where he remained for several years. He returned to Scotland in 1902 at 30 and took a poor paying job in the herbarium of Edinburgh Botanic Gardens. Since he could not abide crowded towns, he walked 6 miles each morning and evening to his country lodging. For 5 hours each day, with Scottish determination, he poured over herbarium specimens from all over the world, dedicated to learn all he possibly could about plants at which he, indeed, became an expert. This work was to be a great asset in his later life as a plant collector of outstanding ability in Yunnan, China.

Two years later, in 1904, he left for Yunnan where he spent 28 years. This area of Tibet and Yunnan Sheng became known as "Forrest's special territory"—he guarded it well and fiercely against other plant hunters. At Yaregong, on the Tibetan border, he met and became friendly with the French missionaries, especially with the missionary-botanist, André Soulié, who was also a skilled physician and linguist fluent in all the difficult frontier dialects. Soulié from his Tibetan marches had sent over 7,000 dried specimens to Paris. While staying at Soulié's mission during a Tibetan border uprising led by Tibetan monks, foreigners were seized, tortured and killed. The mission was set upon; Soulié captured with several other missionaries, was tortured and hacked to death. In the skirmish and murders, Forrest and eighty of the mission staff escaped from Tseku with the monks in pursuit. Eventually all were caught and tortured to death except Forrest who managed to escape. Hiding by day, he fled through the mountains south leaving his boots behind because of their traceable prints. Nearly captured he again escaped, wading a river over his head. Later he wrote. . . . "at the end of eight days I had ceased to care whether I lived or died. My feet were swollen out of all shape, my hands and face torn with thorns, and my whole person was caked in mire and blood."

Starvation drove him to risk approaching a village where he found friendly people for a few days before the Tibetans were again upon him. He fled up river, through canebreaks, changing his directions for 6 days over glacier snows and ice that ribboned his feet. At last when he thought he was safe, he came to a maize field only to step upon a farmer's panji, a sharpened bamboo stake booby-trap. It completely pierced through his foot. He tore the stake loose and after some days he eventually found refuge in a mission house in a town where Chinese soldiers were stationed. It took several months for his foot to be healed sufficiently for him to walk again.

It was here, in Yunnan, that he discovered *S. yunnanensis* in 1906 and sent back seed that introduced it into commerce. A less hearty soul after such trying experiences would have willingly sailed for home, but not George Forrest. He had a deep love for the country of Yunnan, its people and customs and continued on plant hunting for new species for another twenty-four years—years of prolific output. In 1931 from Tonghai (then Teng-yueh), Yunnan, he wrote, "When all are dealt with and packed I expect to have nearly, if not more than, two mule-loads of good clean seed, representing some 4 to 5,000 species, and a mule load means 130 to 150 lbs., that is something like 300 lbs. of seed. . . . If all goes well I shall have made a rather glowing and satisfactory finish to all my past years of labor. . . ." Indeed, it was a glowing finish to the thousands of seeds and plants he had shipped over the 28 years!

As the last parcels were packed and sent on their way, Forrest went snipe hunting which was a favorite hobby. While in the field he developed chest pains and asked to be chair-carried to a low wall. As a snipe drummed overhead George Forrest raised his gun—shot—and fell to the ground dead! He was buried there in Yunnan that he so loved. It was the fall of the year 1931.

Reginald Farrer

Reginald Farrer born in Yorkshire, England, Henry John Elwes, Glouchestershire, England and E. H. M. Cox, another Englishman were in that class of amateur plant collectors who did considerable collecting mostly in Burma and on returning, turned their plant collecting experiences into books of outstanding merit and interest. Although important for their work (Farrer with his 'tea' hunting in Burma) none of them discovered or is particularly noted for plant hunting that included lilacs. They are mentioned only because of their relationship to the plant hunters who did discover or send back seeds of *Syringa* species. Farrer will ever be known for his two books on Gansu Sheng in which he described its northwestern mountains as ". . . stretching across the world from easterly to westerly in one unbroken rank of impregnable 18,000 foot dolomite needles, crags, castles and pinnacles." In his books, *On the Eaves of the World* and *Rainbow Bridge,* Farrer proves to be a master of words and descriptions, especially on the experiences and conditions of plant hunting in the mountainous country. E. H. M. Cox, who accompanied Farrer on his first journey of plant collecting later authored the book *The Plant Introductions of Reginald Farrer* which gives the considerable contributions of this collector. Cox wrote of Farrer's colorful character, ". . . his stocky figure clad in khaki shorts and shirt, tieless and colorless, a faded topee on his head, old boots, and stockings that gradually slipped down and clung around his ankles as the day wore on . . . the constant use of the field glasses which always hung around his neck . . . and his intense satisfaction when a plant was once in his collection bag—his enjoyment of our evening tot of rum . . . his indomitable energy . . . his frame so unlikely for searching and climbing . . ." There has never been his likes as an alpine gardener nor as dashing a character as a plant collector. Farrer had a fine sense of humor despite torrential rains and mountain trails . . . "he set out on his pony (called 'Spotted

Fat') followed by a faithful servant whom he called 'The Dragon'." Although only forty, the climate and harshness of plant journeys caught up with him at his chest. Each day he could do less. Unable to eat he could take only whiskey and soda—eight thousand miles from home, in the unrelenting rains of the Chinese-Burma borderlands he died, as 'The Dragon' wrote to 'Mr. E. H. M. Cox'— ". . . without giving any of us pain or trouble!" (*Bon jardinier, mon ami et amie*—such were the lives of these adventurous men who loved plants and the life-giving search for new species! From them have come our treasured garden lilacs and many other plants that once grew as wild and far away as the mountain valleys of Gansu, Yunnan and Sichuan! Their lives are filled with such wonderful and awesome tales!)

Are there still some undiscovered Chinese species? We have no records of plant explorers for lilacs in far western China, Quinghai Sheng, Xizang Sheng, Xinjiang Shen and its Altun Shan (Altun Mountains), nor have the mountain ranges of Hengduan Shan, Tanggula (Dangla) Shang been explored for lilacs. Surely one should expect some species from these enormously vast, colder areas as from the other provinces of China. There is yet much lilac exploring to be done in China and the vast reaches of Tibet. Perhaps some native Chinese plant explorers will accomplish this and find the fabled home of the legendary *S. afghanica* (to which we deny species status today) or the home of *S. meyeri* (so far found only in Chinese gardens).

The northeastern provinces of Liaoning, Juling and Heilongjang Sheng as well as the mountain areas of Nei Monggol surely have not been exhausted. In time they will be searched out or their plant materials lost forever.

Lilacdom is deeply indebted to the great land of China that has mothered the many species of lilacs among the richness of its native plants. What other discoveries may yet be made remains untold. Meanwhile we glory in what we have obtained from mother China in lilacs! Great strides have been made in hybridizing these many species. They have prospered well both in Canada and in the United States and more recently in Russia. Already their children are named as Prestonian Hybrids, Skinner Hybrids, various late hybrids, multibrids and tetraploids—what wonderful portents for the future.

The Great Botanical and Horticultural Institutions
The Treasures of the Plant Collectors

No account of plant explorations would be complete without mention of the great world horticultural herbariums, gardens and arboreta that often were the recipients, the guardians of herbarium materials obtained in these difficult expeditions and which, most often, kept careful account by number of each seedling sent them. It was through these great educational-horticultural institutions that most of the plant introductions were made and preserved for our gardens. No price can be placed on their work and value.

Foremost one must mention the horticultural nursery firm of Veitch in England. Singly they undertook to send plant collectors to the Orient on several occasions and perhaps were the most significant nursery in acquiring and selling new plants from the Orient. They trained and undertook the financial burdens of extensive explorations. Wilson's first two explorations in China were under their auspices.

Although several horticultural institutions became the deposits of these plant treasures (in England, Scotland, France, Austria, Germany, Italy, Russia, Sweden and the United States), I would specifically point out the tremendous contributions in the history of the lilacs of the Royal Botanical Gardens at Kew, England, perhaps the paternal institution of longest horticultural standing and outstanding reputation; the magnificent work in horticulture, plant research and archival and herbarium materials of The Arnold Arboretum, Jamaica Plains, Massachusetts, U.S.A. (so dear and close to me) and the long and renowned work and herbarium, archival materials of the Library at St. Petersburg, now the University of Leningrad, formerly the Library at St. Petersburg, U.S.S.R., which has for centuries been the repository for many famous European and Asian botanists and plant explorers. To these must be added the name of the Jardin in Paris, France, whose archives and herbarium materials are replete with botanical writings and specimens collected by countless scholars. Most active in present day plant explorations appear to be The Arnold Arboretum, The Royal Botanical Gardens at Kew and the University of Tokyo, Japan. The activities of other institutions are not as well known to me.

Arnold Arboretum Plant Expedition, July 30, 1926. Campsite by the Jo-Shui (Ruo Shui River), Yobehung Valley, Gansu Sheng, China. ". . . a place of grandeur and filled with botanical treasures . . . a plant hunters' paradise . . ." (Photo by J. F. Rock, courtesy Archives of Arnold Arboretum.)

The 'Lilac Walk" of Harvard University's famous Arnold Arboretum, the mother and pre-eminent arboretum of American gardens in plant materials, research, plant explorations, and plant archives. (Photo Archives of Arnold Arboretum.)

In the United States I wish to draw attention to the specialized work of The Arnold Arboretum for the past century on behalf of the lilac. It has not only kept one of the finest herbariums of *Syringa* species but also has maintained a magnificent collection of growing plants. Many of the original introductions of lilac species are still to be found in this fine collection. For lilacs it is the 'mother' institution in America. From this single source have come most of the species in commerce in North America and countless named cultivars. To me it is the greatest repository of living, authentic lilac materials in the world.

More recently introductions of lilacs have been made from South Korea through the explorations of the U.S. National Arboretum at Washington, D.C. (*S. oblata donaldii*) and the University of New Hampshire at Durham, N.H., introductions from Korean *S. patula* seed and the *S. vulgaris* seed collecting of Dr. Radcliffe Pike. In the past few years additional seed has been collected in China by several individuals, among them Peter Bristol of the Holden Arboretum, and Roger Luce of Hampden Highland, Maine. For several years the Royal Botanical Gardens at Hamilton, Ontario, Canada, has disseminated the *S. vulgaris* hybrids and species hybrids more recently developed in the U.S.S.R. as has the National Arboretum at Washington, D.C. which perhaps has the largest number of Russian and Polish lilac introductions.

Mrs. McKelvey gives more explicit taxonomical information from many plant botanists and taxonomists. For those interested in updating her materials the archives of the institutions mentioned give much pertinent information on the lilac.

Chronological Listing of Principal *Syringa* Explorations in China and Japan

1742—Pierre d'Incarville of France found *S. pekinensis* in the Beijing Mountains.

1750—Pierre d'Incarville, a French Jesuit botanist, discovered *S. villosa* in the Beijing Mountains

1831—Alexander Bunge, a Russian botanist, explored the areas of China around Beijing and sent lilac specimens back to St. Petersburg.

1831—R. Blinkworth, an Englishman working for the East India Co., collected *S. emodi* in the Kurum Valley of Afghanistan.

1831—P. V. Kirilov, a Russian botanist and explorer discovered *S. pekinensis* in the Beijing Mountains and sent seed to St. Petersburg.

1835—P. V. Kirilov rediscovered *S. villosa* and sent plant materials back to St. Petersburg.

1840—P. V. Kirilov discovered *S. pubescens* in Hebei Sheng.

1853–1856—Robert Fortune of England on his third exploration to China sent the first live plants of *S. oblata* and *S. oblata* var. *alba* gathered from Chinese gardens back to England.

1855—Richard Maack and Karl Ivan Maximowicz, Russian botanists, independently each discovered *S. reticulata* var. *amurensis*.

1863—Père Armand David collected *S. pekinensis* in the Beijing Mountains and is credited as its discoverer.

1870—Major J. E. T. Aitchison from England discovered the mysterious *S. afghanica* in the Kurum Valley of Afghanistan.

1875—Karl Ivan Maximowicz collected *S. reticulata* var. *reticulata* in Japan calling it *S. japonica*.

1885—Grigori A. Potanin, a Russian, collected *S. oblata* var. *giraldii* in Shaanxi Sheng and also discovered *S. potaninii* in Gansu Sheng.

1887—Abbé Jean Marie Delavay, A Frenchman, discovered *S. yunnanensis* growing in the wooded areas around Lake Lanking in Yunnan Sheng.

1891–1894—Grigori A. Potanin discovered *S. komarowii* in Sichuan Sheng.

1891—Rev. Guiseppe Giraldi, an Italian missionary and botanist, gathered and identified *S. oblata* var. *giraldii* in Shaanxi Sheng.

1891—M. Bonvolat and Prince Henry of Orleans, travelers from France, discovered *S. tomentella* in Sichuan Sheng.

1893–1895—V. L. Komorov, a Russian botanist, sent seed of *S. wolfii* to St. Petersburg.

1895—Miss A. Sontag, of the Russian Legation, first collected *S. patula* near Seoul, Korea.

1896—Rev. Guiseppe Giraldi found *S. microphylla* growing in Shaanxi Sheng.

1901—Ernest H. Wilson, an Englishman, discovered *S. julianae* in Hebei Sheng and *S. reflexa* in western Hubei Sheng.

1904—E. H. Wilson working for the Veitch Firm discovered *S. pinnatifolia* in western Sichuan Sheng and sent seed of *S. sweginzowii.*

1906—George Forrest, a Scot, from his plant explorations in Yunnan Sheng brought back seed of *S. yunnanensis* and introduced this species into commerce.

1907–1908—E. H. Wilson made his third plant exploration for the Arnold Arboretum bringing back additional seed of already discovered species.

1908—Frank N. Meyer, an American, found *S. meyeri* growing in gardens at Fengtai, Henon Sheng and brought back cuttings to the United States, as well as *S. oblata* var. *alba.*

1909–1911—William Purdom, an Englishman, sent additional information and plant materials on already discovered species.

1910–1911—E. H. Wilson made a fourth exploration on behalf of the Arnold Arboretum sending back additional seed and pictures of already discovered species.

1913–1915—Frank N. Meyer sent back additional materials and seed of already discovered species.

1917—E. H. Wilson on his fifth trip sent back seed of *S. oblata* var. *dilatata* found in Korea.

1922–1923—Joseph Hers, a Belgian, sent specimens of *S. microphylla* and *S. julianae* 'Hers' to Europe and the United States.

1924–1925—E. H. Wilson on his sixth trip to China sent back seed of *S. pinnatifolia* and other previously discovered species to the Arnold Arboretum.

1925–1926—J. F. Rock, an American working for the Arnold Arboretum Expedition, sent back lilac specimens and seed of already discovered species from southwestern China.

1934—H. Smith, a Swede, discovered *S. tigerstedtii* in Sichuan Sheng introducing the species at the University of Uppsala, Sweden.

1947—Professor E. M. Meader, of the University of New Hampshire, N.H., United States, collected seed of *S. patula* in the Pouk Han Mountains, Korea, from which he raised the cultivar *S. patula* 'Miss Kim'.

1977—Robert and Jelena de Belder brought *S. debelderi* from South Korea.

1977–78—The U.S. Dept. of Agriculture, Division of Forestry from an expedition in South Korea's Mt. Sorak National Park regions brought back for the National Arboretum, Washington, D.C. seed of a new subspecies, *S. oblata* var. *donaldii.*

1980—Peter Bristol from plant explorations in Sichuan Sheng for the Holden Alboretum, Mentor, Ohio, U.S.A., brought back seed of *S. oblata.*

1981—The Arnold Arboretum plant explorations brought back several already collected species.

There are undoubtedly other plant explorations to China that included species and cultivars of *Syringa* of which the author is unaware. It is significant that the many species and cultivars of lilacs were discovered and introduced over a period covering more than 240 years by men and women from many nations making it, indeed, an international shrub. Even the most recent explorations have found new species that have enriched lilacdom with additional cultivars. Perhaps somewhere in the vastness of mother China there still remain some few undiscovered species and rare cultivars.

The Species Lilacs from China, India, The Isles of Japan and Korea

In the following pages are presented the different species of lilacs that are readily accepted as such by most authorities today (with the exception of *S. debelderi*, which is so new as to be described for the first time botanically in this book). The accepted names for each species are given according to the latest nomenclature. Their older, not acceptable, taxonomical names are also given for those who may have lilacs known to them only by these older names. The only two non-verified species given are *S. afghanica* and *S. pinetorum*, which the author does believe are in cultivation. They are included so that the reasons for their non-acceptance might be given. Most species are presented with at least one color photo, or more. Some because of their rarity are difficult to find and to photograph. I am deeply indebted to the Arnold Arboretum for pictures from their Archives and to Charles Holetich, of the Royal Botanical Gardens Staff, Hamilton, Ontario, Canada, for those pictures used that were better than my own or which I did not have. Without their contributions the picture part of this chapter would not be possible.

Bon jardinier, there are many lovely hybrids that I have not been able to present in color photos but know that they are indeed lovely and, where possible, worthy to be in the finest gardens.

SYRINGA AFGHANICA—Lilac of Legend and Mystery

In 1870 Major J. E. T. Aitchison collected in the Kuram Valley on the low outer hills near Shalizan, Afghanistan, at 7500 ft., a single specimen of a lilac that has remained an enigma to taxonomists and lilac specialists to this day. Aitchison called it *S. persica*. It was, as Schneider later wrote, "A wild plant as a small gnarled and much ramified dwarf shrub, with very finely leaved foliage; also the inflorescences are small, dense, terminal, compound panicles, lengthened and composed of terminal and lateral panicles... the flowers a lilac (color)..." From the Aitchison specimen Schneider is describing the plant he calls *S. afghanica*. The description seems to be in many ways quite identical with what was called *S.* × *persica laciniata*, then thought to be a hybrid plant and not a species, but now recognized as *S. laciniata* (which is a species).

From the fact that no other plant, or seeds of this plant have been found or introduced and from the somewhat sketchy specimen of Aitchison, one could and perhaps might wonder if there ever was a separate species *S. afghanica*. Aitchison's single plant could well have been a dwarfed, misshapen plant of another species or hybrid (e.g. *S. laciniata* or the hybrid *S.* × *persica*). There are today a few specimens known under the name of *S. afghanica*. In earlier lilac writings there was much confusion about *S. laciniata* as it was not considered a species. Mrs. McKelvey in her monograph seems to confuse *S. laciniata*, the species, with the hybrid *S.* × *persica*. Today we recognize *S. laciniata* as a true species and *S.* × *persica* as a hybrid, while we consider *S. afghanica* to be a somewhat difficult species as no cultivated plants exist.

If all this naming and describing of lilacs seems confusing, it is! Dr. James Pringle writing in 1978 sheds considerable light on the causes of the original confusion, concluding that *S. laciniata* has been most often confused for *S. afghanica*. He concludes that since there are no existing plants of the so called "true *S. afghanica*" it should be equated as an unacceptable name for *S. laciniata*. However, for 'historical reasons' he shows some reluctance to exclude it from his list of lilac species. Your author has not included *S. afghanica* as a true species, yet believes that there might be a lilac species of *S. afghanica*. Studies of the Aitchinson specimens are quite convincing. Recently, Dr. Peter Green, Kew Gardens, has done extensive work showing that this species does exist in the wilds of the Kurum Valley in Pakistan, and is a valid species.

However, if we do not accept *S. afghanica* as a true species, then what is the parentage of the sterile hybrid named *S.* × *persica* which we know has existed for a century as one of our fine garden shrubs? It had traditionally been called a hybrid of *S. afghanica* × *S. laciniata*. I suggest that it is probably a difficult hybrid of the Series Vulgares (perhaps var. *rhodopea* or of *S. oblata* or one of the newer species.) (*Bon jardinier,* do not trouble your head about these matters! Leave them to the taxonomists! Often the yarn does not come so easily from the ball, especially when there are knots and tangles that need unravelling! Only do not ask for a lilac called 'afghanica' in any nursery or expect to see it in any bona fide botanical garden or collection. I once had such a named plant that was given to me by one of our most prestigious arboreta—today we have both long since discarded it as a misnomer.)

SYRINGA DEBELDERI

What appears to be a new species of lilac was found by Robert and Jelena de Belder of Belgium while collecting plant materials in the Mt. Sorak National Park in South Korea. Seed labelled *S. Mt. Sorak* was sent by de Belder to both the Arnold Arboretum and the U.S. National Arboretum, Washington, D.C. in 1977. From plants grown at the National Arboretum plants were obtained for the lilac collection at Falconskeape, Medina, Ohio, from which the following description is made. I have chosen to call it *S. debelderi* to honor the de Belders.

Syringa debelderi belongs to the Series *Pubescentes*. The bush is extremely dwarf to about 70 cm high (6-year-old plants) and no more than 40 cm wide; canes and branches are slender, slow-growing and somewhat twiggy; leaves are small, opposite, intermediate in shape between those of *S. meyeri* and *S. patula*, with apices narrowly acuminate rather than obtuse, elliptic-ovate to oblong, bases broad-cuneate to rounded and of a dull medium-green, slightly pubescent to glabrous above, slightly whitish pubescent beneath, no more than 7 cm long and 5 cm wide. The primary veins and veinlets are conspicuous and raised on the underside. The inflorescences coming from both terminal and lateral buds, are small with panicles to 6 cm long and no more than 3–3.5 cm wide; buds are a lavender-purple with tubes of a paler lavender about 4 mm long; florets are single, opening to a medium to pale lavender-purple with a slight fragrance but not pronounced. Seed capsules are from 1–1.4 cm long, warty, often with 4 seeds per capsule. It appears to be entirely hardy to −20°C (at Medina, Ohio) and entirely so at the Arnold and National Arboretums. Herbarium specimens are at both of these arboretums. *S. debelderi* differs from other species of *Syringa* in the Series *Pubescentes* in the extreme dwarfness of the plant (it appears to be the most dwarf of all the *Syringa*), in the small size of the leaves, their unique shape, in the smallness of the inflorescences and in the unique size of the seed capsules. It is self-fertile and readily sets seeds.

The Type plant at the U.S. National Arbortum, Washington, D.C., is N.A. 41179, and at Falconskeep it is N.A. 41179-F3810.

SYRINGA DEBELDERI

Syringa debelderi est nova species collecta a Roberto et Jelena de Belder, Kalmthout, Belgium, in montibus regionibus Montis Sorak, Austra Korea, anno 1977, semina mittantur et ad Arboretum Arnoldianum, Jamaica Plains, Mass., et Arboretum Nationalem, Washington, D.C. sub nomine pro tempore *S. 'Mt. Sorak'*. Nomen *S. debelderi* eligitur ut honoretur familia de Belder, Kalmthout, Belgium. Plantes *S. debelderi*, seriei *Pubescentes*, formae omino minimae usque ad 70 cm altae (in sextis annis) et non maiore 40 cm latae; rames parvae, graciles, tarde crescentes brachyandribusque parvis; foliis parvis, opposite positis, intermediae formae *S. meyeri* et *S. patula*, cum apicibus anguste acuminatis quam obtusis, elliptice-ovatis usque ad oblongis, basibus late cuneatis paulisper rotundis, obscure medii-viridi coloris, pauliter pubescentibus et modice glabris supra, veinibus primariis et veiniculis conspicuis ad infra; modice albescentibus et pubescentibus ad infra, non maiore quam 7 cm longis et 5 cm latis; inflorescentes a gemmis et terminalis et lateralibus, minimae, paniculis 6 cm longis et 3 ad 3.5 cm latis, gemmis purpurea coloris, apertae flores lilaceae palescentes purpureae, minime fragrantes; capsules seminorum 1 cm ad 1.4 cm longae, verrucosae, saepe cum quattuor seminibus; plantes perhiemantes usque ad −20°C (Medina, Ohio) et omnino in arboretis Arnoldianae et in Washington, D.C.; herbarium specimen in utrisque arboretis. *S. debelderi* differt ab omnibus aliis syringarum seriei *Pubescentes* in parvissima forma, singularitate foliis, inflorescentibus et in capsulis seminorum. In his omnibus est omnino singularis. Typus N.A. 41179.

SYRINGA EMODI

In 1831 Nathaniel Wallich, listing the dried specimens of plants of the East India Company's botanic gardens at Calcutta, identified R. Blinkworth as the first to collect *S. emodi*. It was found in the Western Himalayas around Kuram Valley, Afghanistan. A rather tall shrub to 15 feet with upright branches and rather robust branchlets of a gray or olive-brown color. The leaves are oblong to elliptical from 2–9 in. long and from 1–5 in. wide. The primary veins and veinlets are conspicuously tinged with an Indian Purple coloring for half the length of the leaf. Inflorescences are borne on the leafy terminal shoots; color in bud is a pale greenish yellow tinged with pinkish mauve. When the flowers expand they are white. Some early botanists thought it was a form of *S. josikaea*, while others ascribed it to *S. villosa*. Today it appears to be a valid species. E. H. Wilson writing of *S. emodi* states, ". . . in the United States it is less hardy than any other species" and is one of the few lilacs "which thrive better in Great Britian than in New England". (Prof. Wilson did not consider the rest of the country but today it thrives as well in the midwestern U.S. as it does in England or even better.) There is no great difficulty in growing it well without winterkill in the midwest and central U.S. Perhaps the late summer droughts harden its growth more than in the East.

S. emodi, Royal Botanical Gardens, Kew, England. (Photo by E. H. Wilson, courtesy Archives of Arnold Arboretum.)

In late spring its flower buds on occasion may be touched by frosts. It is a broad, round shrub with heavy foliage and large leaves, opening late in the spring and among the last to fall in the autumn. It is a dirty bloomer in that its spent flowers do not fall neatly and there is an uneveness to their opening. Thus there are faded and opening florets on the same raceme giving an untidy appearance. (Alas, this untidy trait it passes on to its offspring! Hybridizers have not been able to do well with it.) In long summer droughts it often sheds many of its leaves. It is a shrub for the well-drained but moist loamy soils of mountain freshets or riverlet banks. Its most striking characteristic is its extremely lenticellate bark marked on the branchlets with long, pale verticle fissures, which on older and grayer branches give a fish-net appearance.

S. emodi, although not an attractive garden and landscape plant, may have some merit to the hybridizer, despite its retention of spent florets, in its strong leaf growth, interesting bark and its ability to transmit its white color to its hybrids. Good white blooming late hybrids are always in demand. It has been used to some extent in some of the multibrids (crosses containing several species) made by recent hybridizers. Its value has yet to be proven. A gold-leaved cultivar obtained as a mutation may have some appeal to those who specialize in oddities. Called *S. emodi* 'aurea' it is probably the best of all the gold-leaved and variegated oddities found in *Syringa*, retaining its gold color for most of the season before turning a pale green. At best it is a lilac for botanical collections. (*Jardinier*, you can do without it! If you must, the best specimen is at Highland Park, Rochester, N.Y., but do not tell them I told you.)

SYRINGA JULIANAE

This beautiful, rather low-growing, broad lilac, about five ft. in height with horizontally spreading branches carrying small velvety leaves was discovered by E. H. Wilson on a mountain cliff in western Hubei Sheng, China in 1901. (The taxonomist Schneider thought so much of it that he named it after his wife.) To this day, although it is one of the loveliest lilac species, *S. julianae* is relatively unknown in our gardens. It blooms a little later than most *S. vulgaris*, generally opening in late May into the first week of June in Ohio and always escapes even the latest frosts. The rather small, fragrant (spicy aromatic) flower clusters are borne in very great profusion all along the slender upper twiggy branches. The flowers of the species are a violet-purple on the outer surfaces of the corolla and petals and white to whitish-blushed the palest lavender within with violet anthers. This contrast of colors is strikingly beautiful. McKelvey notes that the verrucose (warty) seed capsules are now considered to be characteristic of this species (all the varieties have this same wartiness on the seed capsules). It is not unusual to find flowers with 5 or 6 corolla-lobes rather than the customary 4. *S. julianae* should be in every garden where there is space for a corner shrub or specimen! Give it room, as its branches can spread to 5 or 6 feet.

It does not fare well in heavy clay soils but needs a well-drained, gravel-sand, humus enriched location (remember Wilson found it on a mountain cliff). It is most intolerant of water-logged or wet situations but it does seem to accept rather dry sites. Perhaps this is why it is not often found in the heavy clay of the mid-west and central states, whereas it thrives in the soils of New England. We have grown it most successfully on a well-drained site mulched frequently with very well-rotted sawdust to 2 in. It seems to need no pruning and does not appear to be bothered by lilac pests or scale. This does not mean that it is totally immune to them, but in our 35 years with this species we have not experienced difficulties. Here it has been completely hardy to at least −30°F. Although *S. julianae* appears to be somewhat self-sterile it hybridizes freely with *S. microphylla*. (They must be very closely related species.) It is one of the few lilacs that grows in the northern part of Florida where it blooms fairly well but not as profusely as it does in the North.

S. julianae 'Hers'.

A pale-lavender variety of *S. julianae* named 'Hers' was introduced by Joseph Hers, a Belgian, after a plant hunting expedition in China. It has wide weeping branches and forms a much broader bush than the species. Here at Falconskeape this variety has grown rather wide—a 10-year specimen is fully 12 ft. across and about 5 ft. tall. Each spring it is covered with cascading deep purple-violet buds that open a lighter lavender both on the outside and inner side of corolla and petals. And what a lovely fragrance! It is a plant most worthy of a quiet Buddist garden or a prayer house!

The notable difference between the 'Hers' variety and the species *S. julianae* is that the latter carries a flower which is a paler lavender on the outside and a blushed, pale lavender-white on the inside. *S. julianae* 'Hers' has a far deeper purple corolla and outer petals opening to a light lavender floret inside the petals. The 'Hers' form is a notable wide weeper with willowy sweeping branches whereas the species is far more upright although it, too, is a wide shrub. You must ask for it by name! (There are some taxonomists who insist that the species and the 'Hers' variety are the same. They must not have seen them growing side by side.)

S. julianae 'George Eastman'

One of the newest and reddest cultivars of *S. julianae*. Magnificent in its rich wine-red buds and deep cerise-pink flowers it is an upright growing shrub. The rich reddish-pink is the same on the outer and inner sides of both corolla and petals, although the florets do fade to a lighter pink with age. It was a chance seedling of *S. julianae* planted on the gravelly high river bank at Durand-Eastman Park, Rochester, N.Y. (The entire planting demonstrates how lovely a naturalized grouping of this lilac can be). It is a slower growing form than *S. julianae* or the 'Hers' cultivar, needs well-drained gravelly soil and should not be transplanted too often but allowed to develop a good root system. It augurs to be a progenitor of a whole new series of *S. julianae* cultivars. Possibly it is a natural cross of *S. julianae* with *S. potaninii* or *S. microphylla*, although neither of these species were nearby the *S. julianae* original planting.

Recently *S. julianae* is being recognized for its beauty and good habits with hybridizers seeing its worth. For several years it has been hybridized by the author and more recently great strides have been made at the Royal Botanical Gardens, Hamilton, Ontario, Canada, in crossing *S. julianae* with *S. microphylla* 'Superba' and *S. meyeri* 'Palibin'. Several very fine hybrids have been produced from the continuing work of Joan Brown and more recently by Hugh Pearson of the R.B.G. Staff. Certainly our gardens will be filled in the years to come with the beauty found in *S. julianae* and its hybrids!

The Story of S. julianae 'George Eastman'—A Lilac of Serendipity

George Eastman, of Eastman Kodak fame, bestowed a gift upon the City of Rochester that in time became known as Durand-Eastman Park. It is a magnificent piece of property close to Lake Ontario, with hills, rivers and small lakes. If one were looking for a bit of the mountains and hills of China with their mirror lakes, he could not find a more ideal spot in which to plant some of the horticultural wonders of that land. It was in these areas that Bernard Slavin, then Parks Superintendent, mapped out some of Rochester's most beautiful horticultural collections. Here the rare *Davidia involucrata* flourishes with its fluttering dove-like blossoms; the Oriental Crabapples paint the hillsides with color every Spring; magnificent specimens of *Acer griseum* display their cinnamon and bright orange peeling bark! It is a natural park where these transplanted, Oriental treasures growing as if they were native. Here springtime comes gradually and winters are tempered by the great Lake. Along one of the streams, as it rounds a bend paralleled by a curving road, Slavin planted a number of lilac seedlings. For want of a better name they were called *Syringa* species.

In time they grew. Spreading shrubs, slender of branch, arching, they rooted in the well-drained, gravelly-sandy soil high along the stream banks and bloomed in shades of pale and deeper lavenders each year. In the springs of 1971 and 1972, a few plants of their seedlings struck the attention of Park Superintendent, Richard Fennicchia, and Park Taxonomist, Robert B. Clark. Were these dark, reddish-purple lilacs something different? They were shown to the author in 1971, who was given a cutting of one of them (there appeared to be two separate plants, both a slightly different reddish-purple), a rosy, carmine-red budded plant. The cutting was successfully rooted and grown at Medina, Ohio. Meanwhile circumstances forced the widening of the road at Durand-Eastman Park, and the remaining lilacs were removed. Some of the reddish seedlings were propagated at the Park nursery. Happenstance and wet weather worked their way and the seedlings were eventually lost. The remaining survivor was the single plant in Medina at Falconskeape. It was immediately propagated, a plant being sent to the U.S. National Arboretum, another to Birchwood Gardens, Meredith, New Hampshire and one to the Landis Arboretum, Esperance, N.Y. Cuttings were sent to Wedge Nursery and to California. Happenstance or whatever, the National Arboretum, New Hampshire and the Medina plants appear to be the only survivors.

It is a delicate grower requiring perfect drainage and gravelly soil but a wonderful plant in bloom. Correctly it is a form of *S. julianae* (not of *S. microphylla*) as were all the naturalized lilacs in this Durand-Eastman Park planting. It had naturalized itself from seed as lilacs on occasion do. (Another example of naturalized lilacs are the hundreds of *S. reticulata* at Delhi, New York.) a second set of propagations has since been undertaken. Hopefully it will be more widely appreciated and in time made available to the general public. It was dutifully named *S. julianae* var. 'George Eastman' in honor of the generous park patron and to commemorate the Park where it was found naturalized along the river bank.

We owe a special debt to all three men who first discovered it, who pointed it out as unique and outstanding and who kept alive its rooted cuttings. May it prove to be a great milestone to hybridizers (it does set seed and is fertile) and a delight to all who eventually have it in their gardens. Lilacdom is filled with circumstances of serendipity! (*Mon ami*, do not give up hope; it could well happen in your own garden too! But please recognize them.)

S. julianae 'Pink Parasol'

One of the most recent *S. julianae* cultivars (Fiala 1980). It is a dainty baby-pink form with recurved, parasol-like florets on an upright plant. It shows the great diversity obtainable by intensive breeding in this lovely species. *S. julianae* 'Sentinel' and 'Epaulettes' are newer larger headed introductions of *S. julianae* 'Hers' × *S. julianae* 'George Eastman'. 'Epaulettes' has broad-shouldered blooms.

SYRINGA KOMAROWII—'Komarov/Komarof's Lilac'

S. komarowii, one of the finest of the native species from China, was first collected for the Botanic Garden, St. Petersburg, Russia, probably by the plant explorer, A. Potanin, whose materials were sent to the St. Petersburg Garden. Schneider, who described and named it from the Botanical Garden materials, points out that it was collected in Sichuan Province, China, on July 18, 1893 and has, "as a shrub.... older branches gray-brown ... leaves deep green ... inflorescence narrow to large ... flowers violet...." Others describe the flower color as 'reddish-violet or a deeper pale rose-pink with violet tints' (For us at Falconskeape it is a paler tone of light violet over a deeper rose-pink.) Undoubtedly soils have much to do with these differences in coloration.

Since *S. komarowii* closely resembles *S. reflexa*, in early writings there was some confusion as to its rank as a species. E. H. Wilson believed it to be an extreme form of the very variable *S. reflexa*. Today we consider it as a separate species. It has much to offer as a garden plant and as a parent in hybridizing. Many of the plants labeled as *S. komarowii* today do not have the intense drooping character of inflorescence pictured in McKelvey's book. Undoubtedly there are many misnamed lilacs in horticultural collections purportedly this species. An exceptionally fine form of *S. komarowii*, described originally by Sargent as *S. wolfii*, is found at the Arnold Arboretum. In some respects *S. komarowii* in leaf and vigor appears to be a better plant than *S. reflexa* but the latter is better and more showy in bloom.

 S. komarowii is an outstanding species for hybridizing. Recent tribrids of *S. sweginzowii* × *S. tomentella* × *S. komarowii* have given us cultivars such as 'Lark Song' and 'Spellbinder' which is a cross of *S. komarowii* × *S. wolfii*. *S. komarowii* is one of the better species for bloom in landscape use. As a shrub to 10 ft. it is ideal for background plantings. Use *S. komarowii* in mass plantings before Russian Olive. It will not grow too tall and the feathery plumes go so well with the soft-leaved olive. Its summer, good, green leaves are also a fine combination with the silvery background. The contrast of its pinkish-lavender blossom against a background of silvery olive is well worth the effort.

 S. komarowii grows to about 10 ft., a bit more in very good soils, and is more rounded than weeping. It rarely suckers but comes readily from seed, of which there is always an abundance. "The somewhat upright branches are lenticellate, marked with conspicous ridges, color brownish-gray. The leaf scars are much raised, shield-shaped, very conspicuous, large . . . leaves ovate-oblong to oblong-lanceolate . . . 2 to 6 inches long and ½ to 3 inches broad . . . base cuneate, dark dull green, glabrous above, paler pubescent beneath . . . Inflorence is borne on leafy shoots that are terminal, often somewhat nodding or pendulous about 2 to 6 inches long and 2 inches broad." (One observation is that they are slightly larger and broader than Mrs. McKelvey describes.)

 As we have mentioned, the relationship between *S. komarowii* and *S. reflexa* is so close that at some future date taxonomists may classify them as extremes of the same species. However, today they are considered by most as separate species.

SYRINGA LACINIATA (*S. protolaciniata* Green)

 One of the most beautiful and useful species, *S. laciniata*, has had a confusing past because of its unique cutleaf form. *S. laciniata* and its hybrid with whatever lilac it was (*S. vulgaris*, *S. oblata*), called *S.* × *persica*, were taxonomically misplaced. Linnaeus, himself, confused this lilac and made the hybrid *S.* × *persica* the species type, calling it *S. persica*. In modern times Susan McKelvey made a similar mistake calling the species (*S. laciniata*) *S. persica* var. *laciniata*. Today we recognize *S. laciniata* as a true species and *S.* × *persica* as its hybrid.

 Frank Meyer found *S. laciniata* growing wild on January 17, 1915 near Palitang, near Kingchow, Gansu, China. (N-40,709) It was one of the first oriental lilacs to travel. Crossed somewhere along the way (probably with *S. oblata* or one of its varieties), it found its way as the hybrid *S.* × *persica* into Persia long ago. Here the hybrid flourished and was called *S. persica*. Because of its great beauty and ease of culture it was planted everywhere. Even today this hybrid, *S.* × *persica* (the Persian Lilac) waves its two feet of lavender-pink floral wands from the Iranian hill gardens even to our own gardens, parks and estates. So well-known is the hybrid with its massed beauty that it attracts all passers-by. Not so well known is the parent, *S. laciniata*, which in its own right is a lovely and enchanting lilac. (How often, *mon ami*, the child surpasses the parent!)

 S. laciniata (although not quite as showy as its hybrids) is an outstanding species worthy of a place in any garden that has room. It is a rather tall plant to 12 ft., perhaps somewhat less, spreading an equal distance with age. In the spring its willowy, somewhat arched branchlets are covered with lavender-purple buds opening to a lighter pale-lavender bloom. It is a modest shrub, easy of culture, undemanding, a fine annual bloomer and relatively free of pests. The plant bears both full and cut leaves on often the same stem. The leaves of both forms are not large and of a dark to medium green color, mostly free of insect pests. The inflorescenses are borne in many, somewhat small, clusters along the slender branches giving the total effect of a long flowering wand. They are mostly a pale lavender in color. Give your plant good soil, drainage and sunlight and it will be admired in your garden.

 S. laciniata is best known for its two outstanding hybrids, the oldest of which (*S.* × *persica*) is a sterile hybrid. Taxonomists in the past were rather quick to ascribe its parentage to a so called *S. afghanica* × *S. laciniata*. The difficulty with this is that there is no really hard, scientific evidence that there ever was a species *S. afghanica*. The author does accept the evidence for a species called *S. afghanica*—it is one of lilacdom's cherished legends. It would be safer to assume that one of the forms of *S. oblata* (quite possibly a form of *S. oblata dilatata*) crossed with *S. laciniata* and gave us the magnificent sterile hybrid we now call *S.* × *persica*. Both *S. laciniata* and *S. oblata* with its many forms

S. × *persica,* once thought to be a valid species, now is found to be a hybrid of *S. laciniata* and an unknown species (most probably a form of *S. vulgaris* or *S. oblata*). Plant shown is growing on the hillside at the Arnold Arboretum. (Photo, Arnold Arboretum.)

are found in the Gansu Sheng (Kansu Province) and neighboring provinces of China.

The second group of *S. lacinata* hybrids are those called *S.* × *chinensis*, all of which are crosses of *S. laciniata* × *S. vulgaris*. McKelvey misidentified this hybrid as being a cross of *S. persica* and *S. vulgaris*. She writes, "*S. chinensis* is now believed to be a hybrid between the two Linnean species *S. persica* and *S. vulgaris*." It is known to have occurred as a natural hybrid about 1777 at the Botanic Garden at Rouen of which Varin was the director. Varin made no artificial crosses but *LE BON JARDINIER* of 1805 quotes him as stating that after 1777 for a number of years he sowed seed of the cut-leaved Persian Lilac (*S. persica* var. *laciniata* [to McKelvey] and to us the present day species *S. laciniata*) always obtaining this intermediate plant, 'le Lilas Varin'." Varin's Lilac was the first of the crosses. These were first called Rouen Lilac or Chinese Lilac. The official name is now *S.* × *chinensis* due to Wildenow's error in thinking that it came from China. The cross has been made several times since and among the *S.* × *chinensis* hybrids are some of the loveliest and most useful of the garden shrubs. All of the *S. laciniata* clan, with its increasing number of excellent hybrids, are easy growing, from 12–15 ft. high (after many years), form upright rounded bushes equally as wide or wider, sucker very little, have rather slender branchlets and flower from the branch extremities on several lateral buds giving the inflorescence a long flowered effect. They are excellent for mass effect and color, producing enormous amounts of bloom. Some of these *S.* × *chinensis* hybrids that are better known and available are: *S.* × *chinensis* 'alba' similar in every way to Varin's *S.* × *chinensis* 'metensis' a pale lavender (once called 'varina metensis', 'Varin's Lilac' or the 'Rouen Lilac'). (My own specimen from Lemoine was labeled 'varina metensis'.) *S.* × *chinensis* 'Bicolor', introduced by Lemoine, when examined closely has its pale whitish petals offset by a small, but prominent, deep-purple eye making it an outstanding plant for close viewing; *S.* × *chinensis* 'Lavender Lady' a pinkish-lavender; *S.* × *chinensis* 'Red Rothomagensis' (or simply 'Rothomagensis') is another name for the Rouen Lilac. Equally beautiful are *S.* × *chinensis* 'Crayton Red' and *S.* × *chinensis* 'Saugeana' (the reddish cultivar most frequently planted and stocked by nurserymen). Lemoine's *S.* × *chinensis* 'President Hayes' is another reddish form beautiful but little known. Certainly the named cultivars should be more widely propagated by nurserymen and therefore more widely grown. As hybridizers continue to make this cross of *S. laciniata* with newer forms of *S. vulgaris* we can expect exciting hybrids, even doubles.

S. lacinata, S. × *persica,* and the *S.* × *chinensis* hybrids are most useful in larger groups where they give a massive show of color, used as hedges or as single specimens (*mon ami,* they are truly *magnifique!*) An excellent use of *S.* × *chinensis* and *S.* × *persica* can be seen in the Royal Botanical Gardens, Hamilton, Ontario, Canada, and in Highland Park, Rochester, New York. These plantings embody the best that can be achieved with good landscaping design. (I particularly like the unique *S.* × *chinensis* 'Bicolor' on the hillside path at Highland Park). They are all heavy bloomers (perhaps because they produce little or no seed), are not offensively perfumed, are graceful in form and subdued in color range. Should you need a thick boundary hedge, or a screen to hide service areas, play courts or a neighbor's building, they are excellent choices. Small birds delight in building their nests in their slender branches which are too thin for a cat to climb. They sucker very little. All are beautiful and the newest hybrids have not diminished the utility and beauty of the first hybrids of Varin and Lemoine. (Unfortunately, *mon ami,* they are not for a small city lot or very restricted garden, but if you have room by all means plant them all!)

A hybrid cross, unusual because it is interseries described by Rehder in the *Journal of the Arnold Arboretum* (16: 362–1935), (presumably the cross was made in 1947 by Dr. Sax), is that of *S. pinnatifolia* × *S. oblata* (plants of it do not seem now to exist). Another cross made by Dr. Sax in 1947, also called *S.* × *diversifolia* was between *S. pinnatifolia* × *S. laciniata* producing plants..."vigorous and including plants of possible horticultural value." This hybrid may be found at the Arnold Arboretum and Agriculture Canada Research Station, Mordem, Manitoba. Skinner made this cross naming *S.* × *diversifolia* 'William H. Judd', a plant of fine growth with possible benefits if used in hybridization. I have not been able to ascertain the fertility of this cross, as my own plants so far have not set seed; they are quite young and bloom only sparsely. (The only plants I have seen offered are from the plant auction of rare lilacs at the annual International Lilac Conventions. At times *S.* × *diversifolia* has been auctioned.)

SYRINGA MEYERI

The beautiful *S. meyeri* is known only as a cultivated plant. It was first found in the gardens at Fengtai near Beijing in the Province of Henan, China. It is a low, compact shrub growing only to 5 ft. with sturdy upright branches. It flowers in smaller clusters of pale lilac to lilac-purple, even to a whitish-lavender. In some ways it is quite similar to *S. pubescens.* It has never been found in the wild, leading some authorities to believe it may be a hybrid or varietal form of one of the lilacs to which it is so similar. The Chinese call it *Shau ting hsien,* according to Frank N. Meyer, who was the first to send cuttings back to the United States Department of Agriculture in 1909. Meyer relates that it is much used for forcing in China. With the two sets of *S. meyeri* cuttings Meyer sent home, he also notes that one has a slightly different color. "There are two white-flowering ones among them. Keep them protected from heavy frosts. It has a future for the western people as a very graceful, spring-flowering shrub of dwarfy habit."

S. meyeri has proven to be entirely hardy and has the habit, observed in *S. microphylla,* of blooming again in late summer or very early autumn if the season is favorable. The venation of the leaves, paralleling the margins, appears to be the characteristic most clearly distinguishing *S. meyeri* from other closely related lilacs, according to McKelvey.

Joseph Hers, who also collected this species in Chengchow in northern Honan, China, on April 20, 1920, notes that, "There the Chinese call it *Nan-ting-siang* (the South Syringa), that it is a slow grower to only 4 and 5 feet, very scented and a dark lilac, rarely found on its own roots mostly grafted on privet. Its name seems to imply a foreign or southern origin." McKelvey concludes in her consideration of *S. meyeri,* "It is possible that further study may lead to the conclusion that *S. meyeri,* as yet unknown as a wild plant, is merely a selected form of *S. pubescens.*" (*The Lilac,* p. 172). With others, your author would give it separate species status, at least for the present.

S. meyeri var. 'Palibin' is a beautiful, delightful small lilac, at one time called *S. palibiniana* (since 1960 this misnomer no longer prevails). It is the most dwarf of all lilacs reaching up to 4 or 5 ft. only after many years if left unpruned. What a fine deep-green hedge it makes all by itself with or without pruning. It always remains a close growing, twiggy shrub to 3 or 4 ft. Its bright, dark, green leaves, glossy, small and somewhat leathery, give it added value throughout the season. In the spring it is covered with deep purple buds that burst into a lavender-pinkish tinged blue bloom. In blossom alone it bears some similarity to *S. microphylla* which is pinker and a much taller shrub. It spreads moderately by underground suckers and is rather easy to root from early spring shoots taken in the first weeks of June. The plant suckers well if given a good mulch of well-rotted sawdust. It likes loose soil somewhat on the dry side.

This cultivar 'Palibin' has been grown for many years in England as a rock garden shrub, for which purpose it is ideally suited. Here at Falconskeape it annually sets seed rather heavily and the seedlings are easy to grow (our plant is from the Arnold Arboretum). One must give the seedlings some protection for the first winter as they root so shallowly that they are subject to heavy freezing and thawing. After the second or third year they need no extra protection. The seedlings (open pollinated) are somewhat variable, so to assure the dwarf form, cuttings should be rooted. I am certain it will prove an excellent cultivar for hybridists. As a shrub use it for hedges, in the rock garden as a small focal plant and it adapts magnificently as a Japanese bonsai specimen.

(*Mon ami*, remember you do not find this fine lilac growing in any nursery. You must ask for it by name *S. meyeri* var. 'Palibin'! It is, indeed, outstanding! Remember in the past it has been called *S. palbiniana*, *S. meyeri*, Ingwersen's Dwarf, even *S. microphylla minor*.)

Only recently has *S. meyeri* 'Palibin' been used in hybridization. A lovely plant 'Josee', which was introduced from France in 1974 by G. Morel, is a tribrid, (*S. patula* × *S. microphylla*) × *S. meyeri*. The author has hybridized it for several years (see *S. julianae*), and rather extensive hybridization using *S. meyeri* 'Palibin', *S. microphylla* and *S. julianae* continues at the Royal Botanical Gardens, Hamilton, Ontario, Canada, under H. Pearson assisted by Margo Belknac, who are continuing the 1975 work of Joan Brown. Very fine and interesting hybrids are resulting from their work.

SYRINGA MICROPHYLLA—The Littleleaf Lilac

S. microphylla was first described by Ludwig Diels in an article *Die Flora von Central China* written in 1901 for Engler's *BOTANISCHE JAHRBÜCHER*. Diels' description is based on two fruiting specimens collected in October, 1896 by the missionary botanist Rev. Giuseppe Giraldi in the mountains at *Tui-kio-san* in northern Shaanxi Sheng (Shensi Province), China. It had been collected before this date by other plant explorers but not described botanically. Subsequently, it has been located as a native in Shanxi Sheng, Hebei Sheng, Hunan and Gansu Sheng, a very widely distributed lilac species over an enormous area. Diels describes it "—with all new growth short-pilose, leaves small broad-ovate at base, obtuse or acuminate, above a deep green, beneath pale glabrescent, on both sides especially beneath short-pilose with reticulate veins... with panicles 5–7 cm long".

It is an important species, probably first collected by Ludwig Loczy (a Hungarian plant explorer) in 1879 at *Tsing Tschon*, Gansu Sheng (Kansu Province). Several others also collected *S. microphylla*: Dr. Augustine Henry in 1882; G. A. Potanin found it growing near *Hui dui* in western Gansu (Kansu) in May of 1885... "The flower cluster, pedicel and calyx are densely pubescent" ("*S. microphylla* is very similar to *S. pubescens*. In the latter, the pubescence of the leaves is long villose along the midrib, whereas, in *S. microphylla* short pubescent." McKelvey). Giraldi collected it in 1896; Frater Hugh Scallan at *Mt. Miao uan san*, northern Hupeh in 1898; P. C. Silvester found it in Hupeh in 1907 and by William Purdom in Shaanxi Sheng (Shensi) in 1910, while Joseph Hers in 1919 collected many specimens of it in Hunan Sheng (Honan) noting, "The flowers are used as a substitute by the Chinese for tea". In Gansu Province he notes the people call it *Tze ki ting siang* (the Fourseason Lilac) for it is said to flower all year around." (As a fact it will throw intermittent flower heads most of the summer if the season be good, and a fair show of bloom again in the autumn.) In 1925 J. F. Rock found it as a cultivated specimen in a lamasery at Chomi, China, growing as a tree form from 15–20 ft. with pink flowers lacking a strong fragrance (this is the tallest mentioned specimen) a smaller 6–8 ft. shrub had lavender flowers and small leaves." J. Hers (1922–23 expedition) found it much cultivated in Hunan Sheng (Honan Province)... "the Chinese here call it *yeh ting siang* (the wild syringa), the flowers are dark lilac, very sweet scented." He sent specimens from several areas back to the United States.

All in all, it is somewhat slow growing to about 8 ft. and with considerable breadth since many branches spread horizontally. ". . . the branchlets, yellow-green in color, are long, whispy and so slender as to droop under the weight of the flower clusters... flower clusters are small, rarely over 3 in. . . . but produced from lateral buds they appear from many pairs of buds on the same branchlet and intermingle producing what appears to be large and showy inflorescences . . . ten inches or more long . . . the flowers have a very sweet fragrance (the plant has the curious habit of blooming twice in the same season)" (McKelvey). We find the fragrance exquisitely unique, others claim it has little or no fragrance—it is a varied species, so there is little wonder that plants from widely different areas could well differ considerably.

S. microphylla, although the wood is somewhat brittle, is nonetheless a strong grower, but in moist seasons it does not stop growing and the late growth does not ripen leaving a 'twiggy' effect in the spring. (*S. potaninii* has this same messy habit—at least for us.) These dead branchlet tips can be annoying but are soon forgotten as the plant bursts into bloom. It does well in loamy-sandy-gravel. There is little difficulty in starting new plants from early spring cuttings. It does not appear to sucker at all and outside of the slight winter die-back at the tips of the smallest branchlets it requires little if any pruning.

A selected form, *S. microphylla* 'Superba', has a better pinkish blossom and supposedly larger florets. Although it sets much seed as a result of its long blooming period, most of it is sterile. It should prove a fine parent in hybridizing as its pollen is fertile.

S. microphylla flowered for the first time in the United States at the Arnold Arboretum in 1915: "It is far from being one of the handsomest of the lilacs but if it keeps up its habit of flowering a second time in autumn, it will be at least interesting, even if other lilacs are more beautiful." (A. A. Bulletin, Vol. III, p. 64) John Dunbar in his *NOTES* states, "It is a low grower with a loose habit." Upton calls it "A rare and very choice lilac." We would say, "A good lilac species with heavy bloom, a bit untidy but should prove an excellent parent for serious hybridizers. Time will probably tie it closer to some of the species in the Series Pubescentes and we may find some, we consider species today, as extremes of a single species." (Fiala).

SYRINGA OBLATA—The Early Blooming Lilac or the Broadleaf Lilac

S. vulgaris ordinarily blooms from mid-May through to the first week in June. From China and Korea comes a species, *S. oblata*, with several forms, that blooms from a week to nearly two weeks earlier. It is a sturdy lilac and where late frosts are not exceedingly bothersome *S. oblata* (and its many hybrids) can be a real 'Spring Opener'! For us at Medina, Ohio, where late frosts are unpredictable and often devastating, *S. oblata* always manages a delightful early display despite the frosts. Its hybrids with *S. vulgaris* are somewhat less reliable. (*Mon ami*, remember, there will always be a spring when all the lilacs fail because of the frost.) All the *S. oblata* subspecies are strong and healthy growers and seem somewhat less affected by that plague of lilacs, the scale—although they are not footproof!

Even though *S. oblata* and 3 or 4 of its subspecies have been identified we should not believe that 'all' of its forms have been discovered. It is a geographically widespread species occurring in several provinces of China's interior, as well as throughout Korea, and some of the more recent plant collectors have brought back seed that show striking differences from the described subspecies. Early specimens of *S. oblata* came principally from Chinese gardens and so were the first to be described, often with the note 'found only in Chinese gardens'. These were the first introductions of *S. oblata* into commerce. With time the species was discovered growing wild in several areas and many of these are better plants than the specimens propagated, most often, from a single 'Chinese garden plant', which was not always the best representative of this vast species.

The subspecies of *S. oblata* have undergone some taxonomical rearrangement in the last few years and as new forms are being discovered more changes may occur. For the present to clarify the subspecies the following is the order used in this book:

> *Syringa oblata* Rehder
>> var. *oblata*
>> var. *alba* Rehder
>> var. *dilatata* (Nakai) Rehder
>> var. *donaldii* Clark & Fiala

According to Pringle *S. oblata* is said to differ from the subspecies in having a more compact growth habit; smaller leaves and less open inflorescence; and more definitely cordate leaf bases. From var. *alba* it differs further in having smaller, thicker leaves which turn maroon in autumn; larger and pinkish corollas. From var. *dilatata* it differs in having the corolla tube shorter and thicker and the corolla lobes proportionately wider and less recurved. I believe that it also has smaller leaves and

S. oblata growing in the garden of the German legation, Beijing, China (1915).

inflorescences which are also more compact. From var. *donaldii* it differs in having much smaller leaves that are far less leathery and which do not have a whitish pubescence on the underside, also in having far less open inflorescences and smaller florets, the leaves do not have the undulating margins nor do they turn the deep blackish-purple with carmine coloring of var. *donaldii*.

In *S. oblata* there appears to be some difference in the ultimate size of the shrub which appears to be the tallest of the *oblatas*. At one time *S. oblata* was also called *S. oblata* var. *giraldii* with the simple species *S. oblata* being considered the smaller growing and the var. *giraldii* being the taller and the most upright of all the forms. I am not so certain that there are not two clone forms under this one name. What has been in the trade as *S. oblata* var. *giraldii* does appear to be a tall growing, rather spreading form often reaching considerable height in the garden in contrast to *S. oblata* but I do not believe it is a separate subspecies—rather a selected clone.

For the ordinary gardener the var. *dilatata* is far superior in that it is lower-growing and a far better all-around plant. There is no reason for growing the *S. oblata* form except for larger parks and special collections. Even in hybridization the lower-growing *dilatata* is preferable. As a taller background specimen that blooms early, *S. oblata* might have some merit but its many hybrids are better choices than the species. It appears to be the best species for southern gardens, growing and blooming quite well as far south as Ocala in northern Florida.

As a species *S. oblata* is somewhat similar to *S. vulgaris* and belongs to the Series *Vulgares*: it blooms earlier, is more frost resistant, its flowers are far less significant and are borne in loose panicles that have a wonderful fragrance. All the *oblatas* are strong growers with many of them making small, multi-trunked trees.

Once called the Broadleaved Lilac, *S. oblata* is mentioned by Alexander von Bunge as early as 1831 although he mistakenly called it *S. chinensis*. Even then he observed "It is common in Chinese gardens." Robert Fortune on his third trip to China 1853–1856 brought it to England. John Lindley in 1859 quotes Fortune as saying, "The Chinese informed me it came from the north and was common in the gardens of Peking . . . it is more tree-like in general outline; the leaves, also, are very striking, being large, rather fleshy and oblately cordate. The species blooms profusely, and its fine bunches of purple flowers are very ornamental. There is a white variety equally interesting (*S. oblata* var. *alba*) found in the same country which I have succeeded in getting home alive . . . both these varieties will be found perfectly hardy. . . ." Fortune brought back *S. oblata* gathered from Chinese gardens but it was later found growing extensively around Beijing (Peking) and in the provinces of Hebei, Shanxi, Shaanxi, northern Hunan and even in Huangtu Gaoyuan, a diverse and extremely extensive area.

Lindley, J. D. Hooker and Professor C. S. Sargent made note of its close similarity to *S. vulgaris*. Sargent adds, "In gardens this plant becomes a tall, broad shrub, but the brittleness of the branches, which are often broken down by snow or ice reduces its value." (Arnold Arboretum Bulletin No. 23, May 12, 1912) We do not find this so in the midwestern U.S. Although its branches are somewhat more brittle than *S. vulgaris,* it is a fine shrub. Its height, alone, makes it less desirable for home gardens.

McKelvey notes: "It is a smaller shrub or tree to 10 or 12 ft., uprightly branched, sparingly lenticellate twigs, globose winter buds, scales dark reddish brown, leaf scars much raised ... orbicular-ovate leaves to 4 in. and 4½ in. broad, abruptly acuminate with cordate base, somewhat glabrous, when young tinged on margins a Burnt Umber. The flower panicles come from lateral buds, 2–5 in. long and to 3 in. broad and are thin and loose; color in bud a Purplish Lilac (xxxvii) and Pale Lilac (xxxvi) when opened ... " *S. oblata* and many of its hybrids have a pale to deeper purple autumn leaf color which is most attractive in the landscape.

S. oblata 'Giraldii'

A specimen of this form of *S. oblata* was collected by G. Potanin in western Gansu Sheng in 1885 but not identified or described until much later. By then it was found, again, by Rev. Giuseppe Giraldi, an Italian botanist and missionary, in Shaanxi Sheng (Shensi Province), China in 1891 and was described and named as *S. oblata* var. *giraldii* by Sprenger in 1905. Today Peter Green has reduced var. *giraldii* to be one with *S. oblata* var. *oblata* and it no longer holds status as a subspecies. However it is a distinct clone differing in some minor aspects from the species. As a clone which I call, for clarity's sake, *S. oblata* cultivar 'Giraldi'. McKelvey states ... "its leaves are more gradually acuminate, truncate or very broad-cuneate at the base rather than cordate or subcordate, minutely puberulous or sometimes pubescent beneath". (She does not give the leaf size but it is comparable to *S. oblata.*

Its mauve (Argyle Purple) to lavender-pinkish flowers are borne in large, open and only moderately fragrant clusters. As a shrub it is somewhat taller than *S. oblata* generally not exceeding 20 ft. It was used extensively by Victor Lemoine in creating his historic race of × *hyacinthiflora* lilacs, now called Early Hybrids. The hybrids of this 'Giraldi' clone of *S. oblata* are much taller, more vigorous and upright growing than those of *S. oblata* var. *dilatata*. Unless restrained by heavy pruning they become small trees.

Interestingly, in 1909 Bellair wrote that, "I have grown this lilac at Versailles where it flowers, 'blanc lilacé' (a pale lilac) appearing about April 15 to early May. The flower clusters are more numerous than those of *S. oblata* and are not so much affected by the spring frosts." He makes an interesting observation that over the years the early flowers of this variety all appear to be self-sterile and only the top florets (presumedly pollenized by later lilacs) bear seed. This still appears to be true that only the later flowers set seed. The early leaves of this clone are tinged with a heavy bronze and the summer foliage remains green to the end of October. It is not a plant for the small garden for it grows to 18 ft. and almost as wide! On large estates and in arboreta it is one of Spring's finest shrubs, delightfully perfuming the air. (I would not be without it for this very reason!)

S. oblata cv., 'Giraldi' was the first of the *S. oblata* crosses with *S. vulgaris*. Historically, Victor Lemoine used it to pollenize 'Azurea Plena', the puny double *S. vulgaris* of Monsieur Libert of Liege, to produce the outstanding Early Hybrid race he called '*Syringa hyacinthiflora*'. What magnificent hybrids they are, strong growing, singles and heavy doubles, heavily fragrant and early blooming! Generally they do not root sucker as readily as the common lilac. Their leaves, like *oblata,* are often tinged with a reddish-bronze in their early unfolding, are deep-green and robust throughout the season and have a most attractive purplish-red coloration in the autumn. Among some of Lemoine's hybrids are 'Lamartine' (that blossoms so well in St. Louis, Missouri and in the midwestern U.S.), 'Louvois' a massive lavender, 'Buffon' with recurved petals of pinkish-lavender, 'Catinat', 'Fenelon' and 'Turgot' all early pinks.

From his famous mountain nursery in San Jose, California, Walter Bosworth Clarke used *S. oblata* to produce such outstanding beauties as 'Sweetheart', 'Sunset', 'Fantasy' (a beautiful double purple), 'Purple Glory', 'Purple Gem', 'Purple Heart' (lower growing excellent deep purples), 'Bountiful', a magnificent ball panicled beauty, 'Cora Brandt', 'Blue Hyacinth', 'Kate Sessions' a deep red-purple double of exceeding beauty, 'Missimo', 'Pink Spray' and the outstanding 'Esther Staley' and others. Dr. John Rankin added the earliest of all pinks 'Lewis Maddock'.

PLATE 33

Bush and flower of *Syringa komarowii,* one of the finer of the large-leafed late blooming lilacs. It has proven to be an excellent plant for hybridizing and several of the newer late-blooming multibrids have this species in their parentage. It appears to be a better plant than *S. villosa,* not shedding its leaves in late summer and produces smaller growing, more compact hybrids. It should be planted far more extensively in arboreta and parks and on larger estates. There is a form, *S. komarowii* 'Sargent' that has a deeper pink blossom, somewhat larger than the species, that is most attractive.

PLATE 34

S. laciniata displays its pale lavender plumes and cut and whole leaves on one plant. Once called *S. persica laciniata*, today we recognize it as a valid species with *S. × persica* its hybrid. Beautiful in itself it is outdone by its hybrid progeny.

S. × persica (a hybrid of *S. laciniata*) in a wonderful massed planting of heavy bloom along a walkway at the Royal Botanical Gardens, Hamilton, Ontario, Canada, on the way their outstanding rock gardens. An example of magnificer landscaping with lilacs as a tall screen and background.

PLATE 35

S. ×*chinensis* **'Bicolor'**, the beautiful hybrid introduced by Lemoine & Fils in 1853. After 130 years it still remains an outstanding lilac. One must come close to lilacs to see their hidden beauty as in 'Bicolor's' deep purple eye and golden anthers. It is among the finest of the × *chinensis* cultivars.

S. × *chinensis* 'Metensis' growing at Highland Park, Rochester, N.Y. More than 50 years old and still beautiful. Once it was called 'Varin Lilac' or *S. chinensis* 'Varina Metensis'. It blooms a very pale lavender.

PLATE 36

S. ✕ chinensis cultivars are among some of the finest shrubs among the species lilacs. They are large growing but where space permits are excellent as single specimens and background shrubs. They are smaller, fine branched, leafed and flowered than the larger *S. ✕ prestoniae*. The Chinensis Hybrids bloom with the regular lilacs.

S. ✕ *chinensis* 'Hybrida' (also called 'Rouenensis' or 'Rouen') introduced before 1885 (prob. Prince 1884).

S. ✕ *chinensis* 'Alba' (Audibert 1885). Note the pink mutation on plant. This form is exceedingly beautiful.

The beautiful *S. ✕ chinensis* 'Saugeana' (prob. Loudon 1885).

A blossom close-up of *S. ✕ chinensis* 'Alba' showing the delicate flower.

S. ✕ *chinensis* 'Orchid Beauty' (pre 1953).

S. ✕ *chinensis* 'Le Progres'

PLATE 37

S. meyeri var. **'Palibin'** is an outstanding, rather dwarf lilac. It has never been collected in the wild and is known only from the gardens of China. Its glossy leaves make it an excellent shrub all year long.

Plant form of *S. meyeri* 'Palibin' growing at the University of
Guelph Arboretum, Guelph, Ontario, Canada.

PLATE 38

S. mircophylla, with pale pink blossoms, is one of the finest species. Although it blooms heavily in colder climates it has considerable branch-blossom tip dieback.

S. microphylla 'Superba' is a more attractive form of the species. (Photos R.B.G.) It has been used much of late as a pollen parent in hybridizing. As a seed parent it sets no viable seed. (See chapter on Hybridizers, Royal Botanical Gardens, Hamilton, Ontario, Canada.)

S. microphylla 'Superba' (flower close-up)

S. microphylla 'Superba' (bush form)

PLATE 39

Close-up of flower detail of the Early Hybrid 'Fenelon' shows a masterpiece of delicate shades of pink. This *S.* ×
hyacinthiflora (using *S. oblata* 'Giraldii') was introduced by V. Lemoine & Fil in 1938. Still little known and appreciated
except in larger collections it is a work of sheer loveliness for any garden. It is a tall grower needs room and heavy pruning.
Truly one of the earliest harbingers of springtime!

PLATE 40

S. ×hyacinthiflora 'Maureen' (Preston) is an *S. oblata* 'Giraldii' hybrid lovely with florets of lavender-pink, very fragrant and airy. It is a good, strong grower that will please everyone. Give it a bit of room for growth and prune rather heavily. Another lovely Preston *S. ×hyacinthiflora* is her pale lavender 'Grace'.

PLATE 41

Some S. × *hyacinthiflora* hybrids, old and new, of proven merit.

'nnabel' (Hawkins 1948). One of the earliest to bloom.

'Norah' (Preston 1931). A fine light lilac color.

'ewis Maddock' (Rankin 1963). A lovely soft pink, perhaps e earliest to bloom, tall grower, lovely and fragrant.

'auban' (Lemoine 1913). Lovely in bloom, early but it must e considered a background or specimen shrub of con-derable size.

'Buffon' (Lemoine 1921). One of the finest of his Early Hybrids. Recurved petals and a tall grower.

PLATE 42

'Esther Staley' (Clarke 1948) a lavender pink of great beauty. Robust grower, tall.

'Purple Glory' (Clarke 1949)

'Kate Sessions' (Clarke 1942). Very large florets, extremely showy.

'Purple Gem' (Clarke 1960). Very fine low growing deep purple, showy and choice. Like 'Purple Gem' it makes a small shrub.

The hyacinthiflora hybrids of Walter B Clarke, who used both *S. oblata* 'Giraldi' and *S. oblata dilatata,* are a group of extraordinary lilacs of great beauty and massive bloom. All the hyacinthiflorae are early blooming and extremely fragrant. They are all good growing lilacs with new hybrids appearing each year.

Bush form of 'Bountiful' (Clarke 1949) with Prof. Robert Clark showing the size and floriferous nature of this fine cultivar.

A close-up of the very large, unique ball-shaped thrysus. It is one of the better of the hyacinthiflora cultivars and should be planted far more.

PLATE 43

S. oblata dilatata is perhaps one of the best forms of *S. oblata* due to its lower shrub form, floriferous annual bloom and fragrance. It is a fine shrub for the garden and has proven a wonderful parent in hybridizing for Skinner, Clarke, Fiala and others. As modern plant exploration brings new forms of *S. oblata dilatata* to the gardens we can expect even finer and more refined early hybrids.

Shrub form of *S. oblata dilatata* growing at Highland Park, Rochester, N.Y. Dilatata is extremely fragrant and a fine growing form—the best of the oblatas.

'Cheyenne' one of the newer selected cultivars of dilatata made by Hildreth in 1971. Note the abundant bloom and fine shrub form.

Flower of *S. oblata dilatata*.

PLATE 44

S. × hyacinthiflora is the earliest of the lilacs to bloom. There are many excellent cultivars to choose from in a variety of color and fragrance! Pictured are some of the fine hybrids of Skinner using *S. oblata dilatata* as one of the parents giving smaller shrubs of great beauty. (Photos by C. Holetich, R.B.G.)

PLATE 45

THE BEAUTIFUL EARLY HYBRIDS

S. × hyacinthiflora that used the lower form of *S. oblata dilatata* to give us lower, fragrant and beautiful lilacs.

'he Bride' (Skinner)

'Mary Short' (Fiala)

'Melissa Oakes' (Oakes)

'Doctor Chadwick' (Skinner)

'ister Justena' (Skinner)

PLATE 46

S. oblata **var.** *donaldii* a new form introduced by the National Arboretum, Washington D.C. discovered in South Korea in 1979. This new form of the early blooming lilac show many unique characteristics and should prove an asset in hybridizing new plants for our gardens.

The deeper lavender bloom is in open panicles.

Enormous leaves of *S. oblata* var. *donaldii* often reach 12 cms broad and 19 cms long with undulating margins on very heavy, leathery leaves.

New seedlings as 2 year old plants show typical, large leathery leaves with undulating margins that are a rich deep green.

This new form of *S. oblata* has the most outstanding autumn leaf color of all lilacs—rich purples—deep mauves—red burgundys—and deep purple-blacks!

PLATE 47

S. patula, the Korean Lilac, is a mountain species. Somewhat lower growing than most lilacs, it has pale lavender-whitish flowers with a delicate fragrance of spiced honey. In autumn it turns to shades of lavender and reddish leaves.

patula showing the flower close-up.

Fine bush form.

patula 'Excellens' a selection of Lemoine named in 1931.

In 1979 Dr. Owen Rogers, University of New Hampshire, crossed *S. patula* with *S. julianae,* a most interesting cross.

'Josee' a tribrid of G. Morel named in 1974. It combines (*S. patula* × *S. microphylla*) × *S. meyeri* in a rare cross that is very beautiful and refined.

PLATE 48

S. patula **'Miss Kim'**, a fabulous lilac introduced by Professor A. M. Meader, Univ. of New Hampshire, who brought it as seed from the mountains of South Korea in 1947. It is the most outstanding cultivar of *S. patula*. Slow growing, most fragrant, ice-blue lavender flowers, autumn foliage color it is truly outstanding!

Flowers.

Bush form.

S. oblata var. *alba* Rehder

In some early writings *S. oblata* var. *alba* was called *S. oblata affinis* or simply *S. affinis*. Correctly the oldest name *S. oblata* var. *alba* prevails. This white flowering subspecies is similar in all respects to the type except that it is a bit more slender with a more open habit, has smaller leaves heavily truncated at the base and, of course, bears white flowers. A plant of this white lilac was brought back from China by Robert Fortune in 1856—his third exploration. In *LE JARDIN* (VIII, 162, 1894) L. Henry writes of what he believes may be a white form of *S. oblata* without giving it a name. The plants he describes growing at the Museum of Natural History, Paris, were raised from seed sent by Dr. Brethschneider who was attached to the Russian Legation at Beijing. The plants flowered in 1891. Henry notes that the seedlings show no color variations and therefore he looks upon them as a wild form of *S. oblata*. Frank N. Meyer also collected this variety (U.S. Plant Introduction S.P.I. No. 23031, which is a beautiful flowering white lilac still growing near the old greenhouse at the Glendale Plant Introduction Center, USDA, and the original plant from seed sent by Meyer) which was once thought to be known only from Chinese gardens. In his notes Meyer states, "March 1908, from Fengtai, near Peking, Chihli, China.—a medium sized, white flowering lilac... They are drought resistant plants." Whether this plant from F. Meyer seed produces uniform white seedlings and is therefore a true subspecies, I do not know but I believe it does.

Peter S. Green, Royal Botanical Gardens, Kew, England, writing in *THE PLANTSMAN* (VI; 12–13, June 1984) after a recent visit to China and the plant nursery at the 18th century Summer Palace of the Qing Emperors at Chengde, Hebei Sheng, speaks of a ... "lilac with white flowers ... I was able to confirm that this white plant needs to be propagated vegetatively while the other plants referred to above (*S. oblata*) had been raised from seed." He goes on to state, "This white lilac was clearly *Syringa oblata* var. *alba* Hort. ex Rehd. (*S. oblata* var. *affinis* [L. Henry] Lingelsh.), a variety which was lost in cultivation in Britain at one time but may perhaps have been lost in the West, and in need of reintroduction. One suspects that it is entirely dependent on clonal reproduction and is perhaps a cultivar or, botanically, no more than a form." I do not believe that propagation vegetatively alone leads to the conclusion of it being a cultivar since in many species and subspecies there are sufficient incidental variations to merit certain seedlings to be propagated for their superior qualities vegetatively rather than by seed. Also, I do not believe Green was aware of the splendid specimen of *S. oblata* var. *alba* at the Plant Introduction Center, USDA, grown from F. Meyer seed. This, too, may perhaps be merely a selected white seedling that can be propagated only by clonal reproduction.

Thus we have 4 (or 3) known separate plants of a white *S. oblata*: Robert Fortune's introduction, which may or may not be the same as the Chengde white lilac of Peter Green, and two others grown from seeds—those described by L. Henry at the Museum in Paris, and Frank Meyer's seedling growing by the greenhouse at the Plant Introduction Center, Glendale. The latter is a most interesting and beautiful lilac! Because it is such an excellent white *oblata*, I have designated it in this book as *S. oblata alba* 'Frank Meyer' so it will not be lost or misidentified with any other form.

S. oblata var. *alba* does not appear to have been used in hybridizing until only very recently by Dr. Donald Egolf at the National Arboretum where the *S. oblata alba* 'Frank Meyer' introduction was used extensively with dramatic results. There is a great need for good, white Early Hybrids.

S. oblata var. *dilatata*

Dr. Nakai, of Japan, first noted this new variety of *S. oblata* in 1911 in his work *Flora Koreana* but improperly identified it. In 1918 he correctly identified it as *S. oblata* var. *dilatata* and describes it as a ... "shrub 2 m. tall, branching from the base, grayish bark with obscure lenticles, leaves opposite, petioles 2–2.5 cm. long, very broadly ovate, subcordate or truncate at the base, accuminate at the apex, very bright green above, green beneath, 4–5 cm. long by 4.5 cm. broad (7–6, 6.5–4.3, 12–8, 11–8.5, 7.5–7, 7–4), very glabrous, buds ovoid, inflorescences at top of branches of the previous year, commonly from auxiliary pairs of buds... flowers fragrant, calyx acutely toothed, corolla purple-violet, very handsome, stamens inserted." Nakai's specimens were from plants found in the mountains of Korea.

It was not until E. H. Wilson, collecting for the Arnold Arboretum in the Diamond Mountains of Korea in 1917–1918, that seed was gathered and the plant introduced at the Arnold in 1917. From Wilson's seed two separate forms are evident—one without heavy leaves that was at the Arnold Arboretum and one with the characteristic leathery leaves that was grown at the Walter Hunnewell's Estate, Wellesley, Massachusetts (now transplanted to the Arnold). Of this new variety

S. oblata var. *dilatata* on the Walter Hunnewell Estate, Wellesley, Mass. (Photo by E. H. Wilson, May 11, 1924 (M 198), Archives of Arnold Arboretum.) It is one of the loveliest of the species lilacs—delightfully fragrant and earliest to bloom.

of *S. oblata* on a herbarium specimen Wilson notes, ". . . taken from a bush 6 ft. tall with wine colored autumn leaves . . . common on slate rocks and limestone 35 miles west of Yeiko, Korea." Again, in the *Journal of the Arnold Arboretum,* Wilson remarks, "On the mudshales and limestone a little to the northwest of Keijyo (Korea), grows a lilac, *Syringa dilatata* (Nakai), which opens its panicles of palest lilac flowers early in the spring . . . it is a bush of good habit often twelve feet high and nearly as broad, with dark green leathery foliage which colors finely in autumn. Examples two feet high bear flowers." Wilson assumes the leathery-leaved lilac he had found was the same as that described by Nakai. Both Nakai's description and Mrs. McKelvey's do not include this heavy, leathery leaf texture. Could it be that Wilson is in reality describing a different variety of *S. oblata* or a cultivar of *S. oblata* var. *dilatata* different somewhat from the varietal form? I am of the belief that he is describing a different form or cultivar. This heavy, leathery leaf characteristic is not found on *S. oblata* var. *dilatata* plants. It is a most desirable characteristic for garden purposes and the beauty of the plant. Its blossom color is deeper than the description given by Mrs. McKelvey of the plants then growing at the Arnold from Wilson's seed.

McKelvey describes *S. oblata* var. *dilatata* (originally growing at the Arnold Arboretum from Wilson's seed gathering) as: "This variety differs considerably from the type (*S. oblata*) . . . the habit of the plant is more graceful, with many slender branchlets tinged when young Bay (II) . . . leaves glabrous, ovate, long accuminate, and as a rule truncate at the base . . . borne on very slender petioles, frequently an inch long . . . flowers are handsomer with longer and more slender cololla-tube . . . habit of the Korean plant is spreading rather than upright (as in variety *giraldii*). Color of expanded flowers Pale Laelia Pink (XXXXVIII) tinged Hay's Lilac (XXXVII). Winter buds are obovoid with acute apex . . . the leaf scars much raised, shield-shaped, conspicuous, large." (In a footnote she admits she is taking her description from two separate plants—one at the Arboretum and one at the Hunnewell Estate from which she describes the flower.) This leads to some confusion as I feel the Hunnewell specimen represents the native *S. oblata* var. *dilatata* 'Nakai' described by Wilson, whereas the original plants growing at the Arnold fit the typical description of *S. oblata* var. *dilatata*. One has ordinary leaves and pale flowers, the other has leathery leaves and somewhat darker flowers and better bush form altogether.

Of the Hunnewell plant, which I call *S. oblata* var. *dilatata* 'Nakai', McKelvey states . . . "At its best, this is to me one of the most beautiful of all Lilacs" and adds, undoubtedly referring to the Arnold specimens, "although every specimen is not of equal decorative value. Those at the Arnold are inferior up to the present time to a plant growing at the Hunnewell Estate." It is my conviction that the Hunnewell specimen (now at the Arnold) represents a selected strain of *S. oblata* var. *dilatata* which should be designated as a cultivar 'Nakai' (*S. oblata* var. *dilatata* 'Nakai') to prevent it from being lost among the ordinary or inferior seedlings of *S. oblata* var. *dilatata*.

From all that I have been able to find and observe on *S. oblata* var. *dilatata*, it appears that there are several forms or cultivars—all being somewhat similar in lower shrub form, more abundant branching and of a spreading habit of growth; all have glabrous leaves but not the same in texture and shape; all have open inflorescences from several pairs of lateral buds, are fragrant but differ somewhat in depth and shades of lavender-purplish color; all have good autumn leaf color but some are far superior to others.

Syringa oblata var. donaldii

In 1979 a considerable amount of seed was collected in Korea by the U.S. Department of Forestry, among which was that of *Syringa*. Under the direction of Dr. Donald Egolf of the U.S. National Arboretum, Washington, D.C., this *S. oblata* seed was grown, among which was a special group of seedlings of truly outstanding and new characteristics for *S. oblata*. These new plants are somewhat akin to *S. oblata* var. *dilatata* but by no means identical and upon closer observation more like what I call *S. oblata* var. *dilatata* 'Nakai' in their leathery leaves but in other respects appear to be entirely a new varietal form or subspecies. I have chosen to call it *S. oblata* var. *donaldii*. Since the plants are no more than 6 years old it is difficult to ascertain their ultimate height. They are unique in their robust growth, but especially in the giant size of their leaves, far greater than that described for any other subspecies of *S. oblata*. The leatheriness of their leaves is far more than in the cultivar described by Nakai; their autumn color is far deeper black-purple changing to bright reddish mauves and deep purple combinations that far eclipse the coloration found in other forms of *oblata*. Botanically this new subspecies is described as follows:

A NEW SUBSPECIES LILAC

Syringa oblata var. *donaldii* was discovered by plant collectors of the U.S. Division of Forestry in the foothills and mountains of South Korea in 1978–79. This seed was sent to the U.S. National Arboretum, Washington, D.C. and grown by Dr. Donald Egolf. My description is from 5- and 6-year-old plants growing at the National Arboretum which are 3–4 m high, slightly less broad; the bush is well branched from the ground (even moreso than other varieties of *S. oblata*); leaves ovate, long and broad, apex acuminate, leaf base round but at times truncate though less frequently so, very glabrous with margins mostly conspicuously undulating but at times without undulations; leaf texture is extremely heavy similar to leather; leaf size is 10.5 cm broad and 16.8 cm long (individual measurements: 12–19 cm, 10–16cm, 11–18 cm, 9–15 cm, and 10–16 cm, this with good and ordinary culture) a leaf size not found in any other subspecies of *S. oblata*; leaf color is a very dark green above, pale whitish-green often with fine pubescence beneath; inflorescences are both from terminal as well as lateral buds; flowers are moderately fragrant in open-spreading panicles with a modest to sparse number of florets; buds are a purple opening to a pale purplish to a deeper purple color; autumn leaf color is exceptional from a deep black-purple changing to red-purple and shades of carmine with outstandingly glabrous leaves among the last to fall; branches are reddish brown with small but conspicuous lenticels; the plants are especially handsome with deep green glossy foliage in the summer and a very special blackish-purple-carmine in the autumn. This autumn color is among the finest of all lilacs and most distinctive.

This subspecies differs from other *S. oblata* forms in both its unusual leaf size and form, in the undulating leaf margins, round bases and the pale whitish green underside which is often slightly pubescent, the very special leathery thickness and glabrousness of the leaves, in the more abundant lateral inflorescences and in their wider and open form. It also differs in the very intense as well as the density of the black-purple-carmine autumn coloration of the leaves. Its herbarium specimen is at the U.S. National Arboretum, Washington, D.C. Type plant N.A. 39951.

SYRINGA OBLATA VAR. DONALDII

Series *Vulgares*, species *oblata*, semina collecta ad pedem et in montibus Koreae a Departmentale Silvi-culturae, U.S.A., annis 1978–79; semina germinavit Dr. Donald Egolf, Arboreti Nationali, Washington, D.C., U.S.A. Plantes quintorum annorum 3 ad 3.5 m altae, paucae minore latae; formae substantiales cum ramis usque ad terram (multioribus quam in *S. oblata* et eius varietatibus); folia ovata, longa et cum apicibus acuminatis, basis rotundis aliquando truncatis, specialissime glabra cum marginalibus vel conspicue undulatis vel sine undulationibus, texturae specialissime densae similiter coriaceae, 10.4 cm lata et 16.8 cm longa (12–19, 10–16, 11–18, 9–15, 10–16 bene et ordinaria cultura); color foliorum atro-virida supra, pallida-virida albescens aliquando cum foliis subtus minute pubescentibus; inflorescentes et a terminale et a pluribus lateralibus gemmis; flores apertae modice fragrantes cum paniculis late apertis, flores nonnunquam sparsae coloris pallidae-purpuralae usque ad purpuralescentes; color autumnalis foliorum specialissima nigrans-purpurea usque ad rubra-purpurea et carmina, eximie pulchritudine, specialiter glabra et tardissime cadentes; ramis rubrescentibus-brunis cum minute sed conspicuis lentibus; plantes sunt specialiter placentes cum foliis autro-viribus in aestivo et eximie coloratis carminis nigrantibus-purpuris autumno. Inter omnes species syringarum est colorata distinctivissima, foliis coriaceis et magnifice longis et latis.

Differt haec varietas ab aliis *S. oblatae* varietatibus in magnitudine et form foliorum, in undulatibus marginalibus, rotunda basa, subtus in colore albescente subvirida aliquando pubescentis foliis, et speciale in coriacitate et glabritate foliorum, in inflorescentibus ab multioribus lateralibus in paniculis late separatis. Specimen herbarium reposita in Arboreta Nationale, Washington, D.C. Typus N.A. 39951.

Working to produce lower growing plants L. Skinner using *S. oblata* var. *dilatata* added a whole new strain of lower growing Early Hybrids of incomparable beauty among which must be singled out the magnificent pale pink 'Maiden's Blush', the excellent deep violet 'Pocahontas' and the white 'The Bride'. Yet to be named are some magnificent seedlings grown by Dr. Don Egolf at the National Arboretum using the new *S. oblata* var. *donaldii*. (Indeed, *mon ami et amie*, *S. oblata* has been a truly outstanding parent—and its offspring—children worthy of the limelight of lilacdom!) *S. oblata* cultivars selected for their fine autumn coloration include: 'Birchwood' (Clark), 'Cheyenne' (Hildreth) and 'Wild Fire' (Fiala).

Since all the *S. oblatae* and their hybrids bloom earlier than *S. vulgaris* it is essential to avoid planting them in 'frost pockets' or against warm buildings that prematurely advance their already early buds, or in sheltered spots. They need open, well-ventilated sunlit sites. They are not fussy. Since they are excellent growers, strong and robust by nature, do not over-fertilize. Most need little extra help. Use them in the backgrounds (the *S. oblata* 'Giraldii' hybrids) or as early focal shrubs (the *S. oblata* var. *dilatata* or var. *donaldii* hybrids). To keep the taller sorts low one must resort to periodic pruning. If left to grow too tall they become small trees with flower spikes correspondingly smaller and difficult to appreciate. To see these newer Early Hybrids visit your local lilac collections, arboreta and newer parks. (If they do not grow them alert the park superintendent of his oversight.) One must ask for them by name from the better nurseries. You do not find fine lilacs as the Early Hybrids in the nursery container trade; one must buy and consult from a nursery specializing in newer lilacs grown on their own roots. (Do not settle for less, *bon jardinier!* If you do, you deserve the poor lilac you will receive.) Plant explorers have gone through great sacrifices to bring us these species; hybridizers have worked hard for many years to produce new plants. We owe it to our gardens to grow some of these exciting, very fragrant lilacs!

There is one rather rare interseries lilac hybrid between the series *Pinnatifolia* and the series *Vulgares*, *S. pinnatifolia* × *S. oblata* called *S. × diversifolia*. It is not an outstanding garden plant but could well point directions for possible new crosses by hybridizers for the future. The only known cultivar is *S. × diversifolia* 'William H. Judd'. Perhaps hybridizers could make more extensive crosses using other forms of *S. oblata* or even *S. vulgaris* crossed with *S. pinnatifolia*. 'William H. Judd' is a cross of *S. pinnatifolia* with *S. oblata* 'Giraldii'.

SYRINGA PATULA —The Korean Lilac

This lovely lilac species was first collected in Seoul, Korea, by Miss A. Sonntag of the Russian Legation, who found it on May 20, 1895 near Tap Tong. Palibin first labeled it as *Ligustrinum patulum*. Komarov in his writings *Species, Novae Florae Asiae Orientalis* and who collected it as *S. velutina* in northern Korea in 1897, describes it as "a shrub 6–12 feet tall, branched, with slender

S. patula, one of the finer species for the garden, with pale lavender, delicate blossoms with the fragrance of cloves and the added attraction of mauve-purple autumn foliage. (Photo Arnold Arboretum.)

erect branches, with gray bark marked by many lenticels, the leaves papery . . . the inflorescence all densely short-pilose . . . panicles uninterrupted, pyramidal, the pedicels almost lacking or as long as the calyx, the calyx velvety white-pilose . . ." Collecting in different areas Komarov tells us the plant occurs quite frequently among rocks, on rocky slopes, or in mountain gravel. It was also collected in northern Korea by Dr. Takenoshin Nakai and by E. H. Wilson on his expeditions in 1917–1918. Because of Komarov's well described specimens, it was originally named *S. velutina* (McKelvey so lists it in *The Lilac*). Taxonomists in keeping with the rules of nomenclature have returned to its first recorded mention by Palibin who called it *Ligustrinum patulum* but have corrected the genus name. So as Nakai points out, it is today correctly called *S. patula.* In more recent times several individuals have brought back seed from the mountains of Korea and some fine variations of the species are being named. One of the finest among them is from seed collected by Professor E. M. Meader in 1947 who named an outstanding seedling 'Miss Kim'. Several new cultivars and hybrids are soon to be released.

   S. patula is a lovely, modest shrub, neither coarse nor a rampant grower. Its pale, light lavender, feathery blossoms have a delightfully spicy fragrance uniquely its own. Although the flower panicles are not large it is a reasonable heavy bloomer, shortly after the peak of the *S. vulgaris* season. Where room allows one should have several of these medium to smaller sized shrubs simply for their fragrance throughout the garden. It sets seed rather abundantly and should prove to be an excellent source for hybridizing with other species. In the autumn its rather pale-green somewhat smaller leaves turn a beautiful shade of mauve and soft violets. Grown from seed many interesting variations develop that can be intensified by selective breeding. Remember that *S. patula* comes from the high mountains, so give it good, well-drained soil. Here at Falconskeape it appears to grow well even in rather wet but well-drained soil—never water-logged.

S. patula 'Miss Kim'

Professor E. M. Meader of Rochester, New Hampshire, gives this account of how he discovered and named this lovely cultivar of *S. patula*.

It was November 11, 1947, a holiday in Seoul, Korea, where I was stationed as horticulturist for the U.S. Army Military Government, that meant a day free for hiking in the nearby Pouk Han Mountains. Early that morning a companion and I set out through the old city's North Gate with C-rations and canteens tied to our belts.

Up hill and down dale we followed well-trodden trails until we had scaled Paik Un Dae (White Cloud Peak), 892 meters in height. There stunted pines and shrubs grew in crevices where sufficient soil had clung to the craggy granite. On a cliff high above I spotted a lonesome, upright shrub, shoulder high, neatly ensconced in a wide crack of rock. Two inches of snow had collected under the plant despite bare ground at lower elevations. As I examined its twigs and seed pods I knew it must be a lilac. Could the dried capsules still contain any seeds in such a windswept place? A diligent search rewarded me with a few, most had gone with the wind!

Back home in 1948 I planted my twelve precious seeds which I'd collected that previous Veterans' Day in Korea. Seven thrifty seeds sprouted. Five grew into tall upright plants like their parent in the Korean mountains. Two, however, although strong and vigorous enough, were rather dwarf by comparison. All seedlings proved hardy and in time bloomed late, a full week or so after 'James Macfarlane'. The fragrant single flowers, purple in bud and when first open, fade to a blue-ice whiteness before falling.

One of the two low-stature seedlings bore dark green leaves with wavy margins. The foliage remained free of mildew all summer and turned Burgundy red in autumn for a delightful display. I named it 'Miss Kim', since 'Kim' is a most common family name in Korea. There are thousands of Misses Kim, many could easily win a Beauty Contest if such were ever held in that country.

'Miss Kim' was released in 1954 by the New Hampshire Agricultural Experiment Station and became the first named cultivar of *S. patula* (still erroneously called in the nursery trade *S. palibiniana Nakai*, or the older name *S. velutina*). When one contemplates this extremely limited sampling of lilacs growing wild in the Pouk Han Mountains, further plant explorations for valuable germ plasm might well be considered. If one must choose between the species *S. patula* and the cultivar 'Miss Kim' by all means choose the cultivar. (See *mon ami*, a second time we have a most beautiful lilac by serendipity—and a search).

S. patula 'Miss Kim'—a fabulous lilac. It is one of the most outstanding cultivars of *S. patula*. Its use in hybridizing should be a milestone for lilacs.

The "original" 'Miss Kim' seedling planted by Prof. Meader at the University of New Hampshire Lilac Research Plantings, 30 years of age. (Shown with P. Pesata.) Approximately 10 ft. high and 15–17 ft. wide—a most impressive shrub—outstanding in bloom.

Professor E. M. Meader, who brought
back the seed from the mountains of
Korea in 1947.

SYRINGA POTANINII

The Russian plant explorer, G. A. Potanin, while at T'an ch'ang (Tangchang), a small village on the northern effluent of the Hei shui kiang River, on June 18, 1885 (of the old style calendar, but July 1 of our calendar) discovered this species growing in the deeply dissected loess-country of southern Gansu (Kansu) Province in China. Writing some years later Camillo Schneider named this lilac after its discoverer *S. potaninii*. E. H. Wilson collected specimens of it in western Sichuan Sheng (Szechuan) in May of 1904, at Tachien lu (Ta tsien lu) with rose purple flowers whereas the specimen collected by Potanin, as described by Schneider, had "flowers of whitish-lilac pedicels almost lacking; anthers deep violet..." Reginald Farrer while collecting plants near the Tibetan border in 1914 in southeastern Gansu (Kansu), found a lilac (*S. potaninii*) which he describes, ". . . a tall slender, and very graceful lilac of 6–8 feet, which I have only once seen, far up, on the shady side in a collateral of the great Siku Gorge, growing in a big colony amid blocks of mossy detritus from the cliff-wall overhead. Its flowers, so far as I could judge it at the end of June, seemed small and rather poor, in small insignificant panicles; it may however improve in cultivation." Otto Staph writing of a plant grown from seed collected by Farrer and growing in the "chalk garden at Highdown near Goring on the Sea, Sussex, England ... it may be that the 'insignificant panicles were merely the last of the season ... The inflorescences of the plant raised by Major Stern (at Highdown) from Farrer's seed hardly warrant the term 'insignificant'."

Today *S. potaninii* is a very significant lilac although relatively unknown by the general public. It is more upright, vase like in habit rather than spreading. It closely resembles *S. microphylla* (to which it must be very closely related and for which it is often mistaken. In my opinion they could perhaps be the extremes of the same species.) *S. potaninii* is somewhat variable in color from whitish purple to a light rose-purple but with a general over-all appearance of a pinkish that fades to a near white. The calyx is a light purple and the anthers pale purplish yellow. In some soils it flowers more magenta than purplish. The wood is somewhat brittle and the plant should be

S. potaninii, one of the finest species, growing at the Arnold Arboretum.

(Photos Arnold Arboretum.)

Plant form.

encouraged early to form a shrub of more than one main trunk. It does not sucker but cuttings strike easily in the spring. The leaves vary remarkably even on the same branch. Susan McKelvey describes it, "A shrub to 18 feet, branchlets short-pubescent. Leaves broad-elliptic to oblong-elliptic, sometimes rhombic, suborbicular or ovate, 1–2¾ inches long, ½ to 1¾ inches broad . . . rather densely pubescent with short stiff hairs above, densely light-gray villous-pubescent beneath . . . Inflorescence from lateral buds, sometimes fascicled, upright, 3–7 in. long, 2–3 in. broad . . . corolla-tube slender, cylindric ⅜ in. long, corolla-lobes spreading . . . or curling backward . . . usually with a pronounced hook . . . anthers small, yellow." McKelvey does not state the actual color of the flower except in quoting other descriptions of it from a "white flushed purple exterior, fragrant" (E. H. Wilson) whereas he describes another specimen from a different area as "flowers fragrant, pale creamy-rose." Most of the *S. potaninii* plants I have seen (as well as my own specimen) are the creamy-rose to pink type. The buds being a deeper rose and the opening florets a creamy-rose mixed with white. As the flower fades it is more whitish than rose. The branches upright in growth resemble pink flowering plumes. There is such a great similarity between *S. potaninii* and *S. microphylla* that plants growing side by side at Falconskeape are difficult to tell apart except by the shrub habit and close inspection for minute species characteristics. It is also closely related to *S. pubescens* and less to *S. meyeri*.

Like *S. microphylla* it is a long season grower. Often the branchlet tips do not sufficiently harden and are killed by frost, leaving a twiggy, broomy effect in the spring. Since it flowers on lower matured lateral buds, winter kill does not seem to affect the blooming, only the appearance. Perhaps in less fertile soils and with drier summers, late summer growth may not occur. Its natural habitat are gravelly, well-drained mountainsides. It will not tolerate heavy, water-logged soils, so one must make certain it is in well drained loamy-sandy-gravel. It has great tolerance for long, summertime droughts. In the spring it is a most delightful shrub, one for real shrub connoiseurs. It is, unfortunately, not readily available except from some private lilac collections or larger arboreta. Do not expect your local nurseryman to even know what you are asking for as it is rarely offered even in the finest nursery specialties catalogues. It rarely produces seed but does carry sterile seed pods. There are no known selections or hybrids of *S. potaninii*.

Many of the plants labelled as *S. potaninii* today are really *S. microphylla* or *S. pubescens*, both of which it so closely resembles.* If you have *S. potaninii* in your garden, *mon ami*, cherish it dearly and give it a *granddame's* place of distinction.

SYRINGA PINETORUM (A Disavowed Species)

A lilac called *S. pinetorum* was collected by George Forrest in June 1914 in the 'open pine forrests on the Lichiang Range, Yunnan, China'. The specimen was so similar to *S. microphylla* and to *S. julianae*, *S. potaninii* as well as to *S. pubescens* that it cannot today be ascertained as a true species but most likely was a form of one of these related species, in all likelihood *S. microphylla*. Although Mrs. McKelvey listed it as a species in her monograph, she is very uncertain as to its real species status believing the specimen to be that of *S. microphylla*. E. H. Wilson believed that "as a true species it was never introduced and, if it does exist, it must be re-discovered in some remote wilderness." No subsequent plant explorers have been able to locate it, nor is it in any living, authentic collection today. All plants once labeled *S. pinetorum* have been removed as not a true species in most of the best collections and all the lilac arboreta. (Eventually, *mon ami*, the 'status seekers' get weeded out!)

SYRINGA PUBESCENS

P. Y. Kirilov, who traveled through Mongolia in 1831 with the Russian botanist, Alexander von Bunge, is believed to have discovered *S. pubescens* growing on cliffs at the foot of the mountains in northernmost Hebei Sheng, China. Nicolai Turczaninov first described *S. pubescens* in 1840 as "a *Syringa* with ovate acute leaves, pubescent on the midrib beneath, ciliate on margins, with very

---

*Although I have considerable misgivings about the validity of *S. potaninii* as a species distinct from *S. microphylla* and *S. julianae*, I accept them for the present as separate species. However, I would not be surpised if in the near future they may all be classified as one species with several varietal forms. *S. potaninii* and *S. microphylla* rarely, if ever, set seed although pollen fertile. It is difficult to see a valid species perpetuate itself with such great problems of seed setting! (Introgressive Hybridization, McClintock—refer to Chapter on Lilac Propagation/Hybridization.)

S. pubescens is a lovely, dainty lilac with pale violet to lavender blossoms. Never growing too rampant, it is a lovely lilac for the home garden or as a focal plant on the Lilac Walk. (Photos Archives of Arnold Arboretum.)

Shrub form at maturity.

short, obtuse calyx lobes." Bretschneider citing O. V. Moellendorff, who collected this species in China in 1881 in the mountains west of Beijing, and Turczaninov who described the material of Dr. Kirilov and Bunge (1831) states... "This shrub, from 6 to 8 feet high, is found in the lower regions of the mountains, has smaller leaves, 1½ inches long, ovate white beneath, pubescent on the midrib. Flowers are also small. The small seed capsules are covered with warts. In Chinese it is called *Siao ting hiang* (the Clove-like lilac) because of the resemblence of the flower bud to the Clove."

S. *pubescens* belongs to the Series Pubescentes of lilacs, all of which have great similarities. A mature plant at the Arnold Arboretum is some 12 or more ft. high with numerous slender branches, as broad as it is tall. Its foliage and buds unfold early in the spring and it is a dependable and profuse bloomer. Color in bud is a pale purplish-lilac (XXXVII) and the same color when expanded without and within. (McKelvey). We see it mostly as a pale lilac with a pale pinkish wash. The delicate flowers are not showy nor the individual clusters large but since many pairs of buds are produced on the same branchlet the total inflorescence is long. S. *pubescens*, like many of the oriental species, has its own distinct spicy-clove like fragrance. Truly it is a plant for the discriminating lilac collector and hybridizer.

Photographs at the Arnold Arboretum of S. *pubescens* taken by Frank N. Meyer at Hsiao wu tai shan, Chihli, show the difficult conditions under which the species will grow, ... "a medium size wild lilac with rather small leaves found in rocky places at altitudes from 5000 to 8000 feet. It is intolerant of heavy, clay soils."

Soon after its discovery it was introduced into the nursery trade being offered for sale by Dieck, owner of the Zoschen Nursery, near Merseburg, Germany, in 1887. Dr. Bretschneider's seed was received at Kew, England, in 1880 and the plants first bloomed there in 1888; he also sent seed to the Arnold Arboretum in 1882 and there the seedlings bloomed first in 1886. S. *pubescens* is not known to be a heavy seed setter (the plant at the Arnold is said not to produce seed or very little); elsewhere it either produces no seed or a very small quantity.

At Kew, Sir Joseph Dalton Hooker reports the plant to be hardy but Bean in *Trees and Shrubs Hardy in the British Isles* states: "It is only a second-rate lilac in this country, owing to the frequent injury of the young growths and panicles by late frosts. In the United States, where the summer heat is greater, and the seasons better defined, it is very beautiful." So it is, one of our finer lilacs and a choice specimen for any garden.

To date there appear to be no validly known hybrids of this species except the reported crosses made by Isabella Preston who crossed S. *vulgaris* with S. *pubescens*. In June 1928 she states, "I examined the seedlings raised and could find no evidence of S. *pubescens* influence." A reported cross made by Frank Skinner named S. × *skinneri*, a cross of S. *patula* (*velutina*) × S. *pubescens* in 1945 was successful. His reported cross of S. *pubescens* × S. *oblata* var. *dilatata* in 1962 was never introduced. It would seem that the possibility of crosses among the similar species S. *pubescens*, S. *microphylla*, S. *potaninii* and S. *julianae* might not be as difficult and could produce some exciting hybrids. (It is the author's sincere belief that some of these species will prove to be extreme forms of a single species. Time and scholarly research will unravel the problem.)

At one time S. *pubescens* was called S. *villosa* var. *pubescens*. Today we know it as a species with no varietal forms.

SYRINGA REFLEXA

Certainly one of the princes of Lilacdom must be S. *reflexa*. It was found wild in its native Hebei Sheng (Hupeh Province) in Central China in 1901 by the plant explorer E. H. Wilson. In his book *Aristocrats of the Garden* Wilson states, "The most distinct of all lilacs is the new S. *reflexa* with narrow or broad flower clusters from nine to twelve inches long, suberect, nodding or pendent and sometimes hanging downward like the inflorescence of the *Wisteria*... It is native of the margin woods and thickets on the mountains of western Hupeh (Hebei), Central China." He describes the flower buds as a deep bright red, expanding to pale rose color in early and mid June. It is rather strong growing from 8–12 ft. high at best with erect stems and oblong, large lance-shaped leaves. McKelvey's description adds, ". . . the winter buds ½ in. long are keeled, forming a distinctly four-sided bud... leaf scars much raised... leaves ovate-oblong to oblong-lanceolate, 3–8 in. long, 1–2 in. broad... dull green, glabrous above... villous beneath... color of floret expanded Rhodonite Pink (XXXVIII) without, Light Buff (XV) or white within... anthers yellow." Wilson in collecting this species again in 1907 near Fang hsien notes at one location the flowers were reddish while at another they were a rosy-pink. Seed collected by him in October 1910 was sent to the Arnold

S. reflexa. Variations of quality of inflorescences and color of bloom are considerable in seed collected in the wild, even from the same plant, showing the need to select and preserve the finest cultivars. (Photos Archives of Arnold Arboretum.)

A1469, a much better form, from seed collected by Wilson.

Arboretum and from there to England and Kew. This was the first introduction of the species from China. In 1910 Schneider describing and naming the species remarks "*S. reflexa* is a shrub related to *S. villosa* . . . with large inflorescence, flower violet."

Lemoine et Fils Nursery were the first to offer *S. reflexa* for sale in 1917 describing it as having, ". . . reflexed lobes of a soft mauve." It is a species of wide variation not only in color but in flower and inflorescence. McKelvey cites four excellent specimens of *S. reflexa* at Holm Lea, Brookline, Mass. . . . "In one the flower clusters are narrow, in the other three they branch widely at the base; three have large flowers, one has small ones; the flowers when expanded are various shades of color from Rhodonite Pink to Vinaceous Pale Purple with Pale Pink to Light Buff and white within." (Three of these are now in the Arnold nos. 20,450, 20,451, 20,452)

The foliage to McKelvey is "large and handsome, somewhat rough to the touch, unfolds late in spring, falls early in autumn." Emile Lemoine in 1925 writing to Mrs. McKelvey questioned if *S. reflexa, S. komarovii* and *S. villosa* might not be all varieties of one species? (The question remains unanswered but it is generally agreed they are each a separate species.)

Schneider who first described this species taxonomically distinguishes it by its warty, reflexed fruit panicles from *S. villosa*. Because of this character, rather than the reflexed, pendulous flower clusters, he called it *S. reflexa*. (Others do not find the fruit more reflexed than in *S. villosa*, yet it remains properly named if we consider the flower clusters rather than the seed.)

E. H. Wilson in *Aristocrats of the Garden* suggests that in the hands of the hybridist *S. reflexa* "may be the forerunner of a race totally different in aspect from present day Lilacs." In 1920 Isabella Preston, at the Central Experiment Farm, Ottawa, Canada, made her famous cross of *S. villosa* × *S. reflexa* (the pollen plant) creating her famous *S.* × *prestoniae* hyrids and also the cross *S. reflexa* × *S. josikaea*. A white form *S. reflexa* 'Alba', was discovered by Upton growing in his nursery at Goodrich, Michigan as a seedling variant and was introduced by him. The flowers are a clear, creamy-white with both narrow and drooping clusters typical of the species. In habit it is identical to the pink form except that the leaves are a bit paler green. When *S. reflexa* is grown from protected, selfed seed, there is some variation in the seedlings as to color and degree of drooping inflorescence—

shades of light pinks, tinged mauve to a pale lavender show it is a rather variable species. Some plants are quite a bit more showy than others. It is a wonderful shrub for both the garden and the hybridist! Truly it is one of our choicest lilacs.

Often one sees 'typical' species plants of lilacs that were grown from seed sent back by plant explorers—perhaps only a few seed and descriptions are made from a rather poor representative of the species. I feel strongly that this has been the case with *S. reflexa*. The black and white pictures from the Arnold Archives clearly indicate the variability of *S. reflexa* seedlings. Not only does this hold in plant vigor and form, but especially in floriferousness, size of blossom thrysus and various shades of color. One of the loveliest forms of *S. reflexa* I have seen is a seedling grown by the late Bernard Slavin when Superintendent at Highland Park, Rochester, N.Y. There is in the lilac collection a splendid form which I designate *S. reflexa* 'Slavin' (Park No. Slavin #1) so that it may not be lost. It is most worthy of propagation. Some might argue that it is a hyrid but I believe it to be a superior selection of *S. reflexa*. So far we have had no large population of controlled self pollinated *S. reflexa* (or many other species). Some far superior seedlings would undoubtedly be found if this self pollination were to occur.

Wilson discovered it growing along the margins of the forest and mountain wood thickets. It does not relish hardpan, clay or undrained soils. It will not grow in them. As a native of forest borders give it well drained, woodsy loam, mixed with gravel and a little drier hillside. Use it as a

S. reflexa, actual photo taken by E. H. Wilson at Fang Hsien, western Hebei Sheng. "Flowers rosy pink in pendulous panicles, bush 12 feet, altitude 6500 feet." E. H. Wilson, June 16, 1910. Wilson had discovered *S. reflexa* in 1901, but no seed was then available. This photo was taken on a subsequent exploration, when seed was sent back to the Arnold Arboretum. (Photo Archives of Arnold Arboretum.)

focal plant in your garden. (*Mon Ami,* when one has a Prince in the garden, he must be properly enthroned!)

Recently (1977 *Baileya,* Vol. 20, Jan. 1977, No. 2) Dr. James Pringle of the Royal Botanical Gardens, Hamilton, Ontario, Canada, described several hybrid crosses made there in the lilac Series *Villosae.* It is the most extensive hybridization program and description of results of so many interspecific crosses that it merits special recognition. He has described the results of the many crosses and discussed the merits of each cross, its potential for hybridizing and its value as a garden plant. Among these crosses were the following involving *S. reflexa* as one of the parents: *S. emodi* × *S. reflexa; S.* × *henryi* × *S. reflexa; S. reflexa* × *S. yunnanensis; S. sweginzowii* × *S. relexa;* "*S. wolfii hybrid*" × *S. reflexa.* In all it is an extraordinary and thorough hybridizing of *S. reflexa* within the series *Villosae.* So far plants remain under number and as yet none have been introduced and named although some appear to be excellent garden plants with considerable promise for hybridizers. I have chosen to name his cross *S. reflexa* × *S. yunnanensis* in this book as *S.* × *pringleiana* not only to honor him for his excellent work but because I feel this cross will eventually add much to the hybridization of the late blooming lilacs and be the progenitor of even finer lilacs to come that will one day fill our gardens with additional beauty.

SYRINGA SWEGINZOWII

In 1910 Koehne and Lingelsheim described *S. sweginzowii* from a living specimen in the arboretum of Max von Slivers, Roemershof, near Riga, Russia, "Branches gray to grayish brown sparingly lenticellate with round lenticels, glabrous... winter buds about 3 mm long, ovate-conical, brown, glabrous. Leaves papery, oblong or ovate... 5–7 cm long, 2–3.5 cm broad, brownish green above, entirely glabrous beneath... Panicles terminal or lateral, loose, elongated, 15–25 cm long. Flowers yellowish-rose, calyx campanulate, subtruncate, 2 mm long... corolla tube narrowly cylindrical, 8 mm long, 2 mm in diameter, lobes oblong-ovate, subacute. Fruit smooth. Plant hardy."

They do not say who discovered this new species but G. N. Potanin, on behalf of the Russian Geographical Society, made an expedition from 1891 through 1894 into western Sichuan Sheng (Szechwan Province). In his company, as zoologist for the expedition, was Michael Michaelovich Berezovski. Potanin brought back seed as did Berezovski, together with specimens of the plant. It is most likely that the plant in Slivers' fine arboretum came from either of these sources and we would be safe to say that *S. sweginzowii* was first discovered by Potanin-Berezovski in 1893 (May and June) in western Sichuan Sheng. It was precisely in this same neighborhood that E. H. Wilson collected specimens and seed of *S. sweginzowii* in 1904. Koehne in 1910 describes the flowers as 'salmon colored'. Wilson relates that *S. sweginzowii* (no 4080) was growing in a ravine at an elevation of 11,000 feet, a bush 6 feet tall... "in a ravine in the descent to the Ya lung River at Nagachuka, Szechwan (Sichuan Sheng)." A second specimen was "in a thicket of lilacs 6 feet tall at altitude 8,000 in northern Szechwan, toward Sunpan, August 1910."

In England, *S. sweginzowii* was exhibited first in June 1915. The Arnold Arboretum received its first plant in November 1910 from the nursery of Regel and Kesselring of St. Petersburg, Russia. It flowered in 1912. "*S. sweginzowii* does not produce the extremely large individual flowers associated with the modern garden forms of the common Lilac, yet they possess a delicacy and refinement which makes them extremely beautiful. It is one of the loveliest of all Lilacs." (Bulletin of Arnold Arboretum, No. 59, 1912) The flowers of the Arnold plant are a pale yellowish-pink. Clusters are open and never crowded and it carries a delicate fragrance.

In our garden, *S. sweginzowii* is a neat, upright growing shrub of about ten feet with somewhat small leaves. Its deep garnet-colored stems (a brownish reddish) are covered in spring with dawn flushed pink florets in open, billowy clusters. The reddish stems and pale pink flowers are a most attractive combination. It is a hardy plant and outstanding garden performer, but somewhat fussy about its location and soil. It is not a rampant grower, nor big-leaved as *S. villosa* or *S. tomentella,* neither does it like open windswept locations (although it is a native mountaineer) nor hard clay soils. Placed in very light shade to protect it from the hottest suns, it thrives wonderfully. Give it well-drained soil or a fertile hilltop that simulate the wide, fertile hills of its native Chinese valleys. It will reward you magnificently with beauty each year at springtime! *S. sweginzowii* belongs to the later blooming species, opening its flowers midway between the last of *S. vulgaris* and the beginnings of the *S. villosa* hybrids. Its fragrance is a haunting, aromatic, spicy scent that brings one back to the spice stalls of the bazaars of old Cathay, altogether unlike the scent of *S. vulgaris.* It is certainly one of our finer lilac species.

If you are a hybridizer you must learn to use it. In 1930 Victor Lemoine et Fils introduced a wonderful hybrid of *S. sweginzowii* × *S. tomentella* named *S. sweginzowii* 'Albida'. It develops into a tall slender plant, flowering at the end of May with a profusion of many branched panicles of most elegant character. The long-tubed flowers with reflexed lobes are a very delicate pale pink passing to white. They, too, are very pleasantly sweet-scented. In more recent years *S. sweginzowii* 'Albida' has been extensively used in hybridizing with *S. komarowii* giving us the beautiful tribrid (three species) cultivar *S.* × 'Lark Song' and with *S. wolfii* in the cultivars *S.* × 'Springtime' and 'Sunrise'. Many new plants with other and more involved species hybrids are presently in hyridizing gardens. *S. sweginzowii* and *S. sweginzowii* 'Albida' are both excellent hybridizing parents and should be more used in crosses with *S.* × *prestoniae* hybrids for their openness of bloom and their out-standing fragrance. Do you not have some special corner for at least one of them in your garden?

In 1977 Dr. James Pringle of the Royal Botanical Gardens, Hamilton, Ontario, Canada, listed a number of excellent hybrids he produced between *S. sweginzowii* 'Albida' and *S.* × *henryi*; between *S. sweginzowii* 'Albida' and *S.* × *prestoniae* 'Isabella'; between *S. emodi* × *S.* × *lemoineiana* 'Albida'; between *S. emodi* × *S. sweginzowii*; between *S.* × *henryi* × *S. sweginzowii*; between *S. sweginzowii* × *S. reflexa*; between *S. sweginzowii* × *S. villosa*; between *S. yunnanensis* × *S. sweginzowii* among all of which were found individual plants of great merit. So far this extensive list of hybrids in series *Villosae* (more than any other hybridizer) have not been named but only numbered. It is hoped that the best cultivars will be named and introduced for garden use and for further hybridization. Although some of the above crosses have previously been made by others, the extent and depth of Pringle's work with this group has not been exceeded by anyone else. I have chosen to call one of the most unique crosses in his work, that of *S. reflexa* × *S. yunnanensis* as *S.* × *pringleiana*, to honor his work in this considerable effort in hybridizing the *Villosae* series of lilacs. One must see these lilacs to fully appreciate the scope and magnitude of his work.

SYRINGA TIGERSTEDTII

A relatively unknown newcomer among the lilac species *S. tigerstedtii* was discovered by K. A. H. Smith of Uppsala, Sweden, growing in Sichuan Sheng, China at 31° N, 102° E when it was in fruit, October 1934. He collected both seeds and herbarium specimens. Smith described the species in 1948 from a 12-year-old plant grown from this seed at the Botanical Garden of the University of Uppsala, Sweden. In 1979 a far more detailed description, history and appraisal of *S. tigerstedtii* was made by Dr. James S. Pringle, Royal Botanical Gardens, Hamilton, Ontario.

S. tigerstedtii, although described and introduced throughout the world within the following 10 years (1950–1960), somehow escaped attention since its original discovery and description appeared in a journal having limited circulation outside Sweden. Pringle states that *S. tigerstedtii* appears to have been brought to the United States on at least 10 occasions, the University of Washington Arboretum, Seattle being the first which received seed from the Hortus Botanicus Bergianus, Stockholm, Sweden, in 1948. The Arnold received its seed of the species from the same institution in 1949 and again in 1952. It was first introduced into Canada at the Agriculture Arboretum and Botanic Garden, Ottawa in 1951. Today it appears in most collections of Botanic Gardens, Arboreta and many private collections.

It is surprising that Smith found it native in an area so much frequented by so many plant explorers and yet it had escaped their attention. Smith's introduction of the seed appears to be the only importation of the species made from China. From the Uppsala planting it has spread throughout the lilac world.

S. tigerstedtii is a rather slender plant, more open than others, somewhat spreading to 8 or more feet and equally as wide. The openness of the plant and the rather thin flowers which are a mauvy-purplish pink to white within have much to recommend it as a garden or landscape plant. Pringle states, ". . . the larger inflorescences are 15–25 cm long" . . . small widely spaced clusters of flowers give the inflorescence an open appearance.

Some question remains as to whether it is really a new species or an extreme isolate of one of the other species it so closely resembles, such as *S. sweginzowii*. I believe it to be a species with growing importance. It appears that *S. tigerstedtii* will probably have its greatest value in programs of hyridization utilizing its slender open form of both plant growth and inflorescence. J. S. Pringle, in appraising the species, points out this hybridizing possibility and recommends the use of crossing the small-leaved, open flowering species with the heavier-blooming, coarser-leaved species such as

Syringa tigerstedtii: 3. Winter twig with terminal floral and lateral vegetative buds; 4. Expanding buds; 5. Inflorescence; 6. Mature fruit; 7. Seeds (scale applies to 3,4,6,7,8); 8. Flowers (a) just before anthesis (b) lateral view (c) top view (d) longitudinal section; 9. Part of inflorescence. (Photos Dr. James Pringle, Royal Botanic Garden.)

S. villosa and its hybrids. "Such hybrids" he finds, "often retained the graceful habit of the small-leaved species, while their denser branching and larger, more densely flowered panicles had considerably more visual impact... *S. tigerstedtii* may contribute not only the graceful habit associated with the small-leaved group generally, but also the tendency toward a lower, more spreading growth habit than would be available in the series *Villosae*." It may also be of value because of its fragrance. Pringle notes that McKelvey described, or cited descriptions of the flowers of all species in series *Villosae* as being either virtually odorless or rather ill-scented, with the exception of *S. sweginzowii* having a "pleasing and delicate fragrance" and *S. yunnanensis* noted by Franchet as having very fragrant flowers. In *S. tigerstedtii* the fragrance is well developed, pleasant "similar to that of carnations but spicier" (Smith 1948).

Smith notes that *S. tigerstedtii* is one of the hardiest of lilacs, easily surviving the very severest winters at Uppsala, Sweden.

Presently it is not a lilac for small gardens and does not produce enough of a flower display to recommend its planting except for the larger estates and botanical gardens. Its hybrids may prove to be good garden plants.

It is my opinion that the plant of *S. tigerstedtii* growing at the Royal Botanical Gardens, Hamilton, Canada, is one of the loveliest species. It has open, white, feathery blossoms and an open plant growth—a most desirable asset to the larger home garden and to the arboreta collections. Its hybrids which are described by Pringle are fine, and selections should be made and named for further use by hybridizers. I cherish the plant I have and the several plants resulting from my hyridization of it. (*Mon ami*, you must seek to have one in your own garden as well!)

Table 1. *Syringa tigerstedtii* contrasted with three closely related species* (Pringle)

	S. tigerstedtii	S. sweginzowii	S. tomentella	S. yunnanensis
Leaves— Lower surface	Pilose along midrib and proximal parts of main secondary veins	Pilose along midrib and proximal parts of main secondary veins	Densely pubescent along primary to quaternary veins	Glabrous
Inflorescence— Branches and pedicels	Glabrous	Glabrous	Usually puberulent, occasionally nearly glabrous	Puberulent
Corolla— Apex in bud	Rounded	Subacute	Subacute	Intermediate
Limb, diameter	7–9.5 mm	8–11.5 mm	6.5–8 mm	9.5–11mm
Tube, length	8–10.5 mm	11–13 mm	10–15 mm	8–11 mm
Anthers, apex	At or up to 0.5 mm below throat	1.5–2 mm below throat	At or slightly above throat	At throat
Capsule	Gradually long-acuminate	Gradually long-acuminate	Gradually long-acuminate	Abruptly short-acuminate

*Based on Krüssmann (1962), McKelvey (1928), Smith (1948), and observations at the Royal Botanical Gardens. Table by Dr. James Pringle, Royal Botanical Gardens, Hamilton, Ontario, Canada

S. TOMENTELLA

Edouard Bureau and Adrien Franchet in their interesting volume (in French) *New Plants of Tibet and Western China Discovered on the Travels of M. Bonvalot and Prince Henry of Orleans*, published in 1891, first described the discovery of *S. tomentella*. This species was collected by these travelers in Sichuan Province, China, on entering To-tsien lu and the borders of Yunan. A somewhat fuller description is given by E. H. Wilson, who also collected this species in 1908 at an altitude of 12,000 ft. He describes it as a bush of 4–10 ft. high, with rose-pink flowers and growing in thickets. At another location he describes it as a bush 12–15 ft. tall, growing at 10,000 ft., with white or pink flowers, again growing in thickets. In his book *Aristocrats of the Garden* Wilson writes, "I saw this plant in flower for the first time on July 9, 1908 on the frontiers of eastern Tibet at an altitude of nine thousand feet, and I thought then that I had never before seen such a handsome species of Lilacs. It had foot high, broad panicles of pink- to rosy-lilac colored flowers and on other bushes they were white. The plants were eight to fifteen feet high, much branched yet compact in habit and the wealth of flower clusters made it conspicuous from afar." The plant of *S. tomentella* at the Arnold Arboretum justifies Wilson's description.

It was not until 1905 that this species was introduced into cultivation. It is a neat, compact shrub of some height, to at least 8–10 ft., with smooth pale gray bark with dark lenticels. Although beautiful in bloom, it is not, in our opinion, quite as handsome as Wilson describes it. McKelvey describes it as... "a shrub to 15 feet, branches upright to branching, slender, gray, smooth lenticelate... Winter buds oblong with acuminate apex... Leaves elliptic to oblong-lanceolate, 1–7 in. long, ½ to 3 in. broad... color of buds Rhodonite Pink (XXXVIII) lobes tinged Olive Buff, when expanded Pale Rhodonite Pink fading to white without, white tinged pink within... anthers Primrose Yellow..."

S. tomentella is very closely related to *S. villosa* for which it is often mistaken, or more often *S. villosa* is sold as *S. tomentella*. Its hybrids are rather fine and it should be used considerably more by hyridizers, especially in crosses with the fine or small-leaved species of the series *Villosae*. To us it is a better species than the summer leaf-shedding *S. villosa*. For larger parks and arboreta *S. tomentella* should be planted more often, especially in mass groupings. It is not a plant for the smaller garden or where premium space is limited. For larger gardens some of its newer hybrids are preferable.

A gold-leaved form of *S. tomentella*, a novelty with gold leaves changing to light green as the season advances with deeper lavender-pink blossoms has been named *S. tomentella* 'Kum-Bum'. It is a chemically induced leaf color mutation with very limited value for small or large gardens. One could well do without it or most lilac leaf variegations.

S. tomentella growing at the Arnold Arboretum, Jamaica Plain, Mass. (Photo Arnold Arboretum.)

Flowering panicle detail of *S. villosa*. (Photo A. W. Gleason, Archives of Arnold Arboretum.)

SYRINGA VILLOSA

Pierre d'Incarville, a Jesuit botanist-missionary, had a keen eye for new plants as well as a zeal for religion. It was he who sent to Paris, somewhere around 1750, a very interesting collection of dried plants and seeds of the Beijing flora. Being a pupil of the great French botanist, Bernard de Jussieu, to whom he sent his plant collection, he carefully separated those plants collected in Beijing from those of the surrounding area. Among the specimens gathered in the Beijing Mountains was that of *S. villosa*. This lilac species was described and named by Vahl in 1804 from d'Incarville's specimen. The species description from this single available specimen of d'Incarville was somewhat inadequate.

S. villosa was rediscovered in 1835 by the Russian botanist, P. V. Krilov, physician to the 11th Ecclesiastical Mission travelling through Mongolia to Beijing who remarked . . . "It is a larger one (lilac) sometimes growing tree-like and inhabiting the higher regions of the mountains." O. V. Moellendorf, in ascending the Siao Wi-t'ai writes . . . "met with large forests of it between 4500 and 6000 feet." Imagine, whole forests of *S. villosa!* Others, such as the missionary Père Armand David, also sent specimens of *S. villosa* from the Beijing plains and the mountains west of the city in 1884. Dr. Bretschneider actually introduced *S. villosa* into cultivatiion in 1889—over a hundred years after its original discovery! Victor Lemoine et Fils, Nancy, France, offered it for sale for the first time under the name of *S. bretschneideri*, from whom they received the seed in 1890.

To distinguish it from other *Syringae* it was termed 'the large-leaved *Syringa*'. McKelvey in *THE LILAC* describes *S. villosa* from a large plant growing at the Arnold Arboretum: "A round-topped shrub of dense habit, up to 12 feet tall, as broad as tall, branches upright, gray, lenticellate . . . Winter-buds ovoid with acute apex, flower bud ½ inch long more or less, lateral leaf buds on each side of terminal bud frequently hardly visible, reddish-brown . . . Leaves oval, broad-elliptic to oblong 2–7 in. long, 1–3 in. broad, acute, glaucescent, usually villose on midrib and primary veins occasionally also on leaf surface . . . Inflorescence borne on leafy shoots, terminal, upright, 3–8 in. long, narrowly pyramidal, nearly cylindric or sometimes with basal subdivisions noticeably longer than those near the apex in which flowers are often fascicled . . . calyx glabrous, rarely villose, with acute teeth . . . corolla tube 3/10–1/2 in. long, slender, cylindric . . . corolla-lobes . . . sometimes with a pronounced hook, color in bud Laelia Pink, corolla-lobes Laelia Pink to Pale Persian Pink (XXXVIII) when expanded without, white tinged pale Persian Lavender within . . . anthers Primrose Yellow . . . capsules oblong, smooth . . ." McKelvey complains that the name *villosa* was poorly chosen by Vahl as the specimens she examined were only slightly villose and only at the midrib. (But so it was named and remains!) Brethschneider, who collected *S. villosa* in several areas around Beijing, reported that natives call it *ting hiang* (the fragrance of cloves). It was he who sent seeds of this species to the Paris Museum Jardin, France, to Kew Gardens, The Arnold Arboretum and to St. Petersburg, Russia. So it was that one of lilacdom's great species was almost simultaneously introduced by one man throughout the world and into the nursery trade, where it was to become in the hands of hybridizers a great progenitor of a newer race of lovely late-blooming lilacs!

In the garden, the flowers of *S. villosa* are distinctly pink, although when using a color chart there is a tinge of bluish-lavender not readily apparent to the unaided eye (but more often captured by color film). In your garden and mine, it is 'pink'! In Europe this species is grown more often as a small tree than in the United States and Canada. (See Chapter on Landscaping with Lilacs—Using Lilacs as Small Trees).

In *THE LILAC* Mrs. McKelvey writes, "While visiting the Central Experimental Farm at Ottawa, Canada, in June 1927, I saw a collection of hedges grown for demonstration purposes. One of *S. villosa*, planted in 1911, is now nearly twenty feet broad and about fifteen feet tall. It forms a handsome hedge, but is not so striking as one of *S. josikaea*." (See Chapter on Using Lilacs as Hedges)

S. villosa is a lovely lilac for backgrounds, hedges and mass plantings in arboreta and large parks or estates. Because of its size it has only limited use in the smaller garden as a tree as in Europe. Its greatest value has been its use in hyridizing at the hands of Isabella Preston and Frank Skinner. They have given us a whole new race of late blooming hybrids. Miss Preston's work is only the beginning of the marvels of genetic wonders these Chinese lilacs hold for future hybridization. Already we are seeing their offspring in the third and fourth generations. What wonderful lilacs we now have for our late blooming gardens! Work now being done with *S. villosa* hybrids under the watchful eye of Dr. Owen Rogers at the University of New Hampshire and by hybridists elsewhere augurs even finer lilacs now growing in seedling rows. Little did the botanist missionaries realize what wonders and blessings they were sending back to the horticultural world! (So be it for missionaries, plant collectors and modern day hyridizers. *Mon ami*, they all work in one great garden!)

THE LATE BLOOMING HYBRIDS *SYRINGA* × *PRESTONIAE*

In 1920 at the Dominion of Canada Central Experimental Farm, Ottawa, Miss Isabella Preston crossed *S. villosa* with the pollen of *S. reflexa* and begot a whole new race of late blooming lilacs now called in her honor *Syringa* × *prestoniae* or simply, the Prestonian Hybrids. (See Chapter on Biographical Sketches of Hybridizers) What a lovely and wonderful race of lilacs they proved to be! For this great work Miss Preston will ever be known as the 'Grand-dame of the Hybrids'! Her many hybrids were mostly named to honor Shakespearian women. One must get acquainted with these lovely lilacs to appreciate the work of this gifted woman. Some may argue that she named too many similar cultivars. Nevertheless, they do make a historic and beautiful contribution to the development of the late blooming lilacs for which all of us are grateful. (Miss Preston named 71 of her initial seedlings; 35 more have been added by others, e.g., Skinner, Bugala, Cuming, Alexander, Yaeger, Rogers, Fiala).

These hybrid beauties, the Prestonians, are noticeably different from their 'French' cousins, *S. vulgaris* cultivars, in flower appearance, in leaf, plant habit and particularly in their own exotic, oriental fragrance. They bloom a week or so later than the *S. vulgaris* sorts. They are large shrubs, even small trees. If space is adequate one should have both the common lilacs and the late blooming hybrids to know and appreciate the whole lilac family. Among the best of the *S.* × *prestoniae* are 'Isabella' (named after Miss Preston), 'Ursula', 'Pauline', 'James Macfarlane' and 'Agnes Smith' (the last two are from the work of the University of New Hampshire hybridizers, Yaeger and Rogers, and are among the finest white late blooming lilacs). Miss Preston considered her hybrid 'W. T. Macoun' as one of the types of her hybrids, the other being 'Isabella'. One of the finest is *S.* × *prestoniae* 'Miss Canada', hybridized by Dr. W. A. Cumming of Morden, Manitoba, Canada, in 1967. (*Mon ami et amie*, it is a priceless lilac treasure!)

Most of the introductions of Miss Preston have pink to lavender pink flowers. Many are quite similar; one type is upright, another more drooping in panicle form. Because of the similarity of color in her hybrids, only a few are carried even by the finest lilac specialty nurseries. I know of no planting that contains all of her named hybrids in one place. Left to themselves these hybrids often are somewhat 'rampant growers'. They do not sucker but are strong, rather tall to 10 or 12 ft. They must not be planted too closely or on small city lots. In limited surroundings they should be treated as a single specimen or a small, focal tree. They are most effective as a single garden tree. Prune them to 3 or no more than 5 trunks when still young and keep them growing upwards, removing all spontaneous lower shoots; soon they will be a small spreading tree. Placed where they will provide shade they do an excellent job for the small patio. They have attractive green foliage mostly free of insects and pests. They are heavy bloomers plagued with an abundance of seed. Keep these clipped if possible (or try some of the newer, lower tetraploid multibrids that do not seed well or at all.) Use one or two *S.* × *prestoniae* on the back boundary line, or to accent a corner, along a garage wall or service area.

Some of these late blooming lilacs, the Prestonians, and their newer relatives bloom as very young plants and are delightful potted in large earthen jars or tubs and set out on the patio as pot-shrubs. Keep them trimmed after blooming and they will perform well for a number of years. They root from green cuttings rather well. Their colors range mostly in the pinks and pale lavender-pinks but among the newer introductions are beautiful whites and deeper purples. Plant one or two if you have the room (or more). Myriads of butterflies and hovering hummingbirds will visit the pale pink, cerise, white and lavender flowers of your lilacs as they begin to unfold in your garden.

S. villosa crossed with *S. reflexa* begot the Prestonian Hybrids . . . and the Prestonian Hybrids crossed with *S. josikaea* begot . . . and with *S. tomentella* begot . . . and with *S. sweginzowii* begot . . . and with *S. wolfii* begot . . . and their progency crossed with *S. yunnanensis* crossed with *S. komarowii* . . . and so we came to have today a whole new race of late blooming multibrids (crosses with several species). The begots begot until we have an array of progeny so numerous that taxonomists can no longer identify, yet alone describe, who begot what and when and by whom. But we do have some marvelous late blooming lilacs despite it all! These combinations of quintobrids and even octobrids are the beginnings of something very fine and fantastic for the future of late blooming lilacs (and a nightmare for taxonomists). Add to these multibrids the newer polyploids and we see the inheritance enhanced even more! What shall become of these new lilac children of science and progress? They must prove themselves to take their place in the garden of the future. Some distinct groupings are beginning to form: the Prestonian Hybrids (the original crosses and their inbred offspring); the New Hampshire Hybrids (from the hybridizing team at the University of New Hampshire); the Multibrids (from several hybridizers); the Polyploids (mostly from Falconskeape). From the original work of Isabella Preston and Frank Skinner, hyridizers like Alexander, Meader, Rogers, Fiala and Bugala continue to add new and beautiful late blooming lilacs to the growing list of newer, cross-bred cultivars. Many are still relatively unknown, even to some of the arboreta and specialized nurseries because of the difficulties of introduction and propagation. Hopefully these obstacles will gradually be overcome. Ordinarily hybridizers are not propagators or commercial nurserymen and it takes time to convince the propagators of the merits of any newer introduction, especially if no one asks for them by name.

The *S.* × *prestoniae* introduced originally by Isabel Preston include the following named cultivars:

'Adrianne' S IV*
'Alice' S VII*
'Ariel' S II
'Beatrice' S V
'Bianca' S IV
'Blanch' S IV
'Caliban' S V
'Calpurnia' S IV*
'Cassandra' S V
'Celia' S IV
'Charmian' S IV
'Cleopatra' S VI*
'Constance' S V
'Coral' S V*
'Cordelia' S IV*
'Cressida' S V
'Dawn' S V*
'Desdemona' S III*
'Diana' S IV*
'Dorcas' S IV
'Elinor' S III*
'Emilia' S IV
'Ethel M. Webster' S V*
'Francisca' S VII
'Freedom' S V
'Gertrude' S IV
'Helene' S IV
'Hermia' S V
'Hermione' S V
'Imogen' S IV
'Isabella' S IV* (the type-1)
'Jacquenetta' S IV
'Jessica' S II*
'Julia' S IV
'Juliet' S VI*
'Katherina' S V
'Kim' S II
'Lavinia' S IV*
'Lucetta' S VI
'Lucinia' S IV
'Lychorida' S V
'Margaret' S V
'Masiana' S IV

'Miranda' S V
'Nocturne' S III*
'Oberon' S V
'Octavia' S V
'Olivia' S VI*
'Ophelia' S V
'Patience' S IV
'Paulina' S VII*
'Perdita' S IV
'Phebe' S V
'Puck' S VI*
'Redwine' S VI*
'Regan' S V
'Romeo' S V*
'Rosalind' S IV
'Silvia' S V
'Swanee' S I*

*cultivars of exceptional merit

'Timandra' S IV
'Ursula' S II*
'Valeria' S II*
'Viola' S VII*
'Virgilia' S VI
'W. T. Macoun' S V* (the type-2)

The *S.* × *josiflexa* hybrids Miss Preston introduced include:
'Bellicent' S V*
'Elaine' S I*
'Enid' S V
'Fountain' S V*
'Geriant' S IV
'Guinevere' S VI* (the type)
'Lynette' S VII*
'Royalty' S VII

S. × *prestoniae*
'Isabella'. (Photo
Arnold Arboretum.)

SYRINGA WOLFII

C. K. Schneider who first described *S. wolfii* in 1910 did so from a living specimen he saw growing at the Forestry Institute in St. Petersburg. To honor the director Egbert Wolf he named it *S. wolfii*. Schneider believed it grew in China although at the time its exact native location was unknown. He states, "... the flowers are as decorative as those of *S. villosa*." V. L. Komarov whose seed collection and plant specimens were sent to St. Petersburg was known to have traveled extensively some years before in Manchuria and Korea and undoubtedly was the first to send seed of *S. wolfii* under the name of *S. villosa* var. *hirsuta* in 1893–95 to Europe. In August of 1917 E. H. Wilson gathered seed in Korea which he sent to the Arnold Arboretum, although previously, in 1906, the Arnold had received seed of *S. wolfii* from Regel and Kesserling in St. Petersburg.

S. wolfii, as Schneider describes it, "is a tall shrub, in habit like *S. villosa*, branches glabrous, rounded, olive colored... leaves elliptic, with margins somewhat paralled, bright green, glabrous above, pale scarcely pillose along the veins or glabrous beneath, 11 × 4 cm to 14 × 6–7 cm. large... inflorescence very large to 28 × 14 cm., large, scarcely minutely pilose, flowers colored lilac, fragrant with erect corolla-lobes, never flattening out, including the lobes 18–20 mm. long, truncate at the margin... fruit obtuse 14 mm. long, non-verrucose." McKelvey making her description from two plants of *S. wolfii* growing at the Arnold Arboretum (from seed collected by Wilson in 1917) states... "... They are open spreading shrubs and rapid growers. Even as young plants they have produced considerable bloom and seed. The flower clusters are pyramidal, with a broad base and narrow top... their lateral branchlets, near the base, droop in a conspicuous fashion; the panicle is borne at the top of a long leafy shoot. On expanding in the spring the young shoots, foliage and inflorescences are tinged with a reddish-brown color. The color of the two plants varies slightly, one being darker than the other. They have a slight but not pleasing fragrance... The foliage expands early in the spring and falls early in the autumn... protruding veins produce a slightly crinkled appearance in the leaf surface..." We have found that the flower color of *S. wolfii* varies in different plants from a pale-lavender to a pale darker purple and in clay soils the same plant is often more pinkish lilac to a pale pink purple. Also some plants bear heavier inflorescence than others when planted from protected selfed seed. It is a somewhat variable species and would appear to be most suited for hybridization and for varietal named selections.

There was some initial confusion on exactly which was the true *S. wolfii* species. The *Bulletin of the Arnold Arboretum,* (Vol. IV, p. 26) first lists it as "cultivated by von Sivers at Riga, Russia, who obtained it from China." This first plant, whatever species it was, does not appear to have been the true *S. wolfii*. Professor Sargent also describes another plant (Bulletin A.A., Vol. I, p. 28), "The handsomest of all the late lilacs is *S. wolfii*, a native of Mongolia. This plant reached the Arnold Arboretum from St. Petersburg in 1906 and before it had received a name. It is related to *S. villosa* which it resembles in its foliage, but it appears to be a larger and more vigorous plant. The small, dark blue-purple or rose-purple flowers are borne in clusters which on a vigorous plant are sometimes two feet long or more, and a foot in diameter, and are produced in great profusion... The flowers, however, lack the fragrance of the Common Lilac and of several of the Chinese species." (Sargent identified this plant as *S. wolfii* which is now known to be incorrect. Actually the plant he described is *S. komarowii*.)

Dr. Nakai in 1917 describes *S. wolfii*, which he collected and called *S. formosissima* found native in central and northern Korea as... "related to *S. josikaea* but differs in the odorless flowers and in the fruit, obtuse or obtusish at the apex, and notes that it is an umbrageous plant growing in fertile soil." Nakai's flowers are darker than those described by Schneider but otherwise the plants correspond in most details. Nakai refers to it as having an additional lobe, five instead of the usual four on many florets. He describes three plants which he called *S. formosissima, S. hirsuta* and *S. robusta* as all closely related. Today we classify Nakai's *S. formosissima* and *S. hirsuta* as more glabrous forms of *S. wolfii*, while his *S. robusta* as probably a form of *S. villosa*. *S. wolfii* var. *hirsuta*, in the arboretum of the University of Guelph, Guelph, Ontario, Canada, is the most beautiful form I have seen. It is most worthy of being in any garden. The Guelph form is the best.

There are strikingly close similarities between *S. wolfii* and *S.josikaea*, although *S. wolfii* is handsomer in bloom than the best forms of *S. josikaea*. In flower color they are much the same from a garden point of view with *S. wolfii* less colored. Some botanists (few taxonomists), both past and present, maintain they are extremes of the same species. McKelvey objects stating, "A vast territory exists between their habitats and *S. wolfii* may be regarded as the Asiatic representative of the European plant." Curiously, as (McKelvey) notes under *S. josikaea*, certain botanists were of the opinion that *S. josikaea* was merely naturalized, and not native in Europe and suggested that it came from northern China.

Differing with Mrs. McKelvey we are strongly of this opinion: historically the Mongol tribes of northern China not only took their families, sheep and household treasures but could also have taken with them in their 'Westward March to Europe' some of the seed and plants they treasured, finally settling in what is today's Hungary many centuries ago. We have seen the long migrations of *S. vulgaris*. Could this not have happened with so great a nation as the Mongol people? Seeds and plants move under strange circumstances! (*Mon ami*, consider just three naturalized plants in America that crossed an ocean and spread thousands of miles: the dandelion (*Taraxacum officinale*), the wild mustard (*Brassica juncea*) and the wild carrot or Queen Anne's Lace (*Daucus carota*)—all of which were brought across the seas by settlers seeking a new land. Although we consider our three examples weeds—could this not have happened with the *Syringa josikaea—wolfii?*)

Whatever, it is a lovely species, not for the small garden and perhaps best in the hands of hybridizers who are making great strides with it as a parent plant. It imparts to many of its hybrids the glossy leaf and dark green color plus vigor. Some of the newest hybrids such as 'Spellbinder' are crosses of *S. komarowii* × *S. wolfii*, a cross known now as *S.* × *clarkiana* containing many fine cultivars.

SYRINGA YUNNANENSIS—The Yunnan Lilac

This relatively unknown species of lilac is closely related to the Himalayan Lilac, *S. emodi*. It was discovered in 1887 by Abbé Jean Marie Delavay of the Missions Estrangeres, growing in the woods by Lake Lankong, near the city of Talifu in Yunnan Sheng (Yunnan Province), southwestern China. An upright, rather narrow shrub it reaches 10–12 ft. in height. The pale whitish-purplish, rose tinted flowers borne on terminal leafy shoots are rather insignificant. Often it has 5 corolla-lobes rather than the usual 4.

Although several plant collectors were in this same area before Delavay-Garnier in 1768, Gill in 1877, Szeczenyi in 1880, Hosie in 1883—no collection of the species was made until Dr. J. Anderson for the first time gathered the plant in 1868. However, it was from Delavay's specimen that Adrien Franchet first described *S. yunnanensis* in 1891. Later the species was collected in western Yunnan by George Forrest in July and August of 1906, who describes it with ". . . flowers pale purplish-rose... growing in shady open situations on the margins of pine forests on the eastern flank of the Tali Range." It was introduced into commerce by Bees Nursery Co., Neston, Cheshire, England, under A. K. Bulley for whom Forrest collected seed, in their offering of lilacs in 1920. Bees Nursery had previously sent plants of *S. yunnanensis* to the Arnold Arboretum in September, 1908. At the Arnold it flowered for the first time in 1913.

McKelvey adds to the description the Arnold plant... "Winter buds oblong with acuminate apex... leaves elliptic-oblong to elliptic-lanceolate, occasionally lanceolate, 1½–3 in. long, ½–1 in. broad, acute or acuminate base cuneate, ciliolate, glabrous above, glaucous beneath... midrib on lower and upper surfaces colored Hay's Maroon (XIII)... Inflorescence borne on leafy shoots, terminal, upright, 6–7 in. long, 4 in. broad... corolla-tube slender, funnel form, 5/16 in. long, color in bud Light Russet-Vinaceous to Pale Vinaceous (XXXIX), expanded Pale Purplish Vinaceous without, lobes marked white with Pale Purplish Vinaceous at throat within, anthers large, Barium Yellow... occasionally protruding... Capsule oblong, smooth..."

S. yunnanensis, like most of the late blooming species, does not sucker. It is easy to root from green cuttings taken after bloomtime.

Until fairly recently *S. yunnanensis* has been little used in hybridizing, as none of its characteristics appear really outstanding except the openess of its inflorescence (this can be found in better species). Of late Pringle has evaluated the possible merits of using some of the smaller-leaved, open flowered species in hybridizing the heavier blossom, large-leaved sorts. The small florets of *S. yunnanensis* are a bane to hybridizers. More recently a tetraploid form under the clonal name of 'Prophecy' has been introduced by Fiala, who has worked with the species for nearly 25 years. The florets of the tetraploid form are considerably larger and a deeper lavender shade, the leaves heavier (thicker) and slightly larger than the diploid form. Otherwise they appear rather identical. *S. yunnanensis* seems to transmit small florets, open inflorescence, narrow growth habit and a deeper lavender color to its progeny. With continued and selective hybridization some few, refined hybrids should appear. It is definitely not a plant for the ordinary garden or even for public parks as it has little, if any, landscape value. In heavy soils it is a rather poor grower and needs a well-drained situation. For very large estates, arboreta or for hybridizers this species has historical or scientific value. Until better hybrids are developed, it is not a lilac to be considered by most. Dr. James Pringle of the Royal Botanical Gardens, Hamilton, has crossed it with *S. reflexa* producing some interesting hybrids which, to honor him, I have called *S.* × *pringleiana*.

In the past it was distributed rather widely as *S. pinetorum* to many arboreta and private collections. (Our own *S. pinetorum* plants all turned out to be *S. yunnanensis* or *S. tigerstedtii*. The species *S. pinetorum* is no longer accepted as valid today.) At best *S. yunnanensis* remains an insignificant lilac species. (Are there not in every family less sparkling individuals?)

SERIES PINNATIFOLIAE

SYRINGA PINNATIFOLIA

In the Genus *Syringa*, Subgenus *Syringa* is a unique Series *Pinnatifoliae* containing a single species of lilac, *S. pinnatifolia*. "It is distinct from all other lilacs," according to W. B. Hemsley, who was the first to describe it in 1906. "At first sight this new lilac might be mistaken . . . for *S. laciniata*, but on closer examination it proves to be a distinct species. It differs in all the leaves being distinctly pinnate, that is, divided to the midrib into separate leaflets; in the lanceolate acute leaflets of much thinner texture, and very minutely fringed on the margin; in the rounded lobes of the calyx; and in the relatively longer corolla-tube. *Syringa pinnatifolia*, as I propose naming it, was imported by Messrs. James Veitch & Sons, through their collector, Mr. E. H. Wilson, who discovered it in the extreme West of China, at an elevation of 9,000 feet. Like many of his discoveries, it appeared to be quite rare, and no seed was collected but a young plant was brought home safely. Mr. Wilson describes it as an elegant bush, six to eight feet high, with very slender branches and white flowers. It has not yet flowered in this country (1906), so far as I know, but judging from the dried specimens I venture to predict that this new Lilac will prove a welcome acquisition." Hemsley notes it as "capsula ignota" (fruit unknown).

Wilson collected for the Veitch firm in May 1904 at Mupin in Sichuan Sheng (Szechuan), China, where he discovered this species. On his Arnold Arboretum expeditions he was back in China in 1907–1908 and in 1910–1911 and again gathered *S. pinnatifolia* at Mupin in June, 1908. He then described the bushes as "seven to ten feet tall with pink flowers, growing in thickets at an altitude of 7,500 feet." Seed of this species collected in October 1910 was received at the Arnold in February 1911; the plant raised from it flowering for the first time in 1917.

In his *Aristocrats of the Garden* Wilson mentions the flowers as being "a pale mauve," whereas previously he called them "pink." Writing in the *Kew Bulletin* (Misc. Inf.)

Bean calls the flowers "white with a slight tinge of lilac." All the plants I have seen in the U.S. and Canada are a creamy white (supposedly they all came from the same specimen at the Arnold Arboretum). The buds on the plant that grew at Rochester Parks were a greenish-pale yellow-white (McKelvey calls it Clear Dull Green-Yellow to Light Chalcedony Yellow (XVII). She notes that most of the plants in cultivation are "white". Lemoine et fils Nancy, France, in their English catalogue for 1923–24 list *S. pinnatifolia* as, "A most curious species of Lilac with very distinct pinnate leaves, small white fowers in terminal panicles." This is incorrect as McKelvey notes "they come from lateral and not terminal buds."

Of the specimen plant of *S. pinnatifolia* at the Arnold Arboretum, McKelvey writes, "From a distance in a general way it resembles in habit and foliage some of the Rose species, such as *Rosa omeiensis* Rolfe. It is a round-topped shrub, five feet tall, with stout, spreading somewhat angular branches and a distinctive bark which peels off in thin, paper-like layers from the old wood. The foliage unfolds early in the spring and is retained until well into autumn and its pinnate character distinguishes it from all other lilacs. The small creamy or pure white flowers, with anthers clearly visible in the wide throat, have a somewhat unpleasant fragrance. The clusters are small and inconspicuous and slightly nodding. They open during the first two weeks in May—or considerably earlier than those of most of the lilac species, and are too small and hidden by the foliage to make the plant of much value as a decorative garden shrub. It is interesting rather than ornamental and, because of its somewhat picturesque habit, might be of value as a tub plant." (The plant she describes is A.A. no. 6860)

It is difficult to find a specimen of *S. pinnatifolia* even in the larger collections. Few if any nurseries list it. *S. × persica* closely resembles this species but only in foliage, being far superior to *S. pinnatifolia* in bloom. It is not a lilac for home gardens but rather for the largest Botanic Gardens and hybridizers. A truly unique hybrid is an interseries cross, *S. pinnatifolia × S. oblata*, called by taxonomists *S. × diversifolia*. Perhaps in the hands of some really patient hybridizer *S. pinnatifolia* may bring forth some yet unknown characteristics. There are a few (your author among them) who speculate in theory that *S. pinnatifolia* may be one of those extremely difficult hybrids such as *S. × persica*, perhaps some seemingly impossible cross made in nature of *S. laciniata* with a form of *S. oblata* or (despite the different time of blooming) even with *S. pekinensis* whence it may have its exfoliating bark. This is all speculation and it is scientifically correct to consider it as a rightful, and valid species on its own. (But *mon ami*—who can be so certain of anything?)

In 1947 Dr. Karl Sax crossed *S. pinnatifolia × S. laciniata*, producing a second but different form of *S. × diversifolia* and described as "vigorous and including plants of possible horticultural value." Plants of this hybrid are at the Arnold Arboretum, Agriculture Canada Research Station, Morden, Manitoba, and at Highland Park, Rochester, New York. It may be a new door to hybridists for the future.

SUBGENUS *LIGUSTRINA*
The Exotic Tree Lilacs

There are two species of late-blooming tree lilacs known to botanists under the Subgenus of *Ligustrina*. The Subgenus being so called because in flower they resemble the privet and at one time were thought by some not to belong to the genus *Syringa*. Today we fully recognize their identity with the lilacs. The Tree Lilacs and their botanical naming have been a troublesome problem for taxonomists for many years. Only very recently have these matters been relatively well worked out (I am not certain that all the varietal forms are finally settled). Today we recognize two separate species of Tree Lilacs *S. pekinensis* and *S. reticulata*. The species *S. reticulata* has at least two varietal forms, *S. reticulata* var. *reticulata* and *S. reticulata* var. *amurensis*. According to Dr. James Pringle the following updating of the more familiar older names is the accepted nomenclature as of May 1983:

S. amurensis (Ruprecht) in the wider sense = *S. reticulata*
in the strict sense = *S. reticulata* var. *amurensis*
S. amurensis var. japonica (Maximovicz) Franchet, Savatier = *S. reticulata* var. *reticulata*
S. fauriei Leveille—questionably distinct from *S. reticulata* var. *amurensis*
S. japonica (Maximowicz) Decaisne = *S. reticulata* var. *reticulata*
S. reticulata var. mandshurica (Maximowicz) Hara = *S. reticulata* var. *amurensis*
S. pekinensis remains *S. pekinensis*

We are grateful for his scholarly and orderly classification and clarifications.

SYRINGA PEKINENSIS

It is quite possible that the Jesuit missionary d'Incarville, who collected in the Beijing mountains and plains in 1742 found the plant, although credit is given to several others, primarily to Père Armand David who in July of 1863 collected specimens of *S. pekinensis* in the mountains north of Beijing in *Ta-Tchiao-chan* and notes, "It is a shrub about 3 meters tall (today we know it to grow to 25 feet and more) with glaucous leaves... with flowers that smell like honey." Kirilov, who also collected in these same mountains from 1831 to 1840, may well have sent the first specimens home to St. Petersburg. It is most probable that it was from his specimens that Ruprecht, the famous botanist of the Russian Flora, first described the species in 1857. Tatarinov also collected in the same area in 1840–1850 but no specific mention is made of a lilac species. Ruprecht, in describing another new species *S. amurensis* adds—". . . it contributes another new section to which can be added yet another new species, *S. pekinesis*" which he describes as having, ". . . leaves heart-shaped, acuminate, very glabrous, the flowers slightly smaller (than *S. amurensis*) and more congested and the primary branches of its panicles naked and longer..."

S. pekinensis was introduced into cultivation by Dr. Bretschneider who collected seed in the same Beijing Mountains. Seed being received in Paris at the Jardin in 1880, in Berlin in 1885, while according to Bean it was received at Kew England in 1881, and on January 23, 1882 it was received at the Arnold Arboretum.

McKelvey's description, a bit more detailed than others, states . . . "it is a large slender, round-topped shrub or small tree to 15 feet (in the wild to 40 feet), bark on old wood fissured, on branchlets reddish-brown, marked by numerous large and conspicuous lenticels, sometimes exfoliating in papery flakes, fissuring early. Winter buds ovoid with acute apex . . . Leaves firm in texture, lanceolate, ovate, ovate-lanceolate, elliptic-ovate . . . 1–3½ in. long, ¾–2¼ in. broad . . . dark green above, paler beneath . . . Inflorescence commonly from one pair of lateral buds at end of branchlet . . . 4–7 in. long, rhachis spreading horizontally . . . corolla-tubes narrow . . . color in bloom Marguerite Yellow (XXX), . . . stamens twice as long as limb, Primrose Yellow . . . capsule ¾ in. long, oblong . . . sparingly verrucose . . ."

For the garden it is a rapidly growing tall shrub or tree with dark leaves and heads of very small creamy-white flowers covering the tree in wonderful clusters in mid to late June (in some localities as late as early July). As the tree ages its most outstanding characteristic is its beautiful peeling bark, which is especially attractive against winter snow. In growing this species from seed some plants are far superior in the peeling, and papery curls of the bark. One must be certain his specimen is from such a plant. Although *S. pekinensis* is a strong and rapid grower in its first decade, it is rather shy blooming. Many complain about the number of years it takes to have a good blooming specimen. Only with age does it begin to show what it is capable of in massive flowering. Perhaps one of the largest and finest specimens is to be found at the Central Agricultural Experiment Farm at Ottawa, Canada. In the U.S. *S. pekinensis* is not planted as extensively as *S. reticulata* and its forms because of its slow flowering. Since *S. reticulata* var. *reticulata* is a far better small tree, with exciting cherry-like bark, better form, and larger blossom, *S. pekinensis* is not the most desirable tree lilac. Leave it to large collections and arboreta where it grows to be a very large, fine specimen.

All the tree lilacs thrive in rich, well-drained soils and need only initial pruning to one stem, if a large tree is desired, or left to 2 or 3 for their interesting branching. (We like to leave several stems and prune all the small branches to a height of 6 to 8 ft. to show the wonderfully interesting bark of both species.) Otherwise it is a healthy tree seldom, if ever, bothered by insects or diseases, needing no real pruning. Its seed panicles are very large and most interesting in the autumn. There is a form of *S. pekinensis* 'Pendula' which is more weeping in name than in actual growth, although I have seen a few specimens that were noticeably so while still very young. The weeping variety must be grafted to retain this characteristic or obtained as rooted cuttings and not from seed. In sprouting the seed it has been noticed to have a very high percentage of albino seedlings, far more so than in any other lilac. The seeds of the tree lilacs species take some weeks longer (a month or more) to germinate and do so over a long period of time, not evenly as does *S. vulgaris* seed. One must be patient with it.

S. amurensis var. *pekinensis*, Hsiao Wu tai shan, Chilhi, China. "Two large old specimens of the North Chinese Tree Lilac. The taller is about 40 feet high and has a trunk over 2 feet in diameter." (Photo, F. W. Meyer, August 8, 1913. Arnold Arboretum.)

Winter trunk. *S. pekinensis* displays an interesting shaggy bark on the old giant trees at Highland Park, Rochester, N.Y. (Photo R. Clark.)

SYRINGA RETICULATA

The finest of the tree lilcs is the species *Syringa reticulata* with its two recognized varietal forms, *S. reticulata* var. *reticulata* and *S. reticulata* var. *amurensis*. Both varieties are quite similar in size, habit, leaf and in inflorescence. McKelvey states that *S. reticulata* var. *reticulata* differs "in its more tree-like habit up to 30 feet, in its later blooming season (in cultivated plants), its slightly larger winter buds, leaves and inflorescence ... and in its usually oblong and verrucose seed capsule." (It is listed in *The Lilac* under *S. amurensis* var. *japonica*).

Syringa reticulata var. reticulata

Ruprecht described this species and varietal form in 1857 and named it *S. amurensis*. Maximowicz, the famous Russian botanist, in 1875 named a variety of tree lilac he collected in Japan as *Syringa japonica*. Actually the Dutch botanist Blume, back in 1850 first described this species of tree lilac from plant material in the Leiden Botanical Museum and named it *Ligustrum reticulatum*. It was not until 1941, however, that the Japanese botanist Hara corrected the species nomenclature, properly identifying *reticulata* in the genus *Syringa* and not *Ligustrum*. Today all lilacs previously classified in the wide sense as *S. amurensis* and particularly those called *S. japonica* or *S. amurensis japonica* are known by the original name *Syringa reticulata*. (It is all really very simple if you are a plant taxonomist—first names simply stick and are always first!) Be assured, according to Pringle, that in *S. reticulata* var. *reticulata*, you may drop the second *reticulata* when speaking of the Old Japanese Tree Lilac and still be very scientifically proper using *S. reticulata* alone.

Of the two forms of *S. reticulata* the variety *reticulata* (the old Japanese Tree Lilac from Japan) is somewhat better than *S. reticulata* var. *amurensis* which is the continental form found native throughout northern China. The variety *reticulata* was collected early, even before Maximowicz (1875), and was introduced as seed sent by W. S. Clark, at that time President of the Agricultural College at Sapporo, Japan, to the Arnold Arboretum in 1876. Plants of this seed bloomed for the first time in 1885 and proved to be outstanding in bloom and form.

It is a lovely, upright growing tree to 30 ft., rather round-topped, dark leaves and large plumes of feathery white blossoms that resemble huge panicles of privet. The protruding yellow anthers give added elegance. It has the same fragrance as *S. pekinensis*, described by David as "*a fleurs blanches exhalant une odeur de miel*." (. . . the white flowers exhale the fragrance of honey). It blooms in June. The bark of both forms of *S. reticulata* have a most appealing reddish-brown much lenticellated glossy bark that peels on younger branches (much like a cherry). It is lovely in the winter landscape. I believe the bark on var. *reticulata* is somewhat more reddish to deep rich brown than on var. *amurensis*. Both are splendid forms of a charming tree that will delight you and all who visit your garden. McKelvey finds very little difference between the two. Try them both if you have room, although I believe you will have great difficulty in finding *S. reticulata* var. *amurensis* as very few nurseries carry it, preferring the *S. reticulata* var. *reticulata* instead. There are two selected upright forms of *S. reticulata* called 'Ivory Silk' and another named 'Cole's Selection' which are somewhat narrower than the type but identical in all other ways.

Syringa reticulata var. amurensis

This fine form of the Tree Lilacs was probably first found in 1855 by two Russians travelling independently, Richard Maack and Karl Johann Maximowicz. Maack states, "It was gathered by me first on June 20 on the right valley wall of the Chingan River, later, now and again, in Central Amur near the mouth of the Garin on the left valley banks of the Ongma Chongko. It grew on the banks of the valleys and at the foot of the banks in mixed forests. I collected it on June 20 in full boom and later on July 26, with unripe and barren fruit in the right valley wall of Sargu by the River Girri. It is called *furagda* by the Goldi at the mouth of the Ussuri and below it." (The book *Journey on the Amur in 1855* in Russian contains an excellent picture of this lilac which Maack called *Ligustrina amurensis*). Maximowicz in his book *Primitiae Florae Amurensis* (New Flora from Amur) in 1859 describes it ... "a tree entirely glabrous, leaves ovate, acuminate, subtruncate ... same color on both sides, the calyx lobes very short..." He notes it as coming from the lower Amur near Borbi and from several places in the Bureja Mountains. In certain of these places he speaks of it as common in deciduous woods, in others as growing on the margins of coniferous forests. Gustav Radde who explored this area in 1855–1859 remarks about *S. amurensis* "with trunks the thickness of a leg, little inclined to grow into a shrub, usually reaching at the most 20–30 feet. It avoids proximity to conifers and was not seen in the interior of the mountains. It only rarely extends to the banks of the rivers (on the left bank of an unknown stream is a gigantic specimen 35 feet tall, hidden however, by *Ulmus*). It is common in the valleys that open to the west and the southwest... it does not appear in the plains." In tree form it is more rounded and broader than *S. reticulata* var. *reticulata*.

The flowers are described by McKelvey as... "Inflorescence from one or more pairs of lateral buds, 4–8 in. long, pedicel glabrous, short, ... calyx glabrous, corolla-tube scarcely longer than calyx, funnelform, corolla-lobes, broad at base, ... color Marguerite Yellow (Ridgeway—XXX) or paler, ... stamens twice the length of the corolla-tube... anthers yellow... capsule obovoid-oblong, smooth, rarely verrucose."

A great number of *S. reticulata* are grown from seed by nurserymen with considerable variation in size, quality of bloom and richness of bark. Some are definitely better than others (whereas some seedlings are poor in all aspects). A great deal of selection needs to be done to develop better cultivars. Those selected should be propagated only by cuttings and not from seed. *S. reticulata* should be grown as one or at most 3 stems. Prune away all lower and smaller branches. (I like 3-trunked trees for the picturesque winter appearance of the bark. Twisted lower branches can be most interesting.) Plant them in front of a background of tall conifers to highlight the display of tree lilac bloom. Place them as a single specimen at the turn of a winding walk, or surround them in a shrub planting with the very latest to bloom *S.* × *prestoniae*. (Often they will overlap in bloom). They are exotic alone or in a triangular planting. As yet no color other than creamy whites (and these vary from cream to very white) has been found among the tree lilacs. Perhaps some color mutation or hybridist's wizardry may give us a light pink or deeper yellow—or a pale lavender!

These lilacs from China and Japan are full of mysteries! Neither of the species, *S. pekinensis* or *S. reticulata* have ever been successfully crossed with any other species although several attempts have been made, some that even produced infertile embryos. Henry in 1900 crossed both species of the tree lilacs with *S. villosa*, *S. pubescens* and *S. vulgaris*, resulting in infertile seed. Sax in 1930 unsuccessfully crossed *S. reticulata* with *S. reflexa*, Clapp attempted an *S. vulgaris* cross, Yaeger in 1950 attempted the cross *S. reticulata* × *S. patula* 'Miss Kim', Schneider in 1964 crossed without success *S. reticulata* × *S. vulgaris* 'Night', Bibikova & Kadryatseva (1969) attempted *S. reticulata* crosses with *S. vulgaris*, *S. josikaea*, *S. oblata*, *S. reflexa*, *S. villosa* and *S. wolfii* without success, Skinner in 1967 tried to cross *S.* × *prestoniae* with *S. reticulata*, Fiala in 1973 attempted the cross of *S. reticulata* × *S. tribrid* (*S. sweginzowii* × *S. tomentella* × *S. wolfii*).

Syringa reticulata var. *reticulata* (once called *S. amurensis* var. *japonica*) makes a most pleasing street tree. We understand it is so used rather extensively in The Netherlands. In Cleveland, Ohio, some decades ago under an enterprising Shade Tree and Parks Director, several streets in the newer developments were planted with *S. reticulata* var. *reticulata*. After 30 years they are lovely small trees requiring practically no pruning or spraying, forming an avenue of bright summer green and are magnificent in bloom. (The one problem is that undisciplined children love to peel their attractive bark.) Excellent advice on using the Tree Lilac for Urban Islands, containers and for city streets is given in the Fall 1984 issue of *Arnoldia* (Vol 44, No. 4, p. 20).

S. reticulata var. *reticulata* showing cherry-like winter bark.

CHAPTER FOUR

Color in Lilacs

The wonderful array of colors found in lilacs makes their description most difficult. Two factors contribute to deeper or lighter hues and to intensity of one color over another when found in combination. These are weather (climatic conditions at blooming) and soil constitution. In cool, damp weather, colors are deeper and more intense, often deeper blue or purple. Hot sun brings out the magenta in the lilac pigmentation and tends to fade them to lighter colors and off-white shades. The gravelly, lighter soils of New England, often heavily enriched with limestone, give different shades and hues than do the heavier clays of the Midwest or the rich loams of the Pacific Northwest. You must see a specimen blooming in your particular area and in your kind of soil to judge accurately what it will look like in your garden. Descriptions given in general accounts are accurate in a wider sense but subtle variations of color and tints arise from the factors mentioned.

A daily change in color hues is found in lilacs as their buds swell and show color, begin to burst into bloom and as the thrysus begins to unfurl its florets, first at the bottom and then a daily march upward until it is in full bloom! This 'unfolding of the colors' is part of the nostalgic magic and captivating charm of the lilac. One may prefer a certain lilac in swelled buds, another in half-bloom with buds of one color and blossoms another, while some prefer the lilac in full bloom. Often the buds, the reverse of the petals or the outer petals are a deeper or entirely different color from the open floret. What lilac connoisseur has not marvelled at the shades of Lemoine's marvelous deep red-budded 'Paul Thirion' as it unfolds from red to delicate shades of pink petticoats (It could have been well named after Madame rather than Paul!) What intriguing shades of deep purple and steel blue combine in the beautiful 'Mrs. Elizabeth Peterson'—is it a true blue or a false purple, or both?

Historical and Technical Considerations of Color

When we go into the lilac garden (or any other garden) the most important attraction is color, then fragrance. Color is the magnetic 'first appeal' of any flower that leads to further appraisal of texture, substance, form, pattern, singleness or doubleness, plant position and surroundings. Colors are never seen alone but in relationship to other colors seen at the same time. One of our best known colorists, Faber-Birren, states, "Beauty is not out there in man's environment, but here within man's brain. The perception of color, including feelings and emotion, is the property of human consciousness." So it is with lilac colors.

When we view lilacs we need to understand certain qualities of color (particularly if we are hybridizing or judging for color). Modern colorists are in fair agreement that there are three qualities of color that are requisite for understanding what we see. Hue is the specific name of a color or, scientifically, hue is measured as dominant wave length and its position in the spectrum recognized as violet (the shortest wave length), blue, green, yellow, orange and red (the longest wave length). The second is saturation, also called chroma or purity, and is the intensity of the color, its brightness or dullness. Tone is a color not at its full intensity. The third characteristic is reflectance or value. Tint is a light value; shade is a dark value. The human eye is able to distinguish about two million different colors, that is, combinations of hue, saturation and reflectance.

There are really no standard colors, but there are standard methods of measuring and defining colors. When we talk of color, lilac colors or otherwise, we are simply saying that we have selected combinations, usually with a logical sequence, so that we have some basis for discussion. We compare unknown colors with known ones in order to identify and classify the unknowns. The simple color classifications devised by John Wister and his Committee to be used in the Lilac Checklist of 1941 and again in 1953 presented a logical sequence of lilac color categories composed of seven basic groups: I—White; II—Violet; III—Bluish; IV—Lilac; V—Pinkish; VI—Magenta; VI—Purple. No attempt was made to describe the hundreds of variations or nuances found in lilacs. Time has proved it a rather successful system of classification for lilac colors by general groups (although for some lilacs even experts might argue as to the appropriate color category).

The history of color is really quite fascinating, and has occupied the attention of thoughtful men beginning with the ancient Greeks. Plato, Pythagoras and the Roman, Pliny, all discoursed on the art of color. Aristotle stated, "Simple colors are the proper colors of the elements—water, fire, air and earth." da Vinci, centuries later wrote, "White for light, yellow for earth, green for water, blue for air, red for fire and black for darkness." Sir Isaac Newton devised the first color wheel; J. C. LeBlon defined the 'red-yellow-blue basic color theory' in 1730—a theory and means of organizing color still favored by artists. (Bon Ami, all this while Lilacs were mixing their own colors in their own secret natural way!)

Harmony in color is a visual acceptance of vibrancy, intensity and complementaries or distinctiveness. Today the color determination system most used by the floriculture and paint industries is the Munsell System. It divides color into steps as the eye would see them and describes color in the meaningful terms of hue, value and chroma. Each of these three qualities is described by a number, hence any color can be described by a simple number standing for the color's relationship to hue, chroma and value.

Now, mind you, all this about color without even having seen a lilac! Perhaps lilacs are one of the most difficult flowers to describe as to color since they represent a limited range of hues, an unlimited number of color chroma or saturations and considerable variety in value or reflectance.

Lilac Pigmentation

Scientists tell us there are no black pigments found in lilacs (or in flowers). The pigmentations which color lilacs are produced by a group of organic compounds known as flavonoids (which include white to yellow flavones) and the chemical group known as anthocyanins (which give the reddish, violet to bluish colors). The dark colors of lilacs (and of most other flowers) are the result of very high concentrations of pigment in the cells of the flower petals. Remember when painting with water colors, if you use too much water the color looks washed-out. Horticulturally this is called lack of substance; in terms of color it is known as low saturation or low chroma. The high saturations of pigmented lilacs look dark; low saturation flowers are a light color. It has been found that in line-breeding of purples or dark violets, the color will tend to get darker. Line-breeding will intensify any color.

Color Dimensions in the Garden

Something should be said of the dimensions of color for landscape values. Incredibly, the eye becomes far-sighted when focusing on red, yellow or orange. Thus, these colors appear closer, whereas greens, browns and violets recede, appearing more distant. Colors also affect size. Light colors tend to expand and therefore, light colored objects appear larger, while the deeper colors contract and appear smaller. In terms of visibility yellow is the brightest hue followed by vibrant orange. Goethe (the German colorist) set up a visibility number scale: yellow—9, orange—8, red—6, green—5, blue—4, violet—3. Most plants depend on flower color to attract insects for pollination. Bees identify four colors, with blue being their preferred color.

Color in lilacs is a magnificent subject since pigmentation is often more intense or entirely different on the outer layer side of the petal than on the inside, giving the floret a two-toned effect.

Clear colors should be preferred to washed-out ones; good saturation to weak. With the many new cultivars and hybrids, plus the intensification of breeding programs together with the new tetraploid lilacs, we are certain to have newer and more distinct combinations of colors. Already the cultivar 'Rochester' used in breeding has given a whole array of new colors, combinations, stripes, stars, eyed and new forms. It has also given us the new 'pearled lilacs, softly iridescent and reflecting like mother-of-pearl. Tetraploids are intensifying the substance, hence deepening the chroma and adding iridescent casts of great beauty.

The next time you walk through the lilacs, stop and look carefully at their wonderful array of colors! They are magnificent and amazing. Incredible is the best description! (*Mon ami et amie*, no wonder these lilac beauties so cast a spell over all of us!)

Recommendation of Lilac Cultivars in the Various Color Classifications

Among the at least 1500 listed lilac cultivars of various colors it would be very difficult for most gardeners, even many experts, to select the 'best' for their gardens without some assistance. In the following pages various lilac cultivars are discussed according to color classifications. I have attempted to present a 'Recommendation List' of each of the color classifications as a guide for those who wish to use it. Over 40 years I have seen many lilac cultivars and have discussed the merits of many of them with lilac experts throughout the country and abroad. I have not seen every single lilac recommended (but most of them). For the few recommended, sight unseen, I depend on authorities far more knowledgeable than myself and the combined judgment of others.

The purpose of these recommendations is to upgrade the selection of lilacs for modern gardens and plantings. Perhaps we are a bit too nostalgic about the 'old sorts'—rootlets gleaned from the old homestead grounds or given by friends, or we simply plant lilacs by 'color only' and have no idea what they are. Over the past 50 years and especially in the last 25, many men and women have sought to greatly improve the lilac for our modern gardens. In great measure they have been wonderfully successful. Today lilacs are no longer called 'French Lilacs' because of the unique work of one man and his son but rather, they are now 'International'. Much work in the past four decades has been done in Canada, The Netherlands, the U.S.S.R. and especially in the United States and to a lesser extent in some of the countries of Europe. It would not be fair nor scientific to ignore this enormous amount of hybridizing skill and achievements of those who have worked to improve the lilac cultivars of *S. vulgaris* and of the many species. Today, lilacs are not limited to the ordinary lilac, *S. vulgaris,* but there are available wonderful plants of the many species and their hybrids.

Be mindful that many on the recommended list are mostly relatively unknown to the vast majority of nurseries. Do not expect to find them in the wholesale nursery outlet stores. They can be found only in specialized nurseries who care to delve into what is new and beautiful and who take time to introduce or grow new lilacs. A great source of information can be had from the International Lilac Society and from its hundreds of members. Also, one should visit the large botanical gardens and arboreta that have lilac collections, walks and feature the lilac. Perhaps, not all have most of the recommended cultivars but you will find there enough to make a practical judgment as to which plants will suit the needs of your own garden. Visit these botanical treasuries often, acquaint yourself with some of the best and newest plant materials.

Likewise, be aware that many extremely fine lilacs have been developed in other countries by lilac enthusiasts and hybridizers, who, unfortunately, are not nurserymen, like the Lemoines, and so cannot propagate their new introductions and given them instant world recognition and saleability, as also is true in this country—but their lilac introductions are indeed beautiful and often superior to many, if not most, of the cherished old varieties. One must continually ask nurserymen for the 'better kinds and named cultivars' and eventually some will respond by propagating them. The recommended list attempts to include as many of the very good cultivars from other countries as possible for what may not be available in the United States may be had in some other country. We are fortunate, indeed, for such a wide choice and variation of cultivars. Elsewhere at the end of this chapter I shall seek to narrow this 'Recommended List' to a dozen or so from each color classification as I have compared lilac cultivars over the past many years.

In the larger, 'Recommended List' the terms used range from: Good; Very Good; Fine; Very Fine; to Excellent which is the most outstanding compliment of all. I have not included any that are Poor; Fair; Average. Only those in the top 20% of all lilac cultivars are rated from Good to Excellent. Individually we are likely to disagree—*de gustibus* and because of climatic and local soil conditions various cultivars respond differently in certain areas. (In the next 20 years, *mon amie* and *ami*, you may be certain a goodly portion of the 'Recommended Cultivars' will have disappeared—either superceded or because no one continued their propagation or could find sources of plants. If the last case were to be true, this would indeed be a real loss to all who love fine lilacs!)

In the recommendation of the various lilac cultivars not only the bloom but also the plant habits, form, vigor, and susceptibility to disease have been given some weighted consideration; e.g. Lemoine's famous 'Mont Blanc' has not been included because it is a rather poor grower with pallid leaves and requires considerable pruning. One of the aims of the International Lilac Society is to make available the better cultivars and to assist in publicizing them to nurseries—how successful they shall be remains to be seen.

White Lilacs: The Essential Element in the Lilac Garden (Color Class I)

White is the one color that co-ordinates and ties together all other colors. A garden planting cannot have too many white lilacs. White is the best color to use when it is necessary to separate clashing colors or to bring out the richness of any color placed close to it. A special kind of unity in the garden is obtained with white lilacs, a kind of fragrant freshness, a sense of restful completeness and of quiet propriety. For a focal point in the garden you can never go wrong with a beautiful white lilac!

White is the color most reflective in the twilight hours. Notice after sundown as shadows fall, the deeper colors in the garden disappear first, then the pinks, then the vibrant lemon-yellows but white somehow remains to reflect the night stars and moonlight. White lilacs give the night garden a whole new dimension as they do in the sunlit hours. White lilacs are a strong 'must' for any garden. What ratio? Are two white lilacs to one colored too many? If you only have three it might be but if your garden or estate is large enough for several, try for a ratio of close to 50% white. You will be surprised—this ratio will never appear excessive. Do not limit yourself to one or two cultivars. Today we have many excellent white lilacs with new introductions appearing almost every year. Be they old or the newest, all have a definite charm and beauty uniquely their own. In planning your lilac plantings remember we have early, midseason and late blooming white lilacs, so you can have flowers from early May to mid June.

Among the earliest to bloom are the *S. hyacinthiflora* hybrids (*S. vulgaris* × *S. oblata* crosses) such as 'Gertrude Leslie', 'Sister Justena' and 'The Bride'. White lilacs, however, come into their glory with the *S. vulgaris* midseason bloomers. Among these are many fine old and new cultivars (many of the newer ones being rather difficult to find on the market). There are some outstanding *S.* × *hyacinthiflora* cultivars developed by Dr. Don Egolf at the National Arboretum, Washington, D.C. that have not as yet been named. Watch for their introduction.

RECOMMENDED LILAC CULTIVARS IN THE COLOR CLASSIFICATION 'WHITE'—I

Historically we have seen that the earliest 'white' lilacs were rather small florets with an ashen or blue-wash cast, not the pure whites we have today. Often they were akin to the old *S. vulgaris* 'Alba', tall, tree-like, with pallid leaves. It was not until the hybridizing genius of Victor Lemoine and his son Emile, who undertook to produce far better white lilacs, that real progress began. Every color the Lemoines touched was remarkably improved. Outstanding whites, single and double, continued to come forth from their nursery for nearly 70 years! Today hybridizers have made even greater strides at improving the white lilacs—working mostly on the foundations of the Lemoine introductions. White has been purified, floret size increased, leaves are now an healthy dark green, the shrub has been lowered to average height and we have many, many exquisite and lovely white cultivars.

There is a uniqueness about each individual cultivar (or it should not be named) that one must study to appreciate. White lilacs, however, are mostly judged by their total mass effect since their contrast to other colors in the garden is so vital and their landscape value so important. I sincerely believe one could plant a whole garden of 100 or more white cultivars (space permitting) and have a most beautiful and varied garden. Elsewhere we have spoken of the need and ratios of white lilacs in a collection. Here we set about the task of recommending the "best".

White lilacs begin with the early hybrids, the *S.* × *hyacinthiflora* cultivars where there are still only a very few, then come the *S. vulgaris* whites—early midseason and later bloomers; finally we close with the white flowering species (very few and a handful of late blooming hybrids. Be mindful of the season of bloom of the whites you select for placing next to the generally later, deep-purple sorts. At most the *S. vulgaris* cultivars will span only a period of 10 days or so from early to late bloomers and enough white buds are beginning to bloom to make a distinctive show for most other colored companion cultivars.

Recommended list of lilac cultivars in the color classification of 'White'—I

S. vulgaris cultivars

'Aloise'—single, Fiala 1964, smaller florets but extremely heavy bloomer annually, fine.
'Angel White'—single, Lammerts 1971, very fine.
'Avalanche'—single, Fiala 1984, large florets, very showy, very fine to excellent.
'Banquise'—double, Lemoine 1905, very good.
'Belle d'Elewyt'—single, Draps 1953, very good.
'Bernard Slavin'—single, Fenicchia 1972, multipetaled, very good.
'Bloemenlust'—single, Piet 1956, fine.
'Candeur'—single, Lemoine 1931, large flowered, very fine to excellent, showy.
'Carley'—single, Havemeyer 1953, large florets, outstanding to excellent.
'Dazzle'—double, Havemeyer-Eaton 1954, very good but difficult to find.
'Early Double White'—double, Clarke 1954, very good, nearly unobtainable.
'Edith Cavell'—double, Lemoine 1916, very showy, excellent.
'Emery Mae Norweb'—double, Fiala 1981, deep creamy buds, excellent.
'Excellent'—single, D. E. Maarse 1939, very showy, fine.
'Flora'—single D. E. Maarse 1953, one of the finest whites, excellent.
'Fraicheur'—single, Lemoine 1946, very fine but most difficult to find.
'Galina Ulanova'—single, Kolesnikov 1976, very showy, fine.
'General Sheridan'—double, Dunbar 1917, very lacey but new shoots obscure bloom, fine.
'Geraldine Smith'—single, Rankin 1963, good to very good.
'Gerrie Schoonenberg'—single, Maarse 1948, very good.
'Gertrude Clark'—single, Fiala 1984, new multipetaled, very fine.
'Glacier'—double, Fiala 1981, new and very showy, very fine.
'Gloire d'Aalsmeer'—single, J. Maarse 1938, very good.
'Heather'—single, Havemeyer 1954, good annual bloomer, medium florets.
'Joan Dunbar'—double, Dunbar 1923, older cultivar but still good.
'Kate Harling'—single, Pfitzer pre-1910, old but good.
'Konign Luise'—single, Pfitzer 1921, very good.
'Krasavitsa Moskvy'—double, Kolesnikov 1974, lavender-rose tinted buds, one of the finest lilacs in commerce, excellent in every way, a Russian introduction.
'Lebedushka'—single, N. Smol'skii, V. Bibikova 1964, very large florets, showy, very fine.
'Madeleine Lemaire'—double, Lemoine 1928, very fine but difficult to obtain.
'Marie Finon'—single, Lemoine 1923, very fine, large florets.
'Marie Legraye'—single, Legray 1840, very old but still good.
'Maud Notcutt'—single, Notcutt 1956, fine.
'Miss Ellen Willmott'—double, Lemoine 1903, very dependable bloomer, fine.
'Mme. Abel Chatenay'—double, Lemoine 1892, old but good.
'Mme. Felix'—single, Felix 1924, very good.
'Mme. Florent Stepman'—single, large spike, very fine, an older cultivar.
'Mme. Lemoine'—double, Lemoine 1896, very good but not Lemoine's finest.
'Mme. Leopold Draps'—single, Draps 1945, very good.
'Monique Lemoine'—double, Lemoine 1939, very fine and showy.
'Monument'—single, Lemoine 1934, one of the last Lemoine whites, very good.
'Mother Louise'—double, Fiala 1969, florets of exceptional quality, very fine.
'Nanook'—single, D. Maarse 1953, very good, difficult to obtain, Dutch origin.
'Oakes Double White'—double, Meader 1963, very good.

'Panni Dorota Golabecka'—double, Karpow 1952, very good, difficult to obtain.

'Primrose'—single, G. Maarse 1949, extraordinary pale yellow color, very good. There are considerable variations of depth of yellow color—among the finest, which must be rooted cuttings, are the A. Lumley plant and the Holden Arboretum selection. Each selection should be numbered 'Primrose L' and 'Primrose H' as both are somewhat different.

'Professor Robert B. Clark'—single, Fiala 1983, large multipetaled florets, excellent.

'Professor E. H. Wilson'—double, Havemeyer 1943, beautiful white rosettes, excellent.

'Riet Bruidegom'—single, D. E. Maarse 1950, very fine Dutch cultivar.

'Rochester'—single, Grant 1971, magnificent multipetaled, outstandingly beautiful, one of the very finest, slow grower, difficult to obtain, excellent.

'Saint Joan'—double, Blacklock 1953, extremely beautiful, among the best, excellent.

'Saint Margaret'—double, Blacklock 1953, beautiful, among the best, excellent.

'Satin Cloud'—single, Fiala 1985, very showy, very fine to excellent.

'Sculptured Ivory'—single, Fiala 1984, very fine.

Seedling (unnamed), Royal Botanical Gardens, Hamilton, Canada—single, No. 7525-17, very showy, excellent.

'Siebold'—double, Lemoine 1906, low growing, pale pink buds, excellent, difficult to find.

'Slater's Elegance'—single, Slater 1974, huge florets, beautiful, excellent, very difficult to obtain but among the very finest single whites.

'Snow Shower'—single, H. Sass 1953, very good, difficult to obtain.

'Souvenir d'Alice Harding'—double, Lemoine 1938, exceptionally fine, excellent, one of the best doubles.

'Souvenir d' Mme. Louis Gielis—single, Gielis 1950, heavy bloomer, very fine.

'Sovetskaya Arktika'—double, Kolesnikov 1974, showy, very fine.

'Swansdown'—single, Fiala 1984, large thrysi, multipetaled, very showy and very fine.

'Taglioni'—double, Lemoine 1905, large white triple slippers, fine.

'Vestale'—single, Lemoine 1910, large florets, moderate bloomer, very good.

'White Lace'—single, Rankin 1964, small florets, extremely showy, very good.

'White Sands'—single, Gardner 1971, very good, difficult to obtain.

'White Swan'—single, Havemeyer 1943, good, dependable bloomer.

WHITE FLOWERING SPECIES AND HYBRIDS

S. × *chinensis* 'Alba'—single, Audibert 1885, large background shrub, very fine. (the white form also occurs very frequently as a 'sport' on the 'Rouen Lilac', (*S.* × *chinensis* hybrida 'Rouen') where it is a creamy white. See chapter 'Mutations'.

× *chinensis* 'Bicolor', single, Lemoine 1928, a lovely white lilac with a pert deep purple eye, a large shrub for backgrounds, very fine.

S. emodi 'Elegantissima'—single, Ottolander 1876, very difficult to obtain.

S. × *hyacinthiflora* 'Gertrude Leslie'—double, Skinner 1954, very early, good.

hyacinthiflora 'Hunting Tower'—single, Skinner 1953, very good.

hyacinthiflora 'Mount Baker'—single, Skinner 1961, very good, showy.

hyacinthiflora 'Sister Justena'—single, Skinner 1956, very fine, showy.

hyacinthiflora 'The Bride'—single, Skinner 1961, very fine, among the best early flowering hybrids of this color.

S. × *josiflexa* 'Anna Amhoff'—single, Yaeger 1958, very fine, late blooming.

josiflexa 'Elaine'—single, Preston 1934, good.

S. oblata alba—single, circa 1763, this form of the species is rather difficult to obtain, good, especially for hybridizers. There is an outstanding form at the National Arboretum, Wash. D.C. (*S. oblata alba* 'Frank Meyer').

S. patula 'Excellens'—single, Lemoine 1931, very fine, most difficult to obtain true cultivar.

S. penkinensis 'Pendula', a medium smaller tree with broad weeping branches, needs ample room for maturity. Colorful leaf change in autumn. Very rare and excellent, Zoschen 1889.

S. × *persica* 'Alba'—single, circa 1770, old form, very good for background shrub.

S. × *prestoniae* 'Agnes Smith'—single, Rogers 1970, one of the finest of the Prestonian Lilacs, magnificent, a choice hybridizer's prize, excellent.

× *prestoniae* 'Snowdrift'—single, Fiala 1983, an abundance of small florets, practically no seed, wonderful glossy leaves, a mixtoploid, fine.

× *prestoniae* 'Summer White'—single, Lape 1973, very fine to excellent, very showy.

× *prestoniae* 'Swanee'—single, Preston 1937, very good.

S. reflexa 'Alba', single, Upton 1939, extremely rare, beautiful hanging racemes, excellent.

S. reticulata var. *reticulata*, single, a medium-sized tree, late blooming, for background use only, very effective, very good.

S. reticulata var. *amurensis*, the species is a smaller tree with cherry-like bark. Seedlings vary in shape and range in bloom from creamy-white to pure white, late blooming.

var. *amurensis* 'Ivory Silk'—single, Slater 1973, very fine upright form.

var. *amurensis* 'Cole's Selection'—single, Cole Nursery 1977, very good.

S. reticulata var. hybrida 'Chinese Magic'—single, Fiala 1978, a cross of *S. reticulata* × var. *amurensis*, creamy flowers, more spreading, small tree, very good for background or naturalizing plantings.

S. sweginzowi 'Albida'—single, Lemoine 1930, tall shrub, slender branchlets, very good (a hybrid of *S. sweginzowii* × *S. tomentella*).

S. tigerstedtii—single, medium shrub, slender with attractive white, feathery blossoms, very fine.

Lavender and Violet Lilacs (Color Classes II and IV)

Lavender or 'lilac' is the original color of *S. vulgaris*. The color named 'lilac' originated from the flowers of this shrub. The first lilacs were designated as *S. vulgaris* 'purpurea' (the lavender, purplish, violet lilac). It is a nostalgic color quickly associated with the lilac flower. No garden should be without at least one lavender or violet lilac. Specifically this color covers two categories in the more modern designation of *Syringa* by color, those identified as 'lilac colored' (IV) and those called 'violet colored' (II). In color charts they are distinct but are both a lavender-purplish. They differ in that those in category II (Violet) are more purple-blue and range from very light to very deep purple; whereas those in category IV (Lilac) are a purple mixed with tones of pinkish or a real lavender shade. We have listed a number of excellent lilacs from both categories mindful that some of the newest cultivars will not be found in nurseries and will be most difficult to obtain but they are well worth all the effort.

In the garden these shades can at times be difficult to co-ordinate with some colors—never with yellows or orange flowers, not too well side by side with blue lilacs and never with red. They are wonderful in bloom as specimens, in rows, or massed in groups of three. Both are excellent beside white lilacs; the violet sorts are outstanding next to the deep purples (VII) whereas the lilac colored do well with pink (V) or magenta (VI) planted alongside of them.

Within the two color categories are found some excellent lilacs, the older sorts being more fragrant than some of the newer ones. It seems that the most fragrant of all the lilacs are found in these color categories—the lavenders, lilacs and soft violets. Older named cultivars, although abundant bloomers, are somewhat smaller in floret size compared to the much larger florets and panicles of the newer ones. Do not overlook this color for the sake of the other more vibrant ones. You will be exceedingly pleased with both their fragrance and their good habits and bloom.

SPECIALLY RECOMMENDED CULTIVARS IN THE COLOR CLASSIFICATION 'VIOLET'—II
S. *vulgaris* cultivars:

'Agincourt Beauty'—single, Slater 1968, very large florets, outstanding very deep purple, excellent.

'Albert F. Holden'—single, Fiala 1981, deep violet with silver reverse, showy, excellent.

'Aleksei Mares'ev'—single, Kolesnikov 1951, large florets, showy, very fine.

'Ambassadeur'—single, Lemoine 1931, lavender-violet with bluish tones, very fine.

'Bertha Dunham'—single, Rankin 1953, large florets very good.

'Beth Turner'—single, Alexander 1970, large florets and panicles, tall grower, very fine.

'Big Blue'—single, introducer unknown—recent, very fine.

'Burgomeester Loggers'—single, D. E.Maarse 1961, very good to fine.

'Cavour'—single, Lemoine 1910, large florets very good.

'Centenaire de la Linneenne'—single, Klettenberg, lavender-violet, good.

'Champlain'—double, Lemoine 1930, very fine.

'De Miribel'—single, Lemoine 1903, long conical clusters with deep bluish tones, very fine.

'Diannah Abbott'—single, Berdeen 1968, very fine to excellent.

'Dr. Edward Mott Moore'—single, Fenicchia 1972, multipetaled, new, showy, excellent.

'Dr. John Rankin'—single, Fiala 1985, very fine, smaller florets.

'Dr. Lemke'—double, Lemke, recent, very fine.

'Eventide'—single, Fiala 1984, large florets, very showy, excellent.

'Flower City'—single, Fenicchia 1983, exceptionally outstanding. One of the finest in a special class, excellent!

'Fred Payne'—single, Havemeyer 1943, large florets, very good.

'Henri Robert'—double, Lemoine 1936, pale violet very fine.

'Hosanna'—double, Fiala 1969, very pale violet, very good.

'Jessie Gardner'—single, Gardner circa 1940, very good.

'Koningsloo'—single, Draps 1953, large florets and showy, very good.

'Kosmos'—single, I Shtan'ko-N. Michailov 1956, very fragrant, showy, very fine.

'Le Notre'—double, Lemoine 1922, very showy and very fine to excellent.

'Leonid Lenov'—single, Kolesnikov 1956, very showy with purplish cast, excellent.

'Lipchanka'—single, V. Romanova—M. Egorova _____, dark violet, heavy bloomer, very fine.

'Lullaby'—double, Fiala 1984, very large thryses, very fine.

'Marechal Lannes'—double, Lemoine 1910—more violet than purple, excellent.

'Marie Marcelin'—double, introducer unknown, 1952, very fine.

'Maximowicz'—double, Lemoine 1901, pale violet shades, showy, excellent.

'Mieczta'—single, Kolesnikov 1941, large florets and panicles with reddish buds, pale violet to lilac, very showy, excellent.

'Mood Indigo'—single, Clarke 1946, fine to excellent.

'Olive Mae Cummings'—double, Berdeen 1979, very good.

'Pauline Fiala'—single, Fiala 1983, dark violet with white eye, very heavy bloomer, very fine to excellent.

'Russkaya Pesnya'—double, N. Vekhov 1953, large florets, showy, fine.

'Souvenir de Mme. Edmond Kenis'—single, Kenis 1936, pale violet, very good.

'Violet Glory'—single, Castle 1969, huge florets of deep violet, excellent.

'Violetta'—double, Lemoine 1916, deep violet, very showy, excellent.

'Zulu'—single, Havemeyer 1954, medium violet, large florets, very showy, excellent.

SPECIES AND HYBRIDS IN COLOR CLASSIFICATION 'VIOLET' II

S. × chinensis 'Duplex'—double, very difficult to find, pale violet, very good.

S. × henryi 'Lutece'—single, Henry pre. 1901, medium violet, large treelike, good.

S. × hyacinthiflora 'Louvois'—single, Lemoine 1921, large florets, very showy, very fine.

   × hyacinthiflora 'Marat Kazei'—single, Smol'skii-Biblikova 1964, very good.

   × hyacinthiflora 'Mood Indigo'—single, Clarke 1946, very good.

   × hyacinthiflora 'Pocahontas'—single, Skinner 1935, better classified as violet than purple, very fine to excellent.

   × hyacinthiflora 'Touch of Spring'—single, Fiala 1982, very floriferous, very fine.

S. josikaea—single, more violet than lavender, one of the better species for the background, very good.

S. josikaea 'Pallida'—single, Jager 1865, good.

S. laciniata—single, very floriferous, tall growing, excellent.

S. meyeri—single, very attractive small leaved shrub, very good.

S. meyeri 'Palibin'—single, deep violet to medium when open—very fine small growing and showy, excellent.

S. patula—single, as a species it is variable as to color and size, very fine.

S. patula 'Miss Kim'—single, Yaeger 1954, very pale violet with lavender-bluish cast this is one of the outstanding selections of this species, excellent.

S. × prestoniae 'Ariel'—single, Preston 1964, good.

   × prestoniae 'Diana'—single, Bugala 1970, 2nd generation hybrid, fine.

   × prestoniae 'Jaga'—single, Bugala 1970, 2nd generation Prestonian, very fine.

   × prestoniae 'Jessica'—single, Preston 1928, very good.

   × prestoniae 'Kim'—single, Preston 1934, good.

× *prestoniae* 'Nike'—single, Bugala 1970.

S. pubescens—single, medium lavender-violet, very fine to excellent.

S. wolfii var. *hirsuta*—single, Schneider pre-1930, very fine to excellent.

SPECIALLY RECOMMENDED LILAC CULTIVARS IN THE COLOR CLASSIFICATION 'LILAC'—IV

'Alice Chieppo'—double, Fiala 1984, very early, fragrant, heavy bloomer, showy, excellent.

'Alice Stofer'—single, Rankin 1963, large florets, fragrant, very fine.

'Alphonse Lavalee'—double, Lemoine 1885, considerable bluish tones, good.

'Ametist 2'—single, Stan'ko-Mikhailov 1956, silvery-lilac, bluish cast, very fine.

'Anna Nickels'—single, Stone 1963, fragrant, large florets, very fine.

'Belorusskie Zori'—single, Smol'skii-Bibikova 1964, very fragrant, large flowered, fine.

'Betty Stone'—single, Stone 1963, fragrant, large florets, very fine.

'Christophe Columb'—single, Lemoine 1905, very fine to excellent.

'Director Dorenboos'—single, D. E. Maarse 1955, very good.

'Gortenziya'—single, Kolesnikov 1930, fragrant, very good.

'Henri Martin'—double, Lemoine 1912, large thrysi, very fine.

'Hippolyte Maringer'—double, Lemoine 1919, very good.

'Izobilie'—double, Kolesnikov 1963, very showy, fine.

'Jacques Callot'—single, V. Lemoine 1876, very fragrant, good.

'Kapriz'—double, Kolesnikov 1952, very good.

'Komsomolka'—double, Kolesnikov 1974, very fine.

'Le Notre'—double, Lemoine 1922, very showy, excellent.

'Leon Gambetta'—double, Lemoine 1907, very showy, excellent.

'Marlyensis Pallida'—single, pre 1864, very fragrant, pale lavender, very good.

'Marshal Zhukov'—single, Kolesnikov 1948, fragrant, showy, very fine.

'Maurice de Vilmorin'—double, Lemoine 1900, very showy, excellent.

'Michel Buchner'—double, V. Lemoine 1885, showy, very fine.

'Mollie Ann'—single, Fiala 1983, large florets, very heavy and showy bloomer, excellent.

'Mrs. John S. Williams'—single, Havemeyer 1953, large florets, showy, excellent.

'Pamyat o S. M. Kirove'—double, Kolesnikov 1943, very fine to excellent.

'Pioner'—single, Kolesnikov 1951, very fragrant, fine.

'Prince of Wales'—single, Dougall 1889, fragrant, recurved, fine to very fine.

'Sesquicentennial'—single, Fenicchia 1972, very heavy bloomer, showy, excellent.

'Silver King'—single, Lemke 1953, silvery-lilac, strikingly beautiful, excellent.

'Sonnet'—single, Fiala 1983, very fine.

'Tadeusz Kosciusko'—double, Karpow-Lipski 1954, very good.

'Victor Lemoine'—double, E. Lemoine 1906, of exceptional merit, showy, excellent.

'William Robinson'—double, Lemoine 1899.

SPECIES AND HYBRID LILACS RECOMMENDED IN COLOR IV—LILAC

S. × *hyacinthiflora* 'Excel'—single, Skinner 1935, very good to fine.

'Nokomis'—single, Skinner 1934, very good to fine.

'Norah'—single, Preston 1931, good.

S. josikaea—single, species, a deep color more purple than lilac, good, fine glossy leaves, somewhat sparse in bloom.

S. julianae,—single, species, soft lilac to pinkish, upright and wide growing, fine.

S. meyeri 'Palibin'—a named cultivar of the species that is low growing, deep purple-reddish buds and lavender flowers, glossy small leaves—excellent.

S. × *persica*—an hybrid of unknown origin that is truly outstanding as a large, background shrub, very showy, fragrant.

S. × *prestoniae* 'Adrianne', single, Preston 1953, very good.

'Charmian', single, Preston 1928, good.

'Diana', single, Bugala 1970, 2nd generation prestoniae, very fine.

'Isabella', single, Preston 1927, very fine to excellent.

'Jagienka', single, Bugala 1971, 2nd generation, very fine.

Lilacs Have the Blues
(Color Class III)

Pure blue is a difficult color to obtain in all the lilac species although many of the earliest lilacs of *Syringa vulgaris* were of a "bluish colour" or a "bluish lavender or light purple color". Undoubtedly the pigment for 'blue' is readily found in lilacs even in the wild *S. vulgaris* on the mountain slopes of modern Romania and Serbia. None of these are a pure or true blue. One of the first named cultivars of *S. vulgaris* was called 'Coerulea Superba' which contains a considerable amount of blue and which undoubtedly, some generations back, has been a parent of many of the new and clearer blues of today. It was used in hybridization by Victor Lemoine who from 1900 made rapid strides in fine new, blue lilacs, both single and doubles of great beauty and refinement which still rank among some of the best blue lilacs. Lemoine, indeed, is the 'Father of the Blues' as far as lilacs are concerned! (*Mon ami,* that Frenchman had a fine eye for hidden colors in lilacs!) In 1932 he introduced 'Firmament' which often is considered the beginning of the fine, new light blues. In rapid succession came a great number of blues—'Ami Schott', a lovely double in 1933 and 'Madame Charles Souchet', a clear, pale blue with but a touch of lavender in 1949—and many other fine blue cultivars before and up to the closing of Lemoine & Fils Nursery. Havemeyer added two outstanding blues with 'Mrs. August Belmont', 1953, and his most beautiful 'True Blue' in 1956 (to your author one of the finest of all the blues to date). These and one other small flowered but deeply genetically blue lilac, once thought to be a species but now relegated to the rank of a cultivar, 'Rhodopea', are the foundation of the modern 'blues'.

Since 1965 the blues were crossed with the magnificent white 'Rochester' which produced a whole new race of outstanding blues, light blues, medium, dark blues, starred blues, eyed and rayed blues and most with the multipetals of that outstanding white lilac from Rochester's Highland Park! Among the first of these was Fenicchia's 'Dwight D. Eisenhower', 1968, an outstanding lilac of medium pale blue tinged with the very slightest lavender. It is truly outstanding! (*Bon amie,* you must have it in your garden!) Then came the medium blue 'Blue Delft', 1980, the unique 'Wedgwood Blue' with pink buds, 1980, 'Porcelain Blue' in 1981, 'Pat Pesata' a wonderful pale blue pearled pink with a white eye and white rays in 1981, 'Rhapsody' a pearled blue on soft pink, 1982, 'Blue Danube' in 1986, and 'Tiffany Blue' with its iridescent shades in 1984. All have the remarkable 'Rochester' as at least once or more in their parentage! 'Sea Storm' a deep blue—almost a navy blue, with violet overtones appeared in 1984 from seedlings of 'Maud Notcutt' crossed with 'Flora' and 'Rhodopea'. Many new forms, colors and shades are combining with large florets and quality bloom with fragrance.

One must not overlook the wonderful blues of Lemoine which by no means have been entirely surpassed by the newer blues. Of outstanding beauty are both the singles and doubles of this great hybridizer such as, 'Olivier de Serres', excellent and real blue, the singles 'Crepuscule', 'Decaisne', 'Saturnale' and the still unsurpassed doubles as 'Georges Claude', 'Marechal Lannes', 'President Grevy', 'Duc de Massa' and the difficult to find 'Savanarole'! (*Bon jardinier,* these alone would have made Lemoine immortal in lilacdom!). In more recent decades there have appeared some outstanding lilacs mostly using Lemoine introductions from the gifted hybridization of Leonid Kolesnikov of the U.S.S.R. and some of his successors. Among these are the doubles 'Nadezhda', 'Pamyat o. S. M. Kirove', 'P. P. Konchalovskii' and the single 'Golubaya'. An exceptional lilac that is a unique silvery-blue is 'Silver King' (Lemke), rare, beautiful and defying description as to color! Some of the Sobek introductions such as 'Blue Boy', 'Descanso King' and Berdeen's 'Lynette Sirois' have a great deal of blue in them. 'Professor Hoser' is a most worthy recent introduction from Europe (the plant at the Royal Botanical Gardens, Hamilton, Ontario, Canada, is outstanding) whereas 'Bluebird', 1968, has unique shades of blue with faint blushes of violet and lavender.

Both the lighter and stronger blues are lovely in the garden surrounded with pale, true pinks or whites. They somewhat clash, but do draw attention, with deep purples and reddish magentas. They seem out of place with lighter violet and lavender cultivars. Do you have a corner in the garden that can be done in soft blue lilacs with white and perhaps a pink one? Try it; you will be delighted! Among good lilacs, perhaps the widest selections are to be found among the 'blue' lilacs.

In the Early Hybrids, *S. × hyacinthiflora* there are few good blues and these have strong hints of lavender in them. Among the late blooming hybrids, *S. × prestoniae,* real blues do not exist but some have a hidden bluish cast—*mon ami*, give the hybridizers time and we will eventually have them! (*Bon jardinier*, you must find special room for a symphony of 'Blues' in your garden!)

There is one other lilac, 'President Lincoln' introduced by Dunbar in 1916 that has held prominence as 'the bluest lilac' for some decades. It is blue but certainly not as blue as many of the Lemoine cultivars. Its importance is the result of touting by garden writers who knew little about blue lilacs (they overlooked Havemeyer's magnificent 'True Blue' altogether!). The fault with 'President Lincoln' is in the rapid development of a bodyguard of new green shoots around the blooming spike thus hiding its beauty and in the tallness and rampant growth of the bush at the expense of heavy bloom. Perhaps modern hybridizers will use it in combination with other blues to preserve its deeper blue tones. Today we have far better blues even in the deeper tones. 'President Lincoln' grows to be an enormous shrub.

SPECIALLY RECOMMENDED LILACS IN THE COLOR CATEGORY 'BLUE—III

S. vulgaris cultivars:

'Ami Schott'—double, Lemoine 1933, medium blue with deeper tones, showy, excellent.

'Bleuatre'—single, Baltet pre-1897, very old, small florets, fragrant, good.

'Blue Angel'—single, Havemeyer-Eaton 1954, difficult to find, good bluish, fine.

'Bluebird'—single, Fiala 1969, large florets medium blue, very showy large spikes, excellent.

'Blue Boy'—single, Sobek 1966, brushed lavender, good.

'Blue Danube'—single, Fiala 1986, the bluest so far, very fine.

'Blue Delft'—single, Fiala 1981, multipetaled, medium to deeper blue, excellent.

'Blue Delight'—single, Castle 1969, very good to fine.

'Blue Giant'—single, Fiala 1968, light blue very fine.

'Boule Azuree'—single, Lemoine 1919, medium sized florets of good blue, very fine.

'Charles Sargent'—double, Lemoine 1905, mixed shades of blue brushed lavender, very fine.

'Crepuscule'—single, Lemoine 1928, large florets, showy, excellent.

'Dawn'—single, Havemeyer 1954, very good to fine.

'Decaisne'—single, Lemoine 1910, darker blue with purple shades, very fine.

'Descanso King'—single, Sobek 1966, blue with lavender tones—very good.

'Diplomate'—single, Lemoine 1915, pale blue dusted lavender, fine.

'Duc de Massa'—double, Lemoine 1905, huge spikes, showy, very fine to excellent.

'Dwight D. Eisenhower'—single, Fenicchia 1968, multipetaled, pale blue brushed lavender, heavy bloomer, very showy, excellent.

'Eleanore Berdeen'—single, Berdeen 1979, excellent.

'Emile Gentile'—double, Lemoine 1915, pale lavender-blue, very fine.

'Fall Baltyku'—double, Karpow 1961, bluish with pale lavender tones, very good.

'Firmament'—single, Lemoine 1932, pale blue of outstanding quality, showy, excellent.

'Flow Blue'—single, Fiala 1980, mixed shades of blue, very good.

'Georges Claude'—double, Lemoine 1935, large thrysi, quality, very fine.

'Golubaya'—single, Kolesnikov 1974, blue dusted lilac-purple, tall grower, showy, very fine.

'Heavenly Blue'—double, Blacklock 1968, difficult to find, very good.

'Hugo Mayer'—single, D. E. Maarse 1950, a Dutch blue with lavender dusting, very fine.

'Jules Simon'—double, Lemoine 1908, very fine.

'Lawrence Wheeler'—single, Gardner 1968, difficult to find, very good.

'Lynette Sirois'—double, Berdeen 1971, blue flushed lavender, very fine.

'Madame Charles Souchet'—single, Lemoine 1949, large florets of outstanding pale to medium blue, showy, quality, excellent.

'Madame Hankar Solvay'—single, Klettenberg 1935, difficult to find, good blue, fine.

'Margot Grunewald'—double, Grunewald 1913, very good.

'Maurice Barres'—single, Lemoine 1917, medium blue of quality, excellent.

'Minister Dab Kociol'—single, Karpow 1961, firm blue color, very good to fine.

'Mrs. August Belmont'—single, Havemeyer 1953, large florets of blue brushed with lavender tones, white eye, very fine.

'Mrs. Elizabeth Peterson'—single, Havemeyer 1953, a unique blue color, deep blue changing to deep violet, very beautiful purple tones, excellent.

'Nadezhda'—double, Kolesnikov prior to 1970, large thrysi, very fine to excellent.

'Nebo Moskovy'—double, Kolesnikov 1963, a blue of great merit, showy, fine.

'Olivier de Serres'—double, Lemoine 1909, large floret of medium to dark blue shades, very showy, excellent.

'Pamyat' o.s.M.Kirove'—double, Kolesnikov 1943, very showy large thrysi, excellent.

'Pat Pesata'—single, Fiala 1981, unique multipetaled blue, medium pink buds, florets edged, starred and eyed white, pearled pink over pale blue, very showy, new, excellent.

'Porcelain Blue'—single, Fiala 1981, multipetaled, pale pearled blue, excellent.

'P. P. Konchalovskii'—double, Kolesnikov 1956, large thrysi, showy, excellent.

'President Grevy'—double, Lemoine 1886, fine blue with large starry florets, immense panicles, excellent.

'President Lincoln'—single, Dunbar 1916, medium blue, tall leafy grower, very good.

'Professor Edmond Jankowski'—single, Karpow 1958, very good.

'Professor Hoser'—double, Hoser circa 1930, showy, full spikes, very fine.

'Rene Jarry Deslogues'—double, Lemoine 1905, very good.

'Rhapsody'—single, Fiala 1982, unique color translucent blue and pearled pink, pink buds, very fine to excellent.

'Rhodopea'—single, prior to 1928 once considered a species thus many forms with varying shades and depth of blue are found under this name, some are truly blue, medium-sized florets, fragrant—fine to very fine depending on individual plants.

'Saturnale'—single, Lemoine 1916, difficult to find, very fine.

'Savonarole'—double, Lemoine 1935, very difficult to find, beautiful shades of blues, very fine to excellent.

'Sea Storm'—single, Fiala 1984, large florets and thrysi of shades of deep blue tinged with violet, showy, recurved petals, heavy bloomer, very fine to excellent.

'S. V. Larov'—double, Larov no date, quality bloom, very good.

'Silver King'—single, Lemke 1953, unique whitish-blue with silvery reverse petals, heavy bloomer, very showy and beautiful, outstanding and excellent!

'Sumerki'—single, Kolesnikov 1954, dark violet-blue of considerable merit, very fine.

'Tiffany Blue'—single, Fiala 1984, outstanding shades of pearled blue colors, showy, large florets, excellent.

'True Blue'—single, Havemeyer c. 1953, large florets and thrysi, outstandingly showy pale blue, one of the finest, excellent!

'Wedgwood Blue'—single, Fiala 1981, wedgwood blue with lilac-pink buds, beautiful hanging racemes, very showy, somewhat lower grower, excellent.

'Woodland Blue'—single, Hancock 1971, difficult to obtain—good to very good.

SPECIES AND HYBRIDS IN THE COLOR CLASSIFICATION 'BLUE'—III

S. × *hyacinthiflora* 'Charles Nordine'—single, Skinner 1960, blushed lavender, very fine.

'Doctor Chadwick'—single, Skinner 1964, lavender tones, fine.

'Konstantin Zasionov'—single, Smol'skii-Bibikova 1964, very good.

'Laurentian'—single, Skinner 1945, lavender tones, very good.

'Peggy'—single, Preston 1931, brushed lavender, very good.

'Spring Dawn'—single, Clarke 1960, toned lavender, very fine.

S. *oblata* var. *dilatata* 'Cheyenne'—single, Hildreth 1971, low growing, very fine.

S. *patula* 'Miss Kim'—single, Yeager 1954, slow growing, excellent, fragrant.

S. × *prestoniae* 'Desdemona'—single, Preston 1927, lavender tones, very fine.

'Elinor'—single, Preston 1928, blushed lavender blue, fine.

Much work remains to be done for far better and clearer blues in both the Early and Late Hybrids. A hybridizer could spend a lifetime improving these and leave a legacy of fine lilacs in blue.

The 'Pink' Lilacs
(Color Class V)

Pink colors in lilacs are very difficult to classify as so many have varying shades of lavender and magenta, with some even having shades of blue in their coloration. True, unadulterated 'pinks' are rare. One must be even aware that the color pink in lilacs is an elusive shade that changes with the weather, with the brightness of the sun, with the pH of soil conditions (acid or alkaline soils have much to do with shades and intensity of color). I have often seen some of the true pinks in colder seasons and in heavier soils become rather lavender or bluish pinks. In all 'Pink' is a difficult classification—especially when one adds the double cultivars with nuances of several shades and colors. One must observe a lilac for some few years and growing in various locations before a 'pink' label can be affixed to a particular cultivar.

Bon jardinier, for the sake of somewhat clarifying this situation and for those who insist on true pink lilacs, I am listing two classifications of 'pink lilacs'. Those that are soft, clear, unadulterated pinks that seem to have no admixture of shades of lavender, violet or blues, and the 'mixed pinks' which are predominantly pink to all appearances but upon closer scrutiny do have tones of lavender, magenta or bluish casts. When the 'mixed pinks' are side by side with the deeper purples, rich magentas, violets, blues or whites, they appear to be real pinks. However, when placed next to the true pinks or lavenders they are not as pink as they appear. Both categories of pinks are very beautiful and many excellent cultivars are found in each. *Mon amie et ami,* you must determine for yourself how pink your lilac cultivar must be. I only seek to list the best of each.

Be mindful that no exhaustive and scientific study has ever been made of the color of lilacs—many are too elusive to be categorized! Pink is also a color classification that needs considerable attention of the hybridizers. Often the florets of the pink sorts are rather small, many of the pink doubles have tightly-knit thrysi with a too compact appearance, many fade to a washed-out white with full sun. Under ideal conditions they are elegant *grandedames* of lilacdom. Give them a soft, filtered umbrella of high shade to retain their delicate tones (*bon jardinier,* they do not like in any way to be sunburnt). In half-bloom they are most beautiful where the contrast of deeper pink buds with the unfolding light pink florets are worthy of the finest garden. Hybridizers are making progress with fine new introductions, yet some of the oldest and finest are well over a century old! 'Lucie Baltet' which was introduced by the Baltet Nursery in 1888, with bronze-pink buds opening to a delicate pale pink is still breathtakingly beautiful and among the finest, and 'Macrostachya', introduced by Lafievre in 1874, with its long, pale-pink clusters is also one of the finer pinks and much used in hybridization.

Among the newer pink introductions are many excellent lilacs. High on this list I would place 'Krasavitsa Moskvy', 'Professor Robert B. Clark', 'Clyde Lucie', 'Marie Chaykowski' and 'Maiden's Blush'. (*Mon ami,* there are others but I have included them in the list that follows!) I must repeat, one must demand (not merely ask for) lilac cultivars by name or else the nursery trade makes no move to reach out to the many very fine newer sorts and continually perpetuates grafts from the old lilac bushes growing by their nursery sheds.

As with all your lilacs, prune the pink sorts heavily so as to get strong young growth on the bush. The pinks have a tendency to be somewhat small flowered and will appear even smaller if you do not prune well. They are exquisite on strong, youthful wood. Keep the beautiful Lemoine doubles low to see their beauty. These massive blooms need heavy pruning and good soil.

Because they are difficult to obtain do not overlook some of the newer introductions, they are well worth all the time and effort. (For many I know of no nursery source other than the originators or the International Lilac Society).

Pink lilacs are for close viewing where their truly delicate shades and tones can best be appreciated. They are resplendent placed against a background of darker conifers or dark purple lilacs. Next to a 'Morheim' Spruce they are a planting to behold! Blanket the foreground with beds of blush early peonies, or beds of some of the newest true-blue leaved *Hosta.* (*Mon jardinier!* It will be a work of artistic genius!)

RECOMMENDED LILAC CULTIVARS IN THE COLOR CLASSIFICATION 'TRUE PINK'—V

S. *vulgaris* cultivars:
'Alenushka'—single, Mikhairov 1956, difficult to obtain, very fragrant, very fine.
'Archiduchesse Charlotte'—single, Brahy 1861, very rare, old, beautiful, very good.

'Burgomeester Voller'—single, D. E. Maarse 1948, slight lavender cast, very good.

'Catawba Pink'—double, Utley 1980, very good.

'Charm'—single, Havemeyer 1948, large florets, very good.

'Clyde Lucie'—single, Utley 1975, an excellent, fine pink selection of 'Lucie Baltet'.

'Cora Lyden'—double, Lyden 1968, a beautiful lilac rating very fine.

'Cynthia'—single, Berdeen 1971, pale pink of great quality, very fine to excellent.

'Emile Lemoine'—double, V. Lemoine 1889, still one of the finest pink-lavender doubles, excellent in every way.

'General Sherman'—single, Dunbar 1917, pearled a pale pinkish turning to a creamy-white, unique large florets, undoubtedly Dunbar's finest, excellent.

'Herman Eilers'—single, de Messemaeker pre-1913, good.

'Holy Maid'—single, Fiala 1984, pale lovely pink, outstandingly beautiful, excellent.

'I. V. Michurin'—double, Kolesnikov 1941, fragrant, very fine.

'Krasavitsa Moskvy'—double, Kolesnikov 1974, one of the finest lilacs grown from the work of a master hybridizer, exceptionally fine, excellent! White pearled pink buds.

'Lee Jewett Walker'—single, Berdeen 1979, very pale pink of exceptional beauty, excellent.

'Lilarosa'—single, Spath pre-1887, very old, very good background, fragrant, small florets but showy, good.

'Lois Amee Utley'—double, Fiala 1986, very showy, very fine to excellent.

'Lourene Wishart'—double, Fiala 1980, very clear, fine pink, heavy bloomer, excellent.

'Lucie Baltet'—single, Baltet 1888, low growing, very fine to excellent.

'Macrostachya'—single, Lafievre 1874, long clusters of pale pink, very fine.

'Maiden's Blush'—single, Skinner 1966, pale to medium pink, outstanding, excellent!

'Maiennacht'—single, Steffen-Heinemann 1948, pale pink very good.

'Marie Chaykowski'—single, Fiala 1983, pale pink multipetaled, very showy, excellent.

'Marshal Vasilevskii'—double, Kolesnikov 1963, very fine quality, very good.

'Martha Kounze'—double, Havemeyer pre-1953, excellent, very showy.

'Melissa Oakes'—single, Oaks 1972, pale pink, very fine to excellent.

'Mme. Antonie Buchner'—double, Lemoine 1909, very fine to excellent.

'Montaigne'—double, Lemoine 1907, high quality, pale pink, very fine.

'Mrs. Harry Bickle'—single, Rolph 1956, pale pink feathery spikes, very fine.

'Olimpiada Kolesnikova'—double, Kolesnikov 1955, very fine.

'Pink Lace'—single, Sass 1953, pale to medium pink, very fine to excellent.

'Pink Mist'—single, Havermeyer-Eaton 1953, large florets, very good.

'Pomarzanka'—single, Karpow 1962, very fine quality, very good.

'Professor Robert B. Clark'—single, Fiala 1982, very large multipetaled florets, white pearled pink, excellent!

'Radiance'—double, Fiala 1983, very fine to excellent.

Rochester Parks, Rochester, NY, USA.

Sdg. No. 1825—single, Fenicchia, very outstanding to excellent.

Sdg. No. 1726—single, Fenicchia, very fine to excellent.

Sdg. No. 1820—single, Fenicchia, very fine.

(These last 3 are soon to be named.)

'Stephanie Rowe'—single, Berdeen 1979, very pale pink long clusters, difficult to obtain, very fine to excellent.

'Siebold'—double, Lemoine 1906, dwarf grower, white with buds tinted pink pearled cream, excellent but most difficult to find.

RECOMMENDED LILAC CULTIVARS IN THE COLOR CLASSIFICATION 'MIXED PINK'—V

S. vulgaris cultivars:

'Capitaine Perrault'—double, Lemoine 1925, very fine.

'Comte Horace de Choiseul'—double, Lemoine 1887, old but still good.

'De Croncels'—single, Baltet pre-1876, very deep lavender toned pink with coppery buds, rather low growing, very floriferous (probably the parent of 'Lucie Baltet' from the same grower and color), bronze-pink, excellent.

'Edward J. Gardner'—double, Gardner pre-1950, pale pink of outstanding beauty, excellent.

'Elsie Lenore'—single, Fiala 1984, enormous florets and panicles, outstandingly showy, a colchicine treated seedling of 'Sensation'—excellent!

'General Pershing'—double, Lemoine 1924, lilac of considerable merit, very fine.

'Katherine Havemeyer'—double, Lemoine 1922, very heavy thrysi, lavender pink, very fine.

'Konstanty Karpow'—double, Karpow 1953, very good.

'Midwest Gem'—double, Sass 1942, medium pink, fine.

'Miriam Cooley'—single, Klager 1931, very fine of great quality.

'Miss Muffet'—single, Fiala 1968, low growing, perhaps should be classified magenta VI. large florets on small bush, very good.

'Romance'—single, Havemeyer-Eaton 1954, large florets of outstanding merit, very fine.

'Roland Mills'—single, Klager 1928, one of her best introductions, a lovely deeper pink, very fine to excellent.

'Ukraina'—single, V. Zhogoleva 1974, large florets, fragrant, very fine and showy.

'Utro Moskvy'—double, Kolesnikov 1938, very fine lilac-pink with silvery tones.

SPECIES AND HYBRID LILACS IN THE COLOR CLASSIFICATION 'PINK'—V

There are some very excellent lilacs among the Early Hybrids in this color, 'Pink'. Some of the earlier introductions of Lemoine are very tall growers unless reduced by heavy pruning. Many of the newer introductions (some not yet named, as are the numbered seedlings at the National Arboretum, Washington, D.C.) are far more refined and better plants for the modest garden of limited space. In a few years we will see many of these newer hybrids.

S. × hyacinthiflora 'Annabel'—double, Hawkins 1948, very early, good.

'Berryer'—double, Lemoine 1913, lavender tones, tall grower, good.

'Bountiful'—single, Clarke 1949, very showy, great quality, excellent.

'Buffon'—single, Lemoine 1921, lavender tones, recurved, very good.

'Catinat'—single, Lemoine 1922, good.

'Churchill'—single, Skinner 1966, very fine.

'Claude Bernard'—double, Lemoine 1915, very fine.

'Daphne Pink'—single, Skinner 1959, very fine.

'Esther Staley'—single, Clarke 1948, lavender tones, excellent!

'Fenelon'—single, Lemoine 1936, good.

'Fraser'—single, Skinner 1945, fine bloomer, very good.

'Kate Sessions'—single, Clarke 1942, large florets—very fine.

'Lewis Maddock'—single, Rankin 1968, very early, very fine pink.

'Orchid Chiffon'—single, Sass 1953, very good.

'Pink Cloud'—single, Clark 1947, lavender-pink, very showy, very fine.

'Vauban'—double, Lemoine 1913, good.

Most of the hyacinthiflora pinks are not pure in color but mixed with lavender.

S. × henryi 'Prairial'—single, Lemoine 1933, medium pink heavy bloomer, very fine.

S. × josiflexa 'Enid'—single, Preston 1934, good.

S. julianae 'Hers'—Hers 1923, more lavender than pink, arching branches, very fine species cultivar, excellent, needs room.

'George Eastman'—single, Clark-Fennicchia 1977, deep carmine buds, outstanding pink, upright grower, excellent.

S. julianae 'Pink Parasol'—single, Fiala 1980, recurved petals of pale pink, fine grower and bloomer, excellent. A seedling of 'George Eastman' but a taller and better grower.

S. komarowii—single, very fine medium pink, excellent.

S. × clarkiana (S. komarowii × S. wolfii) 'Spellbinder'—single, Fiala 1968, very fine pale pink, very floriferous and showy, excellent. Medium sized shrub.

S. microphylla 'Superba'—single, Chenault 1934, very fine, needs good drainage.

S. × prestoniae There are a great number of these hybrids, many very similar, I have selected only a very few—but it is a matter of choice as to their individual merits.

'Alice Rose Foster'—single, Alexander 1968.

'Basia'—single, Bugala 1970, 2nd generation hybrid.

'Coral'—single, Preston 1937, very good.

'Esterka'—single, Bugala 1970, very good.

'Ethel M. Webster'—single, Preston 1934, 2nd generation, very good.

'Fountain'—single, Preston 1934, pale pink, good.

'Goplana'—single, Bugala 1970, very fine.
'Heloise'—single, Skinner 1932, very good.
'Isabella'—single, Preston 1928, excellent.
'James Macfarlane'—single, Yaeger 1959, excellent.
'J. Herbert Alexander'—single, Lyden 1963, good.
'Miss Canada'—single, Cumming 1967, excellent.
'Romeo'—single, Preston 1926, very good.
'Telimena'—single, Bugala 1970, very fine to excellent.
'Ursula'—single, Preston 1928, violet shades, one of the best, excellent.
S. potaninii—single, delicate pink, soft wooded species, blooms over the entire summer.
S. × *quadrobrida* (*S.* × *sweginzowii* 'Albida' × S. × 'Spellbinder (*S. komarowii* × *S. wolfii*) 'Quartet'—single, Fiala 1968, medium sized shrub, extremely floriferous annually, pale pink, excellent.
S. reflexa—single, beautiful hanging racemes, medium to dark pink, to lavender-pink depending on the individual plant selection, outstanding species, excellent!
S. × *swegiflexa* 'Irving'—single, Preston 1953, good to fine.
S. sweginzowii—single, fine species but the hybrids are better.
S. × *sweginzowii* 'Albida'—single, Lemoine 1930, pale feather blooms, fine fragrance, excellent.
S. × *fialiana* 'Springtime'—single, Fiala 1968.
S. sweginzowii 'Albida' × (*S. komarowii* × *S. wolfii*) extremely lovely very floriferous, pale pinkish-white, excellent!
S. × *tribrida* 'Lark Song'—single, Fiala 1968, (*S.* × *swegitella* × *S. komarowii*) medium sized shrub, extremely floriferous, practically no seed pods, excellent.

Magenta and Purple Lilacs
Color Class VI and VII

Having already seen how difficult many lilac cultivars are to classify as to color, the two categories 'Magenta'—VI and 'Purple'—VII have unique problems as both deal with the darkest lilacs. One can clarify and separate these two deep reddish-purple colors if one adheres to their definition colorwise. Magenta denotes a "fuchian, a bright purplish-red color" . . . one with carmine tones, that is, a crimson or purplish-red. In contrast 'Purple' denotes a color having "components of red and blue"—a deep tone of reddish-crimson-blue. (*Mon ami et amie*, you must have the flowers before you to really appreciate the difference a bit of blue can make in these very deep reddish-purple colors! Since very few women are color-blind as to the colors red and blue, as a group they are perhaps better judges as to which cultivar belongs where, but there are also many men who have exceptional color perception in these categories). Nonetheless many lilac cultivars have been classified as 'magenta' which should have been called 'purple'. When we arrive at the deep 'mixed' pinks on through the magentas and then to the purples, we find many cultivars that are misclassified—only a finer chart than the Ridgeway or the Royal Horticultural Color Chart could adequately place their exact shade. (I have always advocated that we adopt the International Color Chart of the Paint Industries as they have a far wider variation and appear more precise for modern use—they also classify colors by a number code which is far easier to ascertain than fancy names for each color.) Forgive me, *bon jardinier*, for I have just cast a stone, a rather large one, into a favorite horticultural 'hornet's nest'—I am most certain to be stung many times!

Albeit! There are many fine cultivars in both the classifications 'Magenta' and 'Purple'—here is my list of some of the better ones.

RECOMMENDED LILAC CULTIVARS IN THE COLOR CLASSIFICATION 'MAGENTA'—CLASS VI

'Amor'—single, Steffen-Heinemann 1948, a deep mixed pink, very good to very fine.
'Andre Csizik'—single, D. E. Maarse 1950, very good.
'Anne Shiach'—single, Havemeyer 1943, very fine to excellent, difficult to find.
'Arch McKean'—single, Fiala 1983, large florets, showy, excellent.
'Atheline Wilbur'—semi-double, Fiala 1979, unique with orchid shades, excellent.
'Botaniste Pauli'—single, Klettenberg 1935, very good, not found in nurseries.
'Bright Centennial'—single, Robinson 1967, deep reddish color, very fine to excellent.
'Capitaine Baltet'—single, Lemoine 1919, large florets, showy, very fine.

'Carolyn Mae'—single, J. Sass 1953, good to very fine, difficult to obtain.
'Charlotte Morgan'—double, Seabury 1928, fine but not readily obtainable.
'Congo'—single, Lemoine 1896, bright deep reddish, heavy bloom, very old but excellent.
'Corrinne'—single, Baltet pre-1900, still very fine.
'De Croncels'—single, Baltet pre-1876, copper buds, low grower, abundant bloom, very fine.
'Downfield'—single, Havemeyer pre-1953, very fine.
'Dzhavakharial Neru'—single, Kolesnikov 1974, good and becoming available.
'Eden'—single, Oliver 1939, deep reddish-purple, fair to good.
'Elizabeth Files'—double, Berdeen 1971, deep reddish, very fine but difficult to obtain.
'Elsie Lenore'—single, Fiala 1983, very large florets and panicles, outstanding, excellent.
'Etoile de Mai'—double, Lemoine 1905, different, combination of pale pink and deep rose, good.
'Frederick Douglass'—single, Fenicchia 1972, multipetaled, very fine.
'Fryderyk Chopin'—single, Karpow 1958, very fine, unobtainable from nurseries.
'Georges Bellair'—double, Lemoine 1900, one of the better deep-red doubles, very fine.
'Gismonda'—double, Lemoine 1939, very fine large thryses (should be class IV-lilac).
'G. J. Baardse'—single, D. E. Maarse 1943, medium florets, very good, showy.
'Glory'—single, Havemeyer 1954, enormous florets, shy bloomer, many suckers, good.
'Henry Wadsworth Longfellow'—double, Dunbar 1920, very good.
'Indiya'—single, Kolesnikov 1955, large florets, fragrant, moderate bloomer, good.
'James Stuart'—single, Havemeyer 1954, large florets, heavy bloomer, very fine.
'Kremlevskie Kuranty'—single, Kolesnikov 1974, large florets, showy, very fine.
'Lady Lindsay'—single, Havemeyer 1943, large recurved florets, very red, fine.
'Leon Wyczolkowski'—single, Karpow 1958, very good.
'Luch Vostoka'—double, C. A. Melnik 19--, large florets, difficult to find.
'Magellan'—double, Lemoine 1915, good reddish, not easily found.
'M. I. Kalinin'—single, Kolesnikov 1941, fragrant large clusters, fine.
'Maitre Georges Herman'—double, Lambrechts 1952, fine reddish-lavender, difficult to find.
'Marceau'—single, Lemoine 1913, very fine, very large deep reddish florets.
'Marechal Foch'—single, Lemoine 1924, very large, reddish-pink florets, tall, excellent.
'Massena'—single, Lemoine 1923, large reddish florets, excellent.
'M. I. Kalinin'—single, Kolesnikov 1941, fragrant large clusters, fine.
'Mister Big'—double, Havermeyer-Eaton 1954, fine, not easily obtainable.
'Mrs. Edward A. Harding'—double, Lemoine 1922, very heavy large spikes, fine.
'Mrs. John W. Davis'—double, Havemeyer 1953, very fine.
'Mrs. Watson Webb'—single, Havemeyer 1954, very fine to excellent, large spikes.
'Paul Deschanel'—double, Lemoine 1924, enormous panicles, large florets, excellent.
'Paul Thirion'—double, Lemoine 1915, very fine, deep reddish-pink, very fine to excellent.
'Planchon'—double, Lemoine 1908, very good.
'Polly Stone'—double, Gardner 1971, very fine, difficult to obtain.
'President Loubet'—double, Lemoine 1901, very fine mixed pinkish-red shades.
'President Poincare'—double, Lemoine 1913, very fine, heavy, large spikes.
'Prince Baudouin'—single, Klettenberg 1935, good to fine.
'Priscilla'—single, Havemeyer 1944, very large florets with lavender cast.
'Radzh Kapur'—single, Kolesnikov 1974, very large florets, fine.
'Reaumur'—single, Lemoine 1904, very fine to excellent.
'Red Feather'—double, Ruliffson 1953, good.
'Rosea Grand Fleur'—single, introducer unknown circa 1945, very showy, very fine to excellent.
'Ruhm von Horstenstein'—single, Wilke 1921, very good.
'Souvenir de Georges Truffaut'—double, Lemoine 1953, fine.
'Souvenir de Louis Chasset'—single, H. Lemoine 1953, very fine.
'St. Jerzy Popieluszko'—single, Fiala 1984, very fine to excellent, showy reddish.
'Stefan Makowiecki'—single, Karpow 1958, fine.
'Talisman'—single, Fiala 1983, very showy, fine to very fine.
'Topaz'—single, V. Zhogoleva 1976, very large florets, very fine.
'Voorzitter Diz'—single, D. E. Maarse 1953, fine.
'Zarya Kommunizma'—single, Kolesnikov 1951, very large deep reddish florets, fine.
'Znamya Lenina'—single, Kolesnikov 1963, one of the finest red lilacs, excellent.

SPECIES AND HYBRIDS IN THE COLOR CLASSIFICATION 'MAGENTA'—VI

S. × *chinensis* 'Crayton Red'—single, Crayton 1953, very fine.

   × *chinensis* 'La Lorraine'—single, Lemoine 1899, fine background shrub.

   × *chinensis* 'Orchid Beauty'—single, cir. 1945, originator unknown.

S. × *henryii* × *tomentella* 'Germinal'—single, Lemoine 1939, fair.

S. × *hyacinthiflora* 'Ada'—single, Preston 1953, good.

   × *hyacinthiflora* 'Alice Eastwood'—double, Clarke 1942, very good.

   × *hyacinthiflora* 'Esther Staley'—single, Clarke 1948, tall grower, heavy bloom, excellent.

   × *hyacinthiflora* 'Fantasy'—double, Clarke 1960, very fine.

   × *hyacinthiflora* 'Katherine Jones'—single, Clarke 1953, good.

   × *hyacinthiflora* 'Missimo'—single, Clarke 1944, very fine.

   × *hyacinthiflora* 'Montesquieu'—single, Lemoine 1926, fine.

   × *hyacinthiflora* 'Patricia'—double, Preston 1931, good.

   × *hyacinthiflora* 'Pink Cloud'—single, Clarke 1947, very fine.

   × *hyacinthiflora* 'Polesskaya Legenda'—single Smoliskii-Bibikova—, fine.

   × *hyacinthiflora* 'Summer Skies'—single, Clarke 1949, very fine.

S. × *hyacinthiflora* 'Sunset'—double, Clarke 1949, very fine to excellent.

   × *hyacinthiflora* 'Sweetheart'—double, Clarke 1953, very fine.

S. × *josiflexa* 'Guinevere'—single, Preston 1934, good.

S. *julianae* 'Epaulette'—single, Fiala 1984, very fine, showy.

S. *julianae* 'George Eastman'—single, Clark-Fenicchia 1977, outstanding color, excellent.

S. *julianae* 'Sentinel'—single, Fiala 1984, upright, very good.

S. *komarowii*—single very fine to excellent, one of the better species, color variations when grown from seed—propagate selected seedlings of merit.

S. × *quatrobrida* 'Dancing Druid' (*S. yunnanensis* × *S. tomentella*) × (*S. komarowii* × *S. sweginzowii* 'Albida')—single, Fiala 1968, very good.

S. × *prestoniae*—(see the recommended list under that title)

S. × *prestoniae* 'Miss Canada'—single, Cumming 1967, exceptionally fine, a truly outstanding late lilac.

S. *wolfii*—single, very good, one of the better species, does have variations of color when grown from seed—propagate selected seedlings only.

RECOMMENDED LILAC CULTIVARS IN THE COLOR CLASSIFICATION 'PURPLE'—VII

These deep purple lilacs always fascinate people and cause a sensation in the garden or at a show. They immediately draw people to them as if they possessed some magical powers. More people will choose the deepest purples over any other color. Be mindful that this is a classification that has several shades of deep purple, mostly the deep reddish-blue-purples. However, it is often difficult to ascertain whether some of the deep violets belong to Class VII or Class II (I have included a few in both for this reason). *Mon amie*—they are beautiful in bloom!

Often their darkness does not carry in the garden and they should be enhanced to be at their best by the contrast of white or light pink lilacs at their sides or behind them. Do NOT place them side by side with lavenders, blues or the magentas which diminish the strength of their color. Too, dark lilacs need to be viewed at rather close range. They lose their effectiveness at any great distance. Use them as a close-up, focal point, come upon them suddenly in the garden as you round a path or have them set as a family heirloom alongside the patio or as a specimen for all to see. They always attract attention, especially with low, white companion plants at their feet. Try a dark lilac underplanted with the newest real blue *Hosta*—a unique combination of color contrasts that is most pleasing.

Many of these really dark lilac beauties are late bloomers, so choose only the late-blooming white or pinks lilacs to accompany them (not just any fine white). It does no good to flank them with whites or pinks that have finished blooming while the deep purples are still in tight bud. Look for later blooming whites such as 'Emery Mae Norweb', 'Prof. E. H. Wilson', 'St. Joan', 'St. Margaret, 'Gertrude Clark' or the delicate pink-shaded whites 'Krasavitsa Moskvy' or 'Professor Robert B. Clark'. (Or use other good late blooming whites and pinks of your own choice.) Do not use the early *oblata* hybrids with the late blooming *S. vulgaris*.

If you are able to shade the deep purples for a few hours from the hottest afternoon sun, they will be so much the better and retain their deep purple color much longer. Hot suns fade their colors to a washed-out purple. These deep purples are particularly beautiful at the Royal Botanical Gardens, Hamilton, Ontario, Canada, where they are grown under the half-shade of tall trees.

Often some of the deep purples (not all) are somewhat fussy growers, slow and at times weak, and need a little extra care with water and weed-free soil. The newest introductions are fine and strong growers. Give them a little extra attention and how they will reward you for this tender love! All the deepest colored lilacs are not found in this VII class alone, many more are in Class II and some would fit in both. Class VII has the deep reddish-blue cast purples, whereas Class II has the deep violets or violet-blues without the admixture of reddish-blue.

The dark lilacs are ideal for contrasting companion plants with *Malus* 'Silver Moon', 'Prairie Rose', 'Prince Georges' or some of the newest *Malus* hybrids that are late bloomers or with many of the low early perennials. Lilacs are garden heirlooms! Choose and buy only the best and let their blessings through the years on you, *mon jardinier*, rest! Please do not settle on any dark lilac when for a few more dollars and shopping for the right nurseryman you can have the finest!

RECOMMENDED LILAC CULTIVARS IN THE COLOR CLASSIFICATION "PURPLE"—VII

'Alesha'—single, A. Sakharova _____ , large florets more cherry red than purple, fine.
'A. B. Lamberton'—double, Dunbar 1916, good.
'Adelaide Dunbar'—double, Dunbar 1916, very good.
'Albert F. Holden'—single, Fiala 1981, deep purple reverse silver, excellent.
'A. M. Brand'—single, Brand 1975, large florets, very fine.
'Andenken an Ludwig Spaeth'—single, Spaeth 1883, good, surpassed by newer cultivars.
'Ann Tighe'—double, Yaeger 1945, very fine.
'Anna Elizabeth Jacquet'—single, Felix & Dykhuis 1924, very fine, very showy heavy bloomers.
'Archeveque'—double, Lemoine 1923, unique color, fine.
'Arthur William Paul'—double, Lemoine 1898, good.
'Bishop Bernard McQuaid'—single, Fenicchia 1972, multipetaled, very fine to excellent.
'Calvin C. Laney'—single, Dunbar 1923, some early hybrid blood, very good.
'Charles Joly'—double, Lemoine 1896, very good, somewhat small thyrses.
'Chris'—single, Berdeen 1963, very good.
'Col. van Ness'—single, introducer and date unknown, very good.
'Col. William Plum'—single, Brand 1953, good.
'Danton'—single, Lemoine 1911, very good.
'Dark Night'—single, Sobek 1966, very good.
'De Saussure'—double, Lemoine 1903, very good.
'Diderot'—single, Lemoine 1915, very good to fine.
'Doctor Brethour'—single, Patterson 1961, very fine to excellent.
'Dusk'—single, Havemeyer 1974, very good.
'Edith Braun'—single, Rankin 1968, one of the finest, excellent.
'Edmond Bossier'—single, Lemoine 1906, very fine.
'Ethel Childs'—single, Childs date unknown, very good.
'Ethel Dupont'—single, Havemeyer 1972, very good.
'Ethiopia'—single, Brand 1945, very good to fine, very dark.
'Etna'—single, Lemoine 1927, very fine to excellent.
'Frank Klager'—single, Klager 1928, very fine.
'Frank Paterson'—single, Paterson 1961, very showy, tall grower, excellent.
'Fuerst Buelow'—single, introduction unknown, very fine and very showy.
'George Ellwanger'—single, Fenicchia 1972, multipetaled very fine.
'Hallelujah'—single, Havemeyer-Eaton 1954, very fine.
'Helen Schloen'—single, Paterson 1962, very fine.
'Jane Day'—single, Havemeyer 1953, very good.
'Krasnaya Moskva'—single, Kolesnikov 1960, fine, moderate bloomer.
'Laplace'—single, Lemoine 1913, good.
'Leonid Leonov'—single, Kolesnikov 1941, very good.
'Leopold III'—single, Klettenberg 1935, very good.
'Margaret Rice Gould'—single, Brand 1953, very good.
'M. I. Kalinin'—single, Kolesnikov 1941, very showy, very fine.
'Mildred Luetta'—double, Hertz 1951, very fine to excellent.

'Miss Aalsmeer'—single, H. Maarse 1953, very fine.

'Mme. Pierre Verhoven'—single, Verhoeven 1936, very good.

'Monge'—single, Lemoine 1913, outstandingly showy, excellent.

'Mrs. Flanders'—single, Havemeyer 1953, smaller florets but outstanding color, excellent.

'Mrs. Robert Gardner'—single, Gardner 1963, very fine.

'Mrs. W. E. Marshall'—single, Havemeyer 1924, small florets but perhaps the darkest colored lilac, almost black—excellent.

'Murillo'—double, Lemoine 1901, very fine.

'Negro'—single, Lemoine 1899, very good.

'Ogni Dombasse'—double, Rubtsov-Zhogoleva-Lyapunouva 1956, very good to fine.

'Ostrander Cooley'—double, Klager 1928, very fine, unique color shades.

'Pasteur'—single, Lemoine 1903, very good.

'Paul Hariot'—double, Lemoine 1902, very fine.

'Prodige'—single, Lemoine 1928, very large florets, excellent.

'Ralph W. Stone'—single, Stone 1971, very fine.

'Sarah Sands'—single, Havemeyer 1943, excellent.

'Roland Mills'—single, Klager 1930, very good.

Seedling No. 75116-16, Royal Botanical Gardens, Hamilton, Ontario, Canada—single, very large floret and very showy, excellent.

'Sensation'—single, D. E. Maarse 1938, outstanding white edged petals, excellent.

'Stadtgartner Rothpletz'—single, Froebel 1905, very fine heavy bloomer (a misnamed double dark lilac is being sold under this name which is not the correct 'Stadtgartner'—the single true cultivar is far superior).

'Toussaint-L'Ouverture'—single, Lemoine 1898, long spikes, very fine.

'Triste Barbaro'—single, originator unknown 1953, very good.

'Vesper'—single, Fleming 1979, excellent, very showy.

'Vesuve'—single, Lemoine 1916, very fine, showy.

'Volcan'—single, Lemoine 1899, showy, very fine.

'Woodland Violet'—single, H. Sass 1971, very good.

S. × *hyacinthiflora* 'Grace'—single, Preston 1934, good.

   × *hyacinthiflora* 'Max Lobner'—single, Steffen-Heinemann 1952, very good.

   × *hyacinthiflora* 'Muriel'—single, Preston 1934, good.

   × *hyacinthiflora* 'Pocahontas'—single, Skinner 1935, excellent, very showy.

   × *hyacinthiflora* 'Purple Gem'—single, Clarke 1949, very fine.

   × *hyacinthiflora* 'Purple Glory'—single, Clarke 1949, very fine to excellent.

   × *hyacinthiflora* 'Purple Heart'—single, Clarke 1949, very fine, showy.

S. × *hyacinthiflora* 'Purple Splendor'—double, Clarke 1975, very fine.

   × *hyacinthiflora* 'Tom Taylor'—double, Skinner 1962, very fine.

S. × *prestoniae* 'Alice'—single, Preston 1941, very good.

   × *prestoniae* 'Donald Wyman'—single, Skinner 1944, very good.

   × *prestoniae* 'Francisca'—single, Preston 1925, very good.

   × *prestoniae* 'Maybelle Farnum'—single, Yaeger 1961, very fine.

   × *prestoniae* 'Nellie Bean'—single, Yaeger 1961, very fine.

   × *prestoniae* 'Paulina'—single, Preston 1927, very good.

   × *prestoniae* 'Viola'—single, Preston 1928, very dark.

S. × *josiflexa* 'Lynette'—single, Preston 1929, very good.

   × *josiflexa* 'Royalty'—single, Preston 1935, good.

S. *vulgaris* × S. *laciniata* 'Lavender Lady'—single, Lammerts 1963, very good.

                  'Lavender Lassie'—single, Lammerts 1967, very good.

PLATE 49

S. potaninii, belonging to the family closely akin to *S. meyeri* and *S. microphylla,* is this feathery lilac. Exotic in bloom—exquisite in fragrance!

The plant form of *S. potaninii* is rather delicately slender and upright. It is filled with the charm and excitement of old Cathay. Blooming over a long period of time it often blooms almost continuously in wet summers, rather well again in late fall. Shelter this beauty from zero weather as the soft late shoots often winterkill. It blooms joyfully each spring—exotic!

PLATE 50

S. reflexa with its drooping flower heads is both handsome and unique. In color it ranges from a whitish-pink to a deeper pink, not infrequently tinged with pale lavender. Native seedlings differ in ornamental value. There is need for selections of the finest seedlings for propagation and hybridization.

A blossom inflorescence while below is a view of the bush form of a specimen growing at the Royal Botanical Gardens, Hamilton, Ontario, Canada.

An outstanding selection. A seedling selection of *S. reflexa* made by B. Slavin, now growing at Highland Park, Rochester, N.Y. I have chosen to call this fine selection *S. reflexa* 'Slavin' so that it may be propagated and not lost.

S. reflexa 'Slavin', bush form.

PLATE 51

sweginzowii comes from the mountains of Sichuan Sheng, ...ina. It is a tall, slender branched shrub, somewhat fragrant ...t not of great garden merit.

Crossed with S. tomentella by Lemoine a beautiful hybrid named 'Albida' was introduced by him in 1930. It is far superior to the species. It is often called *S. sweginzowii* 'Albida' which is incorrect as it is not a selection but an hybrid and should be referred to as *S.* × 'Albida'.

S. × *swegiflexa (S. sweginzowii* × *S. reflexa)* introduced by Hess in 1935.

A beautiful hybrid of *S. villosa* × *S. sweginzowii* made by Skinner and introduced as 'Hedin' in 1935. It is a superior hybrid.

PLATE 52

S. tigerstedtii was recently discovered in Sichuan Sheng, China, by K. A. H. Smith of Uppsala, Sweden. Although it is over 50 years introduced, it has been very little known and distributed. It is a lovely shrub, with blossoms of pale mauvy purply pink tinting a whiter bloom. In growth it is a modest shrub in size, rather slender branched and somewhat spreading as seen in this picture of a specimen growing at the Royal Botanical Gardens, Hamilton, Canada.

One of the few hybrids of *S. tigerstedtii* that has been named is a tribrid called 'Tong Yong' (Fiala 1987) *S. tigerstedtii.* × (*S. yunanensis* × *S.* × *prestoniae* 'Isabella'). It is a heavier branched and flowered plant than the species.

The fine flower of *S. tigerstedtii* which has a strong, pleasing fragrance.

PLATE 53

S. villosa forms a fairly large bush. This specimen is one growing in the lilac collection of Niagara Parks, Niagara, Canada. *S. villosa* has widely been used in hybridizing.

Bush form and flower of *S. villosa* 'Aurea' with golden leaves and beautiful whitish bloom. A very fine form grows at Highland Park.

selected form of *S. villosa* named 'Rosea' was introduced by ew in 1974. There is some degree of color and form varia- on when grown from seed.

PLATE 54

S. ✕ prestoniae **'Miss Canada'** a triumph of Canadian hybridizing for an outstanding beauty of late blooming lilac in shades of deep reddish buds and deep pink blossoms was the hybridizing work of Dr. William A. Cumming, Morden Agricultural Research Center, Morden, Manitoba, Canada, introduced in 1967.

PLATE 55

Syringa × *prestoniae.* The hybridizers are bringing new color shades into the Prestonian Hybrids in outstanding introductions.

...ike' (Bugala 1970)

'Ethel Webster' Preston 1934) a 2nd generation Prestonian.

...oplana' (Bugala 1970)

...lice Rose Foster' (Alexander 1968)

'Hiawatha' (Skinner 1934)

PLATE 56

THE LATE BLOOMING MULTIBRIDS

Mostly introduced by Fiala and a few others are beginning to appear and provide lovely blooming shrubs of lower to moderate size with heavy bloom. Some like *S. × tribrida* 'Lark Song' produce no seed (or very few) hence are better annual bloomers than the heavy seed setters.

'Lark Song' (Fiala 1963). One of finest for heavy bloom-smaller shrub.

S. × clarkiana 'Spellbinder'. Clear light pink feathery bloom. (*S. komarowii × S. wolfii*) (Fiala 1968)

S. × quatrobrida 'Quartet' (Fiala 1980)

S. × quintobrida 'Eventide' ('Garden Peace' × 'Lark Song') (Fiala 1980)

PLATE 57

Syringa wolfii, a lilac for the large gardens and arboreta, also an hybridizer's lilac.

S. wolfii var. *hirsuta* undoubtedly the finest form of *S. wolfii.* One of the best is the plant growing at the University of Guelph Arboretum, Guelph, Ontario, Canada.

'Hagny' (Olsen-Graham, Denmark, 1971). A cross of *S. wolfii* × *S. reflexa.*

Syringa yunanensis, a mediocre lilac not for home gardens but rather for hybridizers and large collections of species lilacs. It is far better in its hybrids.

S. yunanensis growing at Highland Park, Rochester, N.Y., examined by taxonomist, Prof. Robert B. Clark.

'Prophecy' an induced tetraploid form of *S. yunanensis* introduced by Fiala in 1968.

S. yunanensis 'Rosea' is probably one of the best named forms of the species today.

PLATE 58

Syringa pinnatifolia "A most curious species of Lilac with very distinct pinnate leaves and small white flowers." . . . Lemoine. "A lilac that could have much to offer hybridizers" Fiala. *S. pinnatifolia* is extremely difficult to find, even in most large arboreta—never in nurseries. One comes to have it only from rooted cuttings or on occasion at plant auctions of the International Lilac Society.

Shrub form of *S. pinnatifolia* growing at the Brooklyn Botanic Garden, Brooklyn, N.Y.

S. × diversifolia a rare lilac interseries cross of *S. laciniata × S. pinnatifolia* made by Dr. Sax at the Arnold Arboretum in 1935. A vigorous plant so far unused by hybridizers, rare even in arboreta.

PLATE 59

THE 'TREE LILACS'

Although similar in bloom are distinguished quickly by their bark and tree form. *S. pekinensis* is the larger, more spreading tree with exfoliating bark, whereas *S. reticulata* has smooth dark, cherry-like bark and is a somewhat lower growing tree. Both bloom together in June.

The characteristic exfoliating bark of *S. pekinensis* which grows grayer with age.

mooth cherry-like bark of *S. reticulata* var. *reticulata* and *murensis*. *Amurensis* is a smaller and more rounded tree.

Tree form of *S. reticulata* var. *reticulata*. (Falconskeape)

Mature tree form *S. pekinensis*. (Highland Park)

PLATE 60

Syringa reticulata **var.** *reticulata.* The lovely 'Tree Lilacs' are among the latest to bloom, early to mid June. They have their own unique blossoms (all in whites or creamy-white) a lovely cherry-like bark and their own musky fragrance. They are also attractive in autumn with huge yellowish seed pods and pale yellow leaves. They are small to medium trees—plant one if you have space.

Below: the interesting bloom of *S. reticulata* var. *reticulata*

PLATE 61

Syringa reticulata **Variations in Blossoms.** Although the tree lilacs may look very similar in leaf, they present some sharp differences to the careful observer. Far greater selectivity must be made by using cuttings of named cultivars rather than lump all seedlings together as a species that is 'the same'. Selection has not been undertaken to date on *S. reticulata* with the result that little if any improvement has been made in the species.

There is a magnificent round tree specimen at Kingwood Gardens, Mansfield, Ohio, that is worthy of continued propagation. Undoubtedly there are select clones elsewhere worthy of being named or numbered. One must remember that the first *S. vulgaris* were very similar in form and color. Only with intense selection were the present forms evolved.

It is not possible that a species with so great a range in its native habitat over vast expanses of China into Japan, should not have considerable variations of great merit?

COMPARATIVE FLOWER SPIKES

Top: *S. reticulata* var. *amurensis*.

Center: *S. reticulata* var. *reticulata* (formerly var. *japonica*).

Bottom: *S. reticulata* × *S. pekinensis* 'Chinese Magic'. (Varietal forms—Falconskeape)

PLATE 62

In 1843 there appeared in Mons. Libert's garden a small flowered double lilac—a chance seedling that would have gone unnoticed had not Victor Lemoine obtained a rootlet of it for his lilac garden. It went from Libert-Daminont of Leige, Belgium to Lemoine's nursery in Nancy, France, where it grew into an old bush. Some 25 years later Lemoine realized its potential for producing double flowering lilacs—in his skillful hands the magic unfolded into a whole new strain of wonderful lilacs!

'Azurea Plena'. Bush form growing at Highland Park, Rochester, N.Y.

'Azurea Plena'. Close-up of the small, double, insignificant blue-lavender blossoms. Its offspring were magnificent!

'Belle de Nancy' a double pink was introduced in 1891.

The 'Prince de Beauvau', a fine double lavender named in 1897.

PLATE 63

'Victor Lemoine' (E. Lemoine 1906). This truly outstanding double lavender-pink named by a grateful son to honor his gifted father, the lilac 'Victor Lemoine' remains one of the finest to this date.

. . . *bon jardinier,* surely we must find room in our gardens for so fine a lilac and man!

'Emile Lemoine' (Lemoine 1889). The beautiful double lavender-lilac colored 'Emile Lemoine' was named by Victor Lemoine, a hybridizing genius, to honor his only, beloved son, who was to carry on his parents' dreams and visions in lilac hybridization.

. . . mon ami et amie, it was indeed a family of love and deep respect for one another.

PLATE 64

'Maximowicz' (D-II, 1906)

LEMOINE'S FAMOUS DOUBLE LILACS

'Henri Martin' (D-IV, 1912)

'Georges Bellair' (D-VI, 1900)

Elsewhere under *S. vulgaris* by color we have presented many other Lemoine fine lilacs.

'Mme. Antoine Buchner' (D-V, 1909)

'President Poincare' (D-VI, 1913)

'Etoile de Mai' (D-VI, 1905)

A Dozen Best According to Color

One should never recommend the dozen or so best lilacs from his own experience. With thousands of cultivars this is almost an impossible task! Some, however, do stand out as exceptional. What may be outstanding in New England may be average in the Mid-West or poor on the Pacific Coast. Climate and soil play such important roles in the vigor, color and effect a lilac has in any particular garden. From having observed lilacs for over 40 years throughout the United States and in Canada, I mention the following as possible candidates for your garden. Do not ask how I arrived at these choices—bloom effect, hardiness, beauty, color, vigor, form, reliability in flowering and fragrance, all have entered into their appraisal. So while I cannot recommend a dozen, I will offer several dozen I think best. (With tears I passed over much loved cultivars that I insist on in my own garden—but *Bon Jardinier*, we cannot have everything that is beautiful in this world! Can we? Especially if our growing space is limited.) There are some new cultivars that you may find impossible to obtain, especially of the very new multipetaled 'Rochester' hybrids. They are exceedingly lovely and soft colored. One could fill a garden from the work of a single hybridizer but rather, one must seek for a variety of forms both single and double, early and late. Many of the newer lilacs and the Russian introductions are relatively unknown since most cannot be found in nurseries. (Alas, our poor nurseries are so obsolete! *Bon Jardinier*, do not despair! Get a cutting from a lilac collection or from the International Lilac Society).

A DOZEN OR MORE OF THE 'BEST' FROM EACH COLOR CLASSIFICATION

(*Mon ami et amie,* surely you will disagree with me on not including your favorites, but I cannot list them all, and they may not be my favorite lilacs—we are all so different when we come to choosing lilacs for our gardens!)

White Lilacs I
S. vulgaris
'Avalanche'
'Candeur'
'Carley'
'Edith Cavell'
'Flora'
'Krasavitsa Moskvy'
'Monument'
'Mother Louise'
'Professor Robert B. Clark'
'Rochester'
'St. Joan'
'Slater's Elegance'
'Souvenir d' Alice Harding'
'Sovetskaya Artica'
S. chinensis 'Bicolor'
S. × prestoniae 'Agnes Smith'
　'Summer White'
S. reflexa 'Alba'

Violet Lilacs II
S. vulgaris
'Agincourt Beauty'
'Albert F. Holden'
'Beth Turner'
'Dr. Edward Mott Moore'
'Dr. John Rankin'
'Leonid Lenov'
'Marechal Lannes'
'Pauline Fiala'
'Violetta'
'Zulu'

S. hyacinthiflora 'Louvois'
　'Pocahontas'
S. meyeri 'Palibin'
S. patula
S. patula 'Miss Kim'

Blue Lilacs III
S. vulgaris
'Ami Schott'
'Blue Danube'
'Blue Delft'
'Dwight D. Eisenhower'
'Mme. Charles Souchet'
'Mrs. Elizabeth Peterson'
'Olivier de Serres'
'Pat Pesata'
'Porcelain Blue'
'P. P. Konchalovskii'
'Saturnale'
'Sea Storm'
'Sumerki'
'True Blue'
'Wedgwood Blue'
S. × hyacinthiflora 'Laurentian'

Lilac colored Lilacs IV
S. vulgaris
'Le Notre'
'Lullaby'
'Mollie Ann'
'Mrs. John S. Williams'
'Sesquicentennial'

'Silver King'
'Victor Lemoine'
S. julianae
S. × persica
S. × prestoniae 'Isabella'

Pink Lilacs V
S. vulgaris—clear pinks
'Clyde Lucie'
'Edward J. Gardner'
'Emile Lemoine'
'Holy Maid'
'Krasavitsa Moskvy'
'Lee Jewett Walker'
'Lois Amee Utley'
'Lourene Wishart'
'Lucie Baltet'
'Maiden's Blush'
'Marie Chaykowski'
'Mme. Antonie Buchner'
'Professor Robert B. Clark'
S. vulgaris—mixed pinks
'De Croncels'
'Elsie Lenore'
'Romance'
'Roland Mills'
'Utro Moskvy'
S. × hyacinthiflora 'Esther Staley'
　'Lewis Maddox'
　'Pink Cloud'
S. julianae 'Hers'
　'Pink Parasol'

S. komarowii
  S. × *prestoniae* 'Ethel
  Webster'
  'Ursula'
S. × *quadrobrid* 'Lark Song'
  'Springtime'
  'Spellbinder'
S. reflexa

Magenta Lilacs—VI
S. vulgaris
'Anne Shiach'
'Arch McKean'
'Atheline Wilbur'
'Capitaine Baltet'
'De Croncels'
'Elsie Lenore'
'Frederick Douglass'
'Georges Bellaire'

'Marechal Foch'
'Mrs. John W. Davis'
'Mrs. Watson Webb'
'Paul Deschanel'
'Paul Thirion'
'Znamya Lenina'
S. × *chinensis* 'Crayton Red'
S. × *hyacinthiflora* 'Missimo'
  'Mary Short'
  'Sunset'
S. julianae 'Epaulette'
  'George Eastman'
S. komarowii
S. × *prestoniae* 'Miss
  Canada'

Purple Lilacs—VII
S. vulgaris
'Albert F. Holden'
'Doctor Brethour'

'Edith Braun'
'Etna'
'Flower City'
'Frank Paterson'
'Leonid Leonov'
'M. I. Kalinin'
'Monge'
'Mrs. W. E. Marshall'
'Ostrander'
'Prodige'
'Sarah Sands'
'Sensation'
S. × *hyacinthiflora* 'Purple
  Gem'
  'Purple Glory'
  'Tom Taylor'
S. × *prestoniae* 'Donald
  Wyman'
'Nellie Bean'

Lilacs of Special and Unique Color Classifications

There are a few lilacs in a classification all their own, others have some new or unique characteristics not ordinarily found in lilacs. Many could be mentioned for unique combinations of colors but we present here some that are both outstanding and unique.

'Albert F. Holden'—Single, buds deep purple opening deep purple florets, silver reverse giving a deep purple and silver two-color effect.
'Atheline Wilbur'—Semi-double, deep rose-lavender buds, opening to multipetaled florets of orchid, rose and violet.
'Blue Delft'—Single, buds deep blue opening to multipetaled florets that are rayed and striped dark and light blue.
'General Sherman'—Single, buds pale lavender opening to florets of pearled, pale, lavender-white.
'Krasavitsa Moskvy'—Double, buds pinkish-lilac opening to double florets of very pale lavender tint on white.
'Mrs. Trapman'—Single, a unique shade of old-rose and lavender not usually seen in lilacs, somewhat small florets.
'Ostrander Cooley'—Double, outstanding combination of deep carmine with heliotrope and silver.
'Pat Pesata'—Single, buds deep pink-lavender opening to multipetaled florets of pale blue eyed white and rayed blue and white.
'Primrose'—Single, buds butter-cream yellow-green opening to small florets of pale creamy yellow, a yellowish color not found in any other lilac.
'Professor Robert B. Clark'—Single, buds clear pale pink opening to multipetaled florets of pale pearled white. Very effective and unique.
'Sensation'—Single, buds deep purple opening to smaller florets of deep purple edged in white. Outstandingly effective and unique.
'Siebold'—Double, buds deep pink opening to double florets pale pinkish-creamy white. Dwarf.
'Silver King'—Single, bud lavender opening to florets of pearled silvery lavender, unique and very effective.

The rayed and striped patterns in florets are a breakthrough to an entirely new series of pattern colors (mostly from seedlings of 'Rochester').

Autumn Color in Lilacs

Although lilacs, especially the *S. vulgaris* cultivars, are not known for fall leaf coloring, there are a few notable exceptions worth considering. In *S. vulgaris* a few cultivars (mostly in the whites) present a reasonable display of lemon-yellow leaves, e.g., 'White Lace' (Rankin). Among the *S. patula* cultivars autumn color is a most attractive change to soft pastels of reddish and mauve purples. In the cultivar *S. patula* 'Miss Kim' there is a definite and consistent purplish fall color.

S. meyeri var. 'Palibin' has a fine reddish bronze coloration that is most attractive and lasts for some time. Among the *S. hyacinthiflora* hybrids (*S. vulgaris* × *S. oblata*) there are many most attractive fall colorations of wine and bronze shades. The cultivars 'Lamartine' and 'Laurentian' are excellent for fall coloration.

The glory of lilac fall coloring is found in the species *S. oblata. S. oblata dilatata* and the newer *S. oblata donaldii* are both quite striking. They turn a deep purple to a reddish bronze. Probably the finest deep purples are in the new *S. oblata* var. *donaldii* so recently brought by seed from South Korea.

Elsewhere we have mentioned the possibility of developing colorful seed pods on lilacs. Someday, an enterprizing hybridizer will work for both autumn leaf and pod color so the lilac will become a two-season shrub. There are some fair yellow-podded *S. vulgaris* cultivars as well as a few of a light purplish hue. There is much work to be done before a really good, lasting pod color is obtained. It would be well worth the effort.

THE GOLD-LEAVES AND VARIEGATED LILACS

From time to time lilacs with gold, or a combination of gold, white and green variegations in their leaves appear. Most of them are novelties and not of genuine garden value. None is worthy of space in a limited garden. Some few do have places in very large gardens and arboreta.

Among the *S. vulgaris* cultivars *S.* 'Acubaefolia', which is the oldest gold-variegated form, appears to be a variation of the cultivar 'President Grevy'. Some more recent *S. vulgaris* include 'Wittbold's Variegated', introduced by the late Professor Albert Lumley, and 'Dappled Dawn'. The former is more attractive than 'Dappled Dawn'.

Among the other species we find more pure gold-leaved forms such as *S. emodi* 'aurea' and the induced mutation *S. tomentella* aurea 'Kum-Bum' (Fiala). All gold leaved plants need full sun. Most become a pale green as the season advances. Gold-leaved lilacs are a curiosity for the most part and cannot replace the named green-leaved cultivars. If you have large acreage they may be at home in a specialized area. Since there is really no market for the gold-leaved lilacs they are almost impossible to find except as a rootlet or cutting from a large collection, arboretum or lilac specialist.

CHAPTER FIVE

Landscaping with Lilacs

In northern and colder area gardens the lilac is one of the most effective flowering shrubs. Among the earliest to bloom, its flowering period extends over a number of weeks—from colorful buds to full bloom. It is a tough and hardy shrub, not often bothered by frosts and relatively free from major pests and so can be depended upon to be a mainstay of the Spring garden landscape. Lilacs today come in a wide range of colors (except yellows, oranges and bright reds). In size and form they seem to be tailored to meet the needs of all gardens, large or small. They adapt well for a variety of practical needs as screens, hedges, trees and specimen plantings. A well grown lilac in full bloom, no matter what cultivar or color, is a breath-taking sight! Add to their visual beauty their captivating fragrance—so unique and different—nostalgic and you have a garden treasure well worthy of the focal attention in any landscape. For all these reasons lilacs have played a major role over the centuries in garden landscaping.

They are magnificent as single specimens for close viewing and fragrance. They are outstanding where space allows them to be massed in groups of threes or fives. They are gracious used as background shrubs, for framing a view, or for hiding certain areas not desired in the landscape. There is no other spring shrub of such extraordinary beauty that is so versatile for landscape use. To achieve their best effect one must try to understand the lilac's needs, habit of growth and ultimate size. How often one sees beautiful lilacs crowded into a space where only one or two should have been planted instead of several. Throughout this chapter I shall endeavor to give some knowledge on using many of the species and cultivars to enhance your garden no matter how modest or large it may be.

There are certain lilac species and many newer and smaller growing cultivars admirably suited for the more modern one story homes as there are those well adapted for the largest estates and dwellings. Study the many lilacs well and do not make your decisions on what to plant simply on a color label only 'pink' or 'white' found on a nursery offering. (*Mon ami et amie*, remember well, you only plant lilacs but rarely in a lifetime! Choose them well and plant them where they will be most effective and happy! They will be your life-long friends!)

Lilacs are specially well-used if they are planted with companion plants and shrubs that enhance them at bloom time either by forming a fine background for the lilacs in bloom or later in the season providing color against the green leaves of the midsummer lilacs. Several of these companion plants are discussed in another chapter.

Whenever possible plant some of your most scented lilacs where their fragrance might be carried by the prevailing winds across your garden to your patio—your garden sitting and resting place. Their fragrance will delight you. Leave a place or two for one of the spicy perfumed species or late blooming hybrids and your friends will certainly ask what magic you have performed!

In the more modest gardens with limited size, lilacs should be generally treated as specimen shrubs or dwarf hedges—on the larger scale a variety of uses are suggested not only for their bloom but for their attractive deep green color in the landscape during the rest of the year.

Landscaping with Lilacs for the Smaller Garden

Most lilacs, if one carefully selects suitable cultivars and species such as *S. debelderi, S. potaninii, S. julianae, S. meyeri, S. oblata* var. *dilatata, S. patula, S. pubescens* and many low growing and dwarf forms of *S. vulgaris* are rather contained growers lending themselves wonderfully for the smaller garden. Use them as a modest growing background shrub, as corner or accent material, as dwarf hedging (*S. meyeri* 'Palibin') or as a single specimen. They can be effectively used as the flowering mass background of the flower garden. Certainly every small garden can afford space for at least one or two of these magnificent shrubs! Choose those cultivars that are known to be lower growing, less aggressive and need less pruning. Among the *S. vulgaris* cultivars use 'Lucie Baltet', 'Purple Gem', 'Purple Glory', 'Miss Muffett', 'Pixie' or 'Leprechaun'—none of which exceed 5 ft. on their own rootstock. *S. meyeri* 'Palibin' is an outstanding very small lilac of exceptional quality and bloom. There are many other cultivars listed throughout the various chapters that with a little pruning can well be kept at no more than 6–8 ft.—well within the limits of the most modest garden. Do not plant your lilacs under eaves or under windows—all lilacs are too tall or need more sun and water for this kind of planting. Give them an ample amount of room and they will reward you splendidly. I have seen beautiful specimens of *S. meyeri* and some of the other lilacs as potted shrubs on a roof garden or as patio specimens. Some of the lower growing cultivars and species are wonderfully suited for Japanese gardens (*S. julianae* with its arching branches or *S. pubescens* or the newest discovered species *S. debelderi*).

Choosing a Proper Site for a Single Plant, a Lilac Garden or a Collection

Where you plant your lilacs is as important as how you plant them. There is a great difference between planting one lilac and planting a whole collection, a lilac walk or using lilacs in conjunction with other landscape plants. If you plant and have room for a single lilac or a few you must make a thoughtful and wise decision as to what kind of effect you wish: a focal point shrub for a patio or garden, a few scattered shrubs in a border background, a screen of bloom or a lilac tree for a small yard? On the other hand, yours may be a specialty planting of a larger lilac collection, a lilac walk, or lilacs by water or poolside or in a Japanese Garden. Only you can make this decision based on your grounds and landscaping plans. Be mindful that there are lilacs to meet every need, from dwarfs to trees. Select a location with good drainage (the top of a slope rather than the bottom), in mostly full sunlight and not crowded in by other large shrubs and trees. Lilacs must have a reasonably good site.

For a single plant you can generally enrich the soil and provide ample drainage without too much difficulty. For a larger planting of several lilacs you must be more careful to provide the correct site. Always follow the rules for planting lilacs; good drainage—good soil—good sun and care. Your lilacs will repay you with abundant bloom and good growth. Group your lilacs in threes and fives. Use colors that will not clash (always use plenty of white blooming lilacs mixed with other colors). Should your garden be large enough, do not expose all your lilacs in one vista. Save some for an adventure into your garden—for a 'What is around the corner' view, or a winding Lilac Walk. Lilacs are perhaps best when grown with complementary flowering trees, shrubs and plants and with background of choice evergreens that enhance their bloom. Never plant your lilacs in straight rows centered in all directions like an apple orchard! Lilacs abhor regimentation! How could one even think of lining up garden princes and countesses in drill-rows like footsoldiers! Horrors at the thought! Lilacs need attending royalty in the garden and bedecked footservants at their feet with a royal canopy behind them. Then they display their royal mien to its fullest splendor.

In planting a single lilac or a very few, select a site where they can be seen both from a distance and from close range to delight in their beauty and fragrance. Do not plant lilacs under windows or close to doorways; they will outgrow both and you will eventually have to remove them. Give a single lilac adequate space and plant a delightful bed of flowers at its base for summer bloom. A back corner of the yard or against a garage wall often can be made most attractive with one or a few lilacs. Small homes can readily sustain one of the newer medium growing lilacs planted at one corner of the house but somewhat away from it for growth and space. Select an east, south or western side, never a northern side. On smaller properties do not plant a single specimen in the middle of the lawn as its growth soon makes the garden and the eventual landscape appears too small and chopped-up. Plant them to the back of the garden or along a curving side with lawn in front of them.

If you are planting large groupings of lilacs, a walk, collection or an arboretum, then you must visit all the arboreta, parks and large collections possible, especially those in your own area. It will be a delightful bit of homework of great value. Take time to do this, as it is your greatest lesson on what to do and what not to do when planting lilacs. Not everything you see is to be emulated. If one carefully observes lilacs during blooming time in any large collection, you will immediately be able to judge which cultivars and species are pleasing and which are not, what you are able to re-create in your own garden and what, though excellent, is beyond one's means. Take note of the lay of the land, its slopes and vista views, the kind of soil in which lilacs grow best, the drainage and the amount of sun they receive. Notice how some of the best plantings limit what can be appreciated in an eye scan and how they lead one on and on in wonder. There should be no single place where one can stand and take in all the lilac collection or planting at once. A total single view of all the lilacs is not good landscaping. Provide enticing previews from, perchance, a hill-top with the invitation to come down into the sloping glen for a closer view (as at the Katie Osborne Lilac Garden, Hamilton, Ont.). Curve your Lilac Walk for interest, as at The Arnold Arboretum, Jamaica Plains, or at Ewing Park, Des Moines, Iowa, to urge the beholder forward or gradually unfold the lilac wonders with landscaped grassy walks and progressive vistas as at the Holden Arboretum, Mentor, Ohio, or invite the public to come and wander through the lilacs as at Highland Park, Niagara Park or Lilacia Park. These are but a few of the many outstanding lilac collections one should view.

Each of the great collections throughout America, Canada, Russia and Europe present special insights as to how and where one should plant lilacs. Let them be your greatest teachers. Never under any circumstances crowd your lilacs together. This is a beginner's mistake in a misguided effort of getting more plants into a limited space. Forego the numbers and plant fewer plants farther apart. Crowded lilacs in time will reach straight up to the heavens with gangly limbs crying out for vengeance. Then you will have to cut and thin and eliminate some. It is then too late to transplant giant roots. Give a lilac at least ten feet of space or more in each direction (even then they are somewhat crowded). Plan and plant only for the room you have (or you may choose to buy your neighbor's lot, etc. etc. and continue your lilac planting *ad infinitum!*)

Landscaping with Lilacs in Special Situations

LILACS ON HILLSIDES, BY LAKES OR RIVERSIDE

One of the most effective uses of lilacs is to view them in clumped groups on hillsides or slopes reflecting their bloom in a tranquil lake or riverside. Well placed they create pictures never to be forgotten. Do not be misled however, when seeing such a sight, into thinking lilacs will grow if their roots are flooded, even for a brief time, by spring freshets. They will promptly die! The secret of planting lilacs by lakes or riverside is that they absolutely must be on higher ground or atop banks that are well drained at all times of the year. These mountain beauties are not bayou maids! They abhor marshy banks or wet spots. (The only lilac reputed to tolerate some bit of wetness is the species *S. josikaea* and that does not mean a marsh or standing water.) Lilacs must have dry feet, free of flooding and free from the inroads of muskrat tunnels at their roots. Generally a high spot or slope can be found or created along the water's edge where lilacs may hang their panicles over water to be reflected and mirrored in the lake.

White lilacs reflect far better than any other color. I have seen 'Ellen Willmott', the older 'Macrostaycha' and 'Lewis Maddock' with his carmine buds and pale pink blooms simply beautiful in their watery reflections. The blues and dark purples, however, are poor reflectors. Stick to the whites, they are fool-proof at the water's edge! *S. reflexa* 'Alba' is exquisite mirrored in water!

Often some of the species lilacs can be naturalized at the water or river's edge. There used to be a high bank planting of *S. julianae* seedlings made by Bernie Slavin at Durand-Eastman Park (Rochester, New York) that had self-sown and taken over a sweep of the river banks high above the water and had become a thicket of naturalized seedlings. A sight to behold in bloom and a natural landscaping masterpiece. These species lilacs rooted their arching branches and self-sowed the banks. (From one of these seedlings came the beautiful form *S. julianae* 'George Eastman'). Certainly on high banks *S.* × *chinensis*, *S.* × *persica*, the beautiful *S. microphylla*, *S. patula* or *S.*

pubescens could well be used massed in such a waterside, natural planting.

If you have a hillside flaunt it with an array of lilacs. Plan and create a vista there. On gentle, fertile slopes lilacs are a sight to behold, especially if there is the opportunity to look slightly down upon them from an opposite rise or from above. (This is marvelously done at both the Arnold Arboretum and the Royal Botanical Gardens, Hamilton). If there is a natural outcropping of granite or stone or a valley beyond, the vista is even more attractive (as at Lilac Land, Lumley Estate, Amherst, Mass. or the Thomas Chieppo Estate, East Burke, Vermont). One must diligently look for and take advantage of such aspects whenever available. Never plant your lilacs at the bottom of the hill where drainage is not the best; lilacs grow far better on the upper one-third of a hillside or slope. Avoid entirely the north and northwestern sides of slopes; they are generally too cold and receive less sun. Often the wind-chill factor and false spring-bursts damage lilac buds on the very tops of hillsides. It may be that you will have to add some background materials in the form of conifers or flowering trees, such as flowering crabs, or a wind-screen. Where you have the room a wonderful effect is obtained by planting several plants of a single kind of lilac (as at Niagara Park, Niagara Falls, Ont., Canada).

Remember that the very deep purples, which everyone loves so much, have little, if any, carrying power over distance so need an abundance of white lilacs, crabs or silver-leaved shrubs behind them. Although very lovely in themselves, they are for closer viewing and not for distant vistas. Also one must be mindful that most deep purple lilacs are later bloomers when the flowering crabs for the most part have long since passed. Russian Olive (*Elaeagnus angustifolia*) with its silvery leaves is a breath-taking background for dark blooming purple lilacs!

Generally the species lilacs, the later *S.* × *prestoniae* and many of the newer interspecific multibrids lend themselves somewhat better to creating a naturalized effect along hillsides (and watersides) than do the heavier blooming common lilac cultivars of *S. vulgaris*. A planting of lilacs *S.* × *prestoniae* 'Isabella' or 'Ursula' or a massing of tetraploid 'Lark Song', or the truly magnificent 'Agnes Smith', 'Anna Amhoff' or 'Summer White' would be most impressive reflected in a water-side planting or on a hillside or slope. The old hillside plantings of *S.* × *chinensis* 'Bicolor' at Highland Park, Rochester, is an indication of what can be expected from fine cultivars with time. Several parks like Highland Park, The Royal Botanical Gardens, The Arnold Arboretum and the Holden Arboretum are laid out on hillside slopes so one can appreciate what can be accomplished on a smaller scale elsewhere (or perhaps on a larger scale). One must project the landscape vision to what is expected of the lilac plantings at maturity, often twenty or more years later. Mostly we plan and plant for another generation to appreciate and view so it must be planned well both for the beauty of the lilac and for the wonderful fragrance it brings to all the garden.

LILACS FOR THE MINIATURE OR ROCK GARDEN

Most of us think of lilacs as rather large, sometimes unmanageable shrubs. Some of them if left to themselves are large and unkempt. In the last 30 years as hybridizers have transformed the blossom into wonderful size and colors, so they have worked wonders with the form and shape of the lilac bush, producing excellent, tidy miniature lilacs. They have custom tailored the lilac for smaller gardens, even for miniature and rock gardens!

Did you realize that there are now lilacs that rarely grow over 3–4 ft. tall? You can now have the beauty and fragrance of lilacs in your landscape but on a much smaller scale. Foremost are some of the newer species lilacs with dwarf forms, such as *S. meyeri* 'Palibin' (formerly called *S. meyeri* or often *S. palibiniana*). This dwarf grows rather slowly and is easily confined to a height of 4 ft. or less. The ancient Chinese loved it for their small, walled patio gardens. It has delightful lavender blossoms that cover the plant in spring, while throughout the rest of the year it is most attractive with deep green, glossy leaves, similar to a larger boxwood. It is an excellent selection not only for the smaller garden but especially as a neat specimen or a delightful blooming hedge or border. As a rock garden specimen it is excellent. It never looks unkempt, needs very little pruning, is excellent with spring hardy alyssum or rock plants and will occasionally produce a moderate bloom in late summer or early fall if weather conditions are ideal. Placed near an outcropping of a large rock ledge it can be most effective. Try it with the earliest white clematis spilling over rocks at its feet—a picture-card photo indeed! Plant it against an old stone wall where its deep purple buds and lavender blossoms give a splash of bright color to the meandering gray-tan wall with very late yellow daffodils planted around it!

Another of the species lilacs that grows in a dwarf form is *S. oblata dilatata*. There is an especially low form called *S. oblata dilatata* 'nana', although the regular form of *S. oblata dilatata* is not much over 5–6 ft. Very early in spring it is covered with beautiful, feathery lavender-bluish flowers having a most wonderful fragrance. In the fall it has the added attraction of deep reddish-lavender purple leaves (one of the few lilacs with autumn color). Hummingbirds seem to delight in building their small, silky nests in its branches. In winter one sees these miniature nests in the lilac woven as from nylon webbing. *S. oblata dilatata* requires very little pruning, although as is true of all lilacs, they benefit from some trimming and thinning.

The lilac named *S. patula* 'Miss Kim' is a fine selection of the species *S. patula* but is much more attractive, rather dwarf or a slower grower for several years, mostly remaining, under ordinary garden conditions, around 5–6 ft. tall. Its beautiful florets of an ice-bluish lavender exude an aromatic fragrance that is both different and oriental, bespeaking its Korean ancestry in the high mountains of that country. It can be used most successfully in smaller city gardens and especially in the rock garden. A specimen of 'Miss Kim' is outstanding in any garden as a focal point. In the fall it is an added attraction with russet, wine and red-purple leaves, another of the rather few lilacs with very attractive fall coloring.

Some few of the newer late blooming multibrids (crosses of several species) such as 'Lark Song' and some of Roger's University of New Hampshire seedlings (yet to be named) are wonderful additions that are naturally dwarf or low growing, needing little or no pruning to maintain a maximum form of 5–6 ft. These are all admirably suited for smaller gardens, rock and oriental effects.

Among the common lilac, *S. vulgaris* cultivars, are several that are dwarf or low growing and never seem to outgrow their bounds, need little pruning and are magnificently lilac-fragrant and good bloomers. They are enchanting when planted artistically along a miniature garden path, in the rock or Japanese garden. They can be made outstanding focal plants with a bit of creative planning. Among them one should consider the very old favorite, coppery-pink 'Lucie Baltet' (above all get the coppery-pink 'Clyde Lucie' a far better pink), the very deep purple 'Purple Gem', 'Purple Glory' or the more difficult to grow 'L' Oncle Tom'. Bear in mind that all the deep purple dwarfs are very slow growers and a bit more difficult to establish, not tolerating wetness one bit.

There are a host of recently introduced dwarf forms of *S. vulgaris* such as the tetraploid 'Miss Muffet'. Introduced in 1977, it rarely exceeds 3–4 ft. when grown on its own roots. (On grafted rootstock all these dwarfs grow much larger. Obtain them as rooted cuttings and not grafted plants). 'Miss Muffet', although a tetraploid dwarf grower, has a rather large thyrse of deep magenta reddish-violet opening to lavender-pink flowers. Some of the dwarf forms also have smaller florets. A number of the new dwarfs have 'Rochester' as a seed parent and are wonderfully slow growing such as 'White Elf', 'Munchkin' and 'Dwarf Princess'. The cultivar 'Mount Domogled' named by Robert Clark in 1971 is a dwarf form of *S. vulgaris* brought to this country by Edgar Anderson in 1935 and found native near Baile Herculane on the southern face of Mount Domogled in Romania. It is a dwarf form of the common lilac and quite fragrant.

The dwarf forms are all very difficult to find in nurseries which are usually 10–20 years behind the hybridizers. They are most readily obtainable from lilac specialists or the International Lilac Society special introductions. These small lilacs definitely have a place, and an important one, in our modern, smaller gardens. They are lovely combined with the many fine, dwarf conifers and rock plants now available.

Skill in choosing the proper lilac materials, knowledge of the newer introductions and observation of growth habits and forms of the various lilac cultivars will aid considerably in achieving the over-all effect one seeks to create in the smaller, miniature or rock garden. Like all lilacs the dwarf cultivars need excellent drainage, full sun, good soil and very moderate pruning. They are enhanced by combination with suitable companion plants and rock outcroppings or garden walls. It is a pity so beautiful and versatile a shrub as the dwarf or low growing lilac is neglected by so many landscapers due to lack of knowledge of these marvelous, smaller forms and how to effectively use them. They are beautiful indeed. (*Mon bon jardinier*, today the commercial garden landscapers use nursery catalogues for their plant materials and knowledge of newer plants—alas, so very, very few nurseries know the really fine and outstanding lilacs at all! I have never seen the dwarf lilacs offered as such in any nursery catalogue. Have you?)

LILACS IN THE JAPANESE AND ORIENTAL GARDEN

The land of China has given us all but 3 or 4 of the 23 or so species of lilacs. Lilacs are rooted in Chinese and Japanese soil. Why should they not be a part of every oriental garden? How could they be out of place in their own native setting? One must understand that we are speaking of the native species lilacs and not of their heady 'French and American' lilac relatives and hybrids. What could be more 'oriental' than the delicate *S. julianae* or *S. patula*, or the feathery spikes of *S. potaninii* or the captivating fragrance of *S. pubescens*—only the winds, the rains, the soil, hills and rocky outcroppings of their native China that have been their home since creation!

How magnificently the tree lilac, *S. reticulata* var. *reticulata*, blooms in the walled gardens of old Beijing as it has for centuries on the fringes of Chinese mountain forests, shedding white plumed blossoms like a blessing on China's valleys below! It is a marvelous tree for the background or as a single specimen. A variety found in Japan was formerly called *S. japonica* or *S. amurensis japonica*. I believe the Japanese form is somewhat better shaped—a bit rounder. Among the other species that can skillfully be worked into a real oriental garden are the beautiful semi-weeping *S. reflexa* and the showy *S. komarowii*. Both are background shrubs for such gardens as they eventually become too large for a specimen planting. For a Japanese garden one must choose both the plant and its exact location with discretion. Generally the Japanese garden is one of considerable shade and screening, whereas all lilacs demand reasonable amounts of sunshine to perform their best. One or two of the newer very feathery hybrids can often be very proper in such landscaping. Mind you, only a very few! (Might I suggest the very delicate hybrids 'Spellbinder' or 'Sunrise'.) For a distant background, space permitting, what could be more exotic than a fine specimen of *S. pekinensis* 'Pendula' or at a crossing of paths the very rare *S. pinnatifolia*? (If one could only find it?) Both are real lilac treasures!

LILACS IN THE SUBURBAN GARDEN AND COUNTRY ESTATE

If your land is close to an acre or more, it is in a special category where you can do marvelous things with special lilac plantings. (If you do not have a large garden or this amount of land, read this chapter for you may become an expert and so be asked for advice on planting a larger lilac garden or collection.) Suburban gardens and estate property differ from other homesites in that they are too large to be called a city lot or a 'yard' and too beautifully landscaped to be simply dismissed as a 'farm'. They are in a classification all their own that requires creating a larger vista of beauty, offers more opportunities for massed plantings that provide special effects and the challenge of using a wider variety of planting materials. They enable one to develop areas of naturalized landscaping with a beauty that staggers the mind and dazzles the eye resulting from their spaciousness and boldness. Often larger gardens and estates may have lakes, ponds, hillsides or beautiful valleys. Lilacs, especially the grand ones, become the Princelings, Countessae, Duchesse and Ladies of the large estate gardens and have a nobility and grandeur of proper garden royalty and place. In large gardens and estates the lilacs' 'proper place' and how to use them most effectively demand serious consideration. Here lilacs have many uses—as single specimens, in massed plantings, reflected in watersides, as separating hedges, as boundary lines or as a walk of great beauty. Here, too, they can be properly attended by conifers, flowering trees and hosts of other wonderful landscaping materials. Yet the lilacs will reign supreme.

As always they need good drainage, sun, soil and care and they will continue to outperform each previous spring with beauty and fragrance. Lilacs are planted for both close-up beauty and fragrance as well as for creating more distant vistas of color. For close viewing use the larger-flowered kinds, especially some of the newest cultivars that are so striking in their colors and hues. For vistas use 3 to 5 of the same cultivar or color massed as a fulcrum of beauty. An old friend of mine who loves the new large floret and deep colored lilacs which are not always as fragrant as some of the older kinds has solved this problem by planting an occasional very fragrant older lilac in the background to fill her garden with their wonderful scent.

Some *prima donnas* or *gloriosos* of the lilac world are admirably suited for close-up inspection or as focal shrubs. Consider a stately 'Mareschal Foch' standing sentry by a garden path in pale pink epaulettes with deeper carmine chevrons or an 'Emile Lemoine' in similar majesty! Equally outstanding is the ballerina-pink bloom of 'Lucie Baltet' in coppery-pink leotards (l' enfant magnifique)! Do not overlook the Dutch sport so aptly named 'Sensation' with its deep purple florets edged in white Dutch lace! It must be seen to be appreciated! The rayed and starred pale blue of 'Pat Pesata' is both unique and beautiful as is the pale blue of 'Dwight D. Eisenhower'. The pristine whites of such cultivars as 'Carley', 'Flora' or 'Slater's Elegance' or the abundant bloom of 'Aloise' or the double 'Souv. d' Alice Harding', 'St. Joan' or the incomparable beauty of 'Rochester' (if you can wait the many years it requires to reach maturity)—all and many more are lilacs of grandeur for the garden. They are truly outstanding as single specimens for close viewing! In the deep red-purples use as specimens 'Sarah Sands', 'Anne Shiach', 'Arch McKean', or 'Agincourt Beauty'. No large garden can be considered complete without some of these dark-tressed lilacs. Elsewhere we have listed some of the finest by color—all are equally beautiful in their splendor in either single or double blossoms (among the deep purples the single lilacs are the better choice if you prefer large flowers and deep colors).

A GARDEN LILAC WALK

Nothing is more pleasing than to be able to come upon rare specimens of lilacs along a grassy path that winds and opens vistas of beauty. The Arnold Arboretum outside of Boston has for many years had a splendid 'Lilac Walk' of many cultivars and species planted along the roadway and adjacent to a hillside of lilacs. It makes for easy viewing in bloomtime by thousands who come to see the lilacs. Rutgers University has its 'Alice Harding Lilac Walk'. Ewing Park in Des Moines, Iowa and many others have outstanding walks where one can see both the massed effect and the close-up character of individual lilacs. Among the finest private walks are those at the Albert Lumley Estate, Amherst, Mass. and the new plantings at the Thomas Chieppo Estate in East Burke, Vermont. These wind through beautifully natural landscaped gardens, blending into plantings of near woodlands, mountain views or amid rock outcroppings with wonderful planting that urge one on. They are not unduly large but exceedingly well done. The new plantings at the Holden Arboretum are likewise a wonder of excellent planning, careful selection of some of the finest cultivars and ease in viewing. Throughout this country and Canada as well as in Russia and Europe, in arboreta, parks and private collections there are Lilac Walks of great beauty where one can see some of the finest cultivars now available.

In former days Lilac Walks were planted along a winding path, rather close together and for some distance without interplanting of other shrubs or trees. If you prefer your lilacs all together in long walks by all means have them so. They are most beautiful and inspiring when in bloom. The massed continuity of beauty of the different cultivars overwhelms you. But what of the summertime and fall? They are simple green shrubs quickly passed over.

If, however, you feel that your Lilac Walk be 'a la moderne' have your lilacs interplanted with shrubs, flowering trees and conifers for a constant succession of interest in bloom and fruit throughout the year. To achieve this most pleasing effect lilacs need to be grouped in 3, 5 or 7 plants together at vantage points along the walk. Place them where they tempt the visitor to continue on to discover their beauty with new combinations and cultivars along the way. You should place lilacs skillfully in small groupings according to their season of bloom. A group of early blooming lilacs can be separated by a few choice conifers from very late blooming ones, which in turn can be separated by some other flowering trees or shrubs from the midseason kinds. Here and there place groupings of select species on either side. On occasion plant a single outstanding specimen lilac at a focal turn—like 'Sensation' or 'St. Joan' with a garden bench for your guests to rest and view that particular lilac. Interspersed among your many lilac plantings should be massed beds of flowering crabs, conifers, Davidia (if you are so fortunate as to have the right weather conditions and shade), Magnolias (these are wonderful plants), small beds of the newer Aesculus pavia, Viburnum or even beds of Paeonia and Hemerocallis. (See the chapter on Companion Plants for Lilacs). As a background use good conifers; they add much to lilac blooms. With careful choice of cultivars and species one can extend the length of bloom of a good Lilac Walk for several weeks. It is not easy to plan but is well worth the effort. Remember the 'French Belles' will always attract their own crowds when in bloom—traditional walk or moderne, be it long or short—above all do have a Lilac Walk!

LILACS BY THE WOODLAND BORDERS

Often the landscape tie between lawns and gardens with a neighboring woodland is not an easily created transition. Lilacs can assist if they are placed advantageously between the garden and the naturalized forest. The species lilacs especially are the ideal wood's edge planting providing they receive adequate sun. In their native China, many of the species lilacs are precisely shrubs of the forest border where they often form small thickets. *S. vulgaris* in its native Balkan Mountains habitat also is at home in open woodland spaces, among stony outcroppings and rocky areas. In a larger garden or park they can play a similar role. Plant the rather tall, tree-like, Early Hybrids in small clumps of threes, all of one cultivar some 20 or 30 ft. from the woodland's edge. Combine them with intervals of flowering dogwoods or some of the better flowering crabs and you will have a wonderful, natural looking buffer of bloom between the heavy forest and its surrounding areas. One does not look for massive continuous bloom in such cases but for 'pockets of bloom' along the landscape horizon.

White birch trunks with pale pink or lavender lilacs are lovely, indeed! Use lavender Early Hybrids, *S.* × *hyacinthiflora*, like 'Louvois', 'Lamartine' or 'Lewis Maddock' backed by dogwoods and you will have sheer elegance. For this woodsy effect use Early Hybrids and not the heavier flowering *S. vulgaris* cultivars which are too overpowering with their massive bloom. Try some of the Skinner Hybrids or use the species, *S. oblata* var. *dilatata* in pale lavender, feathery drifts. Some of the species like *S. sweginzowii, S. komarowii, S. julianae, S. pubescens* and many of the fine *S.* × *chinensis* hybrids such as 'Bicolor' are excellent choices. Do not crowd them together but leave spaces for open small meadows in which to naturalize huge drifts of spring bulbs, especially the late blooming daffodils and narcissi (for the summer interplant these open spaces with wild flowers, especially daisies and drifts of hardy asters). If you plant some of the *S. oblata* var. *dilatata* hybrids not only will your spring woodland be ecstatically perfumed but in autumn these lilacs will give a display of deep wine and purple foliage. Another fine woodside lilac is *S. patula* with its aromatic fragrance and pale mauve autumn foliage. You are fortunate, indeed, if you have a woodland surrounding your Lilac Walk or gardens. Add an occasional small tree lilac such as *S. reticulata* var. *reticulata*, or a small trio of them if space allows. Many of the late blooming hybrids such as the *S.* × *prestoniae* or the newer multibrids 'Springtime' or 'Summer Song' are excellent when used in this fashion. They will add beauty to your landscaping and delight to your heart! (*Mon ami*, do not overdo the buffer area with lilacs, they do not add anything but green shrubbery the rest of the year—and there are other beautiful shrubs as well that could be planted among them.)

USING LILACS AS SMALL TREES IN THE GARDEN

Most people do not realize that certain lilacs make excellent 'small trees' if trained and pruned for that purpose. There are, of course, the real tree lilacs, *S. reticulata* and *S. pekinensis*, which bloom in late June or early July, but these can become somewhat large for the smaller garden. Instead plant one of the Early Hybrids such as *S. oblata* 'Giraldii' which are more apt to make excellent small trees if trained to 2 or 3 trunks. They are more rangy and taller growing than the *S. oblata* var. *dilatata* hybrids, and range in color from pinks to lavenders with few whites. They do not sucker so readily.

Prune out all the lower and weak branches each year and soon you will have a fine spreading tree for the patio or garden. True, the blossoms will not be at eye level and will be considerably smaller due to minimal pruning but you will have lilacs, their wonderful fragrance and an interesting tree. An occasional specimen treated this way can add charm to your plantings. I have seen such 'lilac trees' as a patio focal point for shade, underplanted with a circle of ferns and Impatiens surrounded by a circular brick mosaic—a truly lovely bit of landscaping!

Early Hybrids do make excellent small patio trees. With age their trunks assume the typical twist so characteristic of *S. vulgaris* and their somewhat shaggy bark is also most attractive. Given a little care, even an occasional borer seems to do little harm if good culture and ordinary pest control are practiced. Some of the taller *S. vulgaris* cultivars also do well treated in this manner. Try 'Sarah Sands', 'Mme. Antonine Buchner', 'Mrs. Trapman' or the unique 'Sensation' and 'Silver King' and you will be delighted. Should you have the room, plant three of these small 'trees' together (20 ft. apart)—prune high and plant a magnificent bed of some of the newest *Hosta* cultivars in their shade. Do not overdo their use in any given area. Lilacs are really for viewing comfortably and for large spikes of exotic bloom and fragrance!

USING LILACS FOR HEDGES AND SCREENS

Lilacs have been used as screens, hedges and backgrounds since they were first planted in gardens. (Sometimes a shoddy way to treat so lovely and royal a shrub!) Their height and density of branches admirably suit them for such purposes. We have seen *S. vulgaris* (mostly in the older lavender or white forms) planted in stately rows between large city lots or on back property lines to assure privacy, or used to hide unsightly barns and buildings—the utilitarian side of the lilacs.

There is, also, an aesthetic use of lilac hedges and screens for their beauty in carrying the eye through long vistas to a garden focal point, to accent a landscape design, or to carry the observer around a special contour to seek what may lie beyond. Most often one can combine both the utilitarian and the aesthetic when using lilacs.

No longer must we depend on the old *Syringa vulgaris* or *Syringa villosa*, for today we have new and excellent materials among the cultivars and species and many new hybrids. Many of the lesser known species make excellent, smaller hedges and screens, such as, *S. microphylla, S. komarowii, S. josikaea* and the newer *S. × prestoniae* hybrids and the multibrids. Large parks and estates must dare to 'create' new uses by boldly incorporating these lovely plants in their landscape themes. Some of the older *S. × chinensis* hybrids have been used with excellent results on the hillsides as a screen at Highland Park, Rochester, New York, while *S. × persica* in a long row is magnificent at The Royal Botanical Gardens in Hamilton. Envision a winding background hedge of the lovely new cultivar 'Agnes Smith' or a screen of a dozen plants of *S. julianae* 'Hers' as a spreading background to smaller plantings of flowers or spring bulbs! Far more use should be made of the best of the *S. × prestoniae* as screens and taller hedges. They are strong and rugged shrubs. Given them room to develop, good ground and a side dressing of compost and fertilizer and they will repay you with a most striking display of bloom.

If you have the room, dare to be an innovator in the use of lilacs. You will never be disappointed. A well planned and planted lilac hedge or screen is a landscape of real beauty. (*Bon jardinier,* one must plant thoughtfully and work patiently to create a work of art—be it on canvas or in the landscape!)

To see lilacs excellently planted both in smaller gardens and on large estates one should visit the Shelburne Museum Estate at Burlington, Vermont, at lilactime to see how many ways lilacs can be used in superb plantings. View, also, the fine old plantings of lilacs at Woodstock, Vermont, or at Cooperstown, N.Y., or at Portsmouth, New Hampshire—these are all grand plantings bequeathed from generation to generation and should be cherished as an historic treasure! (*Mon ami,* these grand plantings should be preserved by law).

A formal clipped hedge of *S. × chinensis.* (Photos C. Holetich, R.B.G.)

Lilacs used as a clipped hedge. At the Royal Botanical gardens, Hamilton, Ontario, Canada, lilacs are displayed as 'clipped hedges' with remarkable success, but it does require some work.

The *S.* × *chinensis* forms a hedge of rare beauty to screen out unwanted areas from view. Highland Park, Rochester, N.Y. *S.* × *chinensis,* where it has room to develop its natural form, is one of the finest of screening shrubs. Leave it unpruned.

How to Design or Remodel a Major Arboretum Lilac Collection

Hopefully in the years ahead several of our large arboreta and parks will be planning and designing for a large collection of lilacs. There is a great need for good landscaping design. During 1979–80 at the Holden Arboretum, Mentor, Ohio, under the far-seeing direction of R. Henry Norweb, Jr., a whole new vision of lilacs in a new arboretum design has been accomplished with astounding, wonderful results—a tribute to the Director and his Staff. I use it as an example of all that is good in large arboreta planning for a lilac collection. Bear in mind that wherever there is a fine collection of lilacs thousands of people will come annually to see them in bloom. A good public collection must be designed with this in mind and must seek to keep its lilacs up-to-date not merely remnants of the nostalgic past.

The complete re-designing and replanting of the Holden Arboretum Lilac Collection was not merely a progressive step of a single arboretum, but provides a useful pattern of interest to any other arboretum, large park (or large private collection) planning a lilac display. From its large collection of lilacs, most of which were 40 or more years old, the new design envisioned a unique kind of Lilac Walk with approximately 125 of the finest lilacs from both the old and the new. Since many of the older specimens were among lilacs to be retained a large transplanting and holding (for several months) operation had to be undertaken, necessitating considerable labor and expense.

In designing an arboretum lilac collection one of the very first projects is to establish parameters of financial expenditures for the entire program. Since the Holden design was envisioned as a new type of Lilac Walk it included many other species of trees and shrubs. Skillfully designed by an outstanding landscape architect (of proven experience and creativity) the entire Walk is laid out on 7 acres. First consideration in design must be given to the following: the natural boundaries, topography, soils, microclimates, existing plantings and the relationship with other areas adjacent to the lilac plantings. These aspects were all analyzed by the architect using systematic sketch plans over existing conditions surveys. All existing features were mapped in relationship to future access requirements. Viewer circulation must be considered together with the developmental growth of plant materials, special views, growing conditions, enframement and generalized masses of the proposed plantings. High and low tree forms and medium and low masses were considered in their relationship to wooded and lawn areas.

As a demonstration garden, as well as a Lilac Walk and collection, there were certain special requirements. First, it must entice visitors to enter; it must provide or suggest, for people concerned about the plantings in their own yards or estates, possible solutions to their problems of landscaping. Secondly it must be attractive at all seasons, especially in the spring and early summer when everyone is aware of growing plants and flowers. Evergreens should be included for winter interest and background for floral displays, as well as other families which are spectacular in fruit or fall foliage. Because of its limited size only the choicest species and cultivars should be displayed. (A working collection elsewhere, should carry the more complete lilac inventory.) Lastly, it should allow for viewing of plant groupings arranged in the most pleasing combination of size, texture and color, not just as specimens, while still permitting close inspection of individual plants for identification and study.

The soil at Holden was found to be a shallow, heavy-clay with shale not too far below the clay. This is a real problem for most plants, but especially for lilacs. To overcome the effect of poor drainage raised planting beds were constructed. Mounds which in cross-section consisted of a 3 in. layer of sandy gravel, 9–12 in. of topsoil, 3 in. of well-rotted manure plus a bark mulch were built.

Criteria for lilac selection included mature height of plant, texture of foliage, color of bloom, hardiness, phenological aspect (bloom date, fall color, if any, etc.) and the several types (species, early, mid or late seasons blooming and hybrids). Special consideration was given to the number of lilacs included, in this case 125.

Landscape design consideration must include circulation criteria (width and gradient of drives, walks and paths), relation of turf panels to planting beds, the possible inclusion of water (pools and/or swales), filler plants among the lilacs, fall and winter effect. Lilacs and permanent plantings were spaced for mature size. Filler plants are expendable and will be removed upon crowding the lilacs.

What a magnificent design it has turned out to be! Each year the plantings grow and provide greater depth to the landscaper's vision and planning. It is this kind of mature and thoughtful design that creates great gardens, not only for the present but that continue on into the future. The combination of trees and other plants adds tremendously to the total effect and interest of the lilac collection. The Walk entices one on to explore the many wonders it provides. This is landscaping at its finest! Many, if not most, of the elements of design mentioned could be reproduced in smaller gardens and especially on larger estates. Many private lilac collections number 300–400 plants—but are they skillfully used in the total landscape design?

The above Landscaping Design for Holden Arboretum resume is presented as the work of C. L. Knight, Landscape Architect, who at Holden designed one of America's latest lilac collections to be a thing of beauty for generations to come and to take its place with other excellently designed lilac collections in the United States and Canada, as, The Arnold Arboretum, The Royal Botanical Gardens at Hamilton, Highland Park at Rochester, New York, Ewing Park, Des Moines, Iowa, the Niagara Parks Lilac Collection, Niagara, Canada and several others.

One should visit these carefully-planned lilac collections and note well their design and attractions. Many are unique in several aspects; all are beautiful and appealing. From their expert design the home-owner and gardener can learn much of landscape art and placing lilacs correctly. Indeed, the observer may well copy a bit or piece from here or there to enhance his personal living space.

A WORD ON LILACS IN THE WINTER LANDSCAPE

Winter is a learning time in the lilac garden for all who care to venture out and discover the lessons taught by plants and shrubs. One should go into the lilac garden in winter to note the diversity of species buds, their bark, especially the rich cherry brown of the Tree Lilac, *S. reticulata*, see the hanging seed pods each unique according to their species. Learn to identify them from their topmost buds, noting how the white flowered lilacs have pale green buds whereas the darker colored kind have deeper purplish ones. Winter too, when leaves have fallen, is the best time to evaluate and examine your lilacs to review their last year's growth. Assess both shaping (pruning) strategies and need for nourishment. Fat, thick growth tells one all is well; thin spindly growth indicates need for pruning and more food.

Be kind to the winter birds and place your feeders on the heaviest lilac branches. Perchance they will return there to nest and warble songs mid the lilac blooms of May. Look also to what insect pest or rodents feast unknown to you upon your lilacs. Scale and borer holes give testimony to your summertime negligence in spraying and pruning. The winter garden is, indeed, a lesson, a lecture and a meditation. Frequent its winter halls of learning often and long!

Winter is a time for marking, with bright tags, lilac root suckers that should be given to friends or used to renew new plants for your own garden. It is perhaps the best of times to mark old lilacs for removal, to plan new beds and see the heavy framework of both trees and shrubs. It is the time for careful assessment outdoors in order to plan the work to be done on paper at the fireside for spring renewal of beds, walks and borders. It is a time to study new cultivars and new ways of using your lilacs to full effect. Winter is a time of wonderful anticipation of the new blooms soon to come with spring!

A word on lilacs in the winter landscape. From their winter nests learn all the birds that in your lilacs find rest. See how they build and tie together mud, twigs and feather.

PLATE 65

More of the **'Grand French Lilacs'** of Lemoine et Fil. No other hybridizer to date has produced so many outstanding lilacs as the family of Lemoine. (Photos by C. Holetich, R.B.G. Hamilton, Canada)

Syringa vulgaris
'Crepuscule'
Lemoine-France-1928

R.B.G. - 1974

Syringa vulgaris
'Monge'
Lemoine-France-1913

R.B.G. - 1974

Syringa vulgaris
'Prodige'
Lemoine-France-1928

R.B.G. - 1974

Syringa vulgaris
'De Mirabel'
Lemoine-France-1903

R.B.G. 1977

Syringa vulgaris
'Archeveque'
France - 1923

R.B.G. 1977

Syringa vulgaris
'President Viger'
Lemoine-France-1900

R.B.G. - 1974

PLATE 66

S. vulgaris **'General Sherman'** a pale, lavender-pearled gem of the seedlings planted by John Dunbar at Highland Park. It, like 'General John Pershing' (top right), was a seedling of the old 'Marylensis Pallida', the 'Marly Flieder' that a century later produced such excellent cultivars.

'General John Pershing'

'General Sherman'

The 'famous' Dunbar Seedlings' still grace the hillside where he planted them a half century ago, from which one of America's famous lilac collections was to grow. From these seedlings Mr. Dunbar selected a dozen or more for naming. Some few still are remarkable garden lilacs as 'General Sherman', 'Joan Dunbar' and his then famous blue lilac, 'President Lincoln'.

. . . the two Generals pictured here are perhaps his best!

PLATE 67

'Fred Payne'

'Nancy Frick'

Mark Eaton examining lilacs.

'Priscilla'

'Professor E. H. Wilson'

PLATE 68

The Havemeyer and the Havemeyer-Eaton Lilacs are amon[g] some of the finest single named lilacs available. With large florets and excellent colors they should be in every good collection. Other fine Havemeyer lilacs are 'Mrs. John Davi[s]', 'Carley' and 'True Blue'.

'Dawn' (S-III, 1954)

'White Swan' (S-I, 1943)

'Lady Lindsay' (S-VI, 1945). One of the reddest lilacs in bud with recurved petals.

'Mrs. Watson Webb' (S-VI, 1954). One of his finest.

'Heather' (S-I, 1954)

'Romance' (S-V, 1954)

PLATE 69

The hybridizing genius of Isabella Preston gave us the Prestonian Hybrids (*S. villosa* × *S. reflexa*). They are large shrubs, very similar in color. Many of these fine hybrids should be used in continued multibrid hybridization.

'Jessica' (S-II, 1928)

'Desdemona' (S-III, 1927)

'Coral' (S-V, 1937)

'Octavia' (S-V, 1928)

'Freedom' (S-V, 1928)

'Calpurnia' (S-VI, 1934)

PLATE 70

Skinner's beautiful *S.* × *hyacinthiflora* 'Maiden's Blush', like most lilacs, shows different colors of pink under soil and climate changes. Upper picture shows 'Maiden's Blush' in lighter soil and warmer weather as a delicate, pale pink devoid of lavender tones. Lower picture shows it under heavier soils and in colder weather containing considerable lavender. Under *S. oblata* many of Skinner's fine hybrids are shown. (Chapter 4)

PLATE 71

'Saint Joan' (Blacklock 1953) is one of several excellent introductions from Blacklock—exquisite Canadian lilacs.

SOME FINE LILACS FROM SEVERAL BREEDERS

'White Lace' (Rankin) showing the delicate thryses,
very heavy bloomer.

'White Lace' (Rankin 1960) in bush form. Its autumn leaves
are bright gold.

'Amor' (Steffin 1948) a fine magenta-pink comes from this
German lilac fancier and is one of several from Europe in
more recent years.

'Prince of Wales' (Dougall 1889). Several fine lilacs, very difficult to find now, came from this early Canadian nurseryman.

PLATE 72

'Primrose' the only pale yellow or cream lilac, was a mutation discovered by D. E. Maarse in the lilac forcing houses in Aalsmeer, The Netherlands. Introduced in 1949 it is still difficult to obtain from nurseries. Plant it next to a pure white lilac to fully appreciate the pale creamy-yellow color. There are a number of forms, some a deeper yellow than others. Two of the best are the plants growing at Holden Arboretum and Lilacland, Pelham, Mass. In chapter 2 under Color VII is pictured the rare 'Sensation' (Maarse 1938) another rare chimera.

'Burgomeester Voller' (Maarse 1948)

'Flora' an excellent white introduced by Maarse in 1953. (Some call it 'Flora 1953')

'Excellent' (Maarse 1939). The pod parent of 'Flora'.

PLATE 73

'*Krasavitsa Moskvy*', one of Kolesnikov's finest lilacs, introduced in 1963. It is, indeed, a 'Queen' among lilacs, a double white with pale lavender tinted buds. Like his excellent 'Pamiat o.S.M. Kirove' it is a seedling of 'Belle de Nancy' × 'I. V. Mitchurin' ('Pamiat o.m. Kirove' and the outstanding 'Znamya Lenina' are pictured in Chapter 2.) 'Krasavitsa Moskvy' is an extremely fine and heavy bloomer and is among the best in the double white lilacs available. *Mon ami et amie*—you must search out and find one for your garden!

The lavender 'Sholokhov' (Kolesnikov, 1963, S-IV) is one of several fine single lilacs introduced in recent years from the U.S.S.R.

'Nadezhda' (Kolesnikov, 1963 D-III) is reminiscent of the fine doubles of Lemoine.

PLATE 74

NEWER LILACS FROM THE U.S.S.R. AND POLAND

In the years of the 1950s through to 1963 several named cultivars appeared from the work of lilac breeders in the U.S.S.R. and in Poland. Undoubtedly much of their work is unknown beyond the U.S.S.R. It appears that lilac breeding for better cultivars there is progressing and, hopefully, the best will find its way to other countries.

Pictures, alone, cannot give the full scope of any one hybridizer's efforts but they represent progress made and the areas of hybridizing concerns.

The finest collection of these lilacs can be found at the Royal Botanical Gardens, Hamilton, Canada and the younger collections at the National Arboretum, Washington, D.C., and the collection at Falconskeape, Medina, Ohio.

'Jubileinaya' (I. Shtan'ko, N. Mikhailov, 1956, S-II, U.S.S.R.)

'Taras Bul'ba' (Rubtsov-Zhogoleva-Lyapunova)

'Kosmos' (I. Shtan'ko, N. Mikhailov, 1956, S-II) seedling of 'Mrs. Edward Harding'.

'Konstanty Karpow' (Karpow-Lipski) from Poland

PLATE 75

LILAC HYBRIDIZERS

etty Stone

Leonard Slater

Dr. Donald Egolf

Walter Oakes

Herbert Alexander

Fred Lape

Dr. Joel Margaretten

William Utley

PLATE 76

THE LILACS OF KENNEBUNK, MAINE

'Eleanore Berdeen' (S-III, 1979)

Ken Berdeen has been breeding for finer lilacs for the past 30 years. His 'Lee Jewett Walker', probably one of the finest light true pink lilacs, and 'Stephanie Rowe' (both shown in Chapter 2 under 'pink lilacs') are evidence of his successes.

Many of the Berdeen introductions are very difficult to obtain as they are not widely propagated but they are well worth the effort to have in your garden. Berdeen was a remarkable man with seedling lilacs of high quality and beauty.

'Diannah Abbott' (S-II, 1965)

'President John F. Kennedy'

'Father Patrick McCabe'

'Olive Mae Cummings' 1979

PLATE 77

LILAC BREEDING AT THE ROYAL BOTANICAL GARDENS, HAMILTON

Although new the program at R.B.G. has produced excellent results. Pringle hybridized a number of unique crosses of species; Brown and Pearson have continued new programs.

Sdg. 7525-17 (Brown 1975) 'Rochester' $\times$ 'Primrose'. Magnificent!

'Big Blue' (Brown 1975). Very fine S. II.

Sdg. 75116-16 (Brown 1975)

S. meyeri 'Palibin' $\times$ *S. microphylla* 'Superba' (Pearson 1986). Excellent bloomer!

New hybrid, *S. villosa* $\times$ *S.* $\times$ *henryi* (Pearson 1986)

PLATE 78

Richard Fenicchia, Highland Park, Rochester, N.Y. has produced some of the finest lilacs yet to be named. His 'Dwight D. Eisenhower' and several named cultivars are outstanding. Among his finest is the pink-magenta Seedling #1825—soon to be named—that ranks among the best of lilacs in this color, a hybridizer's dream! Seedling 'Rochester Strain' #1825 (Fenicchia, S-V, 1987)

PLATE 79

By crossing 'Rochester' with select *S. vulgaris* cultivars Fenicchia created a milestone marking new heights in hybridizing lilacs equal to Lemoine's work to create double flowering lilacs. The new 'multipetaled lilacs' are the most important wave of the future for outstanding cultivars. At the National Arboretum and at Falconskeape they are already being crossed with *S. oblata* for superior *S. × hyacinthiflora* cultivars.

ne of Fenicchia's outstanding whites Seedling #1, yet to be med growing at Slavin Park.

Richard Fenicchia examining some of his Rochester Strain hybrids.

A deep purple S-VII, Sdg. #185, in the planting at Slavin Park.

Fenichia's pink-magenta S-V Seedling #1820 growing in the plantings at Highland Park.

PLATE 80

The University of New Hampshire hybridizers have brought back new plants from Korea, *S. patula* 'Miss Kim' (Meader), and worked extensively to create finer hybrids of late blooming lilacs (Yaeger and Rogers). Their work, though limited, has been of highest quality. Exciting new hybrids continue to be introduced. Roger's work with developing double forms is most promising. Dr. Rogers now heads the lilac work with the excellent late blooming hybrids—mostly *S.* × *josiflexa*.

The fine hybrid 'Agnes Smith' (Rogers, 1970) 'Jessie Hepler' (Rogers 1981) is a new, very fine deep lavender-purple.

Dr. Owen M. Rogers

Two of Yaeger's introductions: left, *S.* × *prestoniae* 'James Macfarlane' (Yaeger 1959), a fine pink; right, *S.* × *prestoniae* 'Nellie Bean' an excellent deep purple (Yaeger 1961).

The Best of the Species Lilacs as Garden and Landscape Shrubs

We have already discussed in the previous chapters the wonderful merits of *S. vulgaris*, the Common Lilac, and its hybrids. They are exceptional garden plants and some cultivars of *S. vulgaris* should be in every garden. For the most part they are unequaled in appearance. It is from this species that the lilac has gained its reputation and renown. Among the Chinese and Japanese cousins and *S. josikaea* from Central Europe are many fine garden plants just as they come from the wild. Some have been considerably enhanced by hybridization while a few are of little or no garden value. In presenting this evaluation of the species as garden plants we have in mind gardens that have enough room to grow one or several of them. If one can only be limited to a single lilac or two, then I would strongly recommended it be one of the finer cultivars of *S. vulgaris*. The very largest arboreta and the botanical gardens should have space enough to carry a good collection of all the species, good or indifferent.

SUBGENUS SYRINGA

Series *Pinnatifoliae*
S. pinnatifolia—an interesting shrub but only for the largest gardens and arboreta. It is rarely seen today even in botanical collections.

Series *Pubescentes* (The little-leaved lilacs)
S. julianae—one of the finest species, excellent for the garden but needs room to develop.
S. meyeri—the cultivar 'Palibin' is outstanding, small and dwarf, excellent.
S. microphylla—the cultivar 'Superba' is probably more showy than the species, excellent for the larger garden, a very heavy bloomer. *S. julianae* is much better.
S. patula—a very delicate, refined species excellent in every way—the cultivar 'Miss Kim' is outstanding.
S. potaninii—for the larger garden only, good cerise buds and intermittent bloom but the wood is too brittle to make it an excellent garden shrub.
S. pubescens—a truly fine lilac for the garden although it needs some width to show its full beauty—very good.

Series *Syringa*
S. laciniata—a fine lilac for the larger garden but its hybrids are much better.
S. oblata—among its varietal forms *S. oblata* var. *dilatata* is the best; it is a lower grower than most of the others. One of the first lilacs to bloom. Wonderful mauve-purple foliage in the autumn. Its hybrids with *S. vulgaris* are among some of the finest lilac cultivars. *S. oblata* var. *alba* 'Frank Meyer' is an outstanding white form grown at the U.S. National Arboretum, Washington, D.C.
S. vulgaris (the Common or French lilacs)—the finest among the species. There are nearly 2,000 named cultivars of all colors and hues. It should be represented in every garden.
S. × chinensis—excellent hybrids for the larger garden as a specimen or for the background. The cultivar *S. × chinensis* 'Bicolor' is outstanding.
S. × hyacinthiflora—all lilacs from the crosses *S. oblata* × *S. vulgaris* and *S. vulgaris* × *S. oblata* are called 'hyacinthiflora'. They are fine garden shrubs blooming a bit earlier than the common lilac and somewhat taller growing.
S. × persica—a very fine hybrid for the larger garden. Most excellent as a background shrub and for a taller hedge.

Series *Villosae* (the large-leaved, late blooming lilacs)
S. emodi—for the largest collections and arboreta only—not for the home garden.
S. josikaea—a fine, deep green-leaved lilac good for the larger garden.
S. komarowii—a fine species for the garden large or small—excellent.
S. reflexa—an excellent species with its showy, drooping blossoms—needs room to show its excellent form. A truly unique lilac. Some of its hybrids are more showy.
S. sweginzowii—slender, tall grower, good accent shrub, very fine. Its hybrid *S. sweginzowii* 'Albida' is better.

S. tigerstedtii—for the largest collections and arboreta and for the larger home garden. Very fine.

S. tomentella—a good plant for the larger gardens, estates and arboreta, not for the home garden.

S. villosa—for the larger gardens only; for the home garden use its hybrids the *S.* × *prestoniae* which are far superior; leave the species for arboreta and botanical gardens (hybridizers).

S. wolfii—a fine plant for the larger garden but its hybrids are far superior. The variety *hirsuta* is very fine.

S. yunnanensis—only for the largest species collections and for hybridizers, a poor plant all around for the home garden.

The late-blooming hybrids

S. × *henryi* (*S. josikaea* × *S. villosa*), good to very good for the larger collections.

S. × *josiflexa* (*S. josikaea* × *S. reflexa*) very good, need room, a fine hybrid.

S. × *nanceiana* (*S.* × *henryi* × *S. sweginzowii*) good to very good for the larger garden.

S. × *prestoniae* (*S. villosa* × *S. reflexa*) or (*S. reflexa* × *S. villosa*) some selected cultivars are exceptionally fine and superior to both parents. They are rather large growers and need some room to show their beauty. The cultivars 'Isabella' and 'Ursula' are among the finest. For all gardens, even the smallest should find room for at least one cultivar. 'Miss Canada' is outstanding.

S. × *swegiflexa* (*S. reflexa* × *S. sweginzowii*)—very good where one has room.

S. × *tribrida* ((*S. sweginzowii* × *S. tomentella*) × *S. komarowii*) very fine for larger gardens, especially fine hybrid 'Lark Song' excellent for all gardens.

((*S. sweginzoeii* × *S. tomentella*) × *S. wolfii*) excellent for all gardens.

((*S. yunannensis* × *S. tomentella*) × *S. komarowii*)—the cultivar 'Dancing Druid' is a very heavy bloomer for larger gardens, very good.

S. × *quatrobrida* ((*S. sweginzowii* × *S. tomentella*) × (*S. komarowii* × *S. wolfii*)) very fine for all gardens in select cultivars.

Interseries hybrids

S. × *diversifolia* (*S. pinnatifolia* × *S. oblata*) good for the larger garden, impossible to obtain.

SUBGENUS LIGUSTRINA

S. pekinensis (*beijinensis*)—a larger tree, fine for the largest gardens, arboreta and botanical gardens, not for the home gardens—too large.

S. reticulata var. *reticulata*—the finest of the tree lilacs makes a small upright tree.

var. *amurensis*—small, more rounded tree, almost identical to var. *reticulata* which is the better form for the home garden. Both are very fine.

CHAPTER SIX

Companion Plants to Lilacs

Lilacs possess a beauty both outstanding and unique! The masses of color, bloom and their captivating fragrance are one of the focal points of Springtime wherever they can be grown. For this reason they are ideal 'focal' plants on their own. However, like a diamond in an exquisite setting they are enhanced by many varieties of 'companion plants'. (*Mon amie* and *ami*, like true garden aristocracy they are made even more forceful and beautiful by those plants that attend them.) Some plants are particularly suited either by their form, background color, their bloom or compatibility and harmony to be grown together with lilacs. We shall consider only a few of the most outstanding that form works of landscape artistry when grown together with lilacs. You may have your own special companions to your lilacs—by all means continue to grow them together as you consider some of the combinations others have used most successfully.

Lilacs Squired by the Magnificent Conifers

Among nature's most beautiful trees one must certainly number the conifers—the pines, spruces, firs, cedars, chamaecyparis, taxus and a host of others. Conifers are splendid additions to any garden large or small.

In large gardens the mature specimens rise like pillars into the storm-tossed skies, bold sentries of the landscape keeping guard and watchful eye over all they survey. Others are magnificent weepers spreading arms of evergreen love farther and farther each year in their protective embrace. Consider, also, their splendid cones! Their subtleties of color, texture and form enhance their presence. One must visit the grand parks and arboreta to see these specimens of wonder. On the other hand there are many that fit admirably into a smaller garden. Whether you are blessed with a modest space or have a large estate or farm, or are in charge of a park, learn to know the conifers well. Choose with care the rightful spot in your landscape and watch them grow—most often to outlive your grandchildren! Used in moderation they can be a tremendous asset as backgrounds to your more intimate plantings and shrub borders, especially for your lilacs.

Not all conifers succeed equally well everywhere. They are a tree for all seasons, but are for special seasons and places in the garden. The Brooklyn Botanic Garden has published an invaluable *Handbook on Conifers*. It is an excellent handbook and some such guide should be read before one plants any conifer or tree. We plant them, as we do lilacs, only once and ought not change our minds (like our wills) too often or at all!

Discover by observation of conifers, as in lilacs, which varieties are best suited for your own location, then proceed with your planning and planting. Some are limited by climate, others by size or space. Realize, also, that there are now available for the home garden many selections of dwarf and miniature evergreens. The Gotelli Collection of Dwarf Conifers at the U.S. National Arboretum in Washington D.C. and the collection at the Arnold Arboretum are among the finest in the world to see these smaller forms ideally suited for limited garden space. By all means try to visit them.

Some conifers like the pines, spruces, hemlocks and firs can be grown in nearly any garden. The selection of a particular variety suited for your location need be your only concern. For backgrounds, property dividers, windbreaks, they have served for centuries, often without respect for their individual character and beauty (like soldiers lined up for duty). In our gardens they must become individuals, respected each for what they are and how they share their grace and character with the whole garden.

Ewing Park, Des Moines, Iowa, and the Royal Botanical Gardens, Hamilton, Ontario, Canada, are among the great lilac collections that use conifers and lilacs together extremely well. Here conifers attend the vistas with their form and beauty. At the private estate of the Vale of Aherlow, East Burke, Vermont, the native spruces have been magnificently combined to enhance the great lilac plantings. Conifers do not dominate these parks and gardens—they 'attend' and 'enhance' thus best serving the lilacs planted around them. Lilacs love this stately accompaniment! You can enhance the blue and pink flowering lilacs with blue-toned conifers—the whites with dark green or even golden backgrounds and the pale lavender tones with medium green conifers. Not so with the deep purple lilacs, these rare beauties with flashing dark tresses must have lighter backgrounds of intermediary, early flowering shrubs or small trees like *Cornus* as primary backgrounds in front of the dark conifers. Their bloom is lost when planted directly against the dark conifers.

Some of the exotic weeping forms of hemlock or the spruces do well as a distant background for lilacs. Remember that all large conifers are really somewhat distant backgrounds for anything planted in front of them. They need room for development. In planting lilacs one can generally use only the eastern, southern and south-western sides of evergreen back-plantings. Their shadow becomes greater with age whereas the lilacs need and love sunlight. Never plant lilacs on the north side of evergreens or other trees.

Consider some of these conifers for your lilac companions: *Abies concolor* (one of the finest), *Abies homolepis umbellata*, *Abies procera* (nobilis), *Abies koreana*, *Cedrus atlantica* 'Glauca' (where winters are not so severe it is excellent), *Chamaecyparis pisifera* 'Boulevard', *Chamaecyparis obtusa* 'Gracilis', *Cryptomeria japonica*, *Juniperus scopulorum* 'Gray Gleam', *Picea pungens* 'Kosteri', *Picea omorika*, *Pinus cembra*, *Pinus bungeana* (the lovely Lace Bark Pine—all clones are not equally as attractive), *Pinus strobus* (one of the best), *Pinus* × *schwerinii*, *Pinus resinosa* and the lovely *Pinus thunbergii* 'Oculis Draconis' (lovely planted behind white lilacs), *Taxus baccata* 'Fastigiata', *Taxus cuspidata* 'Capitata' (these latter two are fine for smaller gardens in place of the taller pines), *Tsuga canadensis* and *Thuja occidentallis* (both of these species are fine for smaller gardens). Ask for them by name and be prepared to pay more for these outstanding selections. Do not settle or accept substitutes— *Bon jardinier*, you plant them only once in a lifetime!

Use Early Hybrid lilacs against an evergreen background since so few other flowering trees are early enough for their bloom. Use the mid-season *S. vulgaris* such as some of the very outstanding newer cultivars listed elsewhere as focal plants flanked by some of the choicest conifers—the combinations are endless and your garden will be a landscaper's delight. Do not forget some of the truly outstanding blue flowering lilacs against the many kinds of new and beautiful Blue Spruce selections. The combination is one of the finest of all conifers!

Lilacs and Flowering Crabs (*Malus*)

Top priority for Spring blossom among flowering shrubs and trees to plant with lilacs must be given to the flowering crabs. Although most flowering crabs bloom a week to 12 days earlier than the peak of lilac bloom, there is enough overlap of expanding buds and bloom in each to make beautiful contrasts and magnificent blooming combinations. What is of particular appeal in this lilac-crab combination is the change in the crabs from brilliant red buds to soft pink and pure white bloom creating a backdrop for the striking colors—blues, lavenders, pinks and deep purples of the lilacs. Without a white or soft pink background much of the lilac's beauty would be lost! One can have a dual combination of lilacs opening against full blown crabs or crabs blooming in front of banks of opening early lilacs.

There are two main groups of flowering crabs (*Malus*). The older cultivars are mostly large and spreading trees while the newer cultivars are much smaller, but heavy blooming and bright fall-fruited trees. The latter are far more adaptable to smaller landscapes, special focal points and generally have more variety of form ranging from upright through round headed to many types of excellent weepers. In addition to their landscape utility, these newer flowering crabs have been selected for disease resistance, and produce much smaller and more colorful autumn fruit. Many of these newer varieties are still difficult to obtain but not impossible. They may cost a bit more but are certainly well worth the effort and expense. They are ideal with lilacs. (*Bon jardinier,* you must see them to appreciate their beauty!).

Well planned combinations of crabs and lilacs can be the showpieces of your Spring garden. They are particularly effective when viewed from a slight distance or when they form a focal point at a curve or opening to a new vista beyond. If they are on a slight rise or hillside so much more the pleasing effect they create.

In planting this excellent combination of crabs with lilacs consideration must be given to the time of bloom of each, as well as the special form of both the crabs and the lilacs. In both we have upright, spreading growers and in the crabs a whole new race of excellent weeping trees. One does not plant the beautiful smaller weeping crabs behind tall, upright growing lilacs but rather in front of them.

Combinations are endless and the more one learns to appreciate both lilacs and the flowering crabs, their forms and color nuances, the more effective the landscaping becomes. Lilacs planted with crabs (as with any other shrubs or trees) must not be planted too closely. Both need room for growth and to develop a handsome form. The intended effect can be easily ruined by jam-planting them on top of each other for a 'quick effect'. The planting ends in one-sided crabs and lilacs, malformed and reaching skyward for air and light. (*Mon ami,* you well know that we never get around soon enough to remove filler shrubs until it is too late!) It is better to plant fillers of bulbs and annuals than shrubs that are never removed. The background planting, be it crabs or lilacs, may be somewhat closer together than the foreground, but not too close. At two-thirds maturity the branches must appear close but not intergrown. Specimens planted in front must have full room for development of total form and must not be a mass with the background. Plant combination groups with the over-all maturity of the planting in view. It is well worth the time waiting for this effect as each year its beauty increases as the total planting matures.

Even given ample growing space some pruning must be done to gain the desired effect. The form and position of mature trunks, especially in flowering crabs, is both a science and an art in the growing landscape. The Japanese gardeners have learned the perfection of appreciating mature trunk and branch forms as a landscaping art. We should emulate their efforts. (*Bon jardinier,* they have thousands of years of landscaping art—we must not be afraid to learn and imitate their best forms!)

On larger estates, country gardens, arboreta and parks this lilac-flowering crab combination is truly magnificent. If well planned and executed one can have flowering crabs with half-opened lilacs at their finest bloom. Remember that most crabs bloom somewhat earlier than *S. vulgaris* and that for these early opening trees the Early Hybrid Lilacs are the best. Be mindful that there are later blooming crabs that are excellent with all the lilacs except the very late blooming sorts. The combinations of crabs and lilacs at various stages of bud, half and full bloom is an art of knowing which cultivars complement each other and where to plant them. Why more of this kind of planting is not done at arboreta and parks is difficult to understand. Certainly it is far more appealing than the long orchard-like rows of either flowering crabs or lilacs which demeans the beauty of both lilacs and crabs. Many park officials are still planting lilacs and crabs of both cultivars and combinations outdated 50 years ago, simply because the newer cultivars of far superior rating are not available from commercial nurseries. Hybridizers have made great strides in both of these genera not only in beauty but in disease resistance in the past few decades.

One must be aware that in planting flowering crabs they are a two season tree—one of beautiful Springtime bloom lasting at most two weeks and another of much longer duration of brilliant colored fall fruit which covers 2–4 months depending on the cultivars selected. They add living color to the fall lilac garden.

In recommending cultivars of flowering crabs (*Malus*) I have deliberately passed over most of the older varieties in favor of the newer more brilliantly fruited, disease resistant cultivars which are far superior all around. Once you study both the many cultivars of the newer *Malus* and *Syringa,* beautiful combinations can be had—but one must pay strict attention to the blooming seasons of each, their ultimate height and special characteristics. Elsewhere we have listed the finest among the *Syringa* cultivars, here we list the best (to the present) of the *Malus.* Leave enough room between them so that one may walk among them in the fall to view the beautiful autumn fruit of the flowering crabs and many of their exotic tree forms. Some of the smaller weepers in the crabs are splendid specimen plants to be surrounded by the lilacs.

Many of the newer crabs are polyploids and hybrids of several species. All are recommended after some testing for disease resistance (not complete but great improvements over many of the older sorts). They are annual bloomers and heavily fruited, somewhat smaller trees and have a heavier textured leaf. You may note that many have originated in Ohio, especially at Falconskeape, where I have pioneered with these newer cultivars and with polyploid crabs for over forty years. They were developed not only at Falconskeape but some at Gardenview Horticultural Park, Strongsville, Ohio under the genius of Henry Ross. Several have originated at the Simpson Nursery, Vincennes, Indiana and individual cultivars at various other places. A wonderful list of some of the fine new flowering crabs can be had from the nursery of J. Frank Schmidt & Son Co., Boring, Oregon. The National Arboretum has several new and very outstanding introductions yet unnamed—watch for them.

By no means do I wish you to discard the many excellent older species such as *M. hupehensis*, *M. floribunda*, *M. sargentii* or cultivars like 'Van Eseltine' or 'Liset', but I do wish to emphasize that if you do not have room for the larger trees by all means seek out some of these newer, smaller growing forms. If you love birds they will flock to your garden in the autumn and hungrily strip the small fruit after it is past its peak in color—often it will be their only food in mid-winter. Some of the newer forms are magnificent weepers far surpassing the older cultivars. Some like *M.* 'Red Swan', 'Firedance', 'White Cascade', 'Lullaby', 'Molten Lava', 'Serenade', 'Egret' (the only pink-white semi-double weeper) have far superior form and are unique as specimens—especially with lilacs. Many of the new introductions, especially among the *M. halliana* and *M. sargentii* selections, are extremely dwarf and are exceptional used as low growing shrubs.

There are not many very late blooming crabs but among them is 'Silver Moon' a fine white and the *M. ioensis* 'Prince Georges' and 'Prairie Rose' (both of which, like all the *M. ioensis* and *M. coronaria*, are greatly subject to fireblight and scab).

I am often asked by gardening friends and landscape architects if there are any fragrant flowering crabapples? To be appraised of those most fragrant, I include the following *Malus* species and cultivars that have varying degrees of many types of fragrance:

M. angustifolia Southern Crab

M. baccata Siberian Crab

M. coronaria dasycalyx—very fragrant and *M. coronaria* 'Nieulandiana', 'Prince Georges'

M. ioensis fimbriata Fringe Petal Crab—very fragrant

M. ioensis 'Plena Bechtel' and 'Prairie Rose'—both fragrant and pleasing (late)

M. hupehensis Tea Crab—mildly fragrant

M. lancifolia Allegheny Crab—mildly fragrant

M. floribunda Japanese Crab—mildly fragrant

M. robusta Cherry Crab

M. sieboldii arborescens Tree Toringo Crab—mildly fragrant

M. sieboldii zumi 'Calocarpa' Redbud Crab

M. sargentii Sargent Crab

M. arnoldiana Arnold Crab

The following hybrid Crabs

'Bob White'

'Brandywine'

'Burgundy' (grape-like fragrance)

'Dolgo'

'Huron'

'Lisa'

'Satin Cloud' very strong and pleasing fragrance of clove-cinnamon.

There may be others but these have been brought to my attention at various times. Be mindful that their fragrance in no way compares in strength with that of the lilacs, except for the *M. ioensis, coronaria* crabs and the cultivar 'Satin Cloud'.

Recommended List of some of the better new (few older) flowering crabs. These have been selected for their disease resistance, flowering beauty, attractive fruit and all-around dependability all year. All are not of equal merit; some fall short in certain categories.

Name	bud color/blossom/ leaf color	tree form/ autumn color leaf	fruit color/ comments
'Adams'	rose/pink	dense rounded	carmine ¾"
'Amberina'	red/white/ dark green	compact rounded/12' bright yellow	brilliant orange-red very persistent ½"
'Ames White'	pink/white	rounded	yellow
'Angel Choir'	blush/white double medium green	low spreading to 12'	red persistent/limited to ⅜"/blooms on spurs
'Autumn Glory'	bright red/white/dark green	low rounded to 12' disease resistant	bright orange-red to ⅜" August to January
M. baccata 'Jackii'	white/white	broad upright (a dwarf form also available	good red ⅜ to ½"
M. × (baccata × robusta) 'Taliak'	pink/white/dark green	rounded upright	bright red to ¾" very heavy annual fruiting
'Bob White'	pink/white/ good green	dense rounded	brown-yellow ½" heavy fruiting, relished by birds
'Bridal Crown'	white/dbl. white very heavy blooming clusters	low rounded	small red very limited ½" blossoms on spurs in heavy clusters
'Burgundy'	deep red/purple- red/deep green	oval upright, vase fine growth	small maroon blossoms faint grape-like frag.
'Centurian'	rose-red/deep rose/dark green	columnar	cherry-red ⅝"
'Christmas Holly'	bright red/white/ deep green	low rounded to 10' bright yellow autumn color	glossy bright red ⅛" Aug.–Jan. very effective
'Coralburst'	coral/rose pink/semi- dbl very small foliage, dk. green	dwarf, low rounded	⅜", few bronze
'Coral Cascade'	coral-red/white/ dark green	low, semi-weeping spreading	brilliant coral-pink ⅜" very showy persistent fruit
'Cotton Candy'	purple-rose/deep pink very double clusters	low, rounded to 10'	very few—brown- green/outstanding in bloom
'David'	pink/white	rounded, compact	scarlet, ½", persistent
'Donald Wyman'	pink/white	rounded	bright red to ¾"
'Doubloons'	red-pink/pink-white dbl. dark green healthy	low rounded to 12'	bright yellow gold, ⅜" very heavy fruited persistent
'Egret' (tetraploid)	deep pink/pale pink dbl./deep green leathery leaves	low refined weeper 8' excellent Japanese gardens	deep red—few ⅜" effec- tive slender tree form
'Fiesta'	carmine/white	semi-weeper, low to 15'	bright red-orange-gold
M. × floribunda	red/white heavy annual bloomer	spreading	yellow and red to ⅜" background specimen
'Gibbs Golden'	pink/white	rounded, small form	light yellow 1", persistent

Name	bud color/blossom/ leaf color	tree form/ autumn color leaf	fruit color/ comments
'Golden Gem'	pink/rose-pink	rounded	yellow to ½" (cultivar BD 115-58)
'Golden Hornet'	pale pink/white	upright to spreading	bright yellow to ¾"
M. halliana 'Parkmanii'	rose-pink/ pink semi-dbl.	oval, rounded 14'	deep reddish—few, small
M. halliana 'N.A. #127'	deep rose/deep pink/fine deep green leaves	dwarf rounded to 10'	red to ⅜" effective in bloom
'Henningii'	white/white/ glossy green	upright-rounded 25'	bright red to ⅝"
M. hupehensis	pink/white/ fine dark leaves	spreading vase—unique outstanding landscape value	yellow-green ½" heavy bloomer alternate years
M. hupehensis 'Donald' tetraploid	deep pink/white dark green leather leaves	wide vase—unique as above better form than hupehensis	reddish-yellow, persistent, ⅜" annual bloomer
'Indian Magic'	red/deep carmine-red/deep reddish green	wide rounded	elongated, red to red-orange, ½" very effective (several clones some not as effective as others)
M. ioensis 'Prince Georges'	deep pink, light pink dbl., very fragrant	rounded to 15' some good leaf color in autumn	absent, moderately subject to fire blight/cedar-apple rust
M. ioensis 'Prairie Rose'	deep pink/light pink dbl, very fragrant latest to bloom	spreading rounded	absent/subject to cedar-apple rust and fire blight. Beautiful in bloom and fragrance
'Jewelberry'	pink/white	dwarf, shrubby/very effective	glossy red to ½", effective
'Joy' tetraploid	deep coral/coral pink red-green leaves	rounded to 15'	deep maroon-red
'Leprechaun'	scarlet/white/dark green/disease resistant	small compact tree 10'	brilliant glossy scarlet to ⅛" persistent to January
'Liset'	bright red/orange-red leaves dark reddish-green	rounded to 20'	dark red to ⅝" very effective in bloom
'Lullaby'	pink/white, large blossoms disease resistant	rounded weeper to 8'	bright yellow to ½"
'Madonna'	deep pink/dbl. white, very large blossoms to 3"	upright to 18'	dark red, ½, sparse effective in bloom
'Maria'	deep crimson/bright rose-red outstanding leathery leaves, slender-long reddish-green, disease resistant	weeper to 15', very effective in form	red to ½"—one of the best deep red weepers

'Mary Potter' (see M. sargentii) S. sargentii × 'Mary Potter'

Name	bud color/blossom/ leaf color	tree form/ autumn color leaf	fruit color/ comments
'Mollie Ann' tetraploid	deep crimson/white leathery leaves dark green	upright semi-weeper to 15' fine branchlets in unique clusters	dark red and yellow to ½" very disease resistant/feathery bloom many small florets
'Molten Lava'	red/white dark green	graceful moderate weeper winter bark yellowish	red-orange ⅜", very effective persistent, disease resistant
Mount Arbor Special'	carmine/deep rose	rounded to 20'	red
'Ormiston Roy'	pink/pinkish white medium green	rounded oval	yellow ⅜", persistent subject to cedar-apple rust
'Pagoda'	bright carmine/white dark green	lower semi-weeper graceful form	brilliant orange-red to ¼" very disease resistant, showy
'Peter Pan'	bright red/white medium green	low rounded to 12' disease resistant	very small bright red to ⅛" persistent to January, very showy heavy annual fruiting
'Pink Spires'	deep pink/pink deep purple foliage	upright oval	maroon to ½"
'Prairifire'	red-purple/red-purple purplish to green	moderately upright	deep purplish-red to ½"
'Professor Sprenger'	pink/white	round oval with many slender branchlets 15'	orange-red to ⅜"
'Profusion'	deep red/ purplish-red	rounded oval moderate	ox-blood red to ½"
'Red Barron'	dark-red/dark red dark reddish-green foliage	narrow columnar fall foliage excellent	dark red, glossy to ⅝" very effective in bloom
'Redbird'	brilliant red/ white disease resistant	upright to 10'	bright red-orange beginning in August, ⅝", very effective
'Red Jewel'	white/white very heavy blooming	upright-spreading 15' horizontal branching	cherry-red to ½", persistent, subject to fire blight
'Red Peacock'	bright red/white very disease resistant	upright broad semi-weeper to 15' as wide	brilliant orange-red ⅜", very effective, heavy fruited
'Red Swan'	pink/creamy-white heavy textured narrow leaves/dark green	Graceful fine twiggy weeper outstanding for Japanese gardens or used as unique fine weeper, 10'	oblong bright red to ¼" wide and ½" long, resembles a weeping cherry in bloom, very effective yellow leaves in autumn and red fruit
'Robinson'	crimson/carmine	oval spreading 25'	dark red to ⅝"
M. sargentii	pink/white	spreading to 8'	dark red to ¼"
M. sargentii 'Lustgarten'	pink/white	multi-stemmed, spreading	red to ⅜" more effective form than species
M. sargentii × 'Mary Potter'	pink/white	broad vase	red to ½", very effective in bloom

Name	bud color/blossom/ leaf color	tree form/ autumn color leaf	fruit color/ comments
M. sargentii 'Tina'	red/white effective display of yellow anthers	very dwarf 4 to 5' oval to round	red to ¼", very effective dwarf, useful for container plantings
'Satin Cloud' octoploid	white/white, large blossoms very unique cinnamon fragrance/leaves unique, small leathery texture, deep green, very disease resistant	very small rounded form to 8', many small branchlets giving clipped appearance/outstanding autumn colors reds, mauves and gold	very small amber-gold ⅜", unique and outstanding, slower grower increasingly beautiful with age, persistent fruit, drought resistant plant
'Selkirk'	deep red/carmine red-green foliage	tall rounded to 25'	brilliant glossy red to ¾" (like large cherries—very effective early color)
'Sentinel'	pale pink/pink	narrow upright	bright red to ½" begins color in August
'Serenade'	bright red/blush white/deep green disease resistant	upright semi-weeping 12' graceful arching branches to 15' wide	eliptical ⅜", yellow turning orange with red cheeks, very effective
'Shaker Gold'	carmine-pink/white/medium green disease resistant	upright rounded to 16' and spreading	yellow-orange with orange-red cheeks, very effective even after heavy frosts ¾"
M. sieboldii 'Fuji'	purple-red/dbl. white flowers 1¾" wide, good leaf color	broad, round-headed 38' by 40" wide	orange ½", very effective
M. sieboldii 'Henry Kohankie'	pink/white/large blossoms to 1½" disease resistant	rounded tree	ellipsoidal, red to 1¼"
'Silver Moon'	pinkish-white/white dark green, very disease resistant	vase upright to oval	bright red in cluster, ⅜" persistent/one of the lates to bloom (very effective with lilacs)
'Sinai Fire'	bright red/white, large deep green foliage/very disease resistant	upright weeper to 10' unique downward branching	brilliant orange-red to ¼" persistent and very showy
'Snowdrift'	red/white lustrous green foliage	broad rounded 18'	orange-red to ⅜" subject to scab/fire blight
'Spring Song'	deep pink/bright pink, very large blossoms to 2" dark green leaves/disease resistant	smaller rounded to 12' compact upright grower	deep gold to ⅜", very heavy fruited
M. tschnowskii	white/white—sparse new leaves white to gray to green, white pubescence	upright, oval 30' outstanding autumn color purples to reds	green to 1"—sparse outstanding for its leaf color
'Van Eseltine'	dark rose/dbl pink glossy green	upright columnar	brown to ½"—ineffective/outstanding for mass double bloom only
M. veitchii	mini white odd clusters narrow petals and rose pistils	upright narrow	purple-brown in clusters

Name	bud color/blossom/ leaf color	tree form/ autumn color leaf	fruit color/ comments
'White Angel'	pink/white medium green/disease resistant	upright spreading	scarlet-red ½", one of best white flowering crabs
'White Cascade'	pink/white	fine textured weeper 15'	lime-yellow to ⅜", very fine
'Wintergold'	carmine/white 1" late bloomer/medium green foliage	rounded to 20'	yellow to ½ outstanding in fruit and lateness of bloom

The following National Arboretum numbered selections appear to have outstanding merit: 54936, 54937, 54938 (red leaved), 54939, 54941 (very small leaved), 54942 (red leaved), 54943, 54988.

Cornus florida (Flowering Dogwood) and Lilacs

Where the northern winters are somewhat less severe the *Cornus florida* (Dogwood) stands out as one of the outstanding native trees that awaken spring with bracts of white. They are also an outstanding autumn foliage tree with scarlet, orange-gold intermingled with brilliant red berried fruit. Flowering Dogwoods are excellent companions for early blooming lilacs!

Today there are several outstanding, selected white *Cornus* cultivars. By all means purchase one of these newer selections for greater mass of bloom. You will never regret your purchase. Dogwoods are somewhat difficult to get started. They need woodsy hillsides, extremely good drainage and rather light-sandy-gravelly soil. In fact what suits lilacs is good for dogwoods too! Dogwoods, however, are smaller trees of the forest's edge and do better with a bit of shade, although they will take full sun. Start them in the spring as small plants. Do not waste money on specimen trees that are most difficult to transplant. Be certain they are own-rooted, if at all possible, and come in their own unbroken ball. (Never, *mon ami*, buy them bare rooted. You will lose most, if not all of them and have to confess my advice was correct.)

Dogwoods are excellent at a wood's edge leading into a lilac path or garden. They are the perfect intermediary between the deeper woods, especially if they be of pines, hemlocks or other conifers. Plant them as nature would in small groups of three or as a single specimen—never in rows! Horrors to even think of dogwoods planted like a line of Lombardy poplars! From the native eastern dogwood *Cornus florida*, several choice white flowering cultivars have been derived and include 'Cloud 9', 'Eddie's Wonder', 'Gigantea', 'New Hampshire', 'Cherokee Princess', and 'White Cloud'. Among the pink and red flowering dogwoods are some fine specimens—'Cherokee Chief', a fine deeper pink-red, 'Sweetwater', 'Apple Blossom', 'Spring Song' and 'Super Red'. There are also some very pale blush-pinks and some having a creamy-yellowish tint when placed next to the pure whites. Use as many as you are able, they are all lovely. (*Bon jardinier*, of course use more lilacs than dogwoods! *Merci*, I am writing a book on *Syringa* and not *Cornus!*)

Should you have your own native seedlings, remember they can be enhanced by grafting with some of the better flowering sorts or pinks. If possible leave a large dogwood where it is growing rather than transplant it and plan your landscaping around it. (You cannot do this? Nothing is impossible!) On planning a landscape using dogwoods with lilacs, one must project into the future and picture ultimate sizes of the fully grown specimens. Dogwoods, like lilacs, do no like to be crowded into tight spaces. They will survive but will sulk and lose their magnificent bushy tree form.

If you have an area where you wish to naturalize your plantings, try the combination of native dogwoods with some of the species lilacs such as *S. julianae* 'Hers' or underplant the dogwoods with drifts of *S. pubescens* with its fragrant bloom. A lovely combination is *S. potaninii* backed by dogwoods. Try drifts of *S.* × *chinensis* intermingled with dogwoods frolicking along the forest edges—magnificent! Avoid using the late flowering species and hybrids with dogwoods as they bloom when dogwoods are long past. The pale blues and lavenders of the Early Hybrid lilacs are excellent with dogwoods, although these lilacs in time, too, can become trees. The species *S. oblata dilatata* is excellent with early dogwoods.

Where climate is not extreme there are some other species of *Cornus* that are also extremely showy with early lilacs. *C. kousa* is excellent planted with lilacs and gives a wonderful display, whereas *C. mas* and *C. nuttalli* do well and on the Pacific northwest coast. Try them with your lilac plantings.

Recently some excellent cultivars of *Cornus kousa* have been named and introduced by Mrs. Julian (Polly) Hill of Barnard's Inn Farm, Vineyard Haven, Massachusetts, these include: *Cornus Kousa* var. *chinensis* cultivars 'Big Apple' with very showy bloom and really outstanding fruit (for which it is named), 'Gay Head' with showy bloom and fruit, 'Square Dance' a more vertical than spreading tree with spectacular bloom and fruit. 'Madame Butterfly' a cultivar of *Cornus kousa* selected by David Leach, Madison, Ohio, flaunts bracts that resemble swarms of butterflies. All are marvelous companions with the Early Hybrid lilacs and with *S. oblata* cultivars. (AABGA Bulletin, July 1984). (*Mon amie,* I have tried to surround your lilacs with the royalty of the finest companions which are well worthy of being searched out and purchased as lifetime members of your garden family.)

Lilacs with *Prunus* (Flowering Cherries)

As with dogwoods, where your soil is sandy-gravel and your winters less severe, flowering cherries are excellent companions with the early lilacs. What applies to dogwoods seems to be good advice for flowering cherries. They make a fine display with the very earliest lilacs, *S. oblata* and its hybrids. Cherries do not last long enough to be in bloom during the regular lilac season. With the white and pale pinks of the flowering cherries use the Early Hybrids such as 'Maureen', 'Pink Cloud', 'Sunset', 'Lewis Maddock', 'Fenelon', 'Lamartine' or the deeper purple of 'Pocahontas'. There is a new flowering cherry, somewhat hardier and more rugged that we have developed here at Falconskeape that suckers rather profusely and forms clumps, if allowed, which is a lovely, brilliant white with a somewhat longer blooming season called 'Silver Cloud' that is rather showy with the early lilacs and the flowering crab 'Selkirk'. You may wish to try it, if you have trouble with the less hardy and grafted oriental cherries. It seems to do well in heavier soils and clays.

With the really outstanding flowering *Prunus* one must use the earliest of the lilac hybrids but the combination is truly a 'Spring creation of beauty'! Most cherries are at their peak when the lilacs are still in bud but there are a few of the earliest to combine their bloom. A delightful double flowering cherry is the outstanding *Prunus* 'Hally Jolivette' with its pale pinkish to white blossoms and rather low growing form it is excellent with *S. oblata dilatata*. (They seem to bloom together here in Ohio). The newest *Prunus' mume* hybrids are magnificent!

Peonies and Lilacs

Whether yours be a small city garden or an estate, or a park displaying the finest in horticultural design, then by all means have a special area for some lilacs surrounded by a well kept bed of peonies at their sides. Use beds of the finest herbaceous peonies, the newer Ito Hybrids and, of course, if possible, the magnificent Tree Peonies. The Lilac nobility loves to have the charming little princes and princesses of the herbaceous plantdom blooming at their feet! It is indeed a regal display provided you choose the right colors and the appropriate lilacs and peonies. First one must choose both lilacs and peonies that bloom together.

For Early Hybrids lilacs, the *S. oblata* 'Giraldi' and *S. oblata dilatata* hybrids, use the earliest species peonies and their hybrids such as *P. mlokosewitschii, P. officinalis*, the hybrids 'Playmate', 'Moonlight' and several of the Saunder's Hybrids. Lilacs look best among a bed of peonies if all the peonies are of one cultivar. Too many varieties give a spotted effect. The mass of a single color is far more attractive than individual cultivars of varying heights and colors. A single, choice lilac surrounded by a well kept bed of 7–10 choice peonies all of one kind is a sight not easily forgotten! (You do not acquire this kind of landscaping in 1 or 2 years. You plan and wait for it to develop. Suddenly it is there!)

Another fine example would be the grand old lilac 'Lucie Baltet' with its delicate shades of coppery-pink surrounded by a massed bed of choice Hybrid Peonies in pink or red! With specimen lilacs in pink or a dazzling white use the brilliant hybrid red peonies like 'Carina',

'Alexander Woollcott', the outstanding 'James Cousins', 'America' a large scarlet, 'Burma Midnight', 'Coral Charm', 'Coral Sunset', 'Camellia', 'Chalice, 'Ballerina' a wonderful double, the pale yellow 'Claire De Lune', 'Cytheria', the exotic 'Early Windflower', 'Marie Fischer', the excellent 'Moonrise', the brilliant red 'Cardinal's Robe', or the very rare 'Burgundy' a real gem! For pinks that are always wonderful companions with most lilacs use 'Pageant', 'Frosted Rose', 'Laura Magnuson', 'Louise', 'Victoria Lincoln', 'Sylvia Saunders' or 'Starlight'—or a host of others.

Among the *P. lactiflora* cultivars (the common peony) are many wonderful choices: ranging from white, through pinks, oranges, reds and shades of lavender. Consider some of the newest and the finest as: 'Angel Cheeks', 'Ann Cousins', 'Best Man', 'Bonanza', 'Bridal Gown', 'Bridal Icing', 'Cheddar Gold', 'Cheddar Surprise', 'Dinner Plate', 'Elk Grove', 'Emma Klehm', 'Ethel Mars', 'Fairy's Petticoat', 'Goshen Beauty', 'Helen Hayes', 'Highlight', 'Honey Gold', 'Jay Cee', 'Moon River', 'Minnie Shaylor' (old but good), 'Mister Ed', 'Paul Bunyan', 'Pink Jazz', 'Princess Margaret', 'Raspberry Ice', 'Snow Mountain', 'Sylver', 'Top Brass' or 'Vivid Rose'. (There are a host of others that can be supplied with information on growing them from the American Peony Society.)

There are so many simply wonderful herbaceous peonies and hybrids that one must study the peony catalogues and visit peony gardens to see what is available. Do not settle for the older sorts sold by color only.

THE INTERSPECIFIC PEONY HYBRIDS

A really beautiful bit of landscaping can be made using some of the newer white lilacs such as the deep yellow-creamy budded white 'Emery Mae Norweb', or 'Rochester', 'Souv. d' Alice Harding', 'Flora', 'Carley', 'Mother Louise', or 'Slater's Elegance' and surround them with an entire bed of the new Ito Hybrids. These hybrids are a cross between the Tree Peony × the herbaceous Peony and come in vigorous plants with striking deep yellow flowers. They are well worth the cost. (The difficulty is in finding a nursery specializing in peonies that has them, but there are a few.) These Hybrids are named: 'Yellow Crown', 'Yellow Dream', 'Yellow Emperor', 'Yellow Heaven'. Sheer elegance that increases in beauty as the years pass! (*Mon ami*, you say you cannot afford them! Buy one and divide it as soon as you can. This is a lifetime investment. I am writing this book to introduce you to the finest in both lilacs and companions. Surely you would not surround your regal lilacs with ordinary plants!)

THE MAGNIFICENT TREE PEONIES

Another fine companion to lilacs are the Tree Peonies, both the Japanese, Chinese and the beautiful Saunder's Hybrids. What wonderful combinations some of them make. Use the finest of the newer lilacs in whatever shade pleases you and you will find simply superb Tree Peonies to accompany them. For instance if you use lilacs such as 'Victor Lemoine', 'Atheline Wilbur', 'Albert F. Holden', 'Monge', 'Agincourt Beauty', or a host of other outstanding ones, surround them with white tree peony 'Stolen Heaven', 'Gessekai', 'Renkaku', 'Shiro Kagura', 'Wings of the Morning', or 'Chichibu'. You might wish to use a bed of one of the very fine pale lavender Tree Peonies such as 'Guardian of the Monastery', 'Mt. Fuji', 'Kenreimon' or 'Marie Laurincen' (one of the very finest of all).

For something very choice use the deep purple edged white lilac 'Sensation' as the focal plant surrounded by a bed of the very rare herbaceous hybrid peony 'Picotee' (white with a purple-pink edging) or by the pure white of 'Early or Late Windflower' (they are indistinguishable late or early) and are truly magnificent rarities, or the beautiful 'White Innocence'. Another focal point is lilac 'Maiden's Blush' surrounded by the early hybrid peony 'Rose Crystal', 'Ballerina' or 'Pink Lady' or, if one can find it and divide it enough, the very, very rare 'Eclipse'! Lilacs and Peonies are a wonderful combination when cultivars are used that bloom together. They are a total loss when the combination is not well chosen. Beds of mixed peonies give a very spotted effect—avoid this. Since your garden may be small and you may be able to plant only a few lilacs and peonies, select only the very best. Be prepared to pay more for a newer or choice named variety. (*Mon ami*, avoid dealers who shuffle off their wares by color and have no regard for names that are correct and guaranteed. *Merci*, you do not want your garden to become a home for runaway plants!)

Lilacs and the Showy Magnolias

One of the early spring flowering shrubs outstanding with lilacs is the Magnolia. They grow well together throughout Zone 5 and in sheltered areas of Zone 4. Not all magnolias are equally hardy and one must select them with care. They are found in pure whites, pinks, lavenders, rich red-purples and soft creams and one deep yellow. *M. loebneri* 'Merrill' in pure white blooms early enough to plant with the Early Hybrid lilacs. Together they put on a real show. Most of the choicest magnolias bloom later, just in time for *S. vulgaris*. The newer *Magnolia* hybrids are excellent, *belles* of the garden with lilacs. One must see this combination to really appreciate its outstanding beauty. They like the same deep, well-drained, enriched loam. The only drawback is that one may have too many larger shrubs all blooming together, if this be a hinderance at all. After all Spring is the time for bloom and beauty!

Among the best and some of the hardiest Magnolias do not overlook the following:

The National Arboretum introductions of DeVos and Kosar: DeVos Hybrida, 'Ann', 'Judy', 'Randy', 'Ricki'. Kosar Hybrids, 'Betty', 'Susan', 'Jane' and 'Pinkie' all in various tones of lavender, pink and red-purples. They are excellent with the white lilacs.

Many of the *M. soulangiana* hybrids are excellent, 'Amabilis' pure white, 'Lennei' with enormous deep purple flowers and 'Verbanica' white flushed pink. All are excellent with most colors of lilacs.

M. loebneri 'Ballerina' a magnificent rose blushed white, 'Spring Snow' truly outstanding white, 'Woodsman' and the newest 'Pristine' with 'Elizabeth' a pale cream-yellow. Indeed you are fortunate if you can obtain any of these beauties!

M. liliflora 'O'Neill' a deep wine-purple, *M. watsoni* (*wieseneri*), or the cherished *M. denudata* (Yulan Magnolia) so revered as a classic in China. Some of the less publicized and obtainable, yet beautiful magnolias, include *M. × denudata* 'Royal Crown', *M. salicifolia,* thoroughly hardy and beautiful, *M. sprengeri* 'Diva' a pink-lavender and *M. thompsoniana* 'Urbana'.

M. sieboldi 'Oyama'—exquisite in bloom—a small tree or large shrub, very outstanding.

A real eye-opener is the rare, deep yellow *M. acuminata* 'Miss Honeybee'! What a show it puts on next to the newer white lilacs! It is a rather large shrub that in time may become a small tree. It is new, rare and outstanding.

Like lilacs the newest and best are difficult to obtain except from a few magnolia specialists and must be asked for by name. They are well worth the efforts!

Using Bright Yellows and Oranges with Lilacs

Bright yellows and oranges with lilacs might seem a contradiction but they, too, can be very effective if the right combinations are made. There are only two colors in lilacs that go well with these bright colors, the white lilacs and the very deep purple ones. Since most of the bright yellow and orange spring flowering shrubs are rather early and most of the deep purple lilacs are rather late it is a rare combination. Mostly we are left with the white lilacs.

The deep yellow *Magnolia acuminata* 'Miss Honeybee' is excellent with the white-cream lilacs such as 'St. Joan', 'Aloise', 'Souv. d' Alice Harding', 'Prof. E. H. Wilson', 'Mother Louise', 'Flora', 'Maud Notcutt' or 'Carley'. Or surround these excellent white lilacs with the bright yellow of azaleas as 'Klondyke', 'Gold Dust' or 'Golden Oriel' or 'Toucan' or the brilliant orange of 'Gibraltar'— beautiful landscaping in bloom. Your lilacs will grow equally well in the acid bed of the azaleas, especially if it be made of well rotted sawdust or peat mixed with sand. If fearful you can always make the lilac area to the back in somewhat less acid soil than made for the azaleas.

White lilacs surrounded by the princely Tree Peonies in colors of yellow are equally a magnificent focal point. Use either the new yellow Ito Hybrids or the Saunder's Hybrids in their wonderful shades of yellow and flares. We like Saunder's 'Age of Gold', 'Roman Gold', 'Silver Sails' and the mixed colors of the indescribably 'Savage Splendor'.

We have seen beautiful specimens of white lilacs surrounded by a bed of *Aurinia (Alyssum) saxatilis* that made a most memorable picture well worth duplication. If your lilacs be on a somewhat raised level with a short stone wall for *A. idaeum* to spill over, the combination is outstanding. Many of the early flowering perennials are wonderful companions to lilacs. One may have to interplant them with something else, as *Hemerocallis,* for later bloom. The daylilies then use the dark lilacs as background for their grand summer parade.

Hosta and *Lilacs*

On the north and west side of lilacs why not plant a glorious bed or beds of *Hosta*? (Not for the south or the east sides.)

Have you ever watched *Hosta* plants in the spring unpack their ship-shape, squared-away leaves as they come popping from their winter rest? It is a sight to behold! Their busy unfurling, unfolding suddenly erupts in a clump of bright new leaves, rich greens, blues and blue-greens and greys, golden leaves with white, white with bright green or gold—large broad leaves, puckered and crinkled leaves, small lanceolate leaves—what a marvelous study in colors, textures and leaves! Why not let this spring magic unfold together with your lilac buds? The two, lilacs and hosta, go well together. Some combinations of hosta blend fantastically with the colors of lilac blooms.

The giant leaved *H. seiboldiana elegans* (that is what it is, an elegant hosta) with its broad, rounded leaves overlaid with a heavy blue luster, is a real conversation piece when well grown. Imagine seven to eight of these plants around some of the beautiful new blue lilacs! Do not be content with the older, so called blue lilacs like 'President Lincoln'. Use really blue lilacs like 'Porcelain Blue', 'Blue Delft', 'True Blue', 'Dwight D. Eisenhower', 'Pat Pesata', 'Prof. Hoser', 'Crepuscule', or 'Ami Schott' among others. Then get out your *Hosta* specialty catalogues and consider the blue cast hostas: 'Rough Waters' with its blue-gray, puckered leaves, 'Krossas Regal' with large blue-gray leaves (and summer spikes to 6 ft.), or the magnificent 'President's Choice', 'Rembrant', 'Blue Waterford', 'Big Daddy', 'Blue Umbrellas', 'Fringe Benefit', *tokudama* 'True', 'True Blue', 'Sumi' and 'River Nile'! For a low blue, flat glaucous mound use the flattering 'Blue Boy'. Place the lower ones up front and the large-leaved to the base of the lilacs but not too close. Remember that both hosta and lilac revel in rich soils with good moisture during the hot summer months.

For white lilacs (and lavenders) use the gold-leaved *Hostas* or those with gold and green. Two fine, neat, gold hostas for edging are 'Gold Drop' and 'Gold Edger'—there are others perhaps even more elegant. 'Ellerbroek L-7' is a wide deep green with leaves edged in gold, marvelous before a bush of white lilacs. Some of the bright green hostas are a lovely foundation for the lilac parade. 'Birchwood Green', 'Corduroy', or 'Century One' are all excellent bright greens which later in the season will give delightful displays of flowering spikes.

Hosta cultivars are an excellent companion plant because it is their leaves and not the blossom that is the companion to the flowering lilacs. Among lilacs to go with *Hosta* do not overlook some of the species and their newer hybrids such as *S. sweginzowi* 'Albida' so lovely and fragrant, or the beauty of *S. julianae* 'Hers' or the later flowering *S.* × *prestoniae* 'Agnes Smith' or 'Anna Amhoff' or 'Summer White' or the hybrid 'Lark Song'.

Remember that *Hostas* are shade loving, need good moisture (summer mulches and heavy manuring—all of which are good for lilacs) and should be planted on the north or shaded sides of lilacs. They appreciate filtered sun or high shade. They crowd out grass and weeds, are rather low maintenance. Keep them free from slugs. A list of better and newer *Hosta* cultivars are:

'Gold Standard'—dark green leaf border surrounds a light green center

H. lancifolia 'Kabitan'—low border form narrow, lance leaves yellowish edged green.

H. sieboldiani 'Aurea Marginata'—large leaves pale green edged deep green.

'Cardwell Yellow'—and 'Samuel Blue'—both newer and excellent.

'Celebration'—rock garden or low growing groundcover—green margins on cream base.

'Fascination'—show-stopping, a marvel of variegation, green blotched white-yellow.

'Sun and Substance'—huge, heavily substanced gold leaves, pest-proof—excellent.

'Flamboyant'—broad cream margins dabs of green, chartreuse, white and yellow!

'Big Boy'—giant hosta with green leaves.

'Louisa'—small narrow leaves edged in white (excellent with white lilacs).

'Royal Standard'—old standby, takes sun well—green leaves.

'August Moon'—yellow leaves—holds well—seersuckered leaves, excellent.

H. sieboldiana 'Frances Williams'—large irregular yellow margins on heavy seersuckered blue-green leaves—terrific when established around lilac 'Primrose', 'Rochester' or 'Emery Mae Norweb'.

'Golden Sport'—gold sport of 'Frances Williams'—excellent—use with lilac 'Flora'.

(Hosta Society members could add many more worthwhile names. Plant them with lilacs by leaf color. Later the Hosta will put on a blooming show of their own!

Aesculus Pavia—A Unique Companion Shrub for Lilacs

One of the ever useful and unusual flowering shrubs, or small tree, that can be most successfully combined with certain, but not all, colors of lilacs is the shrubby form of *Aersulus Pavia*. Generally it is found in red shades, but new developments have brought out brilliant reds, soft carmines, deep pinks and salmon suffused coral with varying shades between. These newer *A. pavia* cultivars are excellent and brilliant companions to the mid-season blooming lilacs—mostly *S. vulgaris* and the species lilacs. Combine the white and pink lilacs with the red's of *A. pavia* as a background and it will be a memorable sight indeed! A clump of 3 *A. pavias* kept in shrub form and planted rather close surrounded by 5 or 7 white lilacs behind and to their side can be an outstanding focal point in any landscape. Use coral and pink *Aesculus pavia* with blue lilacs, the palest pinks with the violet and lavender tones lilacs.

The Early Hybrid Lilacs are a bit too early to bloom with *A. pavia* but many of the species, *S. potanini, S. microphylla, S. sweginzowi, S. pubescens* and some of the late blooming Hybrids, Prestoniae and the newer multibrids, are excellent when chosen in correct color shades (use 'Isabella', 'Fountain', 'Dawn' or 'Lark Song' or 'Springtime', and 'Agnes Smith'). Once you realize the effectiveness of this combination of *A. pavia* and Lilacs you will devise combinations of your own. *A. pavia* is somewhat tender in the harsher areas of Zone 5—so needs some protection from the very cold sub-zero temperatures. Why not try to grow it from seed? It blooms at a very early age, often when a foot high, is attractive and will last for years. Its buckeye-like fruit is also attractive.

There are a great number of additional perennial shrubs and flowering trees that go well with lilacs in bloom. The few that have been mentioned are to whet your creative appetite and to excite gardeners not to be content with the ordinary. Should one have room for only one or two lilacs they can well be the focal points for some truly exceptional landscaping. (Please, *mon ami*, do not forsake them but give them beautiful and complementary companions!) Our gardens are limited in space and to contents, consequently we need plant them with the finest design possible which reflects a bit of our own personalities and likes.

Perhaps you may wish to change your planting combinations from year to year. Do this with either bulbs, especially lilies, annuals and the bounteous array of perennials. Many of the late flowering tulips put on a wonderful display with lilacs as a background. Most annuals are not early enough but among the perennials the combinations appear endless. Often a green bed surrounding blooming lilacs can be most effective, especially if it be *Hemerocallis* cultivars that later will parade a show of their own in mid-summer with the green of lilacs as their display curtains. Learn by observing what is in bloom at lilactime or what plant could benefit with a background of green when in bloom later on. One combination I shall always remember was a bed of *Ajuga genevensis* with thousands of blue-purple flowers carpeting a magnificent blooming lilac 'Olivier de Serres'—a picture one hopes to achieve in landscaping! May your combinations be ever as elegant!

PLATE 81

'Professor Robert Clark' (Fiala 1982) is a lovely, multipetaled, long spiked white with a tint of pale pink buds and large florets. Named to honor a lilac authority and long friend, Prof. Robert B. Clark of Meredith, New Hampshire, one of the founders of the International Lilac Society. Being a double cross of 'Rochester' this lilac should be used for hybridizing. ('Rochester' × 'Edward Gardner') × 'Rochester'.

PLATE 90

The modern Flowering Crabs add springtime glory to the lilacs and in fall surround them with from 2 to 3 months of wonderfully colorful fruit.

Malus 'Prairie Rose' (left). Late blooming goes very well with late blue lilac 'Boule Azuree' (Lemoine 1919), (right).

S. × hyacinthiflora 'Pocahontas' (left) is excellent with Malus × 'Red Swan' (Fiala) (right).

The beautiful crab, Malus × 'Burgundy' (Simpson) is beautiful with white or pink early lilacs.

Autumn fruit of Malus × 'Firecracker' is a showy background of red buds opening white in Spring and a blanket of red-fruit in Fall. The new crabs are two season companions, fruiting in reds, orange, gold, yellow and chartruse lemons—even to blue-purple!

PLATE 81

'Professor Robert Clark' (Fiala 1982) is a lovely, multipetaled, long spiked white with a tint of pale pink buds and large florets. Named to honor a lilac authority and long friend, Prof. Robert B. Clark of Meredith, New Hampshire, one of the founders of the International Lilac Society. Being a double cross of 'Rochester' this lilac should be used for hybridizing. ('Rochester' × 'Edward Gardner') × 'Rochester .

PLATE 82

The Lilacs from Falconskeape cover a wide range in hybridizing—from early to late blooming multibrids. Many blue introductions have been named here, the darkest blue is 'Wedgwood Blue', while the brightest blue is 'Blue Danube'.

'Alice Chieppo' *S. × hyacinthiflora* (D-IV, 1984)

'Arch McKean' (1984)

'Pat Pesata' (1981)

'Aloise' (1986)

'Albert Holden' (1980)

'Holy Maid' (1984). Huge florets of pale pink.

PLATE 83

PLANTING LILACS AS SINGLE SPECIMENS

One of their most useful values in landscaping
is as garden specimens.

S. vulgaris 'Flora' is a well chosen specimen for home gardens.

× *hyacinthiflora* 'Assissippi' (Skinner) at the M. Peterson
tate, Meadowlark Hill, Ogallala, Nebraska.

S. × *chinensis* 'Rouenensis' at Highland Park, Rochester, N.Y.

× *prestoniae* 'Calpurnia' makes a beautiful late blooming
ecimen for the garden, Niagara Parks, Niagara, Canada.

S. vulgaris 'Mme. F. Morel'

PLATE 84

LANDSCAPING USES OF LILACS

The versatile lilac adapts itself to many landscaping uses where its beauty adds greatly to the spring garden in either the small home planting of one or two lilacs, or to the larger estate or arboreta vistas of color.

In rock gardens Many lilacs are well suited for Rock Gardens—especially the little-leafed species such as *S. julianae* or *S. pubescens.* Photo is of lilacs at Royal Botanical Gardens, Hamilton, Canada

By the waterside By watersides, pools, small lakes, planted on a h where their roots are not waterlogged, lilacs are supre reflecting their image in water. Use white ones. (Lilacl Lumley Estate, Pelham, Mass.)

With woodlands Lilacs are excellent as intermediate plantings from gardens to woodlands. Use *S. × hyacinthiflora* with dogwoods (*Cornus*). Lumley Estate, Pelham, Mass.

As small trees Pictured is *S. × hyacinthiflora* 'Lamartine' pruned tree form at The John J. Tyler Arboretum, Lima, Pennsylvania.

In miniature or Japanese gardens

Choose small growing dwarfs, or low growing *S. vulgaris* 'Little Miss Muffet' (own root please or else they grow tall).

Al Fordham, Arnold Arboretum, examines the dwarf lilac *S. meyeri* 'Palibin' which is ideally suited for miniatu gardens.

PLATE 85

LILACS ON HILLSIDES, ON LARGE ESTATES, AND IN ARBORETA PLANTINGS

Ideally lilacs are at their best in mass plantings with plenty of room—here they excel.

Lilac 'Monge' planted to perfection at the Katie Osborne Garden, Royal Botanical Gardens, Hamilton, Canada.

Mass planting of lilacs, Shelburne, Burlington, Vermont. Outstanding lilacs!

A home hillside planting, Woodstock, Vermont, that is excellent.

Hillside lilacs at Butternut Ridge, R. Luce Estate, Hampden Highlands, Maine.

Young hillside planting at Highland Park, Rochester, N.Y.

Mass plantings of 'Miss Kim' at Niagara Parks, Niagara, Canada. A wonderful lilac collection!

PLATE 86

VARIETY IN 'LILAC WALKS'

Lilacia Park, Lyle, Illinois, retains Col. Plum's original barn amid wonderful walks of lilacs.

Lilac Walk at The Arnold Arboretum, one of the most famous and original plantings.

Longenecker Gardens lilac display, University of Wisconsin Arboretum.

Part of the Lilac Walk at Falconskeape, Medina, Ohio.

The magnificent Lilac Walk at Meadowlark Hill, estate of Mr. and Mrs. Max Petersen, Ogallala, Nebraska, one of the largest and finest lilac collections in the world.

PLATE 87

LILACS USED AS HEDGES AND SCREENS

Most lilac species can be used as screens, some few can be useful as clipped hedges.

S. × persica makes a wonderful border screen at the Royal
Botanical Gardens, Hamilton.

microphylla 'Superba' used as a formal, clipped hedge,
oyal Botanical Gardens.

S. vulgaris used as a property screen from the highway, Rt. 23, south of
Cooperstown, N.Y. Such screens are most effective and beautiful.

meyeri 'Palibin' makes a natural low growing hedge,
niversity of Guelph, Guelph, Canada.

S. × chinensis 'Metensis' and *S. × chinensis* 'Bicolor' form an attractive
hedge-screen along the older Lilac Walk at Highland Park, Rochester,
N.Y. It is beautiful and most effective.

PLATE 88

THE MASS EFFECT OF LARGE PLANTINGS OF LILACS

One cannot escape the landscape effect of very large plantings of massed lilac groups. Only an Arboretum or large Estate has room for this kind of planting. Where possible it should be encouraged—especially if one can look down upon the massed bloom.

The Grape Hill Gardens planting of lilacs in large massed groups is both breath taking in its beauty and extremely well done.

    Mon ami et amie—you MUST see this planting in the spring. It is at Clyde, New York, in the last week of May.

One of the world's finest massed plantings is at Highland Park, Rochester, N.Y. The 3rd–last week of May is peak bloom. This is one of the world's finest together with the Royal Botanical Gardens at Hamilton, Canada. There are many very fine lilac collections closer to home—search them out.

PLATE 89

One of the finest companions to the Early Hybrid Lilacs (*S.* × *hyacinthiflora*) is the flower crabs (*Malus*). Great progress has been made in recent decades to improve the flowering crabs making them a two-seasons ornamental—spring flowering and long-lasting, small-fruited colorful trees in autumn.

M. × 'White Cascade' (Ross) semi-weeper of highest quality with gold fruit.

S. vulgaris 'Lilasrosa' with *Malus baccata,* one of the larger species, in the background at Grapehill Gardens, Clyde, N.Y.

M. × 'Dorthea' (Sax.) One of the fine older crabs with my Grandmere Louise—it was her favorite.

M. × 'Doubloons' (Fiala 1984). An excellent double with gold fruit. Small tree.

S. × *hyacinthiflora* 'Pink Cloud' (Clarke 1947) is an excellent choice with all crabs of any color especially with the white or carmine such as *M.* × 'Silver Moon' (Simpson)

M. × 'Silver Moon'. Timing of bloom with the particular variety of both crab and lilac is most important for effective landscaping.

PLATE 90

The modern Flowering Crabs add springtime glory to the lilacs and in fall surround them with from 2 to 3 months of wonderfully colorful fruit.

Malus 'Prairie Rose' (left). Late blooming goes very well with late blue lilac 'Boule Azuree' (Lemoine 1919), (right).

S. × hyacinthiflora 'Pocahontas' (left) is excellent with Malus × 'Red Swan' (Fiala) (right).

The beautiful crab, Malus × 'Burgundy' (Simpson) is beautiful with white or pink early lilacs.

Autumn fruit of Malus × 'Firecracker' is a showy background of red buds opening white in Spring and a blanket of
red-fruit in Fall. The new crabs are two season companions,
fruiting in reds, orange, gold, yellow and chartruse lemons—
even to blue-purple!

PLATE 91

Hosta are ideal companion plants for lilacs. As their beautifully colored leaves unfold they provide a complementary carpet of interesting enhancement to the lilac bloom. Later, when lilacs are out of bloom, the *Hosta* put on their own flower show. The Bernard McLaughlin Estate, S. Paris, Maine, is a wonderful display of lilacs surrounded by hundreds of combinations of different *Hosta,* outstanding in the world. One must see it!

Hosta also are excellent with the species lilacs and late blooming Prestonians and Josiflexa Hybrids. Try one of the new variegated *Hosta* with *S. julianae, S. tigerstedtii* or *S. potaninii. Mon amie,* you will have sheer elegance! Remember, all the *Hosta* of one kind—not patchwork of several varieties.

Hosta 'Sunpower' (left) would be an excellent groundcover for lilac 'Primrose' (right).

Lilac 'Professor Hoser' (left) or any of the true blue lilacs are ideally matched with any of the real blue *Hosta* as 'Krossa Regal' (right) or others such as 'August Blue', *H. seiboldiana* or 'Blue Giant'.

lac 'Capitaine Baltet' footed with *Hosta* at the McLaughlin state.

H. *fluctans* 'Variegata' (left) or 'Ground Master' (right) give colorful zest as companions to most any colored lilacs such as S. vulgaris 'Virginia Becker' (center).

PLATE 92

COMPANION PLANTS TO LILACS

Among the many fine companion plants, some common and some exotic, is beautiful *Veronica rupestris* 'Heavenly Blue'. It goes well with white or blue or pink lilacs but must be kept within limits. Can be mowed.

A bed of lilac 'Sensation' is planted with deep purple *Ajuga* at Highland Park, Rochester, N.Y. It will grow in beauty as the *Ajuga* spreads and lilacs mature.

Conifers are always excellent backgrounds for all lilacs. A fine planting as seen at the Royal Botanical Gardens, Hamilton, Ontario. Note also the excellent low underplanting.

The white lilacs do very well with yellow and orange Exbury Azaleas or with *A. mollis*. Avoid other colors of lilacs that would clash with the colorful azaleas. Pictured is lilac 'Mme. Lemoine' with choice Exbury azaleas at the Bernard McLaughlin Gardens, S. Paris, Maine.

Early spring bulbs, especially Tulips, are an annual feature with the hundreds of blooming lilacs at Lilacia Park, Lyle, Illinois. Perhaps no other display of superb lilacs and tulips can be found anywhere else!

Sedums, hemerocallis and many choice perennials are companions to lilacs at the McLaughlin Gardens. Late blooming perennials give early greenery to lilac bloom and a later display of their own with the good green of lilacs as a background.

PLATE 93

TRANSPLANTING AND REJUVENATING 30 YEAR OLD LILACS

The Holden Arboretum Story. Lilacs, even very old lilacs, can be successfully replanted as at Holden Arboretum, Mentor, Ohio in 1979–1980. (Photos by C. Gauci, Holden Arboretum)

ckhoe used to dig lilac balls and to lift them onto wooden llets.

Lifting root ball

Transfer to wooden pallets

oot formation in holding bed of wood-chips and river ravel and straw.

At Holden lilacs were first planted in a wood chip holding bed and then transplanted, after heavy root formation, to their permanent location.

A transplanted, pruned 'Alphonse Lavalee' after 2 years.

PLATE 94

GOOD AND REGULAR PRUNING

One of the most essential requirements for growing good lilacs. There is nothing that deteriorates lilacs and the size and quality of their bloom as neglected pruning. Not to make it a horrendous chore, some pruning of each bush should be made each year, thus gradually rejuvenating the whole bush for strong, healthy growth.

A 30 year old plant of 'Mauve Mist' after it had been renewe[...] 2 years before by drastic cutting back to the ground and encouraged to grow new suckers.

Most very old lilacs are best renewed somewhat gradually as pictured here at Ewing Park, Des Moines, Iowa, where the whole lilac collection was successfully renewed by careful pruning. Only the best younger canes should be retained and the strongest suckers encouraged to grow.

PLATE 95

DISEASES THAT AFFLICT THE LILAC

Perhaps the most serious disease of lilacs is Lilac Blight since it destroys the current bloom and disfigures the lilacs when they should be at their best. Cold spring rains and frosts bring about conditions that favor lilac blight.

Frost damage blasts buds that seem not to have been affected but never grow. Note the many unopened buds on 'Lucie Baltet', these will never open.

Branches of *S. × prestoniae* 'Royalty' afflicted with the 'Brooming Disease' (Witches Broom). Note the many little branchlets that arise from a single bud. These brooms will eventually die. 'Brooming' appears to be a systemic virus and its only known control is to destroy the entire plant to prevent spreading. It is not commonly found on *S. vulgaris* as it is on the *S. × prestoniae*.

PLATE 96

Japanese Beetle

Cicada laying eggs on lilac

Oyster Shell Scale-adults

Oyster Shell Scale. Cottony young as they move about.

Webworm on lilacs.

Giant Hornet Nest

Stripping bark work of the Giant Hornet. Branches will die.

Damaged lilac canes by deer rutting and horn rubbing. All damaged canes will die.

CHAPTER SEVEN

Lilac Culture

As beautiful and useful as lilacs are, people are surprised to learn how undemanding are their cultural requirements. Nor are these splendid plants particularly susceptible to disease or pests. There are but four basics for good lilac culture: good drainage, good soil, good sunlight, and good pruning. Given these your lilac bushes will grow and blossom each year with little other care.

GOOD DRAINAGE

Lilacs above all are shrubs or small trees requiring good drainage. They are children of the fertile hills and the shrub borders that once fringed mountain woodlands. In their native habitat they never venture into swampy areas nor are they found where drainage is not perfect at all times of the year. They are exuberant growers in sandy, gravelly loams that have good drainage. Under such conditions they send forth strong shoots and luxuriant foliage.

If one can control drainage and possesses a gravelly-sandy loam, then lilacs may be planted with no further thought or work in soil resembling that of their native home. In such well-drained soils simply dig an ample hole, about twice the diameter of the rootball, enrich the soil at the bottom with organic matter, plant the lilac and add additional rich soil to cover the crown, mounding the lilac very slightly.

Not so in clays and heavy soils! In such sites, a planting hole as just described, no matter how large or how much enriched soil is returned, is fatal. The clay walls make an underground crypt that holds water and saturates whatever soil has been put into it. Planting, or rather entombing, a lilac in such a clay crypt is 'certain death'! The clay walls make an impenetrable barrier for collected water. The roots of the lilac soon begin to decay and in a matter of a few weeks they are a mass of blackened fibers and rotting roots. This does not mean you cannot grow lilacs, and grow them well, in clay and heavy soils, but it does mean you cannot plant them in the traditional way and expect them to survive. In heavy soils, enriched clays and clay-loams or soils that have heavy clay or rock understrata, one must plant lilacs 'on top of the soil' rather than in it! (*Bon jardinier*—do not despair—I will tell you how.)

In these more difficult soils, drainage must be the first consideration. If one has a hillside or slope, it would be wise to plant the lilac plantings on them (always in the top third and never in the lower half of the slope, as lower slopes weep from the water moving from the top down). When one is not lucky enough to have a slope and so must plant lilacs on a level, poorly drained site, place a layer, 6–8 in. deep, of gravelly-sand directly on the surface of the heavier soil. Over this add a gentle mound-like layer of good, sandy-gravelly loam to a depth of at least 6 in. Then add 4–6 in. of rotted manure or humus. Over this organic layer place another 6 in. of good soil mix. Use good, well-drained, organically enriched garden soil with plenty of sandy gravel (pea size) in it. Slope the sides gently for easy mowing or care. Then plant your lilacs on top of the mound, adding another foot of good soil over their roots capping off your special lilac bed to a height of 3 ft. or so. Remember, this mound will settle several inches with time but at least your lilacs will have excellent drainage and good soil! Eventually some roots will reach the heavier soil below but not the fibrous feeding and nourishing roots which the lilac needs to survive and flourish. (*Bon jardinier*, it is a bit of work but lilacs are planted only a few times in one's life! Do it well!)

In this way one can make excellent 'raised beds' for lilacs, gently sloping the sides so that the grass of underplantings look natural and at home. Do not plant lilacs on man-made mountain peaks that look like ancient burial grounds. Let your raised planting areas appear to naturally rise from the ground as a slight mound or rolling terrain. If one must use this manner of planting, it is more economical to make a longer raised-bed that will accommodate several lilacs in 2 or 3 alternately spaced rows. Always plant the tallest growing varieties in the background and to the middle with the lower growing kinds to the front and sides. The lowest growing ones, like 'Lucie Baltet', 'Little Miss Muffet', 'Purple Glory' and 'Purple Gem' and some of the newer dwarfs are always placed up front.

Every 3 or 4 years add medium to your raised areas in the form of mulches and good top-dressing. Lilacs will thrive beautifully in such mounded plantings. They must have at least 6 in. of good soil covering their root areas. You may prefer to plant them far apart, enough for a mowed grassy walk between them, or a bit closer and underplant them with fine companion plants. Be mindful that your lilacs will spread with age (like most of us). The whole story about this Balkan beauty, *Syringa vulgaris*, and its Chinese cousins, the species lilacs, can be summed up by pointing out that they may on occasion have their feet in swift flowing mountain freshets and streams, but they never, absolutely never, will stand in rice paddies or swamps! (No, *mon bon jardinier*, never! *Madame* must always have dry feet!)

GOOD SOIL

Lilacs thrive, exuberate, luxuriate and radiate beauty and health when they have well-drained, good soils! It need not necessarily be the 'best' but at least good corn-growing, potato-producing, flower-blooming soil. It should be fairly rich in organic matter if lilacs are expected to grow well and bloom for many years. No, a bushel or so of sphagnum or peat will not do. An abundance of good garden soil is required to allow your lilac to grow for many years. You cannot expect good bloom without strong, annual growth of shoots. Unlike flowering crabs and many shrubs, lilacs do not bloom from blossom spurs that remain year after year. New shoots carry the lilac blossom load for each coming spring. A fine display of flowers is obtained from good growth and by pruning.

When well established, new growth will exceed 6 in. of pencil-thick shoots. Such shoots will produce fat, strong flowering buds for the next season. If growth is thin and long (16 or more inches in one season) it may be that the lilacs are in too rich a soil, suffer too much shade and are reaching for the sun, or need pruning and thinning. In any case these thin shoots often do not bloom and if they do the flowers are thin, small and tend to droop. In the common lilac, *S. vulgaris*, and the Early Hybrids, next spring's flowers are set early on this year's spring-summer growth. Whereas in the late blooming species and their hybrids, the bloom comes from the new spring growth. In both cases the bloom depends on the health of last year's growth and vegetative buds.

Soil is better when enriched with high, organic materials that give it tilth, rather than commercial fertilizers. The latter, although they add nutrients, do not build up the tilth (tone or texture) of the soil which provides drainage capacity, air-holding ability and the environment needed by beneficial soil organisms. Of course, moderate fertilization is far better than allowing the soil to become depleted of nitrogen, phosphorous and potash—soil so poor that not even weeds will grow in it.

A word about weeds—good healthy weeds. They are a fine indicator of good soil. Spindly weeds, especially those with reddish and off-color leaves, are an indication of poor soil—hard-pan clays and mineral deficient ground that will not grow good lilacs. (Better to use such soils for parking areas or tennis courts.)

Do not despair if you have poor soil. Enrich it with mulches and mix sand-gravel with it. Plant rye or wheat to turn under, when a foot high, building up organic content. Get stable manure, straw, sawdust, add nitrogen fertilizer to help them rot and let set for a year after rototilling them into the soil. Repeat this performance a few years in a row and "Lo!" your tennis area or parking lot is magically transformed into garden soil! Be mindful it takes blood, sweat and constant effort but it wins the war against clay, hard-pan and just no-good soils! (*Mon ami*, now you know why your lilacs and other plants will not grow in the excavated ground from your basement piled around the foundation of your home with a two inch topping of 'garden soil'!)

Should your soil be too sandy or stony, beware. It may lack sufficient humus or organic matter for things to grow really well. In hot weather nutrients leach out of sandy soils quickly and roots dry up readily. But again, organic matter will save the soil and you must incorporate large

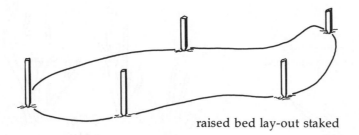

raised bed lay-out staked

on ground level — 6" sand-gravel

6" sand-gravel plus 6–8" garden loam

6" gravel plus 6–8" loam plus 3–4" manure

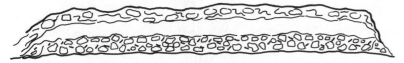

add 6" special soil mix and plant lilacs on top

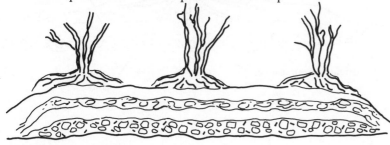

cover lilac roots with 8" special soil mix
mulch with 3–4" wood-chips, sawdust-straw etc.

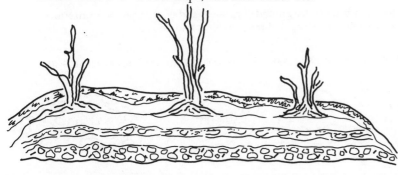

(Drawings by J. Fiala)

PREPARING AN ABOVE GROUND LILAC BED
A Necessity in Heavy Clay and Hardpan Soils
Steps:

1. Stake out the bed and its contours. Note that it drain well and not stand in any natural waterways.
2. Lay a good foundation of sand and gravel at least 6–8 inches.
3. Cover with at least 6 inches of good garden loam mixed with sand-gravel.
4. Cover this foundation with 3 to 6 inches of well rotted stable manure or good humus. If manure is used it must be 2 year rotted, better 3 years, NEVER fresh. Mix it with rotted wood-chips or rotted sawdust—half and half.
5. Cover well rotted stable manure (cow or horse) with 6 to 8 inches good soil mix (⅓ good loam, ⅓ sharp sand, ⅓ humus).
6. Plant lilacs on top of this and cover them to 8 inches with the same good soil mix (loam-sand-humus). Do not plant lilacs in manure layer—let their roots grow down into it.
7. This approximately 30 inches will settle 6 inches. In large areas raise your bed to 3 feet or more.
8. For plants on top of the mounded area leave a dish basin around them for water as it will otherwise run off.
9. Do not make the sides steep. There will be no erosion and the mound will fit more comfortably in the landscape.
10. Watch your lilacs grow!

In well-drained gravel-sandy soils you may plant directly in the ground. Enrich the hole with good soil.

In clay or heavy soil make planting beds above the ground with a good gravel base covered with 2 to 3 feet of good loam.

Always this kind of planting for heavy clay soils—

IN HEAVY CLAY SOILS
Never dig a hole; it becomes a water-casket for the lilac to rot in.

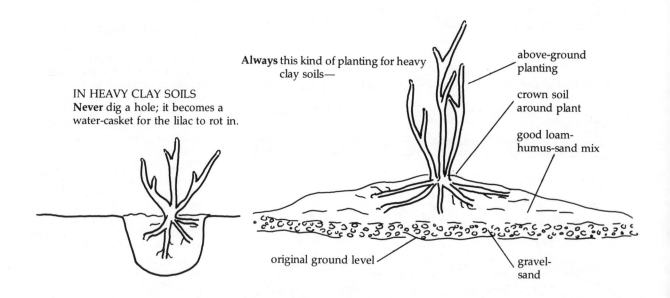

above-ground planting

crown soil around plant

good loam-humus-sand mix

original ground level

gravel-sand

(Drawings by J. Fiala)

Grandmere's old 'kitchen garden' where kitchen garbage, coffee grounds, egg shells and a few bones found their final rest, provided the built-up soil for her magnificently flowering and fragrant lilacs and flowers!

SAND AND GRAVEL + ORGANIC MATTER + GARDEN LOAM + HANDFUL LIME = IDEAL LILAC SOIL

amounts of organic matter such as straw, manure, compost, wood chips and sawdust adding nitrogen to aid their decay. Clay soil owners are not the only ones who must learn to work miracles in building up their soil tilth; even sand dunes succumb to hard and persistent enrichment. I have seen beautiful lilacs growing all along the coast of Maine in sandy soils that have been enriched by nature and by man, despite salt winds and cold northeasterlies!

WETTING SOIL AMENDMENTS

When adding large volumes of dry, organic materials to your soils, such as dry peat, shredded barks, sawdust, wood-chips and dry straws, always remember that these materials take a long time before they absorb water. They are resistant to wetting, so small plants, seedling lilacs, small rooted cuttings or newly planted lilacs can quickly dry out for lack of moisture, especially on hot days (even though you may have watered them very recently). These soil amendments do not initially hold water readily. Research has shown that 70–78% moisture saturation is achieved within 5 days with peat-vermiculite medium, but 45 days are required for milled pine bark medium to achieve a saturation of 58–78%. This difference accounts for the failure of lilacs in some nurseries using holding beds composed of such mixes. Allow a lot more time for these amendments to become wettable before planting. It is well to have them piled for a year and beginning to decay before adding them to your soil. (*Bon jardinier,* you do not want to lose all your fine lilac seedlings or rooted cuttings, do you?)

FULL SUN—THE LILACS' LIMELIGHT

Visiting the truly magnificent lilacs of the Katie Osborne Lilac Garden at the Royal Botanical Gardens at Hamilton, Ontario, Canada, and seeing beautiful specimen lilacs grown with loving care in partial high shade can be deceiving. This carefully grown garden is an exception. Lilacs love full sun for at least two-thirds of the day. They will sulk and refuse to set their flower buds well, if relegated to a place in the shadows. No, lilacs are 'star performers', they insist on having the leading place in the sun! They do not like the shade nor root competition from greedy trees or rapacious shrubs. (*Madame* needs room, air and sunlight to display her majesty!)

If one has good ground, rolling slopes and trees trimmed to cast high shade for a small part of the day only, then one can replicate the splendid plantings at the Katie Osborne Lilac Garden at the Royal Botanical in Hamilton. Theirs is superb culture. It requires work that many gardeners cannot undertake, a knowledge of root systems and splendid selection of individual sites. The limited shade does keep the darker colors of lilacs from fading and in excellent condition. However, for most lilac growers the rule must be, plant your lilacs in nearly full sun. They will be beautiful, bloom their hearts out and never disappoint you come May and June!

TRANSPLANTING LILACS

Lilacs, even 40-year-old plants, can be transplanted at most any time of the year if done properly. The best time, however, is when they are dormant or not growing, generally in the fall, late summer or early spring (in that order of preference). Tests have shown that late fall and the hot days of late July-August are excellent times to transplant lilacs, even better than early spring. However, you must be alert to what you are doing and to after-care.

When transplanting lilacs take as many of the fibrous, close-to-the-surface feeding roots as possible. Lilacs are rather shallowly rooted and top feeders. Most of their feeding roots are in the top foot and a half of soil; their anchoring roots go deeper but are not as necessary as the feeding roots. In transplanting, a small portion of the roots will necessarily be lost. Compensate for this loss by removing a proportionate part of the top of the plant cutting it back or heavily pruning it.

Tests during the gigantic re-landscaping of the excellent lilac collection at the Holden Arboretum in Kirtland-Mentor, Ohio, produced some amazing insights into transplanting lilacs. Gauci and Martin found that lilacs, even 40-year-old bushes, lifted by forklifts, and held for several months in a gravel-sand bed, mulched with straw continued to grow excellent fibrous feeding roots. After being replanted several months later they continued excellent growth. They were watered daily in the heat of the summer while in the straw-gravel mulch holding beds. The summer root growth in these beds was phenomenal!

In the home garden the same results can be had if lilacs are given excellent drainage after transplanting (gravel-sand), are watered frequently and moderately top pruned. Excellent drainage and a good flow of water-air around the roots is a necessity. Gravel-woodchips-straw mulch immediately on the roots does much to provide this. Do not just pack good soil, tramped down, that is water saturated on the roots. They need moist air-drainage too. The key to successful transplanting of lilacs rests in a good soil ball of undamaged fibrous roots, good drainage, a good sand-gravel underlay and good watering. Lilacs will not transplant well if they are set in a water hole for any length of time. Avoid water-saturated, soil-filled, mud-holes at all times. Firm your lilacs down after transplanting but do not trample them. (*Mon ami,* you are moving beloved friends, not tramping out grapes for wine!)

Fibrous growth of lilacs held in a special holding bed until replanted 6 months later indicates the need of lilacs for sand-gravel at their roots. Between 11–22 in. of fibrous roots developed in this kind of mulch. It is an indication that perhaps we are not planting our lilacs with enough sand-gravel at their roots for adequate drainage, air-flow, and growth. (Photo Gauci-Martin, Holden Arboretum.)

Root growth measured 8 weeks after transplanting: 11 inches.

Root growth measured in April, 1979 at 28 inches.

PRUNING LILACS

How shall you prune your lilacs? First one must consider what landscaping effect is to be achieved? Tall, background lilac trees are pruned differently from shrubs that are to be used as single specimens or in massed effect. Whereas smaller, eye-level shrubs usually require more severe pruning. Each purpose demands a somewhat slightly different approach, yet prune one must!

Can one get away with no or very little pruning? Certainly, witness the fact that many wild growing lilacs bloom around abandoned or burnt-out buildings or have kept faith over a stone cellar whose frame house has long vanished. Yet, through it all "Lilacs still by the dooryard bloom!" They will bloom, but how? Not in a magnificent and grand style, neither at their best nor in full beauty. For good bloom a certain amount of pruning is required—even if it be cutting lilacs when in bloom with longer than usual stems.

How much should one prune in any one season? Certainly prune out all diseased or infested canes, all old, unnecessary and declining stems, wild, thin suckers and all twiggy small branches. (Twiggy small branches are a sign of poor growth and indicate a need for nourishment and pruning.) The next good rule of thumb is to cut out ¼ to ⅓ of the oldest branches and suckers each year. This allows your bush to renew itself with good strong canes and growth every 4 years. Leave the strongest trunks that will form the frame of the shrub. Eliminate all but the strongest of the suckers. (Some lilacs sucker a great deal, others only rarely.) Leave a few of the strongest to replace older canes and for new plants that will be later separated from the plant. Prune some of the height off so that your bush will not become a tree. Keep the bloom at eye-level by holding the height to about 8 or 9 ft.

Please do not let your pruning go for a decade before you are forced into it. It then becomes a horrendous, major job, hard work and a considerable disfigurement to the landscape. If you have been derelict, by all means do it. (The lilacs will certainly survive, but you may not!)

REJUVENATING OLDER LILACS

When older bushes begin to decline—main trunks are filled with borers, growth is poor, blossoms are small and new wood is sparse—then drastic measures aimed at rejuvenation must be undertaken. First, look to the soil conditions. Are they growing in poor, depleted, worn-out soil? This is the principal reason for lilac decline in plants 30 or more years old. Over the years without mulches and care the soil not only is depleted but is compacted and thus poorly drained. The lilacs have taken a heavy toll on the available soil nutrients. Hand-in-hand with rejuvenating pruning one must also do some serious soil improvement adding manures, mulches and top-dressing in abundance. Feed your older lilacs well.

At times lilacs fail with age because unnoticed changes have been made in drainage and roots begin to decay. Seek out these changes in your lilac plantings. Pollution, soil depletion, age, and disease are all factors in decline. Each must be considered individually. However, drastic rejuvenation by cutting old lilacs to the ground together with soil enrichment most often is all that is needed for a whole new plant.

After attending to the soil one must often cut out all the oldest wood to the ground to allow the lilac to renew itself by growing new suckers. If you perform this pruning over a 3-year period, the plant will not look so forlorn. Never underestimate the stamina of old lilacs. Most often they will renew themselves vigorously and in a few years you will have a new, young shrub. Pruning does not always work. Then you have to say to your lilac friend, "Alas, poor Yorick, I knew you well"—as you dig out the dead centenarian root. (*Mon ami,* one can never quite tell, as with people, if the lilac is merely old or actually dying.)

Caution and beware!! If your lilacs are of that unhappy kind grafted on privet or common lilac rootstock, you cannot prune or rejuvenate them by cutting back to the ground. Alas, you will, if so foolish as to buy such grafts, find the chicanery of plant magic has transformed your once beautiful lilac into a privet shrub or a French lilac into a common lilac bloom. How? Because you have removed the grafted cultivar top and the understock is all you have left! Someone may ask what kind of lilac you have as they gaze at a privet, *S. villosa* or *S. persica* plant upon which your choice lilac once grew. This is very good reason why one should plant only own-root lilacs. If you buy grafted lilacs, which the gods forbid, but if you insist, then you must plant them deep to form their own roots above the graft and remove any rootstock growth from below the graft. This undergrowth from the mothering root-stock left unremoved will soon starve off the grafted top.

(*Sacre Bleu!* May this never happen to you!).

OTHER GOOD CULTURAL PRACTICES

Keep your lilacs free of weeds; give them room to grow; avoid competitive trees and shrubs; plant them out of wind-swept locations and avoid unusually warm sites that force buds into premature bloom. (*Madame* Lilac does not like false cues for her debut or the false sun's flirting eye. Ah, such progeny is all misshapen, frost-bitten, undeveloped buds! Nothing but dismay and grief!)

Add to all the above advice a couple of handfuls of ground limestone every third year around each lilac and they will remain happy. Give them the 'four goods'—drainage, soil, sunlight and pruning plus attention to pests and then may you live to see your lilacs blooming 'to the third and fourth generations' with fat lilac buds and heavy bloom around your festive garden. Lilacs have only these simple cultural needs, but they need ALL of them. They will not settle for two or three. They demand all the above! As you see them flourish and repay your efforts, then and only then . . .

Rejuvenating nearly century old lilacs at Highland Park, Rochester, New York. After decades of beauty and performance old lilacs begin to wane. Their flowers, though many, decrease considerably in size for lack of young wood needed for top bloom. You may wish to preserve a gnarled, twisting trunk, but if you prefer good lilac bloom you had better do some rejuvenating as they did some years ago at Highland Park.

The pictures above show before and two and three years after pictures. When such drastic cutting back must be done, one will have to sacrifice some bloom for a few years, although not all. What a wonderful joy to have the old replaced by a youthful shrub full of new growth and heavy with large blossoms!

These pruning techniques done at large Parks and Arboreta collections can be duplicated (in fact should, on a smaller scale) in the home garden and estate.

For really good lilacs you simply MUST prune! Many lilacs can go years without drastic pruning. If you prune a little each year you never need resort to heavy and drastic measures. (Picture at lower right.)

Remember together with pruning one must also enrich and replace old, depleted ground that has settled and become void of nutrients. Good new growth is dependent on good soil.

(Photos by Robert B. Clark)

'until death shall ye part' with them! (*Bon jardinier,* these lilacs are a 'love story' of work, sacrifice and exquisite beauty!)

When lilacs cease growing well they begin to 'blueberry' or 'twig' their annual growth. This short stubby growth produces small flowers or none at all. When this happens it is time to consider removing the whole main stem and let the newer stronger suckers take over. As we have mentioned, before making such a pruning decision look to the condition of the soil and consider the need for good growing conditions. 'Blueberrying' is frequently a sign of compacted, waterlogged soils with insufficient tilth, air and drainage. Often the more drastic measures of improving the plant's environment must be taken rather than pruning.

If you are seeking lilacs as trees or background plants, then pruning is usually directed to retaining only 2 or 3 main stems and cutting off all other shoots, removing all lower branches and allowing the plant to grow upward, tree-like. Certain cultivars such as the *S. oblata* 'Giraldii' and the Late Hybrids *S.* × *prestoniae* are best suited for this kind of background use (although *S.* × *prestoniae* make wonderful shrub specimens pruned as most lilacs to lower form). *S. vulgaris,* excepting only the oldest common lavender and white forms (*S. vulgaris purpurea* and *alba*) do not make good small trees. If used as background or hedge materials, they are best pruned at the base to a moderate but higher bush form, cutting away suckers and weaker growth. Many of the dwarf and low-growing lilacs require little pruning except to keep them from getting too old by replacing the oldest trunks with newer shoots.

Generally all lilacs are greatly improved by annual pruning and rejuvenation. Cutting off old seed pods scores no points as pruning, this does not count as sufficient removal of actually growing old wood. It is tidy, cosmetic work, helpful if done immediately after blooming, but it is not pruning.

CHAPTER EIGHT

Lilac Diseases, Pests and Problems

Diseases of Lilacs

Generally the diseases affecting lilacs are not as serious nor do they cause as much trouble as insect pests. There are, however, a few diseases that, when they strike, can be rather devastating. The most serious are the bacterial blights.

BACTERIAL BLIGHT (*Bacterium pseudomonas syringea*)

'Lilac Blight', as it is generally called, is the most serious disease of lilacs. It is not a problem every year nor in every locality, but enough of it is being seen in lilac plantings to arouse concern and require both a knowledge and method for dealing with it. It is more common in the moist Pacific Northwest and throughout the heavier clay soils of the Midwest than in New England, the Eastern States and Canada. I believe it to be associated with the longer, more variable, frost-pocketed springs experienced in those areas compared to the more even advance and later coming of springtime in the East. It is definitely associated with wet, humid, frosty nights and warm days associated with cold spring rains. The general symptoms resemble those of fire blight (also a bacterial disease).

Initial symptoms resemble water-soaked blotches on the new foliage. A bit later these areas begin to wilt and turn dark brown. Affected areas and blossoms may also turn black. Early symptoms on young shoots are a black striping around the shoot or a blackening of one side of the shoot. Ordinarily the discoloration does not extend very far but enough to wilt, then blacken the new growth, leaves and buds. The affected shoots have a noticeable black, droopy quality.

One means of controlling bacterial blight is pruning out stems to provide better air circulation. Sterilize tools in alcohol or strong bleach, since you are dealing with a bacterial disease that enters the plant through wounds. Bacteria ooze from the infected tissue, especially in rainy weather, so it is best to avoid any kind of pruning during wet, humid conditions. We have found that apart from appearance, once the infection has set in, immediate pruning is of no real value. Where adverse environmental conditions prevail, avoid using high nitrogen fertilizers in the spring that cause an excess of soft, flush new growth.

The only control spray recommended and cleared for use on lilacs under these conditions is Bordeaux mixture used at the rate of 2-2-50 (2 pounds copper sulfate, 2 pounds hydrated lime mixed thoroughly with 50 gallons of water). Apply it as soon as you see any symptoms of blight. After the weather warms up and the blight is past, cut off all dead and blackened areas and burn them. The lilacs will respond with new growth and should be fine in the coming year. Tidy up and prune for more open plants and watch for overcrowding from other shrubs that block air flow. Plants when young, with plenty of space between them are not so readily infected as when older and they begin to crowd for space. This blight results in the loss of both leaves and blooming buds.

PHYTOPHTHORA BLIGHT (*Phytophthora syringea*)

Phytophtora Blight is less often seen in lilacs but is similar to Bacterial Blight. Its lesions are brown rather than black. It kills shoots and root sprouts to a greater extent, very often to the ground line. It is a soil-borne fungus and is typically a wet-weather disease, although after long periods of drought it can also do serious damage. Plants under stress appear more susceptible to the disease pathogen.

For some control, pruning and thinning is recommended. Susceptible plants may be sprayed with Bordeaux mixture when the leaves are opening and again when they are fully opened. This precaution need not be taken unless the disease has been serious in the previous year. Often pruning or removing excessive foliage both of the afflicted plant and adjacent shrubs to create air flow is the best measure. A good practice is to avoid growing lilacs in mixed plantings or in close proximity to rhododendrons or elderberry, both of which are highly susceptible to phytophthora infection. Considerable spread of the disease may occur in such mixed plantings.

STEM BLIGHT (*Ascochyta syringea*)

This particular blight is reportedly common in South England but not in North America. Treat as for other blights.

VERTICILLIUM WILT (*Verticillium albo-atrum*)

Verticillium Wilt is not common in lilacs but is found in other plants. Initial symptoms are a loss of glossiness of leaves which later turn pale and wilt. Premature defoliation of branches is common, with affected branches dying to the ground. Ordinarily there is some discoloration of the wood or xylem of the affected stem. It differs from phytophthora blight in that there are no external lesions on wilting stems. Sudden wilting occurs with no external symptoms. You must cut into the bark to detect the infection. The fungus is soil-borne. No preventive measure is known. Remove and burn the entire plant—which in time will die anyway. Do not replant lilacs in soils where verticillium thrives.

FROST CHILLING OR FREEZING OF LILACS

A rather common problem in the West and Midwest is damage to leaves and buds caused by chilling and freezing. In these areas unseasonably warm weather often pushes buds beyond a safe level, so subsequent frosts damage the leaves and particularly the small buds. This generally occurs when the buds are not yet in the real color stage. The buds appear to be in good form but fail to advance. It may be a week before one realizes that they have been frozen and will not open. Often part of the bud will freeze and the upper portions continue to advance resulting in a misshapened and partially floreted thyrse. Some lilac cultivars appear to be more susceptible to frost damage than others. Many of the Early Hybrids seem to escape this damage, whereas some of the earlier *S. vulgaris* are very prone to freeze damage in the bud stages. Generally neither leaves nor buds turn brown, but the leaves have a characteristic curl or pinched effect around the edges where they have frozen which hinders the development of the leaf. There is no remedy for the vagaries of the weather, but in some gardens improvement of air-flow may alleviate this damage by eliminating frost pockets.

Lilac blights, wilts, frozen buds and frost damage all seem to appear together in a given spring. All are results of radical temperature fluctuations. In the Midwest it is not uncommon to have early spring days in the 50°–60°F. range while night temperatures drop suddenly to 25°F. This is the kind of weather, especially if accompanied by rains and sleets, that accelerate these plant diseases and troubles. It is amazing how sturdy lilacs really are in coping with such extremes. The eastern seaboard does not appear to have such radical day-night variations, although they do on occasion have killing frosts. Theirs is a milder and later entrance of Spring!

WIND CHILL CHART

Wind Speed 0 MPH	Actual thermometer readings at						
	40°	30°	20°	10°	0°	−10°	−20°
5 MPH	37°	27°	16°	7°	−6°	−15°	−26°
10 MPH	28°	16°	2°	−9°	−22°	−31°	−45°
15 MPH	22°	11°	−6°	−18°	−33°	−45°	−60°
20 MPH	18°	3°	−9°	−24°	−40°	−52°	−68°
25 MPH	16°	0°	−15°	−29°	−45°	−58°	−75°
30 MPH	13°	−2°	−18°	−33°	−49°	−63°	−78°
35 MPH	11°	−4°	−20°	−35°	−52°	−67°	−83°
40 MPH	10°	−6°	−22°	−36°	−54°	−69°	−87°

Although lilacs are very rugged and withstand extremely cold weather, premature balmy days of spring do cause some troubles. Avoid planting lilacs in warm areas near the house that will prematurely force buds; see to good air flow and a location that has a windbreak from wind-chill. Often it is colder than one may think in wind-chill areas. A good windbreak will do marvels for lilacs.

MILDEW ON LILACS (*Microsphaera alni*)

Mildew, the fungus *Microsphera alni*, named for the alder (*Alnus*) on which it was first discovered, affects many plants, among which is the lilac. Spores germinate on the leaf surface and the fungus growth called 'mycelium' continues mostly on the surface although it will invade the leaf surface to draw nourishment from the epidermal layer, generally entering through a leaf stomate.

In late summer and fall mildew often appears as a white, powdery film on lilac leaves. Usually it is associated with damp, wet weather and warm humid nights. If it appears in the flush of the growing season it can somewhat stunt the growth of and cause a yellowing of the leaves, but this is not the ordinary picture. Mostly older leaves are affected with the white, sometimes cottony film. It is not difficult to control but rather bothersome. Rarely does it do any harm to an otherwise healthy plant.

To get rid of mildew effectively use wettable sulphur at the rate of 3 pounds in 100 gals of water, or Karathane at ½ pound to 100 gallons of water. For complete control 2 or 3 applications should be made beginning as soon as the fungus spots appear, then again at 3-week intervals. Noticeable results are evident with one spraying but 2 or 3 are recommended for complete kill of late fungus spores.

At most it is a superficial disease, although it may be very unsightly on a focal doorway plant or patio specimen. Extensive tests made at the National Arboretum by Dr. Donald Egolf clearly prove that all lilacs can host mildew, with some cultivars far more susceptible than others. In growing lilac seedlings, one can detect at a very early age those that are highly susceptible among the seedlings and discard them. Generally *S. vulgaris* cultivars appear to be more susceptible than the other species and their hybrids. Rarely does one find mildew on the tree lilacs, *S. pekinensis* and *S. reticulata*.

Dr. Owen Rogers, University of New Hampshire, an authority on lilacs, summarizes mildew on lilacs very well:

1. Leave it alone. The plant will survive if otherwise healthy.
2. Spray with chemicals if the shrub is very visible or valuable.
3. Replace the cultivar with one that is more resistant.

All this advice is excellent. You must be the ultimate judge as to how disturbed you wish to become about mildew. Some very beautiful cultivars, such as Lemoine's 'Rosace', are extremely susceptible, others are relatively immune.

Mildew on lilacs.

Left, Microsphaera alni (mildew) on *S. vulgaris* with mature cleistothecia (× 407, T-68°, wd 22.9). *Right, Microsphaera alni* on *Syringa vulgaris* showing stomate with mycelium (20kv-1360x). (Photos Dr. Owen Rogers, Plant Science, Univ. of New Hampshire.)

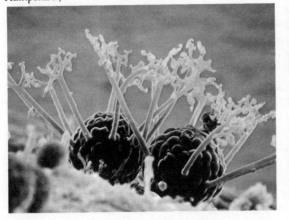 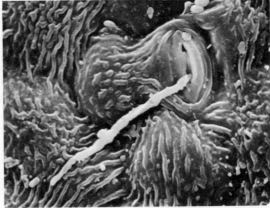

Insect Enemies of the Lilac

LILAC SCALES (Oyster Scale, *Lepidosaphes ulmi*, and San Jose Scale, *Aspidiotus perniciosus*)

Scale is the Number One enemy of lilacs. Left unattended it can destroy a whole garden of lilacs. It is a small insect, gray or brown in color that lives under a tough shell very reminiscent of a very, very small oyster shell, hence its common name, Oyster Shell Scale. There is another form, the San Jose Scale which is a bit larger, rounder and scalloped, that occasionally infests lilacs, but the common Oyster Scale is by far the most prevalent. Since scales of all kinds thrive on a variety of hosts, especially ash and willows, they are constantly being introduced into the garden by wind-blown mites and on the feet of birds as they hop from branch to branch. One must be on constant guard to attack this troublesome pest as soon as it manifests itself either on lilacs or any of the many host trees and shrubs. Since it is almost impossible to eliminate scale from large growing ash or willows, do not plant your lilacs in close proximity to or on the windward side of these hosts.

For some unknown reason scale seems to more rapidly infect plants that are in a some-what weakened condition, those that are poor growers, those surrounded by weeds or neglected. An infestation often follows a heavy application of cow manure. They start slowly on a twig or at the base of a cane and soon spread over the whole plant. Mostly they invade the 2- or 3-year-old canes at their base then quickly climb upward, sideways and anywhere they can crawl. Do not be mistaken that they are permanently encrusted in one section because you cannot see them moving. On days when temperatures are above 60°F they loosen hold and very slowly begin to travel. In the mite stage, when they are nearly microscopic white wooly specks, they are great little travelers both on the host shrub and as wind-borne air travelers, ever seeking new plants to infest. If left alone they soon encircle a cane, particularly at the branch junctures, and so sap its vitality that the cane and often the whole plant soon dies. They are particularly noticeable in the fall after the leaves are gone and reveal the full infestation.

Make no mistake, scale is one of the toughest insects to fight. When it is not on the move it will not die under its protective shield no matter how it is sprayed. The shell appears glued to the branch and cannot be washed away. If, perchance, it should die it seems always to leave enough eggs to continue the infestation, hidden in a bark crevice or under a branch juncture. Hence control must always include more than one spraying.

If there are only a very few scales they can be effectively rubbed off with a sharp stick, blade or plastic label. For a larger infestation an inclusive spray must be used for the adult scale in its crawling stage and for the emerging mites as well. Such spraying must be applied at the right time in spring (or fall) when the scale begins to move about at above 60°F. For serious infestations (all scale is serious) spray in late May with Diazinon, Malathion or Ethion-in-oil at the rate of 1 qt. to 100 gal. of water (or 2 tsp. to 1 gal. of water). Diazinon, Malathion and Ethion-in-oil have home clearance. Dimethoate and Cygon, although somewhat more effective, are not yet cleared for home use. Always follow directions on whatever scalecide or insecticide you use. (Be careful not to stand over chemical mixtures inhaling their fumes and do not mix them by hand.) Spray again in late summer, August or early September, to catch later mites. Often the May spray should be followed with a summer scalecide in June to catch eggs and mites hatched after the May spraying. If the control is rather complete in the Spring and there appear to be no more scale infestations the fall spray may be omitted. (We have found dormant oil spray to be ineffective in controlling scale.)

Often scale appears rather suddenly as a white cottony mass that has taken over a whole lilac cane. Whole plants become infected with these crawly white mites. Drastic measures must be taken at once. With severe infestations the most practical measure, and the best, is to remove the infested canes to the ground. If done early enough the plant will recover with new growth in time. After cutting out diseased canes be certain to clean up the area by removing dried grass, weeds, etc. that might be hiding infestations closer to the ground.

Bon jardinier, because you have had no trouble with scale for a year or two, do not feel your lilacs are secure or immune. They are not! Suddenly it will come upon you when you least expect. One must be vigilant and continued examination of all plants regularly is essential. Especially in the winter can one see the inroads of infestations when all leaves are gone. Part of the program of ridding your garden of scale should include not only regular spraying, but removal of grass and weeds around the plants that harbor scale.

I know of no reason why well-rotted cow manure should be blamed for subsequent scale attacks, but the two seem to go hand in hand. Invariably after heavy manuring, a plant appears

Scale - the number 1 enemy of lilacs

Upper left: Adult Scale in dormant period. It is useless to spray at this time as Scale is not active and moving—sprays cannot reach them. Cut and prune away old Scale infested canes.

Upper right: Warmer weather makes Scale active—May–June and again in early September. Spray with a scalecide at this stage.

Lower left: Young cottony-like Scale on the move—spray with scalecide.

filled with scale. Some old lilac growers are so fearful of cow manure that they refuse to use it at all. This of course is pure nonsense but vigilance must be practiced at all times. Perhaps it will be found that some element in the sap is the special attractant to scale both in lilacs and other plants such as ash and willow.

Spray and prune for an open, healthy shrub! Often people ask why some particular cultivar always seems to be infested with scale. It may be that they are using an ineffective spray at the proper time, or one that may be effective but used at the wrong time—when scale are not moving. There are, however, some lilac cultivars, lovely as they may be, that always seem to harbor scale, 'White Hyacinth', 'Lady Lindsay' and a few others are always infested. It is our feeling that birds transmit a considerable amount of scale (especially English sparrows) in the mite stage but I suggest that this scale-proneness of specific cultivars is an area ripe for experimentation. Early Hybrids appear less susceptible to scale than the ordinary *S. vulgaris* cultivars. The late species hybrids, *S. × prestoniae* and some of the newer hybrids are not altogether immune from scale. The species *S. patula, S. julianae, S. potaninii* and *S. microphylla* seem to be very little bothered as are the tree lilacs, *S. pekinensis* and *S. reticulata.*

THE LILAC BORER (*Podosesia syringae,* The Clearwing Moth—Lepidoptera: *Sesiidae*)

Inspect your lilacs carefully in June, especially the older canes and heavy branches. Look close to the ground on old shaggy trunks, particularly around old wounds. If you see a very roughened area with a tiny bit of sawdust floss coming from a small hole or wound, you have found the work and home of the Lilac Borer. Should you be able to open that tiny hole, you would find comfortably ensconced the larva of the lilac borer—a little worm-like, cream-colored creature, grub-like, with a brown head. It overwinters in its burrow. It spends the summer eating out galleries to make its way, becoming fat on the growing green-wood of the cambium of the lilac. Very late the following May (early June in the East) it emerges as a wasp-like adult leaving the casting of its pupa, the winter coat, hanging near the hole. The pupal case is its Spring calling card stuck to a lilac bark-shred or branch (often on one of your finest plants)! The adult borer waspy-looking moths are out and mating, ready to lay their eggs. You must spray immediately and will have excellent results at mating time. Adult emergence varies according to different locations, mid-June in the midwestern U.S. and perhaps into early July farther North and East.

The adult borer looks very much like a wasp and would be mistaken for one by most people although in reality it is a clearwing moth. They are day fliers camouflaged by using the defense of looking and acting like a wasp. Their wings are rather purplish with rusty colored wing-bases. Soon after emerging they mate and begin to lay their eggs on the heavier trunks, canes and branches (there is really nothing for them to bore into or overwinter on new shoots or thinner canes). They love ready-made open wounds, especially those inflicted by mowers close to the base of the shrubs. The tiny, yellowish eggs hatch in 7 to 10 days and the lively little larvae immediately begin to burrow into the heartwood of the cane. At first, being small, they work closely under the outer layer of the cambium bark and then, as they grow stronger, they attack the heartwood and move deeper within.

Often, during the month of late May to early June, if you were to open last year's borer hole you will find also where the borer has worked a small cocoon. This cocoon contains a small parasitic enemy of the lilac borer, the *ichneumon* wasp. It, too, will emerge from its cocoon about the same time as the borers and lay its eggs to hatch and feed attached to the growing lilac borer larva, which will eventually die. In a survey at Ohio State University, about 37% of lilac borer larvae were infected with this *ichneumon* wasp parasite. (At times Nature does work in favor of the lilac grower.) One can hope that the *ichneumon* wasp inhabits the garden but you cannot count on perfect control. If it is present and the borers are few, do not spray lest you rid the garden of one of its most useful parasites.

An effective control of the lilac borer (which kills the *ichneumon* wasp as well) is to spray the trunks and nest sites with Thiodan 2E (it is sold under the tradename of 'Endosulfan'). Use it at the rate of 1 qt. to 100 gal. of water (equivalent for lesser needs is 2 tsp. to 1 gal. of water). Apply about 2 weeks after the adult borer moths emerge (thus giving time for the moths to mate and ready their egg laying processes). It is important that this solution be applied to the heavier branches and canes, not on leaves or small twigs. Saturate the trunks, especially at the base and the junctures of the heaviest branches where the borer is most likely to infest the lilac wood. After you have located several borer holes you will become expert in spraying the correct areas. Thiodan 2E

Larva of the Lilac Borer, *Podosesia syringae*, working a lilac cane. (Photo courtesy Dr. D. Nielson, Ohio Agri. Research and Development.)

Lilac Borer male moth.   Lilac Borer female moth.

Podosesia syringae (Photos Dr. D. Nielson, Ohio Agri. Research and Development.)

Calling (=pheromone emitting) virgin female of the Banded Ash Clearwing, *Podosesia aureocincta*. This borer species attacks ash, but has been confused with the very similar Lilac Borer that attacks both lilacs and ash. (Photo courtesy Dr. D. Nielson, Ohio Agri. Research and Development.)

is rated as 18 on the toxicity chart, very highly toxic. Therefore use this chemical carefully, following directions and wear rubber gloves. Should you get any spray on your skin, wash it off immediately with hot, soapy water! Note that Malathion has a rating of 1,000, a very low toxicity rating. For Oyster Scale you can use Malathion, but for borer control use Thiodan 2E. Dursban, soon to be cleared for lilac use, is even more effective than Thiodan 2E. Look and ask for Dursban first.

One of the very best controls for the lilac borer, which avoids harmful chemicals or the killing of the *ichneumon* wasp, is the new pheromone attractant pioneered at the Ohio Agricultural Research Center, Wooster, Ohio. Lilac borers, like other clearwing borers, use a sex pheromone attractant, a powerful, volatile chemical attractant, produced by the female to attract a mate. The compound 18 carbon acetate is highly attractive to lilac borer males that are then caught in pheromone traps set throughout the garden. It will not only entrap the lilac borer but also several other kinds of borers, greatly reducing mating success and eliminating the need for strong chemicals. Ask for such pheromone traps at your garden nursery stores before applying heavy chemical sprays.

Most lilacs can withstand a few lilac borers but when they increase in number the gardener had better do something to control them. With the newer means of borer control they should pose practically no problem to the lilac grower.

THE CICADA (Cicadiae: *Cicada septendecim*—the 17-, 20- or whatever-year Locust)

In the years of the emerging Cicadas (Locust) severe damage can be done to the Lilacs, as well as to many other trees and shrubs, especially on 1- and 2-year-old wood. Cicadae do not damage older wood or bark as it is too hard and rough for their egg laying process. The Cicada lives in the ground as a fat white grub for a considerable number of years (10–17 or 20, depending upon the particular variety) eating rootlets below the freezing level often slowing the growth process of the plant considerably (in the central and midwestern U.S. where Cicadae are common, as many as a hundred or more grubs may be feeding on a single plant or tree). As upon a signal, in the proper year they begin their ascent, usually in late July and August. Emerging in their pupal form they crawl upon the nearest weeds, small shrubs and trees, where they shed their pupal case and emerge as adults. The adult is a very large, strong, horse-fly-like insect, with clear wire wings and fierce red eyes. They converge in hordes, hundreds hanging on tall weeds, and smaller shrubs, with a fearful droning sound that can be heard for great distances, made by rubbing their coarse wings together, as they seek to mate. When disturbed they are rapid in flight making a strong whirring sound that frightens even birds, who rarely eat them.

The female finds a tender 1- or 2-year-old branchlet of particular shrubs or trees (some species are preferred to others; lilacs are an acceptable species but not preferred). These she slits, razor-like longitudinally, laying her eggs into the slits and then, in her downward descent, she scores the branch around, weakening it. Soon it will brown and die then be broken by the wind and fall to the ground bringing with it the now hatched larvae. These will crawl from their nesting branch, burrow into the soil, eating plant roots as they descend into the soil below the frost level. They can and, where plentiful, do considerable damage to the growing roots. Thus two-fold damage is experienced: the damaged branches which either die or are totally disfigured by slit scars and eventually must be removed, and by the loss of the feeding roots. Lilacs are rarely totally killed. They are greatly damaged for that year with the loss of next spring's buds as the damage occurs so late in the summer that new growth rarely can be renewed.

'Katydid' may be nostalgic music to some few poets, but the Cicada's deafening dirge is a death-roll for garden shrubs! Do not ask me, "What Katydid did?" You will see for yourself the destruction in split, old branches that either die or may be temporarily healed but later will eventually be weak or deformed and must be removed.

There is no known, effective spray control as the adults are so numerous and so active in flight and movement. If you have any choice lilacs (or other small trees or shrubs), at the warning from your extension agent as to the time of emergence, cover them with cheesecloth until the mating and egg-laying are over—about three weeks. Where damage has been done cut off the egg bearing branches as soon as possible and burn before the larvae emerge or the branch begins to brown.

There are few natural enemies of so formidable, hard shelled and noisy an insect. Most birds are afraid of them. A variety of the Digger Wasp (*Sphecius speciosa*) black or rust colored, with a yellow-banded abdomen, preys on Cicadas with which it provisions its nest. Unfortunately in horde years there are too few Digger Wasps to amount to any kind of control. One or two off-year Cicadae, and there are always a few, like humans, who are out of tune with the species, sterilely rubbing their humming wings in the high trees in late summer, are harmless. When they appear in hordes, by the thousands, then gardener, beware!

THE LILAC LEAF MINER (*Gracillaria syringella*)

In some parts of France and England but rarely in the Americas, this moth can be a vexing problem. It lays its eggs in groups of 3–12 on the underside of lilac leaves (and some other choice species) where in 6 days the young caterpillars emerge and make their way into the leaf between the lower and upper surfaces, mining them as they gorge on tissue and destroy the chlorophyll. If one separates the two surfaces, the small caterpillars can readily be seen. In a few weeks they emerge, roll up the leaf surface with webs of thread until they are fully grown. They let themselves down to earth by silken threads, enter the ground where they spin cocoons and pupate. The adult, small moths reappear in about 14 days, mate, lay their eggs on the underside of the leaf and the cycle repeats. As many as three generations may appear, one in April, May and another in August. Malathion spray as the caterpillars emerge from the eggs is probably the most effective control.

NEMATODES AND LILACS (*Pratylenchus*)

Rarely are root nematodes mentioned as any danger to lilacs. Generally they are not. However, a recent examination of S. × *persica* roots at the University of Illinois found an extremely high population of the lesion nematode, *Pratylenchus*—indeed some of the highest populations of nematodes ever seen. The plants were moved to another field and have not been markedly infested since. No other reports of nematodes found on any other lilac species or cultivar of lilacs are known. It may be a meaningful caution for not using S. × *persica* as an understock on lilac grafts (as is the practice in some nurseries).

THE EUROPEAN HORNET OR THE GREAT HORNET (*Vespa crabro* var. *germana*)

This inch long hornet, resembling a yellow-jacket, with orange markings over a reddish-brown abdomen has proved to be a real lilac pest in some parts of the Eastern United States (especially in New Jersey and eastern Pennsylvania). So far this hornet has not been reported in the West, Midwest or Canada. Although it comes from Europe little is heard of damage there. In late summer and early fall, this Giant Hornet singles out mostly two year old lilac canes, slits, strips and peels them carrying off the tender bark to insulate their nests. They are amazing to watch. The great diligence and vigor with which they work in cutting away the bark is astonishing. Often they girdle and strip whole branches, which of course die. Since they do not eat the bark but use it in nest protection and building, they do not seem to be affected at all by poison sprays. They are rather vicious in their work, brook no interference and have a nasty sting. The only effective control appears to be to identify their nest by following their flight, usually in a tree hollow, but as often in the ground or hanging in a high tree or bush. At night, so as to include all the colony, and to keep from their stings, the nest should be burnt and destroyed.

Although a single colony of this hornet is comparatively small, they do considerable damage to a planting of lilacs in a very short time. They do not necessarily limit themselves to lilacs, but there is a definite preference for lilac bark if available at all. The ravished canes are entirely lost but the plant will send up new shoots the following spring. However, if one does not destroy the colony the same damage recurs each year with a total loss of bloom. They are not a hornet to be taken lightly! (*Madame*, please leave their eradication for *monseiur le jardinier*, their sting results are awesome!)

THE JAPANESE BEETLE (*Popillia japonica*)—a scarabaeld beetle

This beetle is a most discouraging garden pest which fortunately is not usually interested in lilacs but in heavy infestations is likely to turn upon them and cause some moderate damage to young shoots and leaves. The beetle skeletonizes the leaves by devouring all the leaf tissue possible and where extremely tender the whole shoot. It is a scarab-like beetle, ½ to ¾ in. long. Its hard wing-covers and head are a lustrous greenish copper color. In severe infestations it can quickly divest a whole plant of its leaves.

Not only do the adult beetles do considerable leaf damage but their larval grubs live on in the soil doing considerable damage to both grass and plant rootlets. The larvae are plump, white grubs that if not poisoned in the soil soon lead to an infestation of garden moles which feed upon the underground grubs.

Special sprays for this beetle have been developed and are readily available under several names but a most effective control measure is the new beetle trap using a sex pheromone attractant. There is a small parasite that lives on the larvae in spore-form that has some possibility for killing the grubs but one cannot count on its effectiveness as total control. It is purchased in garden stores under the name of Dylox or Dasanit (granules).

THE FALL WEBWORM OF THE PYRALID MOTH (*Hyphantria cunea*)

Fall webworms are a disfiguring nuisance to all shrubs on which they settle; unfortunately lilac are attractive to them. The moths lay their eggs in late summer and early autumn on the undersides of the leaves. The eggs soon hatch into tiny caterpillars that immediately begin to spin a silky, protective web around themselves and their supply of food leaves. When they devour all the leaf material within the first web they enlarge it both to include greater pastures and also for night protection where they return each evening. As the caterpillars grow, eventually to 1½ in. long, they are seen as a mass of greenish, gray-brown worms moving in a dirty silken nest filled with their debris. They forage beyond their tents in the daytime, denuding and devouring whole branches of leaves, with their nests high in the outer extremities, often beyond reach. Birds fear becoming entangled in the web so give them wide berth. Several large webs may be found on a single shrub. Eventually the caterpillars fall to the ground, enter a pupal stage and soon another generation is ready to emerge, mate and the whole egg-laying process repeats as often as 2 or 3 times in good weather.

An easy method of control where there are not too many webs is to gather the nest tents toward evening, when all the pests have returned for protection, into a large paper bag and burn them. Thus the entire colony is destroyed. Where infestations are high and difficult to reach and while still very small the best control is to spray the leaves with Malathion, Sevin, Dursban 2E or some such webworm poison. Look for the tiny eggs and caterpillars in mid to late summer. Mostly they go unnoticed until their web, which begins as a silken mass in the crotch of a branch, becomes enlarged and unsightly. (*Bon jardinier*, they are an extremely unsightly and messy bunch!)

OTHER LESSER INSECT PESTS

There are a few other insect pests that on occasion will injure lilacs, but they are really not specific to lilacs. Damage occurs when in a large infestation they attack several species of plants. Two, that are sometimes mentioned as troublesome in Europe but unknown in America, are *Otiorhynchus lugdunensis*, a beaked insect, nocturnal in habit, that at times does considerable damage to leaves and buds, mostly in England, and *Lytta versicatoria* that comes in swarms destroying foliage in some parts of England. Kolesnikov states that "the worst of the lilac pests is *Cetonia aurata* L., a species of bronze beetle which devours the florets of lilacs especially the white flowering varieties."

Miscellaneous Problems of Lilacs

Lilacs are sturdy plants and will stand a great deal of abuse, attack of disease or insects and come back if given proper treatment. A few environmental conditions do, however, exist that must be considered. Among these are air-borne pollutants, animal-rodent problems and man-made hazards.

AIR POLLUTION AND LEAF-ROLL NECROSIS

Leaf-Roll Necrosis is an air-borne condition caused, as far as can be ascertained, by pollution. Studies at the Brooklyn Botanical Garden and Morton Arboretum have shown that lilacs, as well as many other ornamental shrubs and trees, deteriorate due to sulphur-dioxide and other toxic gases which are the product of both motor traffic and industrialization. Plants suffering from leaf-roll necrosis show a marked leaf curl around the leaf margins, gradual defoliation and an unthrifty condition of the entire plant. Eventually they die. In areas of heavy pollution, as experienced in the central areas of most large cities, only a very limited number of extremely pollution-tolerant shrubs and trees will grow. Sadly lilacs are not among them. (Lilacs are mountain maidens, they never tolerate anything but good fresh air!) All their species and cultivars are more or less susceptible to pollution but some few are more tolerant than others. This does not mean that if one plants only the less susceptible cultivars that all will not eventually fall victim to pollution.

Heroic and regulatory efforts to curb and lessen pollution are the only preventive measures. Not only lilacs, but most of our finest flowering trees and shrubs, are victims of encroaching pollution along highways and city streets. The cost of industrial modernization appears to be a marked reduction in places and kinds of trees and shrubs one may safely plant. Sites for large arboreta should be selected away from freeways and urban pollutants.

'WITCHES' BROOM'

A 'Witches' Broom' is a condition wherein the plant forms thick, twiggy growths in large masses at the branch ends. The appearance of this brushy, twiggy growth gives the condition its name. It occurs in a wide variety of shrubs and trees. Often these 'Witches' Brooms' hanging from one to hundreds on larger trees and shrubs, may look singularly attractive, especially in the winter landscape and on trees—but not on lilacs! It is definitely an unhealthy condition! The tree or shrub soon becomes a mass of twiggy, broom growths, fails to bloom and gradually weakens until it dies. The 'brooms' usually die back during the winter, leaving no new growth or terminal buds for the following year.

Most of this brooming is, again, caused by pollution, although some authorities maintain that true 'brooming disease' is initiated by a virus attack on the plant. One occasionally finds a broom caused by mite or insect infestations. However, along one of the oldest Interstate Highways in the United States, the Pennsylvania Turnpike, one can see hundreds of thousands of trees and shrubs along the highway in every stage and condition of 'pollution brooming'. Some are rather interesting especially if you travel in the winter when all the leaves are gone and can see the 'brooms' clearly. It seems to affect every species of tree and shrub growing along this old Pike. (The various kinds and types of 'brooming' would make an interesting folio of silhouettes.)

In some of the older arboreta experiencing urban pollution, we are seeing an increased incidence of leaf-roll necrosis and 'brooming'. Insect and virus brooming on lilacs is rare. I have seen some incidence of it on mixtoploid plants when working with colchicine. It appears to be a problem of radical chromosome disruption. Much work at the Arnold Arboretum selecting seed of 'Witches' Broom' on pines has resulted in an interesting and valuable collection of dwarf pines and conifers. It would be interesting to see if 'broom seed' in lilacs might not also produce natural dwarfs.

Witches'-broom on *S. × prestoniae* 'Francisca'. (Photo R. Clark.)

Recent studies conducted by Dr. Craig R. Hibben, Research Plant Pathologist, Brooklyn Botanic Garden Research Center, Ossining, New York, indicate that in Lilac, Witches'-Brooms (which include proliferations of axillary shoots, shortened internodes as well as stunted leaves) may be caused by Mycoplasmal organisms (which he calls MLO). These MLO plant pathogens resembling bacteria without a cell wall which he has detected in phloem sieve tubes of leaves stained by Dienes' stain and viewed via transmission electron microscopy. He has found an increasing number of cases of LWB (Lilac Witches'-Broom) in the late blooming *S. × prestoniae* (select cultivars) and especially in *S. × josiflexa* 'Royalty'.

Hibben's research also indicates a similarity between LWB and ash yellows in *Fraxinus americana*. "Ash yellows is a widespread and lethal disease in northeastern United States of ash, and it is also caused by MLO," Hibben states. His on-going research should contribute much to the knowledge of the spreading and fatal disease of 'Witches'-Broom' in lilacs. (*Bon jardinier*, this learned man's research will do much to keep our gardens beautiful with the excellent late hybrids. We must appreciate it!) Ideally it will point to the cause and possible cure or preventative methods. *S. vulgaris* and *S. oblata* appear to be somewhat, but not entirely, untouched by the disease, which is most present in the *Villosae* series, especially in the hybrids.

We have seen an increase of it, perhaps coincidental, in a few years after heavy damage to lilacs by Cicadae penetration for egg-laying in the branches of lilacs (they prefer the late hybrids for their egg-laying and the ash).

When one finds the disease the plants should be destroyed—this is the most practical method of preventing the spread of the disease.

GRAFT INCOMPATIBILITY

Often an older grafted lilac begins to languish. First branches do not renew themselves with new growth, soon the bottom branches and finally the main trunk die for no apparent reason. This usually occurs in older, single trunked lilacs that have never formed their own root system. If you dig out the old root you will find that at the line of the lilac graft upon privet rootstock, the scion lilac has out-grown the union with the rootstock and is marked by a large knob. This over-growth has disturbed the union and prevented the passage of food from the root to the upper plant. You will find no roots have developed on the upper part of the union.

Either the graft was made too high or the plant was planted too shallowly. This provides a good reason not to plant grafted, but rather own-root, lilacs. However, not all grafted lilacs are the same. Good nurseries graft on white ash rootstock that is merely a nurse-root for a year and replant grafts deeper to form own roots. They do not offer it for sale until the lilac has formed a set of own roots. There is no problem with this procedure since before you receive the lilac the understock is cut away (or in ash has already fallen away). If you do have to plant grafted lilacs, always plant them so that the graft union is at least 4 in. below the soil surface. In this way, with time, the lilac can possibly develop its own root system. (*Bon jardinier*, so you wanted a one trunked, grafted lilac that would not sucker! Now you know better!)

Animal and Rodent Damage

Several kinds of animal or rodent damage are frequently seen on lilacs. Most or all of the damage can be prevented or reduced if we understand the nature of the predator and take the appropriate action.

DEER DAMAGE

Undoubtedly the greatest amount of damage done by animals is that done by deer where they are numerous, especially in late fall and winter. Deer browse-damage lilacs by eating the tips of young branches (those most likely to bloom well) even to a foot or a foot and a half. Great damage is done by the bucks in the fall and early winter during the "velvet" time and the rutting season. They then viciously attack lilac shrubs, stripping the main trunk of its bark with their antlers, totally ruining the shrub for the next few years until it is able to grow back from the ground. The shrub always dies back to good wood, usually to the ground. When deer are numerous considerable damage is done. Fortunately they prefer arborvitae to lilacs.

There are several remedies. The best is extensive hunting. If you prefer less vigorous measures and have only a few bushes you can erect a three-legged tepee made of 4 in. boards (sturdy enough so wind and deer do not knock it over). Deer are reputed to fear the smell of blood or clipped human hair. Dried blood or hair clippings may be tied in nylon bags and placed at strategic points on the shrubs. Most garden stores carry dried blood repellent (clipped hair can be obtained from your barber). At best they are half-measures and must be applied before the fall rains and the deeper freezes begin, and renewed after heavy rains. Some deer-repellent sprays have been developed with limited value. In Maryland where deer pests have reached epidemic proportions, some control has been had by mixing hot sauces with spray. Fill a spray tank one-half with water, add 2 oz. Vapor-Guard per gal., mix thoroughly, then add hot sauce, 2–4 oz. per gal. This solution *must* be mixed in this order. If not the hot sauce does not emulsify and washes off the plant. Should this happen what residue is left may act as an attractant rather than a repellent. Vapor-Guard is used as an emulsifying agent that has excellent sticking properties. Use only Vapor-Guard. If mixed properly it should stay in solution for 2 hours within which time you must spray your plants. (Louisiana Hot Sauce is available through food distributors.) Apply the spray only when temperatures are above 40°F.

Some claim aluminum foil hung in the branches to blow in the wind frightens deer. Take your choice, but nothing is as effective as hunting the deer where allowed. What the bucks miss with their horns and simulated battle antics, the does and yearlings delight in browsing, just to let you know they have been there and done your winter pruning—their way! All in all, beautiful and innocent looking, deer are a real nuisance!

RABBIT, MOUSE AND MOLE DAMAGE

When your lilacs are older, three or more years, damage done them by rodents will be minimal. However, as small plants or young seedlings whose succulent bark can be reached, especially as the snow mounds over them and rabbits can reach the outer more tender branches and buds, expect damage unless you spray them in advance with 'Hot Sauce Spray', some other rodent repellent or have placed small wire fencing around them. Rabbits cut yearling growth just to sharpen and keep their teeth from over-growing. Being rodents they must constantly have their teeth trimmed through use, otherwise they will overgrow and the rabbit will starve to death as the overly long teeth make it impossible for them to properly open their jaws and feed. Lilacs are ideal winter teeth conditioners for them.

Field mice and moles nibble and debark the canes under the snow and weeds. Their winter feasting is not revealed until Spring, when leaf buds fail to swell and begin to dry. On close examination one sees their girdling work on the lowest branches and cane base near the ground. How one then wishes he had cleared away the sod from small plants and protected them with wire, foil or the newer anti-rodent tubes available in garden stores! Very small plants may not recover, well rooted ones most often put forth new shoots from below the ground in spring. Use bait treated with zinc phosphide to kill mice (trade names under Rozol, Chempar and Ramik).

Occasionally 'Woody Woodchuck' coming out of hibernation in the spring will polish and sharpen his teeth and long claws on a near-by lilac bush, stripping and ripping its bark, gnawing and being rather fearsome in the damage done. Never plant a lilac close to a woodchuck (ground-hog) hole, or any other small tree or shrub. He will not allow them to grow! Woodchucks have absolutely no feeling for lilac fragrance. Unthinkable! A woodchuck smelling like a lilac! Like deer they will shred your lilac plants, not stopping at one. They are, however, more controllable. This time the woodchuck has to go! How? That is your problem, *mon ami*. I merely point out the culprit and the damage he does.

In lilac seedbeds, nurseries and lilac beds that are heavily mulched with rich humus and good soil, beware of moles! How moles revel in seedbeds! They glory in undermining the choicest seedlings, as they widen and plough open their underground burrows with their furry little snouts and clawed paws until you wonder why your seedlings and young lilacs have wilted and dried. Moles can do a great deal of damage in a few hours. They especially delight in well watered, cooler ground in the heat of summer. They are really after the grubs in the rich soils.

Use mole bait, poison peanuts, poison anything, but get those darned moles out! Of course they are after the grubs in the soil, so rid your soil of grubs and you will have no moles, the experts say. Not necessarily so—moles are really out to get seedlings and small lilacs or to undermine with air pockets your choicest plants! Some advocate using a 'Klippy-Klopp' wooden windmill or a wooden 'Flapping Bird'. This is supposed to make moles nervous so they move away. (From experience I vouch moles have nerves of steel—or have none at all!) Whatever you use, poison bait, traps, 'klippy-klopps', you must get rid of moles. A word of caution in getting rid of rodent pests, be careful of your own animal pets. You may catch or poison dear 'Ole Rags' or 'Kitty Kat' if you are not careful. Since mole runs have so many exits, cyanide gas and smoke bombs are not of much use. (Cyanide gas is extremely dangerous). Your best bets are the commercial poisoned peanuts or pellets which must be used over a long period of time.

Then There Is Man

LILAC DAMAGE DONE BY MOWERS

Considerable damage can be found in every arboretum or lilac garden due to misuse of mowers. Often canes and trunks are skinned and damaged by hurried attempts at coming too close to plants in an effort to save time. One of the great advantages of having a large weed-free circle of mulched soil around each plant is that it prevents needless attempts at coming too close to plants with mowers. These nicks, cuts, debarkings can be tolerated on rare occasions by more robust trees or shrubs but not by lilacs. Usually they do not show the injury damage until a week or so later when the whole cane begins to wither and die.

Do not let careless or nearsighted maintenance men close to your lilacs with mowers. Far more damage is done to plants than is imagined. When grass and weeds surround lilacs it is difficult to see where the actual trunk is, as often it may twist or turn close to the ground. This advice also holds for hand grass blades and for twine power whips that can quickly debark a tender lilac cane. Lilac bark, except on the oldest trunks, is easily injured. Small lilacs should be staked or marked with tall white markers that can be easily seen from a tractor or mower. Only park superintendents know how many choice plants and trees have been eliminated by mowers when not adequately marked. (Now you know why the large arboreta always plant specimens in threes!) Fortunately most healthy, larger lilacs will sprout again from the roots, but not all!

CHEMICAL WEED KILLERS

You can kill the weed in your garden as well as all your lilacs in one clean swoop if you are not careful with the use of weed-killers. Some weed-killers are fine for the first year or two, but you cannot continue to use them without gradually building up in the soil a toxicity that eventually will take its toll on plants, especially your lilacs. Read carefully all instructions before buying or using any weed-killers. Consult your extension agent or your arboretum or parks supervisors as to what is safe for what plants in your own area. They are a better source of advice than the store or garden center clerk who is anxious for a sale.

Damage from weed-killers shows itself initially as undeveloped, curled, deformed new growth with chlorosis (yellowing) of the leaves. The yellow or white leaves fall from older branches as well. Plants languish and die! Once the chemical is within the plant there is no cure, even by moving or soaking it. Be careful of the chemical mists that winds carry over to your lilac plantings (and to all your garden) from roadside spraying crews. There should be a national law forbidding roadside spraying. It can be devastating to the homeowner due to drift and to the often rude and untrained spraying crews. Here you must be adamant! Put up 'NO SPRAYING' signs well in advance of summer road spraying programs and in front of your garden. County road crews are notorious for their inability to see and read signs. If you know the day they are to spray your area, stand at attention on your property line and forbid such spraying. Protect your plantings, your garden as well as your family. (The drift from careless spraying crews one year caused the death of a whole line of lilacs and older flowering crabs for the author—even with posted signs!)

If you must use weed-killers at all, follow directions most carefully. Use a face mask for your own safety, spray only on windless days and close to the ground. If you wish to clear a small area a somewhat safe way we have found is to attach securely an old hand towel to a garden rake, or a paint roller with a long handle and drag it over the weeds you wish to eliminate being careful not to touch any plant parts or root suckers. It works. Be forewarned, if you find your plants turning yellow or white before autumn, do not think you have discovered a new leaf mutation, my friend, you probably have discovered an overdose or misuse of weed-killer at work. One should remember not all weed-killers are for the same plants; weed-killers are generally cumulative in the soil and eventually can build up lethal proportions; they kill by entering the plant through any portion of it; they are dangerous chemicals for humans as well; they are easily carried as fine mist by the wind to plants and the air you breathe; they remain lethal in the spraying tank no matter how you clean it. (*Mon ami,* if you cannot follow this sound advice you perhaps ought not be a gardener at all! Buy your lilacs from the florist or enjoy them at the park or nearest arboretum.)

IMBEDDED TAGGING WIRES

Often smaller lilacs are wire-tagged rather tightly. As the shrub grows, small branches soon become trunks. The wires become ingrown and girdle the cane or branch. It may die but ordinarily an unsightly bulge develops where the plant seeks to overgrow the enmeshed wire. This does not have to be. Tags should always be loose and allow for growth. Place all your name tags on the same side of all your trees, north, south etc. for ease in finding them.

Also, one must be careful in staking plants so that the tie is firm. Wind tossed and shaken canes can often be debarked and damaged by loose ties.

ENCROACHING PLANTS, TREES AND SHRUBS

Where there are large beds of lilacs, especially if they must be hand mowed or weeded, one must be on guard for encroaching plants. There are certain plants, shrubs and trees that can be a real nuisance, either from seedlings or by runners. Particularly difficult are the brambles, Black Locust, Sumac, multiflora rose, Robinia and weed Vinca or wild morning-glory and some other pushy garden pests. They must be dealt with forthright and totally eliminated. (Your author well remembers a four year struggle with a sumac that seemed to have endless underground runners.) Lilacs do not tolerate being pushed off-stage by some ne'er-do-well! They will fret and pout about such intrusions into their space. In eliminating such bold intruders, if it be by weed-killer spray, beware lest your lilac depart with them!

AN 'EPILOGUE' FOR GOAT LOVERS

Should you be one of those 'back to nature people' who love goats for their own sake or for the healthful milk they produce, you must never, absolutely never, admire your lilacs in front of your goats (or even pretend to tolerate lilacs). Goats, above all other animals, are envious and spiteful if they know you have a favorite shrub. Somehow they will find it out and, perhaps weeks later, get to it shredding its buds and growth! Unlike their cousins the deer, they have no interest in eating it for hunger's sake. They do it to humiliate, desecrate and eliminate lilacs! A word to the wise goat-keeper is sufficient, so I have included this timely note in my scholarly book. Never, never have the Granddames of Lilacdom tolerated goat herds! They scorn goats and this enmity is reciprocated. This feud is centuries old having origins in the mountains of old Romania and Moldovia where lilacs and goats never prospered together. Mountain gypsies tell tales of noble princesses who were turned into beautiful lilac bushes and of spurned bandits who were changed into nasty goats! Be it whatever, the enmity is there and eternal! (*Mon ami et amie,* Dr. Radcliff Pike told me this story gleaned from the gypsies of old Romania where he collected *S. vulgaris* seed.)

Tagging Your Lilacs and Record Keeping

Always tag your lilacs with their correct names: when they were planted, where you obtained them, who was the originator, their species or hybrid parentage. Not only you, but friends and visitors will want to know what that beautiful shrub is called.

There are two kinds of tagging and record keeping that should be kept up in any large or refined collection of lilacs. First, you should have a name tag on each shrub itself. A good, durable tag that will last a long time as we do not get around to renew tags often. Some long-lasting tags which are embossed and individually stamped are rather expensive. For most this is not feasible. A good plastic disc-tag is available that can be fastened by coated wire to the shrub's outer branches. I have found a round, 4-inch, bright yellow plastic disc is ideal. It has ample room on which to write with ordinary pencil that lasts some few years and can be re-written with ease, is easily seen because of the bright color and can be used on both sides. In time it needs to be re-written—about every three years. Set these tags on the same sides of all your shrubs and trees—mine are on the southeast side of my plants. When looking for a tag on a rather large shrub it can more readily be found. Fasten the tags securely yet loose enough to allow continued growth of substantial branches without becoming embedded—not on weak branches that will be later pruned away. Use both sides of the tag and include: species, cultivar name, hybrid-cross, introducer, source of plant material or whatever other information you wish. (Introduce your garden shrubs with class and due respect—calling each by their proper name! They are offended if treated as nobodies!)

As to wire ties, they must be plastic coated wire—for some reason copper wire and other wires wear through and often cut branches—plastic-coated wire lasts indefinitely.

The second kind of record one should always have, and it is more important than tagging, is a book which records all your plants and exactly where each is planted—a garden log. Herein by map, by card or by number, you should record the exact location, species, name, source, graft/cutting, bud or seedling, originator, date planted, nursery from which it was purchased and all pertinent information on hybridization of that plant, its offspring, etc. This record is the nerve-center of your collection and knowledge. (It should be passed on to each new owner of your collection.)

If your collection is large enough assign a special number to each plant (acquisition number). Many large arboreta keep an indexed file for each individual plant. If you are an hybridizer, I do not have to tell you how important accurate record keeping is. You may even wish to include a photo close-up of each flower in color, plant form etc. Seedlings must always be marked 'Seedling of' and not given their seed parent's name. Never label a plant with a name that is not certain or whose origin is doubtful, e.g. today there are several *S. vulgaris* 'Lucie Baltet'—each a bit different but all beautiful. Are they mutations of the original plant, or are they seedlings? When similar lilacs are given the same name, nothing but confusion ensues and your whole garden becomes suspect.

When friends want a rootlet of an unnamed seedling, simply tell them, "It is an unnamed seedling", and do not even mention the parent as they will soon call it by the parent's name. Try to avoid buying lilacs just by color and then adding your own name from a description you read in a catalog. Keep your own 'Garden Record Book' with information as accurate as you would have in your own family ancestry—your garden friends are part of your family history—teach your children and family members to call their favorite lilacs by their proper names. Pass your Record Book on with your property. (*Mon ami et amie*, it is a sacred trust—are they not the garden friends you once planted with loving care?)

International Lilac Society, Inc.

LILAC PERFORMANCE FORM

BOTANICAL AND CULTIVAR NAME _____

PLANT OBTAINED FROM _____

LOCATION — Specimen observed at _____

_____

AGE (if known) _____ yrs.   Height _____ m   Spread _____ m: GROWING SPACE: _____ m.

BRANCHING HABIT: Strongly ascending [ ]   Moderately ascending [ ]   Spreading [ ]

DENSITY: Thick [ ]   Moderate [ ]   Thin [ ]

GROWTH: Long (40+ cm/yr) [ ]   Moderate (20-40 cm/yr) [ ]   Short (1-20 cm/yr) [ ]

PRUNED OR THINNED: Regularly [[Occasionally [ ]   Never [ ];   REJUVENATED Yes [ ] No [ ]

PROPAGATION OF SPECIMEN: Grafted [ ]   Budded [ ]   On own roots [ ]   Unknown [ ]

FLOWERS: Single [ ]   Double [ ]   Diameter of corolla (average) _____ cm.

AVERAGE NUMBER OF COROLLA LOBES: 4 [ ]   8 [ ]   12 [ ]   Other _____

TIP OF COROLLA LOBE: Pointed [ ]   Rounded [ ]   Other _____

SHAPE OF COROLLA LOBES AT PEAK OF BLOOM: Cupped [ ]   Flat [ ]   Reflexed [ ]

FRAGRANCE: Strong [ ]   Moderate [ ]   Slight [ ]   Lacking [ ]

FLOWER CLUSTER: Length _____ cm   Width at the base _____ cm.

Rigid [ ]   Lax [ ]   Dense [ ]   Sparse [ ]

Pointed [ ]   Rounded [ ]   Other _____

VISUAL COLOR DESCRIPTION: — — — — — — — —   Bud _____

Flower cluster in bloom _____

Corolla tube _____   Lobes _____   Lobe margins _____

COLOR CHART DESIGNATION: RHS [ ]   Nickerson [ ]   Munsell [ ]   Other _____   Code _____

AMOUNT OF BLOOM: 40 + clusters [ ]   20-40 [ ]   Fewer than 20 [ ]

FLOWERING HABITS: Good annually [ ]   Alternately [ ]   Good occasionally [ ]   Unknown [ ]

BLOOMING TIME: from _____ to _____ (from opening of first to fading of last cluster)

LASTING QUALITY OF CUT BLOOM: 5 days [ ]   3 days [ ]   1 day [ ]   Unknown [ ]

LEAF SIZE (from medium length shoot):   Average length _____ cm.   Average width _____ cm.

SOIL AT CULTIVAR SITE: Clay [ ]   Sandy [ ]   Loamy [ ]   Other _____

DRAINAGE: Good [ ]   Poor [ ]:   SOIL pH (if known) _____

EXPOSURE: Sunny [ ]   Semi-shade [ ]   Shade [ ]

East [ ]   South [ ]   North [ ]   West [ ]   Level ground [ ]

PESTS AND DISEASES OBSERVED DURING PAST 5 YEARS:

Borer [ ]   Hornet [ ]   Scale [ ]   Mildew [ ]   Other _____

EXTREME MINIMUM TEMPERATURE AT OR NEAR THE COLLECTION _____ °F   or _____ °C

AS OBSERVED IN PAST _____ years.

OTHER COMMENTS _____

_____

_____

_____

_____

Completed by _____

Address _____   Date _____

C. Holetich, R.B.G.

CHAPTER NINE

The Propagation of Lilacs

Lilacs from Seed

Seed sowing is nature's most common means of plant propagation. A plant's blossom is pollenized, either by itself (selfed), or by pollen blown by the wind, carried by insects or by man. The seed once set ripens and falls to the ground. Some is eaten by birds, animals, insects or worms. Some few not discovered by hungry enemies are covered by leaves or sheltered in an earthen crevice. Of these a few remain intact and find a germination spot at some place beneath or at some distance from the mother plant. Those eventually finding a suitable place freeze and thaw in moist conditions. This hard treatment by the elements breaks any inherent dormancy of the seeds. (Nature's way often seems hard and inscrutable but it is the path to new life.) The following spring a tiny percentage of all the seed produced by a plant actually sprouts and new plants are begun. (*Mon ami*, if they all grew the world would be covered by lilacs!)

If self-pollinated, the seedlings are true to the mother plant's characteristics and genetic make-up, with the offspring being the same as the original plant. If crossed with pollen from a plant of different characteristics, the offspring is a 'hybrid', different in many ways from each plant parent yet retaining half the original genes and inheritance of both. In a selfed seed the plant is identical but often the gene pool in that species is so great (as in *S. vulgaris*) that the color or conformation may be quite different from the mother plant and a new cultivar is obtained. Inherently the cultivar is of the same species, varying only in minor traits. In the case of *S. vulgaris* thousands of cultivars have been named that are selected variations in color or flower form. Hybrids, in contrast, are an entirely new kind of plant that is only half-like both of its original parents as each is of a different species.

When one picks seed from any given plant, there is no way of knowing if the plant coming from that seed will be a selfed or a hybrid seedling. Most of the time in open-pollinated seed it is nearly impossible to determine who the willy-nilly pollen parent may have been. In man-made crosses, which exclude all but the selected pollen and are protected after being pollinized the parents are known and certain. Usually man-made crosses yield seedlings equal or inferior to their parents, but a few, perhaps no more than 8–10%, show some rare and exceptional traits that have been recessive in the parent plants and are now brought to light for the first time.

Among the 8–10% wonderful results can come forth. This is true especially in man-made crosses where exceptionally fine parents (often the product of hand-pollination themselves) have been chosen. In this way real progress in creating better lilacs has been made. In the rare exception of very superior parent plants with outstandingly unique characteristics the percentage of outstanding seedlings from them may reach as high as 30%. This is very rare and often it is a horticultural break-through caused by some unusual chromosome or genetic structures. (An excellent example is the *S. vulgaris* cultivar 'Azurea plena' used by Lemoine or more recently the *S. vulgaris* cultivar 'Rochester').

HYBRIDS AND SPECIAL CROSSES

To offset the hit-and-miss results in merely planting open-pollinated seed, hybridizers select two outstanding parents and carefully plan the cross, protecting the pollen and both the unfertilized and then the fertilized pistil from all other pollen except that desired in the cross. The percentage of superior, high-quality offspring is greatly increased, depending on the quality of the parents in their genetic make-up. (From the author's experience open-pollinated seed gives no more than about 2 to 3% of all seedlings better than the parent plant with the majority 70% being inferior and reverting back to the more native species. For controlled crosses about 8–10% are superior to the parent plants and the majority equal to the parents with about 40% inferior to both parents. In very select and unusual crosses the results may be as high as 30% superior.

In making lilac crosses the flower bud must be carefully opened before any other pollen, including its own, can reach the pistil. It is best just before the bud opens to remove the petals with forceps or tweezers. In many species the pollen-bearing anthers adhere to the petals and are thus removed with them. All anthers must be removed without injury to the pistil which is then dusted with the desired pollen. Pollinize several on the same cluster and remove all other blossoms and buds. After being pollinized the flower pistils are carefully covered, generally with a small paper or glassine bag (a kind of chastity-belt) to prevent unwanted air or insect borne pollen from fertilizing them. As soon as the seed has been fertilized or set, usually a day or so, the bag is removed to prevent high temperatures from forming within and drying the pistil and to prevent the formation of mold due to lack of air. Mold is deadly to seed formation.

If one is making crosses within an already heavily crossed species, as with *S. vulgaris*, dramatic results can be expected, but rarely. Although there are still many wonderful crosses to be made. In *S. vulgaris* colors can be deepened, fragrance increased, substance and resistance to sun-fading strengthened, floret size increased, new color patterns—rayed, eyed, edged, etc.—developed, and a number of other desired characteristics brought forth or increased. All has by no means been accomplished with this single species that is most universally acclaimed among the lilacs.

If, on the other hand, one is crossing two different species, as was Isabel Preston's cross of the late blooming *S. villosa* with *S. reflexa*, the results may be quite unexpected and dramatic. Even more interesting and beautiful plants can arise from crossing several species. Today some lilac hybridizers are no longer working on crosses using two different species (called interspecific hybridization) but are working with hybrid plants that contain two, three to even five or six different species (multibrids). The progeny of these crosses give rise to considerable variety. Indeed it is almost impossible to identify the genetic species in these complicated crosses unless excellent records are kept, e.g. 'Lark Song' is a cross of *S. komarowii* × *S. sweginzowii* 'Albida' (which is a cross of *S. sweginzowii* × *S. tomentella*). Thus 'Lark Song' has the inherent characteristics of three species (a tribrid) in its make-up. 'Springtime' and 'Sunrise' are crosses of *S. sweginzowii* 'Albida' × *S. wolfii*, also tribrids. Crosses of 'Lark Song' × 'Springtime' have four species (quatrobrids). Crosses of their seedlings (quatrobrids) with *S.* × *prestoniae* (*S. villosa* × *S. reflexa*) are sextobrids (they contain six species).

These newest multibrids become increasingly difficult to follow genetically unless well documented. Even the best taxonomists cannot ascertain the number of species they contain. To merely call them 'hybrids' today is inadequate and, more accurately, they should be designated for

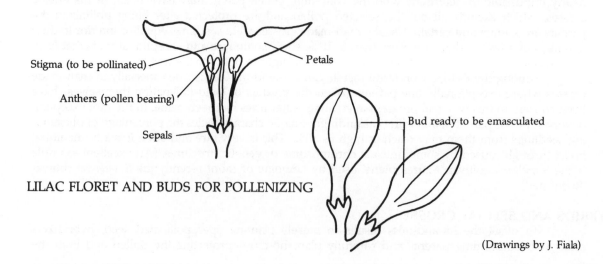

Stigma (to be pollinated)

Anthers (pollen bearing)

Sepals

Petals

Bud ready to be emasculated

LILAC FLORET AND BUDS FOR POLLENIZING

(Drawings by J. Fiala)

brevity, ease and understanding as hybrids (2 species), tribrids (3 species), quatrobrids (4 species), quintobrids (5 species), sextobrids (6 species), septobrids (7 species), octobrids (8 species), nonobrids (9 species), decabrids (10 species) and decaunobrids, decaduobrids, decatriobrids, etc. Hybridists are already working with octobrid plants so the work of interspecificity has broad horizons. But these are only small beginnings. Generations of careful breeding, evaluation and selection are yet to come. To benefit to its greatest extent with this multiple hybridization of species more than 2 or 3 generations of intercrosses need to be made to sufficiently mix the genetic possibilities of selected plants.

How good are all these multibrids as garden plants? Where compatible species have been crossed and re-crossed a veritable 'Pandora's Box' of new forms, color shades and plant variations has been opened—much to the benefit of the gardener. Further recombinations of genetic factors in new ratios will bring forth heretofore recessive factors, never before seen in a plant although as recessives they have always been there. The more species crossed, the wider and more unpredictable the variations. Unpredictable variations or their multiplicity are, however, no guarantee of excellence as a garden plant. What may have value and fascination because of its genetic background to the hybridizer or taxonomist may be worthless to the gardener concerned with landscape effect and to the commercial grower who depends on sales. Unlike *S. vulgaris* which has thousands of selected cultivars after intensive inbreeding, the species lilacs are mostly raw material with little or no inbreeding, hybridization and selectivity of cultivars. It is doubtful that as beautiful as the species are that they will ever approach the intensification of outstanding characteristics found in *S. vulgaris*. (*Mon ami*, they are destined to be the ladies-in-waiting to the *S. vulgaris* cultivars!)

PLANTING THE LILAC SEED

There are several ways to handle lilac seeds depending on the facilities available. The first is to prepare a seed bed early in the fall of good, well drained, sandy-loam soil. Scatter the seed evenly over the bed (the dry seed must be separated from the capsules that cover it, which should always be done or else the capsule will water-log and rot the seed). Cover lightly with ¼ inch of fine soil. After the first freeze cover the entire bed with a very light mulch (an inch or two) of straw or light mulching material to keep it from thawing and freezing. Do not cover too heavily or the mulch will waterlog and so be overly wet all winter (avoid using leaves). In the spring remove the mulch to uncover small seedlings sprouting here and there. Shade your seedbed or frame to exclude direct sunlight at once. Lilac seedling readily scorch from hot suns.

An easier and perhaps surer way is to collect and clean the seed in the fall. Save the seed in a plastic bag in a cool dry place until February. (If refrigerated it should be in a small glass jar and not in plastic to avoid the freon gas most refrigerators emit even in small quantities. It is lethal to dry or growing seed). In February plant the seed in trays containing a sterile, damp medium (one that is not soggy nor holds too much water—but allows good circulation of air) made of sterilized potting soil or milled sphagnum mixed with a bit of sand. Water once, drain well and cover with a clean plastic bag. Place the seed trays in a cool but not freezing place around 55° to 60°F. It is well to dust the seed surface with a fungicide such as Captan. They should begin to sprout in from 2 to 4 weeks depending on the species. After the seeds have begun sprouting (or if you see no sprouts within 3 weeks) move the trays into a sunlight window, under grow-lights or into a greenhouse where the temperature remains between 65°–70°F with ample sun or artificial light. (Or you may leave them, if unsprouted, in the cool area until you place them out of doors. This however faces the risk of rotting and mold if held for any length of time.) Once brought into the sunlight and warmth the seed sprouts and grows rapidly—sprouting should take about 10 days (*S. reticulata* and *S. pekinensis* take about a month to 6 weeks). Remember the trays once growing should be uncovered and remain barely moist, never soggy or all your plants will rot. Dust weekly with Captan or fungicide to prevent dampening off. (The best measure for this disease is good air circulation and not overwatering.) Seed germination varies—*S. villosa* and its hybrids are more precocious than *S. vulgaris*, whereas the tree lilacs require a month or more. If you discover albino seedlings, they have white first leaves and pink stems, do not bother planting them in seedling beds. They have no chlorophyll, so do not drool over them. They are worthless and will all eventually die. Do not confuse them with variegated leaves, those that have some little green in them. The latter will grow and perhaps may be worth saving.

Again, I warn you of the use of a refrigerator for seed or scion storage. Even the smallest

Young seedlings are planted in various containers under lights or in a greenhouse, then moved outside to be planted in a lath or shade house.

Young lilac seedlings transferred into shade house beds where filtered sun and controlled watering will enable them to develop strong roots and where they will be protected from winter extremes of weather. They will be lined out in nursery rows after their second year—spaced about 4 ft. until their third or fourth year bloom, then selected or discarded.

leak of the Freon coolant is lethal to all plant life—seeds or grafts—dry or moist. You may stand in wonderment when none of your seeds sprout or puzzle what went wrong with the germination process or why your carefully grafted scions never grew. You have been forewarned!

You may choose yet another method: store the dry seed in a glass jar in the refrigerator or a cool place. In spring when danger of frost is past, plant the seed directly outdoors in prepared seed beds within a lath house (shade house) or in a shaded area, or in flats that can be moved at will. When planting cover the seed lightly and water well. Keep the seed bed (flats) shaded at all times and watered. Out of doors you must water lightly almost daily, as drying spring winds can cook seedlings. Also cover your seed beds or flats with screen, or those pesky sparrows will soon make a dirt-bath out of your choicest beds. (How these lice-ridden birds love to dirt-dust themselves in the Spring! Forewarned? I have told you beforehand of these 'sparrow tricks'! One dusting sparrow can ruin all your seedbed or flat.) For an earlier start you can plant your lilacs in flats and grow them under artificial lights (Gro-lites) or place them in a sunny window or greenhouse. Dust them every 10 days with fungicide such as Captan. Set out the little plants either in a shade house or in a shaded nursery bed after danger of frost is over.

Once they sprout, lilacs are tough and sturdy little seedlings, rather easy to grow. Cover them with screen or fencing when very small. (Not only birds love to dust and scratch in them but also, perish the thought, kitty cat loves to use the soft lilac seedling bed as a litter box!) Do not set lilac seedlings too close together. Give them a foot and a half at first, even this is a bit close and they will have to be replanted—every other one. Finally, transplant them after their second year to nursery rows in the open where they will have good ground, drainage and sun, about 4–5 ft. apart (slightly closer if you are really pressed for ground) where they should remain until they bloom in about another 2 or 3 years. Do not over-fertilize or you will be misled as to the real quality of the bloom and plant. Reasonably good soil is a test of their real ability both as to bloom and plant. Leave them after first bloom for another 3 years for proper evaluation of flower and form.

Of course there will be some that may be discarded after the second bloom season. Keep evaluating for years. They either get better or worse with age—as do all of us. For open-pollinated seed you will get but a very few that are worthy of being named, some additional ones that are reasonable garden plants, but most should be discarded and destroyed. Do not perpetuate inferior cultivars by giving them away. Your friends may seem thrilled at first with your discards, but in time will come to despise you as a gardener and a lilac grower once they realize what tricks you have played on them. (*Bon jardinier,* you may give away a homely daughter with a large dowry but never give a 'lilac dog' to a friend as a 'gift'! It will come back to bite you!)

Once you begin hybridizing in earnest (not merely planting seed) you are on an endless and consuming, creative venture that grows and grows until it fills all your available time and land. Bon Voyage! May all your progeny not give you heartaches! In the long run you may be better buying the best named varieties at whatever price! But then you will miss all the surprise associated with originating and creating new lilacs!

A NOTE ON SEED COLLECTING

Cut off all unwanted seed pods immediately after blooming. Leave only the few you wish to save or have pollinized for seed. Always mark your seed with the parent seed (pod parent) first and the pollen parent second (pod parent $\times$ pollen parent). Open-pollinated seed should be marked; e.g., pod parent $\times$ open. When seed has been separated from the capsules (if dry this need not be done immediately but can wait for a winter day), store in a bag or container in a cool place away from heat or sunlight after dusting it lightly with a fungicide like Captan. Lilac seed will germinate fairly, even in the second year, but not well thereafter, if at all. Winter picked seed is generally worthless as it has already either fallen from the capsules but mostly has already been attacked by mold and fungus in the wet capsule.

Propagation of Lilacs by Tissue Culture

With the onset of new scientific methods of propagation lilacs for commercial use, it is expected that within the next few years the sole and exclusive method, most profitable to nurserymen and most economical, will be that of micropropagation (tissue culture). There appears to be no species of lilacs that cannot be propagated in this manner. Since it is so new and increasingly important, I suggest that it will be the principal source of own-root lilacs for the gardener within a very few years. Already some nurseries are depending exclusively on this method for lilac propagation. It not only is economical, but it gives own-root plants of saleable size within at most two years. Likewise, we will probably see the cost of the better cultivars lowered and made more readily available to the lilac public. Hence it is the first method of lilac propagation considered. For the few, especially for the home gardener and smaller operations that cannot go into tissue culture laboratory expenses, the older methods of traditional lilac propagation are presented. There will always be a few of us who prefer to propagate some of our lilacs at home in a smaller way.

The consideration of micropropagation is briefly detailed as it is not a technique for the home gardener who is not equipped with sterile laboratory procedures and space. One must bear in mind that the vast majority of our plant materials in the near future, and even in the present, are rapidly being tissue cultured in huge volume and completely changing the nursery trade.

Lilac micropropagation (the new tissue-culture propagation), although not yet perfected, will undoubtedly be the leading type of lilac propagation in the next few years. Great strides have been made in the state of the art of tissue-culture propagation and it is merely a factor of adapting what has been already achieved in other plant species to the lilac to make it economically productive. Large numbers of plants can be easily and simply reproduced in this manner. From the research already done and the existing plants of *Syringa* so far obtained by micropropagation there appear to be no negative factors to prevent this method from becoming the exclusive lilac propagation source for large quantity production in the next few years. Whether nurserymen will find it advantageous to propagate large number of any single cultivars remains to be tested. However, all the elements of successful and profitable tissue-culture propagation of lilacs exist in present-day plant technology and practice. I have in my garden a tissue-culture plant of *S. vulgaris* 'Lucie Baltet' that is equally as rapid-growing as those obtained by any other method. A great advantage for lilacs in tissue-cultured plants is that each is an 'own root' plant. So far there does not appear to be the problem in lilacs of great numbers of mutations because of the tissue-culture process as rarely found in some species, e.g., *Hosta*.

Micropropagation is rapidly becoming a promising source of obtaining uniform, choice and own roots plants in many plant families, e.g., Ericaceae and Rosaceae, *Hemerocallis*, *Hosta* and others. Although the method has been known for over 30 years its practical and commercial application has developed mostly in the past 10 years with annual successes and increased numbers of plants produced. John W. Einset writing in ARNOLDIA gives an excellent presentation of the basic techniques used in micropropagation which is based on control of plant development by phytohormone treatment. Tissue-culture media require over 20 different chemical constituents plus the control of light intensity and temperature needs, but the crucial variable remains the phytohormone content of the medium.

Basically there are three methods of micropropagation: regeneration from callus, somatic embryogenesis and shoot multiplication:

Regeneration from callus, discovered by Skoog and Miller working at the University of Wisconsin with tobacco plants, depends on the kinds and quantities of phytohormones added to the medium, especially the levels of cytokinin and auxin. High cytokinin-to-auxin concentrations result in shoot formation from the callus, low ratios result in root formation, whereas intermediate ratios result in continued callus proliferation. Few plants, however, respond in tissue-culture as tobacco does. Nearly all produce callus but rarely respond to shoot and root culture in phytohormone treatment. For lilacs this method is unproductive.

Somatic embryogenesis which has been successfully used in more than 25 plant families, also depends upon callus formation in its initial stage but using a medium containing *auxin* as the single phytohormone. Callus is then recultured on a medium with *cytokinin* or one lacking phytohormone. Several successive passages are often required in order to form true embryos. The finesse of the tissue culturist plays a considerable part in the success of this technique.

Shoot multiplication, the third tissue-culture technique, is probably considered "the standard methodology" for woody plant micropropagation and the one used for *Syringa*. This method uses a growing shoot tip in a medium of high *cytokinin* concentrations to promote growth and to overcome apical dominance. This produces a many-branched shoot system. The individual shoots are either rooted or used for further shoot development.

Murashige states that all methods of micropropagation involve three basic types of manipulations or stages:

In **Stage 1** an aseptic culture must be established; i.e., an "explant", part of a stock plant, must be cleaned, disinfected and placed on a tissue-culture medium. A growing plant tissue must be obtained free from all microbial contamination. This goal is usually the most difficult aspect to achieve in micropropagation, as simple as it may appear.

In **Stage II,** propagule or shoot multiplication, often coincides with Stage I. Its objective is to obtain rapid increase in shoots or other structures that ultimately give rise to plants. Explants in shoot multiplication almost immediately respond to the high concentration of cytokinin of the medium by proliferating new shoots. (As many as a million shoots a year can be obtained by this method from a single growing tip!)

Stage III involves the processes required to obtain tissue-cultured plants growing in soil. It involves rooting treatment to obtain plantlets, acclimating them to lower humidity, together with the increased light intensity of the greenhouse or outdoor conditions. This hardening process of tender plantlets may last for several weeks.

The medium with its several inorganic and organic components is of primary concern in micropropagation. One should consult several of the leading universities, arboreta and technical papers to assay their use and concentrations. An excellent article published in ARNOLDIA, *A Practical Guide to Woody Plant Micropropagation,* by John W. Einset, Vol. 46, No. 1, Winter 1986, is one of the most comprehensive, well presented informational articles on the state of the art of micropropagation to date. Much of my brief summary or introduction to lilac tissue-culture rests heavily on this summation. In addition to the technical aspects covered by Einset, which include the various methods, medium, explants, rooting and hardening, there is an excellent consideration of the growing economic importance of micropropagation which should be of considerable importance to all who would use this method for lilac propagation. One must obtain a copy of Professor John H. Einset's summary. He is a professor of biology at Harvard University and a staff member of the Arnold Arboretum.

Layering Lilac Branches

Layering is one of the oldest means of propagating plants identical to the mother plant. It depends on covering a branch with soil so that new roots are struck. When the new roots are sturdy enough to support the plant, it is severed and replanted. Occasionally a branch is close enough to the ground or can be bent so that it can be rather easily covered with soil. Nick or wound the bark in 2 or 3 places at the lowest point of the branch, as it will be covered with soil. It is well to dust the wounds with a rooting compound such as Rootone #2 or #3. Around these wounds a heavy white growth of callus cells will develop from which roots will eventually grow. This part of the branch with the nicks or wounds must be buried about 3 or 4 in. in the ground and kept damp so that the callus and root formation will take place. Use enough good soil or compost to prevent drying out in hot weather. If constantly dry no roots will form. I mound the layering site slightly with good soil to which sharp sand has been added, and place a good stone or brick on it to prevent the branch from snapping up out of the soil or from being wind-tossed. Cover this mound with good mulch to help maintain moisture.

In a year roots should have formed, but wait 2 years for a good rooting. Then cut the plant off the branch of the mother plant. After this severing of the branch from the mother plant, I like to leave the layering in place for yet another year to form an excellent root system, then transplant it to a permanent place or a nursery row, or pot it up as a gift to a friend.

Layering is a longer process than propagating by suckers, but for some species and cultivars that do not sucker, it is the only easy way of propagation other than taking cuttings or grafting. Try a few just to be able to say you did it. (*Mon ami*, do not try to layer old, thick branches with heavy bark. Use younger juvenile branches—as always youth is more pliable and ready to strike out with new roots!) Remember that roots form best at the bud so try to make the wound or nick beneath the bud. Most lilacs can be bent so that the branch ends can be layered. Using a branch end you can get 2 or 3 plants in one layering if you make notches 2 or 3 in. apart on the end stem being certain to cover all the notches or wounds with layering soil.

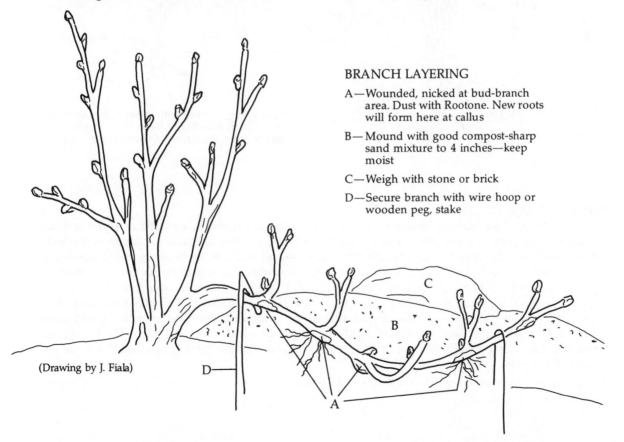

BRANCH LAYERING

A—Wounded, nicked at bud-branch area. Dust with Rootone. New roots will form here at callus

B— Mound with good compost-sharp sand mixture to 4 inches—keep moist

C—Weigh with stone or brick

D—Secure branch with wire hoop or wooden peg, stake

(Drawing by J. Fiala)

LILACS FROM ROOT SHOOTS OR SUCKERS

Most of the cultivars of *S. vulgaris* and its early hybrids produce adventitious buds along the upper root system. Some authorities, e.g. Kolesnikov, in their experiments hold that these bud shoots arise entirely from the lowest portion of the trunk, where it immediately joins the root and that the lilac root, of itself, produces no suckers. Be that as it may, most lilacs are planted below this thin botanical line separating root and stem and do produce root suckers in varying degrees. Some cultivars are notorious in producing root shoots (even to the point of being a nuisance), while other cultivars rarely produce them. If your lilac is not grafted (and this is another good reason why they should not be grafted but be on their own root) these root suckers which appear a short distance from the main trunks are identical in every way to the mother plant.

Root shoots or suckers are an excellent way to propagate choice lilacs on a small scale. It would be totally inadequate for large nursery needs. You must wait a year after the sucker appears to allow it to develop some roots of its own, then cut it off, closer to the main trunk than to the sucker since the roots are not always under the sucker stem directly but often some inches away at an angle. Use a sharp spade as the runner of the suckering shoot often is a few inches below the surface and quite heavy, needing some force of the spade to sever it. You can also clear away some of the soil close to the main stem and sever the runner with pruning shears. After severing it, leave it another year to develop a good root system of its own. The following fall take it up and plant it in a permanent place or a nursery row. Lo! You soon will have a strong, new plant identical in every way to the mother plant. (*Bon jardinier*, do not cut off the shoot when you first see it or, alas, you will have a stem without any root!)

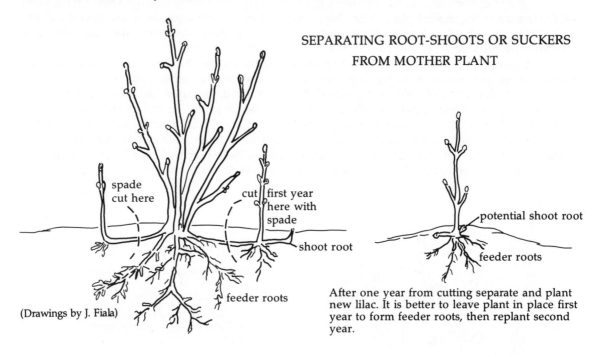

SEPARATING ROOT-SHOOTS OR SUCKERS
FROM MOTHER PLANT

spade cut here

cut first year here with spade

shoot root

feeder roots

(Drawings by J. Fiala)

potential shoot root

feeder roots

After one year from cutting separate and plant new lilac. It is better to leave plant in place first year to form feeder roots, then replant second year.

STOOL LAYERAGE OF LILACS

At the East Malling Research Station, Kent, England, various methods of layering have been the object of considerable research over the years. A number of useful propagation methods have been developed and refined which are of widespread utility in horticulture. Stool layering is an old method which the East Malling Research Staff has refined in light of our better knowledge of plant physiology. It is called the 'Old Wood Method'. It is used to obtain a number of new plants from a single older plant, hence the name 'Old Wood'. Figure 1 shows a plant hilled for layering of older (2 year or more) wood. The bark is nicked, or wounded, then dusted with rooting compound. In 4–6 months over the wound a callus forms from which roots will grow. The hilling soil must be kept damp at all times to provide moisture and air for the rooting process. Plants are left hilled for a year.

PROPAGATION BY STOOL LAYERING

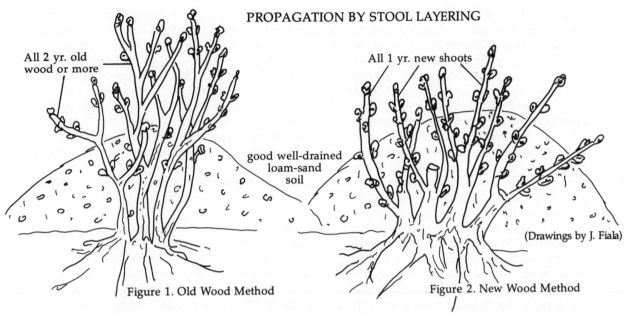

All 2 yr. old
wood or more

All 1 yr. new shoots

good well-drained
loam-sand
soil

(Drawings by J. Fiala)

Figure 1. Old Wood Method

Figure 2. New Wood Method

A newer method developed at East Malling is better, and produces plants sooner, with a stronger root system. The older canes of a strong lilac are pruned back to 4–6 in. stubbs to force the mother plant into strong new growth. Several shoots will sprout and form pencil-thick growth the first year. These are then notched (bark wounded) slightly and dusted with rooting compound. Rooting medium is hilled up around the new, year-old growth some 4–5 in. The medium is kept damp—but not wet—so the forming roots have both adequate air and water. Use a ½ humus (well-rotted leaf mold), ¼ sharp sand and ¼ good garden loam mixture for the medium. Do not pack heavy soils or fine sand around the plant. Hill the plant so that only the top two buds are above ground (up to a foot or more depending on the size of the plant and the growth). Buds close to the medium surface generally do not root as they dry out too much; rather the deeper bud unions send out roots at the callus formations. After rooting is complete (after the first year), separate the new plants and transplant them to a lath or shade house for another year of supervised and watered growth; remove the hilling medium and let the mother plant recover. A strong mother plant can be stool-layered every 3–4 years without harming it. Of course one must sacrifice the bloom from these propagating plants. (*Bon jardinier*—did I not tell you that Madame Lilac for all her splendor is a tough lady!) By this method several handsome plants can be obtained from one hilling without harm to the mother plant.

As with all young, newly rooted plants, pamper these offspring the first year or two with a little extra care—water and some shade—and they will show astounding vigor. (*Bon jardinier*, do not forget the life-giving mother plant—she needs special attention too!) Layered plants, since they are not greenhouse products, are stronger from the beginning and do not need to be hardened-off or acclimated to normal outside temperatures. This method works well not only on lilacs but also with most woody shrubs. The telling point is the correct consistency of the hilling material—not too soggy and not too dry. It must provide both excellent drainage and aeration—as the medium recipe prescribes.

Lilacs from Cuttings

With a little skill and understanding it is possible to grow your new lilacs from green cuttings (same season growth). Choose strong new growth with about 4–5 pairs of buds. Make your cuttings in late spring when new growth can be snapped off by hand and not bend or has begun to harden. In early varieties late May and early June, with most others early to mid-June is the best time for taking green cuttings. Much depends upon the growing weather and the area of the country. Do not expose fresh cut materials to hot winds or sun (place in a stryo-cooler if many are to be made). Keep the length of cuttings rather uniform—to about 5 in. Make a basal cut just below the last pair of leaves. Make clean cuts. Remove the bottom leaves from the lowest two pairs of buds which will be in the cutting medium. (I like to keep 2 pairs of buds in the medium, one pair just at the ground level and two pairs above the medium level.) Treat the cut ends with a rooting compound, such as 'Rootone II', following directions for either a liquid dip or a powder dusting.

Prepare a good propagating medium—such as ⅓ vermiculite, ⅓ sharp (not fine) sand and ⅓ sphagnum or peat. Many very successful propagators use a half-and-half mixture of vermiculite and sand with just a handful of peat or good garden loam. The mixture must be capable of holding moisture and yet have excellent aeration and not become water-logged or the cuttings will rot. Always use a sterile mixture (be certain of this). If vermiculite is used it must be from ⅛ to ¼ in. size (not the finely powdered form, nor must one use fine sand, as both of these compact and provide no aeration or good drainage). Soil aeration is tremendously important for root development so the medium must be able to retain dampness without becoming soggy yet provide for a flow of air that is consistent. If one cannot obtain larger-grained sharp sand then very small pea-gravel can be substituted—never fine sand! Water once and drain well. Now you are ready to set the cuttings.

Place the cuttings vertically in the medium so that the third pair of buds is just even with the surface. Do not pack the medium tightly around the cuttings. cover the entire pot, box or cutting tray with heavy polyethylene or plastic, either a bag or sheet according to size needed. Use strong wire hoops as a frame to prop up the plastic from inside. If you have not overwatered the medium the system will then operate on its own, requiring only light and heat, 70°F daytime and 65° at night. For quickest rooting an even bottom heat of 70° from a pre-set heating cable is excellent. Avoid higher temperatures. If one is setting out only a few cuttings place a larger plastic bag inside a pot and fill the bag to the height of the pot with the medium—insert cuttings as per instructions and then tie the bag at the top tightly thus providing a miniature greenhouse that will provide its own moisture-climate—but beware that you not have the medium too wet—just barely damp to begin with. (*Mon ami*, you are trying to root cuttings and not grow rice!)

Roots begin to form in from 8–12 weeks. Some cultivars and the late-blooming species root a bit faster than *S. vulgaris*. If you notice mold growing or leaves blackening or too much water forming in your little plastic greenhouse—something has gone wrong (non-sterile conditions or decay from some source, too much moisture, not enough soil aeration or too much heat). This must be remedied immediately. Open, air and remove the cause of the mold, dust with Captan or fungicide, then reclose. It is not a bad idea to very lightly dust your cuttings with a fungicide just before you close or cover them with plastic. If cuttings show blackened leaves or buds or stem areas, throw them out and begin all over with more sterile medium and procedures.

Cuttings can be prepared in small pots in a window or on an increasingly larger scale in a greenhouse. In smaller scale place the plastic bags inside the pot (not the pot inside the bag) and

HOW TO MAKE A LILAC SOFTWOOD CUTTING

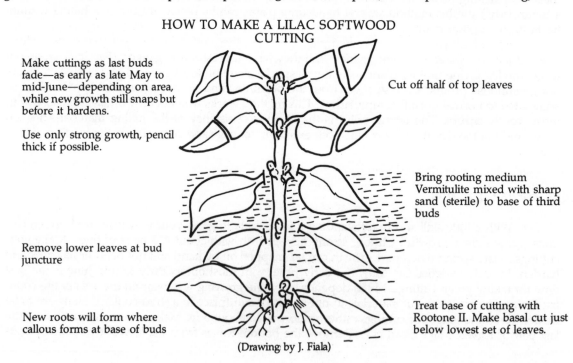

Make cuttings as last buds fade—as early as late May to mid-June—depending on area, while new growth still snaps but before it hardens.

Use only strong growth, pencil thick if possible.

Remove lower leaves at bud juncture

New roots will form where callous forms at base of buds

Cut off half of top leaves

Bring rooting medium Vermitulite mixed with sharp sand (sterile) to base of third buds

Treat base of cutting with Rootone II. Make basal cut just below lowest set of leaves.

(Drawing by J. Fiala)

proceed as previously described. These mini-pot greenhouses will do very well in an east or west window or under artificial lights. If you have a greenhouse, cuttings can be placed in a larger area covered with a large plastic sheet and kept under constant mist which increases the rooting. In a greenhouse make a large wire mesh frame (¼ in. wire) covered with sheet plastic under Grow lights. The wire frame should be at least a foot high to 14 in. from the medium so there is adequate circulation of air—this is necessary. In larger operations a fan should be used to move the air in the frame. If the area is large enough to incorporate one of the newer fine misters then the frame must be at least 2–3 ft. high. Care must be taken to prevent mold—air circulation, excellent drainage and proper medium for aeration are necessary.

If you have a cool lath-house (shade house) with good sharp rooting soil, you can often strike a number of cuttings simply by treating them with rooting compound and sticking them in the soil that is kept damp (not soggy) and shaded. The species and late blooming hybrids do very well this way and a goodly number will root. (This is not a process for commercial growers but for home gardeners who wish to try a few cuttings.) *Bon jardinier,* never drown lilacs—not even as cuttings! These mountain damsels are not water-lilies and despise algae!

After rooting, harden cuttings grown in a window or in the greenhouse to adjust them to the outdoor climate by either keeping them in a controlled greenhouse—not under plastic or by planting them in a shade-house, where they can be sheltered for the first two years from the hot sun and drying winds. When first removed from their plastic incubators they are very susceptible even to the dry air of house temperatures—open their plastic bags gradually—accustom them to room or greenhouse temperatures—then slowly let them get outside air, never direct sunlight which would burn their tender leaves. When hardened-off, they may be set in the protection of a shade-house. Give them air, water and filtered sun in good drained soil—they will soon be strong plants on their own! (*Mon ami,* giving and bringing new life is a traumatic experience for both you and the lilacs—may you both survive!)

ROOTING SMALL NUMBERS OF LILAC CUTTINGS

A small number of lilac cuttings, as few as 2 or 3 in a single pot, can be propagated with comparative ease and very simple materials. One can use any size or shape of container that will fit on a window ledge in a half-shaded window.

Thoroughly wash and sterilize the container by soaking it in a Clorox solution (½ cup Clorox to a gallon of water).

1. Line the container with a clear plastic bag (heavy duty and sterile clean) placing the bag in the container closed end down (the bag will hold all the soil and the container merely provides a substantial form or base). Be certain there are no holes in the plastic. Fill the bag to the height of the container wall with damp, but not wet, rooting medium that has been sterilized. (Small amounts of medium may be sterilized in a 200° oven for 20 to 30 minutes—keep covered so all the moisture does not evaporate.) Use the special mix mentioned previously under 'Cuttings'. It must be damp but not wet and be porous enough to allow for air-flow which is extremely important. Loosen rooting compound as you fill the bag to the proper level. It will take the shape of the container in which the bag is held. (see Fig. 1).

2. Dust your cuttings lightly as per instructions in 'Cuttings' section with a rooting compound such as Rootone II. Making a hole with a pencil or round object, inserting the cuttings into the rooting medium and slightly tighten the area around them left by the hole. If you merely push the cuttings into the loose medium you will rub off all the rooting compound—tamp them slightly as you do not want them in an air pocket either. Do not crowd too many cuttings into one pot (3–4 cuttings to a 5″ pot is enough) but allow for air movement between them.

3. Draw the plastic bag up and close it tightly at the top to make it air-tight. There will be sufficient moisture in the medium to create its own mini-greenhouse atmosphere. Too much water will cause rot and mold. If conditions are correct—do not open the plastic at all. Place in a shaded window with morning or late afternoon sunlight, under Grow-lights or better still in a lath or shade house if you have one. Avoid any direct sunlight as this will overheat the small plastic greenhouse very quickly and cook or kill the cuttings. Remember in this process they have no outside ventilation. (Fig. 2)

4. Ideally, you could construct a simple shade or screen facing north or northeast. (See Fig. 3 and 4) A small 2 or 3 ft. high shade screen will contain several pots. Sink pots into the soil or sand-gravel bottom of the shade house. For a larger model of a shade screen see Fig. 4. A larger

(Drawings by J. Fiala)

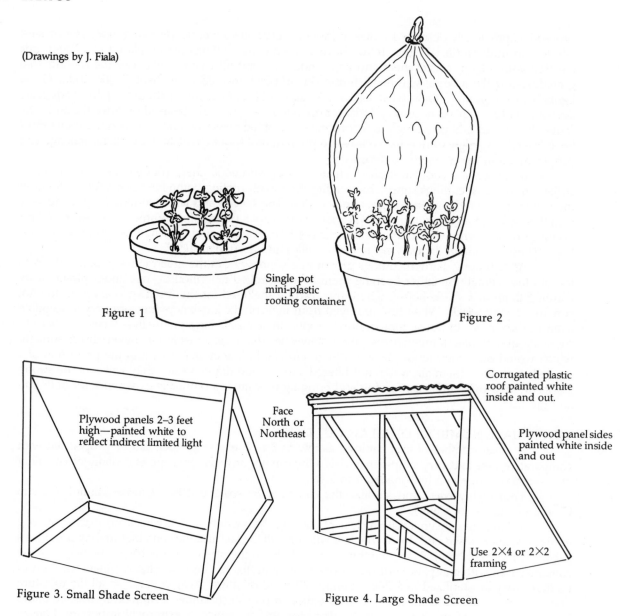

Single pot
mini-plastic
rooting container

Figure 1

Figure 2

Plywood panels 2–3 feet
high—painted white to
reflect indirect limited light

Face
North or
Northeast

Corrugated plastic
roof painted white
inside and out.

Plywood panel sides
painted white inside
and out

Use 2×4 or 2×2
framing

Figure 3. Small Shade Screen

Figure 4. Large Shade Screen

model will provide for several hundred cuttings in trays.

The success of this kind of system rests in using a medium that is only slightly on the damp side, not wet; use sterile rooting medium and good cuttings; also, not overheating with high temperature; no direct sunlight on cuttings. It is relatively simple. It is ideal for rooting a very small number of cuttings in the house in a north or west window. (*Bon jardinier*, do not be discouraged if you fail, try again and learn from your mistakes—soon you will be able to root anything—except pencils!)

AFTER-CARE OF ROOTED CUTTINGS

Some special care is required for rooted cuttings during their first year. All cuttings, especially those rooted under mist, must be gradually hardened off so that adaptation to less moisture and drier soils can be made. The cutting medium must be replaced by a slightly heavier soil with more nutrients. One-third sharp sand-gravel, one-third good garden soil and one-third peat-humus makes an excellent planting medium for rooted cuttings as it drains well and has plenty of nutrients plus an ability to retain some moisture. Never place newly rooted cuttings in heavy clay soils or water-holding sphagnum. They must be watched so that they do not dry out but have a damp but well aerated soil akin to the rooting medium. Avoid mixing fine sand with the soil as it only helps compact the medium—a coarse sand-gravel mix is best. Before watering the cuttings push your

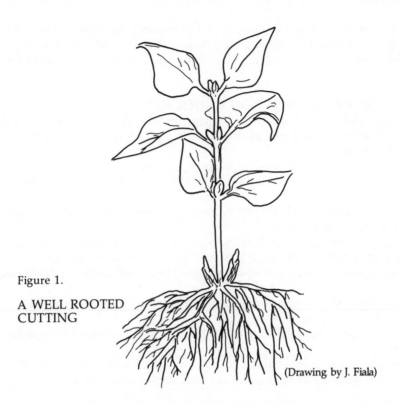

Figure 1.

A WELL ROOTED
CUTTING

(Drawing by J. Fiala)

finger into the soil to ascertain how dry it really is. Often the upper surface appears dry but within a half inch of the surface all is sufficiently damp and not in need of water. It is better to leave plants a little less damp than to be constantly overwatering them. Good leaf growth and color are indicative of healthy conditions. Yellowing leaves, poor color or growth show signs of overwatering, excessive dryness or heavy soils. Rooted cuttings that are not doing well need immediate attention. Things do not get better without help.

If the hardening-off area is in a lath or shade house and there is sufficient room between plants that are growing well, it is best to leave them grow where they are for a second year. This will give larger and stronger plants. Top mulch them with a good balanced mixture of well-rotted humus, or very well rotted manure mixed with a bit of sharp sand. After the second year they should be strong, handsome plants ready to be planted out in the nursery rows or garden and take care of themselves. If, however, they appear weak and have only modest root growth, leave them for a third year. Some cultivars when rooted as cuttings are slow to make good growth and need this extra pampering.

Second year plants grown well may be ready to be potted up and sold for the nursery container trade. They are much smaller than grafted plants but saleable, especially if they are of the newer and special cultivars or species. They should be so labelled as 'Special—Rooted Cutting of New Cultivar'. In the open nursery or Garden Center sales area they must be carefully watered and not allowed to dry out. (I have seen countless container plants dead or dying simply from not having been watered and given proper care—Lilacs will not stand this kind of abuse! No, *mon ami,* you will soon be out of the lilac business if there is not excellent container care.) Container plants always dry out much more quickly if not in a mulched, buried container area. Rooted cuttings are really best kept for a third and fourth year in nursery rows where they can grow and form rather strong plants. Three or four year old, own-root plants handled this way should command a premium price. Always propagate only the better and newer cultivars. Ordinarily the lavender, pinks and blue lilacs grow and root somewhat faster than the whites and very deep purples. Tetraploids and dwarfs are the slowest and most difficult growers initially.

In rooting lilacs, experience has identified certain cultivars that are extremely difficult, if not impossible, to propagate as cuttings (e.g. 'Rochester'), whereas others seem to root no matter when taken and with minimal care. 'Rochester', as beautiful as it is, grows and roots poorly for many years before it is established, thus making it an unattractive prospect for the nursery trade. If one grafts it on white ash and is patient to care for it for 5 or 6 years, it is a most desirable cultivar for any garden and a real showpiece—it should command a premium price. One should not make ease of propagation the main criterion for selecting lilacs to be offered for sale. Do not eliminate some of the most beautiful lilacs on this one score, rather, learn their needs and the skills for successfully rooting them.

THE HALWARD METHOD OF PROPAGATION UNDER MIST

A most successful method of rooting cuttings under constant mist has been developed at the Royal Botanical Gardens, Hamilton, Ontario, Canada, by Ray Halward, Chief Propagator. Briefly the procedure is as follows:

1. The misting system is housed in a fiber-glass, plastic lined house, shaded with 46% shade saran outside plus burlap shade on the inside. Heating cables in the sandbed are set at 70°F during the summer.

2. Cuttings are taken in the latter part of June up to July 10 (cuttings taken this late will not dry out as readily as early taken ones.)

3. Cuttings are wounded on the bottom ⅓ in two places, on each side. As many as two and three sets of leaves are retained, very large leaves at times are reduced in size.

4. The rooting medium is 3 parts sand and 1 part peat. Half and half peat-pearlite is another good mixture.

5. The most successful rooting compound is Seradix No. 3 (which is about 75% I.B.A.); it is mixed with equal parts of Captan 50W.

6. Cuttings are given extra light up to 16 hours a day. They are left until September and then hardened-off.

7. Rooted plants are over-wintered in the same area with cable set at 32°F to prevent freezing. Plants are potted in early spring and are well started when set out.

Grafting Lilacs

Grafting is an old art used in propagating lilacs as well as many other genera. It is mentioned by plant explorers as being used in China to propagate certain species of lilacs as far back as the mid-seventeen hundreds. In Europe grafting lilacs began at about this same time. Whoever made the discovery of grafting lilacs on privet, *Ligustrum ovalifolium*, rootstock is not known, but this dates back also into the late 1700s. In recent years commercial growers have done extensive research, both in America and Europe, to find better rootstocks than privet which had some drawbacks as it does not always allow the graft to form its own root, thus resulting in a single stemmed plant that is subject to injury, borers and eventually incompatibility of scion and understock causing the death of the lilac plant. It has been found by using Ash (*Fraxinus pennsylvanica* or *americana*) rootstock as a 'graft nurse' to start the lilac on its own root, a far better, own-rooted lilac plant results. In the first year the ash understock feeds and supports the lilac scion forcing it to form considerable root callus and its own fibrous roots, after which the ash root falls away and the lilac, now well-rooted, is entirely on its own. In the past lilacs were traditionally grafted upon common privet, *Ligustrum, S. vulgaris, S. villosa* and *S. × persica*. Each proposed difficulties: *S. × persica* rootstock has been found to be a major host of root nematodes; privet is eventually incompatible and somewhat short lived; both privet and *S. vulgaris* send up innumerable understock growth which in *S. vulgaris* grafts is indistinguishable from the top-worked growth and eventually takes over the whole plant leaving the grafted scion dead; *S. villosa* does not allow own-roots to form on the scion and eventually outgrows it with a tree-like root. White or Green Ash appear to be the best and most successful understock for grafting lilacs.

The best type of graft with White Ash understock appears to be either the 'saddle graft' or the 'cleft graft' (see diagram). With both types of grafts enough callus is formed by the lilac to successfully induce own-root formation. After the first year the slight graft incompatibility of the ash rootstock begins to separate it from the lilac graft, now on its own root. At this time the lilacs are lifted, sold or replanted in nursery rows for further growth as 2- or 3-year-old own-root plants. These are ideal for planting by the homeowner or gardener.

In the nursery grafting generally is done in the wintertime, January or February, in the greenhouse where the grafts after they have been made are covered to callus and kept cool to be lined out in early Spring. The small homeowner can make a few grafts and place them in a polybag covered pot in a shady window in a cool place. From one ash root 3 or 4 rootstocks can be made that are 5–8 in. long depending on the caliper of the scion. After the grafts are made they should be placed in a cool place of 65° to 70° (a warm greenhouse or cellar) and covered with a plastic. Keep them out of direct sunlight and heat—they must callus over at the place of the graft. They are then planted out in a cool frame house or stored very slightly damp for later planting. They must not be permitted to mold during the callus formation period of from 4–8 weeks. They must be slightly damp (not wet) to begin the growth process which initiates callus formation. The grafts when made should be dipped into a Clorox solution or dusted with any good garden fungicide. They are best placed or covered with a good sterile sphagnum—more on the dry side than wet.

On a smaller, less commercial scale, success may be had in rooting lilac grafts by the unique process of spring grafting lilac scions on larger ash trees (3–5″ in diameter). Scions are bark-grafted onto the trunk after the top of the tree has been entirely removed, held in place by electrical tape. The strong root of the ash will force these grafts into rapid spring growth (usually done in late April-early May). When these grafts are 6–10″ high with new growth, they are unwrapped and will be found to have heavy white callus growth at the point of their grafting with the tree. Carefully remove the graft with as much white callus adhering as possible and pot plant them as you would a cutting and cover with polybags. Root formation is very quick on such 'green-graft cuttings'. This method is not feasible for large nursery propagations but where a few plants are desired works quite well.

If winter grafting is done in the greenhouse or using a house window for the plants, scions should be collected at the time of grafting—usually in January. Often grafting is done in late September-October and grafts are set out in specially protected beds in a lath or shade house for protection. For scions always use current season growth of pencil size at least 5–6 inches long with at least 3 pairs of buds. Never use weak or immature wood with long internodes (spaces between buds). Do not pack budwood in damp paper, moss, etc. as this will foster mold. Wrap scions in a dry, plastic bag to eliminate air and store in a refrigerator (or snow bank) until grafts are made (beware of freon gas-leaking refrigerators as freon gas (refrigerant) will kill buds on stored scions or seeds). In making the grafts study the diagrams given. Remember no one gets 100% to grow but with practice and proper management of the grafts once they have been made one should expect at least half to grow. For the beginner in propagating lilacs, cuttings are perhaps more successful than grafts.

One should practice making cuts, fitting the cambium layers together (the green growing skin layer just below the bark is the real place all growth takes place in grafting—it is called the cambium layer). This must fit as tightly as possible where the scion meets the understock—upon knitting these two layers together depends the success of the graft. Practice on any two twigs, shaping, and fitting them together using the different kind or styles of grafting pictured. Soon you will feel you are an expert and be ready to tackle the real plant materials of lilacs.

IMPORTANT TERMS IN GRAFTING

Understock—the nurse root upon which another variety is to be grafted

Scion—the budwood, graftwood, or the desired new plant to be grafted onto the understock.

Rooting Compound—a hormonal chemical compound that assists in root formation. (Rootone, Hormo-Root B or C, Hormodin) Use Captan as a disinfectant powder). Always follow instructions on container.

Rubber Tie—are special rubber strips of various widths used in grafting and budding.

Graft union—the places where budwood meets understock on the graft. These areas MUST touch, meet tightly for healing and success. No air spaces please! *Cambium layers must join tightly.*

Callous material—the whitish growth that developes at the graft union and from which roots later form.

PREPARING THE UNDERSTOCK FOR CLEFT GRAFTING

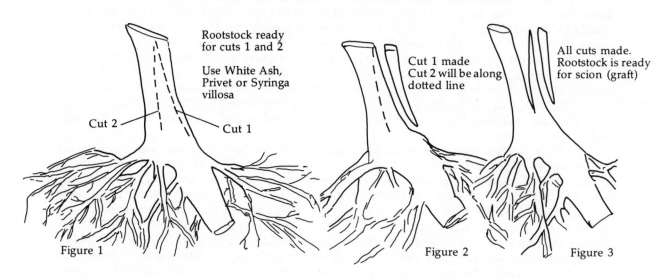

Rootstock ready
for cuts 1 and 2

Use White Ash,
Privet or Syringa
villosa

Cut 2   Cut 1

Figure 1

Cut 1 made
Cut 2 will be along
dotted line

Figure 2

All cuts made.
Rootstock is ready
for scion (graft)

Figure 3

SADDLE GRAFT ON WHITE ASH

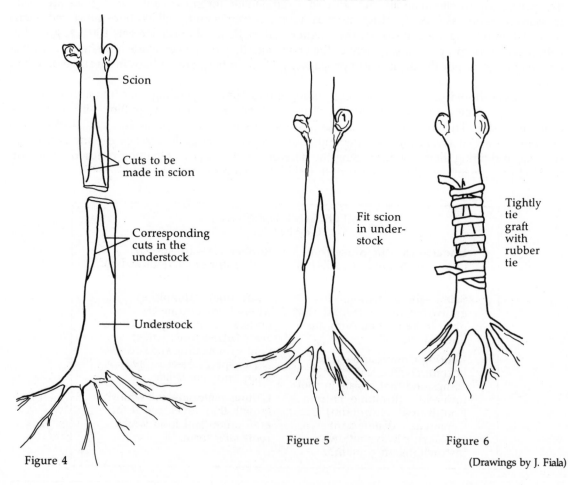

Scion

Cuts to be
made in scion

Corresponding
cuts in the
understock

Understock

Figure 4

Fit scion
in under-
stock

Figure 5

Tightly
tie
graft
with
rubber
tie

Figure 6

(Drawings by J. Fiala)

CLEFT GRAFT

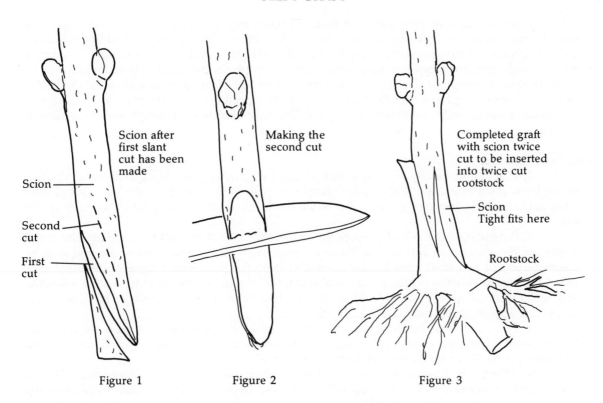

Scion

Second cut

First cut

Scion after first slant cut has been made

Figure 1

Making the second cut

Figure 2

Completed graft with scion twice cut to be inserted into twice cut rootstock

Scion Tight fits here

Rootstock

Figure 3

GRAFTING LILACS

1. Grafting is generally done in late fall or winter (January/February). With a greenhouse the late winter months are most favorable.

2. Select scionwood from past, new growth. Cut on days above freezing. Try to use immediately and store in polyetheleyne bag—no wetting.

3. For rootstock use White Ash, Privet, *Syringa villosa* or *reticulata*.

4. Follow directions in making graft.

5. Allow grafts to callous in damp sphagnum or sawdust or barely damp sand, for a week to 10 days at 70°.

6. When calloused they may be planted out, or cold stored for Spring planting.

7. In field all understock root shoots must be cut off immediately or they will grow up smothering the graft.

8. Be certain to plant up to and including the first buds on scion. Graft must be covered entirely.

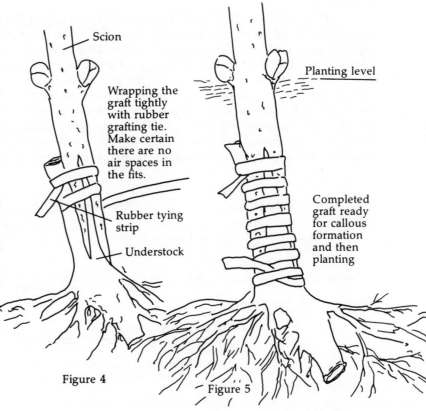

Scion

Wrapping the graft tightly with rubber grafting tie. Make certain there are no air spaces in the fits.

Rubber tying strip

Understock

Figure 4

Planting level

Completed graft ready for callous formation and then planting

Figure 5

(Drawings by J. Fiala)

Budding Lilacs

Lilacs may also be propagated by budding (inserting) a bud-eye onto an understock of a rooted plant—usually of *S. vulgaris* or one of the species of lilacs. The purpose of budding is to use a single bud rather than a substantial length of stem containing several buds. Budding is simply a more cost-effective propagation in cases where many new plants are required from limited mother stock. In time the single bud will grow an entirely new top of the desired cultivar. If the bud is expected to form own-roots later the bud-graft must be placed low, near the root, so that it can be eventually covered with soil in which to root. The following steps have proved successful in budding:

The Budding Process:

1. Lilacs are generally budded in late summer when this year's buds have matured. Only strong buds should be used. With a razor-sharp knife cut off the bud from the bud-stick as indicated in the drawing, leaving a small heel of wood on the bud—do not peel but rather cut it off the wood.

2. Prior to cutting the bud, prepare the understock (privet or lilac) for budding. The major portion of the understock is removed, leaving a portion above the place where the bud is to be inserted—one or two small branches are desired to keep the sap flowing above the budded area. When the bud has knitted or taken, the remaining top of the understock is removed the following year as its vigor or new growth would hinder the bud from developing. Never leave any new shoots that appear on the understock below the bud.

3. Cut only the cambium bark of the understock as shown in the drawing in the form of a T. Make sharp, clean cuts, gently peel or slip back the cambium only enough to insert the prepared bud, drawing the T-cut cambium bark back over the bud.

4. After the bud has been inserted and the cambium layers matched, tighten and wrap the bud securely beginning at the top with either a rubber budding strip or waxed twine, end the wrapping at the bottom of the bud. With practice you can tie the bud in securely either from the top or bottom—most beginners, who start from the bottom first, have a tendency to squeeze the bud too high and out of the slit.

5. Remove the top stock the summer after the bud has united with the understock and begun to grow.

Be careful to make all cuts clean and sharp, not fraying the edges. Make the bud-cut flat, not scooped or dished, as you cut. Fasten the bud tightly with no air pockets and all will be well. Within a short time, a week, one can tell if the bud has taken as it will be plump and green. Shriveled, dry buds are failures. These are due to drying-out of the bud before insertion or allowing too much air in the budding process by not tightening the tie sufficiently; or too much green cambium had been peeled back and the cambium layers failed to meet; faulty and careless, frayed cuts; allowing too much new wild growth to develop on the understock below the bud; or overexposure to hot drying winds and extremely hot suns with little ground moisture for the understock. Do not be discouraged if you have considerable failures—practice makes perfect. (*Bon jardinier*, may all your buds be green and fat and grow next season! Remember buds remain dormant until the next Spring.)

BUDDING LILACS

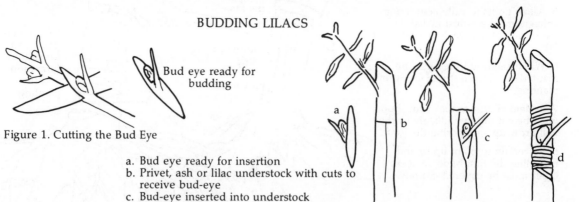

Figure 1. Cutting the Bud Eye

Bud eye ready for budding

a. Bud eye ready for insertion
b. Privet, ash or lilac understock with cuts to receive bud-eye
c. Bud-eye inserted into understock
d. Completed bud bound tight with rubber budding band

(Drawings by J. Fiala)

Figure 2. The Budding Process

Future Prospects for Breeding New and Useful Cultivars of *Syringa*

There are only 3 ways new cultivars of lilacs can be produced—hybridization, genetic chromosome count changes (increasing the number of chromosomes), and mutations (natural or induced). Each is a rather exacting science and art so each is considered separately. Undoubtedly, the greatest number of new cultivars will be produced by hybridization.

HYBRIDIZING LILACS

For those interested in hybridizing lilacs the following suggestions provide a firm basis to proceed in a rational way. There will always be those who gather seed and plant them hoping for an outstanding new cultivar and, indeed, some few, fine seedlings will come forth from these efforts. Real progress in breeding exceptional new lilacs will come from the hands of those who seriously hybridize, i.e. hand-pollinate lilacs with a set purpose of selected parents. Several models or programs are herein proposed.

In every hybridizing design there should be:

1. An hybridizing plan with a specific purpose and with special selection of parent materials: e.g., crossing *S. vulgaris* 'Rochester' with *S. oblata* var *alba* to obtain better large-flowering, early blooming white lilacs; or crossing *S. debelderii* with *S. julianae* to produce low blooming little-leaved lilacs; or a cross of *S. vulgaris* 'Prodige' with 'Rochester' to produce large flowered, multi-petaled deep purple lilacs. Always use only the best gene stock available and be certain of its purity.

2. There be controlled purity of the cross-pollinization with every precaution against any false pollinizations—wind or insect or self-fertilizations.

3. There must be controlled observation of the entire seedling population resulting from the entire seed crop. One specific, singular trait should not be ascribed as a cross characteristic when it appears in only 1 or 2 seedlings. Accurate records should be kept of all cross traits and characteristics with total objectivity as to merit or values.

4. Carefully derived standards for the selection of individual crosses should be established and pursued with complete objectivity, with selection emphasis based both on the merits of genetic inheritance and the general traits of the specific cross. Selectivity for hybridization at times may be quite different from selectivity for the commercial market. Very often a 'winner' on the commercial market may have little to offer future generations of hybrids because it is a poor parent, e.g. 'Sensation' or 'Primrose' as far as color is concerned.

In the area of hybridization 2 main areas are open: one of intensive, selective breeding within a species; the other the careful crossing of different species which results are called interspecific hybrids.

HYBRIDIZING WITHIN A SPECIES (Intraspecies hybridization)

'Inbreeding' within a species is simply crossing different cultivars within the same species—or very strictly crossing the offspring of a special cultivar with each other (sib-crossing). In the thousands of cultivars of *S. vulgaris* certain crosses have been developed with such strong and set characteristics that they could be considered clonal-crosses, e.g. the heavy Lemoine doubles, or the large flowered Havemeyer singles, or the multipetals singles resulting from 'Rochester' ('Rochester Hybrids'), or in the late blooming lilacs the intercrossing of the *S. × prestoniae* hybrids. Intraspecific hybridization seeks to select certain special characteristics—e.g. size of florets or thryses, unique color intensification, low-growing or dwarfness of shrub—and to intensive them by inbreeding. It may also seek to take two different characteristics found one in each parent and combine them with the hope of finding both characteristics in the offspring, e.g. deep purple of 'Prodige' combined with the multipetaled florets and candle-spikes of the white 'Rochester' hoping to result in a deep purple, multipetaled candle-spiked lilac. By this kind of hybridization we seek to intensify or combine unique characteristics—often we are able to deepen the color or clarify its brightness, add fragrance, bring out an earlier or later blooming cultivar. It is interesting to note that Hulda Klager did most of her work with, as she states ". . . only three *S. vulgaris* cultivars!" Any characteristic can be intensified to a certain point with continued careful selectivity and breeding for that factor.

'Back-crossing' involves crossing the end product of any inbred line back to one of the original or very early parents. Frequently some very outstanding results and intensification of an originally sought after factor are thus obtained, e.g. crossing the third and fourth generation 'Rochester Hybrids' back to 'Rochester' would undoubtedly give some very fine 'Rochester' type offspring.

'Out-crossing' within a given species, such as *S. vulgaris*, which has so many diverse cultivars (nearly 2,000 named varieties) involves crossing one clone bred for a special factor—e.g. floret size, to another bred for a different characteristic—e.g. special color. Often the infusion of sufficiently different clonal material gives the offspring 'special vigor (best illustrated by crossing separate species and known as 'hybrid vigor' but also found within a species where there is considerable clonal differences as in *S. vulgaris*). In *S. vulgaris* for example the original and earlier named cultivars of deep-purple were marked by weak and poor growth, with the infusion of strong-growing clonal vigor from other colored lilacs we now have strong-growing very deep purple lilacs such as 'Prodige' and 'Agincourt Beauty' or 'Albert F. Holden'. Extensive hybridization work within the species of *S. vulgaris* has been done by Lemoine, Havemeyer, Maarse, Kolesnikov, Fenicchia (Rochester Strain) and Fiala. Much more still remains to be done.

HYBRIDIZING DIFFERENT SPECIES (Interspecific hybridization)

Interspecific crosses are those made between two species or species hybrids within a genus. To date only interspecific hybridization within a series of lilacs has been successful with the one exception of *S.* × *diversifolia* which is a cross between *S. pinnatifolia* (Series *Pinatifoliae*) and *S. oblata* (Series *Vulgares*)—it is unique as all other attempts at inter-series hybridization have been unsuccessful. The continued interspecific crosses of lilacs will undoubtedly provide some of the most exciting and profitable new lilacs for both hybridists and commercial growers in years to come. These crosses, however, also require some of the most difficult work, selectivity and evaluation as well as being the least profitable commercially in the beginning, but eventually should prove their worth in the third and fourth generations. (*Mon ami*, the great and landmark hybridization done by Isabella Preston in producing the remarkable 'Prestonian Hybrids' enriched her very little, if at all, but it has set a foundation of considerable magnitude for others to build upon.)

All the horticultural world, especially lilac fanciers, should be aware of the interspecific crosses done by Miss Preston, Lemoine and Frank Skinner—they are some of the milestones in lilac hybridizing. Fewer still are aware of the continued work of inbreeding the *S.* × *prestoniae* being done by Dr. W. Bugala, Kornik, Poland; that in progress by Dr. Owen Rogers of the University of New Hampshire; and the outstanding work of Dr. Donald Egolf in producing far superior Early Hybrids at the U.S. National Arboretum, Washington, D.C., in his work with *S.* × *hyacinthiflora*. Dr. Rogers has worked rather extensively with the beginnings of new double forms of *S.* × *prestoniae* and *S.* × *josiflexa;* Dr. James Pringle at the Royal Botanical Gardens, Hamilton, Ontario, Canada, has crossed some relatively little worked with species in new crosses. The author has worked with several different and new crosses, some with multibrids—plants containing 4 and 5 different species. Although all have had some degree of success, not all their work is yet available to the commercial (or private) trade. These efforts should be continued with additional hybridization and considerable selection. There are any number of hybridizing possibilities for young hybridizers in continuing this work of back-crossing, line-breeding, multibrid crossing and selective breeding. In 1972 John C. Wister pointed out to the International Lilac Society, "We have enough work for all the plant hybridists the world can produce to last to the end of this century!"

Often some relatively insignificant species or one of the recently discovered species has a recessive potential that literally 'explodes' when properly hybridized. To date many *Syringa* species have been comparatively 'untouched by hybridists', e.g. *S. pinnatifolia*, *S. potaninii*, *S. patula*, *S. julianae*, *S. reticulata*, the newest *S. debelderii* and *S. oblata* var. *donaldii*. Other species have only been little used. What a treasury of beauty is still to be unfolded!

INDUCING POLYPLOIDS IN THE GENUS *SYRINGA*

Polyploids are plants in which, through some fashion, the chromosomes have been doubled, tripled etc. to varying degrees. This increase in the number of chromosomes causes the plant to have a considerably increased but varying degree of inheritable characteristics. Polyploids appear in some species of plants in nature, but seem to be naturally absent in others. Considerable advance has been made in genera other than *Syringa* with tetraploids and polyploid plants. Many new and superior forms have thus arisen in horticultural plants available for our gardens. To date, no polyploids of the genus *Syringa* have been found in nature.

PLATE 97

INDUCING TETRAPOLOIDS in Lilacs with a .01% colchicine solution.

Pre-germinate seed to first leaf or cotyledon (not true leaves) stage. Germinate in sphagnum moss.

Sprouted seedlings in colchicine solution (several hours).

Treated seedlings removed to clear water wash (several hours and change of water).

Normal untreated seedlings of S. julianae after 4 weeks.

Tetraploid seedlings of S. julianae after 4 weeks.

eedlings of S. pekinensis 'Pendula' rarely roduce healthy green seedlings when self-pollinated. Most f these seedlings are albinos that will die for lack of chlorophyll. or your author 30–1 are white.

Left: Untreated seedlings of late hybrids
Right: Tetraploid seedlings.

PLATE 98

Mutations (Chimeras) generally do not produce superior lilacs but on rare occasions some have been found with considerable merit as in 'Sensation' and 'Primrose'. The lilac 'Sensation' (left) with a pale lavender mutation (chimera or sport). This often happens on 'Sensation'. One can let it grow and root it as a cutting (center) and have a pale lavender lilac of little merit. S. × *chinensis* 'Alba' (right) often has rosy lavender sports. These, if of merit, can be rooted and named. Mutations often are unstable and have more mutations e.g. *S. vulgaris* 'Comtese Horace de Choiseul' has many varied mutations. One must be careful in taking cuttings that the real cultivar is obtained.

MUTATIONS

HYBRIDIZING

Hybridizing Lilacs is by far a more certain way to obtain choice cultivars. In breeding lilacs superior parents must be chosen. After pollinization the pistils must be covered (left). When seed is ripe it must be separated and cleaned (right) and sown as best fits the needs of the breeder, either out-of-doors or indoors.

PLANTING AND AFTERCARE

Preparing the seed for germination (about 3–4 weeks) depending on species.

Normal seedlings of several species crosses.

Only three people of record have worked to the present to produce tetraploids or polyploids in lilacs. Dr. Karl Sax, working at the Arnold Arboretum, produced a tetraploid *S. vulgaris* that has now been lost (his was the first effort in the genus *Syringa*, but as no seedlings were obtained it was an academic but important effort). The author has worked for nearly 40 years with the various species of *Syringa* producing experimental tetraploids, polyploids and mixtaploids. Several tetraploid hybrids were obtained of *S. wolfii, S. komarowii, S. julianae, S. × prestoniae, S. yunnanensis* and several *S. vulgaris* cultivars and crosses with *S. × hyacinthiflora* and *S. oblata*. Some few of these hybrids have been named, mostly for continued hybridization rather than commercial plants, e.g. 'Lark Song', 'Spellbinder', 'Sunrise', 'Prophecy', 'Garden Peace' and 'Eventide'. Several second and third generation seedlings remain under evaluation. Dr. Owen Rogers, University of New Hampshire, has done some limited work in inducing tetraploids, specializing in the *S. × josiflexa* hybrids.

The ordinary (diploid) number of chromosomes in *Syringa* is 44, 46 or 48 (haploid numbers are $x = 22, 23, 24$ depending upon the species (cf. Darlington *Chromosome Atlas*). Elsewhere in this work the diploid number has been listed for each species so far counted (some few remain uncounted). Not only is it important to the hybridist to be able to work with a plant having increased numbers of chromosomes but this increase is visible in the physical appearance of the tetraploid plant—thicker, heavier and more leathery leaves, somewhat larger florets and flower spikes, deeper color and new hues, often with irridescent tones; thicker flower petals which withstand sun and weather better; more buds, at closer intervals; and often more stamina and resistance to certain diseases and viruses. These traits do not generally appear as dominant until fixed in the third and fourth generations of polyploid crossings. Hence it takes considerable time not only to induce a polyploid but also to carry it on through the next generation to an acceptable garden plant. It is a lifetime work! (*Mon ami*, it is not a task for tinkerers or those easily distracted!)

In nature polyploids are induced in a variety of ways, e.g. by seeds or plants frozen in ice under tremendous pressure of weight or by certain natural vacuums, by electrical charges (lightning), and certain chemical reactions which effect the growing plant cells in mitosis (the time of cell division in the growing plant tissue)—one of such naturally produced chemicals is colchicine produced in the juice of the autumn crocus, *Colchicum autumnalis*. In the laboratory various means have been used as well: heat, radiation, gamma rays and several experimental chemicals. For practical purposes in obtaining polyploids with lilacs the best method is the use of the chemical colchicine.

Presently this drug is restricted in its use by Federal regulation; is rather expensive; difficult to obtain; and considerably dangerous to use if its fumes are inhaled or it touches the skin. On the other hand, it is easy to work with (using proper precautions) as it is soluble in water and does not disintegrate or contaminate too rapidly and is reasonably stable in its activity. It is a potent, carcinogenic drug and should not be used by beginners. Best results are obtained by using colchicine at the crucial time of cell division so it is used only on growing material, as sprouting seedlings or expanding new growth. Near-lethal doses produce the necessary disruption that result in chromosome longitudinal splitting thus producing polyploids. Because of the near-lethal dose most of the plants treated will die, approximately 90%. Not all that remain will be polyploids. Those that double their chromosome number are called tetraploids (4x number), quintoploids (5x) etc. Some few will have mixed numbers of unstable chromosomes and will be called mixtaploids; some will divide unevenly and become sterile triploids.

USE OF COLCHICINE IN INDUCING POLYPLOIDS

The author has found that the most economical and effective use of colchicine has been with germinating seed or with emerging growth (inverting the lilac plants in pots lowered to cover the new growth with the colchicine solution. Long new growth is too difficult to treat. Expanding buds and very short new growth should be used. I have found that most *Syringa* seedlings and growing tissue react well in treatment with solutions of colchicine of .048 to .06% of an aequous solution (1 gram of colchicine powder dissolved in 1000 milliliters, equivalent to 100 cc of distilled water [1 liter] which gives a .1% solution; ½ gram to a liter gives a workable .05% solution which is the most effective for treating *Syringa*). Use care to keep this solution from adulteration by any additional water as it will be too weak to be effective. Colchicine solutions hold up rather well if stored in a dark, colored bottle away from sunlight, in a cool place ALWAYS AWAY FROM THE REACH OF ANY CHILDREN. The solution can be reused several times if not diluted.

Pre-germinated *Syringa* seeds in active growth—just as the first true leaves begin to unfold—are the best subjects. It is imperative that hard covered seed-coats, such as in *S. reticulata*, be carefully removed before treatment as they greatly inhibit and soak-up additional chemical to prolong (killing) the process. Allow seeds to swell and as they break, before the cotyledons open fully, treat them. The best way to pre-germinate seed is in sterile milled sphagnum moss with some bottom heat of 65–68°F. Do not wash seedlings prior to treatment.

Heavy test tubes (glass cigar tubes are ideal) are used with the seedlings just covered by the colchicine solution, then corking the tube. Seedlings are left in this solution for 12–36 hours with slight stirring or shaking (the longer the treatment the more lethal the dosage and the more seedlings will die). The solution is poured off (to be reused) and seedlings are rinsed a few times, then placed in a sterile water bath for up to 30 hours or at least equal to the treatment time to rid them of all excess colchicine which will continue to react, if not removed, and kill the seedlings by overexposure.

After washing the seedlings plant them in an absolutely sterile, slightly damp medium (sphagnum ¼, perlite ¼, sharp sand ¼ and good sterile potting soil ¼). Dampen and water only with sterile water. Dust with a fungicide such as Captan. DO NOT OVERWATER or let dry out during the crucial immediate 3 weeks of aftercare. This is the most critical time in which most of the seedlings will die from the overdose of the colchicine in their tissue (resembles the virus of dampening-off). They must not be in a too damp medium; keep them at about 65–70°F, no more and away from hot sunlight, under Grow-Lights. Most of the seedlings will begin to show the effect of colchicine kill and begin to rot and die—remove dying seedlings immediately. The few that survive will have very deep, bright green, thick cotyledons and emerging leaves but will remain static (in inactive growth) for several weeks.

When the first leaves appear they are thick, often misshapened, krinkled and very slow to develop and usually much larger than untreated seedlings which will be on their second and third leaves by the same time. Growth of polyploids is very slow, often not more than one or two leaves the first year. Root growth is also very slow, hence winter care is most important. They are best wintered in a cold greenhouse where the temperatures do not go below freezing. Out of doors or in a lath house they generally freeze out the first winter. (This was learned by sad experience). Only after their second, better the third year, they can be planted out in a sheltered location. Polyploid plants grow very slowly with bud intervals very close together, often several buds are found within the length of an inch and one-half (4 cm). Many polyploid seedlings are only a foot high after ten years (this does not mean they are dwarf but are still recovering from the shock of treatment—eventually they will form stronger roots and begin to grow more normally).

In time they will bloom but you will be most disappointed in the first bloom—expectations are always higher than the reality. Induced tetraploids and polyploids in the first generation still have only the original pattern of chromosomes, these must be recombined and crossed with other tetraploids to bring out the real variety and potential found in their greatly increased genetic capability. The flowers even of the originally treated plants are larger, floret petals thicker and color often much deeper but at times flowers can be smaller in the first generation and heavier—(*mon ami et amie*, these treated plants are very mixed genetically and need to settle down!) Preferably hand-pollinate tetraploids with other tetraploids of a different gene pool for best and fastest results.

I have treated several clones of *S. vulgaris*, the *S.* × *hyacinthiflora* and the following species lilacs: *S. julianae, S. oblata, S. komarowii, S. reflexa, S. sweginzowii* 'Albida', *S. tomentella, S. yunnanensis, S. reticulata, S. wolfii, S. tigerstedti* plus several *S.* × *prestoniae* hybrids and hybrids of the late species. They are all slow growing and somewhat disappointing in their first generations—some few have been lost because they were such poor growers and due to the severity of our harsh winters. A very few tetraploids and mixtoploids have been named not that they are all superior cultivars, but that they may be useful to hybridizers. Some few are exceptionally fine garden plants e.g. *S.* × *tribrida* 'Lark Song', *S.* × *clarkiana* 'Spellbinder', 'Springtime', 'Eventide', 'Garden Peace' and *S. vulgaris* 'Elsie Lenore' whereas 'Little Miss Muffet' is a fine dwarf only if on its own roots.

In these early tetraploids the tissue is not always stable and the hybridizer must be on guard for plants reverting after some years back to the diploid type. All tetraploids and polyploids in *Syringa* are still in an experimental stage but they are on their way to make a name for themselves.

LILAC MUTATIONS

New cultivars of lilacs generally come from hybridization or induced tetraploids, but they do occur as the result of natural bud mutations. Bud mutations are a disruption of the genetic chains in the chromosome (not the doubling of chromosomes as in polyploids). These disruptions are caused in nature by viruses, heat, radiation, electrical shock, pollution or unknown factors. Often bud mutations have arisen in the greenhouse in the process of forcing lilacs for winter bloom by using the hot-water method. Two very outstanding cultivars produced in this way are *S. vulgaris* 'Sensation' (a sport or mutation of 'Hugo de Vries') and 'Primrose'. Both were introduced by D. E. Maarse of The Netherlands. Undoubtedly many bud sports (mutations) occur each year in nature but go unnoticed. Some cultivars, e.g. *S. vulgaris* 'Comtesse Horace de Choiseul', often have several mutations in bloom of different shades and colors on the same plant. But mutations often cause curious results, leaf variegations of green with white or yellow, red leaf colorations, blossom color changes, petal shape or marginal floret variations such as in 'Sensation' with its white margins. Most bud mutations, for various yet not understood reasons, appear to be non-genetic; i.e., their special characteristics are not transferrable through hybridization. However, desirable genetic characteristics may remain as hidden recessives that might be intensified through inbreeding. Bud mutations when found must be either rooted as cuttings or grafted to preserve them. When left on the mother plant they most often die by being outgrown by more aggressive growth around them. The author once asked the noted Dutch hybridist, Dirk E. Maarse, why he seemed to find and introduce proportionately more fine lilac sports than other growers? "Because I look a little longer at my lilacs and at the whole plant. I spend more time looking and thinking", was his reply. "There are probably just as many mutations in every large lilac collection but others do not take them to see them or to root them as a separate plant." (This, *mon ami,* can be said of seedling crosses and indeed of all hybridization!)

Dr. Barbara McClintock's research on "TE's" or ". . . transposable elements that can do unpredictable things in plants and genetics" has shown what can be accomplished by paying attention to minute genetic elements." Her work with color genes in corn shows that (even in lilacs) if we were far more observant, we might discover small changes that could be meaningful in the hybridization of new cultivars. We do not pay enough attention to the structures, shades of color, the eyed and striped patterns of floret petals and do not intensify them in breeding, therefore many improvements go undiscovered and unused. McClintock's studies show that color does not always follow predictable patterns. (It may be that one of these gene unpredictabilities will some day give us a true yellow or bright red lilac!)

CHAPTER TEN

The Lilac Hybridizers of Yesterday and Today

Nature has hidden in the genetic make-up of flowers and growing things, marvelous traits and beauty much of which is yet to be unfolded by the work of nature or discovered by the patient genius of man. The lilac is no exception. Gifted individuals have through their dedicated work, understanding and love of the genus brought forth many new forms, colors and hybrids over the years. Through the efforts of plant explorers who brought back new species and forms of lilacs, of lilac hybridizers and nurserymen in many countries, who have constantly sought new and better ways of propagating and growing lilacs, we have available today more and better lilacs than at any time in history. The doors to even greater lilac riches are wide open to any and all who will carry on the work and projects of earlier hybridists.

In the following pages I seek to give a glimpse into the work of the principal lilac hybridizers—the men and women who have made outstanding contributions to the lilac. Knowing a bit of their efforts we may better appreciate the loveliness and variety that abound in the large family we call 'Lilacs'. Some of these hybridizers have been giants of genius and labor; others have added to or extended work left undone; several have built the foundations needed by others to continue; some few have discovered, perhaps, only a single lilac cultivar, yet one that has made an outstanding contribution in lilac history. In this chapter, historically arranged, we unfold the life of the Lilac, the outstanding cultivars and their international heritage, through their originators. (*Mon ami*, their work is a fascinating story!)

I have endeavored to include the lilac notables of all countries. Some may accuse me of dwelling more on the North American scene (Canada and the United States) than other countries. I plead only that in this century, outside of the U.S.S.R., North America has been the most productive of new developments in hybridization of the Lilac. In recent times considerable work in hybridizing *S. vulgaris* has been done in the U.S.S.R. by Leonid Kolesnikov. The availability of additional plant materials of lilacs from China and Korea in the last few years augurs well for future hybrid development.

Lilac Hybridizers Prior to 1870

Prior to 1870 hybridization of lilacs was relatively rare and poorly understood. The cultivars, mostly of *S. vulgaris*, were selections made from natural crosses of seeds planted by nurserymen and garden enthusiasts. Some of the best seedlings were named and a limited number of colors emerged. Among the most outstanding cultivars, as mentioned in the Chapter on the History of the Lilac, were 'Marie Legraye' (white single), 'Lucie Baltet' (pale pink single), 'Macrostachya' (pale pink), 'Charles X' (a deep purple), 'Lilarosa' (a pale single lavender) and 'Azurea plena' (small double blue).

Mention must be made of some of these early lilac growers, who though not hybridizers, yet introduced some excellent lilacs that have been cherished through the years and remain outstanding today. Many of these earlier cultivars have become the progenitors of our modern day lilacs. Of unknown origin was the old cultivar named 'Marlyensis' (a lavender single) and the more beautiful form used decades later by Dunbar called 'marlyensis pallida', both in commerce before 1855.

The Baltet Nursery, Troyes, France, founded in 1720 and active with lilacs from 1842 to 1900 originated some famous lilacs, 'Bleuatre', 'De Croncels', 'Lucie Baltet' and 'Ville de Troyes'. 'Bleuatre' remains an outstanding blue, much used in hybridizing by Victor Lemoine. Both 'De Croncels' and 'Lucie Baltet' have a rare coppery coloring or flush while in bud. There is every indication that 'De Croncels', being somewhat a dwarf, having a rare coppery color and a deeper pink-lavender bloom was the parent of the lovely light pink 'Lucie Baltet', also a dwarf with the same copper glow that has endeared it to the lilac public ever since. Today, after over a hundred years, it is still one of the most sought after cultivars and a prime choice of hybridists. (*Bon jardinier,* you must have it in your garden!)

The Nursery of Ludwig Spaeth, founded in Berlin in 1720, has given us the outstanding deep magenta lilac named 'Andenken an Ludwig Spaeth'. Francesque Morel Nursery of Lyons, France, selected and grew the outstanding 'Mme. Francesque Morel', for many years one of the largest floret lilacs of a deep magenta color. Stepman de Messemaeker, Brussels, Belgium, introduced 10 lilacs among which was the beautiful 'Mme. Florent Stepman', one of the finest white forcing lilacs in commerce even to this day.

Meanwhile in Canada at the Windsor Nurseries, Windsor, Ontario, John Dougall from several thousand open-pollinated seedlings selected 5 fine cultivars of *S. vulgaris:* 'Prince of Wales' a dark purple, 'Princess Alexandra' a fine double white, 'Queen Victoria' a dark bluish-purple, 'Albert the Good' his finest dark red-purple and 'Azure' also called 'Marchinoess of Lorne', a pale blue. Dougall plants were listed in his 1874 catalogue and are the earliest recorded cultivars introduced in North America. Today they are mostly unavailable as they have been superseded by newer cultivars. (The 'Prince of Wales' growing in my garden still puts on a fine spring show each year.)

In these early years (1720–1770) much confusion obtained with regard to color descriptions and true names (both unhappy problems continue to emerge with modern introductions. (*Bon ami*—do keep good and careful records and refrain from using old names.)

Before 1850 most nurseries were not interested in hybridizing lilacs. Nurserymen were content to plant seeds and if something new appeared they selected it and named the new cultivar. The science of hybridization, although not unknown, was not much practiced in the case of the lilac. Most nurserymen before 1900 did not receive an education in plant genetics but were trained as gardener apprentices—the practice of good garden management, growing and propagating plants. What a college education in botanical genetics is today was relatively unknown to them. Some few, however, such as Victor Lemoine, learned genetics on their own and the results of their more scientific approach are evident in the excellent hybrids they produced. Among lilac breeders it was not until 1870 with the work of Victor Lemoine that hybridization, the actual crossing of two named cultivars, was begun on any large scale and in earnest. It is with him that modern lilac hybridization begins. Even to this day it is very limited. Many cultivars are the result of seed sowing rather than hybridization. The finest are from hybridization.

S. vulgaris 'Marie Legraye', introduced by the Belgian Legraye before 1879, was one of the mainstay white lilacs used by Victor Lemoine to produce his fine line of pure white lilacs. (Photo Archives of Arnold Arboretum.)

A Brief History of the Science of Genetics and Hybridization

Although I am unable to consider in length the discovery of hybridization and breeding of plants, we do know that it is an interesting scientific story that was unravelled by many botanists over the centuries. The first mention of hybridization, or the necessity of having two different kinds of trees, pollen and seed bearing, is found in Assyrian bas-relief tablets around 883–859 B.C. Hand pollinating of date trees was practiced from that time among the Assyrians and Egyptians. It was not until Rudolph Jakob Camerer (Camerarius) (1665–1721) wrote in August of 1694 about his experiments with plants in *De Sexu Plantarum Epistola* (A letter on the Sex of Plants) that the foundation of plant breeding began. This German botanist appears to have been the first to discover by his experiments, that pollen is essential to fertilization, and that pollen-producing plants are essentially male, and seed-bearing plants female. His experiments included several species of plants among which was the newly discovered Indian corn (maize). In 1759 the Imperial Academy of Sciences at St. Petersburg offered a prize for the determination of the problem of sex in plants. (Apparently Camerarius's work went unnoticed until fifty years after he wrote it.) The prize was given to Carl von Linne (Linneaus), who, in his *De Sexu Plantarum*, (On the Sex of Plants) presented many actual accounts of hybridization and their results.

In September of 1761, another German botanical scientist, Joseph Gottlieb Kölrueter (1733–1806), who rightly attributed to Camerarius the first discovery of sex in plants and the results of hybridization, published his *Preliminary Reports On Some Experimentations and Observation Concerning Sex in Plants*. Kölreuter's work was monumental in its scientific exactness, scope, magnitude and conclusions. It is a landmark in plant breeding.

It is suggested that Sir Thomas Milligan, in a lecture on the anatomy of flowers, may have been the first to describe the function of pollen as the 'male' for the generation of seed. The lecture is only reputed to have been given and had no actual experiments to back it, and since his wording is identical to later published materials, Camerarius, and not Milligan, is given as the first scientific discoverer with experiments as to the sex of plants.

Others rapidly followed with published details and experiments on plant sex and hybridization. Philip Miller, from the Chelsea Gardens near London, wrote *The Gardeners' Dictionary* in 1724. James Logan, Supreme Justice of the Provincial Council of Pennsylvania in America in 1739 published a 13-page memoir in Latin in Leiden, Germany, on *De Generatione Plantarum* (On the Breeding of Plants). In 1751 Johann Gottlieb Gleditsch, Director of the Berlin Botanical Gardens, published a well-prepared, scientific account of his plant experiments which still stands as one of the finest of its time. Konrad Sprengel (1750–1816), after five years of intensive study, published his *On the Nature of Flowers* after careful observation of nearly 500 species. Lacking financial means he was forced to give up the publication of his second volume. His first volume contained hundreds of accurate, detailed drawings on plant fertilization in 25 plates—this outstanding scientific work, which ranked among the best, went unnoticed for 43 years until Charles Darwin brought it to recognition in his *Origin of Species*.

Among the early English hybridists must be mentioned the work of Thomas Andrew Knight (1759–1838) who, educated at Oxford, conducted experiments on his estate at Elton, Herefordshire, England, raising new varieties of vegetables and fruits. An account of his work was published in 1795. Like Mendel, he wrote of experiments crossing various colored peas—his being the first recorded instance of color-dominance in peas. In 1809 he presented another paper on *The Influence of Parents, Male and Female, on Their Offspring*. He was the first to observe the effects of cross-pollinating species of flowering crab-apples. William Herbert (1778–1850) who worked with hybridizing flowers and published several extensive papers, outstanding in their depth, followed by John Goss, Alexander Sexton, Thomas Laxton and Patrick Shirreff were all English botanists who added to the knowledge of plant hybridization up to 1873. (*Mon ami et amie,* what has this to do with lilacs? They set the knowledge and scientific basis for plant breeding that was translated into many languages and published in the leading horticultural journals of the day. Certainly our well read friend, Victor Lemoine, read these works and followed in their footsteps in hybridizing hundreds of plant species, among which was the lilac! (*Bon jardinier,* the work of many fine minds and years of scientific experimentation lie behind the art of plant breeding which we take for granted!)

Not only Germans, Russians and Englishmen contributed to the great science of genetics and plant breeding, but high among the experimentations and work were men of France, whom

Victor Lemoine would have known far better, even personally. He has immortalized many of them by naming choice lilacs after them—men like Augustine Sageret (1763—1851) who crossed pickles (*Cucurbitaceae*) on 750 acres of his estate; Charles Naudin (1815–1899), Dominique Alexandre Godron (1807–1880), B. Verlot who published his *Breeding of Plants* in 1865, and the eminent work of the Vilmorin family. From this outstanding family, through 7 generations of father and son, were published more than 360 articles dealing with all aspects of plants, flowers and botany! Perhaps for us in dealing with plant hybridization the most important were the works of Louis de Vilmorin (1816–1860) and his son, Henry Vilmorin (1843–1899). What wonderful hybridizing knowledge came from the works of this father-son team! Among the French writers on hybridizing one must include the works of Henri Lecoq who first published his findings in 1827.

Germans such as Dr. A. F. Wiegmann, writing in 1826, Karl Friedrich von Gärtner (1772–1850), Max Ernest Wichura (1817–1866), Edward August Regel, Carl Wilhelm von Nageli writing in 1865, Wilhelm Olbers Focke who published a 569-page work in 1881 and died in 1922, and Gregor Mendel (1822–1884) all made advanced and substantial contributions to the science of genetics and modern plant breeding. (*Mon ami*, to recount their learned contributions would be another book—fascinating and unique—but such has already been published by Prof. H. F. Roberts of the University of Manitoba.)

Of outstanding merit is the work of Charles Darwin (1809–1882) and his cousin, Sir Francis Galton (1822–1911), J. S. Henslow whose paper was read before the Cambridge Philosophical Society in November of 1831–the first of its kind published in English with excellent illustrations; and James M. Macfarlane whose work was published in the 1890s. (*Mon amie*—a beautiful, late-blooming lilac was named in his honor although he did not work with lilacs.) Certainly among these giants must be numbered Luther Burbank (1840–1926), who worked so successfully in California, U.S.A., with his outstanding hybrids. There are several others, but I have presented the most outstanding who worked to perfect the knowledge of plant heredity and breeding that has helped develop our modern science of hybridizing. Much remains to be done in breeding new lilac forms and cultivars. (*Bon jardinier*, from date-breeding to our modern lilacs we have come a long way over 2,000 years of learning! Wonderful people of many countries have made great contributions. With that background we now turn to consider the very special lilac hybridists of more recent times to the present.)

VICTOR LEMOINE 1823–1911, Plant Genius and Master Hybridizer

Victor Lemoine, the great plant hybridizer and genius was born on October 21, 1823 and died aged eighty-eight, December 11, 1911 at his home in Nancy, France. In the span of his active life as a plantsman, nurseryman and hybridist in his little garden nursery at Nancy, Lorraine Province, France, he probably gave more to the field of horticulture than any other single individual known. He possessed a universal love of plants. He had a near intuitive knowledge of and keen vision into what could be hidden in their genetic make-up. This remarkable mental capacity was coupled with a character given to patience, hard work and persistence. In his lifetime of plant work and hybridizing Victor Lemoine so influenced our plants that hardly a garden today does not have at least one plant that can be traced to his genius in horticulture. Although Lemoine worked with many plant genera, creating new hybrids of magnificent beauty and worth, he is especially known for his work with lilacs.

Victor Lemoine began his lilac work around 1870 when he was 47 years old. During the Franco-Prussian War, when his town of Nancy was occupied by German troops, partly as a diversion from the trials of the times and partly out of his own curiosity, he began to turn his spare time to improving the lilac. In 1843 a little known, small double, bluish lilac *S. vulgaris* 'Azurea plena' had been introduced by Libert-Daminont of Liege, Belgium. A bush of this plant had grown for some years in Lemoine's garden. He had early recognized its merits and acquired the plant for future work and study. Now the opportunity had come. Lemoine determined to cross this insignificant double lilac, first with the best available single cultivars of *S. vulgaris* and then with *Syringa oblata* (an early blooming Chinese species which he had added to his collection).

His eyesight was no longer acute and his hands a bit unsteady from hard work in the nursery, so he enlisted the help of his wife for the actual work as Mme. Lemoine was far more fit than he. Lemoine began this work with about 30 or so named varieties of single *S. vulgaris* and the small *S. vulgaris* double of Libert-Daminont. *S. vulgaris* 'Azurea Plena' was most difficult to work on. The old bush in the Lemoine garden was very tall, while the minute, nearly unworkable, flowers were formed of many petals without stamens and with twisted pistils covered by lobes of interior petals which were mostly deformed and sterile. Yet this was the plant Victor had chosen as the seed bearer. From her perch atop a step-ladder, Mme. Lemoine pursued the very tedious task of uncovering and finding the best of the deformed pistils to cover with the chosen pollen. Pollen came from several of the best *S. vulgaris* singles then available and from *S. oblata*. Results were ever in doubt. From over one hundred flowers crossed that first season, only 7 seeds were produced. What children of promise they were! The following year 30 more fertile seeds were gathered and the work of promise continued!

Their first results were seen in 1876 when three of the seedlings bloomed. The first received the name of *Syringa* 'hybrida hyacinthiflora plena'. It was a true hybrid between *S.* 'azurea plena' and *S. oblata*. The thyrses of the new hybrid were well developed although the flowers were small and a little separated, but they were double, of a lilac-blue color, very fragrant, and bloomed early. The foliage recalled the *S. oblata* autumn purple tints. It was put into trade in 1878. Today it is hardly obtainable except from a specimen at the Arnold Arboretum in Boston, Mass. and perhaps one at Kew Gardens in England.

S. vulgaris 'Lemonei', another cultivar selected from these first seeds, flowered for Lemoine first in 1877 and was already in commerce by 1879. It was not a hybrid of *S. oblata* but simply a cross between *S.* 'azurea plena' and a single *S. vulgaris* cultivar. The flowers of this cultivar were double, of good size and a pure blue-lilac in color. From that same cross resulted the cultivars 'Renoncule' and 'Rubella plena' (1881) and 'Mathieu de Dombasle' (1882).

These 'first doubles' were then crossed without difficulty with the best available singles. In three years this cross produced the wonderful seedlings that were quickly placed into commerce and became known as the 'French Hybrids': 'Alphonse Lavallee' and 'Michel Buchner' (1885), 'Mons. Maxime Cornu', 'President Grevy', 'Pyramidal', 'Lamarck' in 1886; 'Condorcet', 'Virginite', 'Leon Simon', 'La Tour d'Auvergne' in 1888; with 'Jean Bart' and 'Emile Lemoine' introduced in 1889. Most of these cultivars are not available commercially today but can be seen in the very large lilac collections. Some of them have been surpassed by later and newer sorts. But whatever, it was through the genius and work of M. and Mme. Lemoine that a whole new race of giant double lilacs came into being. In their lifetime they had accomplished what seemed an impossible dream!

EMILE LEMOINE 1862–1943, A Most Outstanding Lilac Hybridist

The firm of 'Victor Lemoine et Fils', although founded on the plant genius of the older Victor Lemoine, continued on in greatness through the horticultural skill and ability of Emile Lemoine, son of the founder. This father-son partnership was to prove an outstanding gift to horticulture. Emile developed a deep love for the plants his father hybridized, especially the lilacs. Emile was born to Victor and Madame Lemoine at Nancy, France, in 1862, eight years before the senior Lemoine began his work with lilacs. As a boy he helped his father in the work of hybridizing and learned to know rare plants and species and what could be expected of them. He was a precocious and bright lad.

By the time he was sixteen he was already sufficiently knowledgeable to assist in the work of hybridizing the second generation of lilacs so painstakingly crossed by his parents. His nimble and quick fingers, and his keen eyesight proved to be a considerable asset to his parents. Many of the transitional lilacs coming from that famous garden at Nancy, between the years of 1900 and 1911 were probably the work of Emile under his aging father's guidance rather than the direct work of Victor himself.

It is too easy to forget this gifted son and a tendency to attribute most of the work to Victor Lemoine alone, whereas in reality, the greatest bulk of the introductions and hybridizing appears to be the work of Emile Lemoine. Under the name of Victor as hybridizer, perhaps 67 cultivars were introduced before 1900. From 1900, when Victor was already 78 years old and in failing health, until his death in 1911, another 64 cultivars were introduced. These are some of the most outstanding cultivars. Probably all are fruits of the hybridizing work of Emile. From 1912 to 1933 (ten years before Emile's death) another 62 cultivars were introduced and are clearly the work of Emile Lemoine. From 1933 to 1955 when the firm of Lemoine et Fils closed its doors forever, another 21 cultivars were added, 14 of which were the last work of Emile in collaboration with his son Henri.

After Emile's death in 1943, an additional 7 cultivars were added by Henri Lemoine bringing to a grand total of at least 214 cultivars that originated in this most famous lilac hybridizing nursery over the span of 71 years! Of these 64 should be solely attributed to Victor Lemoine, approximately 140 cultivars to the work of Emile and perhaps 10 as selections of Henri Lemoine. A wonderful legacy from a most outstanding family that has contributed more than any other to the named lilacs of today.

Neither Victor nor son, Emile, left many records of the hybridizing parentage of their outstanding lilacs. It is known that the single, white cultivar 'Marie Legraye' was used as the seed parent crossed with the earliest doubles. From this original cross most of Lemoine's finest white doubles have come. One, his very finest at that time, Victor Lemoine named for his faithful hybridizing student and partner, 'Madame Lemoine'. It is still one of his finest. In 1955, after two wars in which Nancy was a battlefield, with their last named lilac, 'Souv. de Louis Chasset', a magnificent finale, the memorable and historic lilac genius of Lemoine et Fils came to an end!

The Lemoine cultivars encompass every range and shade of color and form. One could plant an entire arboretum of Lemoine lilacs and have one of the most beautiful and outstanding collections found anywhere. From a hybridizer's view, some of the finest blue lilacs are still to be found in the really blue Lemoine introductions. Today, crossed with the most modern cultivars they are showing tremendous promise in pale pastel blues and deeper wedgwood colors. There is a wealth of hybridizing material yet to be discovered in the Lemoine introductions. Beautiful new forms have come from the skilled work of Leonid Kolesnikov in the U.S.S.R., who had dedicated a lifetime to hybridizing principally with Lemoine introductions. One of his finest is 'Krasavista Moskvy' which traces its parentage to Lemoine's delicate vari-pink shaded 'Belle de Nancy'.

Victor Lemoine et Fils Lilac Introductions from 1876 to 1953

'Abel Carriere' D-III, 1896
'Albida' S-I, 1930 (*sweginzowii*)
'Alfred Neuner' D-I, 1842
'Alphonse Lavallee' D-IV, 1885
'Ambassadeur' S-III, 1930
'Ami Schott' D-III, 1933
'Archeveque' D-VII, 1923
'Arthur William Paul' D-VII, 1898
'Banquise' D-I, 1905
'Belle de Nancy' D-V, 1891
'Berryer' D-V, 1913
'Bicolor' S-I, 1928 (× *chinensis*)
'Boule Azuree' S-III, 1919
'Boussingault' D-V, 1896
'Buffon' S-V, 1921
'Candeur' S-I, 1931
'Capitaine Baltet' S-IV, 1919
'Capitaine Perrault' D-V, 1925
'Carmen' D-V, 1918
'Catinat' S-V, 1922
'Cavour' S-II, 1910
'Champlain' D-II, 1930
'Charles Baltet' D-IV, 1893
'Charles Joly' D-VII, 1896
'Charles Sargent' D-III, 1905
'Christophe Colomb' S-IV, 1905
'Claude Bernard' D-V, 1915
'Claude de Lorrain' S-V, 1889
'Colbert' D-VI, 1899
'Comte Adrien de Montebello' D-IV, 1910

'Comte de Kerchove' D-VI, 1899
'Comte Horace de Choiseul' D-V, 1887
'Comtesse Horace de Choiseul' D-V, 1891
'Condorcet' D-VI, 1888
'Congo' S-VI, 1896
'Crampel' S-III, 1899
'Crepuscule' S-III, 1928
'Dame Blanche' D-I, 1903
'Danton' S-VII, 1911
'Decaisne' S-III, 1910
'De Humboldt' D-II, 1892
'De Jussieu' D-IV, 1891
'De Miribel' S-II, 1903
'De Saussure' D-VII, 1903
'Descartes' S-V, 1916
'Desfontaines' D-VI, 1906
'Deuil d'Emile Galle' D-V, 1904
'Diderot' S-VII, 1915
'Diplomate' S-III, 1930
'Doyen Keteleer' D-IV, 1895
'Dr. Maillot' D-IV, 1895
'Dr. Masters' D-V, 1898
'Dr. Troyanowsky' D-IV, 1901
'Duc de Massa' D-III, 1905
'Edith Cavell' D-I, 1916
'Edmond About' D-VI, 1908
'Edmond Boissier' S-VII, 1906
'Edouard Andre' D-V, 1900
'Emile Gentil' D-III, 1915
'Emile Lemoine' D-IV, 1889
'Etna' S-VII, 1927

'Etoile de Mai' D-VI, 1905
'Excellens' S-I, 1931 (*S. velutina*) *S. patula*
'Fenelon' S-V, 1937
'Firmament' S-III, 1932
'Floreal' S-V, 1925 (*nanceiana*)
'Fraicheur' S-I, 1946
'Francisque Morel' D-IV, 1896
'Gaudichaud' D-III, 1903
'General Drouot' S-IV, 1890
'General Pershing' D-V, 1924
'Georges Bellair' D-VI, 1900
'Georges Claude' D-III, 1935
'Germinal' S-VI, 1939 (*henryi* × *tomentella*)
'Gilbert' S-IV, 1911
'Gismonda' D-IV, 1939
'Gloire de Lorraine' S-VI, 1876
'Godron' D-III, 1908
'Grand-Duc Constantin' D-III, 1895
'Guizot' D-IV, 1897
'Henri Martin' D-IV, 1912
'Henri Robert' D-II, 1936
'Henryi Albida' S-V, 1935
'Hippolyte Maringer' D-IV, 1909
'Hyacinthiflora Plena' D-IV, 1878
'Jacques Callot' S-IV, 1876
'Jean Bart' D-V, 1889
'Jean Mace' D-V, 1915
'Jeanne d'Arc' D-I, 1902
'Jules Ferry' D-V, 1907

'Jules Simon' D-III, 1908
'Julien Gerardin' D-IV, 1916
'Katherine Havemeyer' D-V, 1922
'La Lorraine' S-VI, 1899
'Lamarck' D-III, 1886
'Lamartine' S-V, 1911
'La Mauve' D-V, 1893
'Laplace' S-VII, 1913
'La Tour d'Auvergne' D-VI, 1888
'Lavoisier' S-V, 1913
'Le Gaulois' D-IV, 1884
'Lemoinei' D-IV, 1878
'Le Notre' D-II, 1922
'Leon Gambetta' D-IV, 1907
'Leon Simon' D-IV, 1888
'Le Printemps' D-V, 1901
'Le Progres' S-IV, 1903
'Linne' D-VI, 1890
'L'Oncle Tom' S-VII, 1903
'Louis Henry' D-VI, 1894
'Louvois' S-II, 1921
'Madame Charles Souchet' S-III, 1949
'Madeleine Lemaire' D-I, 1928
'Magellan' D-VI, 1915
'Marceau' S-VI, 1913
'Marc Micheli' D-V, 1898
'Marechal de Bassompierre' D-VI, 1897
'Marechal Foch' S-VI, 1924
'Marechal Lannes' D-III, 1910
'Marengo' S-IV, 1923
'Marie Finon' S-I, 1923
'Massena' S-VI, 1923
'Mathieu de Dombasle' D-IV, 1882
'Maurice Barres' S-III, 1917
'Maurice de Vilmorin' D-IV, 1900
'Maximowicz' D-II, 1906
'Michel Buchner' D-IV, 1885
'Milton' S-VII, 1910
'Mirabeau' S-IV, 1911
'Mireille' D-I, 1904
'Miss Ellen Willmott' D-I, 1903
'Mme. Abel Chatenay' D-I, 1892
'Mme. Antonie Buchner' D-V, 1909
'Mme. Casimir Perier' D-I, 1894
'Mme. de Miller' D-I, 1901
'Mme. Jules Finger' D-IV, 1887

'Mme. Lemoine' D-I, 1890
'Mme. Leon Simon' D-IV, 1897
'Monge' S-VII, 1913
'Monique Lemoine' D-I, 1939
'Mons. Lepage' S-III, 1889
'Mons. Maxime Cornu' D-V, 1886
'Montaigne' D-V, 1907
'Mont Blanc' S-I, 1915
'Montesquieu' S-VI, 1926
'Montgolfier' S-VI, 1905
'Monument' S-I, 1934
'Monument Carnot' D-V, 1895
'Mrs. Edward Harding' D-VI, 1922
'Murillo' D-VII, 1901
'Naudin' D-IV, 1913
'Necker' S-V, 1920
'Negro' S-VII, 1899
'Obelisque' D-I, 1894
'Olivier de Serres' D-III, 1909
'Othello' S-VI, 1900
'Pascal' S-IV, 1916
'Pasteur' S-VII, 1903
'Paul Deschanel' D-VI, 1924
'Paul Hariot' D-VII, 1902
'Paul Thirion' D-VI, 1915
'Pierre Joigneaux' D-IV, 1892
'Planchon' D-VI, 1908
'Prairal' S-V, 1933 (henryi × tomentella)
'President Carnot' D-IV, 1890
'President Fallieres' D-IV, 1911
'President Grevy' D-III, 1886
'President Hayes' S-VI, 1899 (× chinensis)
'President Loubet' D-VI, 1901
'President Poincare' D-VI, 1913
'President Viger' D-III, 1900
'Prince de Beauvau' D-IV, 1897
'Prodige' S-VII, 1928
'Pyramidal' D-IV, 1886
'Rabelais' D-I, 1896
'Reaumur' S-VI, 1904
'Reflexa Pallens' S-V, 1931 (reflexa)
'Rene Jarry-Desloges' D-III, 1905
'Renoncule' D-IV, 1881
'Rochambeau' S-VII, 1919
'Ronsard' S-III, 1912
'Rosace' D-IV, 1932
'Rubella Plena' D-VI, 1881

'Rustica' D-IV, 1950
'Rutilant' S-VII, 1931 (nanceiana)
'Saturnale' S-III, 1916
'Savonarole' D-III, 1935
'Senateur Volland' D-VI, 1887
'Siebold' D-I, 1906
'Souvenir d'Alice Harding' D-I, 1938
'Souvenir de Georges Truffaut' D-VI, 1953
'Souvenir de Louis Chasset' S-VI, 1953
'Souvenir de L. Thibaut' D-V, 1893
'Superba' S-V, 1929 (sweginzowii)
'Taglioni' D-I, 1905
'Thunberg' D-IV, 1913
'Tombouctou' S-VII, 1910
'Tournefort' D-II, 1887
'Toussaint-L'Ouverture' S-VII, 1898
'Turenne' S-VII, 1916
'Turgot' S-V, 1921
'Vauban' D-V, 1913
'Vestale' S-I, 1910
'Vesuve' S-VII, 1916
'Victor Lemoine' D-IV, 1906
'Villars' S-IV, 1920
'Violetta' D-II, 1916
'Virginite' D-V, 1888
'Viviand-Morel' D-IV, 1902
'Volcan' S-VII, 1899
'Waldeck-Rousseau' D-V, 1904
'William Robinson' D-IV, 1899

A Selection of Some of the Best 'Lemoine' Lilac Introductions

One is often asked, "What are the best cultivars introduced by Lemoine & Fils?" To choose the 'best' from among the more than 214 introductions is difficult if not impossible. Beauty is in the eye of the beholder and so it is with lilacs. What is particularly appealing to one is less so to another. Color preferences vary considerably. Some prefer large single lilacs whereas others are overwhelmed by the large double lilacs that Lemoine so popularized. When one surveys the various Lemoine cultivars one must be impressed that the finest blue lilacs are their introductions. Fully one-third of all the Lemoine cultivars are blue or predominantly blue. Many of the finest cultivars are of this hue, with lilac or lilac-purple next in prominence, followed by the Lemoine whites.

My list of 'favorite Lemoine Lilacs' numbers forty and are:

'Ambassadeur'—S. blue
'Ami Schott'—D. blue
'Candeur'—S. white
'Capitaine Baltet'—S. magenta-pink
'Capitaine Perrault'—D. pink-lavender
'Congo'—S. magenta-red
'Crepuscule'—S. blue
'De Miribel'—S. blue-deep violet
'Duc de Massa'—D. blue
'Edith Cavell'—D. white
'Ellen Willmott'—D. white
'Emile Lemoine'—D. lilac
'Etna'—S. deep reddish-purple
'Firmament'—S. blue
'George Claude'—D. blue
'Gismonda'—D. bluish magenta

'Lamartine' (early hybrid)—S. pink
'Leon Gambetta'—D. lilac
'Marechal Foch'—S. deep pink
'Maurice Barres'—S. blue
'Maurice de Vilmorin'—D. lilac
'Maximowicz'—D. violet
'Mme. Antoine Buchner'—D. pink
'Mme. Lemoine'—D. white
'Monge'—S. red-purple
'Monument'—S. white
'Mrs. Edward Harding'—D. magenta
'Olivier de Serres'—D. blue
'President Grevy'—D. blue
'President Poincare'—D. magenta

'Prodige'—S. deep reddish-purple
'Rustica'—D. lilac
'Souvenir d'Alice Harding'—D. white
'Violetta'—D. deep violet
'Victor Lemoine'—D. pink-lavender
S. × chinensis 'Bicolor'

Uniquely colored Lemoine lilacs

'Archeveque'—D. deep purplish
'Le Notre'—D. lilac shades
'Savanarole'—D. bluish shades
'Siebold'—D. pinkish-white shades

It is truthfully said that one could plant an entire collection of Lemoine lilacs and have one of the finest plantings that exist. However, one must be aware that many of Lemoine's cultivars have been surpassed by some of the newer hybrids and that many Lemoine hybrids have produced even more outstanding offspring. One would not wish to be without some of the excellent large, single lilacs of Havemeyer, nor without some of the newest 'Rochester Strain' multipetaled, pastel hued lilacs. Nor can any fine collection not contain Lemoine cultivars. Indeed they are outstanding!

JOHN DUNBAR 1859–1927, Pioneer American Lilac Introducer

John Dunbar was a Scots gardener born in Rafford, Elginshire, Scotland on June 4, 1859. After migrating to the United States he eventually became assistant Superintendent of Parks at Rochester, New York. In 1891 he planted about a hundred lilacs at Highland Park and thereby began an odyssey which was to make Rochester a center of lilac cultivars. In four years the first hundred lilacs bloomed with such splendor that they attracted considerable attention. Great crowds soon began to come each May to see the lilacs. Lilacs became an outstanding horticultural success at Rochester (as they are wherever they are grown and displayed).

By 1908 Dunbar raised several lilac seedlings (all open pollinated) of the original French Hybrids he had planted. Six years later he grew a second group from the mostly Lemoine cultivars. All except 'A. B. Lamberton', which was from one of his own seedlings, were from the original lilacs planted at the park.

From his first 75 seedlings which matured just prior to World War I, he selected 19 cultivars to be named (perhaps somewhat too many). Eight were very well received and entered the commercial trade. Among them was his famous bluish lilac, 'President Lincoln' and a deep purple

Pioneer American Hybridizer. John Dunbar and his graddaughter at Highland Park, Rochester, N.Y., June 20, 1922. It was here, at Highland Park, that Dunbar began planting lilacs and created a 'Lilac City and Festival'. Thousands still come each year to see the lilacs and honor his memory.

'Adelaide Dunbar' honoring his wife. From the second group of seedlings he selected about 50 of which 11 were named. Only four reached the commercial market. Of the 30 cultivars Dunbar named in his lifetime, 12 were available at one time or another from nurserymen. This is a remarkably high record for a hybridizer not growing and selling his own plants.

Dunbar's 'President Lincoln' was considered for many decades as the 'bluest lilac known' (his garden writers' fancy and not a true statement as many of Lemoine's lilacs were indeed bluer). Since its introduction many other truer blues of far better quality have been introduced. Although the color of 'President Lincoln' is a unique blue-lavender, its greatest fault is the bodyguard of new green shoots so quickly and vigorously thrown up around the bloom as to hide its real beauty as a garden plant. 'President Lincoln' derived from a seed plant of the old lilac 'Alba Virginalis', itself a vigorous grower, and perhaps some windborne Early Hybrid pollen or of *S. rhodopea* (today considered only a cultivar of *S. vulgaris*).

Of his most prized cultivar, 'General Sherman', Dunbar writes, "We consider this cultivar perhaps one of the most beautiful lilacs in cultivation!" Indeed, this natural seedling of the very old *S. vulgaris* 'Marlyensis pallida' is an outstanding lilac even today and should be included in every worthwhile collection. In bud a deep lavender it opens to a pearled creamy, pale lavender—a treasure of beauty. It was Dunbar's choicest which somehow the garden writers and the commercial nurseries missed. Other named Dunbar lilacs of considerable merit include: 'A. B. Lamberton' a violet-lavender, 'William C. Barry' a pale lavender, 'Joan Dunbar' a double white, 'Adelaide Dunbar' a double purple, 'President Roosevelt' a purplish-red, 'Gen. John Pershing' an azure lilac, 'President John Adams' a double white, 'Henry Clay' a rather showy white, 'Alexander Hamilton' a violet-lavender, and 'General Sheridan' a double lacey white (perhaps his best white).

Although all his lilacs cannot be found at Highland Park, where he made lilacs famous, a Pansy Bed surrounded by choice lilacs harbors a bronze plaque honoring the memory of this staunch Scotsman who made Lilacs and Rochester so famous. He must smile at the annual lilac festivals and parades that pass the spot where he planted the first hundred lilacs and bloomed his seedlings. A row of old 'Dunbar Lilacs' can still be found blooming each spring to greet the lilac enthusiasts as they climb the path high on the hill! The memory of John Dunbar still is strong mid the fragrance of lilacs heavy on the Park's spring air! He retired as Assistant Superintendent and Arboriculturist due to illness in 1926 and died at his Rochester, New York home on June 14, 1927.

HULDA THIEL KLAGER 1864–1960, The 'Lilac Lady of Woodland'

Hulda Thiel was born in Germany in 1864 and spent her first birthday on the high seas enroute to North America. The Thiels pioneered in Wisconsin, then moved on to Minnesota and finally, when Hulda was thirteen, settled in Lewis County, Washington, near the town of Woodland. In her early teens Hulda married Frank Klager and settled down to be a dairyman's wife. Their farm was yearly inundated by the flooding Lewis River so Frank graded a 7 ft high embankment 90 ft. square around their home. The flooding waters brought fertility and on this 'floating island' as Hulda called it, she planted her beloved flowers and garden.

Among her duties as a farm wife and mother, she somehow found time to study botany and read every available gardening book and catalogue. There were but meager funds for new plants and seeds each year, so Hulda crossed and saved her own seeds. In time, with her father's death, she and her husband were able to purchase the old family home on the outskirts of Woodland where she first lived. This became her permanent home and the place where she planted and worked for more than 40 years with her lilacs. She learned from a book of Luther Burbank the great possibilities in cross-pollinating plants. Although she worked with many different kinds of plants she turned her efforts to crossing her lilacs.

It was in 1905 that she first began her work with lilacs and in five years had hybridized 14 new cultivars. She had purchased a collection of 7 named *S. vulgaris* cultivars from an eastern nursery of which she discarded two for poor quality of their flowers, two were trampled and destroyed by the horses so only three remained as the foundation of her breeding lilacs; 'Mme. Casimir Perier' a fine double white, 'President Grevy' a double blue and 'Ludwig Spaeth' an excellent purple. These became her "Magic Three", the cornerstones of all her lilac hybridizing. First she crossed these three and then cross-pollinated and back-crossed their seedlings. She had definite objectives in mind: first, vigorous, disease resistant plants; secondly, to extend their color range into clear blues, pinks and rose; and lastly, for variations in flower cluster forms and in the size of florets.

From her "Magic Three" Hulda Klager originated 62 new cultivars (at one time her seedlings numbered over 300). Many were named after friends, relatives and neighboring cities honoring them as they came to visit her gardens. She knew only the two older Lemoine cultivars she used and it is remarkable that despite her ignorance of any of the newer Lemoine or other introductions she was able, in total isolation, to produce so many new cultivars from an extremely limited gene pool of three lilacs. She was misunderstood as a 'farm woman' without skills by some Eastern lilac fanciers who heard of her work only indirectly, as most of her best lilacs have never been seen in Eastern collections or gardens because of the difficulty in obtaining them.

Of the Klager lilacs R. M. Cooley writes, " 'My Favorite' a double dark purple is probably her most widely distributed introduction. It resembles a bunch of deep purple grapes when the buds are first opening. 'R. M. Mills' ('Roland Mills') is a double, deep pink almost a rose color of astonishing size, 'Mrs. Morgan Cooley' is a semi-double clear orchid that has exceptionally large florets. 'Ostrander Cooley' is probably Mrs. Klager's finest double, a deep carmine with shades of heliotrope and silvery-rose."

After her husband's death, and with the help of her son, Fred, she produced plants commercially so had little time for hybridizing. Her sales were limited to customers who came to her nursery for their plants. Hulda had a considerable number of seedlings, many of considerable merit, ready to be named when the disastrous flood of 1948 destroyed her entire garden—her 'Magic Three' and all their progeny! Her son, Fred, died shortly after the flood. The amazing Hulda declared at the age of eighty-four, "I will remain here where I belong. I will devote the rest of my life in rebuilding the garden, I have faith!"

So she did begin anew. Friends, neighbors and wellwishers sent out the message to bring back her lilacs and helped rebuild the garden. Hulda's beloved lilacs came back as rootlets and plants. And they bloomed as they did before for her twilight years. The garden at Woodland, now a State and National Historic Site, blooms with the radiant colors of the Klager lilacs and the fragrance of peace drifts over her bronze memorial—'The Lilac Lady' of Woodland! She died in Woodland in her ninety-sixth year in 1960.

The Best Klager Lilacs

'Mrs. Morgan Cooley'—double, orchid pink—very fine
'My Favorite'—double, deep magenta-purple (Mrs. Klager's favorite)
'Ostrander'—double, deep carmine-purple—probably her best
'R. M. Mills'—double pink of exceptional size (Syn. 'Roland Mills')

THEODORE A. HAVEMEYER 1868–1936, Originator of Giant, Vibrant Colored Single Lilacs

Theodore Havemeyer was a horticulturist, organizer of plant pursuits, collector of plants *extraordinarie*, garden writer and, above all, an outstanding originator of new cultivars of *S. vulgaris*. Of all his many garden pursuits, lilacs were his greatest favorite. He was as successful with them as he was an industrialist and captain of industry. He was an extraordinary man!

The cultivars he introduced still stand among some of the finest lilacs now grown. His 42-acre Cedar Hill Nursery Estate at Brookville, Long Island, at one time numbered 20,000 lilac plants. John Wister with his wonderful lilac knowledge and experience once wrote of Havemeyer ... "Of all the collections of lilacs I have seen either in this country or abroad none can equal that in the garden nursery of Mr. T. A. Havemeyer at Brookville, Long Island ... It has always seemed to me that the colors of his flowers are brighter than those grown farther inland. Perhaps the moist air from the Sound has much to do with that, for his soil is far from being rich and must require much feeding. His plants are grown in nursery rows and are rather difficult to study because often they are too close together or are difficult to approach through cultivated ground, but all of them are making suberb growth and give flowers finer than any I have ever seen elsewhere." (*Horticulture* 1933)

Havemeyer's interest in lilacs stemmed from a visit made to Victor Lemoine at his famous Nancy Nursery. He returned with some of Lemoine's finest new hybrids of *S. vulgaris,* an abundance of sage Lemoine advice and knowledge and a deep love for lilacs that lasted to the end of his life. M. Victor and Mme. Lemoine made a lasting impression on Havemeyer. When he returned, Havemeyer determined to dedicate the major portion of his horticultural career to improving the lilac. Realizing the exceptional hybridizing work of V. Lemoine he turned to improving both the color and the size of single flowered lilacs. Most of the basic stock he used as 'his beginnings' were the plants he brought from the Lemoines. To these he added the finest plants available from the lilac nurseries of his day.

Like Lemoine, Havemeyer named most of his lilacs after dear horticultural friends, prominent members of society, patrons of horticulture and members of his own family. One of his finest whites was named after one of his tow-headed granddaughters affectionately called 'Carley.' Whether he hand-pollinated or planted open-pollinated seed (which is most likely), and what the parent cross or seed pod was for his named varieties, was not recorded nor did he make mention of these facts. Nowhere does Havemeyer claim to have crossed any two particular cultivars so it is to be assumed he gathered seed from plants that he considered to be outstanding parents and carefully selected the choicest of the thousands of seedlings which resulted. His outstanding success gives testimony to what can be accomplished by trained and careful observation and selection of open-pollinated seedlings. He had a good eye and a fine sense of what he was seeking to accomplish in lilacs. Even in old age when illness forced him to use a wheelchair and he was not able to speak, he selected his lilacs carefully with a nod or shake of his head as he viewed his seedlings. His was a cultivated gift with selecting lilacs!

Havemeyer was a modest, retiring and courteous gentlemen despite the recognition that came to him. He won the regard of all who worked with or who knew him. This great man of lilacs died at his lovely Cedar Hill home on the evening of July 30, 1936 in his 68th year.

His legacy to all who love lilacs are the outstanding introductions he had made. Some of the Havemeyer lilacs are outstanding as parents for hybridizing. 'Sarah Sands' crossed with some of our larger floreted, newer lilacs gives seedlings of magnificent old rose, and rose-purple shades. 'Carley' is an excellent parent for both size and color. 'Mrs. John Davis' is perfection for transmitting both floret size and form. 'True Blue' (considered by John Wister as one of Havemeyer's finest and the best blue lilac) is an exceptional parent for all shades of blue, especially pale and delicate blues. There is a wealth of hybridizing material in the Havemeyer lilacs that has never been used. Many of his finest are relatively unknown after 50 years and should have been offered by nurseries decades ago!

The 'Best' of the Theodore Havemeyer Lilacs

(I am presenting them in the order of my own preference. *Mon ami,* perhaps yours would be different—but I have the advantage of writing the book and have all of them in my garden to help confuse me!)

'True Blue'—single—outstanding pale blue—remarkable!

'Sarah Sands'—single—deep rich, red-purple—late bloomer (named after his sister-in-law).

'Carley'—single—white, enormous panicles—(named after his granddaughter)—outstanding.

'Mrs. W. E. Marshall'—single—deep black-purple, perhaps the darkest lilac—small florets but outstanding in color—slow grower. (*Mon amie*, plant it in front of white lilacs).

'Professor E. H. Wilson—double—white rosettes, very fine.

'Mrs. Elizabeth Peterson'—single—two-toned steel-blue and deep purple reverse.

'Mrs. John S. Williams'—single—bluish-lavender—large florets—enormous panicles—outstanding.

'Mrs. Watson Webb'—single—pink-magenta, large florets

'Lady Lindsay'—single—magenta, reddest lilac in bud—recurved and twisted petals—somewhat difficult to grow well.

'Zulu'—single—dark violet of exceptional size and beauty. Grow on own root.

(*Mon ami*, if you do not care for my selections add these beauties of Havemeyer.)

'Romance'—single—rosy-lavender.

'Mrs. Flanders'—single—dusty, old-rose but with smaller florets—color very fine.

'Mrs. August Belmont'—single—light blue with a pert eye (named after stage star, Eleanor Robson, who became Mr. August Belmont).

'Ethel Dupont'—a single deep purple.

James Stuart'—a single carmine-rose.

'Heather'—a single white.

'Night'—an excellent deep purple single.

'Dawn'—a lovely, single bluish lilac.

'Nancy Frick'—single, pink, of considerable merit.

(*Mon ami et amie*, you can see that I am partial to Mr. Havemeyer's lilacs, as they are all lovely! One could not go astray with a garden of lilacs all from his introductions.)

MISS ISABELLA PRESTON 1881–1965, Pioneer Hybridizer of the Late Lilacs

It was in Lancashire, England that Isabella Preston was born in 1881 and where she graduated from Swanley Horticultural College for Women in 1906. When she was thirty-two she came to Canada and enrolled at Ontario Agricultural College in Guelph, with Prof. J. W. Crowe, the noted lily breeder at the University of Guelph. Here she developed the Creelman lily (later in her lily breeding at Ottawa she introduced the 'Stenographer Series' of lilies). In 1920 she joined the staff of the Horticultural Department of the Central Experimental Farm at Ottawa as an ornamental plant breeder.

Her work in plant breeding included many genera beside lilacs and lilies. The 'Rosybloom' series of flowering crabs, many hardy shrub roses and a series of Siberian Iris named after the Canadian rivers are but some of the results of her work. Perhaps her most outstanding accomplishments were with lilacs. Her principal lilac work included the species *S. villosa* × *S. reflexa* resulting in the cross that now bears her name, *Syringa* × *prestoniae* (*S. villosa* × *S. reflexa*) and the hybrid cross of *Syringa* × *josiflexa* (*S. josikaea* × *S. reflexa*) which she officially described. She named over 50 crosses and eventually introduced 47 new cultivars (she described another 36 which she named but never introduced).

Her original crosses made in the spring of 1920 produced 696 seeds of the *S. villosa* × *S. reflexa* cross and a few seeds in the josiflexa cross. The following spring she lined out 299 seedlings, after discarding all the variegated forms, 60 in number. (Would that she had grown these on!) From the *S. josiflexa* (*S. josikaea* × *S. reflexa*) cross only one seedling survived which she named 'Guinevere' and described as the type for that cross. She named 5 open-pollinated seedlings of 'Guinevere' from 1934 to 1948.

In November of 1925 Miss Preston wrote to Mrs. Susan McKelvey of her progress, "In 1924 the majority bloomed and I think this year they all did." She stirred up keen interest at the Arnold Arboretum for both Mrs. McKelvey and Alfred Rehder visited Ottawa on June 20–21 of 1927 to evaluate her new hybrids. Subsequently, Mrs. McKelvey described the Prestonian Hybrids in her book naming two types, 'Isabella' after the originator and 'W. T. Macoun' for the incumbent Dominion Horticulturist under whom Miss Preston worked. (Note, Mrs. McKelvey used the alphabetical system in recording parentage of *S.* × *prestoniae* as *S. reflexa* × *S. villosa* which causes

PLATE 99

SOME OUTSTANDING CITY AND TOWN PLANTINGS

Governor Wentworth Mansion lilacs. A whole Estate of *S. vulgaris* var. *rosea (rubra)*. Portsmouth, New Hampshire.

Bar Harbor, Maine. Wonderful old Estate lilacs. Pictured is *S. vulgaris* var. *purpurea*.

Fennimore Cooper House, Cooperstown, N.Y. A city of wonderful old lilacs everywhere!

S. vulgaris 'Mme. Lemoine' at the entrance to the courthouse, Delhi, N.Y. A town project of planting lilacs has made it a lilac wonder!

All up and down Main Street, throughout the town of Woodstock, Vermont, there are lilacs planted everywhere! A gorgeous sight!

PLATE 100

LILACS IN FLORAL ARRANGEMENTS

Lilacs make excellent floral arrangements but must be handled and cut in a special way as described by Barbara Laking, Royal Botanical Gardens, Hamilton, Ontario, Canada. Pictured are some of her outstanding arrangements made for the International Lilac Society meeting at R.B.G. She is an expert in handling all types of flowers for arrangements of various kinds. Read her instructions well.

considerable confusion especially to those who are wont to place the female parent first in describing a cross. This nomenclatural convention more easily and more effectively tells the true picture of the cross as *S. villosa* (seed or pod parent) × *S. reflexa* (the pollen parent). From the reciprocal cross of *S. reflexa* × *S. villosa,* also made in 1920, only one seedling selection was named, 'Diana' and that in 1926. 'Romeo' is the better known cultivar of open-pollinated 'Diana.'

Isabella Preston was also successful in crossing the early hybrid species. From *S. vulgaris* 'Negro' × *S. hyacinthiflora* 'Lamartine' she named three cultivars: 'Maureen', 'Muriel' and 'Norah' and from open-pollinated 'Lamartine' two more named 'Peggy' and 'Grace.'

This gifted woman developed single handedly a whole new race of hybrid lilacs, revolutionized the lines of the late blooming hybrids and inaugurated a new era of species hybrids. She was a 'gift' not only to horticulture but also to all who love fine lilacs and other ornamentals. She retired to Georgetown, Ontario, Canada, where she enjoyed many of her own plants in her fine garden. There, in her eighty-fifth year, this outstanding woman of horticulture died in 1965.

The Best of the Prestonian Lilacs (*S. villosa* × *S. reflexa*)
'Isabella'—single pinkish-lavender, very fine
'W. T. Macoun'—single pink
'Ursula'—single pinkish-lavender
'Romeo'—single pink
'Alice'—single—deep purple
'Ethel M. Webster'—single bright magenta-pink—very fine (2nd generation)
'Calpurnia'—single lavender
'Coral'—single pink—fine
'Desdemona'—single blue—fine
'Nocturne'—single blue
'Francisca'—single purple—very good
'Juliet'—single magenta—good
'Viola'—single purple—very fine
'Swanee'—single white (whites are rare among the *Prestoniae* lilacs)
'Redwine'—single bright magenta—good
'Elinor'—single bluish-lavender
'Blanch'—single lavender-violet

Among the prestonian Josiflexa (*S. josikaea* × *S. reflexa*)
'Lynette'—single—dark purple
'Guinevere'—single magenta
'Elaine'—single white—very good
'Carlton'—single pink (*S. reflexa* × *S. sweginzowii*)

There are so many named Prestonian Hybrids that are very similar in color (mostly shades of pink and pinkish-lavender) that it is difficult to distinguish them in a collection. Many I have not personally seen. The above mentioned are a good selection of the varying shades of color and form in these hybrids. Some will be impossible to find. They are in the order of my preference.

DR. FRANK LEITH SKINNER, L.L.D., M.B.E. 1882–1967, A Canadian Hybridizing Pioneer
In 1895, at age thirteen, Frank Skinner sailed from his native Scotland with his parents to settle as a cattle and grain rancher at Dropmore in northwestern Manitoba, Canada. Life in the cold north-west was rugged and demanding, so young Frank received little formal education. An unquenchable interest in and a consuming curiosity about plants was to make him internationally recognized as an horticulturist, plant explorer and plant breeder. He was a genius with plants! He was acknowledged peer of the best trained horticulturists around the world; many were personal friends and all knew him through his extensive correspondence.

Frank contracted pneumonia in 1911 and lost the lower lobe of his right lung. He was advised to avoid strenuous activity so he turned more of his attention to his gardening activities. That year he began his first formal collection of plant materials capable of surviving the harsh prairie conditions. These were the foundations for his hybridizing and world famous Hardy Plant Nursery. From 1911 to 1918 he used all available time from the ranching in learning about horticul-

Dr. Frank Leith Skinner spent a lifetime working to improve the Early Hybrids using *S. oblata* var. *dilatata*. These he called the 'American Lilacs'. They are pictured in the chapter dealing with the species *S. oblata*. (Photo courtesy of the Skinner family.)

ture, collecting new materials, corresponding with horticulturists and developing the basics of hybridizing and nursery techniques. He was a self-taught man who received his government's and horticulturist's highest awards.

Skinner remained a rancher and farmer until 1924–1925 when he decided to commercialize his plant propagating and hybridizing work. Devoting a number of acres of the ranch at Dropmore to his nursery he worked to develop new plants hardy to that location and the extremes of weather. This helped support his plant breeding work. Here he worked with many plant taxa— trees, shrubs, fruits and flowers, producing hardy strains that were rapid-growing as well as drought- and disease-resistant.

In 1947 he married Helen Cumming and had five children, one of whom continues to operate the nursery at Dropmore. Frank Skinner received many awards for his work, among them were the Royal Horticultural Society's (Great Britain) award of merit for his lily 'Dropmore Concolor' and the Society's highest award, the Cory Cup, in 1933. Although he worked with new strains of hardy trees, lilies, roses, ornamental and fruit trees with considerable success, one of his great pursuits was his love for the lilacs. He devoted a considerable time in hybridizing for new, hardier cultivars and hybrids.

On his first visit to the Arnold Arboretum in 1917 Skinner carried back with him some cherished seedlings of *S. oblata dilatata* and *S. patula* given to him by Professor Sargent. The *S. oblata* were from seed collected by E. H. Wilson on the Diamond Mountains of Korea. In the spring of 1920 he made his first lilac crosses using *S. reflexa* pollen from the Arnold (*S. reflexa* is not hardy in the harsh climate of Dropmore as neither is *S. sweginzowii*) on flowers of *S. villosa*. This first effort was unsuccessful. By coincidence in the same year another Canadian, Miss Isabel Preston, working thousands of miles away made the same cross successfully in her first attempt. Skinner had to wait until 1922 when he again received pollen from the Arnold Arboretum to attempt the cross again. This cross was successful. From his first generation of seedlings Skinner selected and named only four cultivars: 'Handel', 'Helen', and 'Hiawatha' all introduced in 1935 and 'Hecla' in 1936. A later open-pollinated seedling named 'Donald Wyman' was introduced in 1944.

In the spring of 1921 the seedlings of *S. oblata dilatata*, obtained from Sargent in 1918 at the Arnold, bloomed. Skinner began his famous early hybrid crosses that he called 'American Hybrids' using various *S. vulgaris* cultivars, which he does not name, as pod parents and *S. oblata dilatata* as the pollen parent. Eleven years later, in 1932, he introduced the first of these crosses, 'Assessippi' and 'Minnehaha.' His last introduction in 1966 was 'Maiden's Blush' which at first he believed to be an interspecific hybrid. Among some of the 20 cultivars he introduced from as he said "the French *S. vulgaris* lilacs and the pollen of *S. oblata dilatata*" the more outstanding include 'Pocahontas' in 1935, 'Gertrude Leslie' and 'Swarthmore' in 1954, 'Sister Justena' in 1956, 'Mount Baker' and 'The Bride' in 1961, 'Dr. Chadwick' in 1962, 'Royal Purple' in 1965 and his outstanding 'Maiden's Blush' in 1966. His 'Grace Mackenzie' introduced in 1942, which he at first believed to be an interspecific hybrid, has since been found to be one of his early hybrids. Although he called his hybrids 'American Lilacs', taxonomists refer to them as *S.* × *hyacinthiflora*. Skinner's *S. oblata dilatata* hybrids are much better garden plants than the *S.* × *hyacinthiflora* that used *S. oblata* 'Giraldii.' They are not as tall and rangy and the buds and flowers appear to be somewhat more hardy than the 'Giraldii' seedlings. Their inflorescence appears more open and abundant. (*Bon jardinier*, if you have room for an early hybrid—and you must find a place for these outstanding lilacs—choose the Skinner hybrids for all around performance. You will be delighted!)

Using *S. patula* pollenized by *S. pubescens*, he produced the hybrid known as *S.* × *skinneri* (an interspecific hybrid—a lovely plant if one can obtain it). In 1936 he introduced another interspecific hybrid of *S. villosa* × *S. sweginzowii* named 'Hedin' (another lovely garden plant).

For over 30 years Frank Skinner enriched lilacdom with his genius, patience and skill. Outside of his nursery his only financial aid was a federal grant given when he was eighty years old to record his life experiences. His book, *HORTICULTURAL HORIZONS* was published only six months before his death at his Dropmore home on August 27, 1967, at the age of eighty-six. Beloved for all of the many plants he introduced, he will probably be best remembered for his outstanding *S. oblata dilatata* hybrids.

The Best of the Skinner Lilacs

S. vulgaris × *S. oblata dilatata* hybrids (I do not believe that one can make a mistake by choosing any of the Skinner early hybrids. They are all fine plants—some a bit better than others).

  'Assessippi'—single lavender-lilac—fine plant
  'Doctor Chadwick'—single bluish—good
  'Charles Nordine'—single blue—very good
  'Grace Mackenzie'—single lavender
  'Laurentian'—single blue—very fine
  'Maiden's Blush'—single light pink—exceptionally fine
  'Minnehaha'—single purple—fine
  'Nokomis'—single lavender—lilac
  'Pocahontas'—single purple—very fine
  'Royal Purple'—double purple—good
  'Sister Justena'—single white, very fine
  'Swarthmore'—double, light purple—fine
  'The Bride'—single white—good
  'Tom Taylor'—double purple—fine

S. villosa × *S. reflexa*

  'Donald Wyman'—single rosy-purple—very fine (an F2 × prestoniae)
  'Helen'—single pink—good
  'Hiawatha'—single magenta—unique flower formation—very fine

S. patula × *S. pubescens*

  'Skinneri'—single white—good, different. (very difficult to find)
(*Mon ami*, you want only one Skinner introduction? Then let it be 'Maiden's Blush'! You will be unhappy unless you add 'Pocahontas' and have a pair of lovely lilac maidens!)

WALTER BOSWORTH CLARKE 1876–1953, A Nurseryman of Distinction

Mr. W. B. Clarke founded and developed the Clarke Nursery of San Jose, California, as a specialty nursery featuring many rare plants, shrubs and trees. In 1931 he began a program of selection and hybridization of flowering peaches and apricots and did extensive work in developing worthwhile lilacs for the California area. He was most successful in introducing many outstanding cultivars of lilacs, especially among the Early Hybrids, from 1931 to 1948. Many of these are still choice garden shrubs to this day.

Walter B. Clarke was the recipient of many horticultural awards for his nursery introductions and hybridization programs. Among these awards were the Jackson Dawson Memorial Gold Medal from the Massachusetts Horticultural Society in 1945, twelve Awards of Merit conferred by the California Horticultural Society, and an award of the Royal Horticultural Society. His work with lilacs covered a span of 35 years in which the following introductions were made:

'Alice Eastwood', 1942, double claret purple, long slim spikes, like 'purple cat-tails'; named to honor Alice Eastwood, dean of California botanists.

'Blue Hyacinth', 1942, single, large hyacinth shaped florets of medium blue.

'Bountiful', 1949, single 'fat clusters' borne on long stems, an outstanding rosy-orchid.

'Clarke's Giant', 1948, the first patented lilac No. 754, a rosy mauve single of enormous floret size, a tall grower.

'Cora Brandt', 1947, double white of great merit, showy compounded clusters in open panicles. Named to honor Cora Brandt, Secretary of California Horticultural Society.

'Early Double White', 1944, double white, good but not outstanding, early.

'Esther Staley', 1948, a lovely single seedling of 'Mme. F. Morel', heavy blooming lilac-pink, outstanding in bloom, tall grower. Named to honor Mrs. Esther Staley, Riverbank, California, who pioneered the introduction of many garden plants in the San Joaquin Valley.

'Fantasy', 1950, double medium to deep purple, very fine and showy.

'Kate Sessions', 1942, single medium purple-mauve to bluish, very large florets; named to honor Miss Kate Olivia Sessions, active nurserywoman who died in 1940, aged 83.

'Missimo', 1944, a single rosy purple with very large florets with recurved and curled petals, florets to 1¼ inches, panicles of great size and beauty. Seedling of 'Mme. F. Morel.'

'Mood Indigo', 1944, single, dark ruddy-purple, florets exceeding 1 in. in 8–9 in. clusters.

'Mountain Haze', 1946, single, purplish-blue of moderate size florets, huge compound clusters in great profusion.

'Pink Cloud', 1947, single, soft lavender-pink, very heavy bloomer in large clusters.

'Pink Spray', 1948, single, soft mauve-pink of considerable quality.

'Purple Gem', 1950, single, deep violet-purple, large florets, outstanding; low grower.

'Purple Heart', 1949, single, very early, purplish-black buds opening to deep violet-purple, florets to 1½ in. borne in huge clusters, outstanding.

'Splendor', 1949, double deep purplish-blue, open clusters of great beauty.

'Summer Skies', 1949, single, orchid buds opening bluish to soft sky-blue, very distinctive with very large clusters.

'Sunset', 1949, double, buds deep mauve-carmine opening rosy-purple, very large florets to 1 in., one of the redder lilacs.

'Sweetheart', 1950, double, heart-shaped panicles of a soft to deep pink, very distinctive and attractive.

'White Hyacinth', 1949, single, counterpart of 'Blue Hyacinth' in white; beautiful but a difficult grower, subject to scale.

ROWANCROFT GARDENS—MARY E. BLACKLOCK and MINERVA S. CASTLE

Under the direction of Miss Mary E. Blacklock (1860–1956) and then under Miss Minerva S. Castle (1890–1976) some outstanding lilacs were introduced from Rowancroft Gardens, Meadowvale, Ontario, Canada. Under the name of M. E. Blacklock the lilac cultivars 'Heavenly Blue', 'St. Joan' and 'St. Margaret' were released. The outstanding quality of the last two 'Saints Joan and Margaret' places them among some of the finest double white lilacs available today. Both should be in every larger garden.

Under the name of Minerva Castle have come all the last lilacs introduced: 'Violet Glory' a wonderfully large floreted deep purple or violet-purple of exceptional merit, 'Pink Perfection', 'White Supreme' and 'Blue Delight.' All are of high quality and substance for which Miss Castle was given an Award of Merit by the International Lilac Society. Both Miss Blacklock and Miss Castle were quiet and retiring individuals, shunning any publicity for their work with lilacs. Many of their fine seedlings were never named or introduced.

The 'Best' of the Rowancroft lilacs
'St. Joan'—double white of outstanding quality.
'St. Margaret'—double white—very fine if not equal to 'St. Joan'.
'Violet Glory'—single deep purple—very large florets—very fine.
'Heavenly Blue'—a double blue of great merit and beauty—difficult to find.

JOHN RANKIN M.D. 1891–1976, The Lilac Doctor of Elyria, Ohio

John Rankin was born on February 13, 1891, in Johnstown, Pennsylvania. He graduated from Ohio Wesleyan College and completed his medical studies at Johns Hopkins Medical School. For several years he taught at Western Reserve Medical School in Cleveland, Ohio. As a bachelor he practiced medicine in Elyria, Ohio, but his avocation was a deep dedication to flowering plants and shrubs. All his life he worked in his spare time in his several acres of gardens. He was a rose enthusiast who early began to collect one of the finest selections of lilac cultivars in the country. At one time his lilac collection numbered over a thousand of the finest cultivars.

Personal acquaintance with the Lemoines, John Dunbar, Theodore Havemeyer, Alice Harding and the lilac growers of his time enabled him to assemble in his collection most of the newest introductions. He often obtained the 'original plant' of an introduction he deemed worthy. Several original Havemeyer plants were tagged with special lead markers on the roots to identify them as 'the original plant'; among them were Havemeyer's 'True Blue', 'Mrs. Flanders', 'Mrs. Watson Webb', 'Mrs. John Davis', and 'Carley.' His collection contained lilacs from nearly every breeder at the time. It was of the highest caliber, especially in cultivars of *S. vulgaris*.

His love for lilacs led him to plant several hundred seedlings in seeking to improve certain color categories suggested to him by John Wister, namely the violet and lilac colors. At bloomtime his Elyria lilac gardens welcomed hundreds of visitors. Among the choicest new lilacs were many splendid old cultivars of exceptional quality rarely seen even in botanical collections. He spent a lifetime collecting, improving and selecting lilacs with no financial or material recognition. It is amazing that his superior collection was so ignored by lilac pundits of his day. It far surpassed most of the botanical collections.

Of the 25 or more cultivars he introduced, only a very few are known and survive today, yet alone obtainable. At one time nearly all of them were in the Rochester Parks Collection. Today the largest number (12 or more) can be found in the gardens of two friends to whom he bequeathed his lilacs, Clare Short of Elyria, Ohio, and the author's garden at Falconskeape, Medina, Ohio.

Most of the Rankin introductions are in the colors of violet and lilac. Perhaps his best known cultivars are 'Edith Braun' a magnificent, dark, rich magenta red-purple (named for his bride-to-be who died shortly before they were to be married) and 'Lewis Maddock' an outstanding pink early hybrid, perhaps the earliest to bloom, (named after a trusted garden-keeper). He spent over 40 years working with and collecting special cultivars of lilacs.

In his late years he spent most of his time with his seedlings and in the company of his dear friends, Mary and Clare Short. At the age of 76, after a long illness, he died on November 27, 1967 in his Elyria home. As a hobby he collected and wrote old American ballads which he sang for various audiences, but his greatest love ever remained his 'lilacs'! (His cultivar 'Caroline Foley' is often used by nurseries as a standard for grafting other species because of its extremely strong annual growth.)

Rankin Introductions

'Alice Stofer'—S IV
'Bertha Dunham'—D II
'Betty Opper'—D V
'Caroline Foley'—S VI
'Dove'—D II
'Edith Braun'
'Edna Dunham'—S I
'Esta'—D IV

'Geraldine Smith'—S I
'Helen Pellage'—S VII
'Inez'—S I
'Jack Smith'—S IV
'Jane'—D IV
'Jane Smith'—D II
'Jennie C. Jones'—D I
'Lewis Maddock'—S V

'Pink Bluet'—S V
'Pinkie'—S V
'Pinkinsun'—S V
'Ralph'—S IV
'Robert Dunham'—S IV
'Two Star General'—D IV
'White Lace'—S I
'White Long Fellow'—S I

The Best of the Rankin Lilacs

'Dove'—double gray-purple—slate gray
'Edith Braun'—single, rich magenta red-purple—outstanding
'Lewis Maddock'—single light pink, early hybrid
'Pinkie'—single, light pink, very fine.
'White Lace'—single white—small florets but very heavy bloomer, heavy suckering.
(*Mon amie*—Dr. Rankin's best is 'Edith Braun' named after his lovely bride-to-be.)

John Rankin, M.D. The 'Lilac Doctor' of Elyria, Ohio, spent a lifetime seeking to improve the cultivars of *S. vulgaris*. His collection of rare lilacs numbered over 500 cultivars of the finest lilacs. (Photo courtesy Clare Short)

DIRK EVELEENS MAARSE 1881–1975, The Newer Dutch Lilac Introductions

Dirk Eveleens Maarse and the horticultural family of Maarse are outstanding lilac culturists in the commercial lilac forcing greenhouse industry of Aalsmeer, The Netherlands. Perhaps there is no other area in the world that produces as many cut-flower lilacs for the commercial flower trade as do the forcing houses of Aalsmeer. Here one sees, especially before the Christmas holidays, vast acres of lilacs in bloom under glass. It was here amid the lilacs of Aalsmeer that Dirk Eveleens Maarse was born and spent his life.

For good results over years of commercial forcing certain special traits are required of the lilac cultivars used. Dirk Eveleens Maarse not only was an excellent lilac forcer but specialized in breeding hybrids especially for the commercial forcing market.

Lilacs are forced under heat which often causes bud mutations or sports. Dirk Eveleens Maarse being a keen observer fostered such natural mutations. When large enough, he rooted or grafted them to produce a new cultivar. His sports (mutations) include the outstanding and unique deep purple lilac edged white, which he named 'Sensation.' This cultivar is much sought after and admired wherever it is grown. Another is a creamy yellow sport named 'Primrose.' Both are outstanding color innovations even if the florets are a bit small. Several clones have arisen from the unique 'Sensation' with varying depths of the purple color from deep to a reddish purple. (I think the very deep purple edged white the more attractive form.) Often 'sports' appear on 'Sensation' with florets purple-edged white mixed with petals of one color, to all pale lavender white petals. These should always be removed entirely. Likewise, certain clones of 'Primrose' have appeared with a deeper yellow shade. Some have argued that it is the soil in which they are planted that causes these color differences. True as it may be that lilac colors are influenced by soil content—in this case plants of 'Primrose' planted in identical soil, side by side, show different coloration. The Albert Lumley strain of 'Primrose' and the Holden Arboretum strain appear to be two of the finest in yellowish coloration.

Maarse continued his lilac hybridization well into his 90's. He died in his ninety-fourth year at Aalsmeer. Most of the Maarse family introductions have been made under the name of Topsvoort Nursery, Aalsmeer, The Netherlands. More than 20 introductions have been made in the past decades from this source alone. Some of his introductions and those of the Maarse family include: 'Flora' a magnificent white single, 'Excellent' a fine white single, 'Burgomeester Voller' a fine single lavender-blue with a white eye, 'Sensation' the outstanding deep purple edged white, 'Primrose' a new pale creamy-yellowish white, 'Miss Aalsmeer', 'Glorie d'Aalsmeer', 'Andre Csizik' and 'G. J. Baardse'.

The Best of the Maarse Introductions

'Sensation'—single, deep purple petals edged white—outstanding.
'Primrose'—single, pale creamy yellow—very pale—different color—florets small.
'Flora'—single white of large floret size—very outstanding.
'Burgomeester Voller'—a large single blue of real quality.
(I have not seen many of these Dutch introductions so am not able to judge them well. The four mentioned above are outstanding and unique.) The complete list of D. E. Maarse lilacs includes:

'Andre Csizik', S VI, 1950
'Burgomeester Voller', S-III, 1948
'Excellent'—S I, 1939
'Flora', S I, 1953
'Gerrie Schoonenberg', S I, 1948
'G. J. Baardse', S VI, 1943
'Gloire d'Aalsmeer', S I, 1938
'Hugo Mayer', S III, 1950
'Johann Mensing', S II, 1939
J. R. Koning, S IV, 1955
'Madame Rosel', S IV, 1963
'Miss Aalsmeer', S VII, 1953
'Nanook', S I, 1953
'Peerless Pink' S IV, 1953
'Primrose', S I, 1949 (pale yellow)
'Sensation', S VII, 1938 (deep purple edged white)
'Voorzitter Dix', S VI, 1953
'White Superior', S I, 1953

All the D. E. Maarse lilacs introduced have proved to be outstanding, and it may well be that his white selections are among the finest. They should be better known and grown. Of the many lilacs Maarse introduced all are singles, perhaps because he was so interested in producing better lilacs for the 'forcing' market of which he wrote:

"To those who know the lilac forcing, cut-flower market, there is no 'other way' to force lilac bloom than the 'Dutch Way'! The methods established by the lilac and flower growers of the Netherlands over the last 60 years have stood the test of producing excellent bloom at the proper season without fail. Unfortunately Americans and Canadians rarely, if ever, see cut lilacs at Christmastime or any other time. The florist market here has commercially spent all its efforts on producing thousands of Pointsettas, whereas in Europe lilacs are a fragrant, traditional Christmas flower. For those who have a special interest, especially for those who could be in the Netherlands shortly before the Christmas season, a visit to the forcing houses and garden center at Aalsmeer is an experience of tremendous interest and of exacting horticultural skills under hundreds of acres of glass. Thousands of lilacs are sold throughout Europe each Christmas. Plants to be forced must be handled with great skill and in a special way, beginning 2 or 3 years in advance with special pruning to produce long-stemmed bloom. These plants are kept in huge pots, or burlapped, or dug at the proper time and brought into the greenhouses for special forcing treatment. Sometimes hot-water baths are used to break dormancy, sometimes a special dormancy-breaking gas is substituted. Plants are exposed for a designated amount of time to controlled heat and light in order to break into peak bloom precisely at Christmas." I include these brief instructions from a 'master lilac bloom' producer. To know how to force lilacs is another book, *mon ami,* and a long working visit and trip to Aalsmeer. Both are worthwhile even if one is not in the flower business.

Not all cultivars are equally good for forcing even though they may produce superior bloom ordinarily. In Aalsmeer lilacs are in bloom at two great seasons, in May for the spring bloom and again at Christmastime! The Seringenpark is outstanding in May—the forcing houses in December.

LEONID ALEKSEEVITCH KOLESNIKOV 1893–1973, Creator of Russian Lilacs and Doyen of Russian Lilac Hybridists

In the U.S.S.R., from Central Asia to the blue waters of the Baltic Sea, throughout the Crimea to the Carpathians and on into Siberia, lilacs bloom in May everywhere. It was on the 18th in this beautiful month, that Leonid Alexseevitch Kolesnikov was born in 1893. In old Russia the lilac was called "seanel" derived from the Russian word "siniy" meaning 'blue'. Leonid Kolesnikov began as an amateur grower of lilacs and rose to become a leading specialist and head of the Experimental and Model Selection Nursery. Although he pioneered in the creation of new cultivars of *S. vulgaris,* he did not limit his work to hybridizing lilacs but devoted himself to every aspect of their growth and culture. Kolesnikov first planted lilacs in his own garden in 1916. Three years later he sowed seeds of his own hybridizing and began a career devoted to improving the lilac his country so loved.

Kolesnikov avidly read and studied every available book on botany, especially on methods of breeding, grafting and planting lilacs. Traveling frequently and widely across the country, he not only acquainted himself with the then known methods of lilac culture and propagation, but was able to observe firsthand what was being done in the largest nurseries of his time, such as those on the estates of Feldman Koratchovsky, Focht and others.

The young Kolesnikov made every effort to extend the number of varieties in his own garden. By 1923 his collection of lilacs had reached over 100 named cultivars and his garden began receiving the attention of specialists and scientific researchers. M. P. Nagibins, a researcher at the Botanical Garden of Moscow University, helped Kolesnikov considerably with botany and botanical

One of the finest lilac collections in Europe can be found at the Moscow Botanical Gardens, where there is an excellent representation of many of Kolesnikov's best selections.

Leonid A. Kolesnikov holding his lilac introduction 'Mechta', a lovely, large-flowered
lavender with tints of blue. Kolesnikov was
the recipient of the highest award for horticulture in the U.S.S.R., as well as the
Directors' Award, the highest award for
hybridizing, given by the International Lilac
Society. (Photos and notes on Kolesnikov's
life, courtesy of Dr. A. Gromov, Moscow,
U.S.S.R.)

research which in turn led him to the work of K. Timiryazev, Prof. N. I. Kitchunov, D. D.
Artzibashev, Ivan Michurin and Luther Burbank.

He used almost exclusively the introductions of the Lemoines, with one exception: 'Congo'
'Alphonse Lavallee', 'Katherine Havemeyer', 'Pasteur', 'Reaumur', 'Monge', 'Buffon', 'Decaisne',
'President Poincare', 'Berryer', 'Mme. Lemoine', 'Belle de Nancy', 'Michel Buchner', 'Emil Lemoine'
and 'Jules Simon', and one other 'Ludwig Spaeth' (his only non-Lemoine parent plant).

After twenty years of patient hybridizing he began to see the real results of his labors. From
his seedlings he selected cultivars like 'Zarya Kommunisma', 'Leonid Leonov', 'K. A. Timiryazev'
and 'Sumerki.' From these first open-pollinated seedlings he then cross-pollinated those seedlings
he deemed best. He particularly liked his named cultivars 'I. V. Mitchurin', 'M. I. Kalinin' and 'Zarya
Kommunisma' as hybridizing materials. He shared with Victor Lemoine a preference for the large
floret double lilacs.

He authored a book 'Lilacs', in 1952 growing out of his work in hybridizing and many
experiments in lilac grafting, transplanting and seed growing. His experiments indicating lilacs
could, and perhaps should, be moved in mid-summer dry weather, radically altered the traditional
and conventional notion on transplanting lilacs. His experiments indicated that flower color of cultivars of light-rose, pinks, lilac-violet and blue shades are best in soil pH close to neutral, otherwise
it is 'muddy.' His fertilizing experiments showed that by using 'green water', a heavily manured
water and lime solution, on lilacs, 5 or 6 flower buds could be induced rather than the traditional 2
or 3. (His 'green water' is made by putting weeds, green cuttings, grass, etc. into water and after all
have decayed using the 'water' as fertilizer.) He determined that one of the best times to transplant
lilacs without sacrificing bloom the following year is from 14–18 days after florescence. His horticultural genius extended to inventing new budding tools, shears, pruning and spraying equipment.

Kolesnikov's work was interupted by wars (as was that of the Lemoines). In 1939 he
participated in the Finnish Campaign. In 1940, his wife, Olympiada Nikolaevna, showed in his
absence some of his varieties at the All-Union Agricultural Exposition where he was awarded the
Diploma of Honor for his work. His return to his peaceful lilac pursuits was brief. In 1942 he was
again on the battlefield for five months, returning home after being wounded. In 1943 he made the
cross with 'I. V. Michturin' and 'Belle de Nancy' which gave him his two best lilacs, the magnificent
double white tinged lavender 'Krasavitsa Moskvy' and the fine double bluish-lilac 'Pamiat' o. S. M.
Kirove.' (After the war began the 'golden years' of his lilac work.)

Leonid Kolesnikov was a wonderfully knowledgeable man, always searching to understand the ways of nature. He read a great deal and understood plants with a kind of sixth sense of
the soul. He was ready to share his knowledge with colleagues and visitors whether amateurs or

Peter Upitis, Latvia, U.S.S.R., Russian hybridizer. (Photo courtesy Freek Vrugtman, R.B.G.)

professionals. Ironically he died before he received the news that he had been awarded the highest award of the International Lilac Society at its meeting in Boston, May of 1973, for his work with lilacs. Like Lemoine, his lilacs will ever remain Leonid Kolesnikov's lasting tribute. (Only recently have some of Kolesnikov's introductions become available in North America. Numbers and sources are as yet very limited.)

The Kolesnikov Lilac Introductions

Among the lilac introductions of Leonid A. Kolesnikov are the following cultivars some of which bear a short description, others are merely listed as to color. Those that I have seen and appear outstanding are marked with an asterisk *.

'Akademik Burdenko', double, lilac-blue

'Akademik Maksimov', double, medium lavender-pink

*'Aleksei Mares'ev', N-443, 'Kapitan Gastello' × (Fuerst Buelow × Sdg. 105), single, bluish

'Andryusha Gromov', double, bluish-shaded lavender

'Bal'zak', double, magenta-reddish

'Bol'shevik', double, violet-pink

*'Dzhavakharial Neru', (D. Neru'), (Ludwig Spath × Sdg. 110) × Sdg. 105, deep violet, an early bloomer

'Emel'yan Yaroslavakii', no description to be found

*'Galina Ulanova', single white, wide clusters, pyramidal

*'Gastello', single violet

*'Golubaya', N 241, Sdg. 11 × (Mechta × Decaisne), single, lilac-blue

*'Gortenziya' (Hortensia), single, warm violet tones, good forcing lilac

*'Indiya', N 124, ('Zarya Kommunizma' × Sdg. 105), single, purple-violet with red coppery tones

'I. V. Mitchurin', N212, double delicate lilac rose

*'Izobilie', N 394, ('Katherine Havemeyer' × 'Reaumur'), double, purple lilac to rose

*'Kapriz', double light pink

'K. A. Timiryazev', N 119, light purple to blue, single

'Kolkhoznitsa', no information

*'Komsomolka', double lavender

*'Krasavitsa Moskvy' N 237, ('Belle de Nancy' × 'I. V. Mitchurin')—double, white pearled lavender pink, exceptionally fine

*'Krasnaya Moskva', N335, ('Pasteur' × 'Congo') × Sdg. 110, single, dark velvet purple

'Kremlevskie Kuranty', N 739, 'Congo' × ('Monge' × Sdg. 105), purple-carmine shades, single

*'Leonid Kolesnikov', double, lavender to lilac shades

*'Leonid Leonov', N201/103, (Sdg. 110 × 'Ludwig Spaeth'), single, two-toned lilac-violet

'Marshal Vasilevskii', double, pinkish-lilac tones

*'Marshal Zhukov', N 530, ('M. I. Kalinin' × Sdg. 105), single, outstanding cherry-violet

*'Mechta', N 230, single, large panicles of lilac slightly blue tinted color

'M. I. Kalinin', N 210, (Sdg. 105 × 'Reaumur'), large panicles of purple-lilac

*'Mirza Galib', single, outstanding purple-lilac to violet, panicles to 45 cm. long

*'Nadezhda', N 728, one of the best in blue shades, double, very large panicles

'Nebo Moskvy', N 508, double, lilac-blue, heavy bloomer

*'Nevesta', N 14, single, 'Buffon' × (Sdg. 411 × 'Mme. Antoine Buchner'), white rose tinted

'Obmanshchitsa', double violet

*'Ogni Moskvy', N 525, (Sdg. 105 × 'Pasteur' XX Sdg. 110 × 'Zarya Kommunizma'), single, a purple-violet to lighter shades of purple, large drooping panicles

*'Olumpiada Kolesnikova', N 86, (named after his wife), ('Berryer' × 'Tamara Kolesnikova'), double, violet purple buds opening to rich magenta-purple

*'Pamiat o.s.M. Kirove', N 384, ('Belle de Nancy' × 'I. V. Mitchurin'), double, lavender to lilac-bluish, outstanding

*'Pioner', N 321, (Sdg. 105 × 'Zarya Kommunizma'), single, rich purple-carmine, large panicles

'Polina Osipenko', double white with a bluish tint

'Pol' Robson', single, lavender-blue to lilac

*'P. P. Konchalovskii', N 388, ('Victor Lemoine' × 'Jules Simon' XX 'Pres. Ponicare'), double, blue to lavender shades, immense panicles

'Radzh Kapur' (Raj Kapur) (Brodyaga), N 745, ('Indiya' × 'Pioner'), single, carmine-purple, twisted petals

'Sholokhov', N 61, ('Alphonse Lavallee' × Sdg. 504), single, lilac-violet to pink shades

'Snezhinka', white

'Sorok Let Komsomola', single blue

*'Sovetskaya Arktika', N 300, 'Mme. Lemoine' × ('Snezhinka' × 'Mme. Casimir Perier') double, pure white, recurved petals

'Sumerki', N 104, ('Pasteur' × Sdg. 401), single, purple-violet and bluish

'Tamara Kolesnikova', double, lilac shades

'Russkaya Krasavista', an outstanding white lilac introduced by the Polish-Russian hybridizer, Stashkevitch, a protege of Kolesnikov working in Poland. It is a free-blooming single with a feathery appearance. Stashkevitch's lilacs are very new and appear to be very fine. (Photo Dr. A. Gromov, Moscow, U.S.S.R.)

'Utro Moskvy', double, lilac pink
'Valentina Grizodubova', double, light pink
'Vesna', double, light purple
'Vnuchka Lenochka'—(no description)
*'Zarya Kommunizma', N 153, Sdg. 110 × ('Ludwig Spaeth' × Sdg. 105), single, purple-red
   with blue-violet tones, very effective
*'Znamya Lenina', N 039, ('Congo' × Sdg. 110) × ('Congo' × Sdg. 105), single, purple-red,
   with cherry shades, outer side of petals purple-lilac, outstanding
'Zaya Kosmodem' yanskaya', single bluish
'40 Let VLKSM', N 176, (Sdg. 105 × 'Congo') × 'Alphonse Lavallee', single, lilac-carmine
   with reddish-magenta overtones

(There is always some difficulty in transliteration of the Russian names from Cyrillic letters to Roman, so spelling may vary.)

(Since I have seen only a small portion of Kolesnikov's many introductions, it would be unfair to use this evaluation as definitive. It does, however, present a certain limited validity. Outside of the U.S.S.R. Botanical Gardens at Moscow, the single largest collection of Russian lilacs is at the Royal Botanical Gardens, Hamilton, Ontario, Canada.)

MIKOLAJ KARPOW-LIPSKI, A Polish hybridizer of distinction

Working at Chelmza, Poland between 1948 and 1962, Mikolaj Karpow-Lipski introduced some 22 lilacs of considerable merit. Most of his lilacs can be seen at the Royal Botanical Gardens, Hamilton, Ontario, Canada, which has the largest collection of Polish lilacs. Many fine cultivars from foreign countries are difficult to obtain—let alone to evaluate—until some decades ater their introduction. Karpow-Lipski's lilacs have many fine cultivars, including many doubles:

'Adam Mickiewicz—D IV—1958
'Anna Karpow'—D I—1958
'Bogdan Przyrzkowski'—D VI—1961
'Dr. W. Bugala'—S V—1962
'Fale Baltyku'—D III—1961
'Irene Karpow-Lipska'—D IV—1958
'Jutrzenka Pomorza'—S V—1961
'Kardynal'—D-VI
'Kobierski'—D IV—1960

'Konstanty Karpow'—D V—1953
'Leon Wyczolkowski'—S VI—1958
'Minister Dab Kociol'—S III—1961
'Niewinnosc'—D V—1960
'Panna Dorota Golabecka'—D I—1952
'Piotr Chosinski'—D VI—1960
'Pomorzanka'—S V—1962
'Prof. Bialobok'—D V—1961

'Prof. Edmund Jankowski'—S III—1958
'Prof. Josef Brzezinski'—D V—S III—1958
'Prof. Roman Kobendza'—D IV—1958
'Rozana Mlodosc'—S V—1960
'Stefan Makowiecki' —S VI—1958
'Tadeusz Kosciusko'—D VI—1953

THE KORNICK ARBORETUM LILAC COLLECTION, Kornik, Poland

The Kornik Arboretum founded about 1850 by Tytus Dzialynski and later enlarged by his son, Jan Dzialynski, contains many old specimen trees and shrubs that are well over 100 years old. The Dzialynski family belonged to the richest class, and the dendrological collection reflects their wealth. Individual taxa then numbered well over 2,000 of all species and cultivars. Lilacs were prominent among them. The present lilac collection was mostly the work of A. Wroblewski beginning in 1926. At the outbreak of the war in 1939, the lilac collection at Kornik numbered 125 taxa. After the war the collection increased with newer introductions from abroad to over 500 named cultivars and species. The Arboretum is located on grounds composed of light, sandy, rather dry and poor soil with underlying peat and clay. It is not a desirable soil for *S. vulgaris*. Annual rainfall averages 500 mm (20 inches), with long periods of dry weather in the summers. Rainless periods of from 4–6 weeks are common. Winters are comparatively easy with temperatures of −15° to −20°C. and with little snow.

In 1952 Director W. Bugala began a serious program of hybridizing *S. × prestoniae*, naming several cultivars in 1970 (see Dr. W. Bugala). The lilac collection at Kornik also contains most of the little known but striking introductions of Mikolaj Karpow-Lipski. Many are outstanding but still little known outside of Poland and mostly unavailable in North America. The Arboretum is well worth a special visit and the extra time when in Poland. The lilac collection is a lesson of what can be accomplished despite difficult soil conditions.

WLADYSLAW BUGALA, Late Blooming Polish Hybrids—Kornik Arboretum, Kornik, Poland

In recent years working at the Kornik Arboretum in Poland, Dr. W. Bugala has introduced several open-pollinated seedlings, selected from a very large planting of late blooming *S.* × *prestoniae*. All are second generation seedlings of named Prestonian cultivars and suggest what can be accomplished by diligent selection among this excellent new strain. Although many thousand seedlings were grown only a very few select cultivars were named and introduced. As yet they are unavailable in North America. Among Bugala's introductions from open-pollinated *S.* × *prestoniae* 'Octavia' and 'Ursula' are the following:

'Telimena', pale pink turning to white, very large, glossy leaves.

'Jaga', light violet fading to lavender, very large panicles.

'Basia', deep pink opening to pink, very showy.

'Jagienka', deep purple opening to lavender-violet—early bloomer.

'Nike', deep purple opening to bright purple, very showy late bloomer.

'Goplana', carmine-pink opening to light pink.

'Esterka', deep carmine-rose opening to light pink—outstanding in color.

'Danusia', deep red buds opening to pink—heavy bloomer.

'Diana', deep purple opening to rosy lilac.

(An excellent hybridizing program could be undertaken by a young lilac breeder using Bugala's model but crossing some of the best Prestonian hybrids, selecting the very best and backcrossing these selections. There is an untapped wealth of genetic materials yet untouched in these fine Prestonian Hybrids. Undoubtedly many very fine cultivars would result.)

N. S. STASHKEVITCH

A protégé of Leonid Kolesnikov working in Poland who originated the fine lilac cultivars named 'Komsomoletz Dvadtzatikh godov', 'Tankist' and 'Russkaya Krasavitsa.' (Little is known of these cultivars except that they are considered as rather outstanding and very recent.)

J. HERBERT ALEXANDER, SR. 189?–1977, An outstanding Lilac grower and nurseryman

Under J. Herbert Alexander, Sr., founder of the Dahliadel Nursery, Middleboro, Mass. a continuing stream of new lilac introductions of distinction, together with new and rare forms of better cultivars were made available to the public. Mr. Alexander not only made rare lilacs available by producing large numbers of plants of the better lilac cultivars but was responsible for several new introductions of his own. The late hybrids, 'Foster Alexander', 'Alexander's Pink', 'Ferna Alexander', 'Alexander's Attraction'—were late hybrids of *Prestoniae* parentage. He also introduced from other breeders 'Beth Turner', 'President John F. Kennedy' and 'Cora Lyden' all *S. vulgaris* cultivars. His was a shrewd eye for lilacs and their inherent qualities. Ever creative and enthusiastic he promoted lilacs wherever possible. His was a kind of nursery where one could find always something unique and different. His mind was an 'encyclopedia' of plant knowledge, especially about the lilacs which he loved.

Plants, shrubs and trees need not only those who work to perfect them by diligent hybridization and careful selection, but especially and foremost, they need those whose skill and ingenuity can promote and bring them to the public and to the attention of the commercial nurserymen. Of the more than 2,000 cultivars and named lilacs, no more than a handful can ever be marketed realistically. Lilacs, like other shrubs and plants, need astute nurserymen to ascertain those of merit, to recognize real quality, old and new, and make them available to the public. This is an art and special gift that only a few have. John H. Alexander, Sr. was one of these few!

MRS. FRANK PATERSON, A Canadian Lilac Fancier

Although she had an extensive lilac garden the introductions made by Mrs. Paterson were limited but all were of outstanding quality. Her three dark purple lilacs, 'Doctor Brethour' (1961), 'Frank Paterson' (1961) and 'Helen Schloen' (1962) remain among the finest with 'Jimmy Howarth' (1961) being the only white she introduced. Fortunately the clonal material she used was continued on in the work of Leonard Slater for a short while after her death.

ALVAN GRANT, A Milestone of Serendipity

As Director of Parks at Rochester, New York, Alvan Grant gathered seed of the *S. vulgaris* cultivar 'Edith Cavell', Emile Lemoine's huge double white, then planted in the Highland Park Nursery. In time several seedlings grew, but it was one—small, slow growing, with a heavily textured leaf—that caught the attention of both Grant and Bernard Harkness, the Park Superintendent.

It turned out to be an amazing plant indeed! The florets were single yet multipetaled, waxlike and magnificent in bloom with long, well-filled spikes. In 1971 it was named 'Rochester' to honor the City. As Grant's single contribution to lilacdom it established a new plateau from which whole new races of lilacs have emerged. 'Rochester' has never been introduced into general commerce because it is difficult to propagate and grows too slowly to suit most gardeners—it remains a small plant after several years. However, once established on its own roots it is truly a most outstanding lilac. (I think it the most outstanding lilac ever produced—both for its intrinsic beauty and also its extraordinary genetic makeup for hybridizing.) Its value was immediately recognized by the International Lilac Society with a special Award of Merit. Today 'Rochester' and its hybrids are being heavily used by hybridizers. It is the foundation of the 'Rochester Strain' of hybrids of Richard Fennicchia and is the center of much of the hybridizing done by Dr. Don Egolf at the U.S. National Arboretum and my own work.

LEONARD SLATER, Originator of the Agincourt Lilacs

Leonard Slater carried on the work of Mrs. Frank Paterson with outstanding, large flowered lilacs. His first introduction, 'Agincourt Beauty' in 1968, is an outstanding lilac of heavy substance with huge deep purple florets, so large they hang like deep purple clusters of immense grapes. Another extremely important introduction was the magnificent, enormous, single white named 'Slater's Elegance' in 1974. Although introduced some years ago, neither has yet appeared on the market so are extremely difficult to obtain.

Slater also selected and named a unique columnar tree lilac, *S. reticulata* 'Ivory Silk' from among seedlings at the Sheridan Nurseries in Canada. His introductions are of exceptional quality. Slater's new white 'Slater's Elegance' will be difficult to equal for many years and like 'Rochester' will set a new mark when used in hybridizing. Leonard Slater was a retiring personality who loved lilacs and set a very high standard for new introductions. He died suddenly in 1982.

MARK EATON Contemporary, The Last of the Havemeyer Introductions

Upon the death of Theodore Havemeyer in 1936, his lilac collection at Cedar Hill was passed on to his friend, Mark Eaton. Under Eaton's direction many of the last unnamed selections of Havemeyer were introduced. Some are among the finest of the Havemeyer lilacs. All are extremely difficult to obtain or even find in the largest collections, but are well worth of a place among the best lilacs. They include: 'Hallelujah', 'Mister Big', 'Dazzle', 'Mauve Mist', 'Serene', 'Snowflake' and 'Tit Tat Toe.'

A debt of gratitude is owed to Mr. Eaton for completing Havemeyer's life work. Most of the Havemeyer lilacs were relatively unknown and unobtainable until they were offered to the public through the efforts and nursery of Mark Eaton. Often a hybridizer's most mature and best work is done towards the end of his life and most frequently the best fruit of his work is lost upon his death. Final and best seedlings are most often not evaluated by trustees of estates and are discarded. Rarely does a team such as Havemeyer-Eaton come forth for the good of all.

For his outstanding work in promoting the lilac, Mark Eaton was awarded the International Lilac Society's Award of Merit. Under his direction "Lilacland" at Glen Head, Long Island became a lilac specialty nursery; one where the very difficult and choice introductions of considerable merit could be found. Today this type of lilac nursery has virtually disappeared for lack of support, replaced by mass production of often inferior cultivars produced for color by commercial growers for higher profits rather than the love of plants. The nurseries of Lilacland, J. Herbert Alexander, Sr. and Henry Hohman were in a distinguished category of love for superior cultivars.... today only the Alexander Nursery remains!

FRED LAPE Contemporary, Director, Landis Arboretum, Esperance, New York

Fred Lape was an author, linguist, horticulturist and a lilac enthusiast. His *A Garden of Trees and Shrubs* (the Landis Arboretum) is a must for estate planters who are beginners. He was the originator of *S. vulgaris* seedlings from 'Kapriz' and the originator of the beautiful late blooming white lilac 'Summer White' for which he received an Award of Merit and commendation for his translation of Russian lilac publications into English. He died suddenly in 1985 at his winter home in Mexico, at the age of 83.

BETTY STONE Contemporary, Ashland, Ohio

Mrs. Betty Stone worked for many years creating an outstanding lilac garden at her farm outside Ashland, Ohio. She obtained some of the newest introductions of Lemoine and other outstanding cultivars. From these she selected seed and planted a number of seedlings. She selected her introductions for beauty of bloom and plant vigor. Her named cultivars include: 'Ralph Stone' (named in 1971 to honor her husband), 'Betty Stone', 'Florence Christine' (1963). All her cultivars are fine and of considerable merit. Age and poor health forced her to retire from lilacs and the farm following her husband's death in 1979. She was presented with an I.L.S. Award of Merit for her work.

CORA LINDSEY LYDEN 1892–1982

A love of lilacs led Cora Lyden to selecting and growing new cultivars from open-pollinated seed. In her Maine garden she developed such varieties as 'J. Herbert Alexander' (1963) a × *prestoniae* hybrid; 'President Eisenhower' (1960), 'Hazel' (1968), 'John's Favorite' (1963), 'Cora Lyden' (1968), a delightful pink, and all cultivars of *S. vulgaris*. When age kept her from her garden, she gave up lilac breeding and moved to California where she died at 90 in 1982. Most of her introductions have not received the public attention they deserve and remain relatively unobtainable.

KEN BERDEEN, The Lilacs from Kennebunk, Maine 1907–1987

Born of Scotch ancestry in Stonington, Maine, in 1907 Ken Berdeen started with five lilacs in 1953 and for the past 30 years has spent all his spare time and in retirement full time with developing new forms of *S. vulgaris*. There are over 2,300 lilacs (mostly his seedlings), on his 60-acre farm, Alewive Rd outside of Kennebunk, Maine. Most of the seedlings are still being evaluated, some of which will soon be released. Among his named introductions since 1963 are: 'Eleanor Berdeen', 'Chris', 'Beth Morrison', 'James Berdeen', 'Kate Bergen', 'Walter's Pink', 'Lynette Sirois', 'Berdeen's Chocolate' a unique deep reddish-brown-purple, and 'President John F. Kennedy' a double white. Berdeen's lilacs deserve far more recognition and should be made available commercially. Many excellent cultivars remain to be selected from the large number of fine seedlings growing in his nursery. His newest 'Lee Jewett Walker' and 'Stephanie Rowe' are outstanding pinks, 'Elizabeth Files' a beautiful magenta! Ken Berdeen died suddenly in January 1987.

WILLIAM and LOIS UTLEY, Grape Hill Farm, Clyde, N.Y.

An outstanding planting and nursery of specialized lilacs, many almost unobtainable, are found in this fine collection. Mr. Utley has introduced a lovely double pink *S. vulgaris* named 'Catawba Pink.' He is also responsible for the discovery and introduction of a very lovely sport (or seedling) of 'Lucie Baltet' considered by many superior and of better coloring than the original plant and named it 'Clyde Lucie.' This collection in its early stages shows how to design a lilac planting for both close and distant viewing. It is well worth a May bloom-time visit. This garden was presented the special Arboretum and Large Estate Award by the International Lilacs Society for its outstanding lilac collection.

DR. WILLIAM A. CUMMING, Lilacs from the Morden Arboretum, Manitoba, Canada

For more than 20 years Dr. William Cumming has been active with new plants and with lilac cultivars at the Morden Arboretum, from which he retired in 1976. While working with a number of genera, shrubs and trees he introduced the excellent multibrid lilacs; 'Minuet' (a tribrid) obtained by crossing *S. josiflexa* 'Redwine' × *S. Prestoniae* 'Donald Wyman.' Thus 'Minuet' has the three species *S. josikaea*, *S. reflexa* and *S. villosa* in its genetic makeup. It is a fine low growing dwarf lilac. Cummings also introduced 'Miss Canada', another tribrid from *S. josiflexa* 'Redwine' × *S. prestoniae* 'Hiawatha.' The latter introduction is a fine china-rose in color. Dr. Cumming is an out-

Dr. William A. Cumming of Morden, Manitoba, Canada, working with the late-blooming lilacs, produced the beautiful 'Minuet' and 'Miss Canada'.

standing lilac authority on the hybridization of lilacs in Canada and on the suitability of various cultivars for the different regions of that great country. He is a recipient of the Award of Merit for his hybrids. He is a brother-in-law of Dr. Frank Leith Skinner, the great Canadian lilac hybridizer.

DR. JOEL MARGARETTEN, Growing Lilacs in Leona Valley, California

Dr. Joel Margaretten, Margaretten Park, Leona Valley, California is known for his cattle, his peonies and especially for his thousands of lilacs. In a seemingly impossible area he produces lilacs for the cut-flower industry, hybridizes lilacs and has developed one of the finest and largest lilac collections in the state. His unusual climatic and soil conditions require a very special way of growing lilacs. He writes:

Because of the unusual climate lilacs blossom early, usually before Easter. They last for a week or two, fade and go to seed. The soil is adobe, muddy in the winter and hard as rock in the summer. Except when the ground is frozen, it is almost impossible to cultivate. If there is no rain a power drill is used to get holes dug for planting the lilacs. Normal rainfall, except for 1969–70 is about 2 inches so there is a continual problem with water. Irrigation is a necessity all summer until August, then it is stopped to let the lilacs go dormant. Continued irrigation after that would bring on a new crop of flowers that would abort after a week. Temperatures, even in the winter, can go from zero F in the morning to 75°F by noon. Snow lasts for a day or two, doing more havoc than good. It bends branches down to the ground, freezes the young shoots necessitating more pruning.

Pruning is usually done in the winter when it is easier and more time is available. Pruning is severe to get rid of all dead and crossed branches. The lilacs are kept at 5–6 ft. in height, partly from cutting long stems for the market and to keep them easier to work with. Fertilizer is side dressed. Diesel oil is used for weed control and also cuts down on scale. It also kills any young suckers coming from the ground (You can't have everything!)

Most of the hybrids are grown on terraces. The *S. vulgaris* are in fields for tractor work and irrigation. The lilacs bloom fabulously!

Indeed his lilacs are fabulous and I have chosen to repeat his account of his system of growing lilacs for those who feel it is not possible under such circumstances to grow lilacs. Not only is Dr. Margaretten an outstanding grower with an excellent collection but he hybridizes lilacs as well. His first introduction, a fine double lavender-violet, is named after his wife 'Tita.'

Note: His system of withholding water during the late summer to induce dormancy may be the answer for many warm latitude lilac lovers who claim lilacs will not bloom for them for want of cold weather. It is my firm belief that they will grow and bloom well with this kind of dry period. In 1982 Dr. Margaretten was presented with the 'President's Award', the highest award of the International Lilac Society, for his work with lilacs.

RICHARD A. FENICCHIA Contemporary, Hybridizer of the New 'Rochester Strain' of Lilacs

The wonderful white, single lilac 'Rochester' (introduced by A. Grant) is a truly magnificent multipetaled lilac, unique in its heavy, wax-like, textured florets, and enormous straight panicles of white standing like upright candles. A seedling of 'Edith Cavell', it was brought to recognition by Richard Fenicchia, who first saw its enormous possibilities and began to hybridize with it while park superintendent at Highland Park, Rochester, New York.

Hybridizing was not new to Fenicchia. He had been involved with new plants and plant selection all his life. Lilacs, however, were a new venture in his hybridizing career. In the greenhouses at the Park he successfully pollinated 'Rochester' with select cultivars such as 'Mme. Charles Souchet', 'Edward J. Gardner', 'Glory' and others. From these seeds came a first generation of new lilacs. They were at first dismissed by John Wister as 'ordinary', but when seen by taxonomist Robert Clark and myself their value was quickly seen as a whole new strain of multipetaled (primrose form) new hued lilacs. Fenicchia was urged to name the best and to exhibit them at the forthcoming International Lilac Society Convention being held in Rochester in 1972. Their merit was universally accepted and the work of Fenicchia recognized as one of the landmarks in lilac hybridization. A revolution in lilac breeding had begun! Six of the first generation lilacs were named: 'Dwight D. Eisenhower', 'Bishop Bernard McQuaid', 'Bernard Slavin', 'Frederick Douglass', 'George Ellwanger', 'Dr. Edward Mott Moore.' A dozen or so more were set aside for future introduction. The seedling rows of these first and second generation 'Rochester' crosses have produced more outstanding and more diverse progeny than any other recorded cross of lilacs to date. His latest, 'Flower City', a single deep purple-violet, is outstanding and landmark in lilac breeding. Several unnamed seedlings are among the best.

Upon his retirement in 1980, the work of hybridization of lilacs at Highland Park stopped. The hoped-for introductions are still to be made. The lasting tribute to Fenicchia is that he first recognized and made this most outstanding cross and opened the way for others to follow. Meanwhile other hybridizers, taking their cue from Fenicchia's genius, have begun to use 'Rochester' (as difficult to obtain as it is) in various other crosses with equal success and with outstanding variations and new hybrids being introduced yearly. Today many new and exciting 'Rochester' seedlings from other hybridizers are showing the great worth of the parent plant.

Fenicchia's first and second generations show amazing color variations, from pale pastels to pearled colors not seen before in lilacs. No pearled-color lilacs were introduced by Fenicchia although several were found in the seedlings. This mother-of-pearl effect is seen on the pale pastel shades of blues and lavenders. Among 'Rochester' seedlings are a number of dwarf and very low growing forms excellent for rock gardens and for the Japanese garden as well. Rarely, perhaps once in several decades, does a genetic break-through such as this occur (or does the 'Rochester' story happen more often with no one to recognize or discover it?) Another such plant in 1843 was Libert's insignificant 'Azurea plena' which was not recognized until 30 years later by Victor Lemoine and it, too, began a whole new race of large, double lilacs. Isabella Preston, also, discovered a major break in hybridization when she combined the two ancient species S. villosa with S. reflexa to make her famous cross.

For his work Richard Fenicchia received the highest hybridizing Award from the International Lilac Society—a richly deserved recognition! All who love lilacs will ever be grateful for the hours of work, insight and genius that have given us this whole new race of 'Rochester Strain' lilacs. (Note: It is my view that several more of the excellent Fenicchia seedlings should have been introduced, as many are indeed among the finest lilacs I have seen.)

DR. OWEN ROGERS And the "TEAM OF LILAC SPECIALISTS", Yeager, Meader and Pike, at the University of New Hampshire

Rarely has a single University or Institution brought forth such a distinguished line of lilac specialists and hybridizers, who have contributed so much to the advancement of a single genus, as has the University of New Hampshire. Their work is unique in both the quality of the plant introductions and in the caliber of their work as research scientists. They have become specialists in the late blooming lilacs and species hybrids.

Under Professor Yeager, new, late blooming lilacs began their forward progress at the University with the introduction of the magnificent white 'Anna Amhoff' (Yaeger 1953). The discovery and introduction of the cultivar *S. patula* 'Miss Kim' (recorded under the species lilacs *S. patula*) has been an exceptional and outstanding contribution to lilacs made by Professor E. M. Meader. (Meader 1954). Lilac work and landscaping continued under the late Dr. Radcliff Pike.

Presently, under the able direction and gifted insights of Dr. Owen Rogers, lilac work at the University has reached new and exciting heights. The excellent cultivar 'Agnes Smith' (Rogers 1970) and 'Jessie Hepler' (1981) are new late hybrids. Under Rogers' direction in the research garden and nurseries are rows of wonderful new "break-throughs": multipetaled, double, late-blooming lilacs of exceptional quality, vigor and unique floret substance, hybrids of outstanding beauty, miniature plants, unique forms and sizes, colors and beauty! A whole new race or races of late-blooming lilacs! Indeed, they should be designated as the "Rogers Lilacs"! (For this work Dr. Rogers was awarded the highest hybridizing honors of the International Lilac Society in 1978.)

Not only does Dr. Owen Rogers head the lilac work currently being done at the University but also he has compiled the most recent Lilac Checklist, *'International Register of Cultivar Names in the Genus Syringa'*, a monumental work. He has been President of the International Lilac Society for several terms and authored many articles on Lilacs. He is one of the world's outstanding lilac authorities today.

It is from continuous building upon one program of breeding lilacs (or any other genus) by several succeeding scientists that such fine progress can be achieved. It is hardly possible in the life-span of one individual. The University of New Hampshire and its Botany-Horticulture programs must be highly commended for the foresight and personnel selection that has made this progress possible. One must visit the lilac plantings at Durham, N.H. to understand the research work in lilacs (New Hampshire's State Flower). One comes away filled with wonder at what is yet to be in the glorious history of the Lilacs!

Lilac introductions from the New Hampshire University Team include:

'Anna Amhoff'—S I, (Yeager 1953) *S.* × *josiflexa*
'Maybelle Farnum'—S VII (Yeager 1961) *S.* × *prestoniae*
'Nellie Bean'—S VII (Yeager 1961) *S.* × *prestoniae*
'Miss Kim'—S II (Meader 1954) *S. patula*
'Agnes Smith'—S I (Rogers 1970) *S.* × *prestoniae*
'Jessie Hepler'—S VI (Rogers 1981) *S.* × *prestoniae*

All are outstanding lilacs, worthy for every garden with space for them.

THE HYBRIDIZING TEAM AT THE ROYAL BOTANICAL GARDENS, Hamilton, Ont., Canada

For several years the hybridizers at the Royal Botanical Gardens have been quietly working to improve *S. vulgaris* cultivars as well as many of the species in series *Villosae* and *Pubescentes*. The extent of their work is tremendous. In 1975 Joan Brown worked at crossing *S. vulgaris* 'Rochester' with 'Primrose' and produced some extraordinary white and colored lilacs with large florets and thryses. None were named, but cultivar No. 7525-17 and No. 75116-16 are among some of the finest lilacs yet produced. These have been further crossed under chief hybridizer Hugh Pearson, assisted by Marjo Belknac, with 'Primrose' in a backcross attempting to capture the elusive 'yellow' of 'Primrose' (work in 1985–1986). Pearson has also continued backcrossing several extremely interesting hybrids of *S. meyeri* × *S. microphylla* 'Superba' and crosses of these with *S. julianae*.

In the late '60s Dr. James Pringle and J. Brown made several interesting crosses of *S. yunannensis* × select cultivars of *S.* × *prestoniae*, *S. reflexa* and *S. tigerstedti* and continued this work under Pringle into the next decade. (These interesting hybrids are described elsewhere under the species lilacs.) Not only are many of these crosses historic, in that some have never been attempted before, but they are extremely well documented and evaluated by Dr. Pringle. Something rarely done by other hybridizers.

When selections of the various crosses are made and named, many new and worthy lilacs should be available for gardens and hybridizers as well. Under the scientific work of Pearson we may yet have large florets and 'yellow'—even if pale yellow—lilacs. (*Mon ami et amie*, keep a watchful eye on this young man's work—it is well worth recognition.)

DR. DONALD EGOLF, A Genius in Hybridizing Plants, U.S. National Arboretum, Washington, D.C.

In the last decade from 1970, almost unnoticed, some very outstanding lilac work has gone forward under the direction of Dr. Donald Egolf at the National Arboretum in Washington D.C. A most extensive survey was made of all available, worthwhile cultivars of *S. vulgaris* and the Early Hybrids, to determine their susceptibility to mildew, a disfiguring, although not fatal, disease of lilacs, which particularly discourages growing them in the warmer middle belt of their range. An effort was made to extend the limits of growing good lilacs farther south by selective hybridization, especially in the Early Flowering Hybrids of *S. vulgaris* × *S. oblata*. In this monumental work Egolf has made exciting crosses using the newest forms of *S. oblata* var. *donaldii* (recently found in Korea) and also *S. oblata* var. *alba*. The latter came from a magnificently flowering clone growing at the National Arboretum from seed brought back some decades ago from China by Frank Meyer, who collected new plants throughout the Far East for the U.S. Department of Agriculture. (See Plant Explorers in China.) These and some of the newest species in the *S. Vulgares* Series Egolf has crossed with the finest of the more recent cultivars of *S. vulgaris*, including 'Rochester.' Although these new Egolf Hybrids have not yet been introduced or critically evaluated, they appear to be among the finest of the Early Hybrids thus far produced. They are in every way equal or superior to the Early Hybrids thus far produced. They are in every way equal or superior to the Early Hybrids of Lemoine and Skinner.

Egolf is one of the country's, if not the world's, leading hybridizers of several genera. His lilac hybridizations have not yet reached the public attention or the acclaim they rightfully deserve. His recent work in growing and selecting several outstanding new forms of *S. oblata* from seed recently collected in Korea and China is exciting for hybridization. These selections I have tentatively call *S. oblata* var. *donaldii* to distinguish them from all other forms of *S. oblata*. Elsewhere I have written of their unique leaf size, texture and deep, rich fall coloring. Continued selection and hybridizing has quietly gone on under the genius of this outstanding plant hybridist. His work with *Viburnum, Lagerstroemia, Pyracantha, Hibiscus* and other plants has been most remarkable and oustanding in its achievements. Truly he is an extraordinary person gifted with rare insights and talents in both plant research and hybridizing. He is the recipient of numerous horticultural awards among which is 'The Directors' Award' of the International Lilac Society, the highest award of the Society for scientific research and hybridizing in Lilacs. The new lilac subspecies, *S. oblata* var. *donaldii*, is tentatively named to honor him for his work with lilacs and many research projects. It is a unique and highly desirable form of *S. oblata*.

REV. FATHER JOHN L. FIALA 1924–
By Professor Robert B. Clark

Reared on an Ohio farm, this "boy", as his father called him, early developed a fondness for plants and horticulture. Before he was sixteen he had already planted his own orchard and had an experimental vegetable and flower garden. At twelve he wrote to Arie den Boer asking him all about flowering crabs, beginning a friendship that lasted until den Boer's death. His professional career was that of a parish priest in the Cleveland diocese, and a professor of Clinical Psychology and Education at John Carroll University for over 21 years. In teaching psychology he needed illustrative materials in genetics, and this brought about the continuation of his early work with plants—especially growing seedlings of controlled pollination, and the use of colchicine in experimenting with tetraploids—with its attendant observation of inheritances.

From his college days he worked with plants on the 'little farm plot' allotted to him from the family acres. Here over 45 years of plant work continued on lilacs, flowering crabs, peonies, hemerocallis, aesculus, various nut trees, oaks and numerous plants—with the lilacs and crabs being the most cherished and receiving the greatest attention. Though his principal duties in education, church administration and as the Bishop's secretary for parishes demanded most of his time—

the work with plants went on. Even after his forced retirement, because of serious illness, in the warmer winters of Florida he continues working with hemerocallis and crape myrtle and grows the seedlings of lilacs and crabs, which are then brought north each April for the spring and summer work in the 'farm acres' known as 'Falconskeape.'

Fr. Fiala is one of the founding directors of the International Lilac Society, which has recognized his work in lilacs with three of its highest awards. He is also the recipient of the Massachusetts Horticultural Society's 'Thomas Roland Medal' for hybridizing achievement. Many of his introductions, being still very new, are not as well known yet but a steady stream of new plants continues to flow from the productive gardens of Falconskeape each year, all of wonderful beauty and outstanding quality. To date over 50 named cultivars of lilacs and 42 named flowering crabs have come from this garden. Hundreds of seedlings are still to be evaluated, many of which are to be introduced, especially in the various hybridization programs that are now seeing some of their peak results. For these we must wait with patient expectation and hope that the good Father's health will permit him to continue his work with plants of all kinds. Most of his introductions are being offered by Ameri-Hort Research Inc. specializing in new plant introductions.

THE LILACS OF FALCONSKEAPE A Postscript by Fr. John L. Fiala

I give but few words on my work with lilacs that have fascinated me in hybridizing for the past forty years. Of the many genera worked with at Falconskeape the Lilacs are among the most interesting. One cannot hybridize any plant without being indebted to an endless number of horticultural and gardening friends who have both built up the gardens with rare plants as well as given encouragement and direction. Thirty-five years ago I read with fascination an article on the use of colchicine on plants to induce polyploids with larger blooms, and the marvelous work done by a Swedish research team using this drug to increase the size of apples. Colchicine was then most difficult to obtain. Despite this, colchicine and I went through a wonderful ten year adventure, filled with false expectations, many disappointments, a great deal of learning and discovering how to use it. Alas, thousands of poor seedlings (some of my best) succumbed to lethal doses in those days! (Elsewhere under 'Plant Propagation' I discuss the use of colchicine on lilacs.) Today only meager results are beginning to show, but I believe in the hands of some younger lilac research hybridist, taking up where an older generation is leaving off, there will still be wonderful results from its use.

One of the great obstacles for anyone working with lilacs, who is not institution affiliated, is the difficulty in obtaining enough species and really fine cultivars to begin a good program of hybridizing. Before the beginnings of the International Lilac Society, it was almost impossible to obtain the lesser known species of lilacs, except for some few offered by exceptional lilac nurseries like Upton's (now defunct) and J. Herbert Alexander. Too many years are wasted in gathering together needed plant materials.

Work with the Lilacs here at Falconskeape over the years (it is an hybridizer's garden and not a display park) has been in several programs: working for new and better cultivars of *S. vulgaris*, especially for a wider range of colors and forms; hybridizing new forms of early hybrids; working with the lesser known species particularly *S. julianae*, *S. komarowii* and *S. wolfii* and their hybrids with other species; the continued work with induced *Syringa* tetraploids and polyploids of all species.

Among the most rewarding and productive has been the work with newer forms of *S. vulgaris* using such cultivars as 'Rochester', 'Agincourt Beauty', 'St. Joan', 'Flora' and several others including some of my own like 'Pat Pesata' and 'Professor Robert B. Clark.' Work has also included the combining of several species in the 'multibrids.' There is much promise in perfecting and selecting the best results of this multibrid hybridizing.

Undoubtedly much improvement will come from using some of the newer forms of *S. oblata* var. *donaldii* and from other sources (The Holden Arboretum, Arnold Arboretum's latest explorations and seed introductions, and from the Roger Luce seedlings). What exciting new Early Hybrids could be had by using 'Rochester' on these newest forms? There is also much to be had from many of the wonderful old cultivars—many of which have rarely or never been used in hybridizing but have wonders locked in their genetic backgrounds—e.g. 'De Croncels' with its copper buds and rose copper petals, 'True Blue' with its magnificent bloom and color, 'Coerulea Superba' with its true blue genes or 'Marlyensis pallida' with its form and soft pastel colors! Today there is so much to work with and so many seedlings to evaluate and countless hybridizing programs to begin—a veritable hybridizer's paradise!

(*Mon ami et amie*, one would wish he were forty years younger—but 'kismet', the ancient Parcae Sisters are still at it—spinning, weaving and cutting off the threads of life ever shorter for us all—would that they take a vacation from it all and leave us to longer work and enjoy our lilacs!)

A goodly number of lilacs, both *S. vulgaris* crosses, hybrids of early and late species, multi-brids and tetraploids have been named and introduced here at Falconskeape. They include the following:

S. vulgaris cultivars

'Albert Holden', 1980, S-II, 'Sarah Sands' × 'Reaumur'
'Aloise', 1968, S-I, 'Flora' × 'Flora'
'Arch McKean', 1984, S-VI, 'Agincourt Beauty' × 'Rochester'
'Atheline Wilbur', 1980, D-Vi, ('Rochester' × 'Edward J. Gardner') × 'Rochester'
'Avalanche', 1983, S-I, 'Flora' × 'Carley'
'Bluebird', 1969, S-III, 'Gismonda' × 'Rustica'
'Blue Danube', 1986, S-III, 'Rochester' × 'True Blue'
'Blue Delft', 1982, S-III, 'Mrs. August Belmont' × 'Rochester'
'Bluets', 1979, S-III, 'General Sherman' × 'Mrs. August Belmont'
'Blue Giant', 1977, S-III, 'Flora' × 'True Blue'
'Dr. Joel Margaretten', 1983, S-VII, 'Prodige' × 'Rochester'
'Dr. John Rankin', 1979, S-II, 'Glory' × 'Flora'
'Drifting Dream', 1985, D-II, 'Rochester' × 'Rochester Seedling'
'Elsie Lenore', 1982, S-VI, tetraploid, 'Sensation' × 'Sensation'
'Emery Mae Norweb', 1980, D-I, 'Gismonda' × 'Flora'
'Flow Blue', 1980, S-III, 'True Blue' × 'Mrs. August Belmont'
'Gertrude Clark', 1984, S-I, 'Rochester' × 'Rochester' Seedling
'Glacier', 1981, D-I, ('Gismonda' × 'Flora') × 'Rochester'
'Holy Maid', 1984, S-V, Macrostachya × 'Rochester'
'Hosanna', 1969, D-II, 'Gismonda' × 'Rustica'
'Joel', 1981, S-V, 'General Sherman' × 'Flora'
'Lalique', 1983, S-III, 'True Blue' × 'Rochester'
'Little Miss Muffet', 1977, S-VI, dwarf, 'Mrs. Edward Harding' × Macrostachya'
'Lois Utley', 1986, D-V, 'Rochester' × 'Mrs. Antoine Buchner'
'Lourene Wishart', 1980, D-V, 'Rochester' × 'Edward J. Gardner'
'Lullaby', 1983, D-IV, 'Rochester' × 'Gismonda'
'Marie Frances', 1983, S-V, 'Edward J. Gardner' × 'Rochester'
'Midnight', 1984, S-VII, 'Agincourt Beauty' × 'Violet Glory'
'Mollie Ann', 1981, S-IV, 'Rochester' × 'Violet Glory'
'Mother Louise', 1969, D-I, 'Carley' × 'Flora'
'Munchkin', 1981, S-III, 'True Blue' × 'Rochester'
'Pat Pesata', 1981, S-III, 'Rochester' × 'True Blue'
'Pauline Fiala', 1983, S-II, 'Sensation' × 'Flora'
'Pixie', 1981, S-I, dwarf, 'Rochester' × 'Rochester'
'Porcelain Blue', 1979, S-III, 'Rochester' × 'Mrs. August Belmont'
'Professor Robert Clark', 1982, S-I, ('Rochester' × 'Edward J. Gardner') × 'Rochester'
'Radiance', 1985, D-V, 'Rochester' × 'Elsie Lenore'
'Rhapsody', 1983, S-III, 'Rochester' × 'Mrs. August Belmont'
'Sacrament', 1985, S-I, 'Rochester' × 'Primrose'
'Saint Jerzy Popieluszko', 1985, S-VI, 'Prodige' × 'Rochester'
'Satin Cloud', 1985, S-I, 'Rochester' × 'Elsie Lenore'
'Sculptured Ivory', 1985, S-I, 'Rochester' × 'Primrose'
'Seafoam', 1985, D-I, 'Rochester' × octoploid seedling
'Sea Storm', 1983, S-III, 'Flora' × 'Mrs. August Belmont'
'Shimmering Sea', 1984, S-III, 'Elsie Lenore' × 'Rochester'
'Snow Cap', 1985, S-I, 'Rochester' × 'Professor Robert Clark'
'Snow Princess', 1984, D-I, 'Rochester' × 'Mother Louise'
'Sonnet', 1982, S-IV, 'Mrs. August Belmont' × 'Flora'
'Spring Parade', 1984, S-IV, 'Rochester' × seedling
'Starlight', 1985, S-I, 'Rochester' × 'Primrose'

'Swansdown', 1983, S-I, 'Rochester' × 'Atheline Wilbur'
'Talisman', 1984, S-VI, 'Sarah Sands' × 'Rochester'
'Thunderbolt', 1985, S-VII, 'Prodige' × 'Rochester'
'Tiffany Blue', 1983, S-III, 'True Blue' × 'Mrs. August Belmont'
'Wedgwood Blue', 1981, S-III, 'Rochester' × 'Mrs. August Belmont'
'Windsong', 1984, S-V, 'Rochester' × 'Elsie Lenore'
'Winner's Circle', 1985, D-VI, 'Rochester' × 'Mrs. W. E. Marshall'
'Yankee Doodle', 1985, S-VII, 'Prodige' × 'Rochester'

S. × hyacinthiflora introductions:
'Alice Chieppo', 1984, D-IV, *S. oblata dilatata* × 'Rochester'
'Mary Short, 1979, D-V, 'Pocahontas' × 'Esther Staley'
'Eventide', 1981, S-II, 'Pocahontas' × 'Marechal Foch'

S. julianae introductions
S. julianae 'Epaulettes, 1984, S-VI, *S. julianae* × *S. julianae* 'George Eastman'
S. julianae 'Pink Parasol', 1983, S-V, *S. julianae* 'Hers' × *S. julianae* 'George Eastman'
S. julianae 'Sentinel', 1983, S-V, *S. julianae* 'Hers' × *S. julianae* 'George Eastman'

S. oblata 'Wild Fire', 1984, S-IV

Late Lilac Hybrids and Multibrids
S. × 'Eventide', 1980, S-II, 'Garden Peace' × 'Lark Song'
S. × 'Dancing Druid', 1968, S-VI, (*S. yunnanensis* × *S. tomentella*) × *S. komarowii*
S. × 'Garden Peace', 1970, S-V, *S. komarowii* × *S. wolfii*, (*S.* × *clarkiana*)
S. tomentella 'Kum-Bum', 1969, S-II, induced colchicine mutation, golden leaves.
S. × 'Lark Song', 1963, S-V, *S.* × *tribrida*, *S.* × *swegitella* (*S. sweginzowii* × *S. tomentella*)
   × *S. komarowii*. 'Lark Song' is the type for *S.* × *tribrida*
S. yunnanensis 'Prophecy', 1969, S-II, induced tetraploid form
S. × 'Quartet', 1984, S-IV, *S.* × *quadrobrida*
S. × 'Spellbinder', 1968, S-V, *S.* × *clarkiana*, the type, (*S. komarowii* × *S. wolfii*)
S. × 'Springtime', 1968, S-V, *S.* × *fialiana*, the type, (*S.* × *swegitella* × *S. wolfii*)
S. × 'Snowdrift', 1984, S-I, (*S.* × *prestoniae* × *S.* × *josiflexa*) × *S.* × *prestoniae*
S. × 'Sunrise', 1968, S-V, *S.* × *fialiana*
S. × 'Royal Crown', 1958, S-IV, *S. tigerstedtii* × *S.* × *swegitella*
S. × 'Tong Yong', 1985, S-II, *S. tigerstedtii* × (*S. yunnanensis* × *S.* × *prestoniae* 'Isabella')
S. × 'Ling Tong', 1987, S-II, *S. tigerstedtii* × (*S. yunnanensis* × *S.* × *prestoniae* 'Isabella')
S. × 'High Lama', 1987, S-IV, (*S.* × *josiflexa* 'Royalty' × *S. komarowii*)

S. reticulata Hybrid
S. reticulata 'Chinese Magic', 1987, S-I, *S. reticulata* × *S. pekinensis*

Appendices

Appendices

APPENDIX A

Lilacs in Floral Arrangements

Lilacs make excellent floral arrangements. Their beauty is unsurpassed when used skillfully with other spring flowers. However, one must be certain that lilacs as cut flowers are properly prepared. Effective preparation methods have been outlined by Barbara Laking (wife of the former Director of the Royal Botanical Gardens, Hamilton Ontario, Dr. Leslie Laking). She is an authority on handling lilacs. Following is a summary of her preparation of plant materials for fresh flower design.

To prolong the rather short life of cut plant materials in fresh flower designs it is essential to make sure that the rate of transpiration does not exceed the amount of water entering the stem, and that conducting vessels do not become clogged up with bacteria.

Always carry a bucket of warm water into the garden, and place the flowers and foliage as you cut them directly into it. Stems have a greater surface area for water absorption if they are cut on the slant with a sharp knife or sharp secateurs.

Plant material cut at the end of the day will contain maximum food reserves. This enables the detached part to last longer in water, and also gives the maximum time for hardening the material.

All fresh plant material must be hardened before using it in designs. Hardening means placing stems in deep warm (not hot) water for at least four hours, longer if possible. All the foliage and prickles, if present, should be removed from the lower half of the flower stems before placing them in warm water. During the hardening process the material is kept in a cool, dark, humid, draught-free place.

Some material is very difficult to harden and requires an extra treatment, or treatments, to boost water absorption, which is termed conditioning. To condition plant material the following procedures will be helpful:

Flower Stems

Flower stems are usually conditioned according to the type of stem.

1. **Milky stems**   Char freshly cut base of stem with a match or candle, or place freshly cut base of stem in boiling water for ten seconds. Repeat if the stem is re-cut.
2. **Hard stems**   Make a vertical slit 2″ up the stem with a sharp knife or secateurs. Place in warm water.
3. **Woody stems**   Remove bark from the lower 2″ of the stem. Slit vertically with a sharp knife or secateurs, or crush with a hammer the lower 2″ of the stem. Place in warm water.

To reduce water loss through transpiration, plants with woody stems, e.g., buddleia, lilac, philadelphus, should be defoliated, leaving only foliage near the flower heads. Removing some of the foliage from all woody material is a good general practice.

Foliage

Large leaves, e.g. Boston fern, hosta, rhubarb and some trailing plants like ivy, wilt rapidly when cut. As foliage absorbs water through its surface as well as its stem, totally immerse such foliage overnight in cold water before using in designs.

Tulips

To keep tulip stems straight and foliage crisp looking wrap newspaper around the stems up to the flower heads and place in deep warm water.

Wilted Flowers

When a stem is cut from a plant air enters the cut end. The air bubbles increase the longer the stem is out of water. The resultant airlock prevents water from entering the stem. Placing newly cut stems in a bucket of warm water in the garden greatly reduces the formation of airlocks.

To increase the water content of a wilted stem, cut off 1"–2" of the stem under water to remove airlock and then immediately place the end of the stem in 1" of hot water for half an hour. Add warm water to cover as much of the stem as possible.

Flowers and leaves must be protected from steam with tissue paper or a towel before the hot water treatment commences.

(Courtesy of Barbara Laking)

Another method of preparing lilac flowers for exhibition is:
1. Cut flowers late in the evening prior to exhibiting them.
2. Crush 3" of the base stem with a hammer.
3. Place immediately into a mixture of 2 ounces of Clorox (bleach) to 1 gallon of cold water. Leave lilac blooms in this solution overnight.
4. Next morning, prior to exhibiting, place blooms in cold water arranging the floral display. (Clorox solution is more effective than Floral Life and similar products available at floral shops when preparing lilacs.

For holding bloom for shipment the United States Dept. of Agriculture suggests:
1. Choose floral spikes that are in full and beginning-to-open bud (not full blown).
2. In shipping keep flowers at 40° to 50°F. and wrapped in Kraft paper or polyethylene plastic sheeting.
3. Upon arrival flower spikes should be held in 74°F water in which 400 parts per million of the preservative 8—hydroxyquinoline citrate (available commercially) plus 3% sucrose (sugar) has been added.

(This method is entirely new for lilacs, but it does merit the trial for those who must ship lilacs any distance.) It would seem lilacs for shipment should be hardened as per above before preparing for shipment.

APPENDIX B

A List of Lilac Hybridizers and Originators to 1988

The following list incorporates the work of John C. Wister in *'Lilacs for America'* 1953 and my updating working with John Wister from 1969 to 1975, together with additions from contemporary sources to 1988. Only brief identifications are made; dates are not always known or available.

Alexander, John Herbert Sr., (189__–1977) Nurseryman, Middleboro, Mass., U.S.A. Selected and introduced several lilacs.

Anderson, Edgar Shannon (1897–1969), Botanist, U.S.A.

Audibert, Frères, (circa 1831), Nurseryman in Tonnelle near Tarascon, France.

Baldwin, C. E. (no date), Nurseryman, Omaha, Nebraska, U.S.A.

Baltet, (circa 1700) Nurseryman and breeder, founder of famous Baltet Nursery 1720, at Troyes, France.

Barbier, et Fils, Nursery operated from 1845–1931, Orléans, France.

Barnes, Franklin Lockwood and Alice Gee Barnes (Mrs. F. L.) contemporaries, Fruit farmer Julian, California, U.S.A.

Barnes, Laura Legett (Mrs. Albert C.) (1873–1966) Horticulturist, Merion Station, Penn., U.S.A.

Baudriller, (1880s to 1920) Nurseryman, Gennes (Main-et-Loire), France.

Becker, Gilbert, contemporary, Climax, Michigan, U.S.A.

Bensch, Reinhold, (?–1912) Nurseryman, Dürrgoy near Breslau (now Wroclaw), Silesia, Germany (now Poland).

Berdeen, Kenneth (1907–1987) Breeder, Engineer, Kennebunk, Maine, U.S.A.

Berniau, L., (circa 1854) Nurseryman, Orléans, France.

Bibikova, V. F. (contemporary), Horticulturist, Central Botanical Garden, Minsk, Byelorussia, U.S.S.R.

Billiard, M. Charles (no dates), Nurseryman, Fontenay-aux-Roses, near Paris, France.

Blacklock, Mary Eliza, (1860–1956) Horticulturist, Rowancroft Gardens, Meadowvale, Ontario, Canada.

Block, Allan F., (contemporary), Nurseryman, Romulus, Michigan, U.S.A.

Boice, Dorothy Wardell (Mrs. Van Ness L.) (contemporary), Salt Point, New York, U.S.A.

Brahy-Ekenholm, (circa 1850), Nurserymen, Herstal near Liège, Belgium.

Brand, Archie Mack, (1871–1953), Horticulturist and peony breeder, Faribault, Minnesota, U.S.A.

Briot, Pierre Louis ("Charles"), (1804–1888), Nurseryman, Trianon-Versailles near Paris, France.

Brown, Joan, (contemporary), hybridizer, R.B.G. Hamilton, Ont. Canada.

Bruchet, (circa 1890), Nurseryman, St. Rambery-sur-Loire (Loire), France.

Bugala, Wladyslaw (contemporary), Horticulturist and plant breeder, Kornik Arboretum, Kornik, Poland.

Buis, Weduwe C. & Zoon, Nurserymen, Aalsmeer, the Netherlands.

Case, B. O., (?–1936), Vancouver, Washington, U.S.A.

Cassegrain, R., (no dates), Director, Grandes Roseraies du Val & de la Loire, Orléans, France.

Castle, Minerva S., (1890–1976), Horticulturist, Rowancroft Gardens, Meadowvale, Ontario, Canada.

Chenault, Léon, (1853–1930), Nurseryman, Orléans, France.

Child, Harold L., (contemporary), Dixfield, Maine, U.S.A.

Clark Robert Brown, (contemporary), Botanist and horticultural author, Birchwood Garden, Meredith, New Hampshire, U.S.A.

Clarke, Walter Bosworth (1876–1953), Nurseryman and Horticulturist, W. B. Clarke & Co; succeeded by J. Clarke Nursery Co., James F. Clarke (contemporary), Nurseryman, San Jose, California, U.S.A.

Cochet, Pierre (before 1885), Nurseryman, (Grisu-Suisnes, Seine-et-Marne), Suisnes, France.

Crayton, F. M. & Sons, Nursery, Biltmore, North Carolina, U.S.A.

Cumming, William Archibald, (contemporary), Horticulturist and hybridizer, (formerly Research Station), Morden, Manitoba, Canada.

Darimont (see Libert-Darimont)

Dauvesse Nursery, Orléans, France.

deBelder, Robert and Jelena (contemporary), Horticulturists, Kalmthout Arboretum, Kalmthout, Belgium.

Delcor, (circa 1945), Nurseryman, Lebbeke, Belgium.

deWilde, Robert C., (contemporary), Raleigh, North Carolina, U.S.A.

Dougall, James, (1810–1888), Nurseryman, Windsor, Ontario.

Draps, (circa 1945), Nurseryman, Koningsloo near Brussels, Belgium.

Dubois, (no dates), Nurseryman, France.

Dunbar, John, (1859–1927), Horticulturist, Rochester Parks, Rochester, New York, U.S.A.

Eaton, Mark M., (contemporary), formerly of Glen Head, New York, selected and named some of T. A. Havemeyer's originations (Havemeyer & Eaton), Coco Beach, Florida, U.S.A.

Egolf, Dr. Donald, Botanist, hybridizer, Plant Research, U.S. National Arboretum, Washington, D.C., (contemporary), Upper Marlboro, Maryland, U.S.A.

Egorova, M., (contemporary), Horticulturist, U.S.S.R.

Eichler, Moritz, (circa 1862), Nurseryman, Chemnitz (now Karl-Marx-Stadt), Germany.

Ellwanger & Barry, George Ellwanger (1816–1906) & Patrick Barry (1816–1890), Nurserymen, Mount Hope Nursery, Rochester, New York, U.S.A.

Farr, Bertrand, H., (1863–1924), Nurseryman, Farr Nursery Co., Wyomissing, Penn., U.S.A.

Felix & Dykhuis Nursery, Boskoop, the Netherlands.

Fenicchia, Richard A., (contemporary), Horticulturist at Monroe County Parks, Rochester, N.Y., now at Webster, New York. U.S.A.

Fiala, Rev. John Lee, (contemporary), Horticulturist, hybridizer, author, Falconskeape, Medina, Ohio and Ocala, Florida, U.S.A.

Franklin, Alonzo Barry, (1858–1944), Nurseryman, Minneapolis, Minnesota, U.S.A.

Franklin, Mabel Lucille, (contemporary), Horticulturist, Minnetonka, Minnesota, U.S.A.

Froebel, Otto, (1841–1906), Nurseryman, Zürich, Switzerland.

Gardner, Edward J., (1891–1952), & Robert L. Gardner (contemporary), Nurserymen, Horicon, Wisconsin, U.S.A.

Gathoye, (no dates), Nurseryman, Bayards, lez-Liège, Belgium.

Giellis, Louis (no dates), Nurseryman, Brussels, Belgium.

Gireoud, Friedrich August Herman, (1821–18960), Horticulturist, Sagan, Silesia, Germany, (now Zagan, Poland).

Gouchault, Auguste, (1851–1936), Nurseryman, Orléans, France.

Gram, Kai, (1897–1961), Botanist, University of Copenhagen, Denmark.

Grant, Alvan R., (contemporary), Horticulturist, (formerly Director Monroe County Parks, Rochester, N.Y.), Rochester, N.Y., U.S.A.

Grigor'ev, A., (contemporary), Horticulturist, U.S.S.R.

Grunewald, Friedrich, (circa 1910), Nurseryman, Zossen, Brandenburg, Germany.

Hancock, Marcus Leslie, (1892–1977), Nurseryman, Woodland Nursery, Mississauga, Ontario, Canada.

Hathaway Nurseries, Visalia, California, U.S.A.

Hauck, Cornelius John, (1893–1976), Industrialist, Cincinnati, Ohio, U.S.A.

Havemeyer, Theodore Augustus, (1868–1936), Industrialist and horticulturist, hybridizer, nurseryman, Brookville, Long Island, New York, U.S.A. (Havemeyer-Eaton) (Havemeyer-Sears).

Hawkins, Roy Frank, (1886–1972) Farmer, La Porte City, Iowa, U.S.A.

Henry, Louis, (1854–1903), Horticulturist & Director, Museum of Natural History, Paris, France.

Henry Mary Gibson (Mrs. J. Norman Henry), (1885–1967, Horticulturist, Gladwyne, Penn., U.S.A.

Hers, Joseph (in 1920s), Engineer, Belgium.

Hesse, Herman A., (contemporary), Nurseryman, Weemer-Emms, Germany.

Hetz, Charles W., (1906–1953), Nurseryman, Fairview Evergreen Nurseries, Fairview, Penn., U.S.A.

Hilborn, Ernest Carroll, (1876–1953), Nurseryman, Northwest Nursery Co., Valley City, North Dakota, U.S.A.

Hildreth, Audrey Clare, (1893–1975), Horticulturist, Denver, Colorado, U.S.A.

Hohman, Henry J., (189?–1978), Nurseryman, Kingsville Nursery, Kingsville, Maryland, U.S.A.

Hoser, Peter, (1857–1939), Horticulturist, Warsaw, Poland.

Judd, William H., (188?–1946), Horticulturist, botanist, Arnold Arboretum, Jamaica Plains, Massachusetts, U.S.A.

Jurković, Mato, (contemporary) Botanist, University of Zagreb, Zagreb, Yugoslavia.

Karpow-Lipski, Mikolaj, (contemporary), Plant breeder, Konczewice near Chelmza, Poland.

Keesen, K. Jr., (no dates), Flower grower, Aalsmeer, the Netherlands.

Keesen, W. Jr., (contemporary) W. Keesen Jr. & Zonen, Terra Nova Nursery, Aalsmeer, the Netherlands.

Kelsey, Harlan P., (contemporary) Horticulturist, (Boxford, Mass.), U.S.A.

Kenis, Dr. Edmond, (18__–1952), Horticulturist, Essen, Belgium.

Kettler, Fred, (contemporary), Nurseryman, Plattersville, Wisconsin, U.S.A.

Klager, Hulda Thiel, (1865–1960), Horticulturist, and hybridizer, Woodland, Washington, U.S.A.

Klettenberg, A. J., (1867–1937), Nurseryman, Forest near Brussels, Belgium.

Klimenko, V. and Z. Klimenka, (contemporaries), Horticulturists U.S.S.R.

Kolesnikov, Leonid Alekseevitch, (1893–1973), Horticulturist, and hybridizer, Moscow, U.S.S.R.

Koster, M. & Sons, (contemporary), Nurserymen, Boskoop, the Netherlands.

Kravchenko, L., (contemporary), Horticulturist, U.S.S.R.

Lambert, Peter, (1859–1939), Nurseryman and rose hybridizer, Trier, Germany.

Lambrechts, Pierre, (contemporary), Waterloo, Belgium.

Lammerts, Walter Edwards, (contemporary), Plant breeder, Freedom, California, U.S.A.

Lape, Fred, (1891–1985), Horticulturist, George Landis Arboretum, Esperance, New York, U.S.A.

Lavrov, S. V., (contemporary), Horticulturist, Kharkov, Ukraine, U.S.S.R.

Lecointe, (circa 1890), Nurseryman, Louveciennes, France.

Lefievre, Adolphe, (circa 1874), Nurseryman, Nantes, France.

Legraye, Mme. Marie, (1840–1879), Florist, Liège, Belgium.

Lemke, A. H., (1868–1946), Horticulturist, Wausau, Wisconsin, U.S.A.

Lemoine, Emile, (1862–1943), Horticulturist and Nurseryman, V. Lemoine et Fil, Nancy, France.

Lemoine, Henri, (contemporary), Nurseryman, V. Lemoine et Fil (firm closed 1954), Nancy, France.

Lemoine, Mons. Victor et Madame, (Victor 1823–1911), Horticulturists, hybridizer, Nurseryman, founder V. Lemoine et Fil Nursery, Nancy, France.

Leroy, André, (1801–1875), Nurseryman, Angers, France.

Leslie, William Russel, (contemporary), Horticulturist, (formerly at Research Station), Morden, Manitoba, Canada.

Libert-Darimont, (circa 1843), Horticulturist, Thiers-a-Liège, Belgium.

Liberton, Leon, (no dates), Louvain, Belgium.

Löbner, Max, (1869–1947), Horticulturist, Bonn, Germany.

Loddiges, Conrad, (1738–1826), Nurseryman, Hackney near London, England.

Lombarts, Petrus (Pierre) Arnoldes Franciskus Maria, (1873–1949), Nurseryman, Zundert, the Netherlands.

Lumley, Prof. Albert Ernest, (1904–1979), Horticulturist, Pelham near Amherst, Massachusetts, U.S.A.

Lyapunova, N. A., (contemporary), Horticulturist, Central Republic's Botanical Garden, Kiev, Ukraine, U.S.S.R. (see Rubtzov, Zhogoleva & Lyapunova).

Lyden, Cora Lindsey, (1892–1982), Plant grower, North Monmouth, Massachusetts and late of San Diego, California, U.S.A.

Maarse, Dirk Eveleens, (1881–1975), Nurseryman and hybridizer, Aalsmeer, the Netherlands.

Maarse, Gerrit (no dates), Nurseryman, Aalsmeer, the Netherlands.

Maarse, H., (no dates), Nurseryman, Aalsmeer, the Netherlands.

Maarse, J. D. & Son, Nurserymen, Aalsmeer, the Netherlands.

Maarse, P. & G., Maarse Bros. (no date), Nurserymen, Aalsmeer, the Netherlands.

Machet & Josem Nursery, (no dates), Châlons-sur-Marne, France.

Mahaux, Jean (contemporary), Horticulturist, Brussels, Belgium.

Makoy, Jacob & Co. (contemporary), Nurserymen, Liège, Belgium.

Margaretten, Dr. Joel, (contemporary), Horticulturists and Flower Grower, Leona Valley, California, U.S.A.

Mathieu, Leon, (?–1916), Nurseryman, Louvain, Belgium.

Meader, Elwyn M., (contemporary), Horticulturist and hybridizer, Univ. of New Hampshire, Durham, and Rochester, New Hampshire, U.S.A.

Mel'nik, A., (contemporary), Horticulturist, U.S.S.R.

Mikhailov, Nikolai L., (contemporary), Horticulturist, Main Botanical Garden, Moscow, U.S.S.R. (see Shtan'ko & Mikhailov).

Miller, Philip, (1691–1771) Horticulturist, Chelsea Physic Garden, London, England.

Morel, Francesque, (operated circa 1880–1910), Nurseryman, Lyons, France.

Morel, Georges Michel, (1916–1973), Plant physiologist, Le Chesnay, France.

Morren, Charles Jacques Edouard, (1833–1886), Botanist-horticulturist, Liège, Belgium.

Nelen, Louis, (no dates), Nurseryman, Essen, Belgium.

Nelson, Dr. Caspar L., (1886–1970), formerly of North Dakota Agricultural College, Fargo, North Dakota, U.S.A.

Niemetz, C. F., (no dates), Horticulturist, Temesvár, Hungary.

Notcutt, R. C., (contemporary) R. C. Notcutt Ltd. Nurseryman, Woodbridge, Suffolk, England.

Oakes, Walter (contemporary), Dixfield, Maine, U.S.A.

Oliemans Brothers, (no date), Nurserymen, Aalsmeer, the Netherlands.

Oliver, A. A., (contemporary), Mt. Eden, California, U.S.A.

Olsen, Aksel, (contemporary), Nurseryman, Kolding, Denmark, (Olsen & Gram).

Oudin, P. den, (operating circa 1846), Nurseryman, Lisieux (Calvados), France.

Paterson, Mrs. Frank, (d. circa 1967), horticulturist and hybridizer, Scarborough, Ontario, Canada.

Pfitzer, Wilhelm, (1821–1905), Nurseryman, Stuttgart, Germany.

Phair, Philip D., (contemporary), Grower, Presque Isle, Maine, U.S.A.

Piet, Gebroeders Piet Nursery, (contemporary), Aalsmeer, the Netherlands.

Pillow, James, (contemporary), Cold Spring-on Hudson, New York, U.S.A.

Pokluda, Joseph John, (contemporary), Nurseryman, Sheridan Nurseries, Norval, Ontario, Canada.

Polin, Edward Gustav, (1881–1965), Grower, Charlestown, New York, U.S.A.

Potutova, E., (contemporary), Horticulturist, U.S.S.R.

Preston, Isabella, (1881–1965), Horticulturist and hybridizer, Central Experimental Farm, Ottawa, Ontario, Canada.

Prince, William Robert, (1795–1869), Nurseryman, Flushing, Long Island, New York, U.S.A.

Pringle, Dr. James, (contemporary), Taxonomist, R.B.G. Hamilton, Canada.

Proefstation voor de Bloemisterij (Research Station for Floriculture), Aalsmeer, the Netherlands.

Radermacher, Peter, (contemporary), Nurseryman, Bonn, Germany.

Rankin, Dr. John Paul, (1891–1967), Physician, horticulturist, Elyria, Ohio, U.S.A.

Renaud, (no dates), Horticulturist, Nantes, France.

Robinson, Edward George, (contemporary), Nurseryman, Gaybird Nursery, Wawanesa, Manitoba, Canada.

Rogers, Dr. Owen Maurice, (contemporary), Horticulturist, hybridizer, author, plant research, University of New Hampshire, Durham, New Hampshire, U.S.A.

Rolph, Henry ("Harry") Macdonald, (1886–1977), Farmer, Markham, Ontario, Canada.

Romanova, V., (contemporary), Horticulturist, U.S.S.R.

Rottert, H., (no dates), Nurseryman, Stenger & Rottert, Erfurt, Germany.

Rubtzov, L. I., (contemporary), Horticulturist, Central Republic's Botanical Garden, Kiev, Ukraine, U.S.S.R. (Rubtzov, Zhogoleva & Lyapunova).

Ruliffson, Raymond J., (contemporary), Rochester, New York, U.S.A.

Sakharova, A., (contemporary), Horticulturist, U.S.S.R.

Santa Ines Nursery, Nos near Santiago, Chile.

Sass, Henry E., (contemporary), Farmer and plant breeder, Benson Station, Omaha, Nebraska, U.S.A.

Sass, Hans Peter, (1868–1949), Farmer and plant breeder, Midwest Gardens, Elkhorn, Nebraska, U.S.A.

Sass, Jacob, (1872–1945), Farmer and plant breeder, Benson Station, Omaha, Nebraska, U.S.A.

Schloen, John, (?–1978), Horticulturist, Brooklin, Ontario, Canada.

Scott, Edith Wilder (Mrs. Authur Hoyt), (1875–1960), Media, Pennsylvania, U.S.A.

Seabury, Alton, (contemporary), Little Compton, Rhode Island, U.S.A.

Sears, Thomas V., (contemporary), Horticulturist, formerly Glen Head, New York, U.S.A., selected and named some of T. A. Havemeyer's introductions (Havemeyer & Sears).

Shtan'ko, I. I., (contemporary), Horticulturist Principal Botanic Garden, Moscow, U.S.S.R.

Simon, Francisque Henri, (no dates), Nurseryman, Charbonnières-les-Bains (Rhône), France.

Simon-Louis, Leon Louis, (Leon Louis Simon-Louis), (1834–1913), Nurseryman, Simon-Louis Frères & Cie, Bruyères-le-Chatel, Alsace, France.

Sinai, Friedrich, (1863–1930), Frankfort on Main, Germany.

Skinner, Dr. Frank Leith, (1882–1967), Horticulturist hybridizer, nurseryman, Skinner's Nursery, Dropmore, Manitoba, Canada.

Slater, Leonard Kelvey, (19__–1982), Amateur horticulturist, Agincourt, Ontario, Canada.

Slock, Jette St. Pierre, (contemporary), Horticulturist, Central Botanical Garden, Minsk, Byelorussia, U.S.S.R. (see Bibikova, Smol'skii & Bibikova)

Sobeck, John (contemporary), Grower, California, U.S.A.

Späth, Ludwig, (nursery founded 1720, now defunct), Nurseryman, Berlin, Germany.

Stashkevitch, N. S., (contemporary), Horticulturist, U.S.S.R.

Steffen, Alexander, (contemporary), Erfurt, Germany.

Stepman-de Messemaeker Nursery, Florent Stepman (died before 1917), Nurseryman, Brussels, Belgium.

Stone, Elizabeth (Mrs. Ralph Stone), (contemporary), Breeder, gardener, Ashland, Ohio, U.S.A.

Temple, F. L., (contemporary), Nurseryman, Shady HIll Nursery, defunct, Cambridge, Massachusetts, U.S.A.

Theidel, R., (contemporary), Nurseryman, Hinsdale Nursery, Hinsdale, Illinois, U.S.A.

Timm, (W. Germany).

Towson, Towson Nursery, Towson, Maryland, U.S.A.

Transon Frères Nursery, Orleans, France.

Tulp, P. Tulp & Son Nursery, (contemporary), Aalsmeer, the Netherlands.

Upitis, Peteris, (1896–1976), Plant breeder, Dobele, Latvia, S.S.R.

Upton, Edward A., (1875–1959), Horticulturist, plant breeder, nurseryman, Upton Nursery (defunct), Detroit, Michigan, U.S.A.

Utley, William A. & Lois Devereaux Utley, (contemporaries), Growers, Grape Hill Gardens, Clyde, New York, U.S.A.

Vaigla, Adolph, (contemporary), Horticulturist, College of Horticulture, Räpina, Estonia, S.S.R.

Vandendriessche, Henri, (no dates), Nivelles, Belgium.

van der Bom, Th., (no dates), Oudenbosch, the Netherlands.

van Houtte, Louis, (1810–1876), Horticulturist, Ghent, Belgium.

van Nes, C. B. & Sons, Nurserymen, (contemporary), Boskoop, the Netherlands.

van Tol, Jan, (no dates), Nurseryman, Boskoop, the Netherlands.

Varin, H., (lived circa 1777), Horticulturist, Botanical Gardens, Rouen, France.

Vekhov, N., (contemporary), Horticulturist, U.S.S.R.

Verhoeven, Henri, (no dates), Brussels, Belgium.

Vukićević, (contemporary) Botanist, Botanical Gardens, Zagreb, Yugoslavia.

Wallace, John A., (contemporary), Nurseryman, Beaverlodge Nursery, Beaverlodge, Alberta, Canada.

Wiles, H. N., (contemporary), Dayton, Ohio, U.S.A.

Wilke, Rudolph, (no dates), Nurseryman, Hortensteiner Baumschullen, Berlin, Germany.

Wilson, Ernest H., (1876–1930), Plant explorer, horticulturist, Arnold Arboretum, Jamaica Plain, Massachusetts, U.S.A.

Willmott, J. Jr., (no dates), England.

Yaeger, Albert Franklin, (1892–1961), Plant breeder, University of New Hampshire, Durham, New Hampshire, U.S.A.

Zhogoleva, Valentina Grigorivna, (contemporary), Horticulturist, Central Republic's Botanical Garden, Kiev, Ukraine, U.S.S.R. (see Rubtzov, Zhogoleva & Lyapunova).

Noted Lilac Species Discoveries, Plant Explorers, Introducers of Species or Lilac Botanists

Anderson, Edgar, 1897–1969, botanist and writer, U.S.A.

Belon, Pierre, lived around 1554, botanical author of 'Observations', France.

Berezovski, Michael Michaelovich, Russian botanist and plant explorer, zoologist of Grigor Potanin's expedition into China in 1891 to 1894, (U.S.S.R.).

Bretschneider, Dr. Emil, physician to the Russian legation in Peking; plantsman, botanical descriptions of new species, lived 1833–1901, (U.S.S.R.).

Bunge, Alexander, Russian botanist and plant explorer in Northern China in 1831, (U.S.S.R.).

David, Armand, 1826–1900, French Jesuit missionary and botanist explorer in China, France.

deBelder, Robert and Jelena, contemporary, horticulturists, Kalmthout Arboretum, Kalmthout, Belgium.

Delavay, Abbé Jeân Marie, 1834–1895, French Jesuit missionary-botanist, plant explorer in China, France.

D'Incarville, Pierre, 1706–1757, French Jesuit missionary-botanist, plant explorer in China's interior provinces, France.

Egolf, Donald, Plant research, National Arboretum, Washington, D.C., U.S.A.

Farrer, Reginald, plant explorer in China in 1914, from England.

Forrest, George, collected plants including lilacs in Yunnan Province, China in 1906; from Scotland.

Fortune, Robert, made four plant explorations to China and Asia from 1845 to 1860, from England.

Giraldi, Fr. Giuseppe, missionary, botanist, plant collector working in Shensi Province, China, from 1890 to 1895; from Italy.

Hers, Joseph, plant explorer and businessman collecting plants in China from 1912 to 1924; from Brussels, Belgium.

Kirilov, P. V., Russian plant explorer in China around 1835, (U.S.S.R.).

Komarov, Vladimir Leontyevitch, lived from 1869 to 1945, botanized extensively in China's northern regions; from (U.S.S.R.).

Linne, Carl von (Carolus Linnaeus), taxonomical botanist, lived from 1707 to 1778; Sweden.

Maack, Richard K., 1825–1886 d., plant botanist in China and Asia.

Maximowicz (Maksimovitch), K. I., Russian botanist and author, (U.S.S.R.).

Meyer, Frank N., plant explorer in China and Asia; Dutch-American.

Nakai, Takenoshi, died 1882, botanist, taxonomist, plant explorer in Islands of Japan, from Japan.

Potanin, Grigor N., Siberian-Russian plant explorer in China from 1891 to 1894; prolific author; (U.S.S.R.).

Purdom, William, lived 1880 to 1921, plant explorer in China and Asia; from England.

Rock, Joseph F., plant explorer for the Arnold Arboretum in China from 1915 to 1925; U.S.A.

Ruprecht (Rubrekhtov), Franz, lived from 1814 to 1870, Russian botanist, (U.S.S.R.).

Schneider, Camillo K., botanist and lilac authority lived from 1876 to 1951, Austrian.

Soulie, Abbé Jean Marie, French Jesuit botanist collected in Yunnan Province, China from 1900 to 1910: killed in Yunnan, from France.

Turczaninow (Turchaninov), Nicolai Stepanovitch, lived from 1796 to 1864, Russian botanist and lilac authority, (U.S.S.R.).

Veitch, James and Sons, Nurserymen and introducers of new species from China, active from 1900 to 1924, from England.

Wallich, Dr. Nathaniel, botanist and plant explorer in Asia in 1828; from England.

Ward, F. Kingdon, lived 1885 to 195__ , plant explorer in China around 1913, from England.

Wilson, Prof. Ernest Henry, lived 1876 to 1930, plant explorer for Veitch & Sons and later for the Arnold Arboretum in China and Asia, made several explorations in China from 1891 to 1914; and English-American, U.S.A.

APPENDIX D

Outstanding Contemporary
Lilac Notables

(Other than Hybridizers/Species Introducers)

Information on many foreign, European and Asian lilac notables was not available to the author; this listing does not mean to overlook their work and lilac knowledge.

Alexander, John H. III, plant propagator, Arnold Arboretum, lilac writer and authority, Middleboro, Massachusetts, U.S.A.

Astrov, Prof., horticultural writer on lilacs, Moscow, U.S.S.R.

Bartrum, Douglas, author of book on lilacs, London, England.

Bristol, Peter, horticulturist, Holden Arboretum, Mentor, Ohio, plant explorations in China 1981 and 1984; U.S.A.

Clark, Robert B., horticultural taxonomist, lilac authority, 3rd President of the International Lilac Society, Editor *Lilac Proceedings*, Meredith, New Hampshire, U.S.A.

Eickhorst, Walter E., former Supt. Morton Arboretum, 4th President Int, Lilac Society, lilac authority, Naperville, Illinois, U.S.A.

Green, Dr. Peter, taxonomist and horticultural-botanical author, Kew Gardens, England.

Gromov, Andrey, Horticulturist, writer, lilac authority, Moscow, U.S.S.R.

Harding, Alice (Mrs. Edward), author book on lilacs, horticulturist.

Harkness, Bernard, former Supt, Rochester Parks, N.Y., horticultural writer, 2nd President Int. Lilac Society, Geneva, New York, U.S.A.

Holetich, Charles D., horticulturist, Royal Botanical Gardens, Hamilton, Ontario, Canada; outstanding lilac authority, horticultural writer, Canada. 7th President of Int. Lilac Society.

Luce, Roger, horticulturist, plant explorations to China in 1982, lilac authority, Hampten Highlands, Maine, U.S.A.

Martin, Winifried H., Supt. Holden Arboretum, Mentor, Ohio, lilac authority, U.S.A.

McKean, Arch, lilac authority, Grand Beach, New Buffalo, Michigan, U.S.A.

McKelvey, Susan Delano, author of lilac book, formerly taxonomist Arnold Arboretum, lilac authority, Jamaica Plains, Massachusetts, U.S.A.

Michurin (Mitchurin), Ivan, noted Russian botanical writer and authority, U.S.S.R.

Moore, N. Hudson, author of lilac book, early authority (c. 1904), New York, N.Y., U.S.A.

Norweb, R. Henry Jr., former Director Holden Arboretum, plantsman and lilac authority, horticulturist, Mentor, Ohio, U.S.A.

Oakes, Walter, lilac authority, lilac writer, Rumford, Maine, U.S.A.

Pringle, Dr. James S., taxonomist, Royal Botanical Gardens, Hamilton, Ontario, lilac authority and foremost botanical writer on lilac species; Canada.

Sargent, Charles Sprague, former Director Arnold Arboretum, author, horticultural authority, Massachusetts, U.S.A.

Steward, Orville, lilac authority, 1st President of International Lilac Society, Plymouth Vermont, U.S.A.

Tsitsin, N. V., contemporary Russian lilac authority, writer, Moscow, U.S.S.R.

Vrugtman, Freek, International Registrar for Lilacs (Genus *Syringa*), Royal Botanical Gardens, Hamilton, Ontario, Canada, lilac authority and writer on lilac cultivars, Canada.

Wister, John Caspar, outstanding horticulturist and horticultural writer, author of books on lilacs, author of first, second and third *Checklist of Lilac Species and Cultivars*, outstanding lilac authority.

Zucker, Isabel, horticultural author and authority, lilac authority and horticulturist, editor of the *Lilac Pipeline*, Bloomfield Hills, Michigan.

APPENDIX E

The World's Outstanding Lilac Collections and Gardens

Since I have not been able to visit many of the foreign countries to view their fine collections or do not have knowledge of all of them, some fine plantings of lilacs may be inadvertently omitted. I welcome information, pictures and the invitation to see these fine lilac gardens in the future. The following collections of lilacs in various countries throughout the world are listed so that readers may view lilacs in their own areas and perhaps even visit those farther away when opportunity makes this possible. It is a wonderful experience to view old lilac friends in far away places!

ARBORETUMS AND BOTANICAL GARDENS AND PRIVATE COLLECTIONS (listed by country) (Land Grant Colleges and Gov. Agricultural Experimental Stations/Parks Collections)

Austria
> International Gardens, Vienna, Austria

Belgium
> Kalmthout Arboretum, Robert deBelder, Kalmthout, Belgium

Canada
> Jardin Botanique de Montreal, Montreal, Quebec, Canada
> Royal Botanical Gardens, Hamilton, Ontario, Canada (Katie Osborne Lilac Garden)
> Agriculture Canada Central Experiment Farm, Ottawa, Ontario, Canada
> Agriculture Canada Research Station, Morden, Manitoba, Canada
> University of Guelph Arboretum Centennial Center, Guelph, Ontario, Canada
> University of Manitoba, Dept. Plant Sciences, Winnipeg, Manitoba, Canada
> University of Alberta Devonian Botanical Garden, Edmonton, Alberta, Canada
> Niagara Parks Commission Centennial Lilac Garden and School of Horticulture, Niagara Falls, Ontario, Canada.

Czechoslovakia
> University of Agriculture, Dept. of Horticulture, Prague (Praha), Czechoslovakia

England
> Brighton Parks, Brighton, England
> Royal Botanical Gardens, Kew, England

France
> Jardin Botanique, Museum Histoire Naturelle, Paris, France

F.D.R. (West Germany)
> Dortmund-Brunninghausen botanischer Garten, A.Z.R. Deutshe Baumschule, Aachen, F.D.R.

Hungary
Falskolai Tanszek, Budapest, Hungary

Poland
Kornik Arboretum, Kornik, Poland

The Netherlands
Het Seringenpark, Aalsmeer, The Netherlands

U.S.S.R.—Union of Soviet Socialist Republics (number of species and cultivars)
Principal Botanic Garden, Academy of Science, Moscow (400)
Central Botanical Garden, Ukrainian Academy of Science, Kiev, (141)
Central Botanical Garden, Belorussian Academy of Science, Minsk (176)
Central Botanical Garden, Kazakhsk Academy of Science, Alma-Ata (113)
Botanical Garden, Institute of Botanical Academy of Science, Frunze (109)
Botanical Garden, Institute of Botanical Academy of Science, Dushanbe (106)
Central Botanical Garden, Gruzinsk Academy of Science, Tbilisi (99)
Leostepnaya Experimental Breeding Station, Meshchersk, Lipetzk Region (99)
Science Research Institute of Siberian Botanical Gardens, Barnoul (102)
Botanical Garden of Moscow State University, Moscow (72)
Central Botanical Garden, Uzbeksk Academy of Science, Tashkent (72)
Botanical Garden of Rostov State University, Rostov-on-Don, Dendropark Trostyanetz (61)
Ukrainian Academy of Science, Ichnya, Chernigovsk Region (55)
Botanical Garden Estonian Academy of Science, Tallin, (47)
Botanical Garden, Moldavsk Academy of Science, Kishinev (45)
Nikitsk State Botanical Gardens, Yalta (43)
Botanical Garden Forest-Technical Academy, Leningrad (39)
(There are a number of other Botanical Gardens with a lesser number of cultivars grown)
Subtropical Botanical Garden, Batumi (22) of particular interest to those in warmer areas
Latvian Academy of Science, Salospics, Rizhsk Region
Botanical Garden, Latvian State University, Riga

Yugoslavia
Zagreb Botanical Garden, Zagreb, Yugoslavia.

UNITED STATES OF AMERICA
Arboretums and Botanical Gardens: (many growing from 300 to 500 species and cultivars)
Arnold Arboretum, Harvard University, Jamaica Plains, Massachusetts
Arthur Hoyt Scott Horticultural Foundation, Swarthmore College, Swarthmore, Pennsylvania
Bayard Cutting Arboretum, Long Island, New York
Boerner Botanical Gardens, Milwaukee County Parks Commission, Hales Corner, Wisconsin
Brooklyn Botanic Garden, Brooklyn, New York
Cary Arboretum, Millbrook, New York
Chicago Horticultural Society Gardens, Glencoe, Illinois
Denver Botanic Garden, Denver, Colorado
Freilinghausen Arboretum, Morris County Parks Commission, Morristown, New Jersey
George Landis Arboretum, Esperance, New York
Holden Arboretum, Mentor, Ohio
Howard Taylor Memorial Lilac Arboretum, State Park Commission, Millbrook, New York
John J. Tyler Arboretum, Lima, Pennsylvania
Morton Arboretum, Lisle, Illinois
New York Botanical Garden, Bronx, New York
Tennessee Botanical Gardens, Nashville, Tennessee
United States National Arboretum, Washington, D.C.

Lilac Collections at Land Grant Colleges and Agricultural Experiment Stations

Alice Harding Memorial Lilac Walk, Rutgers-State University, New Brunswick, New Jersey
Harris Memorial Lilac Walk, Cornell Plantations, C.U., Ithaca, New York
Hidden Lake Arboretum, Michigan State University, Tipton, Michigan
Landscape Arboretum, Minnesota State University, St. Paul Minnesota
Purdue University, Horticultural Bldg., Lafayette, Indiana
University of Maine, Plant & Soil Sciences, Deering Hall, Orono, Maine
University of California Botanical Garden, Riverside, California
University of Nebraska, Maxwell Arboretum, Lincoln, Nebraska
University of New Hampshire, Plant Sciences, Nesmith Hall, Durham, New Hampshire
University of Washington Arboretum, Seattle, Washington
University of Wisconsin Arboretum, Madison, Wisconsin

Lilac Collections at Outstanding Public Parks

Elmhurst Park Commission, Elmhurst, Illinois
Ewing Park, Des Moines, Iowa
Highland Park, Monroe County Parks Department, Rochester, New York
Lilacia Park, Lombard Parks Dept., Lombard, Illinois
Skylands Botanical Garden, Ringwood State Park, Ringwood, New Jersey
Somerset County Parks Commission, North Branch, New Jersey

Outstanding Lilac Plantings in Cities and Towns (Whole town private plantings)

Camden, Maine
Cooperstown, New York
Delhi, New York
Mackinac City, Mackinac Island, Michigan
Portsmouth, New Hampshire
Wiscasset, Maine
Woodstock, Vermont

OUTSTANDING PRIVATE COLLECTIONS AND LILAC GARDENS (many with several hundred cultivars and species in their collections)

Aherlow (Vale of Aherlow)—Alice and Thomas Chieppo Estate, East Burke, Vermont
Barnard's Inn Farm, Polly and Julian Hill, Vineyard Haven, Massachusetts
Ken Berdeen, Kennebunk, Maine
Bickelhaupt Arboretum, Clinton, Iowa
Birchwood, Robert B. Clark, Meredith, New Hampshire
Hon. F. W. Bliss Estate, Middleburgh, New York
Butternut Hill Farm, Roger Luce Estate, Newburg, Maine
Falconskeape, Fr. John L. Fiala, and Dr. Karen and Peter Murray, Medina, Ohio
Gardenview Horticultural Park, Henry Ross, Strongsville, Ohio
Grape Hill Gardens, Lois and William Utley Estate, Clyde, New York
Hamesbest Arboretum, Gertrude Hodgdon, Randolph Center, Vermont
Hulda Klager Lilac Garden, Hulda Klager Lilac Society, Woodland, Washington
Lammerts, Dr. Walter E., Estate, Freedom, California
Lilac Land, Estate of Mrs. A. E. Lumley, Pelham, Massachusetts
Lilac Manor Farm, Mrs. Charlotte Bass, South LaPorte, Indiana
Lockwood, Maurice, Mallow Way Farm, Ghent, New York
Longwood Gardens, Kennett Square, Pennsylvania
Lupold, Donald, Muncy, Pennsylvania
Margaretten Park, Estate of Dr. Joel & Tina Margaretten, Leona Valley, California
McLaughlin, Bernard, South Paris, Maine
Meadowby Arboretum, R. O. Pawling, Lewisburg, Pennsylvania
Meadowlark Hill, Max Peterson Estate, Ogallala, Nebraska
Murray, Dr. Karen and Peter, Ameri-Hort Research, Medina, Ohio
Walter W. Oakes, Dixville, Maine
Shelburne Museum Estate, Shelburne (Burlington) Vermont

Clare E. Short, Elyria, Ohio
Stampe Lilac Garden, W. W. Stampe, Davenport, Iowa
Strawbery Banke, Portsmouth, New Hampshire
Stanley M. Rowe Arboretum, Cincinnati, Ohio
Lourene Wishart, Lincoln, Nebraska

Lilac Nurseries

Alexander, John H. III, Dahlia Gardens, Middleboro, Massachusetts
Ameri-Hort Research, Inc., Peter and Karen Murray, P.O. Box 1529, Medina, Ohio
Bakerview Nursery, Inc., Robert W. Clark, Bellingham, Washington
Caprice Farms, A. L. & D. D. Rogers, Sherwood, Oregon
Carroll Gardens, P. Donofrio, Westminister, Maryland
Tom Dilatush Nursery, Robbinsville, New Jersey
Eaglesfile Gardens, P. E. Barnhart, Eugene, Oregon
Erickson's Nurseries, E. E. Erickson, Brainerd, Minnesota
Heard Gardens, Ltd., Wm. R. Heard, Des Moines, Iowa
William H. Horman, 246 Chalmers, Detroit, Michigan
Inter-State Nursery, Hamburg, Iowa
Iris Country, Roger R. Nelson, Wayne, Nebraska
Charles Klehm & Son Nursery, Carl H. Klehm, Arlington Heights, Illinois
Dr. Karen and Peter Murray, Ameri-Hort Research, Medina, Ohio
Penny's Green Thumb, Penny Bufis, Richland, Washington
Reath, Dr. David, Vulcan, Michigan
The Willot, James R. Harlow, Quinque, Virginia
Trautman Nurseries, Herbert F. Trautman, Franklinville, Wisconsin
Wedge Nurseries, Don Wedge, Albert Lea, Minnesota
White Flower Farm, Eliot Wadsworth, Litchfield, Connecticut
Sheridan Nurseries, Ltd., Etobicoke, Ontario, Canada
Mellbye Plantskole, Lennart Mellbye, Nes Hedmark, Norway

Col. William R. Plum, founder of Lilacia Park, Lyle, Illinois.

Lilacia Park, Lyle, Illinois
Col. Plum working in his original lilac garden. (Photos courtesy Lilacia Park Library)

BIBLIOGRAPHY

Bibliography of Lilacs (Syringa)

edited for the author by Robert B. Clark (for whose assistance I am ever grateful)

A. HISTORY
1. Fossil
Andreanaszky, G., Reste d'un lilas du Sarmatian hongrois. (English Summary) *Acta Bot.* 14 (1–2):1–4. 1968
Skoflew, I., Quarternäre Syringa-arten von Vertessyöllös und Monosobel.(English Summary) *Acta Bot.* 14 (1–2): 133–145. 1968
2. Plant Hunting
Anderson, E., A visit to the home of the lilac. *Arnold Arboretum Bull.* Pop. Info., Ser. 4, 3(1):1–4. Mar. 22, 1935
Anon. Grigeri Nikolaievich Potanin (1835–1920). *New York Times* (Russian Section) Nov. 25, 1916
Bristol, P., Unpublished accounts and lectures on plant explorations in China. The Holden Arboretum. Sept. 9–21, 1981; revised Apr. 1982. 4 pp. (mimeo.).
Harkness, B. (ed.), *Charles Sprague Sargent Letters to Rochester Park Personnel.* Rochester Chapbooks. Rochester, N.Y., 1961.
Harkness, B., A Patron for the International Lilac Society? (O. G. de Busbecq). *I.L.S. Proceedings* 5(1):6–8. 1976.
Hedrick, U. P., *A History of Horticulture in America to 1860.* New York, 1950. *Lilacs:*pp. 46–47
Howard, R. A., E. H. Wilson and the nodding lilac. *Lilacs* 9: 13–15. 1980
Meyer, F. N., Notes and photographs on plant explorations to China, 1913–1926. Arnold Arboretum Archives. (Unpublished)
O'Conner, A. H., History of Lilacs in America. *I.L.S. Proceedings,* 5(1):2–3. 1976
Roca-Garcia, H., The lelacke, or pipe tree. *Arnoldia* 31(3): 114–120. May 1971.
Rock, J. F., Notes and photographs on plant explorations to China, 1925–1926. Arnold Arboretum Archives (Unpublished)
Rogers, O. M., Early Lilacs in North America; review of Julia Berrall, *The Garden—an Illustrated History.* Penguin Bks. N.Y., 1978. *Lilac Newsletter* 5(3):9–10. Mar. 1979.
Sussman, V., A plant pioneer, Elwyn O. Meader's search for new varieties has spanned half a century. *Organic Gardening,* pp. 64–71. Sept. 1984.
Wagenknecht, B. L., The Lilacs of New England. *Arnoldia* 19(5): 23–30. May 1959.
Whittle, Tyler, *The Plant Hunters.* Chilton Bk. Co., Phila. 1970.
3. Modern Species of Lilacs
Alexander, J. H. III, The Uncommon Lilac—something old, something new. *Arnoldia* 38(3):65–81. May–June 1978.
Baily Hortorium staff, *Hortus Third.* Macmillan, N.Y. & London. 1976. *Syringa* pp. 1090–1091.
Bartrum D., *Lilac and Laburnum.* John Griffith LTD. London. 175 pp., 1959.
Decaisne, M. J., Monographie des genres *Ligustrum* et *Syringa.* Nouv. Arch. Museum II 2:1–44. 1878.
Green. P. S. (reviser) in Bean's *Trees and Shrubs Hardy in the British Isles.* George Taylor, ed., edition 8. vol. 4. 1980. John Murray LTD, London.

Harding, Alice, *Lilacs in My Garden,* Macmillan, N.Y., 1933

Krüssmann, G., *Handbuch der Laubgehölze.Syringa:*Band II pp. 5–521. Paul Parey, Berlin and Hamburg, 1962

Krüssmann, G., Manual of Cultivated Broad-leaved Trees and Shrubs *Syringa* Volume III. Timber Press, Portland, Oregon, 1986.

Lingelsheim, A. Syringa in Engler, *Das Pflanzenreich.* 72: 74–95, 1920

McKelvey, S. D., *The Lilac,* Macmillan, New York, 1928

Rogers, O. M., Lilacs Today, *I.L.S. Proceedings,* 1(5):23–26, 1972

Starcs, K., Übersicht über die Arten der Gattung Syringa L. *Mitt. Deut. Dend. Ges.,* 1928:31–49.

Wang, Chi-Wu, *The Forests of China,* M. M. Cabot Found. Pub. 5, Harvard Univ. Press, Cambridge, Mass., 1961

Wister, J. C., *Lilac Culture,* Orange Judd Pub. Co., N.Y. 1930

Wyman, D., *Wyman's Gardening Encyclopedia,* Macmillan, N.Y., *Syringa* pp. 1081–1087.

Zucker, I., *Flowering Shrubs, Syringa* pp 307–313, D. van Nostrand Press, N.Y., 1966

B. TAXONOMY

Clark, R. B., and Fiala, J. L., *Lilacs Native to China* (map), I.L.S. Archives, 1982

Dvorak, J. Jr., *Lilac Study of Lilacia Park and Morton Arboretum,* John L. Fiala, ed., 84 pp (line drawings), *I.L.S. Special Pub.* 1978.

Eylar, Mrs. F. B., The Species of Lilacs. *Univ. Wash. Arboretum Bull.,* 14(1): 18–19, 38–39, Spring 1951

Green, P. S., Chinese 'common' Lilac, *The Plantsman,* 6:12–13, 1984.

Green, P. S., Papillate Leaves in Lilacs?, *Lilacs,* 8(1):31–34, 1979.

Hershoff, V. B.and H. Schnitzer, Die subalpinen Birken-Rhododendron Walder im Dagwan-Tal/West-Himalaja, *Mitt. Dtsch. Dendrol. Ges.,* 72:171–186, 1981.

Howard, R. A. and G. K. Brizicky, Translocation and Transliteration of Cultivar Names; With Some Notes on Lilacs. *AABGA Quarterly Newsletter* 64:15–21, October 1965.

Hyypio, P. A., How *Syringa vulgaris* 'Mount Domogled' got its name, *Lilacs,* 8(1):61–64, 1979.

Jurkovic, M., New Varieties of Lilacs (*Syringa vulgaris*), *Lilac Newsletter* 9 (6):10–12, June 1983.

Lenz, L. M., Application of chemosystematics to lilacs, *I.L.S. Proceedings* 3 (1):25–30, 1974.

Pringle, J. S., Concept of the Cultivar, *Royal Bot. Gard. The Gardeners Bull.,* 27 (3):13–27, May 1973.

Pringle, J. S., Notes on confusing and recurrently misapplied names in *Syringa, Lilacs* 7(1):51–70, 1978.

Pringle, J. S., Nomenclatural notes on *Syringa* series Villosae, *Baileya* 20(3):93–103, March 1978.

Pringle, J. S., Notes on *Syringa tigerstedtii, Baileya* 20 (3):104–114, 1978.

Pringle, J. S., Status of alleged intersubgeneric and interseries hybrids in *Syringa, Baileya* 21:101–123, 1981.

Pringle, J. S., Summary of currently accepted nomenclature at the specific and varietal levels, *Lilac Newsletter* 9 (3): 1–6, March 1983.

Pringle, J. S., What is a type specimen? *Lilac Newsletter* 9 (5):1–3, May 1983.

Pringle, J. S., Typical varieties and autonyms, *Lilac Newsletter* 9(6):1–3, June 1983.

Pringle, J. S., Effective and valid publication of botanical names, *Lilac Newsletter* 10(1):2–4, Jan. 1984.

Rehder, A., Notes on some cultivated trees and shrubs, *Jour. Arnold Arboretum* 26:74–77.

Rogers, O. M., The Lilac—taxonomically, *Lilacs* 13(1) 5–8, 1984.

Sax, K., The juvenile characters of trees and shrubs, *Arnoldia* 18 (1):1–6, Feb. 1958.

Smith, M. C., The many shapes of lilac leaves, *Lilac Newsletter* 11(1):3–5, Jan. 1985.

Taylor, H., Cyto-taxonomy and phylogeny of the Oleaceae, *Brittonia* 5(4):337–367, 1945.

Vrugtman, F., Valid publication of new cultivar names of lilacs, *Lilac Newsletter* 10(5):1–3, May 1984.

Vrugtman, F., Cultivar description and cultivar identification, *Lilac Newsletter* 10(5):1–3, May 1984.

C. BREEDING (GENERAL)

Anderson, C., Wonderful World of Color, *Amer. Hemerocallis Soc. Jour.* 34 (4).

Anderson, E., *Introgressive Hybridization,* John Wiley & Sons, N.Y., 1949.

Anderson, E., Lamartine lilacs for St. Louis, *Mo. Bot. Gar. Bull.* 41(5):90–91, May 1953.

Borgenstam, E. Zur Zytologie der Gattung *Syringa* nebst Erörterungen über den Einfluss äusserer Factoren auf die Kernteilungsvergänge, *Arkiv för Botanik* 17:1–27, 1922.

Butler, J. D., and J. B. Gartner, Plant regulators, their use as a hobby, *Univ. Ill. Coop. Ext. Serv. Circ.* 886. 16 pp. reprinted 1973.

Cameron, D. F., *Ornamental plant breeding,* Canada Dept. Agri. Div. Hort., Central Exp. Farm Progress Report, 1934–48, Ottawa, 1950; 1949–53; 1955; 1954–58; 1960. Misc, publ. 1036.

Clarke, W. B., Breeding of Lilacs, *Univ. Wash. Arboretum Bull.* 11(2):13–14, 1948.

Cumming, W. A., Canada Dept. Agric. Research Branch Experimental Farm Progress Rept. 1955–59, *Syringa* p. 27, Morden, Manit. 1961; *Syringa* p. 17, Ottawa, 1977.

Cumming, W. A., Canadian lilac breeders and their introductions, *I.L.S. Proceedings* 3(1):21–24, 1974.

Darlington, C. D., *Chromosome Botany and the Origin of Cultivated Plants,* George, Allen & Unwin, London, 1963.

Derman, H., Colchicine polyploidy and technique, *Bot. Review* 6:599–635, 1940.

Einset, J., Biotechnology at the Arnold Arboretum, *Arnoldia* ( ):27:–33, August.

Emsweller, S. J. and P. Brierley, Colchicine induced tetraploidy in *Lilium, Jour. Heredity* 31:223–230, 1946.

Fenicchia, R. A., Breeding and growing hybrid lilacs from seed, *I.L.S. Newsletter* 2(2):9, 1973.

Fiala, J. L., Lilac research and lilacs of the future. *I.L.S. Proceedings* 1(5):27–31, 38. 1972.

Fiala, J. L., Inducing polyploids in the genus *Syringa, I.L.S. Newsletter* 2(1) 8–11. Spring 1973.

Fiala, J. L., In search of practical programs for hybridizing lilacs, *I.L.S. Newsletter* 2(2):14–15. 1973.

Fiala, J. L., Hybridizing possibilities in the lilac, Brooklyn Bot. Gard. Record Plants and Garden, *Breeding Plants for Home and Garden* Handbook 30(1):64-ff, 1974.

Fiala, J. L., Preview of some lilacs of the future:Fenicchia's 'Rochester' F₃ hybrids, *Lilacs* 4:26–27. 1975.

Fiala, J. L., Lilacs of the future, *I.L.S. Proceedings* 5(1): 14–18, 1976.

Griesbach, R. J. Genetic engineering for the homeowner, *Amer. Rhododendron Soc. Newsletter,* pp. 3–7 (mimeo.), April 1983.

Griesbach, R. J., Breeding for color, *Amer. Rhododendron Soc. Newsletter,* 1984.

Havemeyer, T. A., How the modern lilac came to be:recounting the story of Mons. Lemoine's work. *Garden Mag.* 25:232–234, May 1917.

Henry, L., Crossings made at the Natural History Museum of Paris from 1887 to 1899. *Journal Royal Hort. Soc.* 24:218–236. 1900.

Howard, R. A., A booklet on lilacs from Russia (review of Kolesnikov's 'Lilac' [cit.]). *Arnoldia* 19 (6–7): 31.35, May 1959.

Karpow-Lipski, M., New Polish varieties of lilacs, *Arboretum Kornickie* 3:99–108 (English summary) 1958.

Lammerts, W. A., Warm weather tolerant lilacs, their origin and hybridizing possibilities, *Lilac Newsletter* 9(2):10–17. Feb. 1983.

Lammerts, W. A., Research with interspecific crosses, *Lilac Newsletter* 9(5):10–11, May 1983.

Leach, D. G., The magic of colchicine, *Flower Grower,* 1950.

Lemoine, E., Hybrids between the common lilac and the laciniated Persian lilac. *Jour. Royal Hort. Soc.* 24:299–311, 1900.

Lemoine, V., A new race of lilacs, *Garden and Forest* 2: 326–328, July 10, 1889.

Maarse, D. E., Talk on lilacs, *Deutsche Baumschule* No. 3, March 1953.

Maarse, D. E., Some remarks on my new lilacs, *Dendron* 1: 11–13, 1954.

Macoun, W. T., Report of the Dominion Horticulturist for 1928, *Syringa* pp. 53–58, Canada Dept. Agric. Div. Hort., Ottawa, 1928.

Norton, C., Hybrid Lilacs, *N.Y. Bot. Gard. Garden Jour.* 5: 129–230, July 1955.

Patek, J. M., Standardization of lilac colors, *I.L.S. Proceedings* 1(5):32–37, 1972.

Pease, O. H., African Violets transformed, *Flower Grower,* 1950.

Preston, I., New ornamental plants originated in the Division of Horticulture, Canada Dept. Agric. Rept. of Dominion Horticulturist for 1928, *Syringa* pp. 53–58. Ottawa, 1930; *Syringa* pp. 67–68, 1931.

Pringle, J. S., Interspecific hybridization experiments in *Syringa* series Villosae at the Royal

Botanical Gardens, *I.L.S. Proceedings* 3(1):15–19, 1974; *Baileya* 20 (2):49–91, Jan. 1977.

Roberts, H. F., *Plant Hybridization Before Mendel*, Hafner Publ. Co., N.Y. 1965.

Rogers, O. M., Lilac hybridization, *I.L.S. Proceedings* 3(1): 37–39, 1974.

Santamour, F. S. Jr., Arboreta, genes and plant improvement, *Arnoldia* 33(2):127–134, Mar.–April 1973.

Sax, K., Chromosome number and behavior in the genus Syringa, *Jour. Arnold Arboretum* 11:7–14, 1930.

Sax, K., Lilac species hybrids, *Jour. Arnold Arboretum* 26: 79–84, 1945.

Solberg, O. T., Chromosome cytology and arboreta, a marriage of convenience, *Arnoldia* 33(2):135–146, Mar.–Apr. 1973.

Skinner, F. L., Hybrid lilacs, *Univ. Wash. Arboretum Bull.* 11(2):14–16, Summer 1948.

Skinner, F. L., New American lilacs, *Brooklyn Bot. Gard. Rept. Plants & Gardens*, 4(1):22–24, Spring 1948.

Skinner, F. L., A famous lilac breeder writes about new lilacs, *Horticulture* 27(5):181, May 1949.

Skinner, F. L., *Horticultural Horizons*—plant breeding and introductions at Dropmore, Manitoba, Dept. Agric. and Cons., *Syringa* pp. 106–111, Ottawa, Canada, 1966.

Tischler, G., Über die Bastardnatur des persischen Flieders, Zeit für Bot. 23:150–162.

(anon) *Standard Color Names Based on Munsell*, United States National Bureau of Standards, circ. 553.

Ware, E. H., How to develop new plants with colchicine, *Popular Gard.* 1950

Wilson, E. H., Plant hybrids of *Syringa vulgaris*, Arnold Arboretum Bull, Pop. Info. ser. 3. 2:29–32, May 26, 1928.

Wright, P. H., The latest in hybrid lilacs. *Horticulture*, p. 174.

Yeager, A. F., E. B. Risley, E. M. Meader and R. B.Pike, Breeding and improving ornamentals, *Univ. New Hampshire Agric. Exp. Sta. Bull.* 461, *Syringa* pp. 11–13, Durham, N.H., May 1959.

1. Lilacs (General)

Buckley, A. R., Lilacs will cast a spell in your garden, *Canada Agric. Garden Notes*, Ottawa, Mar. 1971; reprinted *Lilac Newsletter* 7(6):7–10, June 1981

Bunge, S., Lilacs, *Univ. Wash. Arboretum Bull.* 19(1):16–18, Spring 1956.

Davis, M. B., and I. Preston, The lilac in Canada, *Ornamental Flowering Trees and Shrubs*, Rept. of Royal Hort. Soc. Conf., pp. 135–140, 1938.

Downer, H. E., The good lilacs, *Home Garden*, 11:32–38, May 1948.

Downer, H. E., The lilac, America's favorite flowering shrub, *Home Garden*, 13:48–54, Nov, 1950.

Dunbar, J., Seven weeks of lilac bloom, *Garden Magazine*, 1(5):232–234, June 1905.

Dunbar, J., The latest news about the lilac, a review of the acceptable methods of propagation, notes on cultural methods and an analysis of some of the choicer forms and varieties, *Florists' Exchange* 56(12):799, 830–831, Sept. 1923.

Fisher, G. M., Too many lilacs! *Amer. Nurseryman* 80(9): 5–6, Nov. 1944.

Frost, E. B., Lilacs up-to-date, *Hort. Science Bull.*, 11: 3–4, Sept. 1961.

Green, James L, Lilac . . . Year-round cut flower? Dual-purpose Plant?, *Ornamental Northwestern Newsletter*, 8(2):13, Apr–June 1984.

Gromov, A., *Syringa*, 247 pp., Moskovskii Babochii, Moscow, 1963.

Hansell, D. E., The very best shrub of all:May-time is lilac-time, *Horticulture*, :189, 208, May 1948.

Harkness, B., 'I leave thee lilac with heartshaped leaves . . .', *N.Y. Bot. Gard. Garden Jour.* 2(3):84–86, May-June 1952.

Harkness, B., Lilacs for northern gardens, *Rochester Garden Center Bull.* 11(9):May 1956.

Harkness, B., Lilacs old and new varieties, *Horticulture* 34: 484–490, Sept. 1956.

Harkness, B., May-time—Lilac-time, *N.Y. Nursery Notes*, No. 134, p. 10, May 1958.

Heard, C. H., Better lilacs, *N.Y. Bot. Gard. Garden Jour*, 7:180, Nov. 1957.

Holetich, C. D., The dark ones (flower buds), *Lilac Newsletter* 9(11):2, Nov. 1983.

Holetich, C. D., Guidelines to I.L.S. Lilac Evaluation Form, *Lilac Newsletter* 10(8):7–8, Aug. 1984.

Hollandicus, Report on lilacs, being an evaluation of lilac cultivars in three color classes both singles and doubles. Personal communication of H. den Ouden to Brown Bros.

Nursery, Rochester, N.Y., ca. 1950.

Hudson, C. J., Jr., Succession bloom in the lilac, *Country Life* 66:103–109, May 1934.

Kammerer, E. L., Extending 'Lilac Time' until July, *Morton Arboretum Bull.* 25(7):27–30, July 1950.

Kammerer, E. L., Lilacs for the small garden; miscellaneous notes on lilac species and hybrids, *Morton Arboretum Bull.* 28(6): 23–26, June 1953.

Krammerer, E. L., Lilacs from early till late, *Morton Arboretum Bull.* 32(6):25–30, June 1957.

Knight, F. P., Lilacs, *Royal Hort. Soc. Jour.* 84: 486–499, Nov. 1959.

Lipp, L., Lilac comeback, *Holden Arboretum Leaves* 8(2): 4–5, Spring 1966.

Nilson, S., Observations about lilacs, *Horticulture* 39: 474, Sept. 1961.

Rogers, O. M., Lilacs from early spring to mid-summer, *NH Agric. Exp. Sta. Progress Report* 7:18, Apr. 1961.

Rothman, A. D., Know your lilacs, *Horticulture* 32, 414–415, 437, 442, Sept. 1954.

Shedesky, P., Consider these lilacs for modern settings, *Horticulture* 39:515, Oct. 1961.

Vrugtman, F., The garden lilac, *Royal Bot. Gard. The Gardener's Bull.* 27(1):1–6, Feb. 1973.

Wilson, E. H., Lilacdom, *Garden Magazine,* 23:153–155, April 1916.

Wilson, E. H., *Aristocrats of the Garden,* Stratford, Boston, Mass. 1926.

Wilson, E. H., Lilacs wild and otherwise, *House and Garden,* 55:116–117, 181, 182, 186, 212, May 1929.

Wister, J. C., Lilacs, *Univ. Wash. Arboretum Bull.* 11(2): 3–9, 37, Summer 1948.

Wister, J. C., Lilac preferences are like horse races, *Horticulture,* 28(6):219–220, June 1950.

Wister, J. C., Lilacs, *Brooklyn Bot. Gard. Record Plants and Gardens,* 7(1):4–11, 1951.

Wister, J. C., Planting shrubs this autumn? Try some lilac species, *Horticulture* 28:374–375, Oct. 1950.

Wister, J. C., Lilacs and Peonies, *N.Y. Bot. Gard. Garden Jour.,* :37–38, March-April 1954.

Wister, J. C., Every garden needs a lilac, *Flower Grower* 43: 58–59, April 1956.

Wister, J. C., Our garden lilacs, *N.Y. Bot. Gard. Garden Jour.* 9:103–105, May 1959.

Wister, J. C., Lilacs in cultivation, *I.L.S. Proceedings* 1(5):19–22, 38, 1972.

Wister, J. C., What lilacs should our members plant (and where oh where are they going to get them?), *I.L.S. Newsletter,* 2(1):5–7, Spring 1973.

Wyman, O., Use several varieties to lengthen lilac time, *Horticulture,* 25(10):278, May 1947.

Wyman, D., Lilacs, *Arnoldia* 9(4):13–16, May 6, 1949.

Wyman, D., Lilacs get better, *Horticulture,* :268, 289, May 1959.

2. Lilac Cultivars According to Series and Species

Series Vulgares

Syringa vulgaris

Anon. A yellow lilac (editorial), *Gard. Chron.* (London), 126(3260):1, July 1949.

Barron, L., Mr. Havemeyer's lilacs, *Country Life* 66:66–67, May 1934.

Brizicky, G. K., 'Whim'—an overlooked cultivar of *Syringa, AABG Quarterly Newsletter* No. 64:22, 1965.

Clark, R. B., Forty dark-toned lilacs mostly with large and sometimes double florets, *Lilac Newsletter* 6(11):1–5, Nov. 1980.

Clark, R. B., A pair of lilac novelties from Falconskeape, *Lilac Newsletter* 10(9):1984.

Clark, R. B., Havemeyer's 'Glory', what a name, *Lilac Newsletter* 9(4):14–16, April 1983.

Clark, R. B., The new 'Rochester' Strain of lilacs, *I.L.S. Newsletter Convention Issue,* pp. 5–7, May 1972.

Clark, R. B., The 'Dwight D. Eisenhower' lilac, *Lilac Newsletter* 10(8):3–4, Aug. 1984.

Curtis, R. W., Twenty-six lilacs, *Cornell Plantations* 6(3): 35–38, Spring 1950.

Fiala, J. L., ed., The Governor Wentworth lilac, *I.L.S. Proceedings* 2(4):10, May, 1974.

Franklin, M., The Franklin lilacs, *I.L.S. Newsletter* 2(2): 17, 1973.

Gardner' R. L., Blue and pink lilacs, *Lilacs* 12:26–28, 1983.

Harkness, B., In Memoriam:white lilacs, *Rochester Gard. Center. Bull.* 20(9):May, 1965.

Harkness, B., Choose fragrant lilacs, *Amer. Home.* pp. 10, 84, Sept. 1964.

Kammerer, E. L., Notes on some of the newer lilacs, *Morton Arb. Bull.* 36(6):27–29, June 1961.

Maarse, D. E., Rapport . . . der keuring, *De Boomwekerij* 11(15): 119, 1956.

Margaretten, J., Hulda Klager lilacs, *Lilac Newsletter*, 8(5):2–4, May 1982.

Short, C. E., A symphony of lilacs, *I.L.S. Proceedings* 2(4): 5–7, May 1974.

Vrugtman, F., and W. E. Eickhorst, The history of *Syringa vulgaris* 'Primrose', *Lilacs* 9:28–30, 1980.

Wyman, D., *Syringa* 'Vestale', *Amer. Nurseryman* (cover). (date lacking)

Syringa oblata

Clark, R. B., The Korean early lilac, *Lilac Newsletter* 9(7): 1, July 1983.

Green, P. S., The Chinese 'common' lilac, *The Plantsman* 6:12–13, June 1984.

Skinner, F. L., Lilacs for cold climates, *Horticulture* 30(10): 381, October 1952.

Series Pubescentes

Clark, R. B., Little-leaved lilacs at Birchwood, *Lilac Newsletter*, 10(3):6–8, Mar.1984.

Syringa meyeri

Free, M., Meyer's Lilac, *Flower Grower* 46:20, Sept. 1959.

Green, P. S., *Syringa meyeri* cv. 'Palibin', *Lilacs* 8(1): 36–39, 1979.

Kvaalen, R., 'Palibin' dwarf lilac, *Lilac Newsletter* 9(1): 2–8, Jan. 1983.

Syringa microphylla

Chadwick, L. C., *Syringa microphylla* (cover), Amer. Nurseryman, Oct. 1950.

Cumming, W. A., *Syringa microphylla* Diels 'Minor', *Canada Dept. Agric. Research Report*, 1963–1965, p. 13, Morden, Manitoba, 1967.

Syringa patula

Regelson R., An unusual lilac (*Syringa patula*), *Florists Exchange* 98(25):10, June 20, 1942

Meader, E. M., The 'Miss Kim' lilac, *Lilacs* 4:28, 1975.

Syringa × *persica*

Van Melle, P. J., Syringa persica—Persian Lilac, *Flower Grower*, p. 6, Oct. 1951.

Wein, K., Die Geschichte der *Syringa persica*, *Mitt. Dtsch. Dendrol. Ges.* 245–257. 1928.

Syringa villosa

Eagan, W. C., *Syringa villosa*, *Gardening* 4:295–296, 1896.

Syringa × *prestoniae*

Anon. Syringa 'James Macfarlane' (*S. reflexa* × *S. villosa*), *Horticulture* 38(1):37, 1960.

Bugala, W., The Ottawa lilac and its varieties, *Arb. Kornickie* 1:131–141, 1955. (in Polish).

Bugala, W., New varieties of *Syringa Prestoniae* obtained in the Kornik Arboretum, *I.L.S. Newsletter*, 2(1) 15–16, Spring 1973.

Cumming, W. A., Late-flowering lilacs for the prairies. *Prairie Gard.* 20:95, Feb. 1963.

Cumming, W. A., Syringa 'Miss Canada' (*S. reflexa* 'Redwine' × *S. prestoniae* 'Hiawatha'), *Canada Dept. Agric. Research Report 1966*, p. 9, Morden, Manitoba, 1967.

Lape. F., 'Summer White' late lilac, *I.L.S. Proceedings* 5(1):25, 1976.

Oliver, R. W., Canadian late-flowering lilac hybrids, *Greenhouse-Garden-Grass*, 3(1&2):15–17, 1962.

Wyman, D., Syringa Prestoniae, *Arnoldia* 8(7):29–36, 1948.

Wyman, D., The Preston lilacs, *Amer. Nurseryman* 132(11): 10–12, 1970.

Syringa tigerstedtii

Wyman, D., Plants of possible merit? *Arnoldia*, 2(2):9–16, 1960.

Syringa reticulata

Anon., Bad-smelling lilacs, *Country Life*, 24:100–102, July 1913.

Blackburn, B. Syringa, tree lilac, *Flower Grower*, 36:594, July 1949.

Clute, W. N., The tree lilac, *Amer. Botanist* 48:75–76, July 1942.

Dunbar, J., Japanese tree lilac, *Gardening* 4, 293–294, June 15, 1896.

Flemer, W., III, Island and Median-strip Planting (*S. reticulata*), *Arnoldia*, 44(4):20, Fall 1984.

Gerling, J., *Syringa amurensis japonica*, *Amer. Nurseryman* (cover, Vol. 117 (3-bis) Feb. 15, 1963.

Gleaves, C. T., Japanese Tree Lilac, *Lilac Newsletter* 9(3):9–10, March 1983.

Ronald, W. G., 'Ivory Silk' lilac, *Lilac Newsletter* 5(11):13–14, Nov. 1979.

Stiles, W. A., *Syringa pekinensis* blooming at Arnold Arboretum, probably for first time in (American) cultivation. *Garden and Forest* 2:300, June 19, 1889; p. 348, July 17, 1889.

Trumpy, J. R., Lilacs, *Gardening* 1:310, June 15, 1893.

3. Lilacs According to Geographical Regions of Bloom

Anon., Many lilac types suitable for California, ex Greeley (CO) *Daily Tribune,* August 18, 1981, reprinted *Lilac Newsletter* 7(10):1–2, Oct. 1981

Baker, F. Lilac time in Ukiah, Mondicino Co., California, *Lilac Newsletter,* 6(11); 7–9, Nov. 1980.

Borchers, W. C., Lilacs, *Calif. Hort. Soc. Jour.* 9(4):168–173, Oct., 1948.

Borchers, W. C., Lilacs and flowering quince for California gardens, *Calif. Hort. Soc. Jour.* 27(1):13–17, Jan. 1966.

Bugala, W., Lilac varieties, *Owoce Warzywa Kwiaty* 3(11): 16–17, June 1/15, 1963 (in Polish).

Bugala, W. Little known and beautiful varieties of lilacs, *Owoce Warzywa Kwiaty* 3(10):14–15, May 15/31, 1963. (In Polish)

Harkness, B., Favorite lilacs at Rochester, *Flower Grower* 39(9):34–35.

Holetich, C. D., The newest and best of Royal Botanical Gardens Lilacs, *Lilacs* 8(1):1–4, 1979.

Holetich, C. D., Lilac species and cultivars in cultivation in the U.S.S.R., *Lilacs,* 11(2):38 pp., Special issue, Dec. 1982, English translation of a Russian booklet by L. I. Rubtzov et al, qq.v.

Jongkind, M., *Lilacs and Forsythia, Aalsmeer proefsta. Bloemistery Jaarverslag,* 1966, 141pp.(In Dutch).

Krüssmann, E., Das Syringa-sortiment *der AZR Deutsche Baumschule* 10(3):1–2 (Aachen) Mar. 1958.

Lavchyan, H., Which lilacs to plant? *Tsvetovodstvo* 4:10–11, 1968 (In Russian).

Lundstein, A. S. New approved lilacs, *Haven* 67(9): 327, Sept. 1967 (In Danish).

Oakes, W. W., Maine choices (some of my 35 favorite lilacs), *Lilac Newsletter* 10(3):1–4, Mar. 1984.

Romer, L. B., A member writes re Ukiah, California lilacs, *Lilac Newsletter,* 7(1):2–4, Jan. 1981.

Rubtzov, L. I., N. L. Mikhailov and V. G. Zhogoleva, *Lilac Species and Cultivars In Cultivation in the S.S.S.R.,* Naukova Dumka, Kiev, 1980.(In Russian).

Slensker, Mrs. L. J., Lilacs in Casper, Wyoming, *Lilac Newsletter* 7(10):5, Oct. 1981.

Vukicevic, E., Shrubberies of lilac (*Syringa vulgaris* L.) on Goc Movulain, (Serbian) *Liemarstvo* 21(3–4) 17–23, 1968.

Wilson, E. H., Now is lilac time in the Arboretum, *Arnold Arb. Bull. Pop. Info.* ser. 3; 2:21–24, May 18, 1929.

Wister, J. C., Where the country's finest lilacs grew in 1933, *Horticulture.* Nov. 15, 1933. Reprinted in Lilac Newsletter 8(9):4–7, Sept. 1982.

Wister, J. C., A general plan for lilac collections in public gardens, *Univ. Wash. Arboretum Bull.,* Mar. 1944, reprinted in *Lilac Newsletter* 7(2):2–9, Feb. 1981.

Wyman, D., The Arnold Arboretum lilacs in their order of bloom, *Arnoldia* 15(4):17–23, May 13, 1955.

Wyman, D., A spring walk through the Arnold Arboretum, *Arnoldia* 18(3):13–16, May 1958.

D. PHENOLOGY

Anon., Humphrey lilacs injured by Spring frosts (Butler, Pennslyvania), *Horticulture* 28(7):258, July 1950.

Anon., Lilacs intrigue scientists, *Co-op County News,* St. Paul, Minnesota, May 1981.

Caprio, J. M., Phenology of lilac bloom in Montana, *Science* 126(3287):1344–1545, 1957.

Caprio, J. M., Phenological patterns and their use as climatic indicators. *Ground Level Climatology,* AAAS pp. 17–43, 1967.

Caprio, J. M., M. D. Magnuson and H. N. Metcalf, Instructions for phenological observations of purple common lilac and red-berry honeysuckle, *Western Reg. Res. Publ.* Circ. 250, Mont. Agric. Exper. Sta., Bozeman, 1970.

Clark, R. B., Autumn foliage colour in lilacs, *Lilac Newsletter* 9(10):1, Nov. 1983.

Clark, R. B., Lilacs with autumn colour. *Lilac Newsletter* 10(11):7, Nov. 1984.

Holetich, C. D., Frost damage on lilac flowers in Katie Osborne Collection of Royal Botanical Gardens, *Lilacs* 10:24–29, 1981.

Holetich, C. D., Effect of another unusual spring on lilac bloom, *Lilacs,* 12:62–63, 1983.

Hopp, R. J., M. T. Vittum and N. L. Canfield, Instructions for phenological observation of Persian lilac (*S. persica*)cv. 'Red Rothomagensis' (sic) *NE Region Res. Publ.* Pamphlet 36, 8 pp., Vermont Agric. Exper. Sta., Burlington, Vermont, Feb. 1969.

Hopp, R. J., M. T. Vittum, N. L. Canfield and B. E. Dethier, Regional phenological studies with Persian lilac (*S. persica*) (sic.), *N.Y. Food and Life Science Bull.* 17, 1972, Plant Sci. Veg. Crops, Geneva, N.Y., No. 3.

Perenyi, E., Partly cloudy, *Green Thoughts:*a writer in the garden. Random House, Oct. 1981, reprinted *Lilac Newsletter* 8(1):5–10, Jan. 1982.

Perry, L, Riding the green wave, *Lilacs,* 13(1):11–13, 1984.

Vittum, M. T., and R. J. Hopp, The Northeast-95 Lilac phenology network, *Lilacs* 8(1):65–71, 1979.

E.   CHECK LISTS AND REGISTRATIONS

Rogers, O. M., *Tentative International Register of Cultivar Names in the Genus Syringa,* 81 pp. New Hampshire Agric. Exper. Sta. Research Report 49, Durham, N.H., Apr. 1976.

Wister, J. C., *A Lilac Check List,* National Horticulture Mag. 6:1–16, 1927.

Wister, J. C., *Lilacs for America,* Report of 1941 survey conducted by the comm. on Hort. vars. of Amer., Assoc. of Bot. Gardens and Arboreta, A. H. Scott Hort. Foundation, Swarthmore College, Swarthmore, Penn., 1942.

Wister, J. C., *Lilacs for America,* Rept. of 1953 lilac survey Comm. AABGA, 48 pp., A. H. Scott Hort. Foundation, Swarthmore College, Swarthmore, Penn., 1953.

Wister, J. C., Supplementary registration list of cultivar names in *Syringa* L., registered 1963. *Arnoldia* 23(4):77–83.

Wister, J. C., More plant registrations, Lilac registrations. *Arnoldia* 26:13–14, 1966.

Wister, J. C., More plant registrations, *Syringa, Arnoldia* 27:65–66, 1967.

Wister, J. C., Lilac registrations, *Arnoldia* 31(3):121–126, 1971.

Vrugtman, F., Lilac registrations, *Lilacs* 6(1):14–17, 1976.

Vrugtman, F., Lilac registrations, *Lilacs* 7(1):35–37, 1978.

Vrugtman, F., Lilac registrations, *Lilacs* 9:26–27, 1980.

Vrugtman, F., Lilac registrations, *AABGA Bull.* 15(3):71–72, 1980.

Vrugtman, F., Lilac registrations, *AABGA Bull.* 16(4):131–132, 1981.

Vrugtman, F., Lilac registrations, *AABGA Bull.* 17(3):67–69, 1982.

Vrugtman, F., Lilac registration and its implications, *Lilac Newsletter* 4:13–15, 1975.

F.   PHYSIOLOGY

Bibikova, V. F., The effect of boron on the germination of pollen and growth of pollen tubes of some varieties of Syringa, *Mensh. Beloruskaya Akad. Navuk. Veslsi,* Ser. Biyal, Navuk. 3:41–45, 1945. (in Russian)

Borisovskaya, G. M., The development of the vascular bundle in the leaves of the lilac. (*Syringa vulgaris* L.) and the horsechestnut (*Aesculus hippocastanum* L.), *Leningrad Univ. Vestnik Ser. Biol.,* 9(2):40–60, 1966 (in Russian).

Chu, C., Structure and cytogenesis of the shoot apex of *Syringa oblata* var. *affinis* Lingelsh., *Acta Bot. Sinica* 13(3):240–255, 1965 (in Chinese).

Clapp, H. S., The lime and acid tolerance of the common lilac in New Hampshire soils, *Amer. Soc. Hort. Sci. Proc.* 42: 638–640, May 1943.

Costigan, M., When lilacs won't bloom, *Organic Gardening & Farming* 11(2) 51–53, Feb. 1964.

Dluzewaka, W. V., and M. Stokowaha, Effect of gibberillin on the development of lilac seedlings (*Syringa vulgaris* L.), *Acta Agrobot.* 14:217–223, 1963 (In Polish with English summary).

Dochinger, L. S., and T. A. Seliga, Acid precipitation and the forest ecosystem, *Bioscience* 26(9):564–565, Sept. 1976.

Dochinger, L. S. and J. G. Calvert, Air pollution sources: general effects and trends, *Pro. 32nd Ann. Meeting Soil Conserv. Ser. of Amer.,* pp. 187–193, Richmond, Virginia. Aug. 7–10, 1977.

Dostol, R. Effect of gibberillic acid on the initiation of buds in lilacs, *Nature* 201(4921):843–844, London, Feb. 22, 1964.

Fan, Y. H., and S. Y. Tsang, Research on the viability and storage of pollen, *Chinese Acad. Sciences,* Inst. Bot., Botanical Garden, Beijing, pp. 112–129, 1965. (In Chinese with English summary).

Favreau, J., Attempts to force cut branches of lilac, *French Hort.* 197:38–51, April 1967. (In French).

Fiala, J. L., Inducing polyploids in the genus *Syringa, I.L.S. Newsletter,* 2(1):8–11, Spring 1973.

Garrison, R., Origin and development of axillary buds: *Syringa vulgaris* L., *Amer. Jour. Bot.,* 36:205–213, 1949.

Garrison, R. and R. H. Wetmore, Studies in shoot-tip abortion: *Syringa vulgaris* L., *Amer. Jour. Bot.,* 48:789–795, Oct. 1961.

Goodwin, T. W., ed., *Chemistry and Biochemistry of Plant Pigments,* Academic Press, N.Y. and London, 1965.

Gracya, P., The development of the pistil in *Syringa vulgaris* L., *Acta Agron. Akad. Sci. Hungariae* 16(3–4): 439–442, Budapest, 1967.

Holetich, C. D., How to keep cut lilacs fresh for longer periods of time, *I.L.S. Newsletter* 2(3); 9, 1973.

Hjelinquist, H., Eine periklinalchimäre in der gattung *Syringa, Heriditas* 33:367–376 1947.

Jongkind, M., Cold treatment of lilac and forsythia, *Aalsmeer Proefstation voor da Bloemisterij Jaarsverslag.* p. 121, 1965. (In Dutch).

Leeke, H. and R. Law, The effect of gibberillic acid and kinetin on dormant terminal buds of *Syringa vulgaris* L., *Flora Abt. A. Physiol. Biochem.,* 157(S):467–470, 1967. (In German).

Luneva, Z., Crown formation. *Tsvetovodstvo* 4:14, 1967. (In Russian).

Mandy, G., Studies in lilac inflorescences, *Acta Biol. Hungariae* 1:179–205, 1950.

Mihalyfi, J. P., The effect of mechanical wounding on the catalase activity of lilac leaves, *Acta. Biolog. Hungariae* 16(1):51–56, 1965.

Nihous, M., Developpement experimental des Bourgeonsde *Syringa vulgaris* L.(Lilas), *Soc. de Biol. Compt. Rend.* 137: 253, Paris, 1943.

Rogers, O. M., Dwarf lilacs by radiation, *New Hamp. Agric. Sta. Prog. Report* 7:15–16 April 1961.

Rusker, R., Teratological cases in *Ligustrum vulqare, Syringa vulgaris* and *Rhododendron kotschyi, Revista Padurilor* 82(1): 37–39, Jan. 1967. (In Romanian).

Sussex, I. M. et al, Extraction and biological properties of antifungal fraction of woody plant tissue, *Bot. Gaz.,* 121: 171–175, 1960.

Smol'skii, N. V. and V. F. Bibilova, Long term storage of lilac pollen for purposes of hybridization, *Akad. Nauk. Belorusskii SSR. Dok.* 9(2):122–124, Feb. 1965. (In Russian with English summary).

Syrovatko, E. E., Effect of an ultrahigh frequency electric field petroleum growth substance and heteroauxin on the rooting of green cuttings of *Syringa vulgaris* L., *Les. Zh.* 6:20–21, 1965. (In Russian).

Systema, W., Forcing out branches, *Aalsmeer Proefsta. u. de Bloelesterij Jaarveslag* 123–125, 1962. (In Dutch).

Systema, W., Influence of spraying with B-9 on some shrubs for forcing, *Aalsmeer* Proefsta. Bloemisterig Jaarvestag 122–123, 1965 (In Dutch).

Taylor, P. L., Studies on the effect of floral initiation and development on rooting of cuttings of *Syringa vulgaris* 'Charles Joly' and 'Congo', *Dissertation Abstracts* (O.S.Univ.) 19(12):3080, 1959.

Trip, P., C. D. Nelson and G. Krothov, Selective and preferential translocation of C.[14]-labeled sugars in white ash and lilac, *Plant Physiology* 40(4):740–747, July 1965.

Anon. Air pollution and landscape plants, *Nat. Landscape Assoc. Tech Notes,* 8 pp. Washington, D.C., Dec. 10, 1970 (mimeo).

G. PROPAGATION

Anon., Hot-callus method speeds up grafting, *Lilac Newsletter* 10(5):5–6, May 1984.

Alexander, J. H. III, Grafting techniques for the lilac, *Lilacs* 8(1):5–8, 1979.

Berdeen, K., Practice, planting and care of lilac seedlings, *I.L.S. Newsletter* 1(1):9–10, F/W 1972.

Bibikova, V. P., Spring grafting of *Syringa, Tsvetovodstvo* 2:13, 1963 (In Russian).

Boddy, B., The propagation of lilacs (*Syringa*), *Plant Propagators Soc. Proc.* 1962, pp. 254–256.

Bojarczuk, K., Propagation of lilacs (*Syringa vulgaris*) cultivars from green cuttings using various root-stimulating factors, *Lilacs* 8(1):24–30, 1979.

Coggeshall, R. G., Hybrid lilacs from softwood cuttings, *Amer. Nurseryman,* pp. 7–8, June 15, 1962.

Congdon, M., Timing and its relation to cutting selection, *Int. Plant Propagators Soc. Comb. Proc. E/W Regions* 15:230–232, 1965.

de Wilde, R. C., Production and breeding of lilacs, *Int. Plant Propagators Soc. Comb. Proc. E/W Regions* 14:107–113, 1964.

Dunbar, J., Can we raise our own lilacs? *Florists Exch.* 47(23):1137, June 7, 1919.

Einset, John W., A Practical Guide to Woody Plant Micropropagation, *Arnoldia,* 46 (1):36–44, Winter 1986.

Fordham, A. J., Propagation and care of lilacs, *Arnoldia* 17(6–7):36–45, May 22, 1959.

Fourrier, B., Propagation of lilacs at McKay Nursery, *Lilacs* 12:33–37, 1983.

Hilldebrandt, V. and P. M. Harney, *In vitro* propagation of *Syringa vulgaris* 'Vesper' *Lilacs* 12: 48–53, 1983. Reprinted from *Hort. Science* 18:432–434, Aug. 1983.

Holetich, C. D., Collecting, packing and mailing of lilac scions, *Lilac Newsletter* 8(5):5–6, May 1982.

Hughes, R. D., Twelve kinds of lilacs on one bush, *Amer. Home* 45: 34–35, Feb. 1951.

Leiss, J., Propagation of *Syringa reticulata* and forms, *Lilac Newsletter* 8(11):2–5, Nov. 1982.

Luce, R. F., Growing lilacs from seed, *Lilac Newsletter* 9(2): 5–8, Feb. 1983.

McCoun, B., Micropropagation of ornamental plants, *Lilacs* 12: 38–48, 1983.

Minocha, S. C., Lilacs in test-tubes:potential for cloning of lilacs by cell and tissue culture, *Lilacs* 8(1):12–19, 1979.

Pearson, J. L., Propagation of late blooming lilacs, *New Hamp. Agric. Exper. Station Progress Rept.* 7:7–8, April 1961.

Pringle, J. S., Some effects of thermal-neutron radiation on seeds of *Syringa, I.L.S. Newsletter* 5(1):1–24, March 1976.

Sax, K. Rootstock for lilacs, *Arnoldia* 10(9):57–60, July 14, 1950.

Smith, M. C., The case for grafted lilacs, *Lilac Newsletter* 8(4):1–3, April 1982.

Wedge, D., Lilac production at Wedge Nursery, *Int. Plant Propagators Soc. Comb. Proceedings E/W Regions* 14:166–169, 1964.

Wedge, D., Comments concerning grafted lilacs, *Lilac Newsletter* 8(10):7, Oct. 1982.

Weiting C., Lilacs from cuttings, *Northwest Gardens and Homes* 15(3):6, May 1947.

Wister, J. C., Lilac propagation, *Lilac Newsletter* 8(2):2–7, Feb. 1982.

H. CULTURE

Anon., How to grow fine lilacs, *Better Homes & Gardens* 31:331–332, May 1953.

Anon., Growing Lilacs, *U.S.D.A. Home & Garden Bulletin* 199, 9 pp., August 1973.

Brown, J., A member writes from Princeton, Ont., Canada, *Lilac Newsletter* 10(11):4–6 November 1984.

Buckley, A. R., Garden notes from the Plant Research Inst. Ottawa, Oct. 21, 1968. Reprinted in *Lilac Newsletter* 7(11): 9–12, Nov. 1981.

Clark, R. B., Lilac culture, *Lilacs* 13(1): 14–20, 1984.

Duncan, J. W., Early lilac work in Spokane, *Northwest Gardens & Homes* 15(3):19, 1947.

Eaton, M., Cultural hints on lilacs and varieties to try in your own garden, *Flower Grower* p. 33, October 1951.

Eubank, Mrs. A., Growing lilacs in Pratt, Kansas, *Lilac Newsletter* 10(4):1–2, Apr. 1984.

Free, M., Pruning lilacs, *Home Garden* 4:20–21, Nov. 1944.

Free, M., All you need to know about growing lilacs, *Home Garden* 8:38–44, Sept. 1948.

Gauci, C. A., Transplanting lilacs at the Holden Arboretum, *Lilacs* 9:9–12, 1980.

Hagerman, L. W., Lilacs and their culture, *Parks and Recreation* 28(4):208–211, July–August 1945.

Harkness, B., New lilacs from old, *Popular Gardening* 4(3): 59,100, March 1953.

Jongkind, M. Fertilizer trials with the lilac 'Madame Florent Stepman', *Aalsmeer Proefsta. Bloemisterij Jaarsverslag* 1965:112. (In Dutch).

Jongkind, M., Forcing of cold treated lilacs, *Aalsmeer Proefsta. Bloemisterij Jaarsverslag* 1961:118–122, 1962. (In Dutch).

Lape, F., Successes and failures, an assessment of winter damage, 1980–1981, *Lilacs* 11:55–64, 1982.

Leighton, R. S., Enjoy your lilacs, *Univ. Wash. Arboretum Bull.* 12(2):67, Summer 1960. Reprinted from June 1944.

Leighton, R. S., Lilac culture on the west side (of Washington State), *Northwest Gardens and Homes* 15(3):21–22, May 1947.

Leighton, R. S., and G. M. Leighton, Winter care of lilacs, *Univ. Wash. Arbor. Bull.* 32(2):68, Summer 1960. Reprinted from Sept. 1954.

Lowe, A., Lilac culture on the east side (of Washington State), *Northwest Gardens and Homes* 15(1):20, May 1947.

Lumley, A. E., An amateur lilac grower reports, *Lilac Newsletter* 2(4):19, May 1974.

Lupold, D. M., A member writes, *Lilac Newsletter* 5(3): 1–4, March 1979.

Maarse, D. E., Sr., De Seringencultuur in Aalsmeer, *Het Seringenpark te Aalsmeer.* pp. 17–19, 1951.

Margaretten, J., Growing lilacs in Leona Valley, California, *I.L.S. Newsletter* 2(1) Spring 1973.

Margaretten, J., Lilac growing at Margaretten Park, *Lilacs* 10: 3–5, 1981.

Margaretten, J., News from the West Coast, *Lilac Newsletter* 8(3):1–3, March 1982.

Margaretten, J., Helpful hints on lilacs from California, *Lilac Newsletter* 9(2):18, Feb. 1983.

Margaretten, J., Growing lilacs in California, *Lilac Newsletter,* 10(7):2, July 1984.

Oakes, W. W., Lilacs in the Southern States, *Lilac Newsletter* 10(4):4–5, April 1984.

Peterson, M., Planting Lilacs, *Lilac Newsletter* 9(9): 1–4, Sept. 1983.

Rankin, J. P., Growing and trimming lilacs, *Lilac Newsletter* 10(4):5, Apr. 1984.

Tilton, B., Lilacs in Houston, Texas, *Lilac Newsletter* 8(1): 3–4, Jan. 1983.

Wister, J. C., *Lilac Culture,* 123 pp., Orange Judd Publ. Co., N.Y., 1930.

Wood, K. W., Care of the Univ. of Wisc. Lilac Collection, *Lilacs* 4:16–17, 1975.

Wyman, D., Just about lilacs, *Arnold Arb. Bull. Pop. Info.,* series 4; 4(8) 39–49, 1935.

1. Insects

Anon., Ontario Dept. Agric. and Food Pest Control Chart, date lacking.

Appleby, J. E., Insects attacking lilacs and their control, *Lilacs* 4:8–12, 1975.

Filmer, R. S., What about borer control? *Home Garden* 6: 91–95, Sept. 1945.

Klots, A. B. and E. B. Klots, *Living Insects of the World,* Doubleday & Co., Garden City, N.Y., 1961.

Nielson, D. G., New approaches in lilac borer control, *I.L.S. Proceedings* 3(1):31–34, 1974.

Peterson, M., Borer and scale control in western Nebraska, *Lilac Newsletter;* 9(5):4–6, May 1983.

Roselle, B., Control lilac borers, *Nebraska Agric. Exper. Sta. EC 58–1586:*(1), 1959.

2. Diseases

Anon., How to knock out mildew on lilacs, *Amer. Nurseryman* 129(8): 105, April 15, 1969.

Beale, J. H. and H. P. Beale, Transmission of a ringspot virus disease of *Syringa vulgaris* by grafting. *Contrib. Boyce Thompson Institute.* 17(1):1–6, Oct.-Dec. 1952.

Fenicchia, R. A., Susceptibility of lilacs to leaf curl necrosis and powdery mildew, *Lilacs* 7(1):27–49, 1978.

Henry, A. W. and D. Stelfox, *Phytophtora citrocolla* Sawada in relation to shoot blight in lilac (*Syringa vulgaris*) and crown rot of elders (*Sambucus*) in Alberta, Canada, *Canada Plant Disease Survey* 46(4):146, Dec. 1966.

Hibben, C. R. and J. T. Walker, A leaf-roll necrosis complex of lilacs in an urban environment, *Proc. Amer. Soc. Hort. Sci.* 89:636–642, 1966.

Jongkind, M., Chemical control of weeds in lilacs and forsythia, *Aalsmeer proefsta. Bloemisterij Jaarverslag,* 129–130, 1965.

Jongkind, M., Granular herbicides for lilacs, *Ibid.,* 142, 1966.

Maloy, O. C. and C. J. Gould, Plant diseases:lilac blight, *Wash. State Univ. Extension* E.M. 2673, 2 pp., Aug. 1966.

Rogers, O. M., Mildew on lilacs, *I.L.S. Proceedings,* 5(1):19–21, 1976.

Schoeneweiss, D. F., Powdery mildew on lilacs, *Amer. Nurseryman* 124(L):70–71, July 1, 1966.

Systema, W., Effects of spraying lilacs with B-9, *Aalsmeer Proefsta. Bloemisterij Jaarverslag,* 109–110, 1966.

Walker, J. T., C. R. Hibben and J. C. Allison, Cultivar ratings for susceptibility and resistance to the leafroll necrosis disorder of lilacs, *Amer. Soc. Hort. Sci.* 100(6):627–630, 1975.

I.   LANDSCAPE USES

Anon., "Lilacs"—companion plants, *Lilac Newsletter* 8(6): 1–3, June 1982.

Brewer, J. E., L. P. Nichols, C. C. Powell and E. M. Smith, The flowering crabapple, *Co-op Ext. Service North-East States*, N.E. 223, NCR 78, 38 pp. Oct. 1979.

den Boer, A. F., *Ornamental Crabapples*, 1–226 pp., Amer. Assoc. of Nurserymen, 1959.

Hard, C.G., Growing peonies, *Univ. Minn. Agric. Exper. Stat. Hort. No. 2*, Fact Sheet (date lacking).

Harkness, B., *Handbook of Flowering Shrubs*, Brooklyn Bot. Gard. Record Plants and Gardens 20(1):1–64, 1964.

Nichols, L. P., Disease resistant crabapples, a guide for the selection of disease susceptibility and cultural characteristics, *Penn. State Univ. Hort. Bull.* 11 pp. (mimeo.) 1983.

Nichols, L. P., Study of flowering crabapples and disease resistance of cultivars, computer read-outs of cultivars, 1980, 1981, 1982, 1983, 1984, (a continuing research of named cultivars), *Pennsylvania State Univ. Hort. Research Study.*

Perkins, H. O., *Flowering Trees*, Brooklyn Bot. Gard. Record Plants and Gardens, special edition 19(1):1–81, 1957.

Raup, H. M., Notes on the early use of the land in the Arnold Arboretum, *Arnold Arb. Bull. Pop. Info. Ser. 4;* 3:41–70, Dec. 23, 1955.

Smith, M. C., Landscape lilacs, *Lilac Newsletter* 8(11): 8–9, Nov. 1982.

Teuscher, H., ed., *Handbook of Conifers*, Brooklyn Bot. Gard. Record Plants and Gardens 25(1):1–104, 1969.

Hedges

Fiala, J. L., Using new forms of *Syringa* as a hedge, *I.L.S. Newsletter* 2(3):2–3, 1973.

McCormick, M., Lilacs for a hedge, *Horticulture* 27(5); 182, May 1949.

Wagenknecht, B. L., The lilacs of New England, *Arnoldia* 19: 23–30, 1959.

Wister, J. C., Is there a future for fine lilacs? *Amer. Assoc. Bot. and Arb. Bull.* 2:52–53, 1968.

Wyman., D., The hedge demonstration plot twenty years after planting, *Arnoldia* 17(4–5):17–32, Apr. 12, 1957.

Zetterstrom, P., Hungarian lilac (*Syringa josikaea*) an excellent hedge plant. *Lanlbrlidskr. f. Jamtland och Harjedalen* 16(3):18–191, 1963.

J.   LILAC COLLECTIONS (arranged according to geographical site)

California

Margaretten, J., Lilac growing at Margaretten Park, Leona Valley, California, Lilacs 10:3–5, 1981

Iowa

Anon., It's a blooming success:Stampe Lilac Garden, Duck Creek Park, Davenport, Iowa, *The Quad-City Times*, Apr. 30, 1981.

Smith, M. C., Lilacs at the Bickelhaupt Arboretum, Clinton, Iowa, *Lilac Newsletter* 8(4):4–7, Apr. 1982.

Sandahl, P. L., Ewing Park Lilac Arboretum, Des Moines, Iowa, *New York Bot. Garden Journal*, 7:119–121, July 1957.

Illinois

Coen, F. C., Lilacia Park and Memorial Library, gift of Colonel William R. Plum, Lilac time in Lombard, Illinois, 44 pp. date lacking. *Lombard Park Distr. Comm.*

Dvorak, J., Jr., edited J. L. Fiala, *Lilac Study*—a Four Year Study at Lilacia Park Lombard, Ill., and the Morton Arboretum, Lisle, Ill., International Lilac Society Special Publication, 1978.

Eickhorst, W. E., The lilac collection at the Morton Arboretum, Lisle, Illinois, *Lilacs* 4:18–21, 1975.

Hagerman, L. W., A short history of the lilac—Lilac time in Lombard, *Lombard Park District Comm.*, 28 pp, date lacking.

Indiana

Bass, C., Lilacs in Indiana, Lilac Newsletter 8(6):8–10, June 1982.

Maine

Oakes, W. W., Lilacs in Maine, *Lilac Newsletter* 8(6): 4–5, June 1982.

Massachusetts

Wyman, D., *The Arnold Arboretum Garden Book*, Van Nostrand, N.Y., 1954, Lilacs at The Arnold Arboretum, Jamaica Plain, Mass.

Michigan

LaRue, C. D., The lilacs of Mackinac Island, Michigan, *Amer. Midl. Nat.* 39(2):504–408, 1948.

Nebraska

Clark, R. B., Lilac Farm lilac collection, Bennet, Nebraska, *I.L.S. Newsletter* 2(3):6–7, 1973.

Smith, M. C., Wishart garden, a haven in Lincoln, Nebraska, *Lilac Newsletter* 9(10):4, Oct. 1983.

New Hampshire

Clark, R. B., Birchwood's lilac collection, 1973, Meredith, New Hampshire, *Lilac Newsletter* 10(3):9–11, March 1984.

New Jersey

Clark, R. B., The Alice Harding Memorial Lilac Walk, New Brunswick, New Jersey, *I.L.S Newsletter* 1(4):4 F/W 1972.

Trexler, J. Skylands Botanical Garden, Ringwood State Park, New Jersey, *Lilacs* 7(1) 32–34, 1978.

New York

Anon., Havemeyer lilac collection at New York Botanical Gardens, Bronx, N.Y., *Lilac Newsletter* 11(1):6–8, Jan, 1985.

Anon., Howard Taylor Memorial Lilac Arboretum, Millbrook, New York, *Amer. Nurseryman* 14(7);83, 1961.

Clark, R. B., The Highland Park Lilac Collection, *I.L.S Newsletter*, Convention Issue:9–24, May 19, 1972.

Delandic, T. and D. Ryniec, Lilacs bloom at Brooklyn Botanical Garden, *Lilac Newsletter* 10(6):4–10, June 1984.

Ellwanger H. C., Lilacs, peonies and other collections in Highland Park (Rochester, N.Y.), *Gard. Club of Amer. Bull.* 14 (series 7):58–61, March 1941.

Fiala, J. L., The lilacs of Grape Hill Farm, Clyde, N.Y., *Lilacs* 4:27, 1975.

Gunderson, A., ed., Lilacs in the Brooklyn Botanic Garden, *BBG Record* 30:191–224, 1941.

Harkness, B., A checklist of the cultivated woody plants of the Rochester Parks, *Phytologia* 10:254–265, 1964.

Niedz, F. J., Lilacland Revisited, Brookville, N.Y., *I.L.S. Newsletter* 1(4):7–8, F/W 1972.

Robinson, A., Delhi, New York, a 'Lilac Town', *I.L.S. Newsletter* 2(2):18, 1973.

Ohio

Clark, R. B., Falconskeape, its gardens and lilacs, Medina, Ohio, *Lilacs* 9:2–3, 1980.

Clark, R. B., Gardenview Horticultural Park, Strongsville, Ohio, *Lilacs,* 9:4–5, 1980.

Knight, C. L, The Holden Arboretum lilac garden, *Lilacs,* 9: 4–8, 1980.

Pennsylvania

Melrose, D., Swarthmore College and its collections, Swarthmore, Penn., *Lilacs* 7(1):20–23, 1978.

Seibert, R. J., Lilacs at Longwood Gardens, Kennett Sq. Penn., *Lilacs* 7(1):31–32, 1978.

Weber, P., The John Tyler Arboretum, Lima, Penn., *Lilacs* 7(1): 24–26, 1978.

Vermont

Clark, R. B., A visit to Hamebest Nursery, Randolph Center, Vermont, *Lilacs* 4:15, 1975.

Clark, R. B., The Shelburne Museum lilacs, Shelburne, Vermont, *Lilacs* 13(1):24–25, 1984.

Clark, R. B., Lilacs at the Vale of Aherlow, E. Burke, Vermont, *Lilacs* 13(1):21–24, 1984.

Washington State

Anon., Hulda Klager Lilac Gardens (Woodland), *Nat. Gardener* 48(6): 1977.

Duncan, J. W., Early lilac work in Spokane, Washington, *Northwest Gardens and Homes* 15(3):19, May 1947.

Wisconsin

Wood, K. W., The Univ. of Wisconsin Arb. Lilac collection, Madison, Wisconsin, 16 pp. no date, (circa 1974).

Canada

Vick, R., Lilacs at the Devonian Bot. Gardens, Alberta, *I.L.S. Newsletter* 7(11):1–6, Nov. 1981.

Cumming, W. A., The best of the lilacs in 1971, Morden, Manitoba, *I.L.S. Newsletter* 1(2):9–10, Jan. 1972.

Buckley, A. R., *Syringa* taxa growing in the Plant Research Inst. Collection, Ottawa, Ontario, *I.L.S.*

Newsletter 1(2): 11–18, Jan. 1972.

Buckley, A. R., Lilacs at Ottawa, Ontario, *Lilacs* 11:10–20, 1982.

Holetich, C. D., The Royal Botanical Gardens Katie Osborne Lilac Garden, *I.L.S. Newsletter* 1(2):5–8, Jan. 1972.

van Gemeren, J., Lilacs at Montreal Botanical Gardens, *Lilacs* 11:21–27, 1982.

Austria

Kollmer, N., Pflieder in Wien, *Mein Schönoer Garten,* 14–17, Apr. 1974.

Great Britain

Griffin, M., and M. Maunder, The National Lilac Collection, *The Plantsman, England* 7(2):90–113, September 1985.

Rogers, O. M., Lilacs in England, *Lilacs* 6(1):9–11, 1979.

Poland

Bugala, W., Lilacs in the Kornik Arboretum and their acclimatization to date, *Arb. Kornickie* 9:59–95 (in Polish), 9:95–96 (English summary).

The Netherlands

Voller, D. H. P., *Het Seringengenpark te Aalsmeer,* The Netherlands, 24 pp. 1951.

West Germany

Krüssmann, G., Das Syringa-Sortiment der AZR Deutsche Bäumschule, Aachen, F.D.R., 10(3):1–2, March 1, 1958.

Krüssmann, G., Verzeichnis der Bäume und Sträucher des Botanischen Gartens Dortmund-Brunninghausen, *Syringa* pp. 69–70, 1959.

U.S.S.R.

Cronquist, A., Russia's foremost Botanical Garden, *N.Y. Bot. Gard. Garden Jour.,* 16(2):48–53, Mar.–April 1966.

Rubtzov, L. I., N. L. Mikhailov and V. G. Zhogoleva, *Lilac Species and Cultivars in Cultivation in the U.S.S.R.,* (a summary of 42 lilac collections), Naukova Dumka, Kiev, U.S.S.R., 1980. (In Russian)

Holetich, C. D., Lilac Species and Cultivars in Cultivation in U.S.S.R., (Translation into English from the Russian publication), *Lilacs—Special Issue,* 38 pp. International Lilac Society Publication, December 1982.

K. PERSONS (CELEBRITIES OF LILACDOM)

Fiala, J. L., J. Herbert Alexander and grandson Jack, *I.L.S. Newsletter* 2(1):14, Spr. 1973.

Willard, L. F., The Lilac Man—*Ken Berdeen, Yankee Magazine,* pp. 176–177, April 1981.

Wedge, D., A. M. Brand and his peony farm, *Lilacs* 12:29–32, 1983.

Anon., *Dr. W. A. Cumming* honored, *Lilac Newsletter* 7(7):5–6, July 1981.

Vrugtman, P., *James Dougall,* 1810–1888, *Lilacs* 11: 28–32, 1982.

Eickhorst, W. E., *Edward J. Gardner,* 1891–1952, *Lilacs* 12:22–25, 1983.

Hanley, E. E. B., The Lilac Lady of Woodland—*Hulda Klager, Univ. Wash. Arb. Bulletin* 17(2):54 ff., Summer 1954.

Gromov, A., *Leonid Alekseevitch Kolesnikov,* Creator of Russian Lilacs, *I.L.S. Proceedings* 2(4):11–18, May 1974.

Vrugtman, F., *August Henry Lemke,* 1868–1946, *Lilacs* 12:18–21, 1983.

Anon., *Victor Lemoine, Horticulture* pp. 897–899, Dec. 3, 1911; obit. ibid. p. 934, Dec. 30, 1911.

Livian, C., *Victor Lemoine, Gartnerisch Botanis cher Bref.* 78, pp. 53–61, May 1984. (In German).

Frazer, N., *Albert and Mabel Lumley* love Lilacs, *Yankee Magazine,* pp. 42–52, May 1976.

Fiala, J. L., *Dirk Eveleens Maarse, I.L.S. Newsletter* 1(2):19, Jan. 1972.

Cameron, D., *Miss Isabella Preston,* plant breeder extraordinary, *Lilacs* 11(1):3–9, 1982.

Short, Clare and Mary, *Dr. John Rankin*—personal notes, letters and photographs, 1975, *Archives of Int. Lilac Society.*

Moon, M. H., *Frank L. Skinner, Baileya* 5:136–141, Sept. 1957.

Anon., *Dr. Frank Leith Skinner, Manitoba Dept. Cultural Affairs and Historical Resources,* 1981, 11 pp.

Clark, R. B., *Lourene Bratt Wishart, Lilacs* 13:4, 1984.

General Index

Index of Persons

the next classic Lilacs

Look past the common lilac for a worthy group of neater, cleaner shrubs

by PAGE DICKEY

CLOCKWISE FROM LEFT: KAREN FROMENT/GARDEN-PICUTRE.COM, BILL JOHNSON, RICH POMERANTZ

I am tired of reading articles disparaging the lilac.
We are told of its brief period of bloom—a week, two weeks if we're lucky.
We are warned that its leaves become marred by mildew in the summer,
that they contribute no autumn color, and that the shrub possesses an ugly
gangly habit. These articles are referring, of course, to the old-fashioned
common lilac, *Syringa vulgaris*, with its twisted shaggy trunks and glorious
purple and white plumes. A native of Europe, it has nevertheless graced

S. meyeri 'Palibin'

S. pubescens subsp. *patula* 'Miss Kim'

Syringa 'Tinkerbelle'

THE COMMON LILAC (opposite page) may be
the most well known of its kind, but other types
(this page) have much to offer, including smaller,
neater growth habit and mildew-resistant leaves.
They still provide what's expected of a lilac:
showy, fragrant flowers in all shades of purple.

S. vulgaris 'Yankee Doodle'

S. vulgaris 'Madame Lemoine'

the corners of New England and Midwestern farmhouses for more than two centuries. I, for one, will always have it in my garden. I love its appropriateness, its lavish trusses, their unparalleled fragrance. For these pleasures I will suffer less-than-perfect leaves and lack of fall color.

However, what the detractors fail to mention in their articles is that the world of lilacs is richly varied. Today we have available from nurseries a number of other species and their hybrids that offer not only sweet-smelling blooms but splendid habit and leaves that stay fresh and healthy all summer. Some of them also color handsomely in autumn.

FOUR STANDOUTS

The so-called Chinese lilac, *Syringa ×chinensis*, has leaves half the size of those of *S. vulgaris* and looser flowers. In our garden, this billowy shrub has matured to about ten feet high and eight feet wide. Chinese lilac, a hybrid first discovered in France in 1777, does not have the range of flower colors in its cultivars that common lilac does, coming mostly in soft purple and a white tinged with the palest mauve. And the flowers themselves are not quite as showy, being looser and more delicate. However, the plant is more floriferous than the common lilac. With its exceptionally graceful habit, it makes a lovely specimen; planted in quantity, it creates a splendid screen.

The littleleaf lilac, *S. pubescens* subsp. *microphylla* 'Superba', is a favorite of mine, blooming later than both the common and the Chinese. The shrub grows wider than it does tall, maturing at about seven feet wide and six feet high. The flowers start out a vivid red-violet and fade to pale pink. They are intensely fragrant, so much so that a handful of blooms brought inside for a vase will

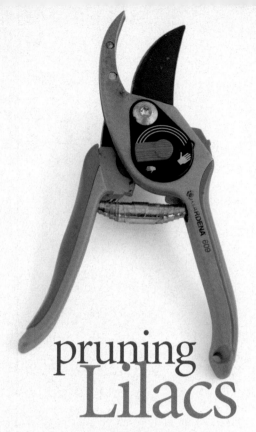

pruning
Lilacs

It is a myth that lilacs won't bloom well if the faded flowers are not clipped. You might want to cut off the dead blooms to tidy the appearance of the plants, but they will bloom the next year whether you do or do not. That said, cutting branches of the flowers for bouquets is the best way to prune the shrubs—and who can resist having large vases full of the luxuriously colored and scented plumes? This strategy also ensures you don't prune too early or too late, both frequent reasons for lack of bloom. Lilacs flower on "old wood"—that is, they form their flower (and leaf) buds during the summer. These open the following spring. If you prune any time from when the buds have developed to when they would open, you remove them. So pruning should take place immediately after the flowers fade, when the new buds haven't yet formed.

Older shrubs that have outgrown their space can be pruned hard in winter, when they are dormant. This sacrifices the year's bloom, but a crowded shrub may not be blooming well anyway. Drastic pruning should be done in stages, taking away some of the old stems over several winters. (Do not remove more than one-third of the plant in one year.) Remove the top branches, then saw off the main stems, one to two feet above the ground. Feed and mulch well in spring. Thin the regrowth in the next winter to leave two or three shoots per stump.—*Ed.*

drive you out of the room. Mildew does not mar the quite small (two-inch) leaves. The most unusual feature of this lilac, however, is its habit of reblooming lightly in August, to everyone's surprise. Butterflies often visit the delicate summer flowers.

The dwarf Korean lilac, *S. meyeri* 'Palibin', deserves its popularity. It has tiny leaves of dark green, not much bigger than a thumbnail, and a densely compact habit, topping out at five feet. It can be kept to three feet. It flowers profusely, covering itself with small mauve-purple trusses that emit a heady fragrance. In October, the foliage turns russet hues, a picturesque addition to the fall garden. Because of its relatively small size and stellar habit, the dwarf Korean lilac works well in the mixed flower border. Underplant it with *Geranium macrorrhizum* and add lavender-colored iris as a companion; they bloom at the same time. Nurseries sometimes sell standards of this lilac—it clips beautifully—and I have seen these used to dramatic effect in garden beds. As an experiment, we have just planted a hedge of 'Palibin' around the herb garden, and I intend to clip it into a formal line each year after it blooms.

Many consider *S. pubescens* subsp. *patula* 'Miss Kim' the finest example of the clan. It grows to about six or seven feet with a graceful habit and healthy foliage that turns a beautiful coppery bronze in autumn. 'Miss Kim' usually blooms in our garden during the first week in June, the last of the lilacs to go. Purple buds open to icy pale blue flowers. One bush that we planted on the terrace just outside the kitchen door fills the air there with its heady fragrance for at least two weeks.

KEEP THE COMMON

As for the common lilac, those of us who are willing to grow it are rewarded with an endless choice of lush colors, ranging from white and creamy yellow to pink, wine red, and the palest and deepest purples. Garden designer and plantsman Hitch Lyman grows 250 cultivars of *S. vulgaris* in his garden in Ithaca, New York. Asked why he remains so obviously partial to this lilac, he explains that in his neutral soil and very cold climate it is the only large-flowered shrub that offers the collector any variety. (The late Fr. John Fiala, a renowned hybridizer, notes there are almost 2,000 named hybrids derived from *S. vulgaris* in his monograph on the genus.)

Varieties of the common lilac seem to bloom more lavishly every other year, like many crab apples. Don't expect them to bloom well in the shade; they love the sun, and they appreciate a little sweetness in the soil. When we empty the ashes from our fireplaces in the spring we spread them under the lilacs. But even with no attention at all, they are astonishingly long-lived, often outlasting the houses at which they were planted. Cherished by the colonists, they are now part of our heritage. My advice is to grow both—the old-fashioned lilac for its extravagant blooms, the novel species for their value as handsome shrubs in the garden. **H**

For sources of plants featured in this article, turn to page 80.

LILACS HOLD their place in gardens. *Syringa vulgaris* (this picture) continues to supply its old-fashioned charm, while less common species find their place in smaller gardens.

S. ×*chinensis*

S. vulgaris 'Monge'

S. pubescens subsp. *microphylla* 'Superba'

HORTICULTURE

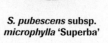

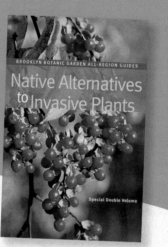

HORTICULTURE